Apartheid's Friends

Apartheid's Friends

The Rise and Fall of South Africa's Secret Service

JAMES SANDERS

JOHN MURRAY

© James Sanders 2006

First published in Great Britain in 2006 by John Murray (Publishers)
A division of Hodder Headline

The right of James Sanders to be identified as the Author of the Work has been asserted by
him in accordance with the Copyright, Designs and Patents Act 1988.

1

A CIP catalogue record for this title is available from the British Library

ISBN-13-0-7195-6675-2
ISBN-10-0-7195-6675-4

Typeset in Monotype Bembo 10.75/13pt
by Servis Filmsetting Ltd, Manchester

Printed and bound by Clays Ltd, St Ives plc

Hodder Headline policy is to use papers that are natural, renewable and recyclable products and
made from wood grown in sustainable forests. The logging and manufacturing processes are
expected to conform to the environmental regulations of the country of origin.

John Murray (Publishers)
338 Euston Road
London NW1 3BH

For my mother

Contents

Illustrations

1. Sir Percy Sillitoe addresses a press conference in the USA, 1951
2. John Vorster and Gordon Winter, early 1960s
3. Jean La Grange, 1970
4. Peter Hain, July 1968
5. Hendrik van den Bergh, Eschel Rhoodie, Yitzhak Rabin and Shimon Peres, April 1974
6. General Magnus Malan, P.W. Botha, and Admiral Bierman in the Caprivi Swamps, Namibia, 1975
7. Hendrik van den Bergh, 1976
8. Eschel Rhoodie and Hendrik van den Bergh, March 1979
9. Lieutenant-General P.W. van der Westhuizen, 1979
10. Niel Barnard, 1980
11. Gerard Ludi, 1981
12. Dieter Gerhardt and Ruth Johr, 1984
13. Craig Williamson at a press conference, 1985
14. Almond Nofemela and Dirk Coetzee, 1997
15. Eugene de Kock, 1999
16. Gideon Nieuwoudt, no date
17. Mac Maharaj, 1992
18. Mike Louw, January 1995
19. Mo Shaik, no date
20. Wouter Basson, March 1999
21. General Meiring, Ronnie Kasrils and Joe Modise, November 1997
22. Bheki Jacobs with two ANC comrades, early 1990s

Picture credits: 1, Unknown; 2, James Soullier; 3, 4, 6 and 7, Gordon Winter; 5, David Rubinger; 8, 10, 11, 13, 15, 16, 17 and 19, Johannesburg *Star*; 9, *Now* magazine; 12, 14, 18 and 21, Johannesburg *Sunday Times*; 20, *Business Day*; 22, Bheki Jacobs

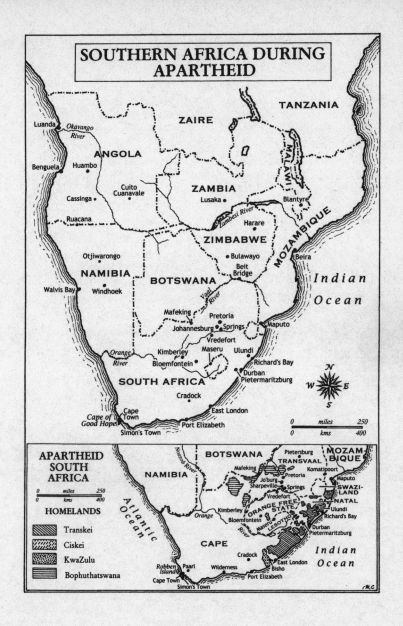

SOUTHERN AFRICA DURING APARTHEID

TANZANIA

Luanda
Okavango River

ZAIRE

ANGOLA

Benguela

Huambo

Cuito
Cuanavale

ZAMBIA

Lusaka

Blantyre

MALAWI

Cassinga

Ruacana

Zambesi River

Harare

MOZAMBIQUE

Otjiwarongo

ZIMBABWE

Bulawayo

Beira

NAMIBIA

BOTSWANA

Beit
Bridge

Indian

Walvis Bay

Windhoek

Vaal River

Ocean

Mafeking

Pretoria

Johannesburg Springs

Maputo

Orange River

Kimberley

Vredefort

Maseru

Ulundi

Bloemfontein

Richard's Bay

SOUTH AFRICA

Durban
Pietermaritzburg

Cradock

N

Cape
Town

East London

W   E

*Cape of
Good Hope*

Simon's Town

Port Elizabeth

S

| 0 | miles | 250 |
| 0 | kms | 400 |

APARTHEID SOUTH AFRICA

| 0 | miles | 250 |
| 0 | kms | 400 |

HOMELANDS

Transkei

Ciskei

KwaZulu

Bophuthatswana

Nossob River

BOTSWANA

Pietersburg

TRANSVAAL

MOZAM-
BIQUE

NAMIBIA

Mafeking

Pretoria

Komatipoort

Jo'burg
Sharpeville Springs

Maputo

SWAZI-
LAND

Vredefort

Atlantic

Orange

Kimberley

ORANGE FREE
STATE

NATAL

Ocean

Bloemfontein

Maseru
LESOTHO

Ulundi
Richard's Bay

River

Durban
Pietermaritzburg

CAPE

Cradock

Indian

*Robben
Island*

Paarl

Wilderness

Bisho

East London

Ocean

Cape Town

Port Elizabeth

Simon's Town

Acknowledgements

Rather than name all the intelligence people who have assisted me with this book over the last six years, I prefer to recognise their need for anonymity with a universal 'thank you'. You all know how appreciative I am for the time, debate and, above all, documentation. In some cases, where the sources were willing, I have named intelligence interviewees in the endnotes, in others I have respected my sources' need for invisibility.

Professor Shula Marks guided my doctoral thesis in the 1990s with care and skill, and has continued to exert an intellectual influence, albeit from a distance. I worked with the late Anthony Sampson from 1996 to 2004 and I remain grateful for the many lessons I learned from him during that period. J.D.F Jones, with whom I have also worked, has become a trusted friend: he came up with the 'Friends' conceit for this book and encouraged John Murray to take a chance on a new author. David Harrison and the BBC provided television research work which permitted me to continue visiting South Africa, as did Robin Benger of the CBC, and Antony Thomas, on behalf of Carlton Television and Channel 4. The Institute of Commonwealth Studies invited me to deliver a seminar at the beginning of my research and Martin Welz of *Noseweek* published a number of my preliminary findings. My particular thanks go to Martin for inviting me to edit *Noseweek* for three months between March and May 2005. Grant McIntyre made the original decision to commission this book for John Murray and Roland Philipps saw it through to its conclusion. Peter James edited with his usual incisive skill and precision, while Rowan Yapp and Caroline Westmore demonstrated endless tolerance for my (many) missed deadlines.

The K Blundell Trust and the Authors' Foundation, which I learned about through the Society of Authors, awarded generous grants which assisted my research. Gordon Winter's archive of clippings, memories and photographs opened my mind to the ambiguities of the 1960s and 1970s and Walter Felgate's security papers revealed the political malevolence at the heart of the violence of the 1980s and 1990s. I have consulted the collections of libraries in South Africa, the United Kingdom and the United States but special thanks must go to the South African History Archive and the Cullen Library at the University of the Witwatersrand, the superb National Security Archive in Washington DC and the Public Record Office (now the National Archive) in London. The often criticised Truth and Reconciliation Commission in South Africa brought numerous important documents to the surface upon which I have fed with a hungry passion.

The following researchers, academics, journalists and authors helped at different times: Piers Pigou, Verne Harris, Will Ferroggiaro, Mervyn Rees, Anthony Butler, Ronald Suresh Roberts, John Murtagh, Mark Israel, Richard Knight, Georgina Sinclair, Ed Stanley, Marion Edmunds, Terry and Barbara Bell, David Beresford, Sam Sole, Stefaans Brummer, Evelyn Groenink, Barbara Jones, Mark Shaw, William Gutteridge, Stephen Ellis, Lateef Parker, Stanley Uys, Peter Stiff, the late Hans Strydom, Liza Key, Sasha Polakow-Suransky, Kevin O'Brien, Peter Younghusband, Mungo Soggot, Mike Popham, Michael Holman and John Carlin.

Steve and Gerlind Bayliss provided a home from home in Johannesburg, as did S.K. Pyne in Bethesda. D.C. Lord and Ralph Tittley know what they contributed. My brother Mark and my father John were useful sounding boards. My girls, Amrit and Izzy, tolerated my absences, supported my endeavours and made day-to-day life a splendid adventure. I am indebted to those people who have already provided corrections and clarifications, while I take full responsibility for any errors that have survived. I will be grateful for any rectifications and suggestions from readers, which can, I hope, be incorporated in later editions.

Abbreviations

A-AM – Anti-Apartheid Movement
ABSA – Amalgamated Banks of South Africa
AFP – Agence France Presse
ANC – African National Congress
ARM – African Resistance Movement, South Africa
ARMSCOR – Armaments Corporation, South Africa
AWB – AfrikanerWeerstandsbeweging, South Africa
BND – Bundesnachrichtendienst, West German intelligence
BOSS – Bureau for State Security, South Africa
BSAP – British South Africa Police, Rhodesia, Central African Federation
CBW – Chemical and Biological Warfare
CCB – Civil Co-operation Bureau, South African military intelligence
CIA – Central Intelligence Agency, USA
CIO – Central Intelligence Organisation, Rhodesia and Zimbabwe
COSATU – Congress of South African Trade Unions, South Africa
CSI – Chief of Staff Intelligence, South African Military Intelligence
DA – Democratic Alliance, South Africa
DCC – Directorate of Covert Collection, South African Military Intelligence
DIS – Department of Intelligence and Security, ANC, later Directorate of
   Intelligence and Security
DMI – Directorate of Military Intelligence, South Africa
DONS – Department for National Security, South Africa
DSO – Directorate of Special Operations, South Africa, the Scorpions
DST – Directorate of Special Tasks, South African Military Intelligence
EO – Executive Outcomes, mercenaries
FBI – Federal Bureau of Investigation, USA
FNLA – Frente Nacional de Libertação de Angola, National Front for the
   Liberation of Angola
FRELIMO – Frente de Libertação de Moçambique, Front for the Liberation
   of Mozambique

GRU – Glavnoye Razvedyvatelnoye Upravleniye, Soviet Military Intelligence
HNP – Herstigte Nasionale Party, South Africa
ID – Intelligence Division, South Africa's post-1995 military intelligence
IDAF – International Defence Fund for Southern Africa
IDSO – International Diamond Smuggling Organisation
IFP – Inkatha Freedom Party, South Africa
IMF – International Monetary Fund
IRA – Irish Republican Army
IUEF – International University Exchange Fund
KGB – Komitet Gosudarstvennoi Bezopasnosti, Soviet intelligence
KIK – Co-ordinating Intelligence Committee, South Africa
KZP – KwaZulu Police
LAKAM – Leshkat Kesher Madai, the Bureau of Scientific Relations, Israeli scientific intelligence
MDM – Mass Democratic Movement, South Africa
MID – Military Intelligence Division, South Africa
MK – Umkhonto we Sizwe, the ANC's military wing
MOD – Ministry of Defence
MPLA – Movimento Popular de Libertação de Angola, Popular Movement for the Liberation of Angola
NAT – Department of National Intelligence and Security, ANC
NATO – North Atlantic Treaty Organisation
NCL – National Committee for Liberation, South Africa
NEC – National Executive Committee
NIA – National Intelligence Agency, South Africa
NICOC – National Intelligence Co-ordinating Committee, South Africa
NIS – National Intelligence Service, South Africa
NP – National Party
NSA – National Security Agency, USA
NSC – National Security Council, USA
NUSAS – National Union of South African Students, South Africa
OAU – Organisation of African Unity
PAC – Pan Africanist Congress, South Africa
PIDE – Portuguese International Police for the Defence of the State
RAU – Rand Afrikaans University
RENAMO – Resistência Nacional Moçambicana, Mozambican National Resistance
RI – Republican Intelligence, South Africa
RSA – Republic of South Africa

SAA – South African Airways
SABC – South African Broadcasting Corporation
SACP – South African Communist Party
SADF – South African Defence Force
SANDF – South African National Defence Force
SAP – South African Police, pre-1995
SAPA – South African Press Association
SAPS – South African Police Service, post-1995
SARS – South African Revenue Service
SAS – Special Air Service, UK, Rhodesia
SASOL – South African Coal, Oil and Gas Corporation
SASS – South African Secret Service
SDECE – Service de Documentation Extérieure et de Contre-Espionage, French foreign intelligence
SIS – Secret Intelligence Service, MI6
SLO – Security Liaison Officer, MI5
SSC – State Security Council, South Africa
SWAPO – South West African People's Organisation, Namibia
TRC – Truth and Reconciliation Commission
TREWITS – Teen-Rewolusionêre Inligting Taakspan, Counter-Revolutionary Information Target Centre, South Africa
UDF – United Democratic Front, South Africa
UDI – Unilateral Declaration of Independence
UNITA – União Nacionale para a Independência Total de Angola, National Union for the Total Liberation of Angola
USSR – Union of Soviet Socialist Republics
WMD – Weapons of Mass Destruction
ZAPU – Zimbabwe African People's Union

Prologue: A Land of Spooks

To articulate the past historically does not mean to recognise it 'the way it really was'. It means to seize hold of a memory as it flashes up at a moment of danger . . . In every era the attempt must be made anew to wrest tradition away from a conformism that is about to overpower it . . . Only that historian will have the gift of fanning the spark of hope in the past who is firmly convinced that *even the dead* will not be safe from the enemy if he wins. And this enemy has not ceased to be victorious.

Walter Benjamin, 'Theses on the Philosophy of History', 1940[1]

It's Johannesburg 1996. It's F.W. De Klerk. He's addressing a breakfast meeting of the American Chamber of Commerce. It's in the same week of another week of the Eugene de Kock trial. Tortures, Third Force hit squads, mutilated bodies. And it's the same story in the same week of another week of the Truth and Reconciliation Commission.

In this same week, then, De Klerk is telling the American Chamber of Commerce: 'Nowhere else in Africa will you find a country in which five large domestic banking conglomerates hold the savings of the population. In no other African country will you find such a developed insurance industry.'

And De Klerk smiles, the practised smile of the practised speaker, to signal 'joke coming up'.

'People talk a lot about a Third Force,' De Klerk says with a twinkle in his eye. 'But in South Africa, the real Third Force is the private sector.' Unquote.

Jeremy Cronin, 'Even The Dead', 1997[2]

SINCE THE EARLY 1960s, South Africa has been a land infested with spies. Some intelligence operatives are essentially civil servants, others are freelance traders in information; some foreign spooks are 'declared', protected by diplomatic immunity, others are 'undeclared' and subject to prosecution if caught. In South Africa over the last half-century, the tentacles of intelligence stretched far and wide, touching students, criminals, bankers and politicians. As a mechanism for exerting discipline on internal stability and providing a crucial 'early-warning system', the South African secret services developed, compromised and controlled many unlikely figures.

An indication of the problems which continue to be raised by apartheid's intelligence legacy in contemporary South Africa can be discerned in the story of a nineteen-year-old 'liberal' who joined the South African Defence Force (SADF) in 1975 for his national service. Our young friend, whose father was a judge and whose second cousin, by marriage, was the editor of the Johannesburg *Sunday Times*, followed his elder brother in being appointed to the staff of the army newspaper *Paratus*. In March 1976, he delivered a propaganda article about the Detention Barracks at Voortrekkerhoogte: 'The truth, and nothing but the truth, about "DB": "We return soldiers, not broken men, to the outside world."' The report was clearly an important story for *Paratus* – it had been produced 'with the assistance of Brig P.W. van der Westhuizen . . . Officer Commanding Northern Transvaal Command'. Van der Westhuizen became one of the most mysterious and powerful intelligence men in South African history: he would serve from 15 June 1978 until 30 June 1985 as Chief of Staff Intelligence (CSI) in the Military Intelligence Division (MID – see page 154). Reports on the detention barracks were not a regular feature of *Paratus*'s journalism. Three decades later, the reporter suggests that 'it was a rather clumsy attempt at some form of glastnost [sic] by the military authorities to show a degree of *faux* openness' but it seems equally possible that something must have happened at Vooktrekkerhoogte that required the ameliorating effect of military propaganda.

The young 'liberal' had a second adventure in July 1976 when, according to a curriculum vitae published a few years later in *Wits Student*, he 'accompanied SAS [South African Ship] President Kruger to American Bi-Centennial'. He did not report for *Paratus* on this intriguing visit by the South African Navy to the United States but apparently 'provided a colour picture for the cover' of the magazine. It would seem likely that at such a sensitive time, a few weeks after the outbreak of the Soweto uprising, the personnel on this trip would have been closely vetted by both the MID and the dominant Department of Information but the military journalist recalls that 'although every officer wanted to go . . . there was only room on the ship for a rating and the editor . . . deemed me to be the best qualified photo journalist for the mission . . . I was chosen with about 24 hours to go'. In November 1976, the budding reporter travelled to Umtata to file a story for *Paratus* on the SADF's role in the 'independence' of the Transkei.[3] South Africa's eagerness to win international acceptance for the 'grand apartheid' policy of establishing independent homelands for Africans within the borders of the country meant that all correspondents were closely monitored by the Secretary for Information Eschel Rhoodie (see page 95). Richard West informed readers of the *Spectator* that journalists who covered the Transkeian 'independence' were 'offered . . . a first class return ticket and some £1,000 in cash for expenses'. Our young friend responds bluntly: 'I received absolutely no increment to go to the Transkei and spent the independence celebrations in a leaking tent.'[4]

While it is possible that each one of these intelligence 'connections' was an accident, those who recall the intense struggle between the Information Department, which was closely linked to the Bureau for State Security, and the MID in the mid-1970s are well aware of the pivotal role that propaganda played in the battle for influence both inside South Africa and overseas. It seems surprising that 'a committed and lifelong champion of liberal democracy . . . [whose] first job was as an organiser for the Progressive party when he was just eighteen' could have casually found himself in such a post at such a time. Indeed, *Paratus* had clearly experienced difficulties in the past; the publication carried a disclaimer on its contents page declaring that 'opinions expressed in articles are not necessarily those of the Defence Staff Council'.[5] Our nineteen-year-old propagandist's name? Tony Leon, the leader of South Africa's Democratic Party (DP) since 1994 and the Leader of the Opposition, Democratic Alliance (DA), since 1999 Leon refutes any suggestion that he could have been compromised during his tenure at *Paratus* and states that he never met van der Westhuizen or Eschel Rhoodie. He is, however, eager to name 'the scholars and exemplars of political correctness in South Africa today who did service in *Paratus* . . . Hugo Cassirer, the son of Nadine Gordimer, or Shaun Johnson, who became Chief Executive of Independent Newspapers and now runs the Mandela Rhodes Trust, or Alan Dunn, currently editor of the *Sunday Tribune* in Durban or Conrad Burke, a very senior journalist at the [South African Broadcasting Corporation]'. Sixteen years after his *Paratus* adventure, Tony Leon, then a freshman MP, suggested a merger between F.W. de Klerk's National Party and the DP. De Klerk's successor, Marthinus van Schalkwyk, whose nickname 'kortbroek' (shortpants) gives some indication of his lack of political gravitas, eventually led the New National Party (NNP) into alliance with the DP in 2000. The *Mail & Guardian* had revealed three years earlier that van Schalkwyk had been 'a paid agent of military intelligence'. The NNP–DP alliance collapsed in 2002 and the NNP was swallowed by the African National Congress (ANC) in 2004.[6]

I started the research for this book in 1999 and on numerous occasions I have wondered why I wanted to write a study of the South African secret services. After all, I am not particularly fascinated by soldiers, policemen or spies. In fact, I have found the chapters in this book which record the appalling brutality and cruelty of the apartheid state the most difficult and uncomfortable to write. I became interested in South African intelligence in the mid-1990s when I was researching and writing a doctoral thesis on the British and American media coverage of South Africa in the 1970s.[7] As I read through the press reports on South Africa for that decade, a task that took more than a year, I stumbled across numerous stories that had run up against South Africa's stringent press censorship laws. Sometimes, these stories were picked up and developed by the foreign press, more often than not they were just left alone: a first draft of history grown brittle with time. In the mid-1990s, I interviewed more than 150 journalists, propagandists and anti-apartheid campaigners and discovered in the process, especially among the reporters, a forgotten history of half-stories, clues, strange happenings and late-night exaggerated fables. Surprisingly often, these fragments of a lost discourse filled gaps in the historical record. The most interesting and difficult to confirm were the intelligence stories.

Back in 1999, intelligence as a popular subject had slipped off the agenda. The main debates were about the encroaching privatisation of the intelligence capacity and the importance of economic intelligence. Who would have imagined that within six years debates about military intelligence (on Iraq), police intelligence (on terrorists) and national intelligence (on al-Qaeda) would have become ubiquitous? One of the most important lessons that we have learned from the war in Iraq and the hunt for weapons of mass destruction is how little American and British foreign intelligence services actually know about countries in the developing world. For many people, it is not a reassuring feeling. A former CIA officer, 'Edward G. Shirley', reported in the *Atlantic Monthly* in February 1998:

> The sad truth about the CIA . . . is that the DO [Directorate of Operations] has for years been running an espionage charade in most countries, deceiving itself and others about the value of its recruited agents and intelligence production. The ugliest DO secret is how the clandestine service encourages decent case officers, gradually and naturally, to evolve into liars about their contribution to America's security. By 1985 . . . the vast majority of the

CIA's foreign agents were mediocre assets at best, put on the payroll because case officers needed high recruitment numbers to get promoted. Long before the Soviet Union collapsed, recruitment and intelligence fraud – the natural product of an insular spy world – had stripped the DO of its integrity and its competence.[8]

The situation is not dramatically different in the United Kingdom. The former British Ambassador to Brazil, Sir Peter Heap, wrote in the *Guardian* in October 2003: 'the whole system of intelligence-gathering is all too often prone to producing inadequate, unreliable and distorted assessments, often at considerable cost'. Nor were the Secret Intelligence Service (SIS) officials particularly discreet, in Heap's experience: 'it normally only took the local British community a few weeks to spot them'. But the most significant problem that Heap raised was the quality of intelligence 'contacts' and sources: 'The role of MI6 officers was to develop [local] contacts . . . who would feed them information. This intelligence was usually paid for in cash . . . MI6 officers also had an incentive to play up the importance or reliability of the sources on which they based their dispatches.' Welcome to the world of secret intelligence, where there is little accountability, rampant hyperbole and incompetence, and information is gathered by paying sources. As former CIA chief William Colby said: 'Intelligence is too damn important and too damn dangerous to be left to the spies, or . . . the government.'[9]

Commercial books on intelligence tend to conform to a series of rather overwrought clichés. The reason for this, John Keegan has succinctly explained, is 'that the public collude . . . the fiction of intelligence, beginning with Childers and Buchan, reaching its apogee in our age with the works of Ian Fleming and John le Carré, has worked so powerfully on the Western imagination that many of its readers, including presidents and prime ministers, have been brought to believe that intelligence solves everything'. The growing academic literature on intelligence is, by its nature, preoccupied with minor episodes in a shadow history; studied in isolation these moments don't seem to connect with the world as we know it. Michael Herman, a former intelligence official who is also a brilliant analyst of intelligence, suggested in 2004 that intelligence's central function during the twentieth century 'has been characterised as "telling truth to power". The idea of "truth" in any absolute sense is open to argument, but crediting intelligence with a professional ethos of *truthfulness* – or at least attempting it – is less controversial.'[10] That sounds acceptable as a theoretical debate in a democratic society, but how would such an 'idea of truth' work in a country like apartheid South Africa, where an entire political philosophy and intelligence culture was based on a 'lie': that people of different races cannot coexist in relative peace and harmony?

There is a substantial gap in the literature, both academic and commercial, on intelligence in Latin American, African and Asian countries. There is no standard work on South African intelligence that the reader can turn to for basic factual details. In Britain, most journalists continued calling the National Intelligence Service (NIS) 'BOSS' years after the name had changed. Few reporters had any idea of the difference between police, civilian or military intelligence. Without understanding the structures within which intelligence power operated, we don't have the slightest hope of avoiding the mistakes and the abuses that have despoiled the past. In the late 1990s, South Africa underwent an extended experiment in 'talking truth to itself': the Truth and Reconciliation Commission, for all its failings, impressively resisted apartheid's dying attempt to erase all evidence of its existence. But time, as well as being a great healer, is a destroyer of memory and we are beginning to forget the neo-colonial horrors of apartheid. As early as June 1997, R.W. Johnson stated in *Prospect* that 'apartheid was . . . a relatively mild historical experience'.[11] In contemporary South Africa, many South Africans feel little responsibility for the past, and yet the history continues to influence the present.

One of the legacies of apartheid is that a stable 'South African' identity is still a long way off. No international company, non-governmental organisation, academic institution or, indeed, political party could hope to understand all of South Africa's innumerable communities. And within each community there are secretive networks: originally formed either to resist apartheid or to benefit from it. Between the 1960s and the 1980s, the only way that the government could hope to retain control of such a disparate society was to flood the land with spies. These problems were magnified in the wider southern African region. On 18 May 1988, as the certainty of negotiation began to sink in, South Africa's Minister of Defence, General Magnus Malan, informed the South African parliament:

> Southern Africa has become a swamp of international agents from Western and communist secret services. It is a grey world about which John Citizen only hears – a world with its own rules and morality. South Africa is, because of its safety needs, also necessarily involved in this grey world. But you must not expect the government to talk publicly about these matters. It would endanger people's lives. Our whole information flow depends on people who are prepared to work with us.[12]

6

This book is by no means the final word on the subject of South Africa's secret services. There will hopefully be many further studies which will examine individual aspects of intelligence history in much greater detail. I have attempted to avoid the macho *Boy's Own* tales of espionage operations in favour of tracking the residual traces of intelligence activity wherever they may lead. My primary interest has been the collision of intelligence and politics, a process which reached its climax in the historic negotiations between the NIS and Nelson Mandela and, later, the exiled ANC. But I have also re-examined a series of extraordinary intelligence-related murders which remain unsolved to the present day. South Africa's intelligence agencies have led me, in my studies of the 1970s, to the Republic's byzantine propaganda operations, and in looking at the 1980s I have followed the connections to the nuclear, chemical and arms sales networks. Throughout, I have employed the available information on the British and American intelligence relationship with South Africa to shine a light on domestic events. Rather than make insupportable leaps to *prove* the unprovable, I have laid out the evidence like a complicated jigsaw puzzle. In 2004 Stephen Ellis stated, correctly, in the *Journal of Modern African Studies* that:

> the most important gap in our historical knowledge of how the apartheid system worked relates to finance. How extensive were the parallel financial systems of the National Party and the Broederbond [the secret Afrikaner establishment network], pioneered in the 1950s by Nico Diederichs, probably the most thorough-going Nazi among all the National Party leaders? How did the Special Defence Account work, the massive slush-fund that was already a major source of illicit funding in the 1970s? What was the role of the Broederbond in the rise of ABSA bank and in the financial machinations of the South African Reserve Bank?[13]

While I haven't answered Ellis's questions – some of which are outside the remit of this study – I have attempted to record the peculiar relationship between South African intelligence and free-market economics. Apartheid South Africa was an isolated bubble which merged aspects of a dying colonial society with features of a vibrant frontier economy; the new South Africa is a 'portal' between worlds, where extreme violence and organised crime collide with vast disparities of wealth to create a science-fiction vision of a dystopic future. Espionage, however incoherent and dishonest, is part of the glue that has held apartheid and post-apartheid society together.

I

Republican Intelligence

'The thing I really wished to see you about, Castle, was, a visit we are going to have in a few weeks' time from a certain Mr Cornelius Muller, one of the head boys in BOSS . . . We are going to let him see some of the material you deal with. Of course, only enough to establish the fact that we *are* cooperating – in a sort of way.'

. . . 'Why do we have to show him anything, sir?'

'Have you ever wondered, Castle, what would happen to the West if the South African gold mines were closed by a racial war? And a losing war perhaps, as in Vietnam. Before the politicians have agreed on a substitute for gold. Russia as the chief source. It would be a bit more complicated than the petrol crisis. And the diamond mines . . . De Beers are more important than General Motors. Diamonds don't age like cars. There are even more serious aspects than gold and diamonds, there's uranium. I don't think you've been told yet of a secret White House paper on an operation they call Uncle Remus.'

'No. There have been rumours . . .'

'Like it or not, we and South Africa and the States are all partners in Uncle Remus. And that means we have to be pleasant to Mr Muller . . . I don't like the idea of Uncle Remus any more than you do. It's what the politicians call a realistic policy, and realism never got anyone very far in the kind of Africa I used to know. My Africa was a sentimental Africa. I really loved Africa, Castle. The Chinese don't, nor do the Russians nor the Americans – but we have to go with the White House and Uncle Remus and Mr Muller. How easy it was in the old days when we dealt with chiefs and witch doctors and bush schools and devils and rain queens. My Africa was still a little like the Africa of Rider Haggard. It wasn't a bad place . . . Oh well, do your best with Muller. He's the personal representative of the big BOSS himself.'

Graham Greene, *The Human Factor*, 1978[1]

The Birth of Apartheid Intelligence

A PARTHEID INTELLIGENCE IN South Africa, like the Greek goddess Athene, had only one parent: Great Britain. On three occasions in 1948 and 1949, the British intelligence Security Liaison Officer (SLO) for Central Africa visited South Africa, where he held meetings with General Palmer (the Commissioner of Police), Major du Plooy (head of the Special Branch), Frans Erasmus (the Minister of Defence) and the British High Commissioner, Sir Evelyn Baring. The SLO reported to London, after his second visit, that 'the South African Police Special Branch did not appear as yet qualified or equipped for tackling security work'. In October 1949, British Prime Minister Clement Attlee wrote to Dr D.F. Malan, the Afrikaner Nationalist Premier:

> I have more recently been turning over in my mind the whole question of maintaining security in the face of the growing and worldwide Communist threat . . . it seems to me that it would be to our mutual advantage if I were to ask Sir Percy Sillitoe, Director-General of our Security Service, to pay a short visit to South Africa to have discussions with your officers . . . I should add, of course, that in the event of your agreeing, we should carefully avoid giving any publicity to it, and I assume this would be your wish also.[2]

Sir Percy Sillitoe, who had started his career in the British South Africa Police (BSAP) of Southern Rhodesia, explained in a letter to 10 Downing Street that his trip should be presented to the South Africans as an opportunity 'to study the experience of the Union authorities in developing an intelligence organisation to investigate indigenous Communist activity'. The focus of Sillitoe's mission was to win the support of 'Blackie' Swart (Minister of Justice) for two objectives: firstly, that members of the Special Branch of the Union CID 'would be relieved of all duties other than those of counter-espionage'; secondly, that 'one or more of the officers of that Branch would be sent to London for at least six months' training'. Upon his arrival in South Africa, Sillitoe visited Dr Malan, who listened with interest to reports of counter-espionage in Britain. Malan 'was friendly, gave expression to his hatred and fear of Communism, and said that the Union Government were anxious to co-operate with the United Kingdom authorities . . . Dr. Malan was clearly impressed, showed no signs of suspicion, made, as usual, sensible comments and appeared anxious to co-operate.'[3]

Following extensive consultations with leaders of the nascent security establishment, Sillitoe wrote to Swart: 'I have found myself in cordial agreement with the South African Police authorities.' He added three recommendations: 'that special attention be paid to the recruitment and training of personnel . . . [that the South African authorities agree to] the loan of an officer from my Service for a limited period for the purpose of lecturing and advising the reorganised Special Branch on technical security matters . . . that the reorganised Special Branch should be given special financial support and should be provided . . . with facilities for the interception of communications for counter espionage and security purposes'. Sir Evelyn Baring reported that, when Sillitoe handed over the document, he 'assured the Minister that it represented no attempt on the part of anyone from the United Kingdom to interfere in domestic affairs in South Africa'. Swart accepted a number of Sillitoe's proposals but demonstrated some reluctance to the idea of committing himself to the posting of a British intelligence instructor in the Union. On the question of funding, Sillitoe explained how these matters were handled in Britain:

> Sir Percy told him that money for the Security Service was provided from the Security Service Vote; that the Prime Minister was responsible for this Vote; and that in the House [of Commons] he refused, in the national interest, to answer questions concerning its use . . . Within the Department of Justice Vote [in South Africa] there was a heading 'Special Services'. Money voted for this head could be increased to meet increased expenditure following reorganisation of the Special Branch. The result would be that inside an open vote there would be a smaller secret vote.[4]

This model is very similar to the method by which money would be supplied for the funding of Connie Mulder's and Eschel Rhoodie's Information Department Secret Projects in the 1970s (see page 97). Two weeks later, having visited east and central Africa, Sillitoe paid a final visit to Swart. They discussed prospective legislation designed to ban the Communist Party of South Africa. Sillitoe suggested 'that this would be a mistake, unless the South African Police could assure [Swart] that they knew all the leaders and would be in a position to seize them, their papers and their funds before any such declaration were made'. Sillitoe agreed to Swart's request that South Africa be kept informed of the security situation in Britain's African territories. Dr Malan appears to have been delighted with the visit of Sir Percy Sillitoe to South Africa. He wrote to Clement Attlee on 31 December 1949: 'I should like you to know how useful, I believe, his visit has been and to thank you for having made his valuable advice and assistance available to us.'[5]

In essence, the British had achieved their aim, which was to exert influence over the Nationalist government through the guise of offering the hand of friendship. Attlee, Sillitoe, Baring and others were engaged in *Realpolitik*: by assisting the new South African government during the early stages of its administration, they could mould the new security structures and influence the development of policy. Beneath the surface of the pleasantries, a complicated display of 'carrot and stick' was taking place: South Africa was being offered access to the intelligence secrets of the Anglo American alliance in exchange for disciplined anti-communism. The 'stick' was the threat of isolation and exclusion. All of this was made clear in a crucial document composed by the British Security Service and dated 14 November 1949:

> Political considerations will almost certainly enter into the build-up of a Security Service organisation in the Union, and it may be too much to hope that such a Department will be able to remain immune from political influences in its subsequent activities. The improper uses to which a Security Service might be put by the Nationalists might well include its employment against the Parliamentary Opposition and against those members of the British community out of sympathy with the Nationalist political programme. It would certainly be used to keep down the black races. In these circumstances, the part that might be played by the Director-General in establishing any form of security organisation in the Union (more particularly if separate from that of the Police) might therefore lay him open to the criticism that he had assisted the Boer Nationalists in implementing their extremist political programme by actively helping in the creation of a Gestapo. It has, however, to be considered whether the above risks are outweighed by wider considerations of Imperial strategy and defence planning. Is it more important that South Africa, whatever its internal political complexion and Republican ambitions, shall be rendered so secure as to allow it to take its proper place in Commonwealth councils and to receive those secrets of American and/or Anglo-American origin which are so vital to that full cooperation?[6]

Despite the wishes of Clement Attlee, Sir Percy Sillitoe's visit to South Africa did attract attention. Anti-apartheid activist Mary Benson later recalled that 'The Minister of Justice . . . announced he was studying the natives' speeches and that, in company with Sir Percy Sillitoe . . . he was going into the question of the growth of communism. Africans saw Sillitoe's presence as one more act of collaboration between the British Government and the Nationalists.' South Africa attended the biannual Commonwealth

Security Conferences from 1949. The British Home Secretary David Maxwell-Fyfe drew Prime Minister Winston Churchill's attention to the fact that the 1951 Conference had facilitated 'the establishment of collaboration and exchange of security information between such incompatible bedfellows as the Union of South Africa, India and Pakistan'.[7] In 1963, when Hendrik van den Bergh created South Africa's Republican Intelligence (RI), he used as one of his models 'a lengthy memorandum gathering dust in Security Police files . . . which included many novel suggestions. One of these was that liberal and left-wing journalists be recruited as secret agents.' The author of the memorandum was Sir Percy Sillitoe.[8]

Sillitoe retired from MI5 in 1953 and purchased a sweet shop in Eastbourne. Six months later, he returned to South Africa to establish the International Diamond Security Organisation (IDSO), investigating international diamond smuggling for Anglo American–De Beers. With the help of a number of former MI5 agents and Fred Kamil (see page 68), Sillitoe stemmed the flow of smuggled diamonds from Sierra Leone. Within three years, his work was done, IDSO was disbanded 'and the Oppenheimer empire set up its own corporate security system'.[9] Sillitoe's exploits were later trumpeted by Ian Fleming in his only non-fiction book, *The Diamond Smugglers*; the spy chief had already had a 'walk-on-part' in Fleming's fictional James Bond story, *Diamonds are Forever*.[10]

Sir Percy Sillitoe noted in his anodyne autobiography *Cloak Without Dagger*, published in 1955, the stringent security including X-rays to which African miners were submitted and the relatively slack examination to which 'European workers' were subject: 'Diamonds still disappear from the South African mines . . . there seems to me to be little doubt that a few Europeans are themselves guilty of theft.' A.W. Cockerill reported in his biography of Sillitoe that the ageing spy chief had been led to believe 'that a Communist-directed diamond-smuggling ring was working in the west on an international scale; its agents, operating from a number of European capitals, were directing the flow of illicit diamonds from the . . . mines . . . to Communist bloc industrial centres . . . Sillitoe's job was to set up an organisation to counteract the ring's operations.' Sillitoe rapidly recruited a number of former colleagues, developed a productive working relationship with Interpol and the police forces of numerous European and African countries and established an African headquarters in Johannesburg. In addition, 'ample funds were made available to recruit local help and to pay informers in a bid to gather diamond intelligence information'. Sillitoe had effectively given De Beers and Anglo American a crash course in contemporary intelligence-gathering.

As time passed, it became clear to Sillitoe, according to Cockerill, 'that there was no evidence of an "international diamond-smuggling ring" – unless one considers those people in Sierra Leone and Liberia exercising their free-enterprise rights . . . Knowing that there was no Communist intrigue, he *must* have reached the conclusion that the organisation he set up was an instrument to serve strictly commercial ends [original emphasis]'.[11] Sillitoe, and by extension British intelligence, had been 'duped' by Sir Ernest Oppenheimer, the mining magnate, who controlled Anglo American and De Beers as his private kingdom. Sillitoe's deputy in IDSO was a former MI5 officer, John Collard; MI5 (the Security Service) was responsible for domestic and colonial/Commonwealth intelligence. It was Collard, in the guise of 'John Blaize', who assisted Ian Fleming with *The Diamond Smugglers*. After the IDSO experience, Sillitoe returned to Eastbourne and Collard abandoned intelligence and became a solicitor. One of Collard's final statements in Fleming's book was 'I'm sick of crooks and sick of spying on them. All I want is a nice quiet job as a country lawyer . . . or some other job where I can clear all this muck out of my mind.'[12]

On 21 March 1960, the South African Police (SAP) killed sixty-seven African protesters; the incident became known as the 'Sharpeville massacre'. The international response was immediate. The Security Council of the United Nations condemned the slaughter, the US State Department 'deplored' the violence of the apartheid government, the South African stock market collapsed and white South Africans feared that revolution was at hand. Richard Dimbleby described the slaughter on the BBC television programme *Panorama* by drawing comparisons with 'Guernica and Lidice, Belsen and Hola and Little Rock'. As Anthony Sampson, the British journalist and author who had edited *Drum* magazine in the early 1950s and was close to ANC politicians, recalled, 'for ten days after Sharpeville, the iron structure of apartheid seemed to be crumbling', but it turned out to be 'the revolution that wasn't'.[13] On 9 April, Prime Minister Hendrik Verwoerd was shot and wounded by a white farmer, David Beresford Pratt, at the Rand Easter Show, an agricultural convention in Johannesburg. The leading ideologue of apartheid recovered quickly and Pratt was declared insane. Pratt's suicide, eighteen months later, was 'freakish . . . [He] tied two sheets to posts of his bed, inserted his head and then somersaulted over and over again until he managed to strangle himself.'[14]

Seven years earlier, Sir Percy Sillitoe had attempted to recruit MI5's SLO Central Africa, Bob de Quehen, for IDSO. De Quehen turned the offer down because he was negotiating the establishment of the Federal Intelligence and Security Bureau (FISB), the Central African Federation's intelligence structure. (The Central African Federation, which survived from 1953 to 1963, consisted of Northern Rhodesia (Zambia), Southern Rhodesia and Nyasaland (Malawi).) In 1956, de Quehen left MI5 to become the first director of FISB. Dr Philip Murphy, a specialist on colonial intelligence, has unearthed a report from de Quehen to Sir Roy Welensky, the Prime Minister of the Federation, dated 30 April 1960, which captures something of the chaos in post-Sharpeville South Africa.

> De Quehen claimed to have detected a new mood in Pretoria when . . . he met with Colonel Prinsloo, head of the South African special branch ('always a good friend of mine') . . . Prinsloo, claimed de Quehen, was adamant that the Rhodesians 'should stand firm and come along with the Union. To do this, we should think of a firm line across Africa to include Mozambique and Angola, the Federation and the Union of SA. Then he said the Union and the Federation could jointly withstand and defy both the USSR and the USA – or as he expressed it, "we can save ourselves."' De Quehen had been invited to Pretoria to assist special branch in the interrogation of 'some hardcore Communists prominent in recent disturbances'. It was in the course of this visit that Prinsloo made what de Quehen described as 'a remarkable offer of closer co-operation': 'Roughly what he said was this: "I would be quite willing to let you Bob run your agents in South Africa if you declare them to me and let me handle them. I would be prepared to send my agents to the Federation or to other parts of Africa providing you handle them."' The offer was made, on de Quehen's own admission, by a 'quite emotional' Prinsloo after 'a good deal of brandy'.

In August 1962, de Quehen learned that the South Africans 'had plans to establish a central intelligence and security organization, answerable directly to the Prime Minister'. FISB had been 'promised access to long-range South African intelligence' and de Quehen had 'arranged to hold monthly meetings with Brigadier Retief, the officer responsible for creating the new organization'.[15]

During the interim, South Africa's relations with Britain had changed dramatically. In October 1960, South Africa held an all-white referendum on whether the country should become a republic (a long-standing Afrikaner nationalist ambition). From 1910, the Union of South Africa had been a self-governing 'Dominion' within the British Empire, and later within the Commonwealth of Nations. After securing the vote, South Africa was forced to leave the Commonwealth in March 1961. Before the vote to become a republic, South Africa had been the responsibility of Britain's Dominions Office (DO); after the departure from the Commonwealth, the Foreign Office assumed responsibility. In culture, the Dominions and Foreign Offices were very different. The DO behaved as if South Africa were part of the British 'family of nations'. Its general attitude was innocuous and unassuming; British civil servants, for example, did not discuss politics with Africans for fear of offending the Nationalist government. In contrast, the Foreign Office treated the Republic as if it was a foreign land, albeit a country with which Britain had a long history and a substantial trade and which contained many English people. Anthony Verrier records that March 1961 'seemed to mark a more radical process, an agonising reappraisal for Britain of where its true interests lay . . . but the economic realities which also governed British policy in Africa were unchanged'. In June 1961, the British Ambassador to South Africa, Sir John Maud, signalled to diplomats that they 'should "reinsure" against the possibility of a future black government by making discreet contacts with black politicians'.[16]

There was a second significant but unpublicised handover in 1961: MI5, which had previously conducted intelligence liaison with South Africa, handed responsibility for the new Republic to MI6, or Secret Intelligence Service (the British intelligence agency tasked with the coverage of foreign countries). Documents released at the British Public Record Office reveal that MI5 had been monitoring the radical Anglican priest Michael Scott since 'the early 1930s when, according to the files, his "contacts with the [Communist] Party were certainly close". MI5 kept tags on him, liaising with the South African security service 20 years later even though by then he had distanced himself from the Party.' Mary Benson, who worked with Scott for seven years, later recalled that Scott's followers 'suspected me of being a spy. An energetic, highly qualified secretary offering to work without pay and a South African at that!'[17] There would always be at best a cautious wariness, at worst an aggressive paranoia, among the anti-apartheid campaigners in Britain on the subject of South African and British spying. As the evidence slowly emerges from the intelligence archives, the fears of activists are being justified. The tension between the domestic anti-communist agenda of the British Special Branch and MI5 and the more pragmatic international concerns of MI6 exerted a direct influence on South African intelligence activity.

As we have seen with Sir Percy Sillitoe and his early policing career in the BSAP, the 'kith and kin' connection played an important role in confusing the intelligence relationship with South Africa. Stella Rimington, who joined MI5 in 1969, recalled that 'many of the men had come in to MI5 from a first career in the Colonial Service'. Consider, for example, the case of Julian Faux, who served as deputy Director-General of MI5 from 1988 to 1993. Born and educated in South Africa, after Cambridge he joined the Colonial Service and worked for nine years in Swaziland as a district commissioner. In 1968, on the eve of Swaziland's independence, he joined MI5 in London. Both the obituaries, obviously written by the same hand, note that he didn't return to South Africa 'because of his hatred of apartheid'. After his retirement, as the *Daily Telegraph* reports, 'he undertook security consultancy work, mainly in Commonwealth countries. He was never happier than on safari in Africa.'[18] The DO and MI5 in South Africa had not concerned themselves with African politicians because they remained preoccupied with the English–Afrikaner tension which had dominated South African politics since the Anglo-Boer War. In the late 1940s and 1950s, they depended on what Geoffrey Berridge has described as 'the ethnic agent in place . . . senior English-speaking public servants, the vast majority of whom were allowed to retain their posts by the new Malan government'. This was obviously a problem for the new administration, as demonstrated by the fact that within weeks of the National Party's victory in the 1948 election, Colonel C.B. Powell, the English-speaking Director of Military intelligence, 'had been dismissed and his files raided by the CID'. In 1952, British spying was operational, as Berridge observed, noting the War Office's 'possession of an apparently "filched" copy of South Africa's draft Defence Estimates'. But perhaps Britain's closest relationship was with English-speaking South African diplomats, a number of whom went on to become ambassadors in the 1970s.[19]

Another theme of the modern intelligence story of South Africa is the constant struggle for influence between the British and American intelligence agencies. Thomas Borstelmann cites a July 1948 State Department Office of Intelligence Research report which 'warned that "the traditions of the Afrikaans front are completely alien to Anglo American democracy". . . Fortunately, concluded this generally grim intelligence analysis, South Africa's cooling military relationship with Britain would draw it closer to the United States.' In the late 1940s and 1950s, the primary American concern in South Africa was minerals, especially uranium which was needed for nuclear weapons. The Cold War was the dominant context within which CIA and State Department reports should be read; there was little of the anxious post-colonial uncertainty and hypocrisy which coloured British diplomatic reports of the period. In one important respect, the British and American intelligence agencies were very similar: they seemed to have had very little contact with Africans. Joseph Sweeney of the US Embassy in the early 1950s was almost alone in being concerned at the lack of 'effective intelligence about African political organisations and their plans'. In October 1951, he offered the State Department the following perceptive comment: 'It is a reflection on the white South African approach to the Native problem that the simple task of finding out what the Native thinks politically should be such a mystery and require such a secretive approach.'[20]

Mandela's Arrest and the Creation of Republican Intelligence

White anxiety and apprehension at developments within African political organisations inspired the growth of South African intelligence organisation in the early 1960s. During the 1950s, the oldest African political structure, the ANC, under the influence of a group of talented young politicians, Walter Sisulu, Oliver Tambo and Nelson Mandela, had launched the Defiance Campaign (1952) and the Freedom Charter (1955) and had been subjected to the eventually futile Treason trial (1956–61). In 1959, a number of 'Africanist' ANC activists, under the leadership of Robert Sobukwe, had broken with the party over the issues of 'communism' and perceived white dominance, to create the Pan Africanist Congress (PAC). The killing at Sharpeville, and the banning of the ANC and PAC that followed, intensified the South African government's determination to arrest those leaders of the African political parties who had not fled into exile. Meanwhile, the apartheid ideologues persisted with the project of 'grand apartheid' which was designed to establish 'bantustans', later known as 'independent homelands', to which all Africans would technically be attached. Eventually, the grand apartheid plan aimed to remove all Africans, except migrant 'guest' workers, from the Republic.

On 5 August 1962, Nelson Mandela was arrested near the town of Howick in Natal. Mandela was disguised as a chauffeur but he later told his biographer, Fatima Meer, that the policeman saw through the disguise: 'He said he knew that I was Nelson Mandela and he had a warrant for my arrest.'[21] Twenty-four years later, the Johannesburg *Star* reported that 'a retired senior police officer . . . in Paris' had claimed that 'Mandela was "betrayed" by an American diplomat at the United States Consulate in Durban . . . the CIA operative for that region.' Before his departure from

South Africa, the unnamed spy attended a dinner party at mercenary Colonel Mike Hoare's apartment where, 'under the influence of drink', he revealed his role in Mandela's arrest. The spy had been trusted by the ANC and a rendezvous with Mandela had been arranged. At the same time, the CIA man had been 'anxious to supply his government with Pretoria's bantustan plans, and the information he needed was available from Colonel Bester, then head of the Natal police. In exchange for the information, he told Colonel Bester the date, time and route Mandela would be taking.' A further report named Donald Rickard as the CIA officer.[22]

In June 1990, on the eve of Mandela's first visit to the United States, the *Atlanta Journal-Constitution* revived the story: a former employee of the CIA had revealed that within hours of Mandela's arrest, 'Paul Eckel, then a senior CIA operative, walked into his office and said approximately these words: "We have turned Mandela over to the South African security branch. We gave them every detail, what he would be wearing, the time of day, just where he would be. They have picked him up. It is one of our greatest coups." ' The CIA source also said that he had later asked Eckel how the CIA had known Mandela's whereabouts. 'He remembers Mr Eckel telling him that the information had come from a paid CIA inform-ant in South Africa who had been taught to communicate with his CIA superiors there through an elaborate series of indirect contacts known as "cutouts".' Former South African spy Gerard Ludi declared that the agent who informed on Mandela 'provided his American case officer with an ongoing account of ANC activities . . . the case officer was [Ludi's] long-time friend Millard Shirley, whom he identified as the CIA's chief under-cover agent in southern Africa. "Millard was very proud of that operation." ' Interviews conducted by the *Atlanta Journal-Constitution* reporters led the paper to conclude that by 1962 a covert CIA branch in Johannesburg 'devoted more money and expertise to penetrating the ANC than did the fledgling intelligence service of the South African government'.[23]

In *Mandela: The Authorised Biography* (1999), for which I was the researcher, Anthony Sampson commented that the CIA theory 'was cred-ible . . . but . . . cannot be substantiated'. He acknowledged that the car which Mandela was driving was conspicuous; that Mandela had been 'care-less' in Natal (reckless would have been more accurate); and that 'the South Africans could have tracked Mandela through Afrikaner employees in the Bechuanaland police'. The Bechuanaland detail arose when documents, which had been held back under the thirty-year rule and then released at the Public Record Office in London, showed that in 1962 there was extensive cross-border security co-operation regarding the ANC. In addition, the Bechuanaland police force employed a significant number of Afrikaners, who lived in the Republic. In 1997, I spoke with Donald Rickard and he said that we would be 'making a mistake' if we named him as 'the man who shopped Mandela'.[24] Millard Shirley was certainly an American spy, although a very peculiar one. Sampson remembered him from the mid-1950s: 'an engaging and gregarious American who was ostensibly writing a book ("My Mother was a Missionary") but was always turning up at ANC functions'. Shirley worked with Gerard Ludi throughout the 1970s and, after Ludi retired from the South African intelligence service, they went into business as partners. Shirley was a heavy drinker and, with his wife, died in an automobile accident in Swaziland in the 1980s.[25]

Paul Eckel died in 1986, but a DO report dated January 1959 recounts 'two long and interesting chats over nightcaps' that T.W. Aston, a British diplomat, had with him, his 'house guest', when Eckel was the First Secretary at the US Embassy. Eckel said that the Americans had:

> all been making considerable efforts to have contact with the Africans and . . . have received a number of deputations in the American Embassy, entertained many Africans in their homes and claimed to have, in the United States Information Office in Johannesburg, the only place where Africans and Europeans are equally welcome and can be seen sitting down together reading literature. I expressed some surprise that the State Department should, as alleged, be expecting the Embassy to pay less attention to its relations to the Government and more attention to its relations with and assistance to the 'opposition' forces . . . All of this was of course said to me in the strictest confidence and on a personal basis by Mr Eckel and we must be careful he does not in any way get to feel that this confidence (and our friendship) has been breached.[26]

If Eckel, the CIA agent, had invested time and anti-communist energy in 'developing' PAC contacts, it is quite possible that he would have felt that the betrayal of Mandela, the militant 'communist', would have served the Cold War interests of the USA. It is clear from the full report of the 'nightcaps' with the British official that Eckel was both indiscreet and keen to trade information. While gathering research for this book I have spoken with many retired Afrikaner intelligence agents and I have been told on a number of occasions that Hendrik van den Bergh, a senior security policeman in 1962, who would later become the head of South African intelligence, privately admitted that Mandela was 'given' to the Security Police by the CIA. Before June 1961, Mandela had not been considered worthy of a British government 'file'; less than three years later, during the Rivonia trial, J.B. Ure of the Information Research Department, the Foreign Office's anti-communist propaganda vehicle, commented on the 'intelligence angle. Mandela's speech contains evidence of the ANC's collaboration with the Communist movement. The extent and nature of this collaboration is of prime interest to our friends (to whom I am copying these minutes).'[27] 'Our friends' was, of course, Foreign Office code for MI6.

In 1970, the Potgieter Commission of Inquiry into State Security, tasked with examining the creation of the Bureau for State Security (BOSS) in 1969, provided further details on the birth of apartheid intelligence. The report noted that although Professor E.G. Malherbe commanded military intelligence during the Second World War, 'for a number of years [after the war] there was no military intelligence section to speak of in South Africa'. In 1960, military intelligence was reactivated under the control of General Bierman and Brigadier Uys. From 1962, the Directorate of Military Intelligence (DMI) was a subsection of the department of the Chief of the Defence Staff. In the domestic sphere, 'up to 1947 there was virtually no internal intelligence service'. In 1947, Major du Plooy visited Scotland Yard in London to 'study the Special Branch'. In the same year, South Africa's first 'Security Police' was established on the British model. Sixteen years later on 14 January 1963, following the arrest of Mandela, Hendrik van den Bergh was appointed 'head of the Security Police with instructions to reorganise the security set up of the country'.[28] In secret, van den Bergh created Republican Intelligence (RI).

The SAP and the South African Security Police/Special Branch (both titles were used to describe the security capacity) had spied on Africans and communists for many years. It was decided that what was needed was an intelligence 'organisation' that could trade information with foreign powers, develop African 'spies' and recruit friendly journalists; in effect, RI was security policing made proactive. Van den Bergh deployed Colonel Att Spengler to recruit young policemen suitable for intelligence work and willing to pretend that they had left the police. Among the RI recruits were Johan Coetzee and Mike Geldenhuys, both of whom would become major players in South Africa's intelligence world. Spengler established 'a private detective agency' in a small suite of offices in Johannesburg's Commissioner Street and filtered his new RI agents into 'work in other front companies, or . . . jobs in both the private and public sectors'. As Terry Bell has pointed out, 'an added attraction of the new service was that it promised to be cost-effective . . . Agents who worked in "outside" jobs were [only paid] a "top-up" fee which made them cheaper to employ.' A training camp was set up on a farm near Pretoria.[29]

Perhaps, the most famous RI agent was Gerard Ludi who, according to legend, infiltrated the South African Communist Party (SACP) and visited the Soviet Union, and whose cover was exposed when the state decided to use him as a witness in the case against SACP leader Bram Fischer. In his book, *Operation Q-018*, Ludi explained that he was politically uncommitted until he read John Stuart Mill's *On Liberty*. Inspired to fight communism, he contacted the police while he was a student at the University of the Witwatersrand in 1960. Spengler and Coetzee encouraged the young Ludi to 'join the Communist Party'. The SACP had been banned since 1950 and used a 'cell structure' to avoid detection. Ludi worked as a journalist and ingratiated himself 'with the editorial staff of [the left-wing] *New Age*'. His book – published in 1969, long after his exposure – describes the ubiquity of multi-racial lovemaking ('crashing the colour line') among the communists, his trip to the Soviet Union (more travelogue than KGB intelligence-training) and his double life as a journalist–spy: 'intelligence work and journalism are similar in many ways.'[30]

Gordon Winter, who was recruited by RI at the same time as Ludi, suggests that the truth was slightly different. Ludi was 'an intense young leftist reporter' who visited Moscow in 1962 as a genuine member of the Congress of Democrats. He joined the SACP in May 1963 and was arrested one month later: 'Ludi . . . agreed to work with RI to save his own skin when the police caught him in bed with an Indian woman.' Winter's version is partly confirmed by Stephen Clingman in his biography of Bram Fischer: 'The Bernsteins [whose daughter Toni travelled to Moscow with Ludi] . . . found him completely convincing: decades later they insisted that either he wasn't originally a spy but had been "turned" by the police, or else that he was the most consummate actor they had ever come across.' Clingman also records that 'letters [Ludi] had written to a woman identified alternately as Malay and Indian were produced in court'. Winter adds, 'the camouflage story that Ludi had been recruited as a spy way back in 1960 was cleverly mounted. This was done for two reasons. It made the Security Branch appear smart and it ensured that Republican Intelligence and its practice of recruiting journalists would not be mentioned in court.'[31]

Despite Ludi's tendency to embroider the facts in his account, certain passages ring true. Republican Intelligence was a secret intelligence structure and there must have been the usual bureaucratic difficulties regarding command and control, promotion, transport and pay. Ludi noted, for example that 'the transfer of several completely inexperienced officers to our units from the CID in 1963 was a mixed blessing. They were completely strange to what was going on and blundered badly sometimes.' On the issue of transport, Ludi announced that after much argument 'they bought an Alfa Romeo sports car for me, but I had to pay all [the] running costs'. It is hard to think of anything that would have attracted more attention; thirty years later, former BOSS agents still remembered Ludi's car. As far as Bram Fischer is concerned, Ludi quoted him as warning the communist cell of which they were both members: 'I have reason to believe that the police now have an intelligence wing organised on the American pattern, and as the FBI does with the [Communist] Party in America, they will plant agents into our organisations.'[32]

Gerard Ludi's appearance in court in 1964 was the first occasion when the South African public 'became aware [of the existence] of a Secret Branch of the South African Police'. The partial admission of active counter-espionage was a significant sacrifice for van den Bergh, but it would prove worth it. Ludi admitted, 'when compared to the infiltration and espionage coups of sophisticated organisations such as the FBI, CIA and MI6, [it] was nothing spectacular. But when you consider the haphazard atmosphere in which it was launched . . . and the incredible blunders that took place . . . it was more than spectacular – it was a miracle.'[33] Gordon Winter, who later 'defected' and produced the first and only book-length exposé of RI and BOSS, was recruited in June 1963. He was introduced to van den Bergh by the Minister of Justice, John Vorster. He was told that one of RI's 'specific aims' was the 'enlisting of journalists as secret agents'. Like Ludi, Winter's first handler was Johan Coetzee and he was given an RI number, RO17 (Ludi's number was apparently RO18). Winter, who had emigrated from Britain to South Africa in 1960, was oblivious to the rights and wrongs of apartheid, but he was hungry for stories and didn't object to trading information for scoops. By his own account, the early work he did for RI involved 'vetting' potential African spies and foreign journalists and keeping an inquisitive eye on his fellow reporters. RI's determination to recruit journalists is confirmed by *Rand Daily Mail* reporter Benjamin Pogrund, who recalled in his memoirs that he had met van den Bergh in January 1963: 'He invited me for lunch, told me that the country was in peril from Communists and that he was recruiting a range of people, including psychologists in universities, to fend off the danger. He offered me a fulltime job. I laughed.'[34]

By 1965, Republican Intelligence, in conjunction with the Security Police, had destroyed organised resistance. The arrest of the leaders of Umkhonto we Sizwe (MK), the ANC's armed wing, in Rivonia, on information supplied by spies, led to life sentences for Walter Sisulu, Govan Mbeki, Ahmed Kathrada and others on Robben Island. Mandela's original five-year sentence was extended to life imprisonment based upon documents seized at Lilliesleaf Farm. It was feared that Mandela and his colleagues might be sentenced to death, but van den Bergh assured British diplomats that that would not be the case. In the Cape, the PAC's 'Poqo' uprising had its back 'broken with the mass arrests of April–June 1963'. The arrest and eventual imprisonment of Bram Fischer represented the symbolic decapitation of the SACP. Liberal and Trotskyist militancy was silenced by the smashing of the African Resistance Movement (ARM) during 'the fourth of July raids' in 1964.[35]

The last gasp of resistance in South Africa was the 'station bomb' on 24 July 1964. John Harris, a believer in non-violent resistance, had telephoned warnings to the police and to the newspapers. The bomb was placed 'in the middle of the concourse' to attract attention. But the warnings were either not heeded or were consciously ignored. Following the explosion which caused the death of an elderly woman and serious injuries to a child, it emerged that the bomb had been hidden under a bench. Van den Bergh's legendary intuition (a writer in the 1970s described it as 'instinct . . . percipience or deduction') led to the arrest of Harris within hours.[36] Harris was brutally beaten by the police in custody: one policeman is said to have 'practised drop-kicks' on Harris's face, breaking his jaw in the process. Van den Bergh later claimed that Harris 'slipped and fell and broke his jaw' because a lightbulb was missing on the stairs of the Security Police headquarters. Following a trial, during which former ARM member John Lloyd gave evidence to Harris's disadvantage, the 'station bomber' was sentenced to death. Harris was hanged on 1 April 1965.[37] Crushing the anti-apartheid resistance confirmed van den Bergh's leadership of the security establishment; the station bomb was used to justify the draconian and repressive legislation previously instituted by the apartheid state.

Dirty Tricks? Charlie Richardson, Verwoerd's Assassination and Yuriy Loginov

One of the strangest associations in the history of South African intelligence was that between the British gangster Charlie Richardson and Hendrik van den Bergh. Richardson was the leader of a gang that challenged the Krays for control of London's criminal underworld in the early 1960s. But, unlike Ron and Reggie Kray, Richardson did not revel in public notoriety; his primary interests were money and power. In August 1964, he flew to Johannesburg to investigate a mining investment deal with Thomas Waldeck. Richardson and Waldeck established a partnership to prospect for minerals in Namaqualand. Less than a year later, Waldeck was murdered. While in South Africa, Richardson had met Gordon Winter and was attracted to Winter's wife, Jean La Grange. At this time, Winter introduced Richardson to Winnie Mandela, on whom he was spying. Meanwhile, Jean La Grange, who was also engaged in spying operations for RI, introduced the gangster to van den Bergh. Richardson and the spy chief developed the traditional, mutually beneficial, criminal–policeman relationship. As Charlie Richardson's biographer Robert Parker explained:

> The General wanted Charlie to rob the various London offices of anti-apartheid organisations [and] . . . he wanted to know if Charlie could get hold of arms . . . [The] arrangement was excellent for both men. For van den Bergh . . . Charlie was a top villain for whom such robberies would be a doddle . . . If Charlie or his men were caught, who would believe it if he claimed he was working for [van den Bergh]? . . . The arrangement was equally valuable to Charlie . . . For him now to be tied in with the top police in South Africa was wonderfully advantageous, especially in the wake of the Waldeck killing. He felt that he could almost have *carte blanche*.[38]

In the UK, Richardson on behalf of van den Bergh contacted a German arms dealer who offered to supply weapons and spare parts for Centurion tanks to the South African state; it is not clear whether the German understood that he would be assisting apartheid South Africa. Richardson's RI handler in London, 'John', wanted the gangster to 'obtain the blueprints of a missile being made at the British Aircraft Corporation factory at Weybridge' or to raid the anti-apartheid campaigner Canon Collins's private papers at Christian Action, but neither task was practicable. Richardson later told Parker that, on the instruction of van den Bergh, he had halted an assassination plot against Dr Hastings

Banda, the Malawian Prime Minister, which was being hatched in the London underworld. In January 1966, a member of the Richardson gang, John Bradbury, was arrested in South Africa and charged with the murder of Waldeck. Gordon Winter was detained at the same time; without his knowledge, his gun had been used for the killing.[39] Winter would later be released without charge and deported to Britain, where he would continue to spy for RI. Richardson believed that his best form of 'insurance' would prove to be more work for RI in London. On 3 March 1966, he stole 'notebooks, files and address cards' from the Anti-Apartheid Movement's office; on 18 March, he raided the Zimbabwe African People's Union (ZAPU) offices, taking 'subscription lists and all written materials and photographs since 1962'; on 28 March, he burgled the offices of Amnesty International, stealing 'files, cheques, address cards and a parcel addressed to ZAPU'. The *Sunday Telegraph* reported eight months later: 'Secret agents are working in London for the Smith regime and the South African police, and are almost certainly responsible for a series of raids which were disclosed last week on the offices of Anti-Apartheid and African freedom movements.'[40]

John Bradbury was found guilty of the murder of Thomas Waldeck and sentenced to death on 3 May 1966. His sentence was commuted to life imprisonment after he confessed that he had been acting under orders from Charlie Richardson; Bradbury also supplied information to the Scotland Yard detectives who were investigating Richardson. On 30 July 1966, the day of the World Cup football final, Charlie Richardson was arrested in London. He was sentenced to twenty-five years' imprisonment following the 'torture trial'; the 'torture' referred to Richardson's favoured method for punishing his underworld victims. The allegation that, on behalf of RI, Richardson had 'bugged' Harold Wilson's private telephone in the 1960s remains unproven.[41]

On 6 September 1966, Prime Minister Hendrik Verwoerd was stabbed to death in the South African parliamentary chamber. His assassin, Demitrios Tsafendas, was a 'Coloured' parliamentary messenger. Stanley Uys, who witnessed the assassination, later recalled, 'Mr Vorster, unable to intervene, seemed curiously detached.' Seconds later, Defence Minister P.W. Botha screamed at Helen Suzman: 'It's you who did this. It's all you liberals. You incite people. Now we will get you. We will get the lot of you.' As Minister of Justice, Vorster was responsible for the investigation into the murder. He told his biographer, John D'Oliveira, 'We were gravely shocked . . . We wanted to know . . . whether the man was mad or whether this was an organised thing, so I sent for the man best qualified to get to the bottom of it quickly. Van den Bergh questioned him for 48 hours and . . . if a man does not break after 48 hours of van den Bergh's questioning, then you know that he doesn't know a thing. Van den Bergh's diagnosis was that it was a one-man job and that Stafendas [sic] was not responsible for his actions.'[42] A number of right-wing (*verkramptes*) Afrikaners believed that the murder was an assassination. Questions were asked about Vorster's press statement, within hours of the killing, that led to the headline 'No sign of assassination plot. This was the work of a lone killer says Vorster'. The Afrikaans-language paper *Beeld* reported that van den Bergh received Tsafendas's Security Police file within minutes of Verwoerd's death. Van den Bergh denied that any such file existed. Right-wingers claimed that there were, in fact, four files on Demitrios Tsafendas.[43]

Verwoerd's death possessed crucial political symbolism. It is difficult to find many former intelligence agents who will defend F.W. de Klerk ('weak'), P.W. Botha ('a thug') or John Vorster ('a drunk'), but if one mentions Verwoerd, their eyes start to twinkle and they all agree that he was a great man *and* that apartheid could have worked if he had lived. No wonder then that conspiracy theories surround the passing of apartheid's blue-eyed visionary. No copies of the speech that Verwoerd was due to make have survived, encouraging the sense that a conspiracy was at work. More than thirty years later, Paul Heylin, the secretary of Verwoerd's secret research committee, told Terry Bell that 'the speech was to have heralded a major departure from orthodox apartheid . . . Verwoerd [had] decided on the model of a federal South Africa, with a non-racial state along the eastern seaboard . . . The interior and the Cape Province would continue to follow the rules of apartheid.'[44]

Gordon Winter, who was the only journalist permitted to interview Tsafendas in prison, adds to the mystery. Winter reports that in 1971 he was told by BOSS agent A.H. Bouwer that David Pratt (who attempted to assassinate Verwoerd in 1960) and Tsafendas had been treated by the same psychiatrist in London in 1959. In 1961, Winter had interviewed Pratt's lover, Doreen Bilson, for the Johannesburg *Sunday Express*. Bilson said that 'after seeing a psychoanalyst in London, David began behaving abnormally; his epileptic fits became more acute. He suddenly decided to enter the political field.' Ten days before the shooting, Pratt had appeared to be in 'some sort of hypnotic trance'. Bouwer was interested in Winter's 1961 story and contacted Pretoria to enquire whether information should be collected on the London-based psychiatrist. He was instructed that no such investigation should be undertaken. The suggestion is that both Pratt and Tsafendas had been 'programmed' to kill Verwoerd. Tsafendas was, according to this interpretation, South Africa's 'Manchurian candidate'.[45]

The capture of KGB spy Yuriy Loginov on 20 July 1967 was a major achievement for the South African security forces, and another example of van den Bergh's detective skills. Barbara Carr published a book on the subject, *Spy in the Sun: The Story of Yuriy Loginov*, in 1969. She stated in a spirit of full disclosure, 'I make no claim to be knowledgeable in Intelligence matters.' Her account of Loginov's arrest by 'the General/The Chief' (van den Bergh) and 'Colonel X' (Mike Geldenhuys) is high comedy. On the way to Pretoria, they stop for a late-afternoon tea: ' "I'm sure you'd like a cup of coffee and some nice sandwiches," said the General.' The description of van den Bergh is also priceless: 'The Chief was six feet four in his socks and built in such perfect proportions that when not standing near another person, he appeared of normal size. At just over fifty, he gave the impression of a much younger man. He was muscular and fit and gave out an air of physical as well as moral strength.' The breakthrough in the interrogation occurred after seven hours, when the General trapped Loginov into admitting he was a Russian spy by throwing a question at him in German; Loginov answered in Russian.[46] Of course, it was all fiction.

In researching his biography of James Jesus Angleton, *Cold Warrior*, published in 1991, Tom Mangold uncovered the truth about Yuriy Loginov. The Russian was, in fact, a double agent: he worked for the CIA as well as the KGB, and the CIA betrayed him to RI. Loginov, who joined the KGB in 1956, had been 'turned' by the CIA in 1961. He was being prepared by the KGB to be an 'illegal' in the United States. Mangold explains that 'Illegals are carefully trained in the traditional black arts of espionage . . . [they] are then given a "legend"— a completely new identity . . . [and] dispatched to the target country, where they become old-fashioned spies.' The trip to South Africa was intended to be the final stage of Loginov's legend. Angleton, the head of the CIA's Counterintelligence Staff, was an undiagnosed paranoid. In 1967, the CIA was subject to one of Angleton's periodic 'mole-hunts'. Angleton decided that Loginov, among others, was what can only be described as a 'triple agent', still working primarily for the KGB. He was therefore 'dirty' and disposable. John Mertz, the CIA station chief in Pretoria, was asked how RI would react. He answered, 'We could get the South Africans to do anything we wanted . . . if they did not get what [was] wanted from Loginov, there wouldn't be much left of him.' The South Africans were not told that Loginov had been a double agent.

Following Loginov's arrest, the press was informed that he had been seen taking photographs of the Grays, Johannesburg's divisional police headquarters. Apparently, van den Bergh dreamed that up 'while shaving'. Barbara Carr was invited to write a book and was provided with 'doctored photocopies of *official* CIA debriefings with Loginov [original emphasis]'. A disinformation campaign was started, supplying false Loginov 'confessions', written by CIA agents, to newspapers around the world. The 'confessions' were a mixture of Loginov's previous debriefings and CIA information on KGB operations in Europe. Mertz worked very closely with van den Bergh on the operation. Indeed, 'the CIA's offices, in the US Embassy, were literally across the central courtyard from the headquarters of [RI–BOSS]'. Mertz added:

> I met with van den Bergh on most days that I ran this covert operation – for about six weeks. The general was so happy with me that he let me use his special back-door entrance to the part of the building where his office was located. It was an entrance no US official had been allowed to use before. We became quite friendly and compared interrogation techniques. He said he had a method of making prisoners stand on bricks while they were questioned. If they fell off, they were ordered back on. He told me he obtained all his confessions that way.[47]

Van den Bergh's 'brick method' failed to work in the Loginov case: after six months held in solitary confinement, the Russian refused to confess to spying. The head of RI had to report to Langley Park that his interrogation had failed. RI could not prove that Loginov was a KGB agent except by revealing the CIA's documents, which would not be valid in a court of law. There was a further problem: RI 'had no Russian speakers in their service'. In April 1968, a CIA Soviet Division team was sent to South Africa to interview Loginov and secure the confession; this also failed. Loginov was becoming a problem and an embarrassment to both RI and the CIA. Angleton's solution to the problem was extraordinarily cruel. Some months earlier, the German foreign intelligence agency, Bundesnachrichtendienst (BND), had enquired whether it might be possible to exchange Loginov for eleven West German agents held by the East Germans. The CIA approved the swap. This would mean handing a double agent back to the Soviet Union to face almost certain death. There would therefore be no need for a court case.

On 12 July 1969, Mike Geldenhuys and Yuriy Loginov were flown to West Germany for the swap. At the Herleshausen border post, Loginov managed to delay for a few hours, but he was in an impossible position. Geldenhuys recalled that one of the BND agents said: 'There's a bit of a drama going on . . . Loginov doesn't want to go back to Moscow. He seems to want to work for us.' Eventually, Loginov was forced to cross the border in the company of KGB officers. Geldenhuys told Mangold that his last words were: 'Give my regards to the General [van den Bergh].' Geldenhuys told the *Cape Times* a variation of this story in 1984 in which Loginov said him: 'I want to say in front of all these people . . . that you have the best intelligence service in the world. I have never seen the likes of it before.' Loginov's fate is unknown. Following Angleton's retirement in 1975, the CIA reviewed the Loginov case. The investigation confirmed that 'Loginov had been a genuine bona fide defector from the KGB . . . Angleton and his staff had forced Loginov back into Soviet hands . . . Loginov's return had been ordered over the objections of South African intelligence officers.' In March 1989, van den Bergh sent a message to Tom Mangold through Mike Geldenhuys: 'Tell anyone who asks that I can't remember about Loginov, and I don't want to remember. Tell them I do not suffer from verbal diarrhoea. We should stay out of this. We have given the facts to Barbara [Carr], and we must stick to them. Whatever anyone else has been told, they've been told nothing by Angleton. He never talked.'[48]

Loginov was not the only 'KGB' agent interrogated by RI–BOSS in the 1960s. In 1968, Bogdan Stashinsky, the fabled KGB assassin whose defection to West Germany in 1961 had led to the Soviet Politburo 'abandon[ing] assassination by the KGB as a normal instrument of policy outside the Soviet bloc', was secretly granted asylum in apartheid South Africa. Mike Geldenhuys (by then the retiring Commissioner of Police) told the *Cape Times* in 1984 that, after Stashinsky had served six years of an eight-year prison sentence in West Germany, the BND contacted RI 'because they were convinced [that South Africa] was the only country where he would be comparatively safe from KGB agents'. Stashinsky underwent 'intensive cosmetic surgery' and was given a new 'family background legend' and identity. Geldenhuys reported that he was best man at

Stashinsky's marriage to 'a girl from Durban'. Apparently, only Vorster, van den Bergh and Geldenhuys knew of the arrangement. But why did RI–BOSS give asylum to a Russian killer? Geldenhuys told the *Cape Times*: 'As a KGB agent who had been awarded the Order of the Red Banner for carrying out . . . political assassinations for the Soviet government, he had been initiated into the closely guarded secrets of the Soviet intelligence service. He was able to supply our intelligence service with a vast amount of invaluable information.'[49]

Western Intelligence Links, 1963–1969

One of the first instructions that Harold Wilson issued upon becoming Prime Minister in October 1964 was that 'all shipment of arms to South Africa should cease forthwith'. This single act earned Wilson the enmity of the apartheid government despite the fact that all existing contracts were honoured. Just over a year later, in November 1965, Rhodesia made its Unilateral Declaration of Independence (UDI). On 21 December, Wilson attacked the Tory right wing over Rhodesia. Quoting Dante, he said, 'The hottest place in hell is reserved for those who are neutral in a moral crisis.' At the Commonwealth Prime Ministers' Conference in Lagos in January 1966 he announced that the 'cumulative effects of the economic and financial sanctions [imposed on Rhodesia] might well bring the rebellion to an end within a matter of weeks rather than months'. As Ben Pimlott explained in his biography of Wilson, the words 'weeks rather than months' would recur for the rest of his career, 'like a reinfecting wound'.[50] Papers released by the Public Record Office reveal Wilson stating privately at the Lagos summit: 'It was all very well to speak of military intervention and of gunboat diplomacy, but this was not the 19th century and Rhodesia was a land-locked state.' He complained that Britain was 'being treated as if we were a bloody colony' by Commonwealth countries, primarily Zambia, Kenya and Sierra Leone. In 1966, MI6 withdrew its representation in Salisbury, Rhodesia's capital, and relocated to South Africa. Until 1970, British intelligence in Rhodesia depended on the CIA.[51]

With the priority firmly on Rhodesia, the Secret Intelligence Service (SIS–MI6) was under some pressure not to make waves in the Republic in order to remain relatively close to events across the border. Anthony Sampson revealed that there was at least one British intelligence incident in 1965: 'a senior agent of MI6, acting as an Embassy official, was "severely interrogated" about his contacts with the white opposition, and was soon afterwards "PNG'd" – declared *persona non grata* . . . MI6 decided that making links with black opposition leaders would be too risky, and could get them tortured or killed.' In 1968, a 'listening station' was uncovered by RI–BOSS and a significant number of MI6 operatives were quietly expelled.[52] The problem was that Britain would need South Africa's assistance if it was to make sanctions effective in Rhodesia. During the debate on the Queen's Speech in 1966, Wilson answered an interruption by announcing that 'We are in discussion with the South African Government at this time. We have had two series of exchanges, and there will be more exchanges . . . I will not be pushed by the Rt Hon. Gentleman into stirring up trouble with another country.' In 1967, the Labour government considered restarting arms sales to South Africa and plans were made for Admiral Bierman, who would later be appointed Chief of the South African Defence Force (SADF), to visit Britain in mid-December. Eventually pressure from Labour backbenchers and negative press coverage convinced the government to confirm the existing embargo.[53]

The other major problem was 'kith and kin'. A retired British diplomat told the *Guardian* in 1997 that 'the Labour government refused to contemplate military action because "we don't do that sort of thing against white ex-colonials". He also recalled the high number of Rhodesian-born officers in the RAF in the mid-1960s. "It was clear we couldn't ask the RAF to fly air strikes against Rhodesian bases," he said.' The government's Rhodesian difficulty inspired the extreme right: Professor William Gutteridge recalls a 'sinister conference at the Randolph Hotel in Oxford' in the late 1960s where it became apparent that 'high intelligence' was 'angry' with Wilson over Rhodesia. The Rhodesian intelligence chief Ken Flower notes in his memoirs that before the withdrawal of MI6 in 1966 'British Intelligence representatives . . . were usually retired officers.' The reform of British intelligence co-ordination in 1967–8 was inspired, in part, by the perceived failure of the intelligence coverage of Rhodesia. Finally, as the 'oilgate' scandal later revealed, the British Labour government colluded with BP and Shell in turning a blind eye to sanctions-busting.[54] Rhodesia would dominate Britain's concerns in southern Africa for the whole of the 1970s.

As we have seen in the Loginov case, by 1967 the CIA was happy to work closely with RI. The United States had benefited from the British difficulties in Rhodesia. In fact, despite dabbling with the anti-communist PAC in the late 1950s, the National Security Agency (NSA), which co-ordinated US intelligence and supplied recommendations to the President and the State Department, had 'home-ported' its first civilian-manned 'spy ship' in Cape Town. The USNS *Private Jose F. Valdez* was a 'slow, unglamorous, seagoing delivery truck . . . [but it was] also ideal as [an] electronic snooper'. Although the ship was supposed to be monitoring Soviet missile-testing, its 'principle mission was to keep a close ear on the newly emerging nations of postcolonial Africa and on the internal struggles of the colonies that remained'. In March 1961, National Security Advisor McGeorge Bundy called 'for a review of US policy towards South Africa following Prime Minister Verwoerd's withdrawal from the Commonwealth'. In July 1962, the State Department discussed a paper, 'The White Redoubt', which painted a depressing picture:

> The seeds of another Algeria have been sown in Southern Africa. Blacks face Whites across a sea of developing hate . . . The possible collision of these rival forces in a world already full of racial hatreds is highly dangerous. A Black–White confrontation on the southern tip of Africa, particularly in an area where US investments are extensive, and US nationals are numerous, is perilous in terms of US objectives in Africa as a whole.[55]

In May 1963, the CIA distributed a 'Special Report' entitled 'Subversive Movements in South Africa'. The report observed that 'subversive groups in the Republic . . . have recently displayed a growing capability to use sabotage and terrorism to harass the white community'. It noted that ANC and PAC members were 'undergoing training in subversion' in a number of African countries 'and perhaps some countries of the Sino-Soviet bloc as well'. But the CIA assessment also noted the 'power of the South African state'. Kevin Danaher spotted the hidden hypocrisy in US Ambassador to the United Nations Adlai Stevenson's announcement of August 1963 that America would 'unilaterally cease arms sales to South Africa'. Stevenson confirmed that existing contracts would be honoured. In June 1962, two months before Mandela's arrest, the United States had 'established a Defense Department space tracking station in South Africa, in return for which Pretoria was permitted to sign contracts for American weapons'. By the time Stevenson made his announcement, the South Africans had already signed contracts for everything they needed.[56] Under Lyndon Johnson, the United States was primarily concerned with the war in Vietnam: South Africa was very low on the list of American priorities.

Beyond the United States and Britain, where the Anti-Apartheid Movement and others sustained a careful watch on apartheid intelligence activity (see page 60), little is known of South African international spying and intelligence liaison in the 1960s. Ed Stanley's doctoral thesis on the Franco-South African relationship has revealed that in 1963 the South African Ambassador to France 'declared that with Pretoria's British relations "detestable" . . . Pretoria wanted France to become its principal source of international patronage and information'. Two years later, in July 1965, Hendrik van den Bergh visited General Jacquier, the Director General of the Service de Documentation Extérieure et de Contre-Espionage (SDECE), in Paris. A South African aide-mémoire informed the French that van den Bergh wanted to study anti-communist methods, to build links with his counterparts in Europe 'and to examine . . . the possibilities of establishing, on a basis of reciprocity, a "plus large" cooperation'. The SDECE was clearly delighted at the prospect of an intelligence relationship: 'The Ministère sees only advantages in the projects of General van den Bergh.' In 1968, French observers were invited to study Operation Sibasa, a huge anti-insurgency exercise in South Africa, from which the British and the Americans had been pointedly excluded. Interviews with former RI agents suggest that van den Bergh was personally very close to the BND, the German foreign intelligence agency. The Germans apparently nicknamed the General 'God'.[57]

The years 1964 to 1973 appeared to be a golden time for white South Africa: violent unrest had been halted, the buffer states of Rhodesia and Portuguese Africa contributed to regional security, and foreign investment poured into the Republic causing the economy to boom: economic growth of 6 per cent a year in the 1960s was second only to Japan. It was a delusion, of course. In the early 1970s, apartheid would be battered by the re-emergence of trades union activity, the oil crisis of 1973, frontier controversies and the return of militant African resistance. But at the end of the 1960s little of that was imaginable. After all, van den Bergh's spies had eyes and ears everywhere. Anthony Sampson visited South Africa in 1970, after a break of six years, to discover that township life had been transformed: 'I found it much harder now to talk politics with the blacks in Soweto. "You know I don't dare tell my own brother what I'm thinking," said one young black politician. "So you've come to pick up the old threads?" said a veteran campaigner. "Well, they're broken." Informers were everywhere.'[58]

2

Bureau for State Security (BOSS)

The intelligence community hates the government of the day, of whichever party. It juggles all our destinies in the name of protecting them. And it is able to do this because of the secrecy with which it surrounds itself, a secrecy which corrodes a democratic society; it is no accident that as intelligence agencies have expanded, our civil liberties have contracted. There might, just might, be some justification for the intelligence community if it did what it claimed to do: provide timely warnings of threats to national existence. But . . . this claim is exaggerated even in wartime and, in peacetime, intelligence agencies seem to have spent more time trying to score off each other, protecting their budgets and their establishments, and inventing new justifications for their existence, than in gathering intelligence. Perhaps, this is because – when not deep in their fantasy world – the intelligence community knows that open, published information, and that obtained through traditional diplomatic and other overt contacts, have proved this century by far the most useful source of military, political and economic intelligence for both sides.

Phillip Knightley, *The Second Oldest Profession*, 1987[1]

Hendrik van den Bergh

HENDRIK JOHAN VAN den Bergh was born in Vredefort in the Orange Free State in November 1914 – the same year that the National Party was founded. His father was a post office official who later became a building contractor. In 1933, van den Bergh joined the Special Service Battalion, a government-sponsored semi-military organisation created to assist young men during the depression. Although selected for training in the South African army, he preferred to join the police. In 1942, during the Second World War, he was interned in the Koffiefontein camp in the Orange Free State for his suspected membership of the Stormjaers (literally,

Stormhunters), a militant saboteur group linked to the proto-Nazi OssewaBrandwag (OB – Ox-wagon Sentinels). The internment would have a major influence on his life: in the camp, he became close friends with a young lawyer, Balthazar John Vorster.[2] Van den Bergh later claimed that 'in those days with bitter memories of the Anglo-Boer war still strong, we were for anyone or anything opposing the English'. In other interviews, he denied having been a member of the OB, although he was photographed in 1966 at OB Commandant-General Dr Hans van Rensburg's funeral giving the OB salute. In the 1970s, van den Bergh told Ken Flower, Rhodesia's head of intelligence, that 'there was nothing that Hitler did to the Jews in Europe in the last World War that was anything like as bad as the British did to our people in the South African war'.[3]

Following the war, van den Bergh worked as a clerk at the South African Institute of Architects, before being permitted, in 1950, to rejoin the police. He was commissioned in the same year and promoted to captain in 1953. A tall man (six feet four inches), his nickname among his colleagues was 'Lang Hendrik' (Tall Hendrik); those he arrested called him 'Die Lang Man' (the Tall Man). In 1959, he was promoted major. In 1961, John Vorster became minister of justice and van den Bergh was promoted lieutenant-colonel. In January 1963, van den Bergh became a full colonel and head of the Security Police; meanwhile, with the full blessing of Vorster, he created Republican Intelligence (see page 20). He told John Vorster's biographer in the 1970s: 'When I was asked to take over security, I had my conditions. And one of those conditions was that the security police force as it then existed should be disbanded and that I would be able to draw to the new Security Police force the men that I either knew personally or knew of as top policemen.' In 1964, following the convictions of leading members of the ANC in the Rivonia trial, van den Bergh (then aged forty-nine) became the youngest brigadier in the police force. Two years later when Vorster succeeded Hendrik Verwoerd as prime minister, van den Bergh was made major-general and inspector-general of the police. In 1968, he was promoted to lieutenant-general while he secretly laid the foundations for the establishment of the Bureau for State Security. In 1969, he was appointed full general and head of BOSS.[4]

BOSS was a far more substantial organisation than the shadowy RI. It gave van den Bergh technical control of all intelligence gathered inside and outside the Republic and 'legalised' what had previously been a secretive network of spying security men. Apparently the possibility of the acronym 'BOSS' being constructed from the title of the new Bureau had been missed by the spy chief: 'He resents what he insists is the misnomer that abbreviating Bureau *for* State Security as *of* State Security, produces the popular acronym of BOSS, either for the bureau or himself. His resentment, frequently expressed to newspapermen, makes it clear that he regards the BOSS nickname as pejorative.' During a telephone conversation in December 1978, van den Bergh told Anthony Sampson: '"BOSS" is a leftist word.' In 1969, a British diplomat described van den Bergh as follows: 'The head of the new Bureau is clever and far from being devoid of humanity. He suffers, however, from a megalomania and infallibility complex (his staff fawn over his lightest remark); this could be dangerous, particularly when combined with lieutenants who appear to be more remarkable for toughness and dedication than for their regard for the niceties of the law'.[5] Sampson recalled that van den Bergh's 'tall, black-suited figure embodied the austere dedication of the Afrikaners'. Political scientist Dan O'Meara assessed the BOSS chief as personifying 'the most paranoid and most vicious tendencies in Afrikaner nationalism'. Van den Bergh was clearly a peculiar figure: one part old-time folksy Afrikaner farmer, one part Janus-faced modern spy-catcher. He was not without charm, as numerous people testify, but it was a charm with an underbelly of dread. ARM member Hugh Lewin recalls van den Bergh looking into an interrogation room after Lewin had been brutally beaten: 'Tweed-suited, the light glinting on his steel-rimmed spectacles, he noted quite jovially, "pleased to see you're co-operating" and sauntered out.'[6] In 1978, Carel Birkby retold one of van den Bergh's folksy stories:

> Two old Boers . . . were out in the bushveld one evening, amply supplied with brandy for their dop-and-damwater [brandy-and-water] sundowners. After the first bottle, they heard a lion roar, or thought they did . . . 'What will you do if that lion jumps us?' 'Shoot him dead, man.' 'What if you got no bullets?' 'I clobber him with the gun, man.' 'What if you got no gun?' 'I stick him with my knife, man.' 'What if you got no knife?' 'I just climb a tree, man.' 'What if there isn't a tree?' 'Man, there's GOT to be a tree.'

The message of the tale was that there is always a way, 'there are no such words as *can't* or *if* or *maybe*'.[7] Max du Preez, a courageous Afrikaner journalist, was once summoned to see van den Bergh: 'It was a huge, dark, wood-panelled room. Van den Bergh was sitting behind a formidable desk . . . I said, "Good morning General" and extended my hand to greet him. He ignored my hand, looked at me . . . and then said, "*Ja, mannetjie*" [Yes, little man].' When du Preez refused to reveal his source for a damaging story, van den Bergh raged: 'I will lock you up for eighty days, and when you come out, I will ask you again. If you tell me you can't reveal your source, I will lock you up again for eighty days.' Benjamin Pogrund, a veteran *Rand Daily Mail* reporter, tells an amusing story about van den Bergh that reflects something of the ambiguity of the BOSS chief's personality: 'At the *Rand Daily Mail*, staff at editorial conferences had a habit, when discussing sensitive matters, of prefacing what they had to say by looking up at the ceiling and saying "Hope you can hear OK, General." When I recounted this to the General he gave me a tight smile: "Yes, I have heard those remarks and it was not in the ceiling."' During the same five-hour interview in 1992, Pogrund obeyed van den Bergh's instruction 'that I not take any notes or use a tape-recorder', but was forced by circumstance to visit the lavatory continuously in order to scribble notes on any available scrap of paper.[8] Fourteen years after his retirement, two years after Mandela was released from prison, Hendrik van den Bergh retained his steely charm.

Van den Bergh farmed throughout his period as head of BOSS. In May 1972, he was electrocuted in a welding accident on his farm. Ken Flower telephoned him soon afterwards:

HVDB: I could feel I was dying. Nothing could have released me from clinging to that electric cable. Then I realised I was dead, and on the other side, for I heard God say 'Hendrik, your life's work is not finished – I need you back on Earth', and I was restored to life.

KF: But, Hendrik, you must surely acknowledge the part played by your servant, Johannes? By all accounts he had the sense to run several hundred yards to throw the switch, and that was how you were saved!

HVDB: . . . How could any Bantu have the sense to do what he did unless God gave him the right instructions?[9]

Some BOSS agents have suggested that van den Bergh's mind was permanently damaged by the electrocution. Certainly, his behaviour was odd in the mid-1970s. I was told that his BOSS chauffeur regularly transported the farm's produce to market in van den Bergh's official car and on one occasion, when an agent suggested an operation in Africa whereby Afrikaner journalists could double as spies, van den Bergh rejected the scheme, gazing out of his office window and declaring: 'I know everything that happens in Africa.' Gordon Winter recalls asking the spy chief 'whether God approved of spying'. Among a selection of Biblical quotations fired back in response, van den Bergh cited Numbers 13: 17–20: 'And Moses sent them to spy out the land of Canaan . . .' Van den Bergh was certainly eccentric and he appears to have been a megalomaniac (he told the Erasmus Commission, which had been tasked with investigating corruption in South Africa's Department of Information, in 1978, 'nothing happened in South Africa without me knowing about it'), but he understood the rudiments of spy-craft. As he said in an interview: 'I steal with my eyes. I always have stolen with my eyes. Even as a farmer, you know, when I visit some friend's farm I look and watch and see what he does and if he is doing intelligent things I make a note of it. And, of course, I did the same in our Trade.'[10]

BOSS and Bureaucracy

BOSS was created in August 1968, although the official announcement was not made until May 1969. The Potgieter Report discovered that the Cabinet Defence Committee, which had five members including the Prime Minister, John Vorster, and the Defence Minister, P.W. Botha, had recommended that 'a central intelligence organisation [be] established'. Van den Bergh was given the title of security adviser to the Prime Minister. A British Foreign Office report noted, 'There was at this stage no mention of any new bureau, though the General [van den Bergh] himself made no secret to us of plans for such a reorganisation which would give him increased power.' In April 1969, the Estimates of Expenditure for the financial year 1969–1970 allocated an increase of R4 million for 'Secret Services' and an increase of more than R200,000 to the secret services section of the police budget, while the military intelligence budget was reduced from R830,000 to R39,000. One month later, the creation of BOSS was announced in the Public Service Amendment Bill. The Foreign Office observed: 'The Opposition raised no objection . . . [They] are as frightened of any security threats from outside or inside the Republic as the Government,[and] had clearly accepted the Bureau as a new CIA-type organisation, with good precedents abroad, which might be necessary for South Africa's "special circumstances".' By 1975–6, BOSS's budget had ballooned to R11,830,000.[11]

Two state security-related clauses in the General Law Amendment Bill did manage to rouse the ire of the (white) opposition. Clause 10 made it 'an offence to publish any security matter', and Clause 29 authorised the government 'to prohibit the giving of any evidence to any court or other statutory body, if such evidence . . . is "prejudicial to the interests of the State or public security"'. These prompted 'a remarkable volume of criticism' from the South African legal profession. But the most unprecedented and passionate objections emerged from the Afrikaner press: 'The extreme right wing publication "Veg", in trenchant satirical vein, put forward a number of suggested Afrikaans transliterations of BOSS. One of these was "BAAS" which means the same as Boss; the initials would stand for "Buro vir Agtervolging en Afluister van super-Afrikaners" – the Bureau for Persecuting and Eavesdropping on super-Afrikaners (right wingers).' The two clauses would become somewhat embarrassing to British diplomats. As the arguments rumbled on, Vorster declared that the legislation was 'modelled on but less draconian than' the special powers of the Northern Ireland government. This was a favourite justification of the Nationalist government. On 31 July 1969, John Macrae issued a depressing missive from the Central and Southern African Department of the British Foreign Office: 'we do not think this is a subject on which it would be right to speak out to justify our position, because both the controversial points, Clause 10 and Clause 29, are ones on which we are vulnerable.'[12]

In November 1969, Dr Albert Hertzog and 'Jaap' Marais left the governing party to form the right-wing Herstigte Nasionale Party (HNP). At a political meeting on 11 November, Hertzog described the BOSS enabling law as 'one of the most dangerous pieces of legislation to appear on the statute books'. He added that he had heard that the cost of the Bureau was nearer to R50m than the R4m voted by Parliament. Hertzog later attacked BOSS as a 'deadly danger to the general public'. Paul Killick of the British Embassy concluded: 'We have learned Dr Hertzog obtained his information about BOSS funds from two officers in the Directorate of Military Intelligence.'[13]

The Potgieter Report, submitted in 1970 but only published in abbreviated form in 1973, revealed that a State Security Committee (SSC) had been established in 1963 but it had proved ineffective. In 1966, Prime Minister Hendrik Verwoerd reformed the SSC, changing its name to State Security Advisory Committee (SSAC), and created an Intelligence Co-ordinating Section (ICS) to serve the SSAC. By 1968, it became apparent 'that the SSAC and ICS also could not meet the requirements of an efficient intelligence service . . . it had become evident that the obvious solution lay in the creation of a central intelligence agency which should be vested with powers to collect intelligence and should be staffed by intelligence experts in the political, economic, military, ethnological and other appropriate fields'. The report also attempted to define the duties of the DMI, which would be renamed the Military Intelligence Division (MID) in 1970, the Security Police and BOSS. The report explained that in the 1960s there had been tension between the military and the police:

trespassing on each other's fields, which actually had no geographical limits . . . in itself created a dangerous situation for the security of the State because relevant and important intelligence was being withheld in the process by one from the other, with the result that it was lost to one of them and in a sense therefore also to the State. The very confusion as to what was whose field or function was decidedly not conducive [to] the security of the State. In itself, it was a danger to State security . . . before the establishment of the Bureau for State Security, there were serious defects in the intelligence community of the Republic.

Potgieter declared that the function of the Security Police was to 'secure the State against subversion of its existing order'. He cited as 'species of subversion' communism, sabotage and espionage. In truth, the 'existing order' was apartheid, and therefore subversion of apartheid was also the responsibility of the Security Police. The report declared that the DMI's primary function, in terms of the Defence Act of 1957, was the 'defence of the Republic' and 'the prevention or suppression of internal disorder in the Republic'. Potgieter emphasised that BOSS was 'pre-eminently an intelligence organisation with no executive powers such as powers of detaining persons, powers of arrest or any other similar Police powers'. The Bureau, at inception, constituted six divisions:

(i) . . . internal collection and evaluation of intelligence in regard to subversion . . . (ii) . . . covert intelligence and counter-espionage; (iii) . . . political and economic evaluation of intelligence; (iv) . . . military evaluation – determination of the military threat . . . (v) . . . administrative matters . . . (vi) . . . national evaluation, research and special studies.

Potgieter described the threat facing South Africa as 'numerous enemies who are seeking to overthrow the existing order . . . They are active in many spheres.'[14] Van den Bergh announced that he thought the report was 'excellent . . . [it] recommends that I do much more than I am doing at the present time'. *Africa Confidential* commented: 'One niggling doubt was expressed. The Commissioner himself said he didn't want to discount the possibility that a central body controlling intelligence "might in itself pose a threat to the security of the State". However, he said he believed that the Prime Minister and his [State Security Council – SSC] would exercise sufficient control to obviate this.' In practice, the SSC (a government committee including the Prime Minister, the Security Adviser, the Minister of Defence and others) was barely utilised. As part of the inquiry, the Potgieter Commission had examined the activities and structures of

American, Australian, New Zealand, British, Dutch, German, French, Portuguese and Rhodesian intelligence. The final report carried an interesting section on 'The Requirements for an Intelligence Officer':

> The basic requirements for a good intelligence officer – including the secret collector, the evaluator and the interpreter – are the following:
>
> (a) He must be a man of great intellectual integrity . . . He must not pretend to know things that he knows nothing about. He must not present things as facts if they are not . . .
>
> (e) He must be knowledgeable in his field. e.g. politics, economics, the military field, ethnology, subversion, terrorism, etc.
>
> (f) He must have a certain amount of imagination to enable him to predict, on the information at his disposal, what the future may bring . . .
>
> (h) He should preserve anonymity as far as possible, should eschew ambition for power and position, and should not be conceited or suffer from megalomania. He should be self-effacing.[15]

Few BOSS officers would meet such strict standards. During the early 1970s, BOSS was effective at enforcing 'state security' but it rarely faced any substantial challenges. The weakening of regional security with the Portuguese coup d'état in 1974 and the re-emergence of violent African internal resistance in 1976, and its implicit challenge to apartheid, were still in the future. In 1963, when van den Bergh was creating RI, he said, 'My job is security, not politics or diplomacy.' During the 1970s, BOSS would become increasingly active in diplomacy and politics (see paage 102). In July 1969, van den Bergh attended a 'week of talks' in Lisbon with officers of the Portuguese International Police for the Defence of the State (PIDE) and the Rhodesian Security Police. A report in the *Daily Telegraph* suggested that the meeting was 'the most important of its kind . . . and could presage a big drive to undermine the "liberation" movements'. A further 'top-level intelligence conference' was held in Salisbury in February 1971, which led to an agreement 'to establish a joint intelligence steering committee whose broad terms of reference provided for the exchange of intelligence and security information . . . and to permit clandestine executive operations on a trilateral basis. Under this agreement, each service could run agents and informers in each other's territory [and] arrange kidnapping and repatriation of security suspects.'[16] Due to press restrictions in South Africa, very few BOSS stories appeared in the newspapers, which served to bolster the impression of a sinister, efficient, intelligence organisation. This was always a somewhat inflated image.

★

In 1974, BOSS were implicated in the 'Spies in the Sky' incident. A South African Airways (SAA) air hostess claimed that BOSS and the police were employing cabin staff 'to listen in on passengers' conversations and pick up information about their political views'. These claims were at first rejected and then grudgingly confirmed.[17] In 1975, BOSS arrested Breyten Breytenbach, an Afrikaner poet married to a Vietnamese woman, who had entered South Africa in order to organise resistance to the apartheid regime. It has been suggested that Breytenbach was a victim of the airline spies. In 1984, he published *The True Confessions of an Albino Terrorist*, which provided an artist's snapshot of a BOSS interrogation:

> Snaaks and Blue Eyes were BOSS agents. Not only did Snaaks insist, foaming at the mouth, that I'm a KGB man, but that I'm one of an ultra-secret section of killers led by a certain Colonel Unpronounceable . . . Blue Eyes would be BOSS's man with the Security Police proper – and I having been successively (unsuccessfully) a French, British and Israeli agent, would end up being accused of working for the CIA . . . Ah yes, those spies, I'm talking now of the people who have questioned me – they have such wonderfully fertile thumbs. I've always felt that they read too many, far too many spy thrillers. Take Blue Eyes for instance, rolling his shoulders, narrowing his eyelids, combing his moustache, swaggering when walking, muscular: the brute. How he thought himself to be James Bond! I called him Jiems Kont in my mind.[18]

The secret Afrikaner Broederbond (Brotherhood) was a masonic-like elite network of male, Protestant Afrikaners that had played a significant role in the development of Afrikaner nationalism and continued to serve behind the scenes as a powerful ideological guardian defending the purity of apartheid. Van den Bergh and most of the senior officers in BOSS were members of the Broederbond, but van den Bergh was also willing to employ his intelligence power for tactical and political advantage even within such a 'sacred' body. In 1965, 'Security Police officers . . . infiltrated the [right-wing] *Afrikaner-Orde* and [came] back with stories of plotting and dissent . . . an instruction went out that a number of security men must be introduced into the Broederbond without the customary scrutiny by branches'. Van den Bergh drew up the list of names. Ten years later, he circulated a confidential communiqué in which he announced that 'South Africa must abandon its traditional attitude towards Rhodesia; it must accept the inevitability of Black majority rule in that country . . . and it must accept some forms of "integration" inside South Africa as also being inevitable.' The document was read aloud at Broederbond cell meetings throughout the country and then returned to the head office in

Johannesburg.[19] The move was clearly designed to isolate right-wing Afrikaners at a time when the issue of Rhodesia was threatening to create further divisions within the Afrikaner polity.

The election of Richard Nixon as US president in November 1968 ushered in a reassessment of American policy towards southern Africa. From the CIA point of view, this was a good opportunity to take advantage of Britain's deteriorating intelligence and diplomatic influence in the region. The National Security Study Memorandum (NSSM) No. 39 was commissioned by National Security Advisor Henry Kissinger in April 1969, and led to an early version of what would later be called 'constructive engagement'. When NSSM 39 was leaked in 1972, 'Option 2' attracted opprobrium from anti-apartheid campaigners: 'The whites are here to stay and the only way that constructive change can come about is through them.' In the section of the memorandum which assessed the prospects for the region, the author (Winston Lord) stated: 'Political freedom has been progressively curtailed over recent decades. The white minority has a monopoly of force which it does not hesitate to use, and of power which it will not voluntarily yield . . . For the foreseeable future South Africa will be able to maintain internal stability and effectively counter insurgent activity.'

The 'tar baby' option, a US diplomatic joke referring to the Brer Rabbit story (because Washington was 'stuck' with its friends in Pretoria), was followed until the election of Jimmy Carter in 1976. Roger Morris, who worked in Washington's National Security Council (NSC), acknowledged the lack of accurate information available to the NSC from the 'presumably' knowledgeable State Department and CIA. The NSC met to discuss southern Africa in December 1969 and when the CIA Director, Richard Helms, spoke, 'So transparently pro-white was the CIA presentation, so disdainful of black African opposition, so reflective of the views of the white security services on whose reports CIA analysis was based, that at one point even the customarily cynical Kissinger passed a puzzled note to an aide, "Why is he doing this?" At the one-word reply, "Clients," he gave a knowing scowl.' Later in the discussion, Helms suggested it would be 'counterproductive' to close the CIA station in Salisbury, Rhodesia: 'We get blind and buy very little in black Africa.' Following a formal request from Britain in 1970, the CIA station was closed. But Morris recalls, 'The CIA station simply adjourned to the US Embassy in South Africa while some of its agents discreetly became private Americans in Rhodesia.'[20]

An American national intelligence estimate, dated 10 April 1972, reflected similar short-term analysis to NSSM 39: 'We see virtually no prospect that white minority rule over South Africa's 16 million non-whites will be overturned in this decade.' Bearing in mind the CIA's friendly relations with BOSS (CIA Director William Colby would later admit that South African intelligence agents received training in the United States), the lack of publicity on South African spying in the US during the early 1970s makes some sense. John Stockwell, a former CIA officer, noted that Agency activity within South Africa was restricted to liaison until 1974, when '[the CIA] yielded to intense pressure in Washington and expanded the Pretoria station's responsibilities to include covert operations to gather information about the South African nuclear project'. Following a 'clumsy and obvious' spying operation in the summer of 1975 by a young CIA agent, later named as Ernest B. Brant, the CIA personnel responsible were 'quietly expelled' and normal business resumed.[21]

Freedom of Information requests in the late 1970s revealed that the US government permitted Hendrik van den Bergh to visit the United States on four occasions between 1965 and 1975 (July–August 1965, July 1969, concerning Loginov, August–September 1973 and June 1975 'for pleasure'); Admiral Bierman, the Chief of the South African Defence Force, was granted a visa in May 1974; and Brigadier Lothar Neethling (see page 200) visited the US 'for business purposes' six times between 1972 and 1976. Tom Mangold discovered that van den Bergh's friendship with CIA spycatcher James Jesus Angleton was so close that following Angleton's retirement in 1975 'Van den Bergh wanted to offer the former CIA counter-intelligence chief work as a consultant.' A South African diplomatic report of a conversation with an unnamed senior French source in 1970 praised 'The personal action . . . of General van den Bergh and Ambassador [to the US] Taswell who "in a parallel direction and with persistency have been able to inspire complete trust from the political and diplomatic services of the USA".' The report concluded by citing the advice of the French source: 'Make big efforts in propaganda and contacts to win over to the cause of the Whites in Southern Africa, the USA (especially Congress) and even the UK and the Western countries in general.'[22]

The Mandela Escape Plot

Gordon Winter's *Inside BOSS* is full of bizarre stories told in a lip-smacking, tabloid style which offended many critics at the time of publication. The only valid test, more than twenty years later, is whether the stories stand up

to serious examination. I met Gordon Winter in 1997 while I was researching the life of Mandela. I was intrigued by one of the more outlandish tales
in *Inside BOSS*: the story of the Mandela escape plot. I was surprised when
Winter was able to provide a file of documents as supporting evidence. Later,
I followed up the story in South Africa and met the central plotter. The story
is told here, with additional details, as an example of what appears to be a
genuine amateur attempt to assist Mandela's escape from Robben Island,
BOSS's manoeuvres to intercept and later manipulate the operation, and the
inherent chaos of intelligence and counter-intelligence. On 18 March 1969,
Robert Gordon Bruce placed a notice in *The Times*:

> I SEEK A PERSON determined to pursue world embracing loyalties
> beyond national commitments, based London; adventurous; good con-
> tact and liaison; personality, competent organiser, prepared to execute
> unusual work in spare time without financial reward. Box 0579Y. The
> Times

Robert Gordon Bruce was an old friend of Nelson Mandela's – they had
first met as members of Johannesburg's International Club in 1950
(Mandela later took over from Bruce as secretary of the club). Mandela was
the Bruces' solicitor and took care of the ante-nuptial legal agreement for
their wedding. During the 1950s, he regularly visited Bruce and his wife
Ursula, whose family had died in the Holocaust. On one occasion, he
assisted the blind Mrs Bruce across a road; white onlookers were shocked
to see an African 'handling' a white woman. While Mandela was 'living
underground' in 1961, he stayed overnight with the Bruce family.[23] Bruce
was not a communist: he was just an old-fashioned, socialist Englishman
who wanted to help his friend. Winter knew none of this, and BOSS, if it
knew, did not tell him.

Gordon Winter was instructed by van den Bergh to 'find out who had
inserted the notice. He had heard "from a reliable London source" that the
subject [would] involve South Africa.' Winter replied to the advertisement
and received an answer from Bruce using the alias 'Henry Morgan' (some
months later his monicker would be 'Charles Metterlink'). Bruce instructed
Winter to pay for the notice in *The Times*. After three months of correspondence, during which Bruce revealed to Winter the subject of the advertisement's 'unusual work' (the escape of Mandela) and BOSS in
Johannesburg managed to identify the secret plotter (Bruce), Winter was
encouraged to meet a third London-based plotter, Marianne Borman, an

employee of the British government's Central Office of Information. Bruce then sent Winter the replies he had received to *The Times* notice. He encouraged Winter to interview the applicants and select people who would be able to add specialist skills to the mission. Winter was preoccupied with weeding out applicants who were in fact British spies. He had been warned by his London 'handler' that 'at least one, if not two or three, of those replies will be from people working for British intelligence'.[24]

In September 1969, Winter interviewed the British aviatrix Sheila Scott for Forum World Features (a CIA-connected news agency). Later, he renewed contact and, according to Sheila Scott, 'wanted to know if I would be interested in doing something exciting . . . [he] told me that when I got to South Africa I would be contacted by a man called Henry Morgan'. The BOSS plan was simple: 'Mandela would be shot during a dramatic recapture as he was about to board Miss Scott's plane on the remote landing strip in the Cape.' Van den Bergh sent Winter details of a Robben Island warder, Gideon Alwyn Huisamen, who would assist Mandela's escape. Winter concocted a story to justify the involvement of the warder, whom Bruce and Winter codenamed 'the receptionist'. A few weeks later, Scott made a solo flight from London to Cape Town and was contacted by Bruce while she stayed at the Mount Nelson Hotel. One day, she 'found an envelope on a chair with a letter inside addressed to her. It was signed Henry Morgan. The letter [requested that Scott] fly her plane over Robben Island "to have a good look at the island" and investigate the possibility of landing an aircraft there.' Scott was telephoned by a man who wanted to discuss the plan, but she brushed him off. 'The last call to me was in Johannesburg and I told them that they must never phone me again.'[25]

Robert Gordon Bruce was a brave, if naive, man and his next suggestion was that Winter or Borman should approach John Lennon for capital to finance a Mandela escape, as Lennon had previously paid the fines of anti-apartheid demonstrators in London. Bruce contacted Canon Collins (codename 'The Big Gun'), the radical cleric and founder of the International Defence and Aid Fund (IDAF) which sent money to political prisoners in the Republic. Denis Herbstein, Collins's biographer, notes that the Soviet Union was also developing a plan to rescue the political prisoners from Robben Island in 1969 (see page 284).[26] There is no evidence that the two plans were linked. In 1970, Bruce considered the option of employing the IRA: 'Wish we could make contact with Bernadette Devlin [a young Nationalist politician in Northern Ireland who had just become an MP] . . . she might have ideas about channels and ways and means . . . Perhaps a group of IRA men might consider freelancing on the South African job in return for money. Do you know of any types in this category who fly planes?' Above all, Bruce had a vision of a multi-racial South Africa which could set an example for the rest of the world:

> It is my desire to make South Africa the headquarters of a worldwide drive in favour of a world authority to reduce the dangers of total war. I am hoping that our friend [Mandela] may be able to join me in this. The first step is to restore him to political visibility in SA. Hence our operation. Thereafter our efforts will be directed to a rapprochement between moderate elements of right and left . . . a new multi-racial party of national liberation might then become possible. Once in power we could then call for the transfer of the United Nations to South Africa . . . South Africa is a little more remote than other parts of the world from the major power blocks and systems and its moral power would thus be enhanced. I mean the moral power of the UN.[27]

But Bruce had 'fallen among thieves'. While he was dreaming of utopias, van den Bergh was imagining the death of Nelson Mandela which he could blame on the irresponsibility of British radicals. Winter outlines the plan as it was later explained to him: the warder would drug the other guards and free Mandela. They would rendezvous with the Bruce group, plus motorboat, on the beach and they would flee to the mainland, whereupon 'Mandela was to be given a revolver, which would give the police the excuse to shoot him as he arrived at the airstrip to fly away. But the gun would be loaded with blanks so that no police officer could be injured . . . [After Mandela's death], a BOSS man would secretly reload Mandela's gun with live ammunition.' For BOSS, the counter-plot started to disintegrate when, in August 1970, Bruce informed Winter that he had 'met old Chipsie boy [Sir Robert Birley, former headmaster of Eton] a couple of times. He knows our Johnnie [Canon Collins] quite well and says he will be seeing him when he gets back to the big city [London] . . . He wants you to meet him.'[28]

Bruce wrote again two weeks later: 'Chips seems to be aware of your name . . . It is not Mr Chips' intention to go into any detail with the BG [Collins] and he would not indicate that we were planning to approach Len [Lennon] for funds . . . It is *most* important that you see him . . . as instructed . . . This guy is great stuff and could be of great help in certain directions.' Van den Bergh ordered Winter to abandon the operation because Sir Robert Birley was connected to MI6: 'The British firm are displeased that you, a British subject, are recruiting British nationals in

London to help in the Mandela escape plot, knowing full well that they will be arrested in South Africa.'[29] Bruce had no idea how close he had come to disaster. In 1981, when the revelations in *Inside BOSS* were reported by the South African media, the Johannesburg *Star* described Bruce as follows: 'A devoted family man in his mid-50s, anyone less like a James Bond it would be difficult to imagine.' The South African intelligence services couldn't do anything to Bruce because to act would be to admit that there was substance in Winter's account. Nevertheless, in July 1988, Bruce's twenty-five-year-old son David was the first South African to be 'sentenced to the maximum penalty of six years in prison for refusing to do compulsory service in the South African Defence Force'. In 1992, Nelson Mandela attended Robert Gordon Bruce's seventieth birthday party.[30]

BOSS versus MID: Operation Savannah

BOSS's attempts to exert influence over both the Security Police and the DMI–MID created problems from the beginning. Republican Intelligence had been the secret elder brother of the Security Police and BOSS became, as an anti-apartheid pamphlet *BOSS: The First Five Years* pointed out, 'the brains behind the Security Police'. Nevertheless, tensions existed: Lieutenant-General P.J. 'Tiny' Venter, the head of the Security Police, spoke to the Johannesburg *Sunday Times* on the occasion of his retirement in 1974: 'He said that he had been upset that BOSS had enticed members of the Security Police to work for the Bureau, and that in some cases incentives had been offered. "Obviously one does not like losing one's top staff to another department." '[31] Venter's successor was Mike Geldenhuys, previously van den Bergh's deputy at BOSS responsible for foreign espionage. The tension between the two organisations appears to have been based on the downgrading of the Security Police's intelligence capacity. The relationship would deteriorate further following the failure of the security forces to curtail the urban rioting in 1976. Ken Flower recorded in his diary on 28 November 1968: 'Lt. General H. van den Bergh telephoned me from Pretoria . . . He described how Mr Vorster had selected him for a new job, which was to head a new co-ordinated "Intelligence Agency". He said he had taken over the previous "Military Intelligence" and that he was actually speaking from the office of Major-General Loots, the previous Chief of

Military Intelligence.' Following his 'defection' in 1979, former BOSS analyst Arthur McGiven revealed that when 'BOSS moved from its first cramped quarters in Pretoria to offices next to the military intelligence headquarters in the Alphen Building, a check was made for bugs. A microphone was found in the office of BOSS chief General Hendrik van den Bergh. The wire led next door. The military were bugging the spies.' John Fullerton (*Now* magazine) reported that in the early 1970s P.W. Botha attempted to resign after 'van den Bergh and his sidekick, General Mike Geldenhuys . . . simply walked into Military Intelligence head-quarters and physically occupied the premises, to the consternation and fury of the military'. In early 1977, P.W. Botha again offered his resigna-tion to John Vorster after Botha discovered that *his* telephone had been tapped by BOSS. Gordon Winter spelled it out in *Inside BOSS*: 'The top men in Military Intelligence regarded themselves as "non-political purists" who were only interested in vital matters of defence. They despised van den Bergh's men as little peeping toms who crept around looking for people who disagreed with apartheid or Whites who slept with Blacks. And to some extent they were right.' The feeling was mutual. On one occasion, Geldenhuys described the military as 'week-end soldiers'.[32]

The struggle between BOSS and DMI–MID was essentially a bureau-cratic turf war. The argument over who should be responsible for the 'defence' of South Africa stretched back to the early 1960s. The Potgieter Report explained that in November 1963 General Retief, the Director of Military Intelligence, had 'submitted a proposal for a central intelligence bureau' to control military and domestic surveillance.[33] Retief's proposal was rejected in favour of van den Bergh's RI. In 1966, following Vorster's succession to the premiership, an attempt was made to consolidate the vari-ous intelligence structures. General Hein du Toit was deputy-chief of DMI at the time: 'There were a lot of problems between us and [RI] . . . The problems boiled down to the areas each organisation had to cover, particu-larly overseas. Neither one nor the other knew anything about intelligence, so each was feeling its way. The conflict was about who had to do what.' Ken Flower recalled wearily: 'It was depressing for us on our visits to South Africa to have to listen to BOSS reviling the Military, the Military berat-ing BOSS and, towards the end, BOSS railing against the Police – in short, almost everyone denigrating almost everyone else.'[34]

In September 1967, John Vorster sent a detachment of South African policemen to assist the Rhodesian army, following a brief and poorly prepared ANC–ZAPU collaborative infiltration known as the Wankie campaign. General Constand Viljoen later recalled, 'We [the SADF] resented it when Vorster, under pressure from van den Bergh, used the police in Rhodesia . . . We felt it was a military task.' Over the next seven years, numerous South African policemen trained in counter-insurgency operations on the 'Rhodesian Front'. Eugene de Kock, who would become one of the most notorious killers in the South African death squads, 'completed nine tours of duty in Rhodesia' (see page 203).[35] During the same year, according to Eschel Rhoodie, later to be disgraced during the Information scandal, the DMI had interfered in Nigeria: 'General van den Bergh told me . . . that [SA] military intelligence had been largely responsible for planning the secession of Biafra from Nigeria.' Van den Bergh had discovered South African involvement in Biafra when he was questioned by a 'senior representative of the CIA'. Gordon Winter put it somewhat differently: 'I was told at high level in BOSS that Mr Botha had been asked to send the troops by the . . . CIA.' Al Venter reported in 2003 that 'the plan [had been] orchestrated by Jacques Foccart, the Elysée's shadowy *éminence grise* in charge of African affairs for President de Gaulle . . . Contact had originally been made with the future President Botha . . . he delegated responsibility to General Fritz Loots, the original founder of the SA Reconnaissance Commandos.'[36]

The second volume of *The Mitrokhin Archive, The KGB and the World*, reveals that in April 1971 a DMI–MID counter-intelligence officer, code-name 'Mario', contacted the KGB in Lusaka 'and offered information about the South African intelligence community'. Although he was valued by the KGB and Glavnoye Razvedyvatelnoye Upravleniye (GRU – Soviet military intelligence), it became apparent in 1973 that the officer had left the DMI–MID before offering the information.

The collapse of the Portuguese Empire in April 1974 was a shock to the CIA and to most international intelligence agencies. Van den Bergh liked to boast that he had predicted the coup d'état, Secretary of Information Eschel Rhoodie explained in 1979.

> The General showed me a copy of the report which he had sent to the CIA almost a year before the collapse of the Portuguese government in which he predicted that the danger was not in Angola or Mozambique but in a collapse of the government in Portugal itself and in which he predicted that if that were to happen the troops in Angola or Mozambique would either revolt, or pull out. He also showed me a letter from the CIA in which they . . . complimented him for his foresight and stated that he was the only

member of intelligence in the Western community who had been accurate in his assessment.[37]

In reality, van den Bergh received intelligence from the Zambians with whom BOSS were quietly communicating as part of the Department of Information's 'unorthodox diplomacy' (see page 102). The Portuguese withdrawal from Angola and Mozambique would have immediate repercussions on South Africa's border. In late 1974, around 2,000 South African paramilitary police were officially withdrawn from Rhodesia, although a significant number clad in BSAP uniforms remained in Rhodesia until 1980. Nevertheless, according to Rhoodie's testimony, MID, under the control of Defence Minister P.W. Botha, planned and nearly executed interventions in both Rhodesia and Mozambique in 1974. Both operations were halted by van den Bergh and BOSS. Benjamin Pogrund approached van den Bergh to confirm the foiled-intervention story in 1979 after Botha had been elected prime minister and was amazed to witness the former spy chief's reaction: 'His features seemed to disintegrate. "Bennie, promise me you won't put this in the newspaper . . . PW doesn't know about this. If he sees this he will have me killed . . . I will have to leave the country . . . I can't leave, I haven't got a passport. I'll have to kill myself.'[38] Whether this was a performance for Pogrund's benefit, genuine terror or a great story told one too many times, is difficult to assess. But in the mid-1970s the conflict between BOSS and MID was coming to a head; it would reach its climax in Angola.

Operation Savannah, as the South African invasion of Angola in 1975 was codenamed, remains shrouded in mystery. The intervention was described by Dan O'Meara as being 'dictated by ad hoc response to events, rather than by a well-worked-out strategic plan and clear political objectives'. It demonstrated 'a barely credible picture of a total policy vacuum and slovenly decision-making'. The Angolan war was certainly complicated: it pitched three Angolan liberation movements against each other. The left-wing, anti-tribalist Popular Movement for the Liberation of Angola (MPLA) opposed two nationalist liberation forces, Holden Roberto's National Front for the Liberation of Angola (FNLA) and Jonas Savimbi's National Union for the Total Liberation of Angola (UNITA). Eventually, the Cubans would enter the conflict on the side of the MPLA and the South Africans would covertly support UNITA and the FNLA. At the height of the Cold War, at a time when the US was perceived as weak following defeat in Vietnam and the fall of Saigon, Angola also represented a microcosm of the global conflict between the Soviet Union and the United States. Under the surface, BOSS and MID engaged in a battle for political and regional influence. In 1974, Jonas Savimbi appealed to the South Africans for assistance. The MID chief, General du Toit, received the request through BOSS channels but was aware that van den Bergh was opposed to involvement: 'He thought it was completely wrong and never believed South Africa should become involved in any military conflict outside our borders . . . He tried to sabotage everything . . . He did so by not passing on intelligence.'[39] Van den Bergh was trying to protect South Africa by sticking to a long-standing foreign policy which loosely stated: 'We don't intervene in African countries and therefore African countries should not concern themselves with South Africa's domestic policies.' The policy was a sham but it had never before been fully exposed as such.

Du Toit visited Angola to meet Savimbi in October 1974 and it was agreed that weapons would be supplied to UNITA. Further meetings followed in December 1974 and February 1975. One month earlier, the CIA had been instructed to start funding the FNLA, but Washington had 'refused to authorise support for Savimbi'. Between 17 and 24 April 1975, BOSS 'representatives' met Savimbi four times in Gabarone, London and Paris. Once again, Savimbi requested weaponry but this was rejected by the South African government.[40] Meanwhile, Washington 'dithered', to use Secretary of State Henry Kissinger's description. On 4 July, General Constand Viljoen and Gert Rothman (BOSS) met Mobutu Sese Seko, President of Zaire, Holden Roberto and Savimbi in Kinshasa. In Pretoria, van den Bergh approved the list of weapons requested by Viljoen. On 17 July, Kissinger recommended 'the covert program proposed by the CIA'. Some $6 million would be spent on the FNLA and UNITA; the weapons and money would be filtered through Zaire. John Stockwell, the head of the CIA Angola task force, noted in his account that an African-American CIA officer had wanted to take part in the operation but was rejected by CIA Africa Division chief James Potts because 'we had to be very careful about letting blacks into the program, [due to] the South African involvement'.[41]

It is clear that van den Bergh's change of mind over Angola was directly related to the change occurring in Washington. General Viljoen later told South African defence correspondent Hilton Hamann, 'Contact with the CIA was always through BOSS.' The SADF appear to have 'crossed the border' of Angola as early as June 1975, but the full intervention did not take place until August. The first admitted incursion was in order to secure the Calueque-Ruacana hydroelectric dam complex. By the end of the month,

MID had taken charge of the operation: South African soldiers were being ordered to remove all forms of identification including dog-tags and were instructed to wear nondescript uniforms.[42] During September, South African soldiers, 'trainers' and 'special forces' moved deeper into Angola. The official invasion by the South African 'Zulu' column began on 14 October. John Stockwell later recorded: 'South Africa . . . came into the conflict cautiously at first, watching the expanding US program and timing their steps to the CIA's . . . I saw no evidence that the United States formally encouraged them to join the conflict.' Eschel Rhoodie added: 'I do not believe that the CIA had actually encouraged South Africa . . . to attack . . . or move into Angola. I understood from General van den Bergh that he had gone to the United States at a later stage after it had been a fait accompli and that he had then obtained, from the White House, approval for continued South African activity and that the CIA would be supporting them.'[43]

South Africa had entered a nightmare. At first, it appeared that the South African troops would easily sweep through to Luanda, but an assault on the city by the FNLA on 10 November failed. Angolan independence was declared on 11 November and the South African intervention was exposed three days later. Stockwell later admitted that 'the propaganda and political war was lost in that stroke. There was nothing the [CIA] Lusaka station could invent that would be as damaging to the other side as our alliance with the hated South Africans was to our cause.' In the weeks that followed, the South African army became stalled and a massive Cuban airlift reinforced the MPLA. Cuban soldiers operating the dreaded 'Stalin Organs', 122 mm rocket-launchers, forced the SADF to recognise that its weapons were out of date.[44] On 19 December, the US Senate passed the Tunney Amendment to the Defense Appropriations Bill which imposed a complete ban on aid to UNITA and the FNLA. Van den Bergh rapidly 'came out against further South African participation in the Angolan war'; he would later claim that the original intervention was P.W. Botha's sole responsibility. Dan O'Meara points out that 'intelligence gathering and evaluation was the supposed exclusive preserve of BOSS . . . The military High Command held van den Bergh personally accountable "for misleading them about the extent of American support for the covert SADF operation".' Slowly, more than 3,000 South African soldiers began to retreat from Angola; by March 1976, Operation Savannah was over. Eschel Rhoodie later declared, 'From a propaganda point of view the Angolan "mistykie" [little mistake] was, in fact, a godsend to our enemies. Diplomatically speaking it was an equal disaster.'[45]

Angola had been the ultimate intelligence war: MI6, the French SDECE, the CIA and BOSS, among others, had all been involved in manipulating news reports and attempting to secure advantage with neigh-bouring countries. Some very strange journalists appeared in Angola in 1975 – for example, the Australian Robert Moss. One of the leading 'cold warriors' in London in the mid-1970s, Moss edited the *Economist*'s *Confidential Foreign Report*, contributed to the Institute for the Study of Conflict (see page 113), was a spokesman for the National Association for Freedom, and wrote Margaret Thatcher's 'Iron Maiden' speech. Oddly, it was the Angolan war that drew Thatcher's attention to Moss, as she revealed in volume one of her autobiography, *The Path to Power*. In November 1975, Moss visited Jonas Savimbi in Angola and wrote a glow-ing portrait for the *Spectator*, which ignored South African involvement in the war.[46] In January and February 1977 in the *Sunday Telegraph*, Moss pro-duced a four-part history of the Angolan war, based on MID sources. In May 1978, in an article for *Politics Today*, he argued that 'South Africa is not being hounded because it is racist but because its rulers are white and, to compound their offence, anti-Communist.' Moss was something of a chameleon, transforming himself into a novelist in the 1980s. When I spoke to him in 1997, he had abandoned Cold War intrigues and literature in favour of dream workshops. He had little interest in his past, noting only that 'some people change'. When I asked him about his politics, he declared, 'If anything, I would be a Blairite.'[47]

John Stockwell accepted that '[CIA] officers liked the South Africans, who tended to be bluff, aggressive men without guile. They admired South African efficiency.' He also revealed that van den Bergh had visited Washington twice during the Angolan war to meet with James Potts; a further meeting was held with the CIA chief in Paris; and 'nearly all CIA intelligence reports . . . were relayed to Pretoria'. However, although the '[CIA] Pretoria and Paris stations were euphoric, having greater access to BOSS and SDECE . . . representatives than ever in agency history . . . the intelligence exchange was entirely one-sided. The South Africans and French accepted voluminous international reports and detailed briefings from those CIA stations but never reciprocated with much information about what they were doing in Angola.'[48] The South African propaganda magazine *To the Point* (see page 99) commented in December 1975: 'spies and their organisations are going through a tough time. Those that used to co-operate now mostly distrust each other.' In May 1976, in an inter-view with Arnaud de Borchgrave of *Newsweek*, John Vorster was asked whether Kissinger had given a green light to the invasion of Angola. Vorster replied: 'If you say that of your own accord, I will not call you a liar.'[49] The 'Cold War' between BOSS and the MID, which had been such a feature of Operation Savannah, would dominate South African politics until 1979.

3

The British Desk

Mr Formerly raised his dark eyes to Patrick's. 'Lower African Security Service. The ambassador is convinced that they kidnapped Whelk.'

'Why would they want to kidnap him?'

'To learn our secrets . . . I know it does seem rather bizarre but I suppose LASS have secrets of their own and that leads them to think that everyone else must have them too. The ambassador thinks this explains why the police don't seem to be doing very much about Whelk . . . it's at his insistence that we're calling in L and F. They're a sort of insurance outfit that advises people on how to negotiate with kidnappers . . . Call themselves Lost and Found. Rather quaint, isn't it? Most irregular for HMG to get involved with such business, of course . . . It's all terribly hush-hush. We mustn't let the Lower Africans know we're doing it.'

. . . 'Why not? If it is them we won't have lost anything because we won't be able to find him anyway, and if it's not they might be able to help.'

Mr Formerly shook his head as though he had been asked whether it were true that someone long dead had recently been returned to life. 'Possible embarrassment.'

'Embarrassment', Patrick soon learned, was what the Foreign Office feared most.

Alan Judd, Short of Glory, 1984[1]

IN IDEAL TIMES, the function of intelligence agencies is to remain invisible; in times of crisis, intelligence-related events can be seen above the surface like icebergs. Seemingly disconnected, these glimpses of a normally hidden world disguise much more than they reveal. In 1976, the apartheid state hit the metaphorical rocks: South Africa's retreat from Angola was interpreted throughout the region as a military defeat; John Vorster finally abandoned his defence of Rhodesia, and within four years that crucial 'buffer' would be reborn as Zimbabwe; the students of Soweto rose up in protest against the insistence upon Afrikaans-language instruction; and the ideology of 'grand apartheid' began to unravel following the failure of the international community to recognise the Transkei 'bantustan' as an independent state. In retrospect, we can recognise that these events marked the moment when apartheid as an ideology began to be transformed from a cruel theory of racial separation into a defensive, morally redundant slouch towards surrender. Little of this was apparent at the time.

South African intelligence had been converted during the 1960s and early 1970s from what had originally been little more than a clumsy policing operation into a full-blown police state for those opposed to apartheid. The setbacks of 1976 would eventually destroy the Prime Minister, his most likely successor, the Minister of Information Connie Mulder, the Department of Information and BOSS. Following the 'iceberg' principle, the sheer scale of peculiar South African intelligence incidents in Great Britain during the winter of 1975 and the spring of 1976 prefigured the developing crisis within the Republic. As if to emphasise the importance of this moment in South African history, the mining giant Anglo American's usually discreet parallel intelligence structure also featured in the stories.

In the spring of 1976, British politics was unsettled by the resignation of two party leaders: the Labour Prime Minister Harold Wilson and the Liberal Party leader Jeremy Thorpe. Wilson had led Labour since 1963 and had won four general elections; Thorpe had led his party since 1967. Both politicians had condemned apartheid: one of Wilson's first actions upon securing power in 1964 was to impose an arms embargo on the Republic; Thorpe had campaigned on behalf of Nelson Mandela and the Rivonia trialists. It has been suggested that Wilson resigned because he sensed the onset of the Alzheimer's disease which would plague his later years. Thorpe resigned because his homosexual affair in the early 1960s with Norman Scott had come to the public's attention in the aftermath of an attempt on Scott's life. In *Rinkagate: The Rise and Fall of Jeremy Thorpe*, Simon Freeman declared with enviable certainty: ' "the South African connection", as it was dubbed by over-excited journalists, did not exist'.[2]

RI and BOSS in London, 1963–1975

London in the late 1950s and early 1960s was the most popular destination for South Africans who were no longer prepared to tolerate life under apartheid. The ANC, the PAC and the SACP all established offices, and support organisations such as the Anti-Apartheid Movement and International Defence and Aid Fund were also based in the city. 'Nevertheless,' as Mark Israel has observed, 'through much of their time in the United Kingdom, political exiles were subject to . . . physical violence from the South African government.' The violence took many forms, but in the 1960s and 1970s it was mainly 'limited to surveillance, burglary and theft'.[3] Between 1958 and 1967, the Afrikaner journalist Hans Lombard worked in London, ostensibly in opposition to apartheid. He became close to the PAC leader, Potlako Leballo, who said of Lombard that he was 'a true dedicated fighter for African freedom in the PAC ranks'. Throughout the decade, Lombard managed to move with ease in and out of South Africa. In 1966, he invited the leader of SWAPO (the Namibian liberation organisation) Sam Nujoma to a party in London; that same evening, Nujoma's hotel room was robbed. Stolen documents were later submitted as evidence in a South African court case. Not long after the Nujoma burglary, Lombard returned to South Africa to edit the *Financial Gazette*. In 1969, PAC member Matthew Nkoana stated in a pamphlet that 'the extent and volume of the intelligence amassed by Lombard over the years must be staggering'; Lombard denied 'that he was ever a spy.'[4]

According to an unpublished history of the South African Intelligence Service, written in 1972 by former DMI employee T.R. Wade, before the mid-1960s intelligence activity in London was limited to 'very amateur penetration operations against South African black movements' by a member of South Africa's Department of Foreign Affairs. In 1965 DMI took charge, and in 1966 RI sent Petrus Cornelius Schoeman to London. Gordon Winter, who was deported from South Africa following his detention, returned to London in December 1966. For the next seven years, he would spy for RI and BOSS while using journalism as his cover. He quickly found work with CIA-funded Forum World Features while continuing to write for his old paper, the Johannesburg *Sunday Express*. He also represented the black publications *Drum* and *Post* in London. One of his intelligence jobs was 'to cover all public demonstrations held by South African political exiles in London'. Between 1967 and 1974, he sent more than 4,000 photographic negatives to Pretoria. He concentrated on information-gathering: studying publicly available information and recording the addresses and telephone numbers of anti-apartheid activists. Winter joined the Foreign Press Association, the Royal Institute of International Affairs (Chatham House) and the National Union of Journalists (NUJ), of which he became membership secretary, with access to the personal details of all NUJ members. Schoeman told him that he 'should "confess" to being a CIA agent if [he] got into serious trouble with British security'.[5] In 1965, John Fairer-Smith, a former detective sergeant in the BSAP, arrived in England. Within a very short period of time, he established a large network of spies who appear to have been working primarily for Rhodesian Intelligence but who were funded by, and shared their findings with, RI–BOSS. In 1969, Nkoana, in *Crisis in the Revolution*, reported that Fairer-Smith's Chester Square flat contained:

> the paraphernalia of the world of espionage: shortwave radios, pocket transmitters, tape-recorders, cameras of various types, a filing cabinet containing dossiers on . . . about 250 political people who are involved in the liberation movements of South Africa, Rhodesia, Angola, Mozambique and the former British High Commission territories of Basutoland (now Lesotho), Bechuanaland (now Botswana), and Swaziland. The dossiers contained detailed background information about the people concerned, including their sexual habits, police records, at least one case of attempted rape in a political office, and allegations of misappropriation of funds and political disputes of a tribalist nature.

Fairer-Smith's most successful agent was Norman Blackburn, who, although British, had joined the Rhodesian army in 1960 and been recruited into the Rhodesian security service in 1963. Blackburn arrived in the UK in 1966 with a brief to 'infiltrate any African organisation, to recruit informers and to carry out other tasks of surveillance'. Blackburn later admitted that there had been approximately seventy agents working for the spy network in Britain: '315 different concerns in Britain holding anti-South African and anti-Rhodesian views were being watched.' Blackburn met regularly with Fairer-Smith at the Playboy Club or the Zambezi Club in Earls Court.[6] At the beginning of 1967, Fairer-Smith departed for South Africa and Blackburn worked with a new unnamed 'controller' based at the South African Embassy. In May 1967, Blackburn and a young typist in the Cabinet Office, Helen Keenan, were arrested by the Special Branch. During the ensuing court case, it emerged that Keenan had given her shorthand dictation notes on Rhodesia to Blackburn. The official report by the Security Commission led by Lord Justice Winn revealed that Keenan had handed Blackburn 'three or four documents'. Blackburn had 'pretended that his father was a businessman in Rhodesia, who would benefit from knowledge about the Government's plans', and paid Keenan £10 per document. He was imprisoned for five years and Helen Keenan for six months.[7] The Blackburn–Keenan case was the first British court case concerned with southern African espionage. Although Blackburn gave detailed information on Fairer-Smith to the Special Branch, no further action was taken. Blackburn later told the *Observer* that '[Fairer-Smith] was in a special position in the eyes of the British security service. It seemed that he was "not to be touched".' John Fairer-Smith returned to Britain in 1968 and started a private detective agency, Argen, which 'conducted economic and political espionage in the UK and on the continent'. Argen continued to function from London throughout the 1970s.[8]

In addition to apartheid South Africa's influential 'friends' in the British establishment (see page 101), intelligence activities were monitored by a number of resourceful enemies. In the British parliament, two Labour MPs, James Wellbeloved and Paul Rose, both of whom later joined the Social Democratic Party (SDP), concentrated on South African intelligence activity. A number of journalists were also inveterate South Africa House-watchers. In 1971, BBC television and ITV's *World in Action* broadcast documentaries on the subject of South African spies, and the *Observer* carried an investigation into 'a South African spy ring operating in Britain from 1966 until [1970]'. In December 1971, the Conservative Home Secretary Reginald Maudling 'confirmed that [South African] agents were at work here, adding that the activities were not illegal'. He was obviously referring to 'declared' intelligence officers. In August 1972, Mark Carlyle, a junior minister at the Home Office, admitted that 'the appropriate authorities know that the South African Intelligence Service has been active in collecting information about anti-South African organisations and individuals in the United Kingdom and that [the British authorities] are keeping a watchful eye on those activities here'.[9] It was the first time that 'undeclared' BOSS activity in the UK had been acknowledged by the British government.

In 1973, the *Guardian* exposed the presence in the UK of Michael Morris, 'who as a [former] police sergeant in the South African security police . . . is known to a generation of students at [the University of] Cape Town where, as he admitted, he operated as an infiltrator and an informer upon the student leadership'. Morris had published a book, *Terrorism*, in 1971, in which he stated: 'it is the policy of the Rhodesian and South African Forces opposing the insurgents to be superior to them in every way . . . to be better man for man'. He also quoted van den Bergh's observation that 'The day we have to fight [insurgents] on our soil it will be an entirely different kind of war; one where we shall have to drop the defensive and strike hard on the offensive. It will then be a total war.' Morris returned to South Africa after one month's 'research'. He told the *Guardian* 'that whether or not he was working for BOSS or the security police his answer to any question on the matter would be a denial'.[10]

Meanwhile, the harassment and mysterious robberies continued: in 1971, the Anti-Apartheid Movement (A-AM) executive secretary Ethel de Keyser had her address book stolen from the A-AM office; Amnesty International and IDAF were burgled; the Society of Friends Peace Committee Office was robbed and 'a file containing information on the visits of South Africans to Britain' was taken; in 1972, Alexandre and Marie-Jose Moumbaris were arrested in South Africa, and at the ensuing trial documents stolen from their London flat were produced in court as evidence (see page 284); anti-apartheid researcher Barbara Rogers reported that her telephone was being tapped; Astrid Winer complained that her London flat had been broken into and searched, and that her telephone was tapped; in 1975, there were multiple burglaries at the homes of ANC and SWAPO members; in addition, SWAPO's offices were burgled. In 1971, Detective Inspector Donker of the English Special Branch, responsible for liaison with the South African Embassy, was 'removed from his post for having irregular contacts with an Embassy official . . . A.H. Bouwer'. Bouwer was Gordon Winter's handler.[11]

Harold Wilson, Jeremy Thorpe and Peter Hain

Prime Minister Harold Wilson set the touch-paper alight with his response to a question in the House of Commons on 9 March 1976. He asserted that 'I have no doubt at all that there is a strong South African participation in recent activities relating to the Right Honourable Gentleman the leader of the Liberal Party, based on massive reserves of business money and private agents of various kinds and various qualities.' Confusingly, he added that he had 'no evidence at all that the South African government or its agencies or agents have any connection with these unsavoury activities'. But Wilson's response to a further question on South African activities was startling: 'Anyone in the House who is concerned with democracy will feel revolted by the fact that we have to face this sort of thing.'[12] Earlier in the day, he had discussed the subject with Barbara Castle: 'It's been a great detective exercise . . . I've got conclusive evidence that South African money has been involved . . . I shall have to say the South African Government isn't involved, because we need their help over Rhodesia.' Hendrik van den Bergh issued an instant statement: 'I deny these accusations and challenge anyone to show there is any truth in them. I have no fear over the findings of any investigation as I am certain the Bureau is innocent. I deny that my Department or any of its officials is involved in any unlawful activities anywhere in the world.'[13]

Following his resignation a week later, on 16 March, Wilson met George Bush, the newly appointed head of the CIA, to discuss a series of mysterious robberies and the possibility of a link with South African intelligence. On 28 March, Conservative MP Sir Frederick Bennett published an 'open' letter to Harold Wilson: 'So far as my researches indicate . . . there are no precedents at all for a Prime Minister refusing to substantiate accusations made under the protection of absolute parliamentary privilege against individuals or corporate bodies, unless of course Secret Service operations are involved.' Wilson's reply, dated 5 April, stated that 'the revelation of details might put the sources or other individuals at risk.'[14]

On 12 May, following Jeremy Thorpe's resignation, Wilson told a Parliamentary Press Gallery lunch: 'What we have seen in recent years has been the work of an underground and well-heeled organisation which did not scruple to use any weapon against the British politicians and parties of whom they disapproved.' He concluded by suggesting that the story should be examined by Britain's media: 'That would be a constructive form of investigative journalism.' On the same day, he summoned to his Lord North Street house two BBC reporters, Barrie Penrose and Roger Courtiour (later dubbed 'Pencourt' in mocking tribute to the 'Woodstein' of the Watergate journalists Woodward and Bernstein). He was clearly determined to provoke a major investigation into both South African illicit activities in Britain and the role of British intelligence agents in smearing members of his government: 'I am not certain that for the last eight months when I was Prime Minister I knew what was happening, fully, in Security.' He then provided:

> detail about the burglaries that he and some of his Labour colleagues in the Government had suffered. He spoke too about the extraordinary 'dirty tricks' which he said had been aimed against some of his Ministers in order to discredit them. He said the culprits were connected with South Africa and with intelligence circles in Britain itself. There was an important story to be investigated, he said, and more than once he used the name Watergate to describe what had been happening in Britain . . . 'I see myself as the big fat spider in the corner of the room. Sometimes I speak when I'm asleep. You should both listen. Occasionally when we meet I might tell you to go to the Charing Cross Road and kick a blind man standing on the corner. That blind man may tell you something, lead you somewhere.'[15]

The Pencourt investigation failed to unearth conclusive proof of a South African connection, preferring to concentrate on aspects of the Thorpe affair, although the pair admitted: 'Somehow the South African connection would not completely disappear.' Meanwhile, Wilson had experienced a further burglary at his house in Great Missenden, Buckinghamshire. One of the items stolen during this robbery was the manuscript of a book by former judge Gerald Sparrow, 'The Ad Astra Connection', which detailed evidence of Sparrow's involvement in South Africa's propaganda operations. On 24 January 1978, before the publication of their book *The Pencourt File*, the Pencourt duo had one final meeting with Sir Harold Wilson, who admitted gloomily: 'I think that people will see me as naive . . . We all chased the wrong hare.'[16] Abandoned by the BBC, *The Pencourt File* was published to substantial criticism. Sir Charles Curran, the BBC Director-General who had commissioned Pencourt, reviewed the book in the *Listener*: 'When a prime minister accuses external agencies of intervening in British political life . . . when he offers to help journalists in pursuing the question . . . and when he asks for a formal assurance of co-operation at the highest level, that, too, has to be given. The important decision was not whether to accept the offer, but whether to publish the information which resulted from it.' Sir Harold Wilson was reported to have declared that the allegations included in the book were 'cock and bull written by two journalists of limited experience and with so little sense of humour that they cannot distinguish between disclosure and a joke'.[17]

Wilson's somewhat melodramatic intervention regarding South African activities in London became confused with the unstated reasons for his surprise resignation and the mysteries surrounding the Jeremy Thorpe case. As Paul Foot recalled in the *London Review of Books* in 1989:

Many years ago, I was one of many journalists who set sail with high hopes in search of an undiscovered country called Wilsonia. It beckoned from afar across mighty oceans of investigations and tip-offs. The lucky journalist to reach it would be rewarded with arguably the greatest political scoop of our time: he or she would finally reveal why Harold Wilson, to the astonishment of the entire political and journalistic world, suddenly took himself off to obscurity . . . One by one we all drifted back to shore unrewarded. My own voyage had taken me from the Wigan Alps to Bulgarian export/import statistics but had produced not a glimpse of Wilsonia . . . I am prepared to accept, like a reformed gold-digger on the Sierra Madre, that Wilsonia never existed: that there was never a simple, secret explanation for Wilson's resignation. His own explanation was probably true – he *had* had enough.[18]

Peter Wright's *Spycatcher* and former British intelligence officer Colin Wallace's testimony in the mid-1980s confirmed that a faction within MI5 had attempted to destabilise Wilson's premiership. As Stephen Dorril and Robin Ramsay concluded in *Smear! Wilson and the Secret State*: ' "South Africa" was a useful short-hand, almost a metaphor, for the other forces [Wilson] knew were at work against him. His problem was that the evidence he did have was about MI5's activities against him; but this he felt unable to use.' In 1979, following Gordon Winter's 'defection', Wilson said that 'he considered Mr Winter's claims to be a vindication of remarks he made to the House of Commons in 1976 . . . "I know there were BOSS people at work in London . . . An inquiry will be three years too late." ' In 1981, commenting on the publication of *Inside BOSS*, Wilson said that 'if only a quarter of the facts alleged in the book were shown to be true a grave state of affairs would be disclosed'.[19]

Jeremy Thorpe, the leader of the Liberal Party, had been an active opponent of the apartheid state for many years. At one point in the early 1960s he was President of the World Campaign for the Release of South African Political Prisoners. In 1966, at the Liberal Party Assembly he spoke in favour of the use of force against the illegal Rhodesian UDI government: 'Selective bombing of supply lines – for example the rail link from Lourenço Marques which carries much of the oil supply – is something the government should consider.' In 1972, speaking at the University of the Witwatersrand in Johannesburg, he announced that he 'was familiar with Sir Robert Birley's . . . legacy known as Birley's Law. This stated "that the gentlemen from the Special Branch are to be found in the second row". However, reassuringly I noted that the second row was occupied by Mr Oppenheimer, who was Chancellor of [the University of] Cape Town.' Joe Haines, former press secretary to Harold Wilson, has posed the question, 'what possible interest [could] South Africa have in destroying Jeremy Thorpe, whose influence, such as it was, was waning?' This simplistic and anglocentric reading of BOSS's intentions failed to acknowledge that it was Gordon Winter, South African journalist and intelligence asset, who in 1971 uncovered the story of Norman Scott's homosexual relationship with Jeremy Thorpe; it was Winter who supplied British intelligence with Norman Scott's documents; and it was Winter who attempted to sell the story to the *Sunday People* on the eve of the February 1974 general election, at which the Liberals would win more than 6,000,000 votes that gave them significant influence in a hung parliament.[20]

It seems extremely unlikely that BOSS had anything to do with the plot surrounding commercial pilot Andrew 'Gino' Newton's killing of Scott's dog Rinka and the attempted murder of Norman Scott. South African intelligence would have enjoyed the power of possessing damaging information about a political opponent, but having knowledge and engaging in a ridiculous conspiracy are very different things. It is quite possible, however, that Thorpe and his supporters were spurred into action against Scott because they knew that Gordon Winter had touted the potential scandal to the newspapers and that Scott claimed to be writing a book which Winter would assist him in publishing in South Africa. It certainly suited Jeremy Thorpe that the South African connection should be publicised by Harold Wilson, drawing attention away from Norman Scott's allegations.

Thorpe told Cyril Smith, the Liberal Chief Whip, on 3 February 1976: 'It's good. It will be pushed on to South Africa . . . The PM believes that there are South African influences at work.' Six weeks later, Smith asked Thorpe whether he intended to resign. ' "Certainly not," he replied. "I'm bound to win. I have the three most important people in Britain on my side – Harold Wilson, Lord Goodman, and MI5." It was yet another of those unreal remarks. What did it mean?'[21] Perhaps what Thorpe meant was that he had intelligence 'insurance'. It would later emerge that Peter Bessell, former Liberal MP and the person who had calmed and provided money for Norman Scott during the mid-1960s, had links with both British and American intelligence. In South Africa, Gordon Winter was informed by van den Bergh that Jeremy Thorpe had intelligence connections. Harold Wilson demonstrated his willingness to help by timing the announcement of his resignation for the same day as Norman Scott began to give evidence against Andrew Newton in the attempted murder case. Lord Goodman represented both Harold Wilson and Jeremy Thorpe as a lawyer and was an acknowledged master at deflecting unwanted newspaper coverage. Intriguingly, he had relatives in the Republic and had travelled to Rhodesia on five occasions between 1968 and 1971 as an emissary of the British government.[22]

Following his resignation from the Liberal Party leadership, Jeremy Thorpe and a number of his supporters were charged in 1978 with incitement and conspiracy to murder. They were acquitted in 1979 after a sensational trial at the Old Bailey. Andrew Newton, who had been sentenced to two years in prison in 1976, was released on parole in 1977 and after a brief sojourn in Rhodesia returned to appear as a prosecution witness in the Thorpe case.[23] In 1990, *The Times* reported:

> Mr Newton has told a senior Conservative backbench MP that he received a £50,000 payment from MI5 in the form of a bogus win on the Premium Bonds for his part in the trial, according to a Whitehall source. It is understood that Mr Newton wrote to the MP complaining that he was still owed a further payment from MI5 and he threatened to 'blow the whistle' on its involvement in the Thorpe trial. Sir Robin Butler, the Cabinet Secretary, ordered an investigation into the claims. Mr Newton has produced evidence apparently showing he received a £50,000 Premium Bond prize in 1981.[24]

An extraordinary link between the Thorpe case and Peter Hain lies in the date: 24 October 1975. On the very day that Andrew Newton was driving out to Exmoor with Norman Scott, Rinka and the faulty Mauser pistol, Peter Hain was arrested in west London in connection with the theft of £490 from the Putney branch of Barclays Bank. In Angola, the South African Defence Force was engaged in the secret invasion of Angola.[25] On the evidence of two twelve-year-old schoolboys and despite the fact that he claimed to have been nowhere near the bank at the time of the robbery, the police charged Hain with theft. Peter Hain had made his name as a young Liberal anti-apartheid campaigner and had played a pivotal role in the campaign to stop sporting relations between Britain and South Africa. In South Africa, Hain was a thoroughly demonised figure and an undoubted target for BOSS. Indeed, in June 1972 he had received a letter-bomb which failed to explode, and two months later he had been prosecuted for 'conspiracy' in relation to activities during the sports campaign. Hain later recalled:

> The right-wing Society for Individual Freedom (which was closely linked to British Intelligence) backed the prosecution, and Gordon Winter was instructed by BOSS to offer his help and pass over his material on me. This he did, liaising initially with Gerald Howarth, its General Secretary (who entered Parliament in 1983 as a hard-right Conservative close to Margaret Thatcher). In June 1971, the 'Hain Prosecution Fund' was launched to raise £20,000 for [barrister and parliamentary draftsman Francis] Bennion's private prosecution. Howarth was its Treasurer and Ross McWhirter its

Chairman. These two, together with Winter, respectively provided links with the hard right, MI5 and BOSS.[26]

On 3 February 1976, Hain was contacted by Kenneth Wyatt, who explained that he had been requested by Fred Kamil, a former security officer who had worked for Anglo American, 'to inform me that the Putney bank theft had been carried out by a South African agent specially flown over to Britain for the job'. Wyatt added that the Hain robbery case was part of a BOSS campaign to discredit leaders of the Liberal Party. He added: 'action against Thorpe is going according to plan'.

Hain was suspicious of Wyatt, who like the majority of the characters in this story could accurately be described as being of somewhat dubious character. On 17 February, however, news reports confirmed a substantial part of Wyatt's story: Wyatt, among others, was due to appear at a London magistrates' court charged with conspiracy to extort £1 million from Anglo American. Peter Hain swiftly produced a memorandum, 'South African Agent Disruption of Liberal Party', for the beleaguered Jeremy Thorpe: 'Apparently, Anglo American's extensive security service works closely with South Africa's secret service, BOSS, and Kamil's own intelligence contacts in Anglo American thus have access to BOSS.' The memorandum detailed a plot against Liberal politicians: 'the daughter of a Liberal MP ("who lives in the Hampstead/St John's Wood area") had been tricked into appearing in a "blue movie" filmed at the MP's home; the film would be used to discredit the MP.' Thorpe handed the memorandum to Harold Wilson and it provided one of the central sources for the statement that he made in the House of Commons on 9 March.[27]

A few days later, Hain received an envelope with a Johannesburg postmark which contained a photograph of Gordon Winter in a swimming pool with Mary Oppenheimer, the daughter of the head of Anglo American. Hain was soon visited by an American academic, Dan Hughes, who introduced him to Diane Lefevre, a mysterious young British doctor. It transpired that Lefevre already knew about the Gordon Winter photograph, even though Hain and his family had not discussed it with anybody. Lefevre was also keen to boost the credibility of a letter which had been sent to Harold Wilson and senior Labour and Liberal politicians: 'The letter alleged that Anglo American had been dealing in arms for the South African government and that documents revealing a smear campaign against Labour, trade union and Liberal leaders had been taken from the office of the company's security force.' Peter Hain was acquitted at his trial in April

1976 after a witness emerged who could testify that he chased the thief and saw his face. Another witness, Sybil Foreshaw, supported the suspicion of a Hain double: 'I went out shopping at 10 a.m. and saw the familiar face of Peter Hain as I walked down the High Street . . . As he got near to me and as we passed within a yard of each other I realised it wasn't Peter Hain. The difference between the two was almost unnoticeable except that Hain had a heavier build and the shape of the other man's face was longer.' It was still a close run-thing: the jury took nearly five hours to deliver a verdict.[28]

Gordon Winter would later reveal how South African intelligence had framed Peter Hain. His former London handler, Alf Bouwer, informed him that BOSS had employed an Irish youth who looked very similar to Hain: 'A BOSS agent had been watching Hain's home from a parked car near by. The youth who really robbed the bank was . . . a "criminal who had to do as he was told because we had a grappling hook up his back-side".' The youth later settled in South Africa. Following the robbery, BOSS telephoned Scotland Yard and told the police 'that if they checked with Special Branch files they would see that Peter Hain was heavily involved in agitating against Barclays Bank and its investments in South Africa'. Hain confirmed that there 'was an unexplained incident which both confused and intrigued my solicitor . . . At one point during my detention . . . the officer in charge of the investigation referred obliquely to telephone conversations with senior officers in Scotland Yard, and to important evidence they had.' Winter also explained that van den Bergh had sent the photograph of Winter in the Oppenheimer swimming pool: the BOSS chief 'actively encouraged the rumours that Harry Oppenheimer was to blame for the smear plot against the Liberal Party'.[29]

The South African Connection

Fouad 'Flash Fred' Kamil was an Anglo American 'diamond soldier' who had fallen out with his masters. A Lebanese trader turned diamond mercenary, 'he extorted money from [diamond] smugglers on the route that led through the swamps from Sierra Leone to Liberia'. Kamil was recruited in 1956 by Percy Sillitoe's International Diamond Security Organisation (IDSO – see page 12) to break the diamond-smuggling networks in Sierra Leone. The deal between Kamil and the IDSO was that 'he would be supplied with information from undercover informers about the exact movements of dia-mond shipments from Sierra Leone to Liberia to facilitate his ambushes. In return he would turn the diamonds over to a De Beers subsidiary, and he would receive one-third of their value in cash.' It was a bloody business but a very profitable one. Within a year, the smuggling problem in Sierra Leone had been resolved and the IDSO was disbanded. Kamil continued to work in diamond security, eventually arriving in Johannesburg in 1965. For a period he worked for the Diamond Branch of the South African Police before once again being recruited by Anglo American.[30]

Colonel George Visser, the head of Anglo American security in the 1960s, described Kamil as 'the best IDB [Illicit Diamond Buying] agent Anglo ever employed'. In the late 1960s, Kamil went to London on behalf of Anglo American to work on Operation Executive: an investigation into diamond-smuggling by two senior Anglo executives. 'In "Operation Executive" I accidentally came across the point where financiers and politicians meet,' he told South Africa's leading investigative journalist Mervyn Rees in 1976. Having worked for Anglo American for a number of years, in particular with Patrick Weichman, Anglo's intelligence chief, Kamil was abruptly dismissed in 1970. He felt that he was owed substantial funds from his diamond-smuggling intercepts and had retained a file of documents to use as leverage with the company. By 1972, having failed to get the money he was owed, he decided he would hijack a South African Airlines jet on which he believed Gordon Waddell, Harry Oppenheimer's son-in-law, would be travelling and hold him to ransom. But the gang hijacked the wrong aeroplane and Kamil was imprisoned in Malawi.[31]

One year later, Kamil was released from prison and Anglo American attempted to achieve a final settlement with him. He was paid R80,000 by Visser's successor as head of security, Colonel F.A.J. van Zijl. The inimitable Fred Kamil continued to feel that he had been underpaid and on 26 September 1975 an advertisement was placed in *Time Out* on his behalf:

DO YOU WANT MONEY AND ADVENTURE?

> Men and women, race and age immaterial, needed for a
> group of adventurers being formed abroad.
>> Send details and photograph if possible.

Box 289/206.[32]

Kamil recruited Kenneth Wyatt 'to mount an "operation" to force a confrontation with the directors of Anglo American'. He later admitted: 'When I asked Wyatt how he intended to operate, he said that all details must be left to his group. I was the client and would be required to pay only on results.' After a series of threats demanding the payment of £1,100,000 were delivered to members of the Oppenheimer family and Anglo American in London, including the sending of wreaths, hearses and menacing letters, Wyatt approached Peter Hain with his tale of a 'doppel-ganger' and South African interference in Liberal politics. In April, Anita Sassin, who had acted as a courier for Kamil, experienced a mysterious break-in at the office of her solicitor. In May, she was visited 'by a man who claimed to work for the British Government. He told her to keep her mouth shut regarding allegations of bribery of British politicians by South African interests. If she didn't keep quiet, she was told, she would be "put in prison for 15 years". Ms. Sassin claims that he also commented on her face and figure and said "You wouldn't want anything to happen to them, would you?" '[33]

While Wyatt and his colleagues faced trial for intimidation and extortion, Fred Kamil gave a number of fascinating interviews from his hideaway in Barcelona. David Hosenball of *Time Out* reported in May 1976: 'Kamil has no doubts of the extent of South African involvement in this country. Would South African agents have tried to smear Jeremy Thorpe or frame Peter Hain for bank robbery? "They really stop at nothing . . . The average member of the public feels that he lives in a sophisticated, civilised world. Really we are living in the world of Machiavelli." ' During the same month, Kamil told the *Rand Daily Mail*: 'I've got enough enemies already. I do not want to say anything against South Africa. I might change my mind later.'[34]

Three years later, Fred Kamil published *The Diamond Underworld*, in which he declared unequivocally: 'There were no plots by BOSS or Anglo American against any British political groups or leaders.' Kamil's version of events casts himself as the victim of Wyatt's activities. Wyatt and his associates were found guilty and imprisoned. During his trial, Wyatt said 'that he went along with Kamil's schemes only because he was working for an "anti-apartheid organisation", not, he stressed, a British-based one, which was keen to obtain Kamil's dossiers on Anglo American'. Peter Hain adds that Wyatt was clearly surprised to be convicted; 'he had told journalists beforehand that he would be "protected" '. Diane Lefevre, who had corroborated Wyatt's story, reappeared during the Wyatt trial when it was 'openly suggested in court that she was a British intelligence agent'. In March 1973, newspapers had suggested that Lefevre had infiltrated the Palestinian organisation Black September, on behalf of MI6.[35]

*

On 31 January 1976, two days after Norman Scott's declaration in court that 'For years I've been hounded because of my homosexual relationship with Jeremy Thorpe,' the *Daily Mirror* published a front page featuring a photograph of Gordon Winter and the screaming headline 'Thorpe Hunter' in large letters. The story declared: 'Winter is believed to have worked with the South African security service.' Winter's deportation from South Africa in 1966 and his return in 1974 were noted. A newspaper colleague who had worked with him in the 1960s was quoted as saying: 'It was the first time anyone deported in a case like his had been allowed back.'[36] The *Daily Mirror* was on strong ground in asserting that Gordon Winter was involved in the Thorpe case – the paper must have known that he had attempted to sell the story to the *Sunday People* in 1974, but it could not prove he was linked to BOSS.

In May 1976 when the press hysteria over the South African connection was at its peak, *The Times* observed in an editorial:

> There is nothing in the story, as it has publicly unfolded, to support an allegation that South African agents fabricate discreditable rumours about figures or parties in British public life, or that they disseminate them, whether fabricated or not, for the purpose of undermining the position of those who are conceived to oppose the interest of the South African government. The only part of the public record which points at all in that direction is the activity of Mr Gordon Winter. He is a South African journalist who was in Britain for seven years, during which time he assembled a story of Mr Thorpe's relationship with Mr Norman Scott. He then proceeded to hawk it round assiduously. But nothing connects him with the South African government, BOSS or Anglo American, and there is no need to look further for an explanation of his assiduity than any journalist's desire, when he thinks he has a good story, to get it into print.[37]

Despite the fact that Winter had not been exposed, the publicity was not appreciated. Van den Bergh instructed Winter that his 'days [as] a spy in the field were over. He said I should resign from the Johannesburg *Sunday Express*.' Winter was instructed to join the *Citizen*, a newspaper that was being started with secret government funds (see page 99). Three years later, Gordon Winter 'defected' from South Africa and revealed that he had worked for South African intelligence since 1963. Lee Tracey, the former British spy to whom Winter gave the Thorpe–Scott documents in the early 1970s, told journalists: 'In my view Gordon Winter was the best agent BOSS ever had in London.'[38]

*

The change in tone obvious in *The Times* editorial had been caused by two stories which were published in May 1976 and appeared to establish convincing links in the South African chain. In April, Peter Hillmore of the *Guardian* was approached by André Thorne, a twenty-year-old male prostitute. Thorne claimed to have been involved in the shooting of a 'blue' film in which a Liberal MP, dressed as a scoutmaster, engaged 'in acts of gross indecency with young boys'. He said that he had been contacted by a South African diplomat, J.L. Russouw, who was interested in purchasing the film. Hillmore later visited the South African Embassy with Thorne and discussed the film with Russouw, who insisted that 'it was a purely personal interest'. Hillmore revealed that he was a *Guardian* reporter and Russouw terminated the meeting. Later, Chris van der Walt, Director of Information at the Embassy, contacted the *Guardian* to declare that the meeting had been secretly recorded. He said that if the paper 'published a report of the meeting the name of the politician would become known. "The tape is our trump card."' The *Guardian* published the story on 15 May.[39] The Prime Minister James Callaghan, Wilson's successor, said in parliament on 20 May: 'Those of us who have known Sir Harold for many years know he has a great capacity for illuminating the truth long before it becomes apparent to others. In this particular case [the smearing of Liberal politicians] there is no doubt whatever that, as the investigation proceeds and in spite of all the persiflage which surrounds much of it, of course there are attempts being made against individual members of the Liberal Party.' Russouw was swiftly recalled to South Africa, where it was later admitted that he had merely been on secondment to the Embassy in London.[40] It has never been revealed whether he was an intelligence officer.

One week later, the *Sunday People*'s front page featured André Thorne and the headline, 'I Lied About That Blue Film'. Thorne declared in a sworn statement: 'I said that the South Africans had first contacted me . . . That was untrue . . . I know I've told lie after lie . . . The person I feel most sorry for is Mr Russouw . . . I think I've destroyed that man and his family.' The *Sunday People* admitted in their story, 'There can be no guarantee that he is telling the truth even now.' An embarrassed *Guardian* responded: 'The *Guardian* utterly denies any attempt to indulge in a smear campaign against the South African government . . . We have never attempted to link the Russouw affair into any wider context or to draw wider lessons from it. We have said repeatedly that it is "quite separate".'[41]

André Thorne disappeared from the news for a few weeks before reappearing in *Time Out* in August 1976. His story had now changed again.

He admitted that he *had* contacted the South African Embassy and offered a pornographic film featuring a British politician. 'Thorne claims that the South Africans realised the film was phoney very quickly. But, he says, they suggested that he contact the *Guardian* and have some fun with them by selling them a dud anti-South African story that would have the added attraction of smearing the Liberal Party.' After the *Guardian* ran the story, the South Africans encouraged Thorne 'to blow the gaff, choosing the *People* to do so'. Two days after the *Guardian* carried Thorne's story, 'Colonel' Frederick Cheeseman contacted David Steel, the Liberal Chief Whip. Cheeseman claimed to be a former intelligence officer who had visited BOSS headquarters in Pretoria in September 1974 where he was shown a number of dossiers on British politicians, Liberal and Labour, who were to be the targets of a smear campaign. He also reported that he had been interviewed by Hendrik van den Bergh. Cheeseman possessed documents including letters from the South African Embassy which confirmed part of his story. The BBC Nine O'Clock News on 18 May led on the Cheeseman story, which had been prepared by the Pencourt team, and this was followed up by the newspapers the next day. On 20 May, the *Daily Express* front page declared: 'Colonel Bogus: "I admit it – spy tale was all lies". The strange Walter Mitty world of the man who claims to have seen South African secret police "smear dossiers" on the Liberal Party fell apart last night . . . "For years I have lived a lie . . . and one lie led to another." '[42]

While most of the British press enjoyed the BBC's discomfort, the *Sunday Telegraph* observed: 'Intensive inquiries into the affair of "Lieutenant Colonel" Frederick Cheeseman indicate more than ever that BBC news investigators were the victims of an elaborate South African plot aimed at discrediting the British media.' The newspaper revealed that BBC producer Gordon Carr and the Pencourt pair spoke to 'military intelligence officers in South Africa and Embassy officials in London [who] went out of their way to indicate [that] Cheeseman's . . . story was substantially true'. Van den Bergh's response was also interesting: on 20 May he commented: 'I only heard of him this morning . . . The whole story is a fabrication. One lie after another.' He later changed his statement to admit that he had interviewed Cheeseman in 1974. William Raynor and Geoff Allen in their unpublished book 'Smear – The Thorpe Affair' (1978) explained that:

> throughout Cheeseman had told one story to the British press – that he had lived a lie to try and win respect from his neighbours and that the whole charade had got out of control – and another to the South African press to whom he said that he had been a 'pawn sacrificed in a complex diplomatic chessgame.

Someone was needed to relieve the strain on the relationship between Britain and South Africa. But it cost dearly. In personal terms it cost very dearly. Someone had to be crucified.' Later he said that it had been necessary to 'stop the train' of the smear story to normalise Anglo-South African relations before the first Kissinger–Vorster meeting on the future of Southern Africa. He acknowledged, 'It was a brilliant manipulation of the press.'[43]

Peter Hain was told by former British intelligence officer Colin Wallace in 1987: 'The Colonel Cheeseman saga is known in intelligence circles as the "double bubble" because it contains a second dimension in deception and not only deflects attention from the main target, but also "bursts", leaving the investigator doubting everything he has uncovered so far.' Gordon Winter entitled the chapter in *Inside BOSS* that dealt with the Thorne and Cheeseman stories 'Red Herrings'. *Private Eye* summed up the end result in July 1976: 'Ironically the main beneficiary of the plot story is none other than the South African secret police (BOSS) . . . BOSS operates one of the most efficiently organised intelligence systems in the world. A well-known CIA ploy is to "expose" ridiculous figures as CIA agents in order to protect their genuine informants . . . All in all, the only people who have not been discredited in this whole affair are BOSS.'[44]

Erasing the Connection

The popular studies of the Thorpe trial and Harold Wilson's resignation avoid any mention of the South African connection. There are good reasons for this: the Jeremy Thorpe case was an early example of the sex-obsessed celebrity culture that became hegemonic in the 1990s. In 1978, the suggestion that the leader of a political party was a 'promiscuous homosexual' was startling enough. The allegation that he had engaged in a plot to murder a former lover seems unbelievable to this day. Thorpe and his associates were, of course, found to be innocent, but the conduct of the judge – especially in his readiness to express his disgust for Norman Scott: 'I am sure you remember him very well. His hysterically warped personality; an accomplished liar; very skilful at exciting and exploiting sympathy . . . He is a fraud. he is a sponger. He is a whiner. He is a parasite' – was viewed by many as ludicrously biased in favour of the defendants. The speech was swiftly satirised by Peter Cook at 'The Secret Policeman's Ball'.[45]

Two Labour Prime Ministers, the BBC and the *Guardian* were severely embarrassed in 1976 by the South African connection. James Callaghan announced in the House of Commons in the autumn of 1976 that there would be no further official investigation into allegations of South African involvement in British politics. But quietly, without drawing any attention to the move, the Labour government issued a directive, to British intelligence and the Special Branch, cancelling liaison with the South African intelligence services or Security Police on any subject except 'common interest'. In 1977 and 1987 British Prime Ministers Callaghan and Thatcher made parliamentary statements officially clearing MI5 of plotting against Harold Wilson. But in 1996 Sir John Hunt, Cabinet Secretary during Wilson's 1974–6 administration, revealed on television that 'There is absolutely no doubt at all that a few, a very few malcontents in MI5 . . . a lot of them, like Peter Wright, who were right wing, malicious, had serious personal grudges, were giving vent to these and were spreading damaging malicious stories about some members of that Labour government.'[46] It is possible that there was a dreadful clash of interests in 1976 in Britain; this was, after all, a pivotal moment in the collapse of Britain's post-war consensus. For an eight-month period between September 1975 and May 1976, South African activities collided with MI5 and MI6 in the middle of, to use Paul Foot's phrase, 'one of their customary fratricidal quarrels'. Wilson's resignation and Norman Scott's allegations provided the drama, but backstage the performance was much more intense. Peter Hain suggests that the Wyatt episode had been an attempt by MI6 to expose the South African connection 'through a source which could not be traced back':

> Peter Wright testifies that the MI5 faction was openly sympathetic to white South Africa because it was seen as an ally in a mutual war against 'international communism'. Colin Wallace corroborates this, adding that information was regularly 'traded' between MI5 and BOSS . . . by 1975 the battle for power in Northern Ireland between MI5 and MI6 meant that 'they were much more at war with each other than with the IRA' . . . The two intelligence services were also known to have quite different political attitudes towards South Africa. MI6 tended to be more anti-apartheid, reflecting Foreign Office policy.[47]

Peter Bessell wrote of the Thorpe case in the privately published *Cover-Up: The Jeremy Thorpe Affair*. 'The one form of corruption that does exist in British public life cuts across all political, professional, commercial and, to some extent, class barriers. It is the cover-up power of the Establishment.' The hysteria that surrounded the investigations into the South African connection between March and May 1976 was followed by an almost complete erasing of the subject from the public record. Investigations were stopped, political campaigners were refused the oxygen of publicity, television films were abandoned and books were brutally edited or not published.[48] After May 1976, Bessell's 'Establishment' decided that South Africa had become an embarrassing diversion and it was dutifully covered up. Gordon Winter's 'defection' in 1979 should have brought the subject back to life.

Unfortunately, very few of the journalists who investigated the Thorpe case had any first-hand knowledge of apartheid South Africa. William Raynor, who knew South Africa well, and Geoff Allen (*Rand Daily Mail*) persisted longest with the South African angle. In May 1977, as 'Smear' was being prepared for publication, Gordon Winter wrote a damaging story that was published in the *Citizen*: 'A London journalist, the author of several articles criticising South Africa, has secretly arrived in this country on a special mission – to track down "secret agents". He is freelance writer Mr William "Bill" Raynor, who still believes South African "agents" were behind a campaign to smear prominent people in Britain last year.' Raynor did not visit South Africa in 1977. Penguin abandoned the book a few weeks later.[49] One of the many mysteries in this story was how Gordon Winter, living and working in South Africa, received copies of the Peter Hain memorandum (February 1976), a page from a transcript of Tom Mangold's BBC interview with Peter Bessell which was never broadcast, and a copy of Raynor and Allen's unpublished book, 'Smear'. Somebody who had access to both the BBC's current affairs documentary department and the publisher Penguin must have handed the manuscript and the memorandum to Special Branch or MI5, from where they were forwarded to Hendrik van den Bergh in Pretoria and eventually to Gordon Winter in Johannesburg.[50] Such a person may well have perceived their action as patriotic but they could have had no idea how their surveillance operation would be abused.

During 1975 and 1976, South African intelligence had overreached in London. The metaphorical iceberg had towered above the water, dragging Anglo American's intelligence structure with it. It took every trick that BOSS knew and every 'friend' that could be mobilised to remove the South African connection from the Wilson and Thorpe stories. Incredibly, with the unwitting assistance of the embarrassed British establishment, it was achieved.

4

The Z Squad

'We do disagreeable things, but we are *defensive*. That, I think, is still fair. We do disagreeable things so that ordinary people here and elsewhere can sleep safely in their beds at night. Is that too romantic? Of course, we occasionally do very wicked things'; he grinned like a schoolboy. 'And in weighing up the moralities, we rather go in for dishonest comparisons; after all, you can't compare the ideals of one side with the methods of the other . . . I mean you've got to compare method with method, and ideal with ideal. I would say that since the war, our methods – ours and those of the opposition – have become much the same. I mean you can't be less ruthless than the opposition simply because your government's *policy* is benevolent, can you now?' He laughed quietly to himself: 'That would *never* do.'

'Control' in John le Carré, *The Spy Who Came in from the Cold*, 1963[1]

The Soweto Uprising and the Culture of Violence

IN JUNE 1976, the Soweto uprising shook South Africa to the core. The violent unrest challenged almost every aspect of the apartheid state's ideology. It is possible to read South African history and conclude that apartheid's eventual disintegration was predetermined from the moment the first bullet hit thirteen-year-old Hector Peterson. Apartheid's leading propagandist, Eschel Rhoodie, believed that 'had the riots lasted a week and been confined only to Soweto, the media would have dropped the matter'. But the riots spread throughout the country and continued sporadically for the next eight months. The Vorster government's response was, in the words of Dan O'Meara, 'a mixture of vacillation and severe and bitterly cynical repression'.[2] Over the years ahead, the leaders of the Security State would question what had happened and who was to blame. Some believed that the government had been too soft on the rioters. In

August 1976, for example, the Minister of Justice Jimmy Kruger, who had become infamous for his comment that blacks needed to be made 'tame to the gun', suggested to the cabinet that 'this movement must be broken and the police should perhaps act more drastically to bring about more deaths'. Brigadier Theuns 'Rooi Rus' (Red Russian) Swanepoel, chief Security Police interrogator (and torturer) and founder of the counter-insurgency unit which later became Koevoet, commanded the police in Johannesburg during the early days of the rioters. He said in 1986: 'If the police had enough men available on the 16th [June 1976] and used sufficient force – irrespective of the number being killed – we could have stopped them . . . and it wouldn't have spread throughout the country.'[3]

In August 1976, van den Bergh, in an article in the official magazine of the Public Servants' Association described the current situation 'in the words of President Kennedy . . . "Each day the crises multiply. Each day their solution grows more difficult. Each day we draw nearer the hour of maximum danger as the weapons spread and hostile forces grow stronger." ' In October 1976, he told Gordon Winter and the *Citizen*: 'We have sufficient information proving that local agitators are getting directions from known South African communists based in London.' His explanation for the uprising was typically conspiratorial and reflected the intellectual vacuum at the heart of the security establishment:

When the South African Communist Party leader, Braam Fischer, was arrested 10 years ago, a vitally important document was found in his posses-sion. 'This was a directive to all his secret Communist Party section leaders in South Africa' . . . Members of the party were instructed to rebuild the shattered Communist Party and achieve its objectives by psychological con-ditioning of the public. Stress would be placed on the need for change – and by consistent propaganda the public's will to resist could be broken down . . . The directive ordered all communists to 'go to ground' and secretly infiltrate respectable and recognised institutions – particularly women's and students' organisations – and use them to further the aims of communism . . . One large organisation was so successfully penetrated that communists inside it actually started training 'agents for change' in South Africa as instructed in the Fischer directive. The plan was that they were to be fully trained by the middle of 1975, when they would be 'let loose' to carry out their mental subversion in South Africa.[4]

Van den Bergh was strategically stuck in his glory days of the 1960s. He could neither recognise nor understand the leaderless millenarian quality of the insurrection. The document to which he referred has never surfaced. Stephen Ellis has observed: 'Claims that the rising was the product of a political conspiracy, whether made by those seeking to portray anti-government agitation as the result of external aggression, or by political actors claiming credit, provide little explanation.' More than 4,000 students fled South Africa during the uprising; the majority joined the ANC (and the SACP) which offered organisation and leadership in exile. In the first five days of rioting, the security forces admitted, 130 people had died and 1,100 had been injured. By February 1977, around 6,000 people had been arrested. The government's Cillie Commission estimated that 575 people had been killed by this time, with 2,389 injured. In May 1977, the South African Institute of Race Relations reported that 618 people had died. All of these figures are underestimates. It is likely that approximately 1,000 people were killed during the Soweto uprising, with between 10,000 and 15,000 arrested. By the end of 1976, a total of 1,556 people had been convicted of charges linked to the disturbances, 1,122 of whom were under the age of eighteen.[5] The South African police deployed the newly formed riot squads and the Special Task Force during the uprising. These specialist units had been created since 1974 following trips to Argentina 'to study riot control' and following the visit of General Meir Amit, a former head of Israel's foreign intelligence agency, Mossad, who toured South Africa in 1975 giving 'guidance on urban warfare techniques'.[6]

South Africa's Truth and Reconciliation Commission (TRC) was a fascinating but flawed experiment in attempting to heal a damaged nation. Between 1995 and 1998, the TRC held hearings throughout South Africa at which both the victims and the perpetrators of human rights abuses were invited to testify. Perpetrators were offered amnesty for past crimes in exchange for an honest account of what happened. The process attempted to construct an accurate history of apartheid South Africa between 1960 and 1994. In fact, its most successful research was on the period from 1979.

The TRC found that, between 1963 and 1975, there had been twenty-one deaths in police custody: thirteen were listed as 'suicide', five as 'natural causes' and three as 'accidental death'. The accidents were genuinely incredible: 'bronchial pneumonia after slipping in the shower', 'fatal injuries from slipping on a bar of soap' and 'slipped down stairs'. Ahmed Timol, a twenty-nine-year-old activist, was tortured and dropped from the tenth floor of the Security Police headquarters at John Vorster Square on

27 October 1971. It was claimed that he had committed suicide. Policemen would later joke that the only thing that the inquest proved 'was that Indians couldn't fly'.[7] In 1976 and 1977, twenty-eight people died at the hands of the police. The most famous was black-consciousness leader Steve Biko, who in the words of the TRC:

> died in police custody in Pretoria on 12 September 1977. He was detained by the Security Branch in Port Elizabeth twenty-four days earlier, and was subjected to interrogation, during which he sustained serious brain injuries. He was examined by both a district surgeon and a medical specialist . . . He was then transported naked in the back of a police van from Port Elizabeth to Pretoria. He died from brain damage in a prison cell shortly after his arrival in Pretoria. On hearing the news of his death, Minister Kruger said: 'It leaves me cold.'[8]

The Biko case became a cause célèbre, but an indication of the difficulties caused by the number of deaths in custody can be detected in a television statement that van den Bergh made in March 1977. He exonerated the police from blame but noted that 'it was "most decidedly" in the interests of police interrogators that detainees did not commit suicide'. He suggested that sometimes police disclosure of ' "detailed knowledge of his misdeeds or involvement in conspiracy" might unnerve the detainee to the point "where he was capable of doing just about anything" '.[9] Torture had been a familiar feature of South African policing since the early 1960s. In the first half of that decade, van den Bergh, 'Rooi Rus' Swanepoel and six other officers visited France and received 'special training in torture techniques' employed by the French in Algeria. In 1968, Swanepoel led a five-man team to France for 'further training in interrogation and counter-interrogation techniques'. In a passage loaded with racial meaning, Henrik Ellert described Swanepoel interrogating MK soldiers in Rhodesia in 1967: 'Swanepoel was accompanied as always by a tall and malevolent looking Zulu detective-sergeant of whom Swanepoel often boasted "that he would cut your throat at the click of my fingers".' DMI operatives received their interrogation training in Italy.[10]

The origins of BOSS's 'Z Squad' are a little less clear. Gordon Winter suggests that South Africa's first designated death squad was established by van den Bergh in the late 1960s. The unit's name was a macabre joke: 'Z is the final letter in the alphabet.' It is difficult to determine death-squad killings from the excessive violence and occasional 'accidents' of normal policing in South Africa. I have therefore concentrated upon murders where there was either an obvious cover-up or some sort of intelligence link.

In *Inside BOSS*, Winter reported that Keith Wallace, a South African journalist and BOSS spy, was murdered by the Z Squad in February 1970. Wallace was working at the *Daily Mail* in London but was also close to John Fairer-Smith, a Rhodesian spy (see page 59). Following the exposure of Norman Blackburn and Helen Keenan, Wallace was ordered by van den Bergh to dissociate himself from Fairer-Smith. Wallace refused this order and was dismissed. Depressed and suicidal, he threatened to 'go public' in the *Daily Mail*, revealing everything he knew about BOSS activities in London. One week later, 'his body was found at the bottom of a ventilation well outside his Kensington flat . . . The coroner's verdict was accidental death caused by Keith trying to climb through his flat window.' Wallace's identity cards, gun, tape recorder and camera equipment had disappeared from his flat. His father Jock said: 'Keith's full-time job was as an intelligence agent for the South African government. Journalism was only secondary. He was recruited at 18 . . . [and] made several trips to the Continent for the Government . . . in particular to Sweden and Czechoslovakia.'[11] In 1971, the investigative television programme *World in Action* interviewed Don Faires, who had previously worked for Fairer-Smith. Faires was convinced that Wallace had been murdered. He told the reporters: 'The police dropped their enquiries like a hot potato after they had contacted South Africa House.'[12]

The earliest TRC amnesty applications for 'targeted assassinations' were by two BOSS officers. Brigadier W.A.L. du Toit admitted to the production of 'explosive devices intended for unknown victims in 1969 and 1970' and Brigadier Willem Schoon applied for amnesty on the basis of confessing 'the abduction, arrest and killing of two ANC combatants . . . in July 1972'. In February 1974, Abram Tiro, who had fled from South Africa in 1973, was killed by a letter-bomb at St Joseph's Catholic Mission in Khale, Botswana. The package bore the wrapping and postmark of the International University Exchange Fund in Geneva. Twelve days later, John Dube, the ANC representative in Zambia, was also killed by a parcel-bomb. As *BOSS: The First Five Years* explained, 'Besides disposing of known opponents to the South African regime, these assassinations also served both to frighten exiled groups and individuals and disrupt their activities, and to warn [foreign] governments . . . that the support they give to political exiles has its dangers.'[13]

The Smit Murders

There have been numerous political assassinations in South Africa that have never been solved, but perhaps the most mysterious was the death of the National Party (NP) politician Dr Robert Smit and his wife. The killing was of historical significance because, although African politicians had always run the risk of being murdered for their beliefs and liberal whites had occasionally been subjected to physical assault, the Smit murder was the first time a member of the ruling NP was killed. The symbolic nature of the Smit murder and the extreme cruelty with which it was executed exposed the stark reality of the apartheid security state.

On 22 November 1977, Dr Robert Smit and his wife Jean-Cora were murdered in their house in Springs, a town near Johannesburg. This was not the usual run-of-the-mill killing and the Smits were not an average Afrikaner couple. Dr Robert Smit was aged forty-four and he had enjoyed a meteoric rise through Afrikaner society. A Rhodes scholar and the holder of a doctorate in economics from Stellenbosch (his thesis was entitled 'South Africa and International Trade Policies'), he had also played rugby for both the Orange Free State Schools and University. As a civil servant, he had led South Africa's delegation to the GATT trade negotiations in Geneva during the 1960s and been appointed deputy secretary for finance in 1967, the youngest to attain such a post in South African history. From 1971 to 1975, he represented South Africa in the United States, eventually reaching the peculiar post of ambassador to the International Monetary Fund (South Africa was the only country to award ambassadorial rank to this role). At the time of his death, Smit was the managing director of an Afrikaner company, Santam International Limited, and parliamentary candidate for the National Party in the constituency of Springs.[14]

The murder of the Smits was notably gruesome: Dr Smit was shot three times, in the head, neck and chest, and stabbed in the back. Jean-Cora Smit was stabbed fourteen times and shot in the head, chest and right thigh. According to Mervyn Rees (*Rand Daily Mail*), who visited the scene the following morning, 'Apart from the bloodstains in the entrance hall, dining-room, lounge and passageway, there are no signs that the house has been ransacked or broken into.' In the kitchen, the words 'RAU TEM' (or 'TEN') had been spray-painted on the wall in foot-high red letters. Most observers immediately thought of the Manson family murders in California eight years earlier; a dramatised film on the Manson murders, *Helter Skelter*, had recently been showing in Johannesburg cinemas. Rees, a hardened crime reporter, admitted that 'it was unlike any murder he had ever covered. It bore all the hallmarks of a professional killing.' This was reinforced by the fact that nothing had been stolen from the house. There was, however, an appointment in Smit's 'personal notebook' for an 8.00 p.m. meeting at the Smit home with a 'Mr MacDougal' on the day of the killings.[15]

Gordon Winter was one of the first people to enter the crime scene after the police. He recalls that his handler, Jacobus Johannes 'Koos' Kemp, later called him in to BOSS headquarters in Pretoria. Kemp told Winter that the Smits had been killed by two assassins. He explained that at least one of the assassins was a specialist: he had raised his gun above his head, before 'bringing it down in front of his body, so that the bullets were fired repeatedly as the gun travelled downwards'. This explained why the Smits had each been shot three times in a vertical line. An Afrikaner detective re-investigating the case in 1999 told me that the couple had been stabbed with a stiletto; he believed that it was unlikely that the murderer had been a South African because 'no Afrikaner would have killed Mrs Smit like that'. Jean-Cora Smit had been killed at eight o'clock in the evening, whereas Robert Smit did not return home until after midnight, despite having a prior appointment.[16] In 1980, the *Cape Times* revealed that Smit had visited a lover ('Mrs X') in the interim. Kemp informed Winter that 'the Bureau was mounting its own probe into the Smit killings and that this probe would run parallel to the police investigation'. Winter was then instructed to launch an investigation into the organised crime fraternity (particularly illegal gambling) of Johannesburg. Winter's memorandum notes that 'Kemp told me that it was possible than an "overseas group or agency" might have hired a "local" gangster in South Africa to kill the Smits. [He] said it was the kind of thing some "agencies" did, by this he meant the American Central Intelligence Agency.'[17]

The funeral of Robert and Jean-Cora Smit on Saturday 26 November was dominated by an extraordinary sermon, 'based on what the Minister, Dr L.M. le Roux, called "an unusual text for a funeral", an extract from St Paul's Letter to the Ephesians': 'Put on the whole armour of God, that ye may be able to stand against the wiles of the devil. For we wrestle not against flesh and blood, but against principalities, against powers, against the rulers of the darkness of this world, against spiritual wickedness in high places. Therefore take unto you the whole armour of God, that He may be able to withstand in the evil day, and having done all, to stand.' If any of the mourners had imagined that the double murder was the result of random criminal violence, the Minister's sermon, albeit in Biblical code, unambiguously stated that this had been a political killing.

Meanwhile the police investigation into the Smit murder stalled. Within a month of the killings, Kitt Katzin, an investigative journalist for the Johannesburg *Sunday Express*, reported that 'police were considering the possibility that Smit was murdered after he uncovered a foreign currency racket and made it known that he meant to expose the swindlers'. A prominent but unnamed Johannesburg businessman was reported by the Johannesburg *Sunday Times* as fearing for his life because of what he claimed to know about Smit. Mervyn Rees recalled that the South African media was full of speculation: 'Smit was negotiating a R1,000 million Swiss bank loan when he was killed . . . a Czechoslovakian scientist was being questioned by the police; Harold Holtman . . . who apparently committed suicide in controversial circumstances, was said to have close links with Dr Smit and was named as a member of an Afrikaner group being formed to investigate corruption.'[18]

In May 1978, the story was given new life by a report in the Afrikaans-language paper *Rapport* which claimed that the Smit murders were linked to the burgeoning Information scandal (see page 104). The fact that 'Muldergate' also involved corruption and illegal transfers of currency fed a rumour mill of mammoth proportions. Five months later, *Rapport* apologised for this story after the former Minister of Information and the Commissioner of Police appealed to the Press Council; nevertheless, the newspaper declared that 'it had originally obtained its information from sources normally considered irreproachable'. A few days after the original *Rapport* story, the South African delegate to the IMF, Dr B.P. Groenewald, was asked 'whether Pretoria was any closer to solving the murder of Robert Smit'. *Euromoney* reported that rumours 'have persisted that Smit had uncovered a major currency evacuation scheme involving South African cabinet officials, and had been silenced'. The author of the article, James Srodes, later said that Dr Smit had made many friends in Washington DC during his term at the IMF. His murder was the subject of much Georgetown dinner-party gossip; indeed, Smit's death seemed to offend Washington insiders more than the cruel killing of Steve Biko two months earlier.[19]

In November 1978, the Smit murder story began to spin out of control. Kitt Katzin reported that 'General Hendrik van den Bergh . . . believes Dr Smit and his wife were murdered by a foreign assassin.' On 17 November, the Johannesburg *Star* declared that Interpol and the FBI were investigating the possibility that the Smits had been murdered by an assassin, named Schneider, from Baden Baden. The killer was apparently linked to the Red Army Faction (the Baader–Meinhof gang), which had recently been active in West Germany. Two days later, Katzin claimed that in the days before his murder 'Smit had been working day and night on a top level secret investigation for the Government and that he had held talks with senior Cabinet Ministers and the then Prime Minister, Mr B.J. Vorster.'[20] The government responded immediately, Prime Minister P.W. Botha issuing a statement: 'It is untrue that Dr Smit at the time of his death or at any other time was conducting a secret or other investigation on behalf of the Government as is alleged.' Between November 1978 and June 1979, Judge Erasmus headed a Commission set up to examine 'alleged irregularities in the former Department of Information' (see page 108). The Commission issued three reports, the first of which, published in December 1978, deleted a controversial statement from Hendrik van den Bergh's testimony. This defensive censorship was quickly seized upon by the South African press. Paragraph 12.437 of the report revealed: '[Van den Bergh] was in charge of a formidable network of agents whose qualities he described in sinister terms.' Paragraph 11.386 added: '[Van den Bergh] told the Commission arrogantly that if he wanted to do something nobody would stop him and that he would stop at nothing.' Van den Bergh had actually said:

> Mr Commissioner, I really want to tell you, that I am able with my department to do the impossible. This is not bragging . . . I can tell you here today, not for your record, but I can tell you I have enough men to commit murder if I tell them to kill . . . I do not care who the prey is, or how important they are. Those are the kind of men I have. And if I wanted to do something like that to protect the security of the State nobody would stop me. I would stop at nothing. But that is such a damaging admission that . . . for the sake of the South African government, you will be compelled to omit it from your findings.[21]

Eighteen months later, the evidence given to the Erasmus Commission was published and van den Bergh's testimony included the information, clearly intended to balance his own violent statement, that two BOSS undercover agents who had infiltrated anti-apartheid organisations had been murdered. One agent, who had infiltrated Professor Jack Simons's SACP cell and supplied information for eight years, was killed in London, by having his throat cut. The second agent, an Indian, had infiltrated an ANC sabotage cell and appeared as a witness against Indres Naidoo. He was murdered several months later. Brigadier Johan Coetzee added that a further eight undercover policemen had been 'assassinated' in recent years.[22]

In February 1979, journalist Ken Owen testified to the Erasmus Commission that 'an official, a responsible man', had said that ten days before the murders Smit had visited him. Smit had questioned the official 'at length about the overseas activities of the Department of Information. They discussed nothing else . . . After Smit was killed he offered the police his cooperation. They never came to him.' A few days later, Joe Ludorf, a former judge of the Transvaal Supreme Court, announced that he had new evidence on the Smit case. He told the Cape Town *Argus* that he had been approached by a former South African Airways pilot who was in fear of losing his life. The pilot claimed that the killers had been two German mercenaries who were paid £40,000. He had flown 'the two mercenaries from Luton airport to Lanseria airport near Roodepoort and then drove them in his car to the Smits' house near Springs. The two killers who, he said, used to fight with Colonel Mike Hoare's Commando 5 mercenary army in the Congo, were then taken to the airport and flown back to Luton.' The *Guardian* noted that 'Mr Ludorf's statement supports rumours which had been circulating in the London underworld for several months that a contract had been on offer in the UK for the killings.' George King, a denizen of Johannesburg's gambling world, also sought the protection of Ludorf. He claimed that he had given Dr Smit information and evidence on links between the police and organised crime.[23] In May 1979, Mervyn Rees raised the subject in one of his extensive interviews with the former Secretary for Information, Eschel Rhoodie:

MR: Does South Africa have any hit teams?
ER: Not to my knowledge.
MR: Who killed Robert Smit and his wife?
ER: I've got absolutely no idea . . .
MR: There was talk of you having an argument with him, and he was supposed to have told you that he would 'fix' you in Parliament.
ER: I deny that most strongly . . . I know . . . that people said we had shared mistresses, and that we fell out over that. It's all absolute nonsense.

By mid-1979, it was clear that the Smit investigation in South Africa had run its course. Dr Smit's brother Jaan offered a £6,000 reward for information leading to an arrest which was added to the substantial fund on offer by an Afrikaans-language newspaper. The reward money remained unclaimed. In February 1980, the *Sunday News Journal* of Delaware named two professional Cuban assassins as the murderers of the Smits. The report, which cited US government sources, claimed that Dr Smit had discovered a secret South African slush fund of $70 million hidden in United States banks while he was attempting to raise international loans for the Republic. 'According to the CIA and State Department sources, Dr Smit discovered the names of 20 Right-wing American politicians, journalists, and publishers who had received pay-offs and bribes. Some of these people were known to be supporters of the Pinochet regime in Chile, which is said to have close ties with South Africa.'[24]

The *Financial Mail* summed up the Smit case in March 1979: 'The obvious conclusion is that somebody wanted Smit dead, to stop him disclosing some dark secret. What was that secret? Who was it that feared he would be in danger? Until these questions are answered, Smit's ghost will continue to haunt the country.' Gordon Winter attempted to assist disclosure in 1980 but, on his own admission, his knowledge was limited. He said that 'Dr Smit had helped to sluice large amounts of money out of South Africa for the government.' The money was directly linked to the Information Department's secret projects. However, Smit discovered that substantial funds ($33 million) were being diverted to a Swiss bank account allegedly in the name of Dr Nicholas Diederichs, the State President and former Minister of Finance.[25] It had constantly been suggested, but not reported, that Smit was murdered because he had intended to use 'parliamentary privilege' to expose the corruption.

Following up Winter's story, the *Rand Daily Mail* discovered that the Union Bank of Switzerland's Zurich head office did have an account that was linked to Diederichs. The paper also reported that Diederichs had narrowly avoided bankruptcy following his appointment as state president. Two rumours began to circulate: that the bank account contained funds for an Afrikaner government in exile; and that Diederichs had been taking commissions on South African gold sales on the Zurich gold market. In February 1981, the Advocate-General, Justice P.J. van der Walt, announced the findings of his official inquiry. There was a bank account in Switzerland but it was in the name of David Mort (a business acquaintance of Diederichs's son) and the account had never contained more than R20,000. The allegations against Diederichs were 'reprehensible'.[26] And there the trail ended.

In 1992, the Smits' daughter, Liza Grundlingh, engineered a meeting with the retired Hendrik van den Bergh. Their conversation, which was published in the Johannesburg *Star*, makes fascinating reading:

LG: Did you have anything to do with the killing of my father and my mother?

HVDB: God can take my youngest grandchild if I lie. I did not have anything to do with your father's death . . . Robert Smit would often come to my office in [Pretoria] and he would give information about things he had heard on his overseas trips. You could say he worked unofficially for me. Robert Smit and I trusted each other. If he had wanted to tell anybody anything he would have come to me and he never did, not with this rubbish about government money being hid away in overseas bank accounts . . .

LG: Too many people say my parents' deaths were politically motivated for there not to be some truth in the rumours . . .

HVDB: When John Vorster asked me to start an intelligence network in South Africa I went to Allan Dulles [founder of the CIA] and I asked him how I should go about it. He said I would not have problems gathering intelligence here, but that Military Intelligence would be my problem. They will also be your problem.[27]

A few months later, veteran South African journalist Benjamin Pogrund interviewed van den Bergh, and the former spy chief once again denied any responsibility for alleged Z Squad killings ('I challenge anyone to produce the slightest proof that we carried out any of these deeds'). But Pogrund pressed the question: ' "You were the power behind Vorster . . . Is it conceivable that these things could have been done without your knowledge, if not your approval?" To which [van den Bergh] replied: "It all depends on how high up the line the report-back comes." That admission was an early insight into the way in which the Nationalists had set up their security machinery so that those at the top could deny knowledge of deeds done on their behalf.' In 1987, in an interview with Mervyn Rees that was not published until after Rhoodie's death in 1993, the former Secretary for Information suggested that Robert Smit had been 'assassinated' because he had discovered evidence of a defence slush fund for a possible Afrikaner government in exile. Rhoodie revealed that R75 million had been given to the Department of Information for Operation Senekal from the Defence Special Procurement Fund, a secret annual supply of cash for purchasing weapons: 'The fund, which ran into hundreds of millions every year and over the past 15 years probably totalled three billion rand, was not always used for the purchase of weapons.'[28]

The Smit case continued to gnaw at the memories of both politicians and journalists. Martin Welz, editor of *Noseweek*, South Africa's investigative magazine, told me that 'Who killed Robert Smit?' is the question he is most regularly asked by South African politicians. Mike Louw, a BOSS agent who was appointed head of the National Intelligence Service (NIS) in 1992, told me that his first request upon becoming spy chief was to be provided with the full agency information on mystery cases like the Smits. He said that this was so that, if he was asked questions by journalists, he would not look uninformed. He admitted that the NIS did not know who had killed the Smits.[29] The TRC declared in 1998: 'The Commission finds that Robert and Jean-Cora Smit were killed by members of the security forces and that their deaths constitute a gross violation of human rights.' The findings of the TRC are worth quoting at length:

> A number of possible motives have been put forward: that Dr Smit had uncovered massive corruption and fraud involving extremely high-level government sources; that he was in possession of information relating to South Africa's nuclear programme; or that the reason for the killings related to South Africa's sanctions-busting activities, in which Dr Smit had been involved. Several people confirmed at the time that Dr Smit was in possession of information he had described as 'explosive'. Particular suspicion was directed at former members of BOSS's alleged Z Squad and the SAP's Special Task Team. Three names, Dries 'Krullebol' Verwey, Jack Widdowson and Roy Allen have repeatedly been associated with the killings. Verwey subsequently died in uncertain circumstances; both Widdowson and Allen, identified by two independent sources as having been in the area at the time of the killings, were named in the 1992 Steyn Report as being connected to 'third force' [see page 256] activities. In addition it is known that Dr Smit was due to meet with a Mr McDougal on the evening of his death. McDougal was the codename of a former Z Squad operative, Phil Freeman, who has been named as a possible suspect in the Rick Turner killing. Further allegations were that the investigation into the killings, conducted by members of the East Rand Murder and Robbery Squad, sought to cover up security force involvement.

Dr Smit's daughter Liza Grundlingh had pressed the TRC to investigate the deaths of her parents. She experienced death threats during her campaign, which, as the TRC admitted, '[suggests] a contemporary interest in ensuring that the facts surrounding the killings remain hidden, and points to a political agenda or at least one in which powerful – possibly financial – interests are vested'.[30] In 1999, the Johannesburg *Star* reported that Eschel Rhoodie had written a 'mysterious manuscript' before his death and that it had 'surfaced in Cape Town'. The article noted that Rhoodie 'points fingers at those people he held responsible for the murder of the Smit couple'. Rhoodie's widow Katie, speaking from Atlanta, told the newspaper that 'she would sue if anyone tried to publish it'. In 2003, Jerry Dan, in his book *Ultimate Deception: How Stalin Stole the Bomb*, quoted an unnamed intelligence source who reported that he had investigated the Smit murder in 1978 because 'Washington and London suspected foul play.' He added, 'the IMF had been forewarned by [Smit] that a huge scam operated in the Reserve Bank, allowing South African politicians and companies to spirit their wealth out of the country without incurring stringent financial penalties'. The source claimed that the murder had been carried out at the behest of 'an aide to John Vorster'.[31]

It is now nearly three decades since the Smit murder and nobody has been brought to justice. What then can we decipher from the mess of conflicting evidence and unsubstantiated stories that dominate the investigative record in the Smit case? While it is quite possible that Smit discovered evidence of high-level corruption and was murdered in order to guarantee his silence, the murders also served as a symbolic slaughter. They signalled the last gasp of the Vorster–van den Bergh police state which had ruled South Africa since the murder of Hendrik Verwoerd in 1966. In 1999, I interviewed Deneys Rhoodie, a former deputy secretary in the Department of Information (see page 95). When I questioned him about the Smit murder and a possible link to the Information scandal, his hands began to shake and did not stop shaking until we moved off the subject.[32] After November 1977, the Afrikaner political elite in South Africa understood that nobody was safe from the brutality of the state. The murder of Robert Smit stood as an example, a disciplinary paradigm: South Africans would learn to remain silent on a series of subjects. Ironically, in the election which followed the murder of the Smits, the National Party won the biggest election victory in its history.

Richard Turner

Richard Turner, a radical political scientist, was murdered on 8 January 1978. He had been 'banned' in 1973 under the Suppression of Communism

Act, as was his book *The Eye of the Needle*. According to the London *Sunday Times*, 'Turner had broken the most rigorous taboo of apartheid by living openly with his [Muslim] wife.' He had certainly been subject to extraordinary intimidation: 'During his banning . . . [he] had a motorbike set on fire, car tyres slashed, a load of cement delivered to his front door and various other little pleasantries, the final one being a bomb thrown at his house.' He was killed at 12.30 in the evening while putting his two daughters to bed. He heard a knock at the door of his Durban house, looked through the bedroom window and was shot at 'point-blank range'. A few days earlier he had discussed on the telephone with his former wife Barbara (now Barbara Follett, the Labour MP) obtaining passports for his daughters.[33] Was Turner murdered because BOSS, which had his house under surveillance, by means inter alia of a phone-tap, suspected that he intended to flee the country as South African newspaper editor Donald Woods had only days before? And why was the surveillance lifted one week before his death?

After an exhaustive investigation, the TRC was unable to establish the identity of the killer. It did, however, assemble conclusive evidence of a link to BOSS:

> Brigadier Christiaan Earle, the original investigating officer, said he believed that Turner was killed by 'people who were part of the security forces and that they wanted to protect this and not have it known'. He told the Commission that his investigations into the killing led him to suspect the involvement of BOSS operative Martin Dolinchek . . . Former Vlakplaas Commander Eugene de Kock reported that one of his informants, former BOSS member Piet Botha, told him that Dolinchek had killed Turner and that Dolinchek's brother-in-law, Mr Von Scheer, drove the getaway vehicle. When Dolinchek was interviewed by the Commission he handed over a number of BOSS reports prepared by himself or the regional representative of BOSS, most of them concerning Turner. However, he denied having been involved in the killing. A former BOSS member told the Commission he believed BOSS was behind the killing and may have set it up to look like the work of Scorpio, a right-wing group based in Cape Town.[34]

The Scorpio gang were involved in a number of assaults and killings in the Cape in the late 1970s. Gordon Winter commented in *Inside BOSS*: 'In its spare time South Africa's Z Squad also terrorised known opponents of apartheid inside South Africa. Many of these sneak attacks were blamed on "Scorpio", a secret and extreme right-wing group . . .

secret to the public because the police try their hardest not to catch them.' Six weeks after the death of her son, Rick Turner's mother received a telephone call: 'The message was terse, the voice sneering: "Is that you, Jane? There isn't much time left. This is Scorpio."' In April 1978, having written a letter that had appeared in the *Cape Times* on the subject of her son and his friends, Jane Turner received a second call from 'Scorpio': 'I have just read your letter about the young intellectuals. We should have shot the bastards the same way we shot your son, the bunch of commie swine.'[35]

Less than a year later, Progressive Federal Party MP Colin Eglin's secretary also received a call from 'Scorpio': 'Tell your boss we've had enough of him. We're going to do to him what we did to Turner.' On Easter Friday 1979, five bullets were fired through the front door of Eglin's Cape Town home. Eglin was unhurt. Three men were eventually arrested, two of whom, David Beelders and Arnold van der Westhuizen, were later imprisoned. They admitted using the name 'Scorpio'. John Carlin revealed in the *Independent* in 1989: 'When [Beelders] was arrested by the Security Police in Windhoek, Namibia in connection with the Eglin incident, he was absolutely stupefied. This seemed to him to be an inexplicable betrayal. The police – and of this he was certain – had been aware of what he had been doing in the Scorpio gang. Not only that, they had been protecting him.'[36] Breyten Breytenbach met van der Westhuizen in Pollsmoor prison:

> He told me that he had broken all links with Beelders. Beelders, he said, was an out-and-out Nazi with serious identity problems, first because he had difficulty with his homosexuality, and secondly because he was not sure of being a White. It was rumoured that he – a White supremacist – was in fact Coloured! Van der Westhuizen related to me how the two of them, with others of their extreme-right organisation, had been directed by the Security Police as heavies or as thugs to go and terrorise suspected opponents to the government . . . Van der Westhuizen also told me that Beelders had confessed to him that he'd been the one who assassinated Rick Turner.[37]

Violence, intimidation, brutality and murder were functioning components of the apartheid security structure by the 1970s. The 'bumbling copper' that Nelson Mandela and Anthony Sampson remembered from the 1950s had been replaced by van den Bergh's and Vorster's police state. As resistance grew, so the cruelty of the state intensified. Africans had long been aware of this, and the teenagers who rioted during the Soweto upris-ing understood that the cost of freedom would be very high. 'Targeted assassination' remained a shadowy subject, but by the mid-1980s it would become accepted policy.

5

Muldergate: A Quiet Coup

It is possible that over the entire period of Dr Rhoodie's tenure of office, his aggressive and undiplomatic brow-beating of foreign editors, together with a heavy-handed policy of trying to 'manage' and pressure overseas newspapers and their correspondents by various means, caused more harm to South Africa abroad than the revelations confirmed in the Erasmus report . . . The generally held view of the international press fraternity – from editorial executives to correspondents – was that Eschel Rhoodie was a man of considerable energy and ability, but was temperamentally unsuited to the job he held. He also lacked a grasp of the true principles of journalism and the functions of newspapers in democratic societies.

Peter Younghusband, the *Capetonian*, February 1979[1]

BETWEEN 1972 AND 1978, South Africa's Department of Information, in association with BOSS, engineered a programme of propaganda, corruption, dirty tricks and 'unorthodox diplomacy' that was years ahead of its time. Historians have barely started to assess the significance of South Africa's experiment in the 'dark arts of spin'. To a significant extent, 'Info' represented the last gasp of Afrikaner Nationalist political creativity. Intelligence and propaganda have always been well-suited bedfellows; in South Africa, they reflected and fed upon a moral hypocrisy that was rapidly consuming the remnants of Verwoerd's apartheid fantasy.

Information and Intelligence

In 1971, Dr Connie Mulder, who had been appointed minister of information in 1968, had taken an extensive overseas tour. He had returned determined that South Africa 'should immediately and actively get involved in the propaganda war and employ the same methods as its opponents'.

In August 1972, Mulder appointed an ambitious young civil servant to the post of secretary of information. Eschel Mostert Rhoodie was born in 1933 in South Africa's Cape Province. His father was a prison warder; cruel voices would whisper (incorrectly) that he was the prison executioner. The Rhoodie family embraced education: all three sons, Nik, Eschel and Deneys, obtained doctorates at South African universities. Eschel Rhoodie was health-conscious – a non-smoking, teetotal vegetarian who played rugby to provincial level in his youth and tennis in his later years. He had joined the Information Department in the 1950s and had represented South Africa in Australia, the United States and Holland. At the time of his appointment, Rhoodie was assistant editor of *To the Point* magazine, which had been launched with secret government backing. He was determined to stop at nothing to transform apartheid South Africa's international image. He quickly appointed his younger brother Deneys and L.E.S ('Les') de Villiers as deputy secretaries.[2] Rhoodie's inspiration was a mysterious ex-CIA employee, 'Mr Brown', whom he had met in the United States in 1964.

> Brown said that the way to run the campaign was to get more Americans involved . . . the more they got involved, the more they would want to know the facts . . . Brownie told me some of the things that the CIA had done in some countries and how they were influencing people through politics and the media. Brownie gave me a book to read called *The Strategy of Subversion*. Then he introduced me to a number of people who today I believe must have been CIA agents . . . They all had enormous knowledge of what was happening in the student movements and in the media, particularly in Europe and Latin America. Brownie and his friends told me that it was essential to pick potential leaders early, and get to know them so when they got into a position of influence you had a friend there. It is almost impossible, they said, to get close to somebody once he gets to the top . . . They also told me that the best way of handling student movements is not to fight them, but infiltrate them. And with political movements, one must infiltrate them, help finance them and then take them over. Brownie was very brutal about the media. He said it was impossible to break through the brutal-highlight syndrome. The only way to influence the media was to own it, or to own some of the senior people in it . . . Brownie became a real friend.[3]

Paul Blackstock's *The Strategy of Subversion: Manipulating the Politics of Other Nations* was, in essence, a study of intelligence and covert action. Employing case studies drawn from the previous half-century, Blackstock attempted to examine all aspects of covert operations from revolutionary propaganda to mercenary activity, from operational control to Congressional oversight. Ironically, the conclusion predicted the central problem of the Information scandal: 'For centuries the Great Powers have used aggressive, clandestine intervention, i.e., covert operations, as an instrument of statecraft . . . In so doing, however, each of the powers has been faced with the baffling problem of "how to control discreetly a dimly seen instrument, so hot that if not handled with great skill it can burn its user rather than its adversary".' Gordon Winter reported in the Dutch edition of *Inside BOSS* that 'Jeff Brown' was the alias of a CIA 'talent scout'. In 1968, Rhoodie published *The Paper Curtain*, a cunning polemic which suggested that the negative international image of apartheid South Africa could be neutralised 'if it were possible to co-ordinate the activities and contributions of . . . people who are willing to help'. Rhoodie believed that 'a massive transfer of positive information . . . using all possible methods' would have the effect of 'cutting through the myth of "world opinion" '.[4] He also boasted powerful patrons: he had been introduced to John Vorster by his childhood priest, the Prime Minister's brother Koot Vorster. As in the case of Gordon Winter, it was Vorster who introduced Rhoodie to Hendrik van den Bergh. Les de Villiers later recalled:

> Eschel Rhoodie never waited in the antechamber at BOSS headquarters in Pretoria. He stepped right in, usually for lunch in van den Bergh's secluded quarters . . . As early as 1971 Eschel Rhoodie got Hendrik van den Bergh to support the idea of establishing *To The Point* with government funds. In 1972 the Security boss played a decisive role in Eschel's appointment as Secretary of Information amid and despite strong opposition from the public service and even some Cabinet ministers . . . I heard General van den Bergh say about Eschel Rhoodie more than once, 'South Africa will have to build a monument to this man.'[5]

At first, Rhoodie's and Mulder's 'Info' developed slowly: a German public relations specialist, Heinz Behrens, was employed to feed positive stories into the European media; two journalist spies, Bernard Lejeune, a Frenchman, and Karl Breyer, a German, were secretly employed to disseminate propaganda; and two advertising front organisations, the Committee for Fairness in Sport and the Club of Ten, were established to place pro-South African advertisements in international publications. Extra funds of approximately R1 million were provided by BOSS. On 3 December 1973, Mulder and

Rhoodie received the Prime Minister's blessing in the form of a circular letter which was dispatched to cabinet ministers. 'In the execution of his objectives it is left to the Minister of Information to decide what methods, medium and actions, whether public or secret, will be the most effective or necessary.' Rhoodie later reported that he had told John Vorster:

> I want you to approve, not an information asset, but a propaganda war in which no rules or regulations count. If it is necessary for me to bribe some-one, then I would bribe him or her. If it is necessary for me to purchase, for example, a sable mink coat for an editor's wife then I should be in a position to do so. If it is necessary for me to send somebody on a holiday to the Hawaiian Islands with his mistress for a month, then I should be able to do so.[6]

Info was now ready to launch a five-year propaganda campaign and expand its operations in the United States. In January 1974, Mulder and de Villiers visited America, where meetings were held with the Governor of California Ronald Reagan, Vice-President Gerald Ford (facilitated by the American publisher John McGoff) and the editorial board of the *New York Times*. In South Africa, Rhoodie's 'five-year plan' was approved; the estimated funding of R15–25 million would be chan-nelled through the secret (arms procurement) Defence Special Account and then transferred to BOSS and the Information Department. A cabinet subcommittee, 'the Committee of Three' (Vorster, Mulder and the Minister of Finance Nico Diederichs), was created to vet secret projects and approve funding. Van den Bergh was invited to attend the biannual meetings of the subcommittee.[7]

Eschel Rhoodie believed that he was now capable of 'turning back the tide' of what he perceived as the negative coverage of South Africa. When one of his deputies voiced concern at the cost of blueprint projects, Rhoodie replied: 'Money is no problem . . . it's manpower that worries me. Cash doesn't tell tales, but men do and we will have to see to it that we get extra full-time hands from outside whom we can trust.' The money and power quickly went to his head. Among the stranger revelations of Muldergate were the nicknames used within the Department: Eschel Rhoodie was known as 'James Bond', 'Thor' or 'Gadaffi'; Les de Villiers was 'Dirty Harry (either because he looks vaguely like Clint Eastwood or because of his predilection for pretty women)'; van den Bergh was 'Moses' or 'Die Lang Man'; John Vorster was 'Olympus (the God of Gods)'; and P.W. Botha was 'Pangaman' (literally Machete Man), because 'you'd never know when he was going to lash out at you'. Les de Villiers admits that within a year the secret projects were beginning to get out of control:

> By then we had tens of spooks and more than a hundred secret projects under the direction of three of us – Deneys Rhoodie at his own insistence was also allowed by his brother Eschel to dabble in the dirty tricks division. I frequently found that payments had been made and orders given to spooks and front organisations without my knowledge . . . So the secrets slipped and the spooks ventured far from their cupboards and front organisations turned transparent.[8]

Rhoodie's overweening ambition merged with a disdain for the accounting of secret funds to create a conflagration that was sooner or later going to be exposed. The Rhoodies and de Villiers were an early indication of the 'new Afrikaner': none of them was a member of the Broederbond (Les de Villiers told me: 'They took a look at us and we took a look at them and none of us liked what we saw'); Eschel Rhoodie and de Villiers, in particular, were famous ladies' men; and they were thrilled to be living a first-class jetset life in which they could always buy themselves out of trouble. All three had enjoyed living overseas, as information officers, but they had hated having to apologise for South Africa. The Information Department philosophy in simplified form was 'If apartheid couldn't win friends through normal methods, it would buy them.' The American journalist Jim Srodes recalled that, when the new Info approach was introduced in Washington, 'it was crazy. They were throwing money around. It was like "Hey, we're nice people. Have some more champagne."'[9]

But Eschel Rhoodie's extraordinary rise and his intense arrogance alienated many members of the South African civil service and his bullying, intimidating style, with both domestic and foreign journalists, stored up trouble for the future. After his resignation in 1978, one South African journalist summed him up, demonstrating in the process years of pent-up bile:

> Rhoodie dazzled. He knew the difference between the Hotel Georges Cinq and the Crillon in Paris and this impressed people like Connie Mulder and General van den Bergh, who thought he was a sophisticate. Of course, in the world outside, among real sophisticates, Rhoodie didn't rate at all. The two-tone shoes he sometimes wore and his style of clothing was not quite right. His manner was too cocky. He came across too slick – almost spivvish. But how were they to know this in the corridors of the Union Building in Pretoria?[10]

The Secret Projects

Operation Senekal, as the Information Department's secret projects were collectively known, was mind-numbing in its scale and ambition. Political scientist Dan O'Meara suggests that it 'would have beggared the imagination of even the author of the fantasy espionage novels from whose hero Rhoodie acquired his nickname'. *To the Point* magazine was created in January 1972 in association with the Dutch publisher Hubert Jussen. Following the Information scandal, it 'staggered on with the open sponsorship of the South African government until December 1980'; an international version was published between April 1974 and October 1977. Inspired by van den Bergh's assessment that foreign correspondents 'simply cut out reports from the *Rand Daily Mail*, write "from Our Correspondent", put them on the telex and the reports then appear literally word for word in the *Washington Post*, the *Washington Star*, or other newspapers', Rhoodie and the Afrikaner fertiliser millionaire Louis Luyt considered buying the Anglo American-controlled South African Associated Newspapers (publisher of the *Rand Daily Mail* and other 'opposition' papers) in 1975.[11] On 7 September 1976, the *Citizen* was launched, ostensibly under the ownership of Luyt but in fact funded to the amount of R13 million by the Information Department. Journalist–spies like Gordon Winter and Aida Parker immediately joined the new paper. Parker later recalled that the *Citizen* was 'a loony bin in the early days. Everyone was there! KGB, CIA, all the South African intelligence branches.' After its exposure, the *Citizen* was sold to the Afrikaner publishing group Perskor. Surprisingly, it survives to the present day. The newspaper's editor Johnny Johnson, previously Winter's editor at the Johannesburg *Sunday Express*, continued in post until his retirement in 1999.[12]

Using two South African businessmen, David Abramson and Stuart Pegg, as a front, Info attempted to purchase the famous African magazine *Drum*. When this failed, they started their own version, *Pace*. Moreover, the Department had shares in a second 'black' magazine, *Hit*. Abramson later told the Erasmus Commission that he had been doing 'minor operations' and 'several missions' for van den Bergh and the Finance Minister, Dr Nico Diederichs, since the 1960s. Rhoodie also had ambitions to start a 'moderate black newspaper' in Bophuthatswana: a budget of R100,000 had been prepared.[13] In addition, Info were keen to produce films for the African audience. Mervyn Rees reported, 'It emerged that the black movie project had two broad aims: censorship and indoctrination . . . [The Department] felt that [Hollywood] films were Americanising urban blacks in South Africa and that their scheme could be used to counteract this trend through the creation of local black super heroes, who would be portrayed against an ethnic background.' One mainstream film, *Golden Rendezvous* (1977) starring Richard Harris, is known to have been supported by government money. An amusing parlour game for those with too much time on their hands is to run through the list of motion pictures that were filmed in South Africa between 1972 and 1979 and try to spot the compromised sequences that were introduced to pacify Eschel Rhoodie.[14]

In 1974, the Department had attempted, with its 'friend' the American publisher John McGoff, to buy the *Washington Star* (today's *Washington Times*). Rebuffed, McGoff used Info funds to purchase the tiny-circulation *Sacramento Union*. In 1975, Rhoodie and McGoff bought a controlling 50 per cent share of United Press International Television News (UPITN) from Paramount Films. UPITN supplied news reports to ABC News in the United States. Rhoodie later declared that UPITN distributed films on the 'independence' of the Transkei and Bophuthatswana, and an interview with John Vorster for which Rhoodie had written the questions *and* the answers.[15] In 1977, the American billionaire Richard Mellon Scaife bought a 50 per cent share in McGoff–Info's Californian holdings. In the same year, McGoff considered purchasing the short-lived New York newspaper the *Trib* with Information Department funds. 'Citizen' Scaife would go on to build the huge neo-conservative network of foundations, think-tanks and media that Hillary Clinton described in 1998 as 'a vast right-wing conspiracy'. In 1981, *Columbia Journalism Review* investigative reporter Karen Rothmyer approached Scaife in Boston and asked the straightforward question: 'Mr Scaife, could you explain why you give so much money to the New Right?' The billionaire's reply: 'You fucking communist cunt, get out of here.'[16]

In the United Kingdom, Info, in conjunction with Abramson and Pegg, attempted to buy the *Daily Express* in 1975. As Rhoodie later told Mervyn Rees, 'the Information team intended to get control of the *Evening Standard*, the *Guardian* or the *Observer*'. With the assistance of Arnon Milchan, now a very successful Hollywood film producer, and the Italian Count Ghislieri, Info secured control of the specialist *West Africa* magazine. One year later, the Department purchased 29 per cent of the shares in the publishing group Morgan Grampian. However, it proved impossible to raise the funds for a full takeover. Eschel Rhoodie explained that 'control of a major British publishing house, with contacts and outlets all over the world, [would provide] a possible cover for the agents of General van den Bergh in countries where it would normally be difficult for Bureau agents to operate'. In 1977, an attempt to purchase the *Investors Chronicle* fell through (the South African journalist Stephen Mulholland had been pencilled in as editor) and Info bought a 50 per cent share of the *Investors Review* as consolation.[17]

The political projects were as ambitious as those in the media. The Department of Information and BOSS attempted to bribe Nigerian politicians to recognise Transkeian 'independence'; financed a political party in Norway; sponsored members of the Japanese Diet to oppose Japanese trade union campaigns against apartheid; and financed a British Conservative MP, Sir Frederick Bennett, to arrange tours of South Africa by British MPs and host South African parliamentarians visiting the UK. This particular project was known as Operation Bowler Hat. Two Labour MPs were employed at a cost of £2,000 per year to 'protect our interests and also to provide us with information . . . whenever new pressure groups were formed in England . . . They were really informers more than anything else.' *Private Eye* later suggested a list of possible suspects, although the MPs have never been exposed. In the United States, the Department intervened in at least two domestic American elections by contributing funds to the opponents of Democrat Senators Dick Clark and John Tunney, who co-sponsored the Tunney–Clark amendment in 1975–76 which halted covert CIA activity in Angola. Tunney was defeated in November 1976 and Clark two years later.[18]

Info employed a lobbyist, Donald deKieffer, to promote South Africa's case within the United States. DeKieffer, in conjunction with the Department's polling company Sydney S. Baron, arranged for former President Gerald Ford and former Secretary of the Treasury William Simon to speak at pro-South African business conferences. Ford was paid $10,000 and Simon received $8,000 'for a 30-minute talk in which he talked about gold and investment possibilities in South Africa'. According to Rhoodie, the head of the South African Reserve Bank believed that 'Mr Simon's speech was worth R5 billion to South Africa'. Donald deKieffer was later appointed to a government post in the Reagan administration. Perhaps, Info's slickest and most cynical use of spin was the employment of Andrew Hatcher, the first African-American appointed to be a press spokesman in the Kennedy White House: Hatcher appeared on American television speaking for the apartheid state during the Soweto uprising.[19]

The Information Department's greatest success was in the arena of 'unorthodox diplomacy'. The scheme was an attempt to bypass what was perceived as the 'ethnic agents in place' still dominant within the Department of Foreign Affairs, but the central belief was that 'everybody was buyable'. The determination to establish a détente with Black Africa served obvious security needs: the isolation of the ANC; the possibility of splitting the votes of the Organisation of African Unity (OAU); and the chance of establishing an air corridor for South African Airways (SAA). In the 1970s, SAA had to travel round the 'bulge' of West Africa, adding significantly to its fuel costs. Rhoodie and van den Bergh split the continent: Rhoodie would concentrate on the Francophone countries, while the General would work on east and central Africa. Rhoodie later revealed that 'van den Bergh had travelled extensively in Africa, visiting Zaire, Gabon, Tanzania, Zambia and the Central African Republic . . . [he] was so successful that eventually he needed permission only from Sudan and Egypt'. Anthony Sampson described van den Bergh as:

> more than the traditional Grand Inquisitor: he was an adventurous diplomat . . . He travelled under different passports and names, and he would slip in and out of unlikely black capitals. Nor was it really contradictory, to be the persecutor of the blacks at home, and the conciliator abroad: he could only deal in Realpolitik if neither side questioned the other's internal oppression.[20]

Rhoodie's Info diplomacy in west Africa was organised through the ministrations of Bernard Lejeune and the BOSS representative in Paris, Albie Geldenhuys, the son of Security Police chief Mike Geldenhuys. The Secretary of Information met Léopold Senghor, the father of 'négritude', in a Paris flat in early 1974. He later recalled: 'I praised Senghor as a statesman and as a poet . . I pointed out to President Senghor that if the Americans and Chinese could speak to each other . . . what would there be to prevent two African statesmen also from talking to each other?' Vorster's meetings with President Félix Houphouet-Boigny of the Ivory Coast in September 1974, President William Tolbert of Liberia in February 1975 and President Kenneth Kaunda of Zambia in August 1975 were a significant improvement on the rather weedy 'outward policy' of the late 1960s which produced little apart from a visit by Dr Hastings Banda, the leader of Malawi, in 1971. One ANC diplomat admitted privately that 'by mid-1975 his organisation had began to fear that it might be excluded from every African state south of the Sahara'. Eschel

Rhoodie also travelled to Iran in 1974 and 1975 to secure the supply of oil to South Africa. In 1976, Connie Mulder made an official visit to the Shah's kingdom.[21]

Rhoodie was certainly a superb networker and talent-spotter. He encouraged the golfer Gary Player and the heart surgeon Christiaan Barnard to promote Department of Information propaganda. But he was equally effective with foreigners: in April 1976, Britain's self-appointed chief censor Mary Whitehouse visited South Africa for a month, during which she 'held meetings with senior police officers and . . . Dr Connie Mulder'. She also found time to be interviewed by *To the Point*: 'Throughout her visit she cautioned South Africans against becoming complacent about the kind of moral onslaught to which the British had been subjected for the past two decades . . . She was impressed by the general moral calibre of the Republic, but was concerned that South Africans tended to feel that "it can't happen here".' As Christopher Dunkley commented in the *Financial Times* following Whitehouse's death: 'She saw sex and violence as two sides of the same coin . . . Given half a chance, she would have been a true totalitarian.'[22] Another English figure utilised by the Department was General Sir Walter Walker, the former NATO Commander-in-Chief, Allied Forces, Northern Europe. Walker, a profound reactionary, retired in 1972 and two years later in the *Evening News* 'raised the possibility that the army might have to take over in Britain'. Soon afterwards, he created 'an "anti-chaos" organisation, known at first as Unison, and later as "Civil Assistance" ', which rapidly attracted 100,000 supporters. Info paid for Walker to visit South Africa, facilitated meetings with P.W. Botha, the Chief of the SADF Magnus Malan and MID, and published his anti-communist book *The Bear at the Back Door* through its publishing imprint Valiant Publishers.[23]

Other Information projects included: church organisations in South Africa, the United States, Britain and Germany; two major front organisations in Britain and the US, 'each with more than 30,000 members'; and five institutes overseas. Rhoodie was eventually brought down by petty corruption. Advocate Retief van Rooyen, who would later defend the police at the inquest into the death of Steve Biko, testified to the Erasmus Commission that when Les de Villiers had left the Department of Information he said that 'they [employees of the Department] were stealing left and right from the secret fund'. De Villiers denied saying this. Certainly, the Rhoodie brothers were excited by money and enjoyed the secret budget that was under their control. But it was small scale; none of them appears to be particularly wealthy today. A rumour has circulated for years that Rhoodie and his colleagues stumbled into the corruption. Officials of the Department, according to the rumour, had to make regular trips to African countries in order to pay African leaders for the flyover rights required for SAA. One Friday, an official missed his flight and banked the money; he made the trip on the Monday. Discovering that significant amounts of interest could accrue in very short periods, he and his colleagues began to delay their flights, eventually missing one or two completely.[24] From small acorns . . .

Muldergate – South Africa's Watergate

'Muldergate' (or the Information scandal) was perhaps the most appropriate of the numerous international scandals, following Watergate, to be granted the 'gate' suffix. In late 1976, Auditor-General Gerald Barrie, Rhoodie's immediate predecessor as Secretary of Information, began 'an investigation into irregularities in the Department of Information'. Les de Villiers recalled that in late November Rhoodie 'issued instructions "on the advice of both Prime Minister Vorster and General van den Bergh" that we destroy all "unnecessary documentation . . . unless, of course, you feel that certain documents give us a hold on certain shady characters. Those we should keep."' Reading the writing on the wall, de Villiers accepted the post of vice-chairman with the Department's American public relations company Sydney S. Baron in July 1977.[25] A few weeks later, Mervyn Rees, investigative reporter at the *Rand Daily Mail*, was introduced to one of the two 'deep throats' who would give guidance to the reporter throughout the investigation. 'Daan', a senior civil servant, said 'There was corruption in high places . . . A lot of money was involved. Top people in government were not what they seemed.' He guided the reporter towards the Department of Information and 'he named a woman who had been the mistress of a leading National Party politician'. The bureaucratic cover-up started in August 1977: John Vorster appointed van den Bergh and BOSS special investigator Loot Reynders to 'investigate matters at the Department on the strength of Barrie's report . . . Van den Bergh asked [Reynders] not to put anything in connection with the investigation on paper.'[26]

By the autumn of 1977, Eschel Rhoodie was becoming concerned: 'We . . . had a very strong suspicion that there was a mole right in our midst. We did not know who it was and we did not know how much was being leaked, or why it was being leaked to journalists.' A similar paranoia was occupying BOSS. Gerard Ludi recalled that the Bureau was obsessed with the idea that a communist spy was operating within the BOSS offices in Pretoria. The paranoia became so intense that some BOSS agents actually rented private offices and moved their filing cabinets and documents. Meanwhile, Mervyn Rees sent a friend to 'test the water' with Rhoodie. The Secretary of Information's response was full of clues: 'Tell those bastards I know about them. Tell them I have tape recordings of them. Tell them I know what they're trying to do. Tell them to go to hell.' The mention of 'tape recordings' confirmed 'Daan's' whispers that Rhoodie and van den Bergh were 'like twins'. Following the Smit murder on 22 November (see page 82), Rees received a telephone call from 'Daan':

D: Mervyn, it's me . . . What's all that business out at Springs?
MR: Smit and his wife were killed.
D: Ja, I know that, but why were they killed?
MR: I've got no answers. Have you?
D: No, but be careful.[27]

Within the government, an attempted cover-up was being engineered. In October 1977, one of the Information Department frontmen, Retief van Rooyen, reported his concerns to John Vorster. On the same day, van den Bergh told his colleagues that van Rooyen 'was going to the Prime Minister with stories'. Some days later, Gerald Barrie demanded Deneys Rhoodie's resignation, 'because of what was emerging from the investigations into public accounts'. By this stage, van den Bergh was 'busy negotiating with Barrie over a solution to the problem'. Vorster told van Rooyen that the Information Department would be cleaned up after the election on 30 November; 'he said to me he could face everything, but just not the newspaper [Info's ownership of the *Citizen*]. Those millions had to come back.'[28] In February 1978, Gerald Barrie delivered his report, which criticised two (unnamed) officials of the Department of Information for misuse of public funds. This, of course, set off a press campaign to unravel the mystery. Retief van Rooyen later testified to the Mostert Commission, which was investigating currency contraventions, that van den Bergh had told him in March:

that he had been to see the Prime Minister and Connie Mulder and had told them he had wanted to resign previously, but that he would save them . . . [He would] takeover the evaluations, and would manage project for project for the next two years, if necessary . . . Any matter dealt with by the Bureau for State Security was covered by the Official Secrets Act, and he would therefore inform newspaper editors that any further writings on the matter would be a contravention of the Official Secrets Act. He also said that he would start with project No 1 . . . [and] he would finish them one by one. In other words, he would stretch the thing out for them until the whole thing was dead.

During March 1978, Mervyn Rees had his first meeting with the person who would become the 'Deep Throat No. 1' of the Info story. At first, 'Myrtle', as this source became known, barely communicated: 'The eyes never blinked. "You have a death wish." ' But the Barrie report was slowly leaking to the press, and even van den Bergh and Rhoodie could not keep the Info story suppressed. 'Myrtle', a source 'so close to the centre of Muldergate that it was breathtaking', eventually agreed to talk: 'Things are moving very fast at the moment . . . Everybody is jumpy. Eschel's got a witch-hunt going to find out where the leaks are coming from . . . They're tapping everything, they're watching everybody. The stakes are high, this thing goes right to the top.'[29]

On 6 May, in a desperate attempt to neutralise the press, Rhoodie announced: 'I wish to state that the Department of Information has, for years, been asked by the Government to undertake sensitive and even highly secret operations as a counter-action to the propaganda war being waged against South Africa.' On 8 May, Vorster informed parliament that the Information Department would face 'a total restructuring' and Rhoodie would retire at the end of June. Mulder would lose the Information portfolio but retain his cabinet post as Minister of Plural Relations (formerly Bantu Administration). On 10 May, Mulder stated in parliament: 'The Department of Information and the Government do not give funds to the *Citizen*.'[30] This was a lie and would eventually destroy Mulder's career. Six days later, Gordon Winter entered the fray as the *Citizen* unmasked Roland Hepers, a former Department of Information official, as 'Deep Throat No. 1'. The obfuscation failed because Hepers was only a minor source. In 1980, the *Citizen* settled Hepers's libel action out of court. In June 1978, the *Rand Daily Mail* exposed the Club of Ten as an Info front organisation; once again, BOSS attempted to deploy Gordon Winter to stymie the *Mail* story. The BOSS official who instructed Winter to do this was Jacobus Kemp, who would soon be leading the Kemp Committee tasked by the South African government with investigating Information's secret projects. Meanwhile, van den Bergh visited the Prime Minister for a 'serious, man-to-man, friend-to-friend' discussion. He 'had decided to force Mr Vorster to accept his retirement, something the Prime

Minister had been unwilling to consider'. Van den Bergh and Vorster argued over whether Vorster knew that the *Citizen* was financed by state funds; van den Bergh later reported that he had called the Prime Minister 'a liar'. The head of BOSS tendered his resignation but suggested that he was willing to continue investigating Info. The suggestion was accepted.[31]

On 20 September 1978, John Vorster and Hendrik van den Bergh announced their retirements, although Vorster declared that he would be willing to serve in the ceremonial role of state president. The National Party was about to face the most bitterly fought leadership campaign in its history. 'Myrtle' told Rees: 'Hell, Mervyn, you can't believe what's going on here, man. They're fighting like dogs around a bone . . . Connie's home and dry. It's all over bar the shouting. The General and Eschel have already started rubbing their hands.' 'Daan' also believed that Mulder was going to win. Then, on 23 September, Mulder and van den Bergh made a fatal mistake; they leaked the findings of the BOSS auditor, Loot Reynders, to the Afrikaans-language newspaper the *Transvaler*. The report cleared Mulder and the Information Department: 'I have examined the funds made available to the Department of Information . . . for secret projects from 1 April 1973 to 31 March 1978 . . . it is my opinion that proper account was kept of all receipts and expenditures during the period.'[32]

Retief van Rooyen was horrified by Reynders's findings. He gave evidence of Information Department malfeasance to Foreign Minister Pik Botha, one of the candidates in the forthcoming leadership election; the other candidate was Defence Minister P.W. Botha. Pik Botha circulated the evidence among the leaders of the National Party, and on 25 September John Vorster in his final cabinet meeting informed the cabinet, 'for the first time', of the 'full ramifications of the [Information] affair'. Nevertheless, Vorster had no intention of informing the South African public; Mulder continued to believe that he was invincible. Van Rooyen, however, had also given a sworn statement to Judge Mostert. On 28 September, the day of the National Party leadership election, a rumour circulated among the assembled delegates that Judge Mostert was going to subpoena Mulder to answer questions regarding a R2 million Swiss bank account. The rumour was effective. P.W. Botha won the first round of voting with 78 votes, to Mulder's 72 and Pik Botha's 22. In the second round, the 'Pangaman' won 98 votes to Mulder's 74.[33] P.W. Botha had secured the premiership.

For the first year of P.W. Botha's administration, Muldergate continued to dominate South African political life. At one level, the government attempted to control the revelations and limit the number of political victims; at another, the domestic and the international media slowly pieced together the full scale of Operation Senekal. Van den Bergh and Eschel Rhoodie had already been forced into retirement, BOSS was renamed the Department for National Security (DONS) under the leadership of Alexander van Wyk, and the Department of Information had been subsumed within the Department of Foreign Affairs in July 1978. In November, Judge Mostert released the evidence given to his Commission, the *Rand Daily Mail* ran the transcripts over a dozen pages under the banner headline 'It's all True!', and P.W. Botha abolished the Mostert Commission and established the Erasmus Commission, which would hear evidence *in camera*. Mulder resigned from the cabinet a few days later and, following the first report of the Erasmus Commission in December, was forced to resign from parliament.[34]

The first Erasmus report found that 'there are irrebuttable indications of large-scale irregularities and exploitation of the secret fund', but it exonerated John Vorster and P.W. Botha. The report said of the BOSS chief:

> By virtue of his functions as head of the Bureau, van den Bergh's role, to use his own words, was to know everything that was going on in South Africa and to report it to his Minister, i.e. Mr Vorster. He was the man with his ear to the ground. However, having regard to all the evidence, the Commission is strongly under the impression that van den Bergh did not confine himself to this role, but actually used his office and his personal friendship with Mr Vorster to try to influence the course of events in South Africa himself. He saw himself as the power behind the throne who, through the person of Mr Vorster, tried to manipulate events in the direction that he wanted them to go.[35]

The Erasmus Commission was extended until 30 May 1979 to inquire into further aspects of the Information Department. Meanwhile, Eschel Rhoodie, who was on a 'business trip' in Europe, had his passport withdrawn. He then disappeared from the public gaze, visiting Brazil, Ecuador and the United States before ending up in France. In March, Mervyn Rees of the *Rand Daily Mail* 'debriefed' the former Secretary of Information. In Pretoria, a warrant was issued for Rhoodie's arrest on charges of fraud and theft. Within days, Rhoodie appeared on television telling his story to British viewers. John Vorster immediately declared that he had never been told about the Info secret projects. He accused Rhoodie of lying and claimed that Rhoodie had threatened to 'bring the temple down on us all'. Mulder responded by accusing Vorster of lying.[36] The second, 'Interim' report of the Erasmus Commission was published on 2 April. It stated that no member of P.W. Botha's cabinet knew before September 1978 that the *Citizen* was state-funded. The report said of Dr Mulder's evidence: 'apart from its vagueness, [it] is always in conflict with the real evidence'. Four days later, Mulder was expelled from the National Party, of which he had been a member for thirty-six years. The third and final, 'Supplementary' report of the Erasmus Commission was published in June 1979. It declared without equivocation: 'Mr Vorster knew everything about the basic financial arrangements for the Department's funds.' John Vorster resigned from his position as state president the next day.[37]

Coup and Counter-coup

The Soweto uprising eventually transformed South African politics, but its first invisible effect in July 1976 was that van den Bergh and Eschel Rhoodie decided that John Vorster would have to be removed (or retired). He had become 'the cork in the bottle'. This plot was at the heart of a North American meeting between the head of BOSS and the Secretary of Information during the Montreal Olympics, which had been subject to a boycott by a number of African countries protesting against New Zealand's rugby tour of South Africa. A 'blueprint for change' was discussed which would be instituted upon the removal, retirement or death of the Prime Minister. The assumption, of course, was that Connie Mulder would succeed to the premiership. The blueprint proposed:

> the establishment of a thinktank comprising key civil servants, leaders of commerce and industry, scientists, technologists, political scientists, military strategists, representatives of the country's intelligence and law enforcement services. The thinktank would be responsible for all the country's forward planning on major political, socio-economic and capital works programmes. This thinktank, or supreme council, would make recommendations to the Cabinet – but the Cabinet would not be allowed to make decisions on its own, without the supreme council first discussing the issues.[38]

Rhoodie summed up the 'basic tenet' of the blueprint as being an abandonment of the 'old policy line' (apartheid) and a movement towards seeing 'South Africa as a plurality of peoples, forgetting about the aspect of race and working towards structuring several democracies under a federal system of government'. Rhoodie later outlined more of the vision to

BBC producer David Harrison: 'They would have consolidated the home-lands. The showpiece port of Richards Bay in Natal would have become part of Kwazulu . . . East London would have gone into the Ciskei . . . It might well have meant that the Nats would lose a few farming seats but they had persuaded Connie that it was worth the price . . . They would have made Soweto into a city state like Berlin . . . All these measures would have bought ten years for South Africa and released the pressure.' Van den Bergh would be appointed chairman of the Supreme Council and would 'probably have got a cabinet post'; Rhoodie was to be the 'co-ordinating director of the thinktank'. For two civil servants to be plotting in this manner probably stands as South Africa's ultimate *trahison des clercs*. In 1988, Rhoodie alluded to the plan in an article for the Johannesburg *Star*: 'Ten to 12 years ago the hottest topic on the Government cocktail circuit, in military circles, among National Party MPs and even among Afrikaner aca-demics, was the wish that there could be a dictatorship, which we qualified as "benevolent" or "verlig", to enforce separate development on an imag-inative scale.' This is what Retief van Rooyen was referring to when he warned Mervyn Rees on 26 September 1978: 'I had put my head through the door of potential dictatorship and what I saw there horrified the hell out of me.'[39]

Perhaps, van den Bergh and Rhoodie had realised that the refusal of the African rioters to abandon their protest and, in the words of a *Daily Telegraph* editorial-writer, 'retreat into a sullen passivity' had already finished their careers. How could the country's intelligence chief not have known that riots would break out in June 1976? And why did he not have any plan to halt the unrest? Rhoodie didn't even bother to explain his fail-ure to 'spin' the uprising. In his Department's annual report for 1976, sub-mitted in May 1977, he blamed the product: 'The Prime Minister was described . . . as a man unable to control the direction of events and unable or unwilling to effect those changes in South Africa, which, it was claimed, were necessary to prevent a race war . . . foreign opinion . . . will not easily be moved except by imaginative large scale moves in South Africa . . . away from racial discrimination.'[40]

Or perhaps Rhoodie and van den Bergh simply believed that they could administer apartheid more effectively than the incumbent. In October 1976, just before the celebrations for the Transkei's 'independence', van den Bergh demonstrated his originality of thought in a startling interview with the right-wing journalist Arnaud de Borchgrave of *Newsweek*. The interview, or background briefing, was published without quotations under the title, 'The Way the BOSS Sees It'. De Borchgrave commented: 'The view from BOSS certainly does not reflect the government's position; van den Bergh often dares to disagree with Vorster.' De Borchgrave started the article by suggesting that 'South Africa's position today is similar to the fix that Israel would be in if it lost U.S. support.' Van den Bergh argued that 'separate development' and the 'bantustans' should be transformed into 'a Swiss-style cantonal system under a multiracial federal umbrella'. Blacks and whites in BOSS's new South Africa would 'share a common citizenship – and, therefore, a common national interest'. The federal government would handle defence and foreign affairs, while the cantons would control policing and internal security.

On South Africa's neighbours, van den Bergh reported that there would be a Zimbabwe People's Army victory in Rhodesia–Zimbabwe: 'A Marxist victory in Rhodesia will not jeopardise South Africa's security, the intelligence service concludes . . . Zimbabwe . . . will need South Africa just as much as Rhodesia does now. Mozambique will remain heavily dependent on both Zimbabwe and South Africa. BOSS thinks Pretoria should encourage a pragmatic interdependence.' SWAPO would be victorious in Namibia: 'South Africa should facilitate their coming to power to preserve its mineral interests in the territory.' In Angola, from which South Africa had retreated only eight months previously, van den Bergh believed that UNITA and the FNLA represented 'only a nuisance value'. He advised that 'Zaire and various right-wing groups in Europe should stop supporting anti-government guerrillas . . . South Africa has begun a process of reconciliation through the auspices of the Anglo American Corp.' If van den Bergh's domestic prescription was extraordinary, his reading of the power balance in the front-line states was revolutionary; it was also strangely prophetic, except for the failure to foresee the victory of Robert Mugabe and the Zimbabwe African National Union Patriotic Front (ZANU-PF) in Zimbabwe. The conclusion to de Borchgrave's article demonstrated that van den Bergh was no longer willing to tolerate Vorster's vacillation:

> BOSS believes that Vorster must move quickly to adopt these policy changes. The country's economic situation is already much worse than most people suspect, the intelligence analysts maintain . . . Vorster's position, BOSS thinks, is comparable to the one Charles de Gaulle found himself in when he returned to power in 1958 and inherited the Algerian war. Like de Gaulle, Vorster must ignore his own right wing or face political collapse. And once he has changed South Africa's present suicidal course, BOSS believes that Vorster must make overtures to the Soviet Union in order to

protect his flanks. Will the boss listen to BOSS? Many observers conclude that he will not. Such a display of leadership and imagination, they suspect, is beyond him and they fear that the Prime Minister will drift into authoritarian rule and perhaps into outright Fascism, with its attendant danger of provoking a race war. But BOSS believes that it still is not too late for South Africa to face reality and find a way to live with it. If there is a will, BOSS thinks it knows the way.[41]

Upon publication of the *Newsweek* interview, Arnaud de Borchgrave was immediately expelled from South Africa. Van den Bergh told *To the Point* magazine that de Borchgrave 'must have been dreaming, or off his rocker'. Vorster said that he was 'an untrustworthy journalist' and 'a liar'. De Borchgrave must have been amazed; he had achieved a fantastic scoop and nobody appears to have recognised its significance. But what of Connie Mulder? Surely such a conservative politician could never have accepted the need for change on the scale planned by Rhoodie and van den Bergh? Benjamin Pogrund noted in his memoirs an occasion when he heard Mulder make 'an outrageously right-wing speech' on the impossibility of 'Coloureds' ever being accepted by the white community. Later, he asked the minister about the speech: 'A cunning look crossed his face . . . "On the other hand, of course, you could have total integration of Coloureds with whites."' Mulder explained that 'my people . . . understand that a leader is going to be pushed by events towards the centre . . . it means that if someone wants to be the leader, he must not be seen to be too much in the centre to start with. He must be on the right.'[42]

While P.W. Botha and the generals began to mobilise their forces around the banner of 'total strategy' (see page 145), van den Bergh, Rhoodie and Connie Mulder were equally determined to execute the political equivalent of a coup d'état in South Africa. Angola and Soweto had demonstrated to both Botha and Mulder the imperative of 'adapt or die'; the problem was that neither of them was really prepared to adapt enough.

Having lived relatively openly in France for a number of months in 1979, Eschel Rhoodie was arrested by the French police on 19 July. On 23 August, he was extradited to South Africa to face 'seven charges of fraud, alternatively theft, involving R83,250 of secret funds from the Department of Information'. Rhoodie's trial, which lasted for eight days in September, was something of a damp squib. Connie Mulder testified on his former civil servant's behalf and the retired head of BOSS, Hendrik van den Bergh, 'sat listening intently' in the court room. Rhoodie was found guilty and sentenced to a total of twelve years' imprisonment on 8 October. Bail, pending the appeal, was granted at the exorbitant figure of R90,000. In October 1980, as Rhoodie later wrote, 'the country's highest court passed a unanimous judgement in my favour, rejecting the state's allegations and putting an end to my political persecution'.[43]

Rhoodie emigrated to the United States after his acquittal, just as his colleague Les de Villiers had in 1977. Neither of them ever returned to live in the Republic. Pogrund posed the question: 'Why did the United States let them in?' Gordon Winter provided an answer in the Dutch edition of *Inside BOSS*. He recalled asking Jacobus Kemp, the BOSS official who had been employed to investigate and cover up the Department of Information's secret projects, who was protecting Rhoodie? Kemp's reply was dramatic: 'Eschel has been actively involved with the CIA for years. The bastard actually admitted [it] to me. And he sat there smiling as he said it.' Rhoodie had continued: 'With the CIA behind me, I'm untouchable.'[44] There is some evidence to support Winter's story: Rhoodie, for example, had happily told Mervyn Rees of his friendship with 'Brownie' and his CIA acquaintances in the early 1960s. There were a handful of CIA connections to the Info family. 'Mysterious former CIA agent' Beurt SerVaas, one of the Information Department's partners in the United States, had taken over a firm called International Investigators Incorporated in Indianapolis, Indiana (nicknamed 'the Five Eyes') in 1965 and employed a number of former FBI and CIA agents. He later became owner and publisher of the *Saturday Evening Post*, before being exposed by the author Jim Hougan.[45]

In 1970, the aforementioned Richard Mellon Scaife purchased Kern House Enterprises, the holding company which owned Forum World Features (FWF), the London-based news agency established by Brian Crozier in 1966. Gordon Winter regularly worked for FWF while he was in England. In May 1975, Scaife suddenly closed FWF shortly before British press reports revealed that it was funded by the Congress for Cultural Freedom, an organisation that provided CIA funds to numerous publications. As Frances Stonor Saunders commented in *Who Pays The Piper*, FWF 'was a classic CIA undercover operation'. In his memoirs, *Free Agent*, Brian Crozier confirmed the role of the CIA and detailed his relationship with British intelligence. In 1969, he had founded the Institute for the Study of Conflict (ISC), in order to promote 'anti-communist' propaganda: 'Dick Scaife, as he liked to be called . . . sanctioned a grant of $100,000 a year to [the ISC], from his Scaife Family Charitable Trusts.'[46]

The ISC published Peter Janke's study of southern Africa in 1974. *Time Out* revealed that in 1973 South African 'author' Michael Morris (see page 60) had visited the ISC and in 1974 Janke had visited both Morris in Cape Town and BOSS headquarters in Pretoria. Eschel Rhoodie revealed in his marathon interview with Mervyn Rees that Info had contributed £5,000 to the cost of Janke's research. Wheels within wheels. In 1976, the Information Research Department (IRD), for which Brian Crozier had worked, of the Foreign Office, was asked by the Foreign Secretary Anthony Crosland to 'write a broad philosophical briefing on South Africa. What they came back with was a briefing, *South Africa: the Communist Peril*. It completely ignored the bad behaviour of the Apartheid state.' The IRD was closed by David Owen in 1977. Scaife's funding for the ISC continued into the 1980s.[47]

Neither the involvement of SerVaas nor that of Scaife proves that Rhoodie had a relationship with the CIA, but they certainly suggest the likelihood that it was safer quietly to grant him a green card than have him travelling the world broadcasting the secrets of South Africa's propaganda networks. And there were a lot more secrets that could have been revealed. Rhoodie told the Dutch magazine *Elseviers* that BOSS 'informed me that about 50 projects of the original five year plan would be continued'. The South African Department of Foreign Affairs inherited the secret operations in 1978, handing them on to MID in 1980. A Strategic Communications Branch (Stratcom) document dated 1984 showed hundreds of active propaganda operations. The document described the function of its operations as 'Ensuring the resoluteness and fighting spirit of the population; breaking the will of the enemy; winning the active support of neutral elements; and halting the negative influence against South Africa'. By 1985, the apartheid state and its bantustan minions were reportedly paying more than £3 million annually to thirteen US lobbyist and public relations firms.[48]

In 1983, Eschel Rhoodie published his own account in *The REAL Information Scandal*. It is an infuriating book, more than 900 pages long, without an index and seemingly unedited. Nevertheless, it contains interesting clues to the mysteries of Muldergate. Rhoodie recounts, for example, how, while he was on the run and telling his story to the press, he was visited in Paris in March 1979 by Hendrik van den Bergh:

> General van den Bergh was particularly concerned with the purchase of certain cases of 'tea leaves' to which reference was made in a top secret document

signed by Brand Fourie, approved by Vorster, and of which I had knowledge . . . I told him not to worry . . . 'I am mad as hell at the Botha government . . . [but] I will not do or say something which could endanger the
entire country' . . . I had obtained much of this top secret information for the
simple reason that I was one of the people who pioneered relations with certain states overseas . . . I remember being on the same aircraft which brought
the 'tea leaves' to South Africa . . . I assured [the General] that the various
projects which he was concerned about would never be released unless, I said,
I were to die an unnatural death.[49]

Intelligence legend has it that van den Bergh was not quite so trusting.
He apparently told Rhoodie, 'If you talk, it won't be South African intelligence that you'll have to worry about, it will be Mossad.' David
Dimbleby, whose BBC interview with Rhoodie was delayed by van den
Bergh's visit, commented in the *Observer*: 'It has been suggested that [the
secrets] could be to do with the relationship between South Africa and
Israel, with arms deals, and with the nuclear capability that South Africa is
widely thought to have.' In 1993, after the South African government
admitted to the development of six nuclear weapons, *City Press* reported
that a total of 30 grammes of tritium (a radioactive isotope of hydrogen
necessary to explode a nuclear bomb) had been 'flown to South Africa in
gas form in tiny capsules of one two-and-a-half grammes a time'. The veteran South African journalist Desmond Blow contacted Rhoodie in
Atlanta, Georgia and put it to him that Israel had supplied tritium to South
Africa and 'in return SA secretly provided Israel with "yellow cake" (uranium oxide) to be enriched to make nuclear energy and code named
"Skape" (Mutton)'. Rhoodie replied: 'I'm not denying knowledge . . . just
that I cannot comment on it.' Rhoodie also confirmed that 'threats had
been made against his life'. *City Press*'s source, although they didn't reveal
it, was documentation leaked from the secret trial of Brigadier Johan
Blaauw, which took place in South Africa in 1988.[50]

A former South African Air Force Korean war veteran, Blaauw became
in 1975 'a go-between for Israel and South Africa on military matters'. In
1976, he was requested by an Israeli Nuclear Council member to facilitate
the purchase of South African 'yellow cake'. Blaauw received approval for
the transaction from John Vorster. Van den Bergh asked Blaauw to request
payment for the uranium oxide in the form of the tritium. Eventually,
600 tonnes of 'yellow cake' was delivered to Israel and South Africa
received enough tritium to create twelve nuclear weapons. The American
author William Burrows revealed in *Critical Mass* that the tritium was

transported by 'people like Rhoodie and Benni Blumberg, the head of the secret LAKAM nuclear procurement network started by [Defence Minister Shimon] Peres'. The operation was run by BOSS and LAKAM. It is not known whether the tritium was transported on commercial flights. Blaauw would later play a role in supplying oil from the Middle East to the Republic following the fall of the Shah's regime in 1978. There appears to have been some debate within South African political and military circles whether the development of a nuclear weapon had any deterrent force if the enemies of South Africa were ignorant of its existence. Over the years, there have been numerous clues in public statements by South African officials, for example Connie Mulder's statement to the *Washington Post* in 1977: 'If we are attacked, no rules apply at all if it comes to a question of our existence. We will use all means at our disposal . . . It is true that we have just completed our own pilot plant that uses very advanced technology, and that we have major uranium resources.'[51]

One of the key figures, in what the *Financial Times* called 'the Israeli connection', was Arnon Milchan, who by the early 1970s had become 'Israel's foremost weapons procurer'. In 1974, Shimon Peres introduced Milchan to Rhoodie 'at a reception in Tel Aviv'. Peres informed Rhoodie that Milchan's father and brother, the owners of an Israeli chemical company, had 'done a great service on behalf of Israel's national security'. Burrows reported that in 1977 'the two nations set up a joint secretariat to handle various matters not the least of which was "propaganda and psychological warfare". . . Under the terms of the agreement, Israel would provide input into how to portray both countries' best side. South Africa would provide the money, with each county appointing a secretary to look after its interests.' Rhoodie and Milchan were appointed to the secretariat. At a meeting in Cannes, Milchan's recommendation was that 'the apartheid regime . . . penetrate the American movie business' – something that Milchan himself did very successfully in the 1980s.[52] In 1977, Milchan, who was keen to make a motion picture about the arms business, met Anthony Sampson, who had recently written *The Arms Bazaar*. As Sampson later recalled, Milchan explained to him that 'South Africa was so corrupt and corrupting that it could buy almost every weapon that it needed by paying double the market rate, via impenetrable Swiss banks where Afrikaner officials kept their own secret accounts.'[53]

South Africa's connection with Israel had fluctuated over the years, especially during the early 1960s when Israel tried to develop productive relationships with the decolonised African states. Van den Bergh visited

Israel in 1973, later informing an interviewer: 'I went to Israel recently, and enjoyed every moment there. I told the Prime Minister when I got back that as long as Israel exists we have a hope. If Israel should, God forbid, be destroyed, then South Africa would be in danger of extinction.' In November 1973, the Arab oil embargo was extended to include South Africa, Portugal and Rhodesia. Eschel Rhoodie later commented: 'When the Yom Kippur War began [in October 1973] and all of Africa and various other Third World countries broke off diplomatic relations with Israel, we were ready. General van den Bergh and I began a series of visits to Israel in which we met with scores of opinion formers, including Prime Minister Rabin.' In *The REAL Information Scandal*, Rhoodie published a facsimile of a letter that he received from Shimon Peres, in November 1974:

> Thank you . . . for the great efforts you employed to ensure the success of the meetings which took place in Pretoria on the 13th and 14th of this month. It is to a very large extent due to your perspicacity, foresight and political imagination that a vitally important cooperation between our two countries has been initiated. This cooperation is based not only on common interests and on the determination to resist equally our enemies, but also on the unshakeable foundations of our common hatred of injustice and our refusal to submit to it.[54]

During June 1975, Rhoodie and Mulder paid a secret visit to Israel during which Rabin extended a formal invitation to John Vorster. Eventually, in April 1976, after the South African Prime Minister's customary period of indecision, the former Nazi-sympathiser Balthazar John Vorster made the first 'official visit' by a South African premier to Israel. Andrew and Leslie Cockburn later commented: 'When Vorster laid a wreath at Yad Vashem, Israel's memorial to the Holocaust, it made some observers exceptionally queasy.' It confirmed for others the acuity of the United Nation's juxtaposition of apartheid and Zionism five months before: 'The General Assembly . . . taking note of Resolution 77(XII) adopted by . . . the [OAU] . . . which considered "that the racist regime in occupied Palestine and the racist regimes in Zimbabwe and South Africa have a common imperialist origin" . . . determines that Zionism is a form of racism and racial discrimination.'[55]

John Vorster died in September 1983. His retirement was dominated by his bitterness towards his successor P.W. Botha, whom he refused to allow to visit him when he was on his deathbed. It was rumoured that Vorster had flirted with the idea of supporting the Conservative Party (CP), which included a number of former NP politicians who had abandoned P.W. Botha in 1982. Connie Mulder, who joined the CP, died in 1988 – in Eschel Rhoodie's words, 'victim of as blatant a case of political assassination as South Africa had ever seen'. One of his sons, Pieter, leads the Afrikaner Freedom Front Plus in South Africa's parliament.[56] Eschel Rhoodie settled in Atlanta, Georgia with his wife and children in 1982. He wrote a number of books, worked in risk consultancy and provided business advice to South Africans investing in the United States. In 1986, he declared in the Johannesburg *Star* that 'Mandela should be freed.' Six years later, it was reported that he had offered his services as a public relations consultant to both the Inkatha Freedom Party in South Africa and the government of Mozambique. He died, aged sixty, of a heart attack in July 1993 while playing tennis. (In 1991, he had been the Georgia over-55 champion.) His son later became a pilot in the US Air Force. I spoke to his wife Katie in 1999 to ask what had happened to Rhoodie's papers. She replied that they had been destroyed following a flood in their garage.[57]

Hendrik van den Bergh survived until 1997. He described the Erasmus Report as 'a travesty of justice', and, when a group launched a campaign demanding his prosecution, he made a point of signing the petition himself in front of the cameras. Later he spoke on public platforms within South Africa arguing against the 'total onslaught' strategy which P.W. Botha and his military advisers were in the process of developing. The General believed that the task of government should be 'to establish the proper climate for negotiation with the black majority [in order to] ensure the geopolitical integrity of the white population'. From his point of view, South Africa was in a 'pre-revolutionary' situation: 'I am afraid that if the whites of this country do not act in concert and very decisively then they will, like the Portuguese in Angola and Mozambique, also lose their place at the table and they will have to settle for the crumbs on the floor.' In 1985, he produced a manuscript entitled 'No Boats in the Harbour', but it was never published. Summing up South African politics since 1970, he wrote: 'The procrastination of the 1970s to a great extent emasculated the Verwoerdian plan of action to give a territorial basis for separate political freedoms . . . It also resulted in the almost frenzied urgency displayed in the early 1980s by Prime Minister P.W. Botha . . . The result, I am afraid to say, was the creation of a political time bomb.'

Mervyn Rees's 'Deep Throats' have, unlike the famous Watergate original, never been exposed. Most observers at the time believed that 'Daan', the senior civil servant, was connected either to military intelligence or to Pik Botha. 'Myrtle', I am reliably informed, was a female lover of one of the Information Department's protagonists.[58]

6

Intelligence Interregnum

Defectors, even the most intelligent and best educated . . . must be used with caution . . . In the first place, the individual who defects usually does so out of desperation, and he suffers not only from personal trauma but also from 'culture shock' when placed in an alien environment. The ideological defector is a deviant from the norm of his own society. He is atypical, or he would not have been sufficiently repelled by the system in which he has been reared to leave it. And like émigrés generally, his usefulness decreases rapidly with the passage of time.

Paul W. Blackstock, *The Strategy of Subversion*, 1964[1]

Department for National Security (DONS)

HENDRIK VAN DEN Bergh's retirement from BOSS in June 1978 heralded a brief period in which South African intelligence was reshuffled between the police, the military, foreign affairs and 'the analysts'. In August 1978, van den Bergh told Carel Birkby that 'one of the weaknesses in any intelligence organisation . . . is the possibility of eventual disloyalty to the Trade'. Commenting with distaste on the number of books by former CIA agents, he said: 'I detest what they have done and written . . . What I know and what my chaps know, we carry in our heads, and we will carry it to our graves.' What van den Bergh clearly did not understand was that intelligence agencies 'leak' when they are either weak or incapable of responding to threats against the state. He would soon find this out. BOSS was certainly in a parlous condition during van den Bergh's last days. Mervyn Rees reported in 1980 that the agency had been afflicted by bureaucratic envy and entropy:

Some men . . . returned to the Security Police – apparently feeling that a power clique was being formed by General van den Bergh . . . Resentment was also building up over what was interpreted as the rapid, and frequently meteoric, promotions of men who were said to have attracted the General's eye. Reports and rumours were circulating that Broederbonders were being recruited into the organisation – some of them ill-equipped to perform intelligence work – and were being given preferential treatment . . . Two of the General's family . . . were said to be stationed abroad.[2]

On the same day that van den Bergh retired, the *Government Gazette* carried the text of the Bureau for State Security Act 1978. This rarely discussed document possessed two intriguing sections among the morass of standard bureaucratic detail. Section 21 stated: 'every member shall place the whole of his time at the disposal of the State . . . no member shall perform or engage himself to perform any remunerative work outside his employment in the Bureau'. Obviously, the days when BOSS agents could freelance or employ freelancers as 'agents' were over. The second Section, 27, warned that 'Any person, not being a member of the Bureau, who . . . by words, conduct or demeanour pretends that he is such a member . . . shall be guilty of an offence and liable on conviction to a fine not exceeding one thousand rand or imprisonment for a period not exceeding six months.'[3] Van den Bergh's sloppy approach to bureaucratic detail was clearly being clamped down on with his departure.

Van den Bergh's successor, his colleague since 1963 and his deputy since 1974, Alexander 'Alec' van Wyk, aged fifty-eight, was little known beyond the police and the bureaucracy. One newspaper described him as 'a strapping, straight-talking . . . public servant with the craggy face of a trawlerman'. When BOSS was created in 1969, van Wyk had been responsible for the Africa desk; later, he 'became the head of external operations . . . in control of foreign agents'. In July 1977, van Wyk, then deputy head of BOSS, spoke to the Johannesburg *Sunday Times*. The bulk of the interview concerned Harold Wilson's allegations that BOSS had burgled his London home and colluded with a pro-South African faction within MI5 (see page 61). But van Wyk also admitted that South Africa 'has undercover agents working in Britain, America and other countries. They are highly trained – in America and West Germany – and have been working abroad for more than five years.' He added, 'most Western countries have undercover agents here – I know those from America, Britain, France and Germany. Every now and then we get together and discuss our mutual interests.' He explained that BOSS was similar to MI6 or the CIA in its concern with external security; 'internal security is looked after by the Security Police'.[4] Former BOSS officers suggest that van Wyk was a reasonable, unassuming man in comparison to his predecessor. Some of this is borne out by the clumsy indiscretions in his 1977 interview:

> We would never commit a criminal act to get hold of documents . . . If you arrive in South Africa with a suitcase, and I want to know what it contains, I don't steal it. If I did I would be telling you I am aware of your presence, and you will skip the country. Instead I find a way to open the suitcase while you are out, and photograph the contents . . . We do tap telephones, but only if we are instructed to or have good reason to believe the person using a phone may be a threat to State security. It is one thing to tape-record a telephone conversation. But a transcript of a 30-minute conversation takes about four hours of work – and then it may contain nothing of significance.[5]

Van Wyk's interview was not appreciated by van den Bergh. Within days, van Wyk claimed that he had been misquoted: 'I have been in the intelligence service for 30 years and I know a statement like that would be very foolish. I even had a telephone call from the British service asking if I had gone mad.' In the process of denial, the indiscretions continued, not least the suggestion that South Africa's Special Branch in the 1950s had considered their work to be 'intelligence'. Upon his appointment in 1978, van Wyk was faced with a number of serious problems: questions were beginning to be asked about the role of BOSS in the mounting Information scandal; van den Bergh had not completely retired (he was investigating Operation Senekal's secret projects for John Vorster); and relations with the CIA were at an all-time low. BOSS agents and officials were certainly anxious by September 1978. First, the title, Bureau for State Security, was changed to the Department for National Security (creating the mafiaesque acronym, DONS). The anti-government press in South Africa were quick to utilise a grotesque abbreviation, even though 'DFNS' would have been the accurate form. Then P.W. Botha was elected prime minister, while retaining the Defence portfolio – an event that 'was greeted with despair' as a result of 'concern over the future of . . . jobs and Botha's reputation for impulsiveness, even instability'. Without van den Bergh as a protector, DONS would have to 'prove its loyalty' to the new regime. A Johannesburg *Sunday Times* story on 22 October reported that:

> After years . . . in the cold, the . . . [MID] has been restored to its 'rightful place' in the South African intelligence community . . . [The MID]'s star has risen with Mr P.W. Botha. The point was emphasised this week when the Chief of the Defence Force, General Magnus Malan, was included in the negotiations with the Western Big Five over South West Africa. In the old

days, it was . . . van den Bergh who was always at Mr Vorster's elbow . . . Mr Botha has consolidated his own control of the intelligence services by appointing Mr Kobie Coetsee MP . . . as Deputy Defence Minister and of National Security. This brings both DONS and [MID] under Mr Coetsee's direct control, and under the control of Mr Botha himself.[6]

Arthur McGiven later recalled that 'a ton of documents [were sent] to Cape Town, where Deputy Secretary Gert Rothman produced them to a committee under Deputy Minister of Defence "Kobie" Coetsee. The committee included senior military and security police officers and was formed to examine the role of the three security forces.' DONS officials had to answer 'trivial questions . . . from Coetsee and his military advisors'. The questions usually related to military matters: a theologian who had published an essay on conscientious objection or a professor who had called for a 'multiracial ambulance service [manned] by conscientious objectors'. Within a year, according to the journalist (and later MI6 agent) John Fullerton, DONS had been relocated to 'the capital's Armscor building', and the agency had been 'stripped to a skeleton of its former self'. The fact that the civilian intelligence agency was housed within the state's arms development and procurement capacity symbolised the dominance of the generals. The conclusion to the article in *Now* magazine was entirely accurate: 'The battle of the spies has put the military in charge of South Africa's destiny for a long time to come.'[7]

CIA Trouble

Van den Bergh had always treasured his relationship with American intelligence, but following the débâcle in Angola, his American friends had become something of a liability. The MID had engineered a masterful 'spin' operation in South Africa which had managed to convince the (white) public that the invasion would have been a success if the SADF had not been 'let down' by the unreliable CIA. Moreover, Washington DC was going through one of its periodic panics regarding the activities of the CIA: in 1975, three separate investigating bodies, the Rockefeller Commission, the (Senate) Select Committee, chaired by Frank Church, and the (House) Select Committee on Intelligence, chaired by Otis Pike, were appointed to investigate US intelligence. The result of the three investigations was that CIA oversight became much stricter. In November 1976, Jimmy Carter was elected president and during 1977 US–South African relations deteriorated.

In April, the US Ambassador to the United Nations Andrew Young gave an offhand reply, 'Yeah,' to the question 'Is the South African government illegitimate?' In May, Vice-President Walter Mondale made an ambiguous statement in favour of 'full political participation' in South Africa.[8]

In June 1977, President Carter issued 'Presidential Directive/NSC-5' which directed the entire government to adopt a new policy on South Africa'. A secret State Department document 'called on the South African Government to adopt a "progressive transformation" of its society. Future US policy would be based on what South Africa did with regard to race relations.' Richard Moose, Assistant Secretary for African Affairs at the State Department in the Carter administration, told an interviewer that at the beginning of 1977:

> We formally ended all forms of intelligence cooperation with the South African government . . . We ended all kinds of government exchanges and that was reasonably effective. I believe it was 99 percent effective. In retrospect, I believe that some of our US intelligence agencies without the knowledge of the President and against his explicit direction nevertheless maintained some level of clandestine exchange with the South Africans, providing some types of information about Soviet bloc activities around the area. It was outside the law. It was the kind of thing that, unfortunately, the CIA has done from time to time. The CIA and our military intelligence believed that it was very important for them to maintain some of the ties because the South Africans were the only really effective non-African intelligence operation in the area. But that was totally illegal.[9]

In 1978, van den Bergh's visa application to visit the United States was rejected. *The Times*, citing *Rapport*'s Washington correspondent, reported that the rejected visit was 'in connection with an investigation into the covert overseas activities of . . . [the] Department of Information'. Two months later, the retiring spy chief reflected his irritation in an offhand assessment of the capabilities of foreign intelligence agencies: 'The British [are] the best in the business. The Russians are past-masters at espionage, but the British are still tops. The Americans? Well, without being rude, not so hot. The KGB has penetrated them thoroughly.' In January 1979, when Anthony Sampson suggested to van den Bergh 'that the CIA might have become less friendly, he replied, "That's a lot of bull. On the contrary, only today I had lunch with a friend of mine who is back here on holiday, who is *very* senior in the CIA."'[10] In reality, relations between the CIA and BOSS–DONS were in a perilous condition; there would be no recovery before January 1981.

In July 1977, the Department of Information-owned newspaper the *Citizen* published an eight-part series of articles detailing the 'Secret US War against South Africa'. The author was the remarkable Aida Parker. Born in 1918 in England, she emigrated to South Africa in the 1930s. She 'revered former Prime Minister Hendrik Verwoerd, describing him as "an absolute gentleman with a giant intellect"'. Parker was an independently wealthy journalist–spy who was happy to trade information with anybody (BOSS, MID, CIA, MI6) so long as the recipient was, or could pretend to be, equally right-wing. In old age (she died in 2003), Aida Parker became increasingly indiscreet and was happy to discuss and name her intelligence contacts and handlers. She said that General Tienie Groenewald was her MID handler and claimed to have been friendly with Ted Shackley, the famous CIA 'Blond Ghost', who was deputy director, responsible for worldwide covert intelligence, under George Bush in 1976. She famously spoke of 'good Germans' and 'bad Germans'; in Aida's interpretation, good meant fascist. The series of articles in 1977, later republished as a pamphlet, were based upon documents supplied by BOSS agent Piet Swanepoel, on the direct orders of Alexander van Wyk.[11] The articles were conspiratorial but sprinkled with fragments of truth. Take, for example, the following claim:

> A number of Western intelligence agencies and newspapers have recently claimed that CIA destabilisation 'specialists' who were in Chili [sic] in 1973, Portugal in 1974 and Mozambique just before it received independence are now in South Africa. Writing in the influential Israeli newspaper, *Ma'ariv*, published in Tel Aviv, commentator Daniel Drooz said 'Their appearance in South Africa at this time is not coincidental. It is a warning that the American "nutcracker" is applying pressure, that the US has begun an active effort to undermine the South African government.'[12]

The allegation that CIA agents visited South Africa after the Soweto uprising is not surprising, but the quote from Daniel Drooz reveals something of a riddle. Drooz arrived in South Africa in 1976 and joined the newly formed Foreign Correspondents' Association claiming to represent *Ma'ariv*, the *Chicago Sun-Times* and *US News and World Report*. He appears to have filed hardly any copy for the American publications. Even one of his own media colleagues thought he might be a spy. In the following year, Drooz was accused by a South African government official 'of spying for both the Central Intelligence Agency and the Israelis'. He was expelled in 1978.[13] One of Parker's targets was the United States Information Service 'reading room' which had opened in Orlando East, Soweto in November 1975. As usual, she makes too many connections and imagines a world in which 'a' always leads directly to 'b':

> Old CIA watchers are not too surprised at the Soweto 'cultural' development. 'It is a classic case of history repeating itself,' one former intelligence officer told me. A facility with a remarkable resemblance to the Soweto operation opened in London in January 1962. This facility, known as the Transcription Centre, was advertised as a 'non-profit making organisation supported by a direct grant from the Farfield Foundation' . . . Prominently involved in the whole exercise was an American, Mr Melvin John Lasky, a director of Transcription Features Services Ltd. Lasky was also a director of Encounter Ltd, which financed such avant-garde magazines as the British socialist publication, *Encounter*. Oddly enough, *Encounter* was also financed by the CIA via the Congress of Cultural Freedom which in turn financed Roland [sic] Segal's *Africa South* and *Africa South in Exile*.[14]

Aida Parker's classification of the anti-communist *Encounter* as 'socialist' demonstrated both how right wing and how unhinged she was. Between 1977 and 1979, a number of odd, 'pro-South African' Americans passed through the hands of Aida Parker and Gordon Winter at the *Citizen*: Ralph Moss, a black campaigner 'trying to drum up Black American support for . . . [the] embattled Rhodesian Government'; the Reverend Lester Kinsolving, accused by the '[US] National Council of Churches [of being] a "secret agent" for the South African Government'; Donald McAlvany, who formed an organisation called Americans Concerned About South Africa (later revealed by Eschel Rhoodie to have been funded 'to the tune of $120,000'); and Dr Billy James Hargis, 'America's number one opponent of communism'. On 29 September 1978, William Rourke Jordan, an American citizen resident in South Africa since 1975, was arrested for being in illegal possession of eight 'firearms and more than 1000 rounds of ammunition'. He claimed to be a former brigadier-general in the US Marines. US officials in South Africa accepted that he was a former member of the armed forces, but the Pentagon 'denied all knowledge of the man'. Jordan was found guilty of the charges and deported. Aida Parker suggested that Jordan had been a senior CIA covert operative who was close friends with Hendrik van den Bergh.[15] Jordan was arrested within twenty-four hours of P.W. Botha's election as prime minister.

In January 1979, Gordon Winter was supplied with a copy of a letter from US diplomat Sally Shelton to a high-profile 'struggle lawyer', Shun Chetty. The ANC activist Murphy Morobe recalled in Chetty's obituary in 2000: 'Ask any member of the then notorious John Vorster Square security establishment. He would not leave them in peace. To them he was . . . that hard-nosed lawyer.' The letter on Department of State letter-headed paper made clear that Shelton and Chetty were lovers. On 2 February 1979, the *Citizen* headlined the story, 'US Envoy in Love with SA Lawyer'. The punch came in the final paragraphs, 'Mr Chetty has some very powerful American friends.' The report named the US Ambassador to South Africa, William Edmondson, and noted that in the 1950s and 1960s Edmondson had served with the CIA. It also named William McKinley Johnson, US Consul-General in Johannesburg, and underlined his period in the CIA. The publication of the Shelton–Chetty story was an indication of the collapse in relations between BOSS–DONS and the CIA. The Johannesburg *Star* reported that Shelton's first reaction to the story was 'that the information . . . had originated from clandestine sources in Pretoria'. Chetty fled South Africa in August 1979 citing 'intensified harassment by the security police'. Shelton was appointed US ambassador to Barbados in May that year. Five years later, she married the former Director of the CIA William Colby.[16]

The crisis in US–South African relations reached its nadir in April 1979 with a genuine diplomatic incident. On 4 April, a MID intelligence operation was executed during which an American 'espionage plane' was intercepted at the remote Upington airport. While the pilots 'slept in a nearby hotel, the agents dismantled a 70mm camera hidden in the belly of the plane to remove a spool of film'. The film was developed and found to contain hundreds of images which indicated that the US had been engaging in a 'systematic surveillance of strategic regions . . . including Pelindaba, site of South Africa's top-secret uranium enrichment plant'. The South African government expelled the pilot and his crew, and P.W. Botha announced that they 'had been under [South African] surveillance for more than six months'. The US government retaliated by expelling South Africa's military and naval attachés. Foreign Minister Pik Botha said on American television, 'The expulsion of the two South African officials was openly intimidatory . . . Instead of apologising, America "seems to want to blame me for what they have done".'[17] Two weeks later, demonstrating the product of South Africa's intelligence blackmail, the *Daily Telegraph* reported that 'photographs taken by an American ambassadorial aircraft of installations in Zambia, Angola and Tanzania have been passed to South Africa in exchange for information obtained by South African intelligence agents'. In July 1979, Rhodesian spy chief Ken Flower visited Washington with Bishop Muzorewa. He was greeted by the Director of the CIA 'like a long-lost brother. Given a spy satellite photo . . . showing our home in Salisbury, recording changes in the surroundings every 103 minutes – perhaps to remind us that Big Brother is always watching!'[18]

On 22 September 1979, one of the US Vela satellites detected 'a double pulse of light, characteristic of a nuclear explosion' in the Indian Ocean. The suspected explosion was widely reported and the American government was caught off guard. Concerted attempts were made to confuse the issue. In late October, the head of the South African Navy made a statement in which he suggested that the 'possible nuclear detonation . . . may have been caused by an accident aboard a Soviet nuclear submarine'. A few days later, sources in the US Air Force proposed that the flash could have been caused by 'a "superbolt" . . . a lightning flash so powerful that it can release as much energy as a small nuclear weapon'. Meanwhile, a South African academic, Dr Renfrew Christie, had been arrested under the Terrorism Act. He had been attempting to pass information to the ANC regarding South Africa's nuclear programme. Christie was imprisoned for seven years. Demonstrating the poor relations with the apartheid regime, the CIA leaked information in January 1980 that the South Africans had tested a nuclear weapon in 1979. In a 'classified report submitted to the National Security Council' in June, the CIA reported that the nuclear blast was 'a direct result of co-operation between Israel and South Africa'.[19]

The Defectors and the Burned

The first major sign of the transformation that was occurring in the 'powerplay' of South African intelligence was the 'defection' of BOSS asset Gordon Winter in June 1979. This was the first publicised intelligence defection in the history of South Africa. Winter, his wife and son arrived in London on 28 May; he carried with him 'suitcases of documents, 18,000 cross-indexed photographic negatives, and tapes of 16 hours of telephone conversations with Bureau for State Security chiefs and other contacts'. He contacted Barrie Penrose, of the Pencourt team, who had previously invited him to appear on a television programme to accompany the Thorpe trial, and declared that he wanted to tell his full story. Winter appeared on London Weekend Television on 29 June and revealed: his role in the Thorpe case (on BOSS instructions, he had tried to sell the story during the February 1974 general election), that BOSS had framed Peter Hain in the 1975 bank robbery case; and that BOSS had murdered Keith Wallace in 1970. He explained that 'Muldergate' and the fall of van den Bergh ('a fabulous man') were among the reasons that he had decided to defect: 'They could have done that to me. So when this Information thing started, I started making tape recordings of everybody, my handlers, the lot.' David Beresford reported the next morning:

> In my presence last night, Mr Penrose telephoned General van den Bergh in Johannesburg with a message from Winter in Europe. Subsequently I telephoned General van den Bergh and informed him that Winter had 'defected' and told him of some of the allegations being made by Winter. The general said the allegations were 'absolute balls' and 'complete tripe'. He said he thought Winter – who he described as an informant rather than an agent – was in South Africa. When I told him that I had been privy to the earlier conversation . . . the general said it was a 'trap' and he ended the interview.[20]

The *Citizen*, the newspaper established by South Africa's Information Department and Winter's erstwhile employer, responded to the defection with a brutal editorial, 'Another Walter Mitty?', composed in an almost staccato style: 'As a journalist he was among the best . . . And there was never any comeback to his stories. In or out of the courts. Since he was meticulously accurate . . . Perhaps the trouble with Winter is that he had begun to believe his own stories. But that can happen in this strange world in which we live. A world in which the Walter Mittys live out their wild fantasies. And ask the rest of us to believe their fantasies are genuine.'[21] Johnny Johnson, the writer of the editorial, was also the editor of the newspaper. He had been Winter's editor at the Johannesburg *Sunday Express* in the 1960s and 1970s. He knew full well that Gordon Winter had a relationship with South African intelligence. In one of our extensive conversations, I asked Winter why he had included the frankly unbelievable chapter at the end of *Inside BOSS* in which he claims that two events convinced him that he must leave South Africa and write a book exposing the agency: the birth of his son, which prompted the realisation that 'Blacks have babies too'; and the torture of his maid's daughter. He replied that, although both events actually happened, the determining factor in his decision to flee apartheid South Africa was his handler Jacobus Kemp's suggestion that he should develop a relationship with the CIA and become a 'double agent'.[22] In the intelligence climate of 1979, Kemp's idea made sense. Winter realised that without van den Bergh's protection, he was beginning to get out of his depth.

While Winter retreated to write what would become *Inside BOSS*, a second 'defector' arrived in Sweden. Alexander Lambert had claimed that he was going 'on holiday' with his wife and six children; 'to prove his *bona fides* to the South African authorities he bought return tickets'. In October 1979, the family were granted permission to remain in Sweden. Lambert, a Coloured (mixed-race) South African, was undoubtedly the most difficult of the defectors to assess. He claimed to work for BOSS but couldn't name other BOSS agents or officers: 'One BOSS agent never knows another . . . We don't even have BOSS contacts, because we always liaise through the security police.' He refused to name people who were under BOSS surveillance, supposedly for their own protection. He told *New African* that BOSS engaged in the kidnap of ANC activists in neighbouring countries.

In *Dagens Nyheter*, a popular Swedish newspaper, Lambert described a favoured interrogation method: 'Injured prisoners were taken up three at a time in helicopters to a thousand metres height. One of the three had his wrists tied with a leather thong to a long rope. He would be knocked out of the helicopter and allowed to fall 20 metres. Then he was allowed to fall to his death. Those remaining would know it was their turn next if they did not speak.' He also claimed that in BOSS's Pietermaritzburg interrogation room, he had seen 'prisoners submerged under water, given electric shocks and having their genitals crushed. When they died their bodies were thrown into a disused mine.' Lambert's 'defection' was not appreciated by the ANC chief representative in Scandinavia, Lindiwe Mabuza, who wrote in an unpublished letter to *Dagens Nyheter*: 'By his own testimony, Lambert is not just an ordinary run-of-the-mill accomplice to the heinous crimes of the apartheid murder squad, BOSS . . . The onus is on Lambert and his sponsors to tell the whole truth.' Dr Zdenek Cervenka, the research director at the Scandinavian Institute for African Studies, suggested that Lambert's testimony could be disinformation: 'defection [is] sometimes just part of the old espionage game'. Alexander Lambert told *New African* that he 'would probably write a book about his experiences.' No book ever appeared.

In one respect, Lambert was no different from Gordon Winter and the later defectors: self-interest was his dominant motivation. Unlike Winter, who was an able communicator who possessed numerous media contacts, if Lambert was telling the truth as he had perceived it, it was the truth of the footsoldier. It is revealing that his stories of torture and brutality are in keeping with what we know happened in South Africa in the 1980s. It is possible that Lambert was an early version of an 'askari', a captured black militant who was turned into a killer for the apartheid regime: Lambert told *Stern* magazine that he had 'been sympathetic to the Black struggle since the early 1960s . . . I decided to be a sort of double agent. At least for myself.' He also said to *New African*, 'I was just a back-up gunman trained to shoot to kill.' It seems likely that Lambert had actually worked for the Security Police but had recognised the iconic power that the BOSS name carried. It is also significant that the only 'black' South African 'defector' was the least reported and least believed. David Beresford reported in December 1979: 'Lambert . . . offered his story to the *Guardian* for £2,500 earlier this month. [He] . . . claimed to know the identity of a BOSS "assassin" who had killed . . . Dr Richard Turner.' He added, that Lambert's story had 'been widely discounted'.[23]

The third South African defector, Arthur McGiven, unlike Winter and Lambert who were essentially operatives, was a BOSS analyst (or what van den Bergh liked to call, but never quite understood, 'an evaluator'). McGiven was able to provide the first view of BOSS from within the bureaucracy. In September 1979, he had quietly resigned from DONS, arriving in London with 'nearly 50 documents' in November 1979. The *Observer* carried his story in three instalments. McGiven had been recruited by BOSS in 1972 while studying at the University of the Witwatersrand. He had spied on fellow students before being instructed to join the overseas propaganda department of the South African Broadcasting Corporation. In 1975, he underwent 'an aptitude test, interview and security clearance' before being appointed a BOSS 'evaluator'. Between 1976 and 1979, he worked in the sections that covered South African and international academics and on the British and United States desks, and ended his brief career as the head of the section covering academics, writers and publishers. The first part of McGiven's testimony, 'Inside BOSS's "super spook" H.Q.', detailed the development of the BOSS–DONS divisional structure:

> Division A . . . white subversion . . . Division B black subversion . . . Division K . . . Coloureds and Asians, the Homelands and Namibian affairs. Division D . . . economic analysis of African states. Division F . . . political analysis of African states . . . Division G performs military evaluations

in liaison with the [MID]. These six divisions constitute the evaluation arm of BOSS . . . they are staffed mainly by ex-policemen (now being phased out in favour of more sophisticated entrants) and more reliable graduates from the Afrikaans Universities. The operational arm consists of four divisions. Division N controls the activities of 14 regional offices within South Africa. Manned largely by ex-policemen, these handle informers [etc.] . . . Division C controls agents operating under diplomatic cover . . . It also controls officials in [the 'independent homelands'] . . . Division V (Covert Operations) operates agents in African States . . . Division O (Counterintelligence and Security) is the 'super spook' department. As part of the spy hunt, it investigates everyone coming to South Africa from a Communist country and monitors the activities of diplomats . . . Other divisions are administrative.

McGiven provided substantial evidence of: BOSS–DONS spying on Progressive Reform Party MP Helen Suzman; transcripts of telephone calls made from the offices of the right-wing HNP, although 'Nothing in the HNP reports can be said to constitute a threat to the present South African system of government'; and surveillance of the non-Afrikaner churches and of South African students. In August 1981, the South African state settled out of court with two HNP officials who sued the government for putting taps on their telephones. In particular, McGiven revealed that since 'a change started in the highly conservative Afrikanse Studente Bond [ASB] about two years ago, shortly after the Soweto uprising', BOSS–DONS was tapping the telephone of a theology student, Theuns Eloff, the chairman of the ASB. He added that BOSS–DONS training took place 'at a farm, the so-called Rietvlei complex, south-east of Pretoria'.[24]

The second extract from McGiven's documents revealed that BOSS–DONS kept files on innumerable South Africans and foreigners: Alan Paton, Laurens van der Post, André Brink, Nadine Gordimer, Sir Harold Wilson, Sir Robert Birley, Harry Oppenheimer, Tiny Rowland (owner of the *Observer*), Mike Terry (A-AM), Abdul Minty (ANC), Robert Hughes (British anti-apartheid MP), Albie Sachs (later mutilated in a bombing), Joe Slovo and Ruth First (later murdered by a parcelbomb). 'Files, dating from the early 1970s, [included] President Carter, identified on the computer index as Governor of Alabama (sic), Cyrus Vance, Andrew Young and ex-President Ford.' Files were also kept on religious institutions which had a history of campaigning against apartheid and on the Rockefeller and Carnegie Foundations. McGiven added that continuous operations included Operation Knoopsgat

(Buttonhole) which intercepted the mail; Operation Hanslam (Pet Lamb) which tapped telephones, 'usually at exchanges where tape recorders are installed'; Operation Rystoel (Wheelchair) which carried out bugging; and Operation Ompik (Pick Over) which covered 'a variety of rougher activities ranging from breaking into premises to photograph documents to fake muggings which enable BOSS agents to search a suspect person'. His portrait of BOSS's response to the Soweto uprising was particularly acute:

> The first telex reports started coming in just before lunch-time. At an emergency meeting the top brass tried to formulate advice for Vorster, but in fact they had none to give. For some weeks . . . the search was on for the culprits. At first it was suggested that the CIA had been running a destabilisation operation . . . The spotlight was then turned on the Black Consciousness Movement, and efforts were made to determine where it got its ideas from. Stokely Carmichael, Frans Fanon, Paulo Freire and Herbert Marcuse were read and discussed . . . It took months for BOSS to understand that a whole generation of black students had come to think along the same lines. When it did so, it instinctively decided that there was a subversive network to be eliminated. This led to a 'banning' spree . . . The refusal to consider black grievances continued, reinforced by the convention that BOSS must never embarrass other State departments . . . [A] German researcher . . . had earlier written about a number of problems perceived by blacks in Soweto. The attitude at BOSS headquarters . . . was predictable . . . Who did he think he was trying to teach us our own business? Who was he working for? The BND (West German intelligence)? The Communists?

McGiven also explained that Division V (covert operations in African countries) had been established because, following the collapse of the Portuguese Empire in 1974, 'BOSS found itself without sources in [Angola] to replace its previous cooperation with Salazar's secret police, PIDE.' Operation Indiaman was an 'intelligence pipeline' which employed remnants of PIDE in Mozambique to spy on the SACP in Maputo. Operation Timmerwerk (Carpentry) played a similar role between Botswana and Zambia. The third part of McGiven's testimony reported on the inter-agency turf war between DONS and military intelligence. The report also provided the first detailed analysis of the revived State Security Council, which had failed to perform the 'watchdog' role imagined in the Potgieter Report (see page 40). McGiven's stories also recorded the emergence of South African intelligence's coming man, the twenty-nine-year-old Professor Niel Barnard.[25]

In South Africa, DONS did not deny that McGiven had been an intelligence officer. Alexander van Wyk commented that McGiven had 'misused his position . . . to steal scraps of untested and unevaluated material and to use it for his own gain'. He did not challenge the provenance of the documents but added that 'allegations were made . . . about [McGiven's] private life which gave reason for concern. When he indicated . . . that he wished to leave the service, the department was relatively relieved. Before he resigned, he approached his superiors with a proposal that he would like to . . . work abroad for the department in a covert capacity . . . this request was turned down.' The reference in van Wyk's statement to McGiven's 'private life' was later explained by Craig Williamson: '[the] counter-intelligence guys learned McGiven was living with a man . . . He was abused [and] told he was a security risk.' Van den Bergh also gave a revealing interview to the *Rand Daily Mail*: 'I can do nothing but take serious offence at the South African Press because they blindly accepted the untested treasonable allegations of a self-confessed traitor . . . Just as in the so-called cases of Colonel Cheeseman and Gordon Winter they allowed themselves to be caught out.'[26]

Although McGiven's testimony had an immediate impact – the 'burning' (exposing) of Security Police spy Craig Williamson (see below) – the incident did not rebound to the defector's credit. His admission to the *Observer* that he had 'disclaimed knowledge' of Williamson because 'his personal safety had not been assured . . . [and] innocent IUEF collaborators . . . might be imperilled' did not really hold up. By way of recompense, he named Karl Edwards as a BOSS agent involved with Williamson and the International University Exchange Fund (IUEF), a Geneva-based organisation with Scandinavian backing which covertly assisted the black consciousness movement inside South Africa. McGiven related that Edwards and Williamson 'did not initially know about each other. They once lunched together at a Johannesburg steakhouse, and afterwards each submitted a report on the conversation to their superiors. Both reports landed simultaneously on McGiven's desk, much to his amusement.' Anti-apartheid activists and journalists felt that the former evaluator was playing a complicated 'double game' and that Williamson's exposure had been an overreaction by the Security Police. Labour MP Robert Hughes captured the mood:

> In the parlance of intelligence services, this information can be seen as chickenfeed. One wonders if it is not being used to obscure much more serious things BOSS/DONS have done in the United Kingdom and in Western

Europe . . . There is almost a smell of 'cover up' as these disclosures affect South Africa's security operations in the UK . . . I have a feeling that this is a bit like a magician's trick, where the number of a card is noted while something else is happening without observation . . . I'd like to see some hard information and also see McGiven volunteer his services to the British security services and to the A-AM.[27]

The *Guardian* diary contributed a vicious coda to the McGiven story. It noted that South Africans had responded 'with great caution and suspicion to the renegade BOSS agent'. In July 1969, McGiven had published a poem, 'Informer?', in the poetry magazine *Ophir*. In the poem, McGiven 'discourses on a friend who had been approached by the security police and asked to work . . . as a campus grass'. The student, anti-apartheid activist Horst Kleinschmidt, immediately publicised the incident. However, McGiven's poem:

> pondered sceptically:
> > *how do I know YOU aren't watching ME?*
> > *after all THEY are all over.*
> > *You too my friend?. . .*
> > *(Christ I wish I hated you because now I won't be certain*
> > *unless those bastards shoot you dead.)*
>
> . . . it nicely sums up the attitude now held towards him by his fellow-countrymen over here.[28]

*

The final 'defector' was Ivan Himmelhoch. He left South Africa in June 1980 and his story appeared in the *New Statesman* that August. Four years earlier, he had been recruited by Gordon Winter's occasional handler 'Jack' Kemp. Himmelhoch, 'who was about to leave South Africa to study law in Britain', was introduced to Kemp by 'a leader in the Jewish community in Cape Town'. Kemp 'wanted detailed unbiased reports on the exile community in Britain'. He did not offer any payment for Himmelhoch's information but he did arrange to have his military service deferred. For two years between September 1976 and November 1978, Himmelhoch engaged in (very) small-scale spying operations for Johann Fourie, the First Secretary and head of BOSS at the South African Embassy. He was encouraged to read 'subversive' literature such as the *Leveller* magazine and report on 'factionalism' within the A-AM. Apparently 'BOSS was convinced that "all phone conversations [at the Embassy] were bugged by the British authorities"'. Himmelhoch's desk officer, Ron Shardelow, maintained 'that BOSS had very close links with British intelligence. Shardelow's favourite expression, Himmelhoch recalled, was: "Countries never talk, but Services do." On one occasion he was more specific, saying "BOSS has the closest co-operation from British intelligence. They are very aware of what is going on – and they are certainly happy with it." ' Himmelhoch named one of the current DONS officers in the Embassy as Ben van der Klashorst. It was later revealed that van der Klashorst had 'posed for several years in coloured political circles as a mysterious "Mr Roy Havinga" before being posted to Britain.'[29]

Having ceased to work for BOSS, Himmelhoch concluded his legal studies and, following a short period working in Germany, returned to South Africa. In October 1979, he started work on the Rhodesia–Zimbabwe desk at the Department of Foreign Affairs. 'My mind was finally made up by my impending call-up. On 2 July I was due to begin my military service, and my application for deferment had been turned down.' Following the 'defection', the Johannesburg *Sunday Times* reported that, while Himmelhoch had been employed by Foreign Affairs, he had also been passing documents to two British diplomats. He told Suzanne Vos:

> In my conversations with [the two diplomats] I confessed that while studying in England . . . I had worked as a spy for BOSS. They really spun me around when they replied that they knew this . . . that British intelligence knew I was a BOSS agent . . . I'm a coward. You can say I'm a spineless coward. I should have stayed. But I'm a pacifist. I couldn't join the army . . . I just couldn't fight for apartheid. What I did was gutless. I admit it.[30]

Although Himmelhoch had given the names of the two diplomats to reporters, the names were not published because the British Embassy in Pretoria 'denies that secret information was ever passed on'. Meanwhile, the MP Robert Hughes asked 'the Home and Foreign Secretaries for a guarantee that our security services are not trading information with the South Africans'. Abdul Minty, Secretary of the A-AM, wanted a clear statement that links between the 'respective security services have been severed . . . "The answers have always been evasive." ' On 7 September, the *Observer* confirmed that the Labour government's 1976 directive cancelling liaison with the South African intelligence services or Security Police on any subject except 'common interest' was still adhered to. An 'intelligence source' told the *Observer*: 'Although you might expect the Conservatives to have a more sympathetic attitude towards the South Africans, the order still remains in force today, as far as we know.'[31] The Home Office produced a splendidly elastic reply to Bob Hughes's question:

> I am glad to be able to assure you that contact between the British police and their South African counterparts is restricted to purely criminal matters and to the protection of individuals and property . . . It is not in accordance with our established practice to make any comment on contact between security services. This convention of not commenting on matters affecting security and intelligence has been respected by successive Governments. It is not possible to deny allegations when they are untrue, since that would indicate that a refusal to comment in another case was tantamount to confirmation of the allegation: and this might reveal to other governments and their security and intelligence services our own knowledge of their activities. This reply therefore carries absolutely no implications as to the substance or lack of substance of the claims to which you have referred.

Following the publication of the stories, Ivan Himmelhoch was subjected to similar criticism as the other defectors. Replying to a critic in the *New Statesman*, he asked: 'How is one supposed to react to someone who not only condemns my work for BOSS but also opposes my having spoken out?'[32]

Arthur McGiven's defection had one immediate effect: the Security Police decided to withdraw Craig Williamson, a 'deep cover' spy who was, from 1978, the Deputy Director of IUEF in Geneva. In the second of McGiven's series of articles on BOSS–DONS, he mentioned in passing: 'Attempts have . . . been made to find out who is "behind" the IUEF.' Security Police counter-intelligence specialist Brigadier Johan Coetzee flew to Zurich and met Williamson, and the pair attempted to blackmail Lars-Gunnar Eriksson, the Swedish Director of IUEF: they suggested that Eriksson's creative book-keeping would be exposed and they attempted to convince him that, as anti-communists, 'We are on the same side.' Finally, they speculated that it would not be impossible for an accident to happen to Eriksson's family. Coetzee later described the meeting to anti-apartheid reporter Denis Herbstein: 'The word is blackmail . . . but this is the world of intelligence.'[33] However, the Director of the IUEF refused to be turned. In a state of panic, Eriksson telephoned Hugh Lewin, an anti-apartheid activist who at that time was employed by the *Guardian*. On 23 January 1980, Craig Williamson was exposed:

> Panic buttons have been pressed over the past three days by activists . . . within South Africa and overseas after the allegations that Craig

Williamson, deputy director of a Geneva aid agency, was a South African Security Police spy. Over the past seven years, Williamson has been privy to the secret activities of South Africa's radical student movement and, more recently, to inside details of overseas funding for revolutionary activities in the country. He was so trusted by his former colleagues . . . that they were still expressing disbelief yesterday at the allegations and were mystified at why he should have 'blown his cover'.[34]

Craig Williamson was born in April 1949 and educated at St John's College, a Johannesburg private school. In 1968 he joined the police and was promoted to sergeant in 1970. In mid-1971, he was recruited by Johan Coetzee for a new Security Police intelligence group named Section 4. Terry Bell, South Africa's leading 'spy-hunter', has written an amusing account of Williamson's activities, in which he explained that 'the only special qualifications' required for the 'fat, rich "English" boy' to become a spy and a member of the Special Branch 'in a milieu dominated by poorer working-class Afrikaners' were that 'he was English-speaking and had sufficient schooling to allow him admission to university'. When BOSS was created in 1968, Coetzee (unlike Mike Geldenhuys) had decided to remain with the Security Police; Section 4 was an attempt to recreate the RI of the early 1960s. Student organisations, and in particular those of white students, were infested with police intelligence operatives in the early 1970s. Posing as a radical, Williamson prospered in the student-activist circles at 'Wits' (the University of the Witwatersrand); by 1974, he had been appointed the national finance officer of the white National Union of South African Students (NUSAS). Coetzee's plan was quite simple – he intended to 'follow the money'. Meanwhile, Section 4 had established an 'escape route' for people who wanted to leave South Africa. The route served two functions: it provided the Security Police with evidence on the people who wanted to flee the Republic, and it established the radical 'legend' of a number of police spies, including Williamson. It would also grow into what became known as Operation Daisy.

In 1975, Craig Williamson travelled to Europe with a NUSAS colleague and met leading anti-apartheid activists and members of the ANC. He was also appointed the official IUEF liaison in South Africa. According to Bell, Williamson was 'formally recruited' by Aziz Pahad, 'to provide information on the student movement'. But a number of senior ANC members, particularly Mac Maharaj, were doubtful. Ronnie

Kasrils, later South Africa's Minister of Intelligence, commented in his memoirs:

> Craig Williamson, a puffy-faced, overweight student leader who claimed to have fled South Africa, offered his services . . . when we checked his background [we] discovered that previous colleagues did not trust him. We tested him with stale material, and when a South African newspaper, with security police links, reported our outdated booklets were surfacing in the townships our suspicions increased. We kept him at arms length but he maintained a strong nerve.[35]

In late 1976, Coetzee sent Williamson for training at Rietvlei Farm. His instructors were Tai Minnaar and Att Nel of the MID. Williamson listed the aspects of his training as 'memory; report writing; surveillance and counter-surveillance techniques; secret writing; photography (general); report photography; personal meetings; dead drops – choosing, using etc.; emergency procedures'. In January 1977, he left South Africa, by the police 'escape route'. He travelled with a young journalist, Eric Abraham, who had made a reputation for himself by spotting and writing about intelligence agents. Coetzee's police spies controlling Operation Daisy merrily looted IUEF funds intended for domestic anti-apartheid structures and out of the proceeds even managed to purchase a farm, which they called Daisy Farm. Outside South Africa, Williamson prospered as before. He worked for the IUEF in Switzerland, where 'he was a "vacuum cleaner" siphoning up, collecting and passing on every piece of paper, scrap of information or whisper' that came his way. Working closely with his wife, Ingrid Bacher, they would spy through the night at the IUEF, as they 'photocopied memoranda, receipts, orders and private correspondence, rifling through files and drawers'.

Although he was quickly promoted to the role of deputy director of the IUEF, Williamson failed to penetrate International Defence and Aid, a key Security Police target. He also failed to draw the IUEF, a Scandinavian social democratic organisation, closer to the ANC. Members of the A-AM and the ANC remained suspicious of him, although Williamson later claimed that Thabo Mbeki, then Oliver Tambo's assistant, had signed a letter 'giving assurances that he was not a spy'. By the time he returned to South Africa in 1980, Williamson had embezzled and relocated substantial funds from the IUEF accounts. The money that he left hidden in Swiss bank accounts would fund continuing Daisy operations in Europe in the 1980s. But his real claim to fame within the intelligence establishment was that he passed on the information which led to the arrest and eventual death of black consciousness leader Steve Biko.[36] 'Ann', a BOSS operative, later recalled that 'when it hit the newspapers . . . everybody was happy . . . [at BOSS, it was] like, "Wow, at last. Well, that's one cheeky kaffir out of the way."' Following his departure, *Africa Confidential* reported that 'Eriksson [had] told colleagues to assume that *all* sensitive information had been siphoned off . . . The ANC has been understandably keen to assert that it had been suspicious of Williamson for years . . . That, we believe, is far from the truth.'[37]

The IUEF was closed in March 1981, only a few weeks after the London *Sunday Times* had carried an extended feature on Williamson, in which he had admitted that to be a good spy, in his opinion, 'You've got to play a part . . . to an extent you've got to be – I'm probably cutting my own throat here – a controlled schizophrenic.' Craig Williamson's deification as South Africa's 'super-spy' was more than a little exaggerated. He was, to a significant extent, similar to Gerard Ludi in the 1960s, 'burned' but operational. Guy Berger recalled being interrogated by Williamson, following his arrest in 1980:

> When they took me into the appointed room, he was standing with his back to the door, gazing out the window, hands clasped behind his back, Napoleon-style. I recognised him even before he turned, and met him with the greeting 'Good morning, Captain Williamson.' Maybe I spoke softly, but he didn't hear me. More likely though so intent was he on the dramatic quality of the moment that nothing would disrupt his rehearsed lines: 'Do you know who I am?' came the pompous utterance. It was a pitiful sight.[38]

*

During van den Bergh's 'reign' months would often pass with minimal intelligence reporting in South Africa. One of the most significant repercussions of Muldergate, the 1979 defections and the exposure of Craig Williamson was that, for a short period, the South African press attempted to develop a new and more informative model of intelligence coverage. In February 1980, Mervyn Rees produced a substantial four-part series, 'The BOSS/DONS story', for the *Rand Daily Mail*. He assembled a multitude of voices for his series, but it remained clear that the 'trigger' had been Gordon Winter's and Arthur McGiven's revelations in London. Fourteen months later, on 28 June 1981, Gerard Ludi re-emerged to explain to Rees what had happened following Ludi's appearance in the Bram Fischer trial.

Between 1966 and 1970, he was employed as an Afrikaans-language journalist. In 1970, General Geldenhuys 'persuaded' him to rejoin the 'intelligence community'. Ludi revealed that, for the past eleven years, he had been 'attached to the clandestine division of BOSS and ran massive operations . . . mainly in Black Africa . . . During my last months with the Department, I was an assistant director in the training division.' He added, repeating his observation from the 1960s, 'I ostensibly ran a news agency – simply because intelligence work and news-gathering are essentially the same' (see page 21). Ludi also said that he had posed as a 'visiting lecturer at a West African university'.[39]

In the 1960s and 1970s, no South African intelligence operative had ever willingly 'outed' themselves *inside* the Republic. However, it was not all positive publicity for South Africa's spies. Ludi had left the National Intelligence Service (NIS) because 'certain sections of the intelligence service – as a result of a variety of internal factors – are not functioning as they should'. He announced that he was starting a security company, Gerard Ludi & Associates, with 'a formidable team of former intelligence agents, military and police officers'. One of the directors of the company was Millard Shirley, the CIA agent who had reportedly played a role in Mandela's arrest in 1962. There doesn't appear to have been any attempt to demand that Ludi maintain a lower profile. In January 1982, for example, the *Financial Mail* asked: 'What of the suggestion that Gerard Ludi & Associates is, in its turn, a front?. . . Ludi smiles, skirts around the question, but does eventually reply to the charge: "The National Intelligence Service is worried about bigger things." '[40] Ludi's decision to trade his specialist skills in the private sector predated by a decade the equivalent mass migration of apartheid's policemen, soldiers and spies during the late 1980s and early 1990s.

Shot by Both Sides

Inside BOSS: South Africa's Secret Police by Gordon Winter ('an ex-spy's dramatic and shocking exposé') was published by Penguin Books in October 1981. The advance publicity for the book announced: 'Torturing, lying and bribing . . . BOSS has become feared and hated the world over.' Never one to underperform, Winter appeared on BBC television to promote his book and confessed for the viewers: 'I was responsible for people dying.' *Inside BOSS* attracted immediate criticism. Ronald Segal, South African exile and the founding editor of the Penguin African Library, told the *Observer*: 'I found it deeply disgusting. It's a form of chequebook journalism; the confessions of someone who has done great evil. It gives details of Gordon Winter's victims – some of whom are still alive and active, no thanks to him – for the purpose of deprecating them and disseminating suspicion. I have suggested to Penguin that the book is withdrawn but it is probably too close to publication date now.' Segal had not been consulted on the book; the book's editor, Neil Middleton, explained that this was 'because it is more to do with BOSS activities in England'. Amusingly, there is no reference to Segal in *Inside BOSS*. A spokesperson for the A-AM said: 'We are surprised that reputable publishers should choose to enable Winter to profit from his alleged association with BOSS.' The only person contacted by the *Observer* who spoke in favour of the book was Peter Hain: 'While there is no doubt that Winter is a sordid character, he does reveal much that will be embarrassing to the South African authorities. Above all he reveals the extent of the close links between British intelligence and BOSS.'[41]

The central problem with *Inside BOSS* was the sheer pleasure with which Gordon Winter told his many tales. Although the book carried a disclaimer regarding the 'excerpts . . . from secret BOSS files . . . it is important to emphasize that the BOSS assessment of a person was not always right', Winter rarely challenged inaccuracies in BOSS stories or analysis. In fact, he seemed to have developed the usual spy problem of believing that intelligence organisations are more powerful and all-knowing than is either possible or likely. Intelligence agents, assets, informants, friends, patriots, call them what you will, only ever see fragments of the bigger picture. The agency bureaucrats and managers rarely see the reality on the ground. Everything in intelligence is fragmented; everybody believes somebody else knows the big secrets. Gordon Winter recalled the *Inside BOSS* experience in *Lobster* magazine in 1989: 'I made one great mistake. I did not take any political stand. Naively believing I could now really write without "slanting" (for a change) I spared no side . . . And so that my readers could understand why the South African Government behaved like it did, I gave Pretoria's point of view.'[42] If Winter had 'defected' to the ANC or the A-AM, he would have been hailed as a hero, but his story would have been carefully controlled; a substantial amount of the useful information that is in *Inside BOSS* would have been hidden away in the ANC's intelligence files.

Ronald Segal's intemperate review in the *Guardian* acknowledged that 'there is much serviceable information in the book', but he still described publication as a 'cruel exercise'. Peter Hain praised the book in the *Morning Star*. 'Some of the extraordinary detail in the book's 621 pages is bound to be challenged, and the author himself comes through as a pretty unpleasant figure. But then he is quite open and honest about that: he spares himself no more than the organisation he has exposed. Overall, the book is invaluable – the most damning indictment of apartheid's hatchet force that has appeared, or is likely to.' A few days later, Jan Marsh, an A-AM–IDAF worker and *Anti-Apartheid News* media analyst, entered the argumentative correspondence in the *Guardian*:

> Penguin Books should never have published, unchecked, damaging allegations against named individuals. How is the general reader to tell which bits are true and which false? Then there is the question of motive. If the book reveals a 'twilight world' of distortion, bribery, disruption, torture, etc, the only interests to be served are those of BOSS, whose sinister reputation is thereby enhanced. Mr Winter may thus be doing BOSS a favour. Myself, I find Penguin's fat book full of fantasy – the sort of things BOSS dreamed of doing in Britain but which – apart from a few 'successes' like the framing of Peter Hain – usually failed to come off. BOSS may be bad, but it isn't *that* good.[43]

The *Argus* in Cape Town showed extracts from *Inside BOSS* to 'a former BOSS agent' who confirmed that a number of the BOSS agents named in the book were genuine. The agent acknowledged that '[Winter] appears to have had access to filed information at BOSS headquarters which would have been unthinkable for anyone who was not considered a full-time employee'. Despite selling out its 15,000 print run, *Inside BOSS* was not reprinted. It had been subject to a number of libel challenges. By 1986, Penguin had settled complaints from Peter Bessell, Adelaide Tambo, Barney Zackon, Patty Patience, Harold Soref, Nana Mahomo, Matthew Nkoana, Ben Turok, Stan Winer and Richard Gibson. Copies now change hands on the internet for £100 or more.[44] In South Africa, the book was banned, and, Winter suggested, the intelligence services 'put the rumour out . . . not to worry, Gordon is still a loyal BOSS agent. Ignore his book, its just a cunning cover for something else he's doing.' In effect, Winter was 'shot by both sides'. As a journalist used to communicating with large numbers of readers, he received the ultimate punishment, what we might call the Cassandra syndrome: his words were not believed. Denis Herbstein, writing in the *New Statesman* in 1986, ruminated that 'Gordon Winter's book may or may not be [an] elaborate hoax, an essay in disinformation at its subtlest.'[45] In 2004, I inspected, with Winter's permission, his security file at the National Archive in Pretoria. It contained no more than a dozen press clippings, at least eight of which covered his detention in 1966. There was one news story on *Inside BOSS*. Where were the documents on his deportation in 1966 and his return to the Republic in 1974? It had obviously been weeded.

The fourteen months during which four South African 'defectors' appeared in Europe determined to tell their stories could only have happened in the aftermath of the P.W. Botha takeover. It is telling that the next major media 'defector', the killer Dirk Coetzee in November 1989, also occurred soon after South Africa changed leaders and when another shuffle of intelligence responsibility was taking place. By 1979, the ANC and support organisations had been in exile for nearly twenty years. There was clearly intense resentment of people who were considered to be little better than apologetic war criminals arriving in London and commanding media attention. The whispering South African network in London was quick to suggest that the defectors were part of a BOSS plot to spread disinformation. But as Mervyn Rees explained in the *Rand Daily Mail*: 'Despite the fact that the [South African] authorities dismiss [Winter and McGiven] with contempt and claim that their roles and knowledge were minimal, there is no doubt that they have caused considerable damage to the reputation, operations and credibility of South Africa's intelligence organisations.' Although the 'defectors' didn't help themselves – none as far as I know offered to give their information to the ANC – it is difficult not to conclude that the ANC–A-AM should and could have exploited the potential of the defector moment better. The mythology of the efficient and effective South African intelligence system had been tarnished in 1979–80; it could have been torpedoed. In the mid-1980s, ANC official Essop Pahad visited Gordon Winter and questioned him.[46] It was much too late.

7

The MID Solution

There are five sorts of spies. These are native spies, internal spies, double spies, doomed spies, and surviving spies. When all these five types of spies are at work and their operations are clandestine, it is called the 'divine manipulation of threads' and is the treasure of a sovereign. Native spies are those from the enemy's country people whom we employ. Internal spies are enemy oYcials whom we employ. Double spies are enemy spies whom we employ. Doomed spies are those of our own spies who are deliberately given false information and told to report it to the enemy. Surviving spies are those who return from the enemy camp to report information. Of all those in the army close to the commander, none is more intimate than the spies ... of all matters, none is more confidential than those relating to spy operations. He who is not sage and wise, humane and just, cannot use spies. And he who is not delicate and subtle cannot get the truth out of them.

Sun Tzu, *The Art of War*, c. 500 BC[1]

'Contra' Theories

IN MARCH 1975, Minister of Defence P.W. Botha presented the Defence White Paper to parliament. He insisted: 'Defence strategy embraces much more than military strategy. It involves economy, ideology, technology, and even social matters and can therefore only be meaningful and valid if proper account is taken of all these other spheres . . . This, in fact, is the meaning of "Total Strategy".' In March 1977, Botha outlined the scale of a 'total national strategy'. He emphasised the importance of the strategy being 'applicable at all levels and to all functions of the state structure . . . [because] there are few, if any, government departments which are not concerned with one or other aspect of national security, or which do not contribute to the realisation of national security'. In reality, 'total strategy' was a child of colonial retreat; as Philip Frankel observed in *Pretoria's Praetorians*, 'it is read-ily apparent that South African military leaders have imbibed deeply of the counter-revolutionary experiences of the United States in Vietnam, of the British in Malaya and of the French in both Algeria and Indo-China'.[2] Despite the ANC–SACP assertion that apartheid South Africa exhibited 'colonialism of a special type', the Republic's military analysts were incap-able of developing an original, incisive, theory for their own defence.

During the late 1970s and early 1980s, the work of the French General André Beaufre exerted the dominant influence on South African military thinking; in fact, Beaufre first used the expression 'total strategy' in 1963 soon after his experiences in the Algerian war. He stated that 'nothing is fated to happen in history, provided one knows how to intervene in time . . . It is simply a matter of will and of faith.' He argued that in an era of 'limited war', direct military action should be complemented by and subordinate to 'non-military means'. Adopting the most effective strategy was, in Dan O'Meara's interpretation of Beaufre, '*the* essential moment of successful counter-insurgency'. The psychological 'terrain of battle', for example, was more important than the military arena: '[The] domestic involvement of the "mass media" is crucial. It is they who can mould public opinion to the point of making it accept the necessity of going to war. It is the media who can inculcate demoralisation of the public and make pos-sible the compromises which are the only type of result possible in limited war.' Beaufre's dominant injunction was that 'the political line':

> must be to deprive the enemy of his trump cards. There are two facets to this: we must first maintain and increase our prestige, not merely by show-ing that we have adequate force available but also by showing that the future we hold out has possibilities (progress of our civilization, international aid, etc.); secondly, by thorough-going reforms we must cut the ground from under the feet of the malcontents.[3]

While military strategists consulted André Beaufre, the political class needed theoretical assistance with the 'process of reform'. Luckily, help was at hand: Samuel Huntington of the Center for International Affairs at Harvard, who would later be the author of the 'clash of civilisations' thesis that inspired US politicians in the aftermath of 9/11, visited South Africa in September 1981. Pik Botha had become aware of Huntington's work in the 1970s and introduced him to Prime Minister P.W. Botha. In his lecture at Rand Afrikaans University (RAU) in Johannesburg, Huntington declared that 'the essence of the reformer [is] that he must employ ambiguity, concealment and deception concerning his goals'. He emphasised the importance of 'managed change': transformation from a position of strength. His reforms depended on a 'high concentration of power in the political system' and an ability to 'monopolize counter-revolutionary repression'. In a rather sinister way, Huntington suggested that reform might be attained 'through some form of autocracy . . . [and that] reform and repression may proceed hand-in-hand', a combination he described as 'Fabian strategy and blitzkrieg tactics'. The newspaper editor Tertius Myburgh later announced that Huntington's 'script was being followed to the letter'. Few listeners appear to have paid attention to Huntington's prediction that 'at some point in the next decade or two, some combination of black mobilisation, economic trouble, and external threat are likely to create a crisis within the South African political system that will only be resolved by fundamental change of that system'.[4]

Frankel observed that 'the logical conclusion of total strategy is a more perfectly defined and streamlined version of South Africa's already authoritarian climate. Total strategy legitimises this development, it engenders the psychological and institutional atmosphere conducive to the growth of a garrison state.' In 1984, the same year that Frankel's book was published, a fresh wave of rioting and insurgency engulfed the townships of the Vaal Triangle. South African military theorists appear to have returned their volumes of Beaufre to the library and starting circulating xeroxed copies of former SADF army chief Lieutenant-General Alan 'Pop' Fraser's privately published *Lessons Drawn from Past Revolutionary Wars* (1968). In some respects, Fraser's study was Beaufre with a macho South African twist. He had argued for example that revolutionary war should be fought with a '20 per cent military, 80 per cent political' formula: 'Victory can be obtained by a government only by retaining and, if temporarily lost, by recapturing the support of the masses – and by the complete destruction of the insurgent organisation and the eradication of its influence upon the people . . . The objective for both sides in a revolutionary war is . . . the population itself.' There was, however, a veiled fist hidden within Fraser's *Lessons*, as Stephen Ellis spotted:

> In paragraph 33 of his original work, Fraser noted on terrorism: 'As the goal of modern warfare is the control of the populace, terrorism is a particularly appropriate weapon since it aims directly at the inhabitant.' He went on to caution that it should be used by the counter-revolutionary power only with the greatest circumspection, and only with approval 'at the highest level'. In other words, terrorism, as used by the enemy, could also be used by the state's security forces . . . under appropriate political control.

In September 1986, President P.W. Botha wrote a foreword for an Afrikaans translation of Fraser's book and issued orders that it be circulated to senior officials.[5] At around the same time that Fraser was resurrected by the military theorists, John J. McCuen's *The Art of Counter-Revolutionary War* (1966), with a foreword by Malayan Emergency veteran Sir Robert Thompson, was also compulsory reading in samizdat paraphrased form. The TRC later explained that General Jannie Geldenhuys 'introduced the military to the ideas of . . . McCuen', a former colonel in the US army who promulgated a thesis perfect for what would later be known as the 'dirty war': 'A governing power can defeat any revolutionary movement if it adapts the revolutionary strategy and principles and applies them in reverse to defeat the revolutionaries with their own weapons on their own battlefield.' Under the heading 'Police Action', the pamphlet stated: 'The annihilation of the [enemy political] organization is mainly a police responsibility.' It also urged: 'in areas where terrorism occurs, Government forces must use the same destructive and constructive strategy as the guerrilla.' In another ominous section entitled 'Counter-revolutionary Strategy', the McCuen précis declared: 'Mobilise the masses. The majority of the masses [are] usually neutral and initially uncommitted. Mobilization cannot be brought about through persuasion; it must be preceded by organisation, protection and possible violence.' A circular issued by General Templer, the High Commissioner of Malaya between 1952 and 1954, was quoted in the McCuen document; it captured the mood of the dying apartheid state: 'Any idea that [the] business of normal government and [the] business of the emergency are two separate entities must be killed for good and all. The two activities are completely and utterly interrelated.'[6]

During the late 1970s and early 1980s, a number of significant conferences or 'councils' were held which prepared the ground for the 'militarisation' of South Africa. A conference held at RAU in December 1977, under the banner of the National Development and Manpower Foundation, represented a critical development in the search for a solution to John Vorster's failing 'police state'. In the immediate aftermath of the defeat in Angola, the Soweto uprising, the 'clampdown' on black consciousness groups, the murders of Steve Biko and Robert Smit, and the re-election of the National Party with its largest share of the vote in history, the conference was certainly held at an opportune moment. Dan O'Meara has revealed that 'By the end of 1977 . . . Afrikaner intellectual circles were rife with discussions of the possibility of a *coup d'état*. Indeed, the SADF General Staff reportedly sent a memorandum to their Minister Botha pressing for a change of government and hinting at the possibility of a coup.' The pre-amble to the RAU conference noted that 'Representatives from top management and senior members of the Defence Force were brought together in an attempt to find solutions for the critical problems encoun-tered by both sides in the field of manpower planning. The vital link is obvious – the continuing close communication . . . between management and the military.' The conference was jointly chaired by Major-General Neil Webster, SADF Director of General Resources, and Ian MacKensie, the chairman of Standard Bank, and attended by General Magnus Malan. All the representatives attending were instructed to sign an agreement accepting that they would not disclose details of the aspects of the confer-ence that were held in camera. The relationship between business and the military that would be such a feature of the early 1980s was based on the growth of South Africa's local arms industry and the skills shortage that was most dramatic in the area of 'high technology'. In October 1977 the United Nations had voted in favour of a mandatory arms embargo against the Republic of South Africa, and the RAU conference was, in part, a response to that embargo; it was also as Philip Frankel later argued 'the "take off point" of the local military–industrial complex'.[7]

In 1979, following P.W. Botha's election as prime minister, a conference was held at Fort Klapperkop in Pretoria. In response to intelligence that the ANC had adopted a new military strategy following a visit to Vietnam where leading ANC members consulted General Vo Nguyen Giap, the master tactician who had driven both the French and the Americans from his country, P.W. Botha convened the nascent security state. The Klapperkop Conference approved an expansion of the SADF's Special Forces and authorised military operations in the 'front-line' countries of Angola, Mozambique, Lesotho, Swaziland and Botswana in order to stymie MK's attempts to establish 'rear-bases within striking distance of South Africa'. One year earlier, in May 1978, the SADF had launched a bomb-ing and paratrooper assault on Cassinga, a SWAPO base inside Angola. Operation Reindeer, as the assault was known, led to the deaths of 624 people: 159 men, 167 women and 298 children, and earned SADF chief General Constand Viljoen the anti-apartheid sobriquet 'the butcher of Cassinga'.[8] The creation of Koevoet in South West Africa and the desta-bilisation operations in Rhodesia–Zimbabwe appear to have been the immediate products of Klapperkop.

The Simonstown Council, held at the Simonstown naval base in January 1981, was a conference of security chiefs chaired by Prime Minister P.W. Botha, which delineated intelligence roles throughout the South African security state. The Security Police, for example, was allowed to maintain an overseas intelligence structure as long as it concentrated on South African political organisations like the ANC or the SACP that were engaged in terrorist activity (in apartheid terms 'crime') within the Republic. The responsibilities of DONS, recently renamed the National Intelligence Service (NIS), were political and economic intelligence, overseas 'covert collection' of intelligence, counter-espionage and intelligence 'evaluation'. The NIS also, in theory, supervised diplomatic intelligence; in reality the Department of Foreign Affairs neurotically defended its minor intelligence capacity. The TRC concluded that Simonstown divided 'labour between the police and the military . . . Swaziland was assigned to the SAP while the rest of the world, but more particularly the region, became an SADF responsibility. The agreement also made provision for joint SAP–SADF operations.' Finally, the 1981 conference established a Co-ordinating Intelligence Committee (known by its Afrikaans-language acronym: KIK).[9] Terry Bell has described the meeting at Simonstown as a 'Council of War', and in the context of the newly elected Republican President Reagan, it would appear that (in Craig Williamson's words), 'the security forces [had been] told to "take the gloves off" in the fight against the revolutionary enemy.'[10]

One sign of the growing power of the South African armed forces, and by extension of the MID, was the extraordinary growth in the annual defence budget. In 1958–9 (before Sharpeville), defence accounted for R36 million; by 1969–70, the figure was R272 million; in 1977–8 (after Soweto), this had grown to R1.7 billion; by 1987–8, around R6.7 billion was allocated for defence. This is a staggering level of increase even when inflation is taken into account. In 1969, Lieutenant-General Fraser briefed the Minister of Defence P.W. Botha and other senior generals on the need to develop an SADF 'special forces' capacity. At this time, the SADF had only one specialist unit: 1 Parachute Battalion. Special forces would engage in operations which were described by the SADF Special Forces manual as being designed 'to inflict the maximum disruption on the enemy of the state by means of special actions'. In 1972, 1 Reconnaissance Commando was established in Oudtshoorn under the command of Commandant Jan Breytenbach, who in 1970 had undertaken the freefall parachute course at the age of thirty-nine.[11] 1 Recce, which would later specialise in airborne warfare, relocated to Durban in 1974 and opened the Reconnaissance Commando school in 1977. 1 Recce was placed under the control of the MID shortly after its foundation. Two years after the establishment of 1 Recce, 2 Recce, the Citizen Force (a specialised Territorial Army) unit, was constituted. Both groups of Recce soldiers apparently performed well in Angola in 1975–6 and following the Soweto uprising a decision was made to establish 'a group specialising in the use of black soldiers trained in guerrilla warfare'. In late December, a group of fifteen men under the command of Major P.J. 'Joe' Verster, who would later play a significant role in South Africa's death squads, visited Rhodesia 'for a course . . . in training black men'. In March 1977, Verster's group, which would be known as 5 Recce, was given a base and began to select African commandos from, primarily, Angola and Mozambique. 5 Recce would provide continuous support to RENAMO, the anti-communist force created by the Rhodesians to oppose the FRELIMO government of Mozambique. By this time, Israel's special forces were assisting in the training of the Recces.[12]

In 1978, 4 Recce, which would specialise in seaborne warfare, was established in the Cape, and finally, in 1980, 3 Recce was created to incorporate the substantial number of former Rhodesian special forces soldiers who emigrated to the Republic following the establishment of Zimbabwe. In October 1980, Special Forces headquarters was established at 'Spes Kop', Swartkop Park near Pretoria. On 1 January 1981, the Recce groups were transformed into regiments under the command of the Chief of the SADF. Additional specialised soldiers within the SADF included 32 Battalion, the remnants of Jan Breytenbach's and Daniel Chipenda's southern Angolan FNLA army which had returned to South Africa following the war in 1976. In 1980, Major-General Loots, the commanding officer of the Special Forces, 'personally travelled to Rhodesia in the last days of the Smith regime to screen potential recruits'. Delta 40 or D40 was a secretive organisation established under the command of Garth Barrett, a former Rhodesian. The TRC Report suggested that D40 was 'composed almost exclusively' of Rhodesians. In 1981, D40 was renamed Barnacle; meanwhile, Joe Verster had been appointed staff officer for Special Operations. He later testified to the TRC that his assignment was 'developing a covert force to counter the covert operations of the ANC'.[13] Over the next few years, Barnacle would be at the forefront of 'destabilisation' operations in Mozambique and Zimbabwe. It was the SADF's first death squad, as two examples should demonstrate.

On 30 January 1981, a few days after President Reagan was inaugurated, a South African force drove seventy kilometres to attack three houses in a suburb of Maputo: thirteen ANC activists and a Portuguese electrician, who looked uncannily like SACP leader Joe Slovo, were killed. Two 'South Africans' were killed by the ANC, one of whom 'was wearing a helmet painted with swastikas and the slogan "Sieg Heil"; he turned out to be a British mercenary . . . [who] had moved from the British Army to Rhodesian SAS and then down to South Africa after Zimbabwean independence'. Joseph Hanlon suggested that Washington had approved of the attack in advance. A Mozambican government investigation discovered that two 'agents' within the army general staff and FRELIMO's Central Committee had facilitated the raid.[14]

On 31 July 1981, the ANC's representative in Zimbabwe and newly appointed deputy head of intelligence Joe Gqabi was assassinated outside his house in Harare. The TRC later reported that Gqabi was 'killed by a South African hit squad acting on the basis of intelligence supplied by agents of [MID] operating from inside Zimbabwe's CIO [Central Intelligence Organisation]'. The MID agents were Colin Evans and Philip Hartlebury: they were later exposed and, after interrogation, confessed to their role in Gqabi's killing. In 2004, the Johannesburg *Sunday Times* announced that Gray Branfield, aged fifty-five, had been killed in Iraq where he was was working as a security contractor. The author Peter Stiff confirmed that Branfield was a former detective inspector in the BSAP who had joined the Barnacle death squad after moving to South Africa in 1980. Branfield had privately revealed that he was one of the assassins who had murdered Gqabi twenty-three years earlier.[15]

Testifying before the TRC, Major-General Joubert, the officer who commanded the Special Forces between 1985 and 1989, disclosed that 'in the mid to late eighties', probably 1986, Barnacle was transformed into the Civil Co-operation Bureau (CCB). The CCB was intended to engage in 'clandestine and covert operations' within South Africa. Joubert listed the tasks of the CCB as the destruction of 'ANC facilities and support services' and the elimination of 'ANC leaders' and 'activists, sympathisers, fighters and people who supported them'. The TRC described the CCB as 'a form of operational intelligence with a precedent in the wider world of espionage and covert operations'. The report continued:

Mr Christoffel Nel, who was the CCB's head of intelligence, explained that the CCB was a long-term project which required at least a ten-year gestation period . . . The goal was to create a global subterranean network of companies that would be both legitimate businesses as well as fronts for operational intelligence . . . Joe Verster confirmed the long-term nature of the CCB project. He described the goal as setting up a 'first line of defence' outside the country . . . The intention was that the CCB would be fully functional sometime in the mid-1990s. Based on the experience of other intelligence agencies, it was recognised that it would take that long for a skilled soldier to transform her/himself into a career business person . . . The escalating nature of internal unrest in the late 1980s, the needs generated by the declarations of the states of emergency, and the desire to prevent a SWAPO victory in South West Africa derailed the timetable, and the CCB was pulled into the counter-insurgency effort before it was properly ready and set up.

Members of the CCB were required to resign their commissions in the SADF, whereupon they were rehired 'with all pensions and other benefits'. By 1988, the organisation was headed by a management board, chaired by General Joubert. This was the ultimate marriage of business and warfare, but not exactly what the people who had attended the 1977 RAU Conference had imagined. The organisational structure of ten 'regions' included two for intelligence and finance–administration, and one for International–Europe, the intelligence for which was produced by Eeben Barlow (see page 377); the remaining seven regions were responsible for southern Africa, including one for South Africa itself. The CCB claimed that it had 'aware' and 'unaware' members – 'unaware' meaning employees rather than employers. Joe Verster 'estimated that there were about one hundred aware members and some 150 unaware members'. Within the 'unaware' category, the CCB employed 'international criminals . . . people who were usable for the type of work that was planned'. The CCB's work included sanctions-busting, the spreading of disinformation and sabotage. CCB intelligence chief Christo Nel explained the objective of the organisation as 'the maximal disruption of the enemy'. The TRC quoted a 'CCB planning document [which] described disruption as having five dimensions: death, infiltration, bribery, compromise or blackmail, and destruction'.[16]

The MID, which by the late 1980s would become an enormous organisation controlling or attempting to control front companies, propaganda networks, foreign parallel diplomacy, the war on the front line and the insurrection within the country, was constructed of numerous 'directorates'. The Directorate of Special Tasks (DST), for example, was created in the mid-1970s following the SADF's withdrawal from Angola. Its role was to supervise 'contra-mobilisation' and counter-revolutionary warfare in the neighbouring countries of Mozambique (RENAMO), Angola (UNITA), Zimbabwe (opponents of the ZANU–PF government), Swaziland and Lesotho. DST deployed South Africa's special forces. The TRC later reported that 'in 1985, an internal dimension was added to the functions of the DST with Operations Marion (support for Inkatha) and Katzen (counter-insurgency operations in the Eastern Cape)' (see page 265). The Directorate of Covert Collection was primarily concerned with the covert gathering of intelligence information. The TRC described its responsibilities as counter-intelligence, which concentrated on foreign intelligence agencies; terrorism, especially the activities of MK; and 'International'.[17] In 1986, it began to establish civilian front organisations, one of which would be Craig Williamson's Longreach (see page 189).

Destructive Engagement

Lieutenant-General Pieter Willem van der Westhuizen was the Chief of Staff Intelligence (CSI) of the MID when Botha secured the premiership. A former chief military instructor at the Military Academy and commander of the SADF's Northern Transvaal district, 'Wessie', as he was known to his friends, was described by John Fullerton in 1979 as having 'a reputation for able, vigorous performance'. There is an incredible scarcity of material on van der Westhuizen, but US Assistant Secretary of State Chester Crocker provided a deliciously acidic portrait of 'the darker face of Pretoria's Januslike foreign policy' in *High Noon in Southern Africa*:

> One of the least constructive characters we faced . . . An expert briefer, with a slick manner of stacking the deck, he travelled constantly to ply his trade across Africa, Europe, and the Americas. But he also made many of our negotiating rounds; eventually we came to view those sessions as unsafe for candid discourse . . . A prominent British businessman once compared Southern Africa to a vast warehouse with its share of rats seeking to steal the goods. Continuing the analogy, he noted that anyone in charge of [a] warehouse needs a 'ratcatcher'. Van der Westhuizen was P.W. Botha's ratcatcher. The name caught on with the US team.[18]

In March 1981, van der Westhuizen, Brigadier Nils van Tonder, Admiral Willem du Plessis, the naval attaché who had been expelled from the US during the spy-plane argument in 1979, and two unnamed officers, visited the United States. The MID group entered the United States in New York and passed themselves off as 'Department of Foreign Affairs officials' because their visa applications would otherwise have been rejected. After a meeting with the 'private, conservative' American Security Council, the officers travelled to Washington where, according to the *Rand Daily Mail*, they 'briefed Pentagon and NSC officials, Congressional aides, and possibly a Cabinet Minister'. It was later revealed that they had also spoken to the US Defense Intelligence. A State Department spokesman described their visit as 'just short of fraudulent'. The US Ambassador to the United Nations, Jeane Kirkpatrick, who actually met the MID officers, later said that she had not known who they were, although as the *New Statesman* noted, 'Secretary of State General Alexander Haig intervened to tell the press that Kirkpatrick's meeting with van der Westhuizen had his personal authorisation.' Nevertheless, it had been a clumsy, embarrassing performance. Crocker later suggested that the MID mission was intended 'to undercut the evolving approach [on South Africa] at State, and to discredit its Africa Bureau in the eyes of conservatives'. Van der Westhuizen was reported to have visited the US again in November 1981 and February 1982.[19]

Crocker's, and the US, policy for South Africa in the 1980s was 'constructive engagement': a strategic analysis which would later prioritise a settlement for the continuing Angolan war. Eventually, this would boil down to a proposal that Cuban forces would leave Angola in exchange for South Africa abandoning its illegal, in the eyes of the United Nations, occupation of South West Africa–Namibia. Critics claimed that 'constructive engagement' was no more than an adaptation of Kissinger's Nixonian policy of benign neglect. Crocker's ideas on southern Africa were aired in the policy journal *Foreign Affairs* before his appointment. In the essay, he acknowledged that the 'real choice' of the United States concerned 'our readiness to compete with our global adversary [the Soviet Union] in the politics of a changing region'. He recognised that P.W. Botha had 'been carrying out the equivalent in Afrikaner nationalist terms of a drawn-out coup d'état', but he believed that:

> Today and for some time to come Pretoria will be in a position to punish severely any neighbors that support or tacitly tolerate anything more than a token guerrilla presence. In the major urban centers black townships can be quickly cut off from the means of subsistence – food, water, electricity, communications, transport and jobs. Spontaneous violence is likely to be highly self-destructive and, in any case, is more useful as a mobilizational ... device

than a military tactic. The means for sustained urban terrorism are developing but remain at an embryonic stage ... the balance of coercive power
remains overwhelmingly in favor of the whites.[20]

But the State Department was not the only American influence in the
region. In January 1981, at the start of Ronald Reagan's government, the
CIA remained critical of the apartheid state, reflecting the policies of
the Carter administration, and prescient of the dangers ahead: 'It is clear that
Botha is not working from a blueprint and is moving in an ad hoc manner
that gives him the flexibility to press or back off from given policies as
circumstances require . . . The pace of reform over the next two to three
years will not be sufficient to satisfy Nonwhite demands.' There had always
been positive and negative views on apartheid South Africa within the CIA;
the dominant view tended to depend on the government of the day.
Nevertheless, the alternative view, and related covert activity, could normally be found if one looked closely enough. For example, during the
Angolan war, MID and ARMSCOR, through the mediation of the Israelis
and the CIA, made contact with Dr Gerald Bull of the Space Research
Corporation (SRC) in the United States. The reason for the contact was that
the SADF needed to develop a howitzer 'super-gun' which could match the
power of the Cuban and MPLA firepower. A Senate subcommittee report
in March 1982 revealed that the SRC supplied South Africa with 'approximately 60,000 155 mm extended range artillery shells, at least four 155 mm
guns including three advanced prototypes, technology and technical assistance to establish its own 155 mm gun and ammunition manufacturing and
testing capability.' The development of the SADF's howitzer occurred
during the Carter administration. Bull was later assassinated in Brussels in
1990 while he was attempting to develop Saddam Hussein's 'super-gun'.[21]

In March 1981, in response to perceived CIA support for the South
African raid on Maputo, the government of Mozambique expelled six
Americans, four CIA agents and two 'CIA wives who had taken part
in support operations'. Following President Reagan's appointment of
William J. Casey to the post of director of the CIA, the dominant faction
within the intelligence organisation once again became hawks. Casey, who
had first visited South Africa in 1949, as a hotelier, secretly met P.W. Botha
in September 1982, delivering as a gift a signed copy of his book.
P.W. Botha told Anthony Sampson that 'Casey . . . was a good friend and
a gentleman.'[22] The CIA Director also developed a friendly working relationship with P.W. van der Westhuizen. Bob Woodward commented in

Veil: The Secret Wars of the CIA: 'State was always hostile to the South Africa work the CIA was doing.' In October 1982, a South African diplomat in Washington, Daniel J.J. Opperman, was expelled 'for acts of an intelligence nature'. Newspaper reports suggested that 'he had been connected with "harassment" of American anti-apartheid groups'. Randal Robinson, the head of the African-American lobbying group TransAfrica, told the *Washington Post* that his offices 'have been the target of almost weekly break-ins for several months'.

In November 1982, TransAfrica publicised extracts from a classified CIA report, dated 15 April 1982, which predicted 'more persistent and widespread racial unrest' in South Africa. The report, according to the *Washington Post*, was 'a chronicle of the [ANC] from its beginnings in the early part of this century through its current and considerable revival after . . . the Soweto riots'. It noted the 'improved efficiency and coordination' of recent MK operations: ' "It is clear", the report said, that the ANC "could have inflicted a large number of casualties if it had chosen to do so." '[23] Two years later, South Africa's security forces, under the strategic control of the MID, were beginning to replicate the chaos of the mid- to late 1970s. Chester Crocker recalled a meeting in Cape Verde to discuss Angola:

> The chilling thing about the Cape Verde meeting was the chemistry within, and the behaviour of, the South African delegation . . . My special assistant Robert Cabelly probed SADF military intelligence boss Pieter van der Westhuizen about the signals being sent by his covert operations far north of the border. 'It tells the MPLA you want to kill them, not do a deal,' Cabelly noted. 'I agree,' [replied van der Westhuizen] . . . Twenty or so of the top ranks of Pretoria's national security establishment set a tone somewhere between Club Med and an adult-style *Lord of the Flies*. There was rampant strife in their ranks . . . They disagreed about everything . . . So deeply did they disagree about Mozambique that [Pik] Botha excluded van der Westhuizen from our related discussion of that topic. Later, when Cabelly approached the fuming 'Wessy' to compare notes, he growled: 'You're wasting your time talking to them [Botha, Malan, Fourie, Barnard, Geldenhuys] – *I run Mozambique*.'[24]

The burgeoning insurrection inside South Africa, which had started in the autumn of 1984, was described by the CIA in August 1985 with refreshing accuracy: 'Despite [South African] government allegations, the vast majority [of the rioters] are not under the direct control of the large antigovernment groups.' Andrew Cockburn had asked in the *New York*

Times a few months earlier: 'Can America afford to bank on the long-term popularity of the Boer intelligence agencies? . . . Recent history . . . suggests how foolish that would be.' The turn against the CIA hawks intensified in 1986. In July of that year, the Foreign Affairs Committee of the British House of Commons was informed that the CIA had restarted the covert supply of weapons to UNITA in Angola. The *Weekly Mail* in Johannesburg reported that Casey 'had visited South Africa secretly around mid-March to make the necessary arrangements'.[25] This 'flak' peaked on 23 July with a story by Seymour Hersh, thought by many to be America's finest investigative journalist. The *New York Times* report announced that, in exchange for South African intelligence on Soviet and Cuban 'activities in the region', American and British intelligence had traded 'information' on the ANC. Hersh disclosed:

> American intelligence officials said a special focus of the intelligence shared with the South African [MID] originated from the interception of communications between the [ANC] headquarters in Lusaka, Zambia, its guerrilla training camps in Angola and its offices in Africa and Western Europe . . . 'It all comes down to what you believe about the ANC,' one former senior Reagan administration official said in acknowledging that communications intelligence on the organization had been relayed to South Africa. He described the congress as a dangerous revolutionary organization controlled by Communists and said, 'Our interests require helping the South Africans' – [The NSA] had traditionally relied on the South African [MID] for data on Soviet shipping and submarine activities around the Cape of Good Hope and in the Indian Ocean . . . Most of these reports . . . were relayed through installations of the [British GCHQ].

Hersh reported that an unnamed NSA source had attended a meeting at Government Communications Headquarters (GCHQ) in Cheltenham, the centre for British signals intelligence and electronic surveillance, at which 'senior American and British officials reviewed previous intelligence assignments and future targets – a process known in intelligence jargon as "tasking" '. At the point in the meeting when they started to discuss Africa, 'three South African [MID] officers were ushered into the room'. In exchange for weekly, rather than the usual monthly, reports on the Silvermine (the South African equivalent of GCHQ) monitoring of Soviet and Cuban activity in Angola and Mozambique, the MID representatives asked for 'an extensive array' of information on political, economic, military and diplomatic activity south of the Sahara. They also wanted 'any and all tasking related to the ANC, including the movements of Oliver Tambo', especially 'reports [of] when he was taking flights aboard Soviet and Cuban aircraft'. Hersh's NSA source 'recalled his personal surprise at how "extensive" the cooperation was between the South Africans and the United States and Britain'.[26]

The MID was never credited with the mythical 'power' that observers had attributed to Hendrik van den Bergh and BOSS in the 1970s. That is strange, because the actions and strategies of van der Westhuizen and the MID led to the deaths of many more people. One reason for the lack of spook mythology was that MID did not seek publicity and has so far managed to avoid being held to account for its actions: very few SADF generals sought amnesty from the TRC. Defence Minister Magnus Malan, who had ceased to be a soldier and had become an ambitious politician, spoke for South Africa's armed forces including the MID. But as van der Westhuizen made clear to Crocker's assistant, the MID believed that it handled real power in southern Africa.

Following the Soweto uprising, MK, the ANC's armed wing, restarted operations within South Africa. The first action listed in the ANC's submission to the TRC was a 'skirmish' with the police in the Eastern Transvaal in November 1976, during which two policemen were killed when escaping 'cadres' threw a grenade into a police vehicle. 'Armed propaganda' operations, as they were known by MK, between 1977 and 1980, included sabotage of railway lines, the bombing of police stations, attacks on and skirmishes with the police and retribution delivered to former ANC members believed to be collaborators. In June 1980, an MK 'Special Operations force launched a simultaneous attack on four installations of the South African Coal, Oil and Gas Corporation (SASOL) . . . including oil storage tanks and a refinery . . . It was the underground army's most successful operation to date.' Special Ops were planned and controlled by Joe Slovo. There were no deaths or injuries and the financial cost to the state of the 'spectacular' has been estimated at between R6 million and R70 million. The number of MK operations increased dramatically after the SASOL attack, most of which continued to concentrate on infrastructure targets in order to minimise the number of civilian deaths. On 11 August 1981, the Special Operations unit launched five 122 mm rockets against the SADF's headquarters at the Voortrekkerhoogte military base. Life as an MK cadre in South Africa was certainly 'nasty, brutish and short'. In 1982, the South African Institute of Race Relations recorded twenty-six incidents of 'sabotage'; the police claimed that thirteen suspected MK members were killed in action.[27] As Stephen Ellis commented:

> The death-rate for guerrillas entering the country was alarmingly high and incoming fighters knew they had little chance of getting out alive. In 1980 one fighter, Petrus Jobane, cornered by the police in Soweto, blew himself up with his own grenade rather than be taken alive . . . [MK] fighters romanticised this type of self-sacrifice. They had little sympathy for any of their comrades who allowed themselves to be captured, expecting fighters to take their own lives rather than surrender. Anyone who was captured knew that they would be extensively interrogated, probably tortured, and forced to reveal information, but perhaps most frightening of all was the prospect of being 'turned' [forced to work as a double agent or with the police counter-intelligence units as an 'askari'].[28]

In May 1983, an MK Special Operations unit exploded a car bomb in Pretoria's Church Street, outside the administrative headquarters of the South African Air Force. The explosion killed twenty-one people, and injured 217. Two MK cadres died in the operation, as did eleven members of the South African armed forces. This act of terrorism, in the heart of the security establishment, was later cited by many intelligence and special forces operatives as a justification for the brutality they meted out to enemies of the state. Death-squad commander Eugene de Kock had returned to Pretoria one day before the Church Street bomb and visited the site of the explosion: 'It had a formidable effect on me. I thought that this was nothing but terror against the public. It gave me the impression that we are sitting here with an enemy that would do anything.' Craig Williamson added: 'The day I stood in Church Street among all the bodies, I hated . . . [it] made me want to kill ANC members.' A senior NIS official told me that on the day following the bombing he was so enraged by the wanton destruction that he suggested to NIS chief Niel Barnard that the agency should unleash whatever killing capacity it had at its disposal to find and destroy the bombers. He remains grateful that Barnard did not take up the idea.[29]

The South African doctrine of 'pre-emptive intervention' amounted to nothing more than 'destructive engagement'. During the early 1980s, the apartheid regime sowed chaos throughout the region. Stephen Ellis has suggested that 'the intention was to recreate the pre-1974 buffer'. But the only way that could be done was, in the words of the probably apocryphal American officer in Vietnam, 'destroying the town in order to save it'. In Angola, which had been the scene of South Africa's first visible 'intervention' in 1975, the SADF made periodic assaults on SWAPO or ANC bases. The South African government's intention appeared to be to partition the country and establish a UNITA administration in the south. Major assaults on Angola took place in June 1980 and August 1981 during which South Africa conquered 50,000 square kilometres of Cunene province: the BBC reported that '160,000 Angolan civilians were rendered homeless'. UNITA assumed control of the occupied zone in January 1982. Further SADF operations occurred on an annual basis. In August 1982, the *Economist* commented: 'For the umpteenth time South Africa has launched a major military operation into southern Angola just when the Namibia negotiations have reached a sensitive stage.'[30]

In Zimbabwe, former Rhodesians, working within South Africa's special forces, launched Operation Drama intending to destabilise the country and 'ensure that the [new] government did not provide concrete support to the ANC and PAC'. Zimbabwe was subjected to extraordinary levels of sabotage, terrorism, assassination and arson. The *Washington Post* reported in 1989 that 'a series of recent Zimbabwean court cases have disclosed evidence of South African penetration at the highest reaches of Zimbabwe's domestic intelligence agency . . . They suggest that South African agents, by manipulating intelligence reports and fanning ethnic strife, may have played a larger role than previously suspected in touching off a bitter five-year post-independence bush war in the southwest provinces of Matabeleland.' A number of South African–Rhodesian spies remain in Zimbabwe's prisons to this day. In Mozambique, the SADF developed RENAMO. In Lesotho, Swaziland and Botswana, the SADF intervened with impunity. Among the most appalling assaults were the attacks on Maseru, Lesotho on 9 December 1982, when forty-two people were killed ('30 South Africans and 12 Basotho. Seven of the dead were women; three were children'), and on Gaberone in June 1985, when twelve people were killed. In July 1983, eight of the nine Southern African Development Coordination Conference (SADCC) heads of state admitted that 'South Africa can invade and occupy sovereign states, blow up vital installations, and massacre populations at no apparent cost to its relations with its main allies.'[31]

National Intelligence Service (NIS)

In November 1979, P.W. Botha announced that Professor Lukas Daniel ('Niel') Barnard would be the new head of the Department of National

Security (DONS), following Alec van Wyk's retirement in 1980. Barnard, aged thirty, was a surprise appointment, as he had no history or particular knowledge of intelligence. In 1992, in an interview with *Die Burger*, he admitted that 'to this day' the background to his appointment mystified him. In January 1980, P.W. Botha appointed Rear-Admiral W.N. du Plessis (from Defence Headquarters) and Brigadier F.M.A. Steenkamp (deputy head of the Security Police) to posts within DONS 'to expand the inter-action' between the agency and the police, the SADF 'and some of the other disciplines'.[32] Barnard must have felt besieged. In June 1980, DONS was renamed the National Intelligence Service.

Barnard was born in 1949 in Otjiwarongo in South West Africa–Namibia. His father was originally a junior-school headmaster and later the chief inspector of education for South West Africa. Barnard studied at the (right-wing) University of the Orange Free State where he completed a BA degree in political science and history, an MA including a thesis, 'Modern Theoretical Approaches to the Study of International Relations', and a PhD on 'The Power Factor in International Relations'. He had been appointed lecturer in political science in 1973, senior lecturer in 1977 and professor of political studies in 1978, aged twenty-nine. He was reported to be the author of more than twenty-five articles in special-ist publications, although his style of writing was described as 'congested and constipated' by Professor André Brink. In his spare time, he was a senior officer in the Citizen Force. Peter Younghusband of *Newsweek* described Barnard as:

> a wrathful rhetorician and passionate believer in the righteous use of force. His writing is peppered with biblical allusions to 'the sword of God' and he strongly favours the use of *swaardmagsansie* – the sword-power sanction. Barnard believes Pretoria should develop a nuclear weapon – and make it known to the world as a deterrent . . . Barnard is not all bullets and bom-bast. While he bluntly advocates a 'mailed fist' approach to South Africa's problems with state security and terrorism, he also cautions politicians that the final solution cannot be a military one.[33]

One senior foreign correspondent told me that he had once been given a story on South Africa's nuclear weapons by Barnard, but afterwards the NIS chief tormented the journalist to repay the 'debt'. The reporter felt that he was being pressurised to behave in an ethically inappropriate way. Barnard's academic interest in the role of the nuclear deterrent would have stood him in good favour with a South African government, and especially a prime minister, that 'believed that [the] possibility of a nuclear attack on South Africa existed and . . . built an underground bunker in Pretoria'. Chester Crocker provided a useful snapshot of the young spook at a 1981 session of negotiations on South West Africa–Namibia: 'Barnard said little in plenary meetings . . . he was extremely reserved, even cold, toward my team. This may in part, have been due to my role in discouraging his research in the United States in matters relating to nuclear technology acquisition while I was still at Georgetown University.' He believed that Barnard 'cultivated an image of inscrutability. Once he refused to identify the name of a local cheese being served at a state function – giving rise to hilarity in the US delegation about the discovery of the [NIS]'s new "secret cheese".'[34] But Barnard's difficulties were a little more tortuous than American teasing.

Following the failed mercenary coup in the Seychelles in 1981 (see page 376) which involved an NIS agent, Martin Dolinchek, the South African newspapers were full of stories of 'spy wars'. It seemed that nothing had changed over the previous three years – the MID, the NIS and the Security Police were at each other's throats again. John Battersby noted: 'In the post-Information Department era, NIS had largely been relegated to a think-tank or intelligence evaluation centre.' In May 1982, the *Rand Daily Mail* published a report suggesting that Barnard was 'on the point of resigning'. In a rare intervention, Barnard stated: 'The rumour, if such there be, is devoid of all truth.' The Johannesburg *Sunday Times* claimed under a headline, 'Spook Wars', that the argument between Barnard and van der Westhuizen concerned 'the Government's acceptance of the Rabie Commission recommendation that a new umbrella Ministry of Law and Order be created over two divisions – the South African Police and the Independent Directorate for Security Legislation. Both hierarchies apparently agree that South Africa needs only one intelligence network independent of the police – their own.' The Rabie Commission held its hearings *in camera* and avoided debate in a South African press subject to censorship on security matters. Judge Rabie 'adopted the view that "those who are responsible for the national security must be the sole judges of what the national security requires"'.[35]

Four weeks later, the *Financial Mail* praised Barnard and the NIS's 'stunning come-back'. The magazine acknowledged Barnard's role in the spy-swap of Soviet agent Aleksei Kozlov for Johan van der Mescht, a South African prisoner of SWAPO, and 'eight high-ranking Western agents'. P.W. Botha, who had used the capture of Kozlov in January 1981 to launch a general election, seized the opportunity of the spy-swap to praise Niel Barnard: 'I would therefore like to avail myself of this opportunity to congratulate the

Director-General and his personnel of the [NIS], on the capable manner . . . with which they conducted the difficult and direct negotiations with the . . . KGB.' In another break with his usual style, Barnard was photographed with the returning prisoner. The NIS's improved position in the South African power structure was borne out when the Director-General of the Prime Minister's Office announced that 'The Secretariat of the State Security Council falls under the [NIS] and not under the Office of the Prime Minister.'[36]

In September 1983, Niel Barnard, in a rare public performance, gave the C.R. Swart Lecture at the University of the Orange Free State. His subject: 'National Intelligence Work in International Relations'. He started by announcing that 'intelligence as a profession is an intellectual game of chess in which information is utilised to enable a government . . . to make timeous and knowledgeable decisions'. The 'raison d'être' of a central intelligence service is that 'knowledge is power . . . espionage runs like a golden thread through the weal and woe of world politics'. An important aspect of Barnard's understanding of intelligence was the secrecy associated with the 'need to know' principle. He interpreted this to mean that 'a member of an intelligence service should only have access to the specific intelligence matter which would enable him to perform his duty'. This almost sounded like an intelligence organisation based on a cell structure and it failed to acknowledge the responsibility and potential for either denial or mischief which it provided to the senior officers within any such system. On media relations, Barnard said, 'A confidential working agreement between the media and an intelligence service is highly desirable and should be assiduously cultivated.' He concluded: 'The National Intelligence Service does not wish to bear the mark of Cain. It would like to be considered as belonging to and serving the South African people. The future of the [Republic] of South Africa depends on the measure of success which the intelligence profession achieves.'[37]

Niel Barnard was a completely different kind of spy chief to Hendrik van den Bergh. Where van den Bergh had been hungry to claim every success, Barnard maintained a low profile: he refused to be interviewed, he held one press conference in the 1980s, and he spoke on a public platform only twice. The second public address was in December 1986 when he 'castigated' the ANC at an Afrikaner commemoration at Blood River. Even on that occasion, he requested that journalists should not be present. In contrast to *Africa Confidential*'s 'ice-cold spy', Chester Crocker described a figure who by January 1985, during an 'unannounced visit to

Washington' with Magnus Malan, appeared to be warming: 'Barnard acknowledged the extreme constipation of Afrikaner politics, where change was equated with weakness' and 'especially . . . welcomed our suggestions'. Of equal interest is Crocker's recollection that 'the South Africans talked to us openly of their sputtering dialogue in secret channels with the exiled ANC leadership (a dialogue we were also tracking through our own ANC contacts).'[38]

Exocets and the Falklands War

The MID solution to the problem of apartheid South Africa's survival was a peculiar mixture of 'kill' and 'cure' – 'adapt or die' indeed. Covert military interventions in the front-line states were intended to weaken hostile governments and facilitate a Verwoerdian 'constellation of states', with South Africa of course as the sun. Movement within the Republic towards legalising trade union activity and establishing a tricameral parliament, in order to co-opt the Indian and Coloured communities, was planned to neutralise anti-apartheid resistance. Internationally, the MID had restored the close relationship with the CIA and developed strong links with fascist states in Latin America, hoping to establish a reactionary version of South–South diplomacy. Finally, local capitalists were to be pacified by the massive expansion of ARMSCOR and the South African arms industry, repairing the weakening economy in the process. The contradictions within the MID solution would become apparent during a strange incident involving the sale of weapons to Argentina.

On 24 May 1982, three weeks before the end of the Falklands war, at a time when the Argentine junta was reported to be scouring the world for missiles, the Johannesburg *Star* led on a story which claimed that 'South Africa is supplying arms to Argentina for use against the British fleet.' Peter Sullivan's story, which 'came from a high-level and authoritative source', claimed that South Africa was supplying surface-to-surface Skerpioen (Gabriel) missiles and Mirage fighter-bomber spares: 'They are loaded aboard a Uruguayan D68 airfreighter in a remote corner of Cape Town's D.F. Malan Airport and packed in Cargolux pallets marked "tractor spares".' A South African government spokesman had refused to confirm or deny the story. He stated that the British arms embargo had 'forced South Africa to embark on its own arms manufacture programme'. Although the spokesman said that existing contracts would be met, he also repeated a guarantee, given two weeks earlier following the sinking of HMS *Sheffield* on 4 May, that 'no Exocet missiles would be delivered to Argentina'. In all the furore, few observers noticed that the South African government had admitted that it possessed Exocet missiles. Under the arms embargo, it had previously been assumed that the South African armed forces was not in possession of the French-made weapons system. The South African government had made a declaration of neutrality in the Falklands war on 8 April 1982.[39]

On 25 May, the British newspapers in unison reported the South African missile story. The *Sun*, in a story titled 'Anger at South Africa Missiles', speculated that 'the allegations . . . could trigger off an international row'. Peter Younghusband (*Daily Mail*) explained that 'South Africa is supplying arms and military equipment to Argentina. It is also supplying military equipment to Britain.' He added that 'South African naval intelligence had passed information to Britain that two Russian Bear spy-planes, operating from Angola, are keeping a watch on the fleet at the Falklands.' Conservative MP Nicholas Winterton, an old friend of the apartheid regime, said that he would question the South African Ambassador to Britain, adding: 'I have put my head on the block for South Africa.'[40] The South African government's statements on the matter were certainly contradictory: P.W. Botha declared that the country would 'not disclose from whom we buy weapons or to whom we sell weapons'. He later warned at a 'public rally in Lichtenburg that these rumours are damaging to South Africa both locally and abroad', even though Defence Minister Magnus Malan had announced in parliament: 'Contrary to reports, South Africa has not provided or sold any missiles or aircraft spare parts to Argentina in any way before or during the Falklands conflict.'[41]

The South African arms for Argentina story was a classic 'one-day wonder' in the British press. Coverage of the 'hunt for black-market Exocets' continued, but few reporters returned to the apartheid angle. On 26 May, the *Daily Express*, which regularly sympathised with the apartheid government, commented in a 'bleeding heart' editorial: 'Having forced South Africa to turn away from us, we now find ourselves stung, the biter bit. It is our fault, and a very sad business indeed.' The *Express* columnist John Ellison continued the theme but added: 'whatever denials emerge from Pretoria, these suggestions bear an unmistakable ring of truth . . . The notorious Captain Alfredo Astiz, the Argentine torturer known as Captain Death who commanded the South Georgia garrison . . . was decorated by the Pretoria Government in 1978. At the time he was on a naval course there which plainly went well beyond the basic tenets of seamanship.' Four days later, Adam Raphael (the *Observer*), who nine years earlier had written the celebrated *Guardian* story about British companies in the Republic paying starvation wages to African employees, reported that British 'officials have been voicing incredulity at South Africa's claims to innocence . . . Normally Whitehall's strategy is to enable foreign governments caught red-handed in covert arms dealing to retreat without public loss of face. The fact that on this occasion Britain has chosen to press the matter is an indication of Mrs Thatcher's anger at being stabbed in the back by a so-called friendly ally.'[42] Meanwhile, in South Africa the pot was still bubbling: Martin Welz (Johannesburg *Sunday Express*) quoted a clearly impassioned British Embassy spokesman:

> We have been asking for an undertaking that South Africa will not supply arms, of whatever sort, to Argentina while hostilities continue . . . That [Malan] still has not given us. South Africa can expect serious diplomatic consequences. Every day that South Africa refuses to give that undertaking our men are being killed – in the air, at sea, on the ground – in the Falklands war . . . We have noted General Malan's statement . . . but we have also noted, by experience, that this is a limited assurance. While it might have satisfied the South African Parliament, it has not satisfied us.

The spokesman stated that Britain was not seeking information on arms which South Africa had sold to Argentina in the past. He admitted, 'We were selling arms to Argentina until very recently.' The Johannesburg *Sunday Express* also commented on the fact that three South African cabinet ministers had prior knowledge of the story which appeared in the *Star*: 'None of them took any steps to prevent publication of the report.'[43] This was all the stranger because South Africa had strict censorship laws regarding security matters, including the armed forces, intelligence agencies and the state arms manufacturer, ARMSCOR. The Afrikaans-language press indicated that 'South Africa was preparing to officially demand that Britain state whether it is supplying the banned African National Congress and SWAPO with arms.' On 31 May, it was widely reported that Argentina's final Exocet missiles had been destroyed.[44] There was no more mention of South Africa in relation to the Falklands war. What had it all meant?

In the late 1960s, John Vorster and P.W. Botha had 'mooted the idea of a South Atlantic pact . . . if European nations created a power vacuum in the region.' In May 1969, the South African Foreign Minister Dr Hilgard Muller paid an official visit to Argentina. Following the oil crisis of 1973, South

Africa rapidly extended its diplomatic relations in Latin America. This appears to have been a complementary operation to the 'détente with black Africa'. While Rhoodie and van den Bergh took responsibility for Africa, and by extension for South Africa's regional security, MID played the dominant role in developing ties with the military governments and arms suppliers of Latin America and the Far East – although, as Eschel Rhoodie explained, in 1978 'secret funds of the Department of Information were used to invite army officers from South American countries and their wives'. In April 1974, Paraguay's President General Alfredo Stroessner made a state visit to South Africa. In August the following year, John Vorster visited Paraguay and Uruguay. Rhoodie admitted that this visit 'came as a surprise to me. I was not told . . . beforehand.' During the same period, South Africa also established diplomatic relations with Somoza's Nicaragua, Pinochet's Chile and the military government of Bolivia. As Vorster said in Uruguay: 'We are the same kind of people.' Dan O'Meara relayed a related P.W. Botha story in *Forty Lost Years*: 'While reviewing an immaculate, stony-faced and goose-stepping honour guard on a state visit to Taiwan in the early 1980s, Botha had remarked to an aide: "*These* are my kind of people." '[45]

South African businessmen swiftly followed the soldiers and diplomats. In 1979 a South African–South American Chamber of Commerce was established and 'an exhibition of industrial products "made in South Africa" was held in Buenos Aires'. But the main economic activity was, of course, 'the business of war': the profitable trade in weapons. In the twelve months before the Falklands war, more than twenty Latin American generals visited South Africa, the most notable being General Mario Benjamin Menéndez, later Governor of the occupied 'Malvinas'. In addition, the veteran South African journalist Arthur Gavshon observed that the American 'Ambassador at large' General Vernon Walters, a former deputy director of the CIA, made numerous 'visits . . . to Latin American capitals between June 1981 and February 1982 . . . [He] hoped to rally support for a security system in the South Atlantic with the aim of blocking Soviet penetration of the area. The project for a South Atlantic Treaty Organisation (SATO) supplementing NATO was designed to accommodate South Africa, Uruguay and Argentina.'[46]

Despite Malan's insistence that South Africa would not supply arms to Argentina, James Adams, whose book *The Unnatural Alliance* was published in 1984, stated that Argentina approached twelve countries during the last week of May 1982: 'Of all the countries approached, only two, South Africa and Israel, were willing to co-operate . . . British Intelligence . . . proved', according to Adams, 'that both countries continued to supply ammunition, Gabriel missiles, spares for the Dagger aircraft and bombs for the A4s during the conflict . . . unofficial sources in South Africa have confirmed that the allegations are quite correct.' The British *Sunday Times* reported that at least one shipment of Israeli weapons had been delivered on 24 May – the same day that the Johannesburg *Star* reported on the South African missiles. In the immediate aftermath of the Falklands war, Israel was 'banned from British military exercises and exhibitions because of growing evidence that it supplied Argentina with arms during the . . . campaign'.[47] South Africa was already functioning outside the usual round of arms fairs, so a similar censure would have been meaningless.

The autobiography of Pieter Wolvaardt, a former South African ambassador to Mexico and Latin American specialist, disclosed that on 15 May, nine days *before* the *Star* story, P.W. Botha received a telegram, simultaneously released as a press statement, from the right-wing Monday Club in London: 'It implored "[Botha] not to supply Exocet missiles to Argentina during the Falkland Islands crisis . . . the Club feels sure that if they are supplied sympathies for South Africa held in the West will wither." ' Wolvaardt also revealed that following the furore on 24 May and especially in the wake of comments from a Foreign Office spokesman on 31 May that 'We have noted the limited scope of [the South African] denial and the fact that it concerns only the past and not the present and the future,' there were 'concerns in South African government circles'. These 'concerns' were compounded by a remark from a member of the Conservative Bow Group to a South African Embassy official in London: 'if a single British serviceman is killed or wounded by any weapon delivered by South Africa, the Bow Group's sympathies will be totally destroyed [and] there will be no further contact'.[48]

South Africa had indirectly admitted possession of the Exocet missile during the war, and a brochure issued by the French arms manufacturer Aerospatiale a few months before the war 'boasted that 1,500 Exocet-MM38 missiles had been ordered and 900 delivered to 12 countries'. In September 1982, ARMSCOR announced that it was developing a new missile system based upon the French Exocet. It was later suggested that this programme had been established in conjunction with the Israelis. In July 1983, the French journal *Afrique-Asie* revealed that:

> Armscor [had] managed to acquire the documentation for the MM-38 Exocet missile with the assistance of highly placed French Government officials, but not directly from France. The actual plans were handed over to

agents in Indonesia and Singapore and then to the Armscor import directors in Amsterdam, where these plans plus one missile and a manual of
instructions were examined.[49]

The Johannesburg *Star* reported that the *Afrique-Asie* story refuted 'British
intelligence sources [who] have always claimed that a South African military delegation was in Buenos Aires at the time of the Falklands war . . . it
was feared that South Africa had bought Exocets from France and was
secretly delivering them to Argentina'. Six weeks later, *African Defence*
announced that American diplomatic sources in Cape Town had been the
first to report the 'delivery of South African-produced Exocet missiles to
Argentina'. In November 1983, 'US intelligence sources suddenly reported
that South Africa was *co-producing* the Aerospatiale Exocet missile.' It has
also been claimed that South Africa financed the research and development
of the original Exocet range, in which case as Signe Landgren later
deduced, 'part of [the] missile is South African property'.[50]

A year after the Falklands war, the British government disclosed that
South Africa was to be 'used as a staging post' for the construction of a military airbase on the Falkland Islands. The £215 million contract was issued
to a consortium of Mowlem–Laing–Amey Roadstone Construction. There
were immediate protests, the most detailed of which was issued by Britain's
Anti-Apartheid Movement: 'The Government has given no explanation as
to why it did not insist that an alternative staging post was used.' The A–AM
explained that the development would assist South Africa's economy and
open 'up the prospect for further strategic collaboration between Britain and
South Africa'. It also noted that 'a number of West African sea ports are
served by British airlines and the distance by sea would not be significantly
greater than that from Cape Town to the Falklands. Moreover, none of these
African states enjoy the close military relations which South Africa has with
Argentina.' Answering a question in the House of Commons, Margaret
Thatcher declared: 'The arrangement made for people to get there to fulfil
the contract is a purely commercial matter.'[51]

The strange episode whereby the South African press exposed arms dealing with Argentina during the Falklands war was later retold by Howard
Barrell, then editor of South Africa's *Mail & Guardian*. It was now a
'delightfully executed deception of a South African journalist':

> For a number of years, [Peter Sullivan] . . . maintained a fruitful . . .
> relationship with a locally based British diplomat who was not entirely

unrelated to Her Majesty's Secret Intelligence Service. The spook had given him a number of stories for his newspaper – and the tip-offs had always proven reliable. Then, as the British task force steamed across the Atlantic . . . [Sullivan] was taken to one side by the diplomat and given another confidence. [He] had no reason to doubt what he was told. South Africa, the diplomat whispered, was secretly supplying Argentina with missile technology for use against British forces. From a folder by his side the diplomat drew the evidence. He passed over a series of photographs. They showed crates, bound for Argentina, being loaded on to an aircraft . . . The story was . . . splashed across South African newspapers . . . Magnus Malan . . . rushed to deny that South Africa was supplying arms to Argentina. Under pressure, Malan . . . promised that South Africa would *never* help the Argies in any way . . . That undertaking was all the Brits had wanted. There had never been an ounce of truth to the tale.[52]

Barrell's parable of the gullible hack is certainly plausible. A BBC television documentary in 2001 revealed that the British intelligence services had been so concerned during the Falklands war about the possibility of Argentina sourcing further supplies of Exocet missiles that the Secretary of State for Defence, Sir John Nott, had 'agreed a programme to buy all the Exocets we could find on the world market. We made unlimited funds available to the security services and others: our agents.' The programme was called Operation Denial, and a former MI6 employee, Anthony Divall, was recalled to active service to head an operation designed 'to prevent the Argentines from obtaining from whatever source additional Exocet missiles'. Divall revealed that the price of an Exocet had inflated from $450,000 each to $1 million. MI6 posed as 'buyers' and then stymied the deals in order to keep the missiles off the market. Divall recalled: 'We were getting offers of Exocet missiles from as far apart as Australia and South Africa.'[53]

In the sinister global 'arms bazaar', few traders can complain when the weapons that they sell are employed for nefarious purposes. The same is true of the less closely examined international military liaison. In December 1969, British diplomats discussed the impending visit of Colonel Cockbain of the South African Air Force; the Ministry of Defence had asked whether the South African visitor 'might visit the . . . [MOD] Air Operations Room . . . during the course of [his] two-month visit'. The Foreign Office remarked that, as Cockbain would be meeting 'with Plessey and other producers of electronic equipment' during his trip, a visit to the Operations Room could 'contribute to the possibility of the sale of electronic equipment to the South Africans'. The diplomat stated with obvious relief, 'Previous visits involving co-operation with members of the South African armed forces have not become public and we would try to ensure that this visit, if approved, did not become public either.'[54] The visit was approved. In 1999, former MID official General Tienie Groenewald, told me that the exchange of military information and designs for weapons systems with the British armed forces was a long-standing tradition. He said that, in his experience, a party would be organised at a British military base and, at a certain point during the evening, the British officers would withdraw, leaving the South Africans alone with a photocopying machine and whichever documents or plans were required.[55] In that way, the British officers would not, technically, have given their South African friends the information.

Whatever South Africa supplied to the Argentinians during the Falklands war, the country's ability to ride the criticism and emerge unscathed had been recognised by the CIA. In the mid-1980s, when the CIA facilitated the provision of Eastern-bloc weapons to Nicaragua's Contras, a major supplier was the apartheid regime. As Chester Crocker sarcastically put it: 'The Angolan honeypot was working like a charm.' Steven Emerson observed in *Secret Warriors* that 'although not identified in the Iran-Contra report, [Oliver] North's notebooks reveal that on January 5 1985, CIA official Dewey Clarridge called North to tell him that 200 tons of weapons were being shipped from South Africa to Costa Rica'. Soon afterwards:

> North scribbled in his notebook: 'More S/A delivery from ARDE [a Costa Rica-based Contra force] to FDN' – the Honduras-based contra group . . . The notebooks further disclose that in the fall of 1984, a high-ranking South African official offered North free shipment of RPG [Rocket-propelled] grenade launchers if North arranged payment of the transportation costs. Clarridge, who was in charge of covert operations in Latin America, denied under oath to the Congressional committee that South Africa provided any assistance for the contras.[56]

Apartheid South Africa certainly possessed motive to sell missiles to the Argentinians; it probably possessed the very Exocet missiles that Argentina needed; and far from simply issuing an immediate 'promise', as Barrell implied, the South African government reacted in a contradictory fashion, issuing buried threats from one voice and assurances from another. When I asked General Tienie Groenewald whether South Africa had supplied

Exocets to Argentina, he answered: 'We *also* supplied special "belly tanks" [long-range fuel tanks] to the British air force.' The British 'deception of a South African journalist', if that is what it was, could just as easily have been a moment of genuine panic where diplomatic subtleties and the 'usual channels' were abandoned in favour of a straightforward leak of information which could have resulted in a major diplomatic incident and the expulsion of a number of Foreign Office officials. In June 1988, in the aftermath of South Africa's defeat at the hands of the MPLA and their Cuban allies in the battle of Cuito Cuanavale, the *Independent* reported that 'Argentina is selling Mirage-3 fighter-bombers to South Africa . . . The aircraft, which are vital to South Africa's war in southern Angola, have been seen being unloaded in wooden crates at South African ports in recent months. [Western] Diplomats have confirmed that they are from Argentina, possibly those used against British troops in the Falklands war.'[57]

8

Spy Games

In the pause Mr Vladimir formulated in his mind a series of disparaging remarks concerning Mr Verloc's face and figure. The fellow was unexpectedly vulgar, heavy, and impudently unintelligent. He looked uncommonly like a master plumber come to present his bill . . . This was then the famous and trusty secret agent, so secret that he was never designated otherwise but by the symbol Δ in the late Baron Stott-Wartenheim's official, semi-official, and confidential correspondence; the celebrated agent Δ whose warnings had the power to change the schemes and the dates of royal, imperial, grand-ducal journeys, and sometimes cause them to be put off altogether! This fellow!

Joseph Conrad, *The Secret Agent*, 1907[1]

I never got the impression that it was like the movies . . . where James Bond or somebody gets called in and the Minister says to him: 'I want you to go and kill somebody in the Bahamas but if you are caught we don't know who you are.' I had the feeling that we had the backing of the State and that if necessary they would take the necessary pain.

Craig Williamson, cited in TRC, *Report*, Vol. 6, 2003[2]

IN A FOUR-MONTH period between September 1982 and January 1983, three separate but equally interesting South African intelligence episodes occurred. In each case, the end result was a mysterious lack of clarity, or indeed of honesty. Each case featured different agencies within South Africa's disparate spy world, although the MID has managed to avoid any reference to itself ever appearing in its story. One of the episodes involved South African spies in Britain; the other two involved or pointed to the British and the Soviet intelligence agencies in relation to South Africa. All three episodes stretched back many years and continued to reverberate for many years after their occurrence. Intelligence stories nearly always open up an 'Alice in Wonderland' world where everything is interpretable in a number of different ways.

Anthony Champion de Crespigny: The Professor–Spy

On 10 September 1982, South African newspaper readers were surprised to learn that Anthony de Crespigny, former head of the department of political science at the University of Cape Town and member of P.W. Botha's sixty-strong President's Council, tasked with drawing up proposals for a new constitution, had fled South Africa on 4 August. De Crespigny was a former liberal, whose politics had moved to the right while teaching in the United States. His ex-wife Caroline had been held in solitary confinement in a South African prison for 144 days in 1966. The Afrikaans-language press speculated that 'de Crespigny was an MI6 spy'. Another report added, 'There have been unconfirmed reports that Prof De Crespigny was recently questioned by members of South Africa's National Intelligence Service.' De Crespigny's first response was to issue an 'unsolicited statement from a secret British address declaring: "I am no spy".'[3] Only later, did he inform a South African journalist: 'What's the point in denying that I worked for a foreign intelligence agency? If one makes a denial of that kind, does it increase or diminish the likelihood that people will believe you? It's a Catch-22.'[4]

On 12 September, the Johannesburg *Sunday Times* revealed that the NIS had interviewed de Crespigny on 29 July in relation to 'a list believed to contain the names of members of the banned African National Congress'. The list, which had appeared in London, featured de Crespigny's name. De Crespigny denied that there had been any meeting with intelligence agents and 'said he knew nothing of the alleged ANC document'. Neil Hooper's headline story also explained that de Crespigny had resigned from the President's Council on 11 August, 'for personal and family reasons'. He then contacted the South African Associated Newspapers London office 'saying he wished to issue a statement once the contents of his letter [of resignation] had been made public'. But the contents of the letter were not made public and de Crespigny then 'had a change of heart and said he no longer wished to issue a statement'. Three days later, de Crespigny gave an interview to Stanley Uys in which he admitted that, in fact, he had been interviewed by two NIS officials: 'They were neither offensive, bullying nor intimidating.' De Crespigny said that the NIS had only been interested in 'his views and activities when he was a member of the Liberal Party in

Natal, and particularly his activities in London from 1960 to 1963 when he was studying for his PhD'. He added that Dr Dennis Worrall, a colleague on the Constitutional Committee of the President's Council, had contacted the NIS and received assurances that the NIS had 'no objections to me returning to my post'.[5]

Anthony de Crespigny, the dissembling Professor, did not return to South Africa. But on 26 September 1982, the Johannesburg *Sunday Times* revived the story. It claimed that there was a link between de Crespigny's flight and the arrest in London of Casselton, Wedin and Aspinall in connection with burglaries at the ANC, PAC and SWAPO offices (see page 184). The report also revealed that an academic in Cape Town had 'submitted a 40-page report on Dr de Crespigny, detailing his meetings with known British intelligence agents since 1974'. The de Crespigny mystery disappeared from the newspapers in the weeks that followed except one story which appeared in the *Argus* on 4 December: 'De Crespigny plans to be travel agent'. The last glimpse of de Crespigny was an article and follow-up letter in the *Daily Telegraph* in 1983; the article argued 'against giving blacks an equal voice in South Africa's political system'.[6] 'What had Anthony de Crespigny done, and why, after questioning, had he fled?

In the early 1970s, during a house-search supervised by BOSS, an extraordinary nine-page document had been discovered in Pretoria. It appeared to be a report, dated 7 August 1961, from 'the Group' to an unnamed paymaster accounting for £25,000. The report was labelled 'Top Secret'. The document, described as 'the first report', referred in its opening sentence to an 'arrangement' made in April 1961. The Group claimed to be representing the 'developing underground movement in South Africa'. Its activities 'had largely been directed to the rescue of persons who were victims of apartheid'. The report noted that the Group was unable to 'operate' in Rhodesia or the Portuguese colonies; only Bechuanaland and Swaziland offered 'any degree of freedom'. The Group had purchased a ship and an aircraft and registered 'two private companies with limited liability' as owners in London. The ship, *Torquil*, which could carry '10 to 15 tons of material', had cost £8,000; the aircraft, a Comanche which could seat four passengers, cost £8,896. A further £1,200 had been expended on transporting 'fifteen banishees'. Maintaining the banished people cost £100 a quarter. Two donations of £500 each had been made to the 'organisers of the 31st May strike' and the Pan Africanist Congress. A Cape Coloured Convention had been organised and, at a cost of £1,000, 'a very encouraging unprecedented representative gathering of practically all shades of opinion outside the National Party'. Equipment to make radio broadcasts had been purchased for £800, and a second-hand car, adapted to carry a 'powerful shortwave transmitter', had cost £450. The wage bill of the four full-time members of the Group, two of whom were African, was £220 per month.

While half of the mysterious report detailed money spent, the other half listed suggested future expenditure. Additional funds would be needed for building a 'storeroom, workshop and certain living quarters' near an airstrip in Swaziland; the cost was estimated at £6,000 to purchase the property and £1,500 for renovation. The workshop would need a 'multi-purpose dynamo' to pump water and generate electricity and tools, at an estimated cost of £850. The Group would also need a Land Rover and trailer, approximate cost £1,500. Under the heading 'Communications', the Group requested £600 for four 'transmitter receivers'. Printing facilities could be established in Swaziland for the 'Liberatory Movements' at a cost of £2,000. On the subject of 'Policy', the report states: 'There appears to have been some misunderstanding as to the policy of the Group and it would appear that a suggestion was made that the situation in South Africa had changed and that the Group's policy was therefore to change.' The report asserted that the Group remained committed to 'the ideal objectives arrived at in the memorandum supplied to you when these arrangements were first negotiated'. The Group declared that it had transported fifteen 'banished persons' to Basutoland. Rather desperately, the secret report pleaded for 'plastic explosive . . . [and] diagrammes illustrating suitable detonator mechanisms'. Contact had been made with Duma Nokwe of the ANC in order that there could be 'close liaison between the two organisations'. The remainder of the report listed possible targets for arson and sabotage including rail routes, 'the Shackleton aircraft at Cape Town', telephone lines, police stations, pass offices, tax offices and granaries. An explosives 'instructor from Europe' would be needed to 'run weekly courses' in Swaziland. The report concluded by noting that:

> discussions with your representative here has led to the formulation of an idea emanating from him that . . . the Group should obtain a small merchant's business in Dar-es-Salaam and place its own proprietor in that business. The business should have a warehouse within the customs area and that warehouse could be used for storage purposes . . . it is therefore suggested that a deep consideration should be given to the immediate payment of a further £20,000 . . . You will continue to receive detailed reports of this

nature and you yourself will be the best judge of whether effective use is being made of these monies.[7]

The BOSS–NIS officer Piet Swanepoel, who investigated the mysterious report, later wrote an unpublished sixty-four-page analysis tracing the 1961 document through to de Crespigny's hurried departure from South Africa. His methodology was similar to Woodward and Bernstein's 'follow the money': 'Evaluators of international and even local politics should pay more attention to the ultimate source of the cash which makes political activity possible. Ideologies, professed or real, may, it seems, be ignored.' Swanepoel quickly discovered that 'the Group' was, in fact, directly linked to the National Committee for Liberation (NCL), later known as the African Resistance Movement (ARM – see page 23). Following the money, Swanepoel decided to consult Companies House in London on the two limited-liability companies registered in London as the owners of the ship and the aircraft. Brijit Transport Ltd had been registered on 16 June 1961, in the names of Anthony Rampton and Alexander Warnock Filson; Paul Di Biase was listed as secretary. Ten months later, the first 'subscribers' resigned and they were replaced by Anthony Champion de Crespigny and Caroline McNaghton. On 20 October 1962, de Crespigny and McNaghton resigned and their places were taken by John and Brenda Lang. It was the same pattern of ownership with the second company, Delia Properties Ltd. Swanepoel then checked whether John Lang was registered as the director of any other companies. He was: Gransight Holdings Ltd.

Gransight had a fascinating board of directors: John Lang, Neville Rubin, Marion Friedman and Jeremy Thorpe. The company secretary was Brenda Lang. Past and present members of the company were Christopher Courtauld, Derek Ingram, Timothy Beaumont, Richard Moore and Randolph Vigne. Gransight had been registered as a company on 7 August 1963, and was dissolved on 3 November 1972. Swanepoel's investigation moved on to a study of *New African* magazine, whose controlling companies, Insight Publications (Pty) Ltd and Granite Publications (Pty) Ltd, shared at different times three of the directors and members of Gransight. Swanepoel pointed out that *New African* had admitted in a leading article in 1966 that from its inception in 1962 the magazine had 'obtained its funds . . . from the Congress for Cultural Freedom'. The exposure of the Congress for Cultural Freedom as a CIA front-organisation in *Ramparts* magazine in 1967 encouraged the excited Afrikaner investigator to believe that Rubin, Friedman and Vigne were vehicles for the CIA.[8] That was, of course, ridiculous.

Returning to de Crespigny, Swanepoel studied the Professor's career, noting his 'membership of the Travellers Club in London, an institution particularly favoured by Foreign Office personnel'. This must have been an NIS joke – surely Swanepoel knew that the Travellers Club was a famous haunt of spooks. By the end of his investigation, Swanepoel was convinced that Anthony de Crespigny was a CIA agent. He wrote in the conclusion to his document: 'The intelligence profession . . . is pursued within a set of unwritten, but very binding rules. One of the most important of these is the one which states that "friendly services" cannot just place any of their officers in another country without clearing . . . the matter with the host service. In South Africa these matters have to be taken up with the [NIS].' Two NIS agents, one of whom was Swanepoel, approached de Crespigny with a long list of questions which he failed to answer. The NIS informed him that 'he was now definitely suspected of being either a fraud or an agent of some sort'. De Crespigny fled South Africa four days later. Swanepoel's final comment on the fleeing Professor was that 'the problem is that the Intelligence profession, despite all its academic openness, is still full of all kinds of secrets. Operations people, for example, do not tell anyone outside their own directorate what they know. Their biggest secrets concern their or their opponents' sources, or agents.'[9]

If it remains difficult to prove whether Anthony de Crespigny was connected to British intelligence, it ought, after more than four decades, to be possible to discuss the nine-page memorandum without ancient politics intervening. Former members of the NCL–ARM accept that anti-apartheid activist John Lang was the author of the document. Randolph Vigne in *Liberals against Apartheid* recalled that Lang's 'charm and ebullience had won . . . him a wide range of influential friends and acquaintances in many places'.[10] The political scientist Magnus Gunther, a former South African Liberal and a relative by marriage of Anthony de Crespigny, published an extended essay on the NCL–ARM in 2004. He described Lang as 'an adventurer with bold ideas' and explained that the report was 'an extraordinary mixture of fact and fancy and contains considerable exaggeration as to what the NCL had achieved, plus astonishing claims for more equipment'. Lang told Gunther in 1992 that he had received two payments of £9,000 and £15,000 from Kwame Nkrumah's Ghana. Gunther also stated, rather boldly, that Swanepoel 'erroneously believed that this funding came from Western intelligence sources'. But Gunther himself is hardly convincing. In the body of the text, he stated: '[Leslie] Rubin introduced Lang to [Geoffrey] Bing, and also asked the

Ghanaian Minister of Finance, K.A. Gbedemah, for financial assistance for Lang and the NCL. As a result, the Ghanaian government gave the NCL/ARM its first foreign subvention in April 1961.' Leslie Rubin, the vice-president of South Africa's Liberal Party, had emigrated to Ghana in 1960; Geoffrey Bing, a former British Labour Party MP, 1945–55, had also emigrated to newly independent Ghana, where he was Nkrumah's Attorney-General from 1957 to 1961. In a footnote, Gunther back-pedalled:

In his autobiography, *Reap the Whirlwind* . . . Geoffrey Bing wrote: 'I know personally of a case where some £50,000 was paid to an individual to arrange for the escape from South Africa of political leaders on the run.' Lang's memorandum emphasised the need for rescuing 'victims of apartheid'. Could Lang be Bing's mystery man? I am convinced from other sources that Bing was referring to Lang, but there is no 'smoking gun'.

It is equally possible that MI6 channelled the funds through Ghana. The key is the date of the 'arrangement' between Lang and his invisible backer: April 1961. As stated in Chapter 1, MI5 handed over responsibility for South Africa to MI6 in March 1961 when the Republic left the Commonwealth. Gunther is quite clear that 'the Group' originated in 'a highly secretive, paramilitary organisation' called 'the Horticulturists', founded in 1959. This was 'primarily an anti-republican movement . . . [and] the world in which Lang was apprenticed into the language and logistics of insurrection'.[11] The anti-republicanism would have played well with the British. It is quite possible that in the early weeks of taking over the intelligence coverage of the Republic, and in the spirit of Sir John Maud's 'reinsurance', a bright spark at MI6 decided to finance Lang's plan to smuggle banned people and provide financial assistance to the liberation movements. It would have been quite typical of British activity to try to use a white South African to mediate violent black unrest. But it would also make sense that British funding would dry up when the threat of arson and explosions became real: it is instructive to recognise that there is no evidence that such items were ever delivered. The document noted that the sponsor had a 'representative' in South Africa. Ghana did not have diplomatic or intelligence representation in the Republic in 1961. When the Swanepoel document received some news coverage in 2000 following its partial publication in *Noseweek* magazine, Magnus Gunther was interviewed by the *Mail & Guardian*. He said that he had:

found a document in 1998 in the Ministry of Justice files in Pretoria that showed that the security services had known as early as 1961 that John Lang, the ARM's moneyman, had received money from Ghana. 'The report, which sets out a summary of all the relevant facts the security services knew about Lang, notes that it was *betroubaar vasgestel* (reliably confirmed) that Lang received £5,000 from the Ghanaian government *om plofstowwe en ammunisie aan to koop om in Suid Afrika to gebruik* (to buy explosives and ammunition to use in South Africa). I have no information on whether this led to any action on the part of the security apparatus but had Mr Swanepoel known of this document he clearly would not have written his paper.'[12]

Gunther's essay (not a book, as he had assured the *Mail & Guardian*) on the ARM made no reference to this fascinating document. He also claimed that the Ghanaians funded the ARM because 'it was the "first on the spot" as the Pan Africanist Congress was too divided at the time'. Professor Bernard Leeman, a former PAC member, explained in a letter to the paper: 'the PAC was formed in April 1959, heavily financed by Nkrumah . . . In September 1962 [Robert] Sobukwe smuggled a message to acting PAC president Potlako Leballo, agreeing to armed resistance. Leballo met Nkrumah, who bought a Swedish freighter for the PAC for £124,000 and had it loaded with arms in Egypt. The ship sailed south in early 1963 . . . to assist the Poqo rising. It never arrived.'[13] Gunther's essay avoided placing these complicated debates on funding into context. One of the odder aspects of what is a very peculiar story is that, following van den Bergh's retirement in 1978, the Johannesburg *Sunday Times* disclosed that one of the reasons for the RI–DMI argument in the 1960s involved the ARM: 'In the early 1960s . . . [DMI] withheld its knowledge of the [ARM] . . . from the security police. It pursued its own investigations using an agent called David Plotz to try to infiltrate the organisation in Cape Town . . . The report from Plotz was handed to [DMI] in December 1962, but details of his cloak and dagger operations . . . were not passed on.'[14]

In September 1998, I tracked Anthony Champion de Crespigny, a five-times-married, large, ruddy-faced man, to a flat in Bath. He was very nervous. Eventually, I asked him outright: 'Were you an intelligence operative? Did you work for MI6 or the CIA?' De Crespigny said that it had all been a terrible mistake; his name had been used for front companies but he barely knew John Lang; and he had had no further involvement with British intelligence after he had flunked his SIS interview in the 1950s. Swanepoel and the NIS had, apparently, put two and two together and made fourteen. De Crespigny fled South Africa because he was terrified and because his work on the Presidential Council was done.[15] I came to the conclusion that he was a 'useful idiot', a man with an unfortunate history that had come back to haunt him. Two years after my meeting with the vanishing Professor, I attended Benjamin Pogrund's London launch for his memoir of his newspaper days *War of Words*. Randolph Vigne, a former ARM member and historian of South Africa's Liberal Party, was present and, without prompting, he told me: 'After you visited Anthony de Crespigny, he telephoned me in a panic: "What are we going to do, Randolph, what are we going to do?" I told him: "It's all water under the bridge. There's nothing anyone can do about it now."' I nodded and didn't comment; it felt as if Vigne was having a little gloat at my expense. I have spoken to Vigne since and he refuses to accept that, as he puts it, 'Lang may have been a hireling of MI6.' But that might be because as Gunther states in his essay: 'Lang's most significant contribution to the NCL[-ARM] was the recruitment of Randolph Vigne.'[16]

In December 2000, I spoke to Professor Neville Rubin, who had been in charge of international affairs for the South African Liberal Party (1962–3). As a member of the ARM he fled South Africa in 1964 and was imprisoned in Mozambique before deportation to Britain. In Britain he worked for Canon Collins's Defence and Aid. Rubin told me that the Thorpe material in the Swanepoel report was designed to 'make salivating Englishmen jump around'. After a few minutes, he admitted that the ARM members had been 'too young and too wet behind the ears to appreciate the difference' between MI5 and MI6. He explained that he had no knowledge of Lang's front companies; that he had seen the boat but not the plane; and that there were too many loose threads in the story to straighten them out now. I told him about my conversation with Randolph Vigne and he responded: 'We may have been patsies but we were legit . . . I regard myself as unwitting.' He then proceeded to make the fair point that in the 1960s before the famous *Ramparts* exposure of CIA front organisations, including the Congress for Cultural Freedom, people had no idea of the sort of activities that international intelligence agencies would engage in.[17] I had never attempted to claim anything else. It should not, of course, be interpreted as a slur on former members of the NCL–ARM to suggest that British intelligence could have played an (invisible) role in the funding of their organisation.

Craig Michael Williamson: The Fat-Spy

With at least £58,000 in start-up funds Major Craig Williamson returned to action in Great Britain; he established a front company in the Isle of

Man in September 1981. African Aviation Consultants employed Peter Casselton, a thirty-seven-year-old British citizen who had been educated in Rhodesia before moving to South Africa and spying in Mozambique for the South African security forces. His 'cover' was that he was a pilot.[18] Six months later, in March 1982, the Security Police exploded a bomb at the ANC's office in London, designed to kill the leadership of the ANC. The operation was planned by Lieutenant-General Johan Coetzee (the head of the Security Police) and Williamson. In late 1981, Joseph Klue (the defence attaché at the South African Embassy) provided Peter Casselton with three metal boxes containing detonators and explosives. One week before the planned attack, Casselton was given 'false passports, details of emergency escape routes out of the United Kingdom, and arms and ammunition'.[19] The other members of the team led by Colonel Piet Goosen, who had supervised the interrogation of Biko in 1977, included Williamson, Major John Adam, Captain Jimmy Taylor, Eugene de Kock, Vic McPherson and Jerry Raven, the explosives expert. Williamson recruited de Kock and Adam from Koevoet in South West Africa–Namibia for the operation. On 14 March 1982, the bomb exploded near the back door of 28 Penton Street, NW1 – the ANC offices. The offices were empty, but the building's caretaker was injured by the explosion.

The evidence suggested that, because the bombing coincided with an international anti-apartheid demonstration, the Security Police had possessed intelligence suggesting that Oliver Tambo would be visiting the ANC's offices at the time of the explosion. According to the TRC report, the team were also carrying 'vials of nerve gas . . . for "added protection"'. The attack had been approved by the Minister of Police, the bomb and other material had been transported in the diplomatic bag and a number of the bombers believed that the Minister of Foreign Affairs, Pik Botha, had approved the operation and assisted in the movement of the explosives. At the TRC Pik Botha 'denied any prior knowledge of the use of the bag'. The bombers were awarded the Police Star for Excellent Service by Louis le Grange, the Minister of Police. The medal ceremony was attended by Johan Coetzee and Mike Geldenhuys. Craig Williamson later informed the *Observer*: 'It was a message to the British government that they were supporting the ANC too much and in times of war there is a spill-over effect.'[20]

A few weeks later, Major Williamson attended an NIS intelligence symposium, where he presented a paper 'on the use of "cover" in secret operations . . . [and] the recruitment of long-term "deep-cover" agents (moles)'. On 17 August 1982, Ruth First was murdered by a parcel-bomb. At the time, she was the research director at the Centre of African Studies at Eduardo Mondlane University in Maputo. Williamson spread a 'smear', later published in the Johannesburg *Star*, that Joe Slovo had murdered Ruth First; Slovo sued the paper and won damages for the unfounded allegation that he had assassinated his own wife.[21] Williamson testified to the TRC that he had been instructed to prepare the bombs and that he 'assigned the task' to his colleague Jerry Raven. In the mid-1990s, Ruth First's daughter Gillian Slovo interviewed Williamson, during which he revealed that '"unbeknown to the ANC, all post from Botswana, Lesotho and Angola was sorted in Johannesburg" . . . He described a cavernous basement room in Jan Smuts airport where retired security branch policemen used specially modified kettles to search the post.' Later, Slovo enquired at the airport and was told by a postal service employee: 'Oh yes . . . I never went there, none of us did, but we had a special name for it. We called it the bomb room.'[22]

On 9 September 1982, Edward Aspinall, a twenty-three-year-old 'professional burglar', was arrested in Liverpool for drunk driving. He 'blurted out all he knew to [the] startled police'. Aspinall told the police that he worked for South African intelligence; he had been employed by Joseph Klue (of the South African Embassy). He believed that Klue had been given his name by a mercenary, John Banks, with whom he had once shared a prison cell. Klue introduced Aspinall to Peter Casselton. In a feeble recreation of van den Bergh's relationship with Charlie Richardson, Aspinall was paid £500 per robbery and he had earned £6,000 including a £4,000 bonus. He understood why the South Africans needed to employ a petty criminal: 'If Casselton opened his mouth it would be political – if I am caught I am just a simple screwsman.' Aspinall led the police to Peter Casselton and tape-recorded a conversation with him before his arrest. Casselton, as soon as he got the opportunity, telephoned Joseph Klue. Aspinall and Casselton were arrested.[23]

The ANC's office in London had been burgled on 20 July 1982. Six weeks later, SWAPO's London base had been similarly invaded. According to an ANC document of the period, 'both burglaries were clearly politically motivated judging from what had been taken'. On 18 September, the ANC learned from 'a South African journalist in London' that Johan Coetzee, head of the Security Police, would be visiting London in connection with the arrest of Aspinall. In fact, Coetzee cancelled his trip. On 16 September, the Anti-Terrorism Squad informed the ANC, and later

SWAPO, that 'there would be a court appearance . . . in connection with the break-ins'. The ANC instructed a solicitor 'to maintain a watching brief' in the case. On 22 September, Detective Chief Inspector Hilton Coles of the Anti-Terrorism Squad informed the ANC's lawyer that three men would appear in court: Peter Casselton and Bertil Wedin, who would be charged with receiving stolen goods. The Inspector believed that they would plead guilty and be fined £50. The third man was Edward Aspinall, who would be charged with the two burglaries; '[his] case would probably take a little longer'. The ANC became concerned that there was going to be an attempt to engineer a 'cover up [to disguise] the political nature of the case and the SA connection'.

On 23 September, the detective 'asked [the court] for a remand pending . . . more serious charges'. Wedin was released on bail and Casselton was remanded in custody; Aspinall had fled. One week later, a charge of 'conspiracy to burgle' was brought against Wedin and Casselton. The ANC observed that 'this is a much more serious charge [which] offers the possibility of the full extent of the SA connection being brought out in evidence'. The Director of Public Prosecutions (DPP) opposed bail, but 'conditional bail' was granted to Wedin. On the same day, a note was discovered in a telephone box near the court. The note was written in Afrikaans, bore the letterhead of a Pretoria law firm and contained instructions for an Afrikaner lawyer. The ANC document revealed that it 'was later discovered that [the lawyer's] name is Goosen'. He was in fact the son of the policeman who had led the operation in March to bomb the ANC's offices.[24] On 26 September, the *Observer* published the story of the telephone-box note and stated perceptively: '[It] has provided a direct link between Pretoria and men being investigated by London police in connection with the bombing of African nationalist offices.'[25]

On 30 September, an NIS agent in the South African Embassy in London, Ben van der Klashorst, was suddenly withdrawn. Van der Klashorst had been named as the chief intelligence operative in Britain in defector Ivan Himmelhoch's *New Statesman* story in 1980 (see page 136). One week later, Casselton and Wedin appeared in court. The DPP informed the magistrate that, although the case involved burglary, it also had 'international and political overtones and concerned intelligence gathering'. Detective Coles said that he believed Casselton to have 'other employers' and that Aspinall 'could [not] have disappeared in the way he has without assistance'. It was also revealed that Casselton had given three false addresses to the police upon his arrest. Aspinall was arrested in Holland a few days later; he was travelling on a false passport and was caught trying to steal a car. The ANC document concluded with a portrait of the three spies; it said of the Swede Bertil Wedin: 'Journalists in [Johannesburg] recognised him as having been in SA in March 1981.'[26]

While the South African spy-ring was awaiting trial, the British liberal newspapers reported on an arms trial at the Old Bailey. It was, as David Pallister commented in the *Guardian*, 'One of the rare occasions when the veil was lifted from South Africa's huge and clandestine efforts to maintain the efficiency of its defence force and to arm anti-government guerrillas in neighbouring black African states.'[27] On 13 October 1982, an A-AM delegation visited the Home Secretary William Whitelaw to ask the government 'to terminate the no-visa agreement with South Africa . . . to expel all South African agents involved in security police operations; and to establish a parliamentary inquiry into the whole subject with a view to making comprehensive recommendations for ending South African intelligence operations in the UK'. The A-AM memorandum delivered to the Home Office 'estimated that one quarter of the "diplomats" at South Africa House were engaged in covert operations on behalf of the [NIS]'.[28]

On 16 December, it was reported that Joseph Klue had returned to South Africa on 23 November, after the Foreign Office had asked the South African Embassy to waive the military attaché's diplomatic immunity and to permit the police 'to interview him in connection with activities against anti-apartheid organisations'. Klue, who had been dubbed 'Inspector Klueseau' by wags in the press, 'had been engaged in activities incompatible with his official status in this country' – the diplomatic euphemism for espionage. The South African response was typically disingenuous. The Embassy 'categorically denied' that any Embassy employee was engaged in spying. Mike Geldenhuys, the Commissioner of Police, said: 'He is not a member of the Security Police.' That was true: Klue was the military attaché – in other words, an MID operative.

On 17 December 1982, Edward Aspinall was imprisoned for eighteen months after pleading guilty to robbery; Peter Casselton was imprisoned for four years after pleading guilty to conspiring to burgle the ANC, PAC and SWAPO London offices. The *Guardian* reported that the prosecuting barrister had said that 'Casselton was a South African agent working in partnership with a man he told the police was called Arthur Clayton. "This man in fact is Major Craig Williamson of the South African Security

Police." ' The court heard that 'maps, documents, photographs, files and address books were stolen from the three offices and Aspinall claimed that the South Africans were able to carry out a successful raid on ANC bases in Mozambique on the strength of the information'. Aspinall also said that he had been asked to 'steal documents from a house in Norway' and that Casselton had said to him: 'Money is no object – you know South Africa has a lot of resources.' Mike Terry of the A-AM described the South African Embassy as 'a nest of spies'.[29]

The *Observer* commented: 'MI5 and the Special Branch seem originally to have been indifferent to, or genuinely ignorant of, the "black bag" gang of burglars operating in London . . . British Intelligence also apparently stood by while the South African Embassy . . . arranged big illegal shipments of small arms via London, using dealers well known to MI5 and MI6 in 1980 and 1981'. A London *Sunday Times* editorial declared: 'We do not agree with those calling for the Embassy to be closed. But the spooks and burglars within deserve no more tolerance than those of the KGB.' The Shadow Home Secretary Roy Hattersley said on ITV's *Weekend World*:

> If what is going on, and what we suspect is going on from London – this spying on private and legitimate organisations – if this was going on from an eastern European Embassy I think British security services would take it a great deal more seriously. My worst fear is that in the security services many individuals actually know what is going on and I suspect that some of the activities are, in their crudest form, anti-communist and therefore are activities they don't want to stamp on.[30]

Hattersley's suspicion has been demonstrated to be well founded by recent research under the new Freedom of Information Act which has revealed that the British Special Branch spied on members of the A-AM as late as 1983. The spying involved recording details about A-AM members (such as car registration numbers and telephone numbers) and employing A-AM members to work as 'sources'.[31] In March 1983, General Johan Coetzee visited London. The *Guardian* later reported that 'British intelligence sources believed that the South Africans established a new London burglary team in April'. Bertil Wedin was found not guilty in the same month, although he admitted that he had been paid rent, travelling expenses to Canada and Cyprus and £1,000 monthly for ten months for supplying 'newspaper cuttings, reports and analyses' to African Aviation Consultants. On May Day 1983, the A-AM offices were robbed again:

'The materials taken included files on the recent Old Bailey case of Edward Aspinall.'[32] The imprisonment of Peter Casselton in 1982 was only the second time that a southern African intelligence agent had been sent to prison in Britain; the first was Norman Blackburn sixteen years earlier (see page 59).

On 28 June 1984, ANC member Jeanette Schoon, aged thirty-five, and her daughter Katryn, aged six, were killed by a Security Police letter-bomb in Lubango, Angola. The bomb was apparently intended for her husband, Marius Schoon. As Williamson smugly informed the TRC years later, 'The 11th Commandment was well known' within the security forces: 'Thou shalt not be found out.' He claimed in 1995 that the deaths of Jeanette and Katryn Schoon had 'disillusioned him'. He wrote an article in the *South African Journal of Criminal Law* in which he suggested that:

> using armed force against the civilian population symbolises the end of civil-
> ian government, and 'that was the end of my career. I came to the conclu-
> sion that the war was lost . . . the strategy that was being used was wrong.
> It was getting more and more military and less and less political, and it had
> to go the other way. So I decided to get involved in proper intelligence
> work, especially on the international scene.[33]

It seems far more likely that, in the patronage-driven South African spy world, Williamson had been drawn into the argument between his former handler, General Coetzee, the Commissioner of Police, and the MID. *Work in Progress* reported in 1988 that, when the rioting returned in 1984, Coetzee (of whom Bram Fischer had once said, 'After the revolution, he will be my garden boy') argued for a policy of containment. Coetzee rec-ommended 'that by selectively removing leadership and exploiting tensions in the extraparliamentary opposition, the opposition could be controlled and manipulated without forcing it underground, where control was more difficult'. The declaration of a national state of emergency in June 1986 'marked the demise of Coetzee'. In 1987, the former BOSS official retired one year early. In 1994, Coetzee spoke to Denis Herbstein of 'an ongoing and unresolved debate in the upper reaches of government about the merits of the "Argentinian route" '.[34]

In February 1986, the glossy magazine *Leadership* carried a feature art-icle by Craig Williamson, who the magazine reported had 'resigned from the Security Police last year. He now operates privately as a security ana-lyst.' Williamson's article examined the security condition of South Africa for the year ahead. The report suggested that 'the revolutionary wants to eliminate negotiation. He wants to polarise . . . He attempts to manipulate our society by violence and unrest. He infiltrates organisations, uses radical slogans in political statements, all of which are designed to create increasingly hostile attitudes between black and white.' And the government? 'Through judicious but firm use of state power and the security forces we can protect what needs to be protected and destroy what needs to be destroyed.'[35] Williamson's article illustrated the degree to which the servants of the security state regurgitated their own propaganda and revelled in their own ambiguous violence.

Williamson had only partially entered the private sector; he had also joined the MID. His central MID project was the establishment of Longreach Ltd. He told the *Observer* in 1995 that the company 'gave him cover and access to anywhere he wished to go'. It was also a genuine security company, which in 1986 took over the security for President Albert René of the Seychelles. From 1986, the MID was in effect performing the intelligence function for an independent state. The managing director of Longreach was Mike Irwin, a Falklands war veteran. The *Observer* reported that 'Longreach recruited former Ugandan Army officers and bought a shop near the ANC's Solomon Mahlangu School in Tanzania, where it eavesdropped . . . It used Ghanaians and Malawians to recruit spies in London and Britons to recruit spies in African countries where the ANC was active.' Most people involved 'did not know they were spying for the apartheid regime' because Longreach was ostensibly a British company. Alternatively, as the *Mail & Guardian* announced a year after the *Observer* story, 'Longreach . . . Ltd failed in all its endeavours. It couldn't sell its intelligence reports . . . Mike Irwin . . . said he can't recall performing a single useful task during his two years with the company.'

Longreach did, however, have a relationship with the International Freedom Foundation (IFF), a Washington-based organisation which was effectively run from Johannesburg. IFF was also an MID front. Williamson told the *Observer*: 'We couldn't convince Americans that apartheid was right. The only chance of manipulating things to survive just a little bit longer was to paint the ANC as a product of the international department of the Soviet Communist Party.'[36] The IFF was started by Russell Crystal, a militant South African anti-communist, who simply asked the MID to fund his organisation. In the early 1990s, it was very active in the reports of human rights abuses in the ANC prison camps in Angola, as was *Aida Parker's Newsletter*, the independent publication which Parker produced following her departure from the *Citizen*. Like the Information Department in the 1970s, the MID assisted Jack Abramoff, the foundation's first president, to enter the film business. The motion picture *Red Scorpion* (1989) starring Grace Jones and Dolph Lundgren was funded, in part, with MID money. The Conservative MP for Basingstoke, Andrew Hunter, also had dealings with the IFF. He told the *Observer* that the South African Security Police and the NIS had given him 'intelligence' which he used to produce reports on the links between the ANC and the IRA, 'Hunter's key contact . . . was Colonel Vic McPherson' who had been involved in the bombing of the ANC offices in 1982. Hunter, who joined Ian Paisley's Democratic Unionists before retiring at the 2005 election, said that 'Everything they told me was in the hands of MI5 and MI6 as soon as possible.' The MID funding to the IFF ended in 1992, and the foundation itself closed in 1995.[37]

In December 2005, the *Washington Post* described the former IFF president, Jack Abramoff, as 'the central figure in what could become the biggest congressional corruption scandal in generations'. Abramoff, whose fall caused significant embarrassment to both the Bush administration and the Republican Party, overcharged Native American groups for lobbying and public relations, lavished contributions and gifts on elected politicians and 'quietly paid op-ed columnists thousands of dollars to write favorably about his clients'. Rather than face trial, he pleaded guilty 'to fraud, tax evasion and conspiracy to bribe public officials in a deal that requires him to provide evidence about members of Congress'. Abramoff is expected to receive a prison sentence of at least ten years. In South Africa, the *Mail & Guardian* revealed that Russell Crystal, Abramoff's old IFF colleague, had reinvented himself as 'an influential behind-the-scenes operator' in the white DA opposition. Crystal was apparently 'responsible for making sure every Tony [Leon] event works' (see page 2).[38]

Craig Williamson merged his MID work with that of an Italian millionaire and 'diplomat', Giovanni Mario Ricci. In 1987, Williamson was appointed to a position, as a National Party member, on P.W. Botha's President's Council. But, despite the celebrity attention he has on numerous occasions attracted, Williamson has remained a frightened man. The children of Ruth First and Jeanette Schoon tried to pursue him through the civil courts in 2002, and Peter Hain assured the *Observer* in 1995 that he would be prosecuted for the London bombing if he set foot in Britain.[39] After confessing to an ANC intelligence officer in 1994, he wrote a letter to the Johannesburg *Sunday Independent*. It is the authentic voice of Joseph Conrad's sleazy Mr Verloc:

> A senior member of the ANC and MK recently said to me, 'Craig, the difference between your people and ours is that our people always backed us up which yours do not do. They are too busy sipping champagne with us at cocktail parties and trying to be our friends.' How true his words have proven to be, in the light of the National Party's pathetic performance on the amnesty/indemnity issue. I hope that those politicians, who are in such an incompetent, self-serving, pension-protecting and cowardly way, betraying the members and political heads of the security forces which kept the NP in power for so long, do not think that we have forgotten who gave us the orders to do what was done during the conflicts of the past. Those who sat on the State Security Council, those who chaired the National Security Management System structures, those who signed the orders, those who often begged us to restore order in their ideological apartheid creations must know that we remember them, though they seem too frightened to remember us. I suppose they also believe it was the NP's political brilliance which kept them in power for 46 years and not security force action. We remember too, those who were paid to serve on State-funded gravy train projects – on women, youth, the church, black political groups and others, especially those who are currently serving NP Members of Parliament.[40]

Dieter Gerhardt: The Sailor–Spy

Perhaps the most successful spy in South African history was the naval officer Dieter Gerhardt. Unfortunately for the apartheid intelligence agencies, which didn't even manage to arrest him, Gerhardt was working for the Soviet Union. Between 1962 and 1982, he supplied the most sensitive military secrets of South Africa, Britain, France, Germany, the United States and Israel to his handlers in GRU, Soviet military intelligence. Born in November 1935 in Cape Town, Gerhardt was the son of recent German immigrants to South Africa; his father was interned in Koffiefontein during the war for suspected pro-Nazi sympathies. In 1956, Gerhardt 'passed out as Sword of Honour winner at Simonstown Naval Academy'. He was then sent for further training in London. A British naval colleague later told the *Mail on Sunday*: 'He was certainly a lot more liberal than most white South Africans I met. There was no question about Dieter not sharing with coloured officers on our course. It was at the time a quite open disregard for his country's political views.' In 1958, he met and married Janet Coggin.

Over the next few years, he served as an engineering officer on Royal Navy ships off Cyprus and Iceland and attended: 'HMS *Excellent*, the gunnery school . . . at Portsmouth; HMS *Collingwood*, the electronics and radio training school; HMS *Tenby*, a Type 12 frigate; the RN mine school in Portsmouth; and the Parachute Training Course at Abingdon'.[41]

In the early 1960s, he contacted 'a number of senior figures in the South African Communist Party and told them I wanted to do my part for the blacks' struggle'. After checking that Gerhardt was authentic, Bram Fischer handed his details on to Moscow. The GRU gave Gerhardt the codename Felix. In 1963 and 1964, he spent eighteen months in Britain 'attending advanced weapons courses'. He then went to Switzerland for 'a skiing vacation' while, in reality, travelling to the Soviet Union for training. Gerhardt explained the training to the Israeli journalist Ronen Bergman in 2000:

> He was taught to use miniature photography equipment, how to develop the film and encode it in microscopic negatives that he would affix to the periods and commas in letters he sent to various European addresses. He learned Morse code, surveillance and evasion methods, and was taught how to survive interrogations, including a special course on how to beat polygraph tests. Dozens of photographs were taken of Gerhardt wearing different kinds of clothing, in wigs, and with false beards and moustaches, and these photos were used for the many false passports he was supplied with over the years.[42]

Dieter Gerhardt's marriage to Janet Coggin had broken down, after eight years, in 1966. In 1999, she published a semi-fictionalised account of their marriage, *The Spy's Wife*, in which she revealed that he had confessed his spying and attempted to recruit her. She returned to Europe but remained silent, 'afraid for the lives of their three children'. Coggin paints a picture of Gerhardt as an egotist, who was not remotely interested in the ANC–SACP or the anti-apartheid cause.[43] Gerhardt met his second wife, Ruth Johr, at Klosters, the Swiss ski resort. They were married in 1969. He informed her of his espionage work and she agreed to work with him, undergoing training in Moscow. Two years earlier, he had learned that the South Africans had been told 'that there was a serious security leak in their structures'. His concerned Soviet handlers invented a cover story for him to be used in the event of capture: he was supposed to say 'that he was an operative for the Mossad . . . He had names of Israeli handlers, places in Israel where he had supposedly trained and many more details'. Gerhardt is particularly useful as a witness to the pressures on the intelligence agent:

> I estimate that I devoted something like 45 hours a week to espionage work, more than I spent on my real work . . . It was hell, there is no other word for it . . . On the one hand, the demands from Moscow centre were impossible. They always wanted more and more and more. There was no end to it. Very quickly you become a slave to the shopping list and you effectively lose control of your life. I would call it controlled paranoia. Life is filled with small moments of shock, moments in which you are certain that everything is lost, when everyone understands who you are, and arrest, interrogation, torture and execution are just around the corner.

As Dieter Gerhardt's naval career developed, he had access to a substantial number of military secrets. He is understood to have supplied the GRU with a multitude of documents. These are reported to have included information on: NATO 'smart mines'; the full text of the secret Anglo-American agreement on Diego Garcia, the Indian Ocean island 'which was evacuated [and] turned into a centre of intelligence operations'; specifications of German missiles and helicopters; the archetype of the French Exocet missile (see page 169); the 'shock resistance' of individual Royal Navy ships; Selenia fire and weapon control systems; developments in sonar equipment; the Seacat missile system; technical documentation on the Sea Sparrow surface-to-air missile; and developments in electronic warfare, especially with regard to torpedoes. One of the most interesting subjects on which Gerhardt spied for the Soviet Union was the South African–Israeli nuclear programme. He reported that the apartheid state 'began to develop an independent nuclear option in 1964'. The nuclear programme was driven not by the military but by academics at the Council for Scientific and Industrial Research; the project was codenamed Kerktoring (Church Tower). In the 1970s, Gerhardt managed to arrange a visit to the Kalahari Desert project centre and supplied photographs to the GRU. His espionage led directly to the most dramatic publicisation of South Africa's nuclear ambitions when the Soviet Union raised the subject with the United States. The *Los Angeles Times* reported on 27 August 1977: 'Because of the photographic evidence assembled after the Russians made their concern known, the State Department moved last weekend to seek assurances from Pretoria that no bomb would be set off.'[44]

Soon after the Yom Kippur war (1973), Gerhardt discovered (see page 117) that South Africa was establishing a military alliance with Israel.

He informed the Soviet Union that in November 1974 the Israeli Defence Minister Shimon Peres had held a secret meeting in Geneva with the South African Minister of Defence P.W. Botha. 'A massive document, consisting of hundreds of pages', was distributed for review among South Africa's senior military officers:

> The document . . . dealt with a mutual defence pact between the two countries, according to which each would assist the other in wartime by supplying spare parts and ammunition from its emergency stocks. Each country agreed that its territory would be used to store all types of weapons for the other country. The clause that outraged me most in the agreement was called 'Chalet'. Within its framework, Israel agreed to arm eight Jericho 2 missiles with what were described as 'special warheads'. I asked the chief of staff what that meant and he told me what was obvious: atomic bombs.[45]

A document unearthed by the South African History Archive at the University of the Witwatersrand is entitled 'The Jericho Weapon System' and dated 21 March 1975. The report proposed the purchase of the weapon system and started with the assumption 'that the missiles will be armed with nuclear warheads manufactured in the RSA [Republic of South Africa] or acquired elsewhere'. Under the heading 'The need for a nuclear deterrent', the document noted that an analysis by the Director of Strategic Studies had concluded that 'a direct and/or indirect nuclear threat against the RSA has developed to the point of being a real danger'. Among the 'factors' provided for the proposal was the belief that China might supply a nuclear weapon to a terrorist organisation or an 'OAU "liberation army"'. As ever the cultural cringe towards the West played a role: 'The Director of the United States "Arms Control Agency" maintains that nuclear weapons will become available . . . [to terrorists] within the next ten years.' The military strategists believed that the Jericho system would act as a deterrent: 'Should it become generally known that the RSA possesses a nuclear weapon and that we would use it if we were subjected to nuclear attack, such a deterrent strategy could be used as a positive weapon in our defence.' Finally, the document attached two maps which indicated the distance that a Buccaneer aircraft could travel, 'calculated on the assumption that a bomb load of 8 × 1,000 lb bombs [is] being carried'. Depressingly, the maps were out of date – they had been drawn in the colonial period featuring countries like Nyasaland (Malawi) and Northern Rhodesia (Zambia).[46]

In the late 1970s, Gerhardt served on the 'planning and operations staff' in Pretoria where he had access to the full range of military intelligence secrets. In 1981, he was appointed one of the four commandants, in charge of the docks, of Simonstown naval base. He was also a naval representative 'at the highest levels of the state security apparatus with access to the State Security Council'. At the end of 1982, he went to the United States to attend an advanced mathematics course at Syracuse University. Dieter Gerhardt was captured in a New York hotel room on 8 January 1983: ' "The door burst open to admit agents from the CIA, the FBI and . . . MI6. One of them addressed me by my code name, Felix, and I knew the game was over" . . . Ruth [Gerhardt] was arrested the same night at their home in South Africa. "Good evening, Mrs Rosenberg," the secret service agent said as he opened the door, alluding to the Americans, Julius and Ethel Rosenberg, executed in [1953] for spying for the Soviet Union.' Gerhardt told Bergman that 'at first the Americans tried to double me.' After two weeks he was returned to South Africa.[47]

On 26 January 1983, P.W. Botha announced Gerhardt's arrest. Over the next few weeks, Gerhardt said, 'representatives of foreign intelligence services began to arrive in order to question me about their spheres of interest. The French came and the Germans and the British and, of course, the Israelis.' The South African interrogators were determined to discover the names of other Soviet spies in South Africa. After three months of questioning, Gerhardt said, he gave them the names 'of several officials . . . from the Ministry of Defence and the State President's Office, who were totally uninvolved' in his espionage work. They later discovered that he had 'conveyed . . . between 400,000 and 500,000 pages of documents' to the Soviet Union.[48] Gerhardt's trial started on 5 September 1983. It lasted for four months and was held *in camera* at the Cape Town Supreme Court. Dieter Gerhardt escaped the death sentence for 'high treason', which he had expected, but received life imprisonment. His wife Ruth was sentenced to ten years in prison. It was widely speculated in the South African newspapers that the Gerhardts would soon, like Yuriy Loginov and Major Aleksei Kozlov, be subject to the traditional spy-swap. But they remained in prison in South Africa. F.W. de Klerk released Gerhardt in August 1992, following a personal intervention from the Russian President Boris Yeltsin.[49] Ruth Gerhardt had been released a few years earlier and had waited for her husband. They moved to Switzerland following his release.

In November 1983, the Muldergate investigative journalist Mervyn Rees, who had access to a 'trunkload' of documents relating to Gerhardt, wrote the *Mail on Sunday*'s 'world exclusive' on the subject. One senior intelligence expert told Rees: 'You can take it that anything of significance in the naval field over the past dozen or so years, he knew about . . . He was at least as effective as Philby.' The central British problem, and there were many, was that Gerhardt had compromised the Polaris nuclear deterrent programme. Rees explained:

> As a naval attaché at the South African Embassy in London, he placed advertisements in British newspapers seeking Royal Navy technicians and civilian specialists to join the South African Navy, which was then building a submarine fleet. More than 1,800 men applied. Many were in sensitive posts with access to top secret equipment and documents, but Gerhardt concentrated his efforts on those involved with Polaris. Some of the men appeared during their interviews with Gerhardt to be disenchanted with the Royal Navy, short of money – or both. Gerhardt passed on more than 100 names to his controllers at the Moscow headquarters of the GRU . . . MI5 is now faced with the frightening possibility that some of them were approached by the Russians and that there are undiscovered agents in the Polaris programme. An intelligence man said: 'It was as if Yuri Andropov [the head of the KGB] had come to Britain and put an advertisement in the papers saying "Spy wanted – must have access to Polaris." It was a brilliant and potentially devastating operation.'[50]

The Times rubbished the *Mail on Sunday*'s revelations. All Gerhardt's contacts in the UK 'occurred at least 20 years ago and related to equipment which could now be as much as 30 years old'. The suggestion that the Polaris nuclear submarines could have been 'prejudiced' was countered by a statement from the Ministry of Defence that 'all those associated with the Polaris programme would have been very carefully screened'. The Ministry of Defence added 'that it was confident Commodore Gerhardt did not have access to classified information about the South Atlantic operation [the Falklands war]'.[51] Intriguingly, Mervyn Rees recalled that following the exclusive, which was not offered to the Ministry of Defence for comment before publication, the *Mail on Sunday* was silenced by a government D-Notice. In June 1984, the *Washington Post* reverted to the original story. Quoting a US intelligence official, it reported that Gerhardt had 'one of the most extraordinary careers in modern espionage history . . . [He] is no ordinary spy. He is, in fact, the first flag officer of any country with ties to NATO who has been turned by the Soviets since the start of the Cold War . . . Gerhardt has been a member of "the Club" where there is a lot of camaraderie and information exchange to which he had access. There is no telling what this man might have picked up over the years.' The *Post* also suggested that 'the first tip that Gerhardt was working covertly' was from Mossad.[52]

The apartheid state could not resist one more attempt to rewrite the story of South Africa's genuine 'super-spy'. In February 1992, the South African Police magazine *Servamus* published an article by Marina Conradie on Dieter Gerhardt. She had been granted access to both the court papers and the investigating officers and reported that it was 'a story bordering on a conspiracy in a James Bond movie'. While supporting much of Gerhardt's later testimony, Conradie claimed that he had been driven primarily by financial gain. Interestingly, she sustained the South African untruth that he had been captured in the Republic. Conradie concluded: 'Gerhardt is by no means a political prisoner. His deed of high treason came forth from much more than just ideological differences. He is an egotistical, work-orientated person who, for his own profit, stabbed his country in the back. This is a despicable deed of which the four walls of his cell will remind him every day of his life.'[53]

9

'Take the Pain'

Sentenced to death in September 1987 for murdering a . . . farmer – not a political crime, but a cold-blooded killing – Nofemela had hoped that his colleagues in the security police would save him from the gallows. Senior policemen had sent messages to him in his death cell asking him not to talk about his role in the death squads. They had promised to save his life in return for his absolute silence. Three days before he was due to meet the hangman, he was visited by a security police officer who told him that there was nothing they could do for him. He would have to 'take the pain'. Nofemela realised that he had been betrayed, called his attorney . . . and made an affidavit.

Jacques Pauw, *In the Heart of the Whore*, 1991[1]

TERROR WAS A central feature of the apartheid regime throughout the 1980s. The Smit and Biko murders in 1977 had opened a door that could not be closed. The killing took many forms: the Vlakplaas police death squad, the Civil Co-operation Bureau (CCB), cross-border military operations and the 'targeted assassinations' of ANC members both in South Africa and abroad. The intensity of the brutality would be heightened during the insurrection of the mid-1980s. This chapter also considers three unsolved 'murders': of President Olof Palme of Sweden, who was assassinated in 1986; of the Mozambican President Samora Machel, who died in an aeroplane crash in 1986; and of Dulcie September, the ANC representative in Paris, who was assassinated in 1988. Some writers believe that Machel's death was not a murder, merely the result of 'human error plain and simple', as Hilton Hamann wrote in 2001.[2] Aeroplane crashes are notoriously difficult to explain without the requisite technical knowledge, but I believe that the circumstantial evidence is strong enough to warrant an examination of the case.

Vlakplaas

Dirk Coetzee was born in April 1945, the child of a postal worker. He followed his father into the Post Office in 1963 and was employed in the Investigation Branch until 1969. After nine months of training in the South African Navy, he joined the police. In July 1970, he graduated with distinction from the Police College in Pretoria. By 1973, he had passed the warrant officer's examination and trained as a dog handler and scuba diver. From January to March 1974, he served in Rhodesia as a specialist dog handler. To the animal-loving reader this might appear to be rather a charming job, but it should be remembered that Coetzee's beasts would have been vicious 'attack dogs'. Although not directly involved in engagements with the guerrilla enemy, Coetzee assisted the Rhodesian Special Branch in burying the bodies of dead guerrilla fighters. Returning to South Africa, he passed the examinations to be promoted lieutenant. At the Police College, he attended lectures on the ANC given by Brigadier Neels du Plooy. The lectures were celebrated within the force because of the semi-religious fervour du Plooy brought to his task: 'He entered the room with an arsenal of enemy armoury that gave an ominous and impressive weight to his words. [His] lectures consisted of cycles of emotion. He would start in a calm and collected manner and gradually work himself into a frenzy that left the audience in a trance. He supported his claims with a display of subversive and banned literature that ordinary citizens could never see.'[3]

In June 1976, Coetzee was responsible for guarding 'key points' during the Soweto uprising, particularly the city's mortuary. Within a few months, he was transferred to the small town of Volksrust as the station commander. In 1977, he was recruited to the Security Police and posted to the Swazi border post of Oshoek. Coetzee swiftly adjusted to a world of 'dirty tricks' (proactive attacks on ANC supporters living in Swaziland, including bombings) and petty crime (stealing cars to be supplied to Rhodesian Special Branch and importing pornographic films). Following the MK bombing of the SASOL petroleum plant at Secunda in the Transvaal in June 1980, Coetzee was instructed to exact revenge by blowing up an ANC 'transit house' in Swaziland. The ensuing explosions killed an MK fighter and a small child; fifty-three-houses over a distance of three kilometres were damaged. In August 1980, Dirk Coetzee was promoted to captain and sent to Pretoria to head the Vlakplaas counter-insurgency unit.[4]

Vlakplaas had been founded in 1979, ostensibly as a base for 'askaris'. The term originated in colonial Kenya and referred to loyal troops or security guards. But during the Mau Mau emergency of the 1950s, the British pioneered the development of 'pseudo-terrorists, units of black Africans employed by the colonial government to live exactly like the nationalist guerrillas, to move far behind enemy lines and gather intelligence'. Askaris of this type were widely used in Rhodesia and the Portuguese Empire. The most developed askari force was RENAMO in Mozambique, which eventually grew into a genuine political movement. When Coetzee arrived at Vlakplaas in 1980, there were seventeen South African askaris based in the unit, paid a monthly stipend of R200. In addition three former ZAPU guerrillas worked as labourers on the farm and RENAMO fighters would sometimes visit. As Jacques Pauw, the chronicler of the death squads, explained: 'From beginning to end, the primary function of the Vlakplaas squads was surveillance and the detection of infiltrators. It was inevitable, however, that Vlakplaas would become involved in the secret and unconventional war against the enemy.' Coetzee organised the askaris into four separate squads, introduced white officers and obtained illegal Russian-made weapons.[5]

Captain Dirk Coetzee's experience of death-squad killing started in October 1981. Selby 'Bab' Mavuso, an MK guerrilla, had been abducted during the Matola raid on 30 January 1981 (see page 152). The Security Police hoped to recruit him as an askari, but Mavuso refused to be turned. Enraged by Mavuso's exhortation that the police should 'charge me or shoot me', and lacking solid evidence to bring a charge, it was decided that Vlakplaas would murder the ANC fighter. At the same time, Brigadier Willem Schoon, head of the Security Police's ANC–PAC desk, instructed Coetzee to 'get rid of "poor Peter" as well'. Peter Dlamini had left South Africa in 1978 and joined the ANC, which had sent him to Bulgaria for training. In April 1981, he turned himself in at the South African Embassy in Greece. Returned to the Republic, he was quickly recruited by the Security Police and sent to join the Vlakplaas unit, but, according to Coetzee, he proved a poor askari – hence the decision to hasten his end. Coetzee visited General Lothar Neethling, head of the police forensic laboratory, in order to obtain poison to kill the men. Coetzee attempted to poison his victims three times, increasing the dose on each occasion, but they would not die. Eventually, the pair were shot and their bodies were burned on the banks of the Komati river, close to the border with Mozambique. Near the improvised funeral pyre, Dirk Coetzee and his colleagues lit a second fire, around which they sat drinking beer and enjoying a braai (barbecue). After seven hours, the captives' ashes were disposed of in the river.[6]

The determination to destroy the bodies of death-squad murder victims in South Africa demonstrated that the police were concerned that even a censored press and a compromised judiciary might still be able to expose their activities. Later, death squads would get rid of bodies with dynamite. In neighbouring countries caution was abandoned: Koevoet operative and security policeman Paul Erasmus told the American reporter David Goodman that in South West Africa, 'If you killed, it didn't matter. And they died like flies . . . We beat and [electric] shocked . . . the hell out of people . . . I watched human beings bite their own tongues off.' Coetzee's next 'operation' was a twenty-four-year-old MK soldier who had fallen into the hands of the Security Police. Sizwe Kondile was one of SACP rising star Chris Hani's aides and had been arrested in the Orange Free State, having driven from Lesotho in Hani's car. He was sent to the Eastern Cape for questioning by the Security Police and suffered brain damage during his interrogation. Coetzee later testified that Colonel Nic van Rensburg had explained that 'a doctor had said that Kondile had blood on the brain and if they wanted to avoid a Steve Biko case, they would have to do something'. Van Rensburg met Coetzee at a farm near the Mozambique border where they drugged Kondile with Neethling's 'knockout drops', shot him and cremated the body. Years later, when Coetzee testified at the TRC, he appealed to Kondile's mother for a forgiveness that she refused to grant. She later commented in an interview: 'It is easy for Mandela and Tutu to forgive . . . They lead vindicated lives. In my life nothing, not a single thing, has changed since my son was burnt by barbarians . . . nothing. Therefore, I cannot forgive.'[7]

The murder of the well-known, politically active Durban lawyer Griffiths Mxenge on 19 November 1981 was not so easily disguised. The killers, under the instruction of Captain Dirk Coetzee, poisoned Mxenge's dogs and staged a car-breakdown to entrap the ANC lawyer. One of the killers, Almond Nofemela, later described the hijack in an affidavit: 'Mxenge stopped behind the bakkie [pick-up van] . . . and asked whether he could help us. I opened the car and I said "Yes please". He then switched off his ignition and at the same time I pulled my firearm, a Makarov pistol.' The killers transported Mxenge to the Umlazi football stadium: 'We then all stabbed him several times. He immediately died and we carried on butchering him.' The death squad then stole various items including Mxenge's car, which was later discovered burned out, in order to disguise the murder as a robbery. Each one of the four killers was paid R1,000. Griffiths Mxenge's wife Victoria, also an ANC lawyer, identified the body at the Durban government mortuary and informed the press: 'My husband died in great pain. His throat was slashed, his stomach ripped open and his ears almost cut off. The rest of his body was covered in stab wounds. I don't believe this is the work of ordinary thugs, it was done by someone opposed to what he stood for.' The head of the Security Police, Johan Coetzee, suggested that Mxenge might have been killed by the ANC. This would become a familiar riposte as the death-squad killings grew in number. At Mxenge's burial, the mourners set upon a Transkei security policeman, who was attempting to tape-record the speeches, and killed him.[8]

In December 1981, Dirk Coetzee was transferred from Vlakplaas to the Narcotics Bureau. By 1984, he was in the flying squad, a significant demotion. In December 1984, Coetzee was suspended from the force. Meanwhile, he met two journalists, Martin Welz and Jacques Pauw, who worked for the Afrikaans-language newspaper *Rapport*. They listened to his stories but, lacking international outlets, had no idea how to publicise the death squads in a country where censorship was both a physical reality and an invisible restraint. Pauw recalls that 'Welz suggested that we should keep the knowledge to ourselves until we had an opportunity to publish.'[9] In 1986, Coetzee was discharged from the police. Nearly four years later, askari Almond Nofemela, in rage at being instructed by a former colleague to 'take the pain' for a criminal killing, and in what turned out to be a successful attempt to avoid execution, announced that he had been a member of a South African death squad. As David Beresford wrote in 1989: 'The quotation – "take the pain" – is worth savouring more for the frame of mind which it discloses than the detail . . . It reflects the extraordinary arrogance of police senior officers in imagining that Nofemela would tamely have his neck broken rather than implicate them in murder.' It was even more outrageous because Nofemela had been a good student of the security culture. Later he made a significant statement which drew from the core philosophy of the military–industrial alliance that had given birth to Vlakplaas. He was asked in March 1990 at the Harms Commission which investigated the death squads, 'whether he did not feel that it was wrong to pursue criminal activities under the protection of the police. Nofemela thought for a while. Then he shrugged in the witness box. "Private enterprise," he said.'[10]

Dirk Coetzee rushed to talk 'on the record'. The radical Afrikaans-language paper *Vrye Weekblad* published his story in November 1989 and the former death-squad leader fled to London, where he met Jacob Zuma of the ANC's intelligence wing. Unlike the late 1970s, when the A-AM and the ANC had

failed to exploit the BOSS 'defectors', Zuma recognised that Coetzee's revelations were a crucial propaganda weapon for the ANC. The ANC protected
the former policeman and later found a job for him within the National
Intelligence Agency (NIA – see page 342). Antjie Krog wrote of Dirk Coetzee
that it had been his 'dream to become a member of the elite corps, the cream
of the crop, the hand-picked core of the security forces'. She noted that he 'has
often been accused of stretching stories and fabricating details. Yet it is pre-
cisely these details that make it difficult to dismiss his evidence . . . [he] is an
expert on banal statistics.' Coetzee's description of the cheapness of life in the
hands of Vlakplaas reads like a demented Masonic ritual: 'The orders were
given orally, one to one. No diaries, no written reports. Among ourselves, says
Coetzee, we developed our own body language. The wink of an eye, the nod
of a head, could spell someone's end.'[11]

Eugene Alexander de Kock was born in January 1949 into a typical
Afrikaner family. His father was a magistrate and a member of the
Broederbond. In 1968, he joined the South African Police, where in the
words of his contemporary Paul Erasmus he was indoctrinated in 'a culture of hatred'. Rejected by the elite Special Task Force due to his poor
eyesight, de Kock completed nine tours of duty in Rhodesia between
1968 and 1975. He later observed that he had learned an important lesson
from the Rhodesians: 'Why keep to the Queensberry rules and fight one
boxer when you can kick them in the balls and kill all three?' He also told
Jeremy Gordin: 'In all my years of service I was never given a copy of the
Geneva Convention and never received any training in it.' In January 1977,
Lieutenant de Kock was appointed station commander in Ruacana, South
West Africa–Namibia. Two years later, he joined a newly formed police
counter-insurgency unit, Koevoet (Crowbar), which had been designed
to develop askaris and destroy SWAPO's intelligence and guerrilla networks. De Kock's first task was 'source-handling – that is, intelligence-
gathering'.[12] Koevoet was the perfect training ground for a future
commander of a South African death squad: life in Ovamboland and
across the border in Angola was cheap. Denis Herbstein, in *The Devils are
among Us*, explained:

> These were not 'bobbies in the bush', but bogus policemen trained in the
> art of ambushing, tracking, bush survival and murder. The dirty task of caus-
> ing enemies to disappear had been assigned to a specially groomed squad.
> Its formal title was the cumbersome Special Operations K unit of the South
> African Security Police, alternatively COIN, for Counter-Insurgency Unit,

but its founder [Colonel] Hans Dreyer personally preferred the Koevoet pseudonym. Law and Order Minister Louis le Grange encouraged the name by describing it as 'the crowbar which prises terrorists out of the bushveld like nails from rotten wood'. Off duty, members of Koevoet wore T-shirts proclaiming 'Murder is our business – and business is good'.[13]

The former military commanders have claimed that Koevoet was not a respected unit: General Constand Viljoen later recalled: 'I could never agree with the methods of Koevoet . . . They had a cruelty about them that certainly didn't further the hearts and minds of the people.' General Jannie Geldenhuys, who commanded the SADF in South West Africa, added: 'They would, for example, go into an area, "clean" it up, then collect the bodies and drag them through the town behind their vehicles.' The South African author Peter Stiff, in his panegyric to Koevoet, responded: 'It just didn't happen . . . The closest was when bodies of insurgents were strapped to the mudguards of Casspirs [armoured personnel carriers] and taken to Koevoet bases.' Nevertheless, the official figures revealed that between January 1979 and December 1981 the unit killed 603 'insurgents' and captured 171. As de Kock later made clear, Koevoet was not preoccupied with the need to take prisoners: 'I was told by Colonel Hans Dreyer to kill certain members of SWAPO who had been arrested. Their intelligence uses had been exhausted and he didn't want to be bothered with keeping them alive.' By 1983, when de Kock requested a transfer to Pretoria, 'the members of my own section . . . boasted the highest kill rate of all the Koevoet units'.[14]

Koevoet continued to operate in South West Africa until 1989. Denis Herbstein noted one particularly hideous feature of life in Koevoet: 'Special constables were paid *kopgeld* (literally, head money) for every guerrilla brought in, dead or alive. The amount ranged between R2,000 and R20,000.' Peter Stiff retorted that 'the payments were strictly supervised' and were paid only if the 'insurgent . . . could be linked to a recovered weapon'. Apparently, the *kopgeld* booty was also available to units of the security forces engaged in counter-insurgency in the Republic. In 2000, the *Mail & Guardian* reported that the Koevoet 'old boys' had held a reunion in Paarl. A wine had been 'bottled for the occasion [which] carried labels boasting of the uneven balance in the death toll – 3,861 [SWAPO] members killed compared to 153 members of Koevoet'.[15]

Captain Eugene de Kock joined the Vlakplaas unit in June 1983 but 'very little happened'. Following Dirk Coetzee's departure at the end of 1981, the death squad had been commanded by Brigadier Jack Cronje.

Beyond the car bombing of two ANC activists in Swaziland in June 1982, there had been few murderous operations. Askari Joe Mamasela's first impression of de Kock was ambiguous: 'On the surface he appeared to be a relatively nice chap, but behind that mask lurked a terrible mamba [venomous snake]. He was a brutal man.' In November 1983, de Kock was involved in a raid on Swaziland, in which the main 'target' was Zwelibanzi Nyanda, the MK commander in Natal. De Kock personally killed Nyanda, whose brother Siphiwe Nyanda was later appointed head of the South African National Defence Force (SANDF) in 1998. Stephen Ellis reported in *Comrades against Apartheid* that before his death Zwelibanzi Nyanda had accused 'Comrade Cyril, the Operations chief of the [MK] Natal Military Command', of being a spy. In 1988, 'Cyril' was detained by the MK security men: 'He confessed to being a career security policeman who had been ordered to infiltrate [MK].'[16] On 1 July 1985, de Kock was appointed commander of the Vlakplaas unit.

Under de Kock's control, the Vlakplaas unit branched out into all kinds of murder and mayhem. In September 1985, Colonel, later General, Johan le Roux of the Krugersdorp Security Police requested that Vlakplaas '"steal" – kidnap – a man called Japie Maponya, a security guard'. His crime was that his brother was an MK cadre and Maponya refused to talk. He was kidnapped, tortured ('put into a minibus and teargas was sprayed into it') and 'disappeared' on le Roux's instruction. In December 1985, Vlakplaas killed nine people in a raid on a house in Maseru, Lesotho. One of the victims of the December assault was Morris Seabelo, the regional MK commander, who had been the head of ANC security in Angola. In January 1986, Lesotho's Chief Jonathan was deposed in a coup led by 'pro-Pretoria officers of the Royal Lesotho Defence Force. The new military junta was the first government to be installed by Pretoria in any independent country.' The Vlakplaas unit that had taken part in the Maseru operation were awarded 'the SAP Silver Cross for bravery'.[17] De Kock has admitted that from 1985 Vlakplaas submitted fraudulent financial claims with the complicity of the financial division of the Security Police. The explanation was that 'money was needed for operations . . . [and] had to be generated'. Vlakplaas also 'served as a kind of central weapons depot'; captured guns were stockpiled for distribution among the bodies of victims, and later vigilante groups. On occasion, 'booby-trapped' weapons, such as grenades, were issued to ANC supporters.[18]

With the bulk of the MK intelligence and operational structure expelled from Lesotho, Vlakplaas was instructed to launch attacks on MK structures within Swaziland. In June 1986, de Kock and his colleagues kidnapped Sidney Msibi, a former bodyguard of Oliver Tambo and a leading MK intelligence official. Msibi, in conjunction with Glory Sedibe, Joe Modise's brother-in-law and the MK intelligence chief for the Transvaal, had recruited Warrant Officer Malaza of the Nelspruit Security Police. On information from Malaza, Msibi was trapped and kidnapped by Vlakplaas. De Kock recalled: 'This incident led to a fallout between General Johan van der Merwe [the head of the Security Police] and Niel Barnard . . . [NIS's] networks and informants were put under serious pressure as a result of Msibi's kidnapping.' Vlakplaas 'assaulted' Msibi during his interrogation and handed him on to MID. In August 1986, Vlakplaas kidnapped Glory Sedibe from a Swaziland jail. He was later turned by his Security Police interrogators. Stephen Ellis reported that the information given by Sedibe enabled the Security Police 'virtually to wipe out [MK] in Swaziland'. In July 1987, Vlakplaas killed Cassius Make and Paul Dikeledi, two senior MK commanders in Swaziland.[19]

The significance of Vlakplaas's kidnap and ambush operations is that they were clearly informed by and responsive to Security Police and MID intelligence. De Kock told his biographer that 'It was common knowledge, at the senior level, that C1 [Vlakplaas], the SAP, the Directorate of Covert Collection [MID] and the [SADF] worked together. I knew there existed a written agreement of co-operation between C1 and DCC.' Vlakplaas was not an isolated gang of psychopaths tolerated, from a distance, by the securocrats. It was a state-sanctioned death squad. Eugene de Kock recalled: 'Hardly a Wednesday night . . . passed without generals showing up at the farm for a good time: braais, booze and "war stories".' After one murderous cross-border operation in the mid-1980s during which three 'ANC terrorists' were killed, de Kock and his colleagues went to the home of the Commissioner of Police General Johan Coetzee in Pretoria at 5.30 in the morning: 'Coetzee shook everybody's hand. I remember that he was in his dressing gown. When he got to me, he said that he did not know whether he should touch my hands since they were covered in blood.'

Vlakplaas was also responsible for blowing up two buildings in Johannesburg: Cosatu House, the headquarters of the ANC-aligned trade union federation, in May 1987, and Khotso House, the South African Council of Churches' headquarters, in September 1988. De Kock was told that the order to blow up Cosatu House had come from 'the top', which he understood to mean President P.W. Botha. At the TRC, the Minister of Police Adriaan Vlok and the head of the Security Police (and later Commissioner of Police) General J.V. van der Merwe applied for amnesty for both bombings. While no one had been killed in those incidents, a substantial number were treated for injuries and shock. Adriaan Vlok testified that P.W. Botha had ordered the action against Khotso House: 'Mr Botha . . . told me . . . "We cannot act against the people, you must make that building unusable . . . Whatever you do, you must make sure that no people are killed." He didn't say how it had to be done, he just said what had to be done.' The TRC revealed that 'former President de Klerk had been aware of [the] involvement [of Vlok and van der Merwe] in both the Cosatu and Khotso House bombings'. Eugene de Kock was told that 'if challenged by other policemen who were not in the know' during the bombings, '[he] should simply shoot them'.[20]

Unlike Dirk Coetzee there was to be no escape for Eugene de Kock; he was arrested one week after South Africa's first free election, on 4 May 1994, 'having a quiet drink at the International Police Association club in Pretoria'. He was sentenced in October 1996 to two life sentences and 212 years' imprisonment. His application for amnesty was granted by the TRC, except for the two crimes 'for which he [is] serving a double life sentence'. F.W. de Klerk acknowledged in his memoirs that he had been 'deeply shocked' by the revelations of 'the Vlakplaas Unit's horrifying activities and methods'. Nevertheless, he was forced to admit that de Kock and the askaris had been paid 'special lump-sum payments . . . in lieu of normal police pensions' in 1993. The payments 'ranged from amounts of about R100,000–R200,000 that were paid to ordinary Askaris, to a sum of approximately R1.2 million that was paid to Colonel de Kock'. De Kock claimed that the early retirement 'payout' to eighty-four Vlakplaas 'policemen' amounted to R17,500,000; 'It was arranged, as part of my discharge agreement, that the state would pay my legal costs if I were prosecuted for any offence committed while I was in the service.' In June 1998, de Kock spoke at President P.W. Botha's trial for refusing to testify before the TRC:

> His former masters were cowards, he said. Politicians, especially those from the National Party, had sold out the police and the army. 'They want to eat lamb, but they do not want to see the blood and guts,' he said scornfully . . . 'We did well. We did the fighting I am proud of that,' he declared. But the politicians did not have the moral fibre to accept responsibility for the killing . . . 'I am an Afrikaner,' he said. But it was as cowards that God would deal with the politicians.[21]

More Death Squads

If Vlakplaas became the most infamous of the South African Police death squads, it was closely followed by the Security Police in the Port Elizabeth area. The most notorious policeman in the Eastern Cape was Gideon Nieuwoudt, who appears in so many death-squad cases that he almost represented an 'angel of death'. Nieuwoudt was described by the *Mail & Guardian* in 1999 as the 'priest from hell' because he 'would don a dog collar to visit the families of police torture victims'. He was born in February 1951 in the Eastern Cape. His father was a detective and Nieuwoudt joined the police upon leaving school. Two influential moments in his life were the visit to his school of an anti-communist preacher, who spoke of the torture he had experienced in a Romanian prison, and his own conversion to born-again Christianity in 1972. He eventually rose to the rank of colonel in the Security Police. In 1977, Nieuwoudt administered the beating with a 'hose pipe' that destroyed Biko's brain. Four years later, Siphiwe Mthimkulu, a nineteen-year-old ANC activist, was arrested and brutalised. Following his release, he attempted to press charges against the Minister of Police for torture. He fell seriously ill and was diagnosed as having been poisoned with the heavy-metal chemical, thallium. In April 1982, he attempted to make a second claim, for poisoning, against the minister. Two weeks later, Nieuwoudt abducted Mthimkulu and a fellow campaigner, Tobekile 'Topsy' Madaka. The TRC later revealed that they were 'taken to Post Chalmers, an abandoned police station near Cradock, where they were interrogated, drugged and finally shot in the head. Their bodies were burnt on a wooden pyre and their remains thrown in the Fish River.' The two murders were the responsibility of the Port Elizabeth Security Police.[22]

The Vaal Triangle insurrection, which began in September 1984, was a more powerful demonstration of revolutionary unrest than the Soweto uprising. As it spread through the Republic in 1985, the government and its intelligence structures had little to offer in response beyond increased brutality. The minutes of a meeting of the Joint Security Staff's intelligence structure concluded ambiguously on 2 May 1985: 'The feeling of this [structure] is that before a riot situation can be effectively defused, the ringleaders must be selectively eliminated . . . The idea around elimination is twofold: 1. The physical gunning-down of leaders in riot situations . . . 2. The removal of intimidators.' The language used in State Security Council (SSC) documents also demonstrated the intensified repression. On 18 July 1985, one SSC minute reported: 'The chairman [President P.W.

Botha] points out that he is convinced that the brain behind the unrest situation is situated inside South Africa, and that it must be found and destroyed.' As the TRC report noted, 'there was a marked shift in the terminology used in SSC and related documentation. Words such as "*neutraliseer*" (neutralise), "*vernietig*" (destroy), "*elimineer*" (eliminate), "*uit te wis*" (wipe out) and so forth became common parlance.'

The PEBCO Three – Sipho Hashe, Champion Galela and Qaqawuli Godolozi – were members of the Port Elizabeth Black Civic Organisation (PEBCO), an organisation aligned to the United Democratic Front (UDF), an umbrella group of South Africans opposed to apartheid. In May 1985, as the Eastern Cape was convulsed in insurrection, President Botha, Defence Minister Malan and Deputy Minister of Defence (and Law and Order) Vlok visited the region and instructed the local security forces that the area had to be, as the TRC put it, 'stabilised at all costs'. Nieuwoudt and 'an English-speaking Security [Police] member, posing as a British Embassy official', contacted the PEBCO Three and requested that they meet him at the local airport. Later evidence received by the TRC suggested that it was possible that 'a person attached to the British Embassy may well have been involved in setting up the meeting' but did not divulge the name of the official. The exact fate of the three activists remains unclear:

> [Port Elizabeth] Security [Police] members, with the help of Vlakplaas *askaris*, abducted them before they entered the [airport] terminal. They were then taken to Post Chalmers [see above] where, according to the Security [Police] members, they were given sedatives in coffee, then executed. This version is contradicted by the evidence of *askaris*. The *askaris*' version is that Galela was interrogated and tortured to death. With his body in full view, Hashe was brought out and subjected to unremitting torture until he, too, died. Godolozi spent the night in a garage with the bodies of Galela and Hashe and the following morning suffered the same fate. Their bodies were thrown in the Fish River.[23]

The askari Joe Mamesela put it even more graphically in his original TRC interview: 'Nieuwoudt beat them up with an iron pipe . . . they were kicked, they were punched, they were stomped . . . and they were killed . . . They died one by one . . . It was terrible. I have never seen anything like that . . . it was a blazing hell on earth.' Six weeks later, Matthew Goniwe, Sparrow Mkhonto, Fort Calata and Sicelo Mhlawuli, collectively known as the Cradock Four, were abducted near Port Elizabeth by the Eastern Cape Security Branch. They were stabbed to death and their bodies were mutilated and burned. Goniwe, a suspended school teacher, was a militant rural organiser for the UDF; Mkhonto and Calata were active within the Cradock Residents' Association; and Mhlawuli was a member of the Oudtshoorn Youth Organisation. In 1992, the *New Nation* published a military signal that had been dispatched by Brigadier Joffel van der Westhuizen, at the time the military commander of the Eastern Cape, later the head of MID. Three weeks before the abduction of the Cradock Four, van der Westhuizen discussed the activists with General Hans Janse van Rensburg, a senior officer on the SSC. Van der Westhuizen's signal recommended that Goniwe and Calata should 'as a matter of urgency be permanently removed from society . . . Widespread reaction can be expected locally as well as nationally, because of the importance of these persons.'[24]

On 5 July 1985, the *Rand Daily Mail*'s successor, the *Weekly Mail*, printed the words 'Death squad' in a headline for the first time in connection with the death of an activist. In 1999, Mungo Soggot revealed that the State Security Council had discussed Matthew Goniwe's 'removal' more than a year before his actual death. At a meeting which was attended by P.W. Botha, Pik Botha and F.W. de Klerk, who would later release Mandela from prison and unban the ANC, Barend du Plessis, then Minister of Black Education, said: 'In Cradock there are two ex-teachers who are acting as agitators. It would be good if they could be removed.' A former security policeman, Jaap van Jaarsveld, told the TRC in 1998 that 'during the middle of 1984, I received an order from Mr Craig Williamson to investigate whether it would be possible to take out Matthew Goniwe – that means kill'.[25]

On 11 August 1985, the *Guardian*, in London, employed the expression 'death squad' in the headline of a news report about the murder of Victoria Mxenge ten days earlier. She was the widow of Griffiths Mxenge, murdered by Vlakplaas in 1981. Mrs Mxenge had said after her husband's death: 'I'll continue where he left off. If by killing my husband they thought the work he was doing would come to an end, they have made a mistake. I'll continue even if it means I must also die.' At the funeral of the Cradock Four, attended by 50,000 people, she had declared: 'Go well, peacemakers. Tell your great-grandfathers we are coming because we are prepared to die for Africa.' At the time of her assassination, Mrs Mxenge had been the instructing attorney representing sixteen members of the UDF in a trial in Natal. She was murdered by a group of four men who 'came rushing from the bushes across the road' from her home. She 'fled down the driveway, screaming for help' before being shot twice. She died on the way to hospital. The UDF said that it had been a 'cold-blooded assassination' aimed at 'wiping out all leading UDF cadres'. The US State Department, in one of the earliest American comments on the use of death squads in South Africa, stated: 'Mrs Mxenge was well known in South Africa and to many American diplomats . . . Her killing is a heinous and horrible crime.' Her murder remains unsolved. The TRC found that she 'was killed by, or on the orders of, unknown members of the security forces'.[26]

In early 1986, Major-General Abraham 'Joep' Joubert, the head of Special Forces, later deputy head of MID, was informed by the Chief of the SADF, General Jannie Geldenhuys, that the government intended to extend and expand the state of emergency. Geldenhuys 'instructed him to draw up a plan showing how Special Forces could provide support for the Security Branch internally'. Joubert informed the TRC that 'everybody of import-ance had realised that the unconventional and revolutionary methods pro-vided the only hope of success . . . [that] the ANC was not going to be stopped by normal conventional methods and that revolutionary methods would have to be used'. As the TRC summarised it: 'Joubert's plan involved killing ANC leaders and others making a substantial contribution to the struggle.' The Security Branch would identify 'potential targets for killing' and once the police and the SADF had chosen a 'modus operandi' and received authorisation, the murder 'would be executed by Special Forces'. The plan was intended for three 'hotspots: the Northern Transvaal, the Witwatersrand and the Eastern Cape'. Joubert claimed that the plan was approved by General Geldenhuys and General Johan Coetzee, in 'April or May 1986'. Questioned by the TRC, both Geldenhuys and Coetzee denied authorising the plan.[27]

In August 1986, the SSC accepted a document entitled 'Strategy for the combating of the ANC' which recommended the following: 'to neutralise the ANC leadership . . . to neutralise the power and influence of key per-sons in the ANC, and their fellow-travellers'. On 1 December 1986, the SSC adopted a document which the TRC later described as 'probably . . . the definitive strategy document for the late 1980s phase of counter-revolutionary warfare'. The document stated bluntly, 'Intimidators must be neutralised by way of formal and informal policing.' A further document, dated 24 January 1987 suggested that the SSC strategy should be to 'identify and eliminate the revolutionary leaders, especially those with charisma'. The reactionary philosophy of the mid-1980s was that violence should be met with greater violence and the methods of the enemy should be turned upon the enemy. The killing that had moved up a gear between the mid-1970s and the early 1980s was being ratcheted up again. In effect, the apartheid state had adopted a scorched-earth policy. Before 1986, the 'identification of targets was done by the different security force components separately and often on an event basis', as the TRC explained. But in September 1986 the Co-ordinating Intelligence Committee (KIK, chaired by Niel Barnard) decided to create the Counter-Revolutionary Information Target Centre (TREWITS). The NIS would later submit to the TRC that the purpose of TREWITS was 'to coordinate tactical information with regard to the . . . liberation movements in neighbouring countries. This included detail on facilities, movement of personnel, training camps, infiltrations and planned military operations. TREWITS, however, had no mandate to get involved in the identification and execution of operations.'

In contrast, a KIK document dated 4 February 1987, three weeks after TREWITS started to function, described the new organisation as a 'joint effort . . . to bring about a solid information base for meaningful counter-revolutionary operational action'. Two of the founding members of TREWITS had been involved in operational activity in the past. Lieutenant-Colonel 'Callie' Steijn had been described in an SADF document in March 1986 as 'very operationally orientated and ought to be applied in that respect'. Although located within the Security Police's 'Terrorism Investigations', the target development group was dominated by members of MID and the Special Forces. Captain Henri van der Westhuizen (MID), who worked closely with Vlakplaas, informed the TRC that 'Targets . . . included ANC personnel and not just those associated with MK.' Captain H.C. Nel (Special Forces) revealed that 'the entire NEC [National Executive Committee of the ANC] was considered a target, for whom specific authorisation for any action was not required'. While there is some evidence that TREWITS started with a focus on external operations, it appears to have quickly been drawn to targets within the country. Captain Nel explained: 'The policemen in the Western Transvaal knew what [was] wanted . . . If they give me a target, I can take it like that to the Special Forces and it was 99% complete because the co-operation between Special Forces and the police dated back to the early 1980s – They fitted into the TREWITS liaison system . . . very easily.' Despite the suggestion that 'the functioning of TREWITS may have declined . . . after 1988, as a result of internal conflicts and political developments', the TRC was damning in its assessment of Niel Barnard and the securocrats:

> The Commission rejects the standpoint of former NIS Director General Niel
> Barnard and other former NIS operatives who have denied involvement

and/or knowledge that intelligence gathered was put to operational uses that included elimination. In evidence before the Commission, Dr Barnard conceded that information was provided both to the Security Branch and the SADF but claimed that 'The Defence Force was not under my responsibility neither [was] the police. What the police or the army did with the information I do not know.' The Commission finds his viewpoint that the manner in which intelligence supplied by his agency was used, was not his concern, unacceptable . . . The Commission finds the following structures and individuals to be accountable for the extra-judicial killing of political opponents: the State President, Ministers of Law and Order, Defence, Foreign Affairs, Commissioners of Police, Chiefs of the Security Branch and Heads of C Section, Chiefs of the Defence Force . . . Special Forces, Chair of the SADF General Command Council, CSI, General Manager CCB, Director General NIS. Further all members of the Cabinet and the SSC are found to be indirectly accountable.[28]

Following Dr Neil Aggett's death on 5 February 1982 at the hands of the police, accurately described as 'induced suicide' by anti-apartheid advocate George Bizos at the inquest, the number of 'suicides' in police custody reduced significantly. One reason was because the security forces discovered that it attracted less attention if activists were simply murdered. A memorable *Weekly Mail* front page on 22 August 1986 shouted, 'Vanished: The people police say weren't detained'.[29] From this time, with strict censorship of the press, it became far more difficult to keep a record of who was killed by the security forces. Years later, families would report missing loved ones to the TRC but there was no evidence of what had happened. On a much smaller scale, this was South Africa's version of Argentina's 'disappeared'.

On 1 May 1989 Dr David Webster, a forty-four-year-old anthropology lecturer at the University of the Witwatersrand, was shot dead 'while [walking] home with his girlfriend, Maggie Friedman'. John Carlin, who had recently arrived from central America, reported in the *Independent* that 'this was the first time a white activist had been murdered in South Africa since 1978, when another lecturer, Rick Turner, was shot'. An essay completed before his death by Webster and Friedman, later published as 'Suppressing Apartheid's Opponents: The State of Emergency – June 1987 to March 1989', examined the full panoply of state repression. The essay described 'vigilante' groups as 'South African Contras' and noted that 'assassinations [are] carried out by clandestine groups or death squads, referred to many years ago as the "Z" squad – though their name has probably changed'. On assassinations, it stated: 'Assassinations have the effect of controlling government opposition when all other methods . . . have failed. It is very rare that such assassinations are solved.' The conclusion was depressing but, in the short term at least, accurate: 'repression is bound to intensify, in all its forms'.[30]

One of Webster's colleagues, Dr Max Coleman, told Carlin that 'he believed those responsible formed part of "groups some steps removed from higher government but beyond the law, kept at arm's length but who can count on the non-intervention of the security forces" – in other words, similar to death squads in countries such as Guatemala and El Salvador'. In 1993, an inquest into the death of David Webster failed to prove that the suspect, former CCB agent Ferdinand Barnard, was responsible for the murder. Mr Justice Stegman said that the evidence against Barnard had come from 'trained, skilled and accomplished liars . . . [Barnard was] entitled to the benefit of the doubt.' In 1997, Ferdinand Barnard was imprisoned for life for the murder of David Webster. The TRC report said that 'Webster went on regular field trips to Kosi Bay in Northern Natal and it was rumoured that he had possibly stumbled on evidence of the ongoing supply of weapons to RENAMO or of ivory smuggling. The Hiemstra Commission, set up to investigate a spy-ring with military links in the Johannesburg City Council, heard evidence that Dr Webster had been under surveillance.'[31]

By 1989, the members of South Africa's death squads were beginning to turn on their own. During June, Phumelo Moses Nthelang was beaten to death by members of his own Vlakplaas unit, after he told Eugene de Kock that he had lost his weapon. The assault, which de Kock initiated when he 'struck Nthelang with a snooker cue and, when that broke, with his open hand', ended with Nthelang being 'tubed' – a 'form of torture in which a tube is held tightly over the victim's mouth, preventing him . . . from breathing'. In December 1989, following the death-squad revelations in *Vyre Weekblad*, Gideon Nieuwoudt became concerned that three African security policemen in the Eastern Cape were going to defect to the ANC and provide evidence on the killing of the Cradock Four, in which he had played a role. Working with members of Vlakplaas, Nieuwoudt exploded a bomb with a radio-controlled device which killed all three of his African colleagues and an informer, who happened to be with them. Nieuwoudt was later found guilty of this crime and sentenced to twenty years' imprisonment; he was out on bail awaiting the decision on his TRC amnesty application when he died of lung cancer in August 2005. At the end of the

1980s, *SA Barometer* published a list of the victims of death squads prepared by the Human Rights Commission and the David Webster Trust Fund. Although sources were limited, the list named 111 people, including 62 assassinated ANC members and MK cadres.[32] There had been an explosion of state murder during the second half of the 1980s.

Olof Palme, Samora Machel and Dulcie September

Olof Palme, the Social Democrat Prime Minister of Sweden, was assassinated in Stockholm on 28 February 1986. He had dismissed his bodyguards and attended a film with his wife before walking home. Palme was shot twice in the back, at close range. The gunman was not captured. Like the murder of John F. Kennedy in the United States, the killing of Palme has haunted his country's politics ever since – the subject has attracted a legion of conspiracy theories. By contemporary standards, Palme was a very radical Social Democrat: he spoke, for example, in favour of communist Cuba and the Sandinista revolution in Nicaragua and against Latin American military dictators and South African apartheid. Between 1969 and 1976, Palme had been prime minister of Sweden and led his party through two election defeats between 1976 and 1982, whereupon he returned to the premiership. Christer Pettersson, a minor criminal, was convicted of Palme's murder in 1989 but acquitted by an appeal court. He had been identified as the gunman by Palme's widow, but her evidence was later dismissed. Pettersson confessed that he was the killer to one newspaper and then retracted his statement. He died in 2004. The Swedish newspaper *Expressen* concluded: 'The murder of Olof Palme will now probably remain unsolved.' Six months after Palme's assassination, a bomb exploded near the Stockholm building housing the ANC's Swedish office. Extensive damage was caused but nobody was injured.[33]

There have always been rumours that the killing of Palme was linked to South African intelligence. Craig Williamson's penetration of the Swedish-funded IUEF in the 1970s and his involvement in the London bombing of the ANC offices in 1982 had established a climate of suspicion with regard to the activities of the South Africa security forces, which normally proved to be well justified. But the assassination of the leader of another country was thought to be out of the apartheid regime's league. There was circumstantial evidence, nonetheless, which suggested that a South African connection was a possibility. One week before his death, Olof Palme had made a fiery speech condemning apartheid at the 'Swedish People's Parliament Against Apartheid', which was attended by Oliver Tambo and Thabo Mbeki. In the early days of the police investigation into the assassination, journalist Per Wastberg 'reported that, according to one of her South African sources, the murder . . . had been the handiwork of three South African agents. They had purchased a station wagon converted into a camper in Germany and lived in this vehicle after entering Sweden.' Wastberg's information was ignored by the Swedish police.[34]

The Swedish investigation, led by Police Commissioner Hans Holmer, followed a number of leads before concentrating upon a theory which suggested that Palme had been murdered by members of the Kurdish separatist movement Partiya Karkeren Kurdistan (PKK). The PKK had bases in West Germany and Stockholm and in recent years had assassinated two Kurdish opponents in Sweden, after which it had been declared a 'terrorist organisation'. The PKK theory failed to provide an answer to the Palme murder and Holmer was forced to resign in March 1987. One of the earliest proponents of the PKK thesis was Bertil Wedin, who had been a minor member of the apartheid London spy-ring in 1982 (see page 185). Wedin was living in Cyprus at the time of the murder, where he presented a radio programme.[35]

More than ten years after Palme's murder, Eugene de Kock testifying in a Pretoria court declared that he had informed the South African Attorney-General of numerous apartheid crimes, notably the assassination of Palme, which was 'one of Craig Williamson's "Operation Longreach" projects . . . I wanted it to be investigated before it was covered up.' The accusation attracted the attention of numerous Scandinavian journalists hungry to solve Sweden's most intractable case; but there were problems in de Kock's statement, not least the fact that Williamson's MID front company, Longreach, had not been registered until April 1986, some weeks after Palme's death.[36] Peter Casselton, having served two years for his role in the London robberies, returned to South Africa. In 1990, Williamson visited de Kock to express his concern that 'Casselton drank too much and that he would talk'. He suggested that de Kock 'take Casselton to Swaziland and . . . "make a plan with him"'. Making a plan with somebody was death-squad patois for murder. De Kock later said to his biographer: 'I told Williamson he could kill Casselton himself if he wanted to do so . . . In the end, Casselton went to work for Williamson as a pilot. Relationships in the intelligence community were as mercurial and theatrical as those of teenage girls.' In 1996, Casselton 'accused Williamson of ordering Palme's assassination. He claimed that Wedin admitted to being the assassin, although there is no reliable evidence that Wedin ever made such an admission. Casselton died in strange circumstances in 1997: 'he was working on a truck when it suddenly started moving and squashed him against a wall. Friends said that he had been drinking since early that morning, but that he wasn't drunk.'[37]

In the same year, 'Nigel Barnett' was arrested for smuggling and arson in Maputo. But 'Barnett' was far more than just a smuggler, as the TRC later confirmed, 'MI[D] infiltrated a [Directorate of Covert Collection] operative, Mr Nigel Barnett (aka Henry William Bacon, Nicho Esslin and H.W. Otto), into Mozambique in 1983. He was still operating there under cover fourteen years later.' During the investigation into Nigel Barnett a number of fascinating details emerged: he possessed 'an arsenal of firearms', he knew both Craig Williamson and the recently deceased Peter Casselton; as a child, he had been adopted by a family with Swedish antecedents; he had visited Sweden on a number of occasions; he could speak Swedish; and among his possession were videotapes of television documentaries concerning the Palme murder, an airline ticket stub, dated 9 May 1986, from Johannesburg to Stockholm and photographs of various Swedish buildings, people and 'a Saab station wagon that had been converted to a camper van'. The Mozambican police subjected Barnett to a polygraph test which registered a lie when he denied that he was the person who murdered Olof Palme. There was, however, no evidence to suggest that he had been in Stockholm during February 1986 and, as Jan Bondeson concluded, 'the investigation regarding him was closed, perhaps prematurely'.[38]

Terry Bell's *Unfinished Business* provided more detail on the mysterious Nigel Barnett. He was born in the Eastern Cape in May 1949 and was named Leon van der Westhuizen. Within a few months, he was adopted by Jeffrey Bacon and his Swedish-born wife and renamed Henry William Bacon. He served his conscription in the South African Navy from 1969 to 1971, specialising as a diver, before joining the BSAP in Rhodesia. During the 1970s, he appears to have experienced all facets of counter-intelligence life in the Rhodesian Special Branch. In October 1979 he was awarded 'a citation for "gallantry" . . . for his conduct "while engaged in anti-terrorist operations"'. Following Zimbabwean independence, Bacon returned to the Republic and was attached to the MID's DCC. In 1981, he rejoined the navy but resigned in December 1982, whereupon he changed his name to Nicho Esslin. Following a further name change, to Nigel Barnett – the name appears to have been lifted from a Rhodesian sapper who was 'killed in action' on 6 July 1979 – he re-emerged in Maputo. As Bell put it, Barnett 'was "Mr 200 per cent", one of that rare kind who excel as both agents – spies – operatives or "men of action"'. Following his arrest and interrogation in 1997, Nigel Barnett was quietly released and returned to South Africa. *Africa Analysis* reported in February 2003 that the SANDF's Military Intelligence had given Barnett 'an early retirement package'.[39]

Samora Machel, the President of Mozambique, died in a plane crash on 19 October 1986. The Tupelov 134A aeroplane crashed in mountainous terrain near Komatipoort, close to where the borders of Swaziland, Mozambique and South Africa meet. The Soviet plane, piloted by a Russian crew, was supposed to be following a VHF omnidirectional radio signal issued from Maputo airport. Machel was returning from a meeting in Lusaka 'which had focused on the liberation of the region'. There were two investigations into the crash. The first, the South African Margo Commission of Inquiry, found that the crash was due to 'pilot error and negligence'; the second, by a Soviet team, 'concluded that a decoy beacon had caused the plane to stray off-course before it crashed into the mountains'. Of the forty-four people on board the aeroplane, nine survived. Members of the public who attempted to offer assistance testified that 'security force officers were seen rummaging through the wreckage and confiscating documents'. Pik Botha and Niel Barnard later informed the TRC that documents had been removed from the crash site. Mozambican officials contacted the South African security forces when they realised that the plane had disappeared, but they were not informed of the crash until more than nine hours had passed.[40]

Although Machel had signed the Nkomati Accord, designed to halt FRELIMO support for the ANC and South African support for RENAMO, with the South African government in March 1984, Mozambique had received little benefit. While P.W. Botha travelled to Europe in May–June at the invitation of Margaret Thatcher, for the first official visit to Britain since Verwoerd in 1961, the MID continued to support and secretly arm RENAMO, which established bases in Swaziland. On Botha's European vacation, he also visited West Germany, France, Portugal, Belgium, Switzerland and the Vatican. One of the central victims of Nkomati was the ANC, which had lost an important route of infiltration into South Africa at the same time as it was experiencing mutinies among the MK cadres in the Angolan camps.[41]

By 1986, relations between South Africa and Mozambique were strained. On 11 September, Machel visited Blantyre, Malawi with Robert

Mugabe and Kenneth Kaunda to lodge a complaint about South African and Malawian support for RENAMO. In Maputo, Machel told the press: 'We will place missiles along the border with Malawi if support to the bandits is not ended. And we will close the border to traffic between Malawi and South Africa going through Mozambique.' Within days of Machel's threat, RENAMO forces, including white soldiers believed to be South African special forces, invaded Mozambique from Malawi. Machel blamed Malawian ministers, soldiers, policemen and security forces who he claimed had 'been bought by the South Africans and other countries.' On 6 October, thirteen days before the plane crash, the South African Defence Minister Magnus Malan accused the FRELIMO government of planting a landmine in South Africa, which had caused injuries to six SADF soldiers: 'If President Machel chooses landmines, South Africa will react accordingly. If he allows a Moscow-inspired revolutionary war against South Africa, he must also be prepared to take responsibility. If he chooses terrorism and revolution, he will clash head on with South Africa.'[42]

Following the plane crash and Machel's death, the Mozambican newspaper *Noticias* wondered in a front-page editorial: 'Can anyone still have doubts about who was responsible?' Carlos Cardosa, a celebrated Mozambican investigative journalist who was assassinated in 2000, revealed that during a press conference on 11 October 1986 Machel had been asked whether the apartheid regime 'might try to murder him. Machel . . . smiled and replied "they've already tried". He said that a plot had been uncovered in November 1985, when South Africa had infiltrated bazookas into Mozambique that were to be used in an assassination attempt . . . "I'm in their way." ' One of the survivors of the crash, Vasco Langa, returned to Maputo on 30 October, where he announced that, while in hospital in Nelspruit, South African security men had tried to recruit him for RENAMO: 'We want you to join the group that's working to liberate Mozambique.'[43] Paul Fauvet of the Mozambique News Agency also revealed that within a few hours of hearing news of the crash he had spoken with a United Press International (UPI) correspondent in Johannesburg. The *Guardian* reported on 13 November:

> The flood of news coverage from South Africa did not include notice of an anonymous phone call to [UPI] in South Africa on the morning of the crash, in which the caller said he was a South African Air Force captain who knew that Pretoria had 'placed a decoy beacon inside Mozambican territory to lure the presidential plane off course' . . . The mysterious phone call is

known to others in South Africa, but the conditions of military censorship have made it impossible to report it. Also unreported is the order of a full military alert for South African forces made on October 18 to cover the next 48 hours, confirmed by intelligence sources in South Africa and the front line states . . . The President's journey had been made public a week in advance.[44]

Machel's widow, Graca, who married Nelson Mandela in 1998, has privately stated that she knows who was involved in the murder of her first husband but 'has pointedly refused to name any suspects'. She 'gave moving testimony' at the TRC and confirmed that Machel was 'engaged in a radical restructuring of both his cabinet and the military' at the time of his death. The TRC stated bluntly: 'Although the plane entered a military and operational zone (a "special restricted airspace") which was under twenty-four hour radar surveillance by a highly sophisticated Plessey system, no warning was given that the plane was off-course.' The TRC also discovered that 'a large number of South African Special Forces . . . converged in the area of Komatipoort/Mbuzini on the night of the crash'. An unnamed former MID officer testified in a closed hearing of the TRC that the Security Police shared a 'base' at Skwamans with MID operatives. The MID officer added 'that a number of high-ranking security force officials converged on Skwamans for a meeting and a *braai* the day before the crash. They left late that night in a small plane and some returned after the crash had taken place.' He named General Kat Liebenberg, Pik Botha, General van der Westhuizen (MID), Eastern Transvaal MID chief Captain Wayne Lelly 'and about fifteen others'. Lelly 'confirmed his presence on the scene, but claimed it was for another operation'. Regardless of what was a mountain of fragmentary evidence, the TRC report merely stated that 'the matter requires further investigation by an appropriate structure'.[45]

Sixteen years after Machel's death, Hans Louw, a former CCB operative, confessed to *Sowetan Sunday World* reporter Mpikeleni Duma that he had been 'part of the back-up team, armed with portable surface-to-air missiles', instructed to 'shoot down the plane if the first plan failed'. The 'first plan', the false beacon, worked and the missiles were not required. A second *Sowetan Sunday World* article reported that a doctor was said to have arrived at the scene thirty minutes after the crash. The report alleged that Samora Machel, 'who was apparently still alive, was injected with poison'. Debora Patta, in an investigation of the Machel case in 1995, recorded that 'General Lothar Neethling . . . is shown, in original police footage of the accident, tramping through the wreckage.'[46] Iain Christie, Machel's biographer, noted that the South African security and medical forces 'made incisions in the necks of some of the people on board'. On 6 April 2003, the *Sunday World* returned to the story when former MID official General Tienie Groenewald revealed:

> 'I . . . have two impeccable sources in Maputo who can corroborate that senior FRELIMO party political bureau members, including [President] Chissano and his henchmen, were familiar with the plans to execute Machel.' Groenewald . . . said the shutting down of a Maputo Airport navigational beacon was supervised by a top officer of the Mozambican Air Force. He said junior officers at the Maputo control tower could not have executed such an operation without supervision . . . '[The Mozambicans] knew from the first day to the last about the plane crash. There is no way they could not have known that Machel would die on 19 October 1986 because they had close relations with elements of the apartheid government and CCB . . . Chissano and the FRELIMO politbureau know that they have a story to tell in connection with the death of Machel.'[47]

This was the first time that a senior securocrat had admitted that the apartheid regime had killed a foreign head of state. Groenewald retracted his statement on the day after publication in the classical apartheid style by claiming that the reporter had made it up. Two weeks before Groenewald made his dramatic statement, his son Pieter had been sentenced to twenty years' imprisonment for the murder of two Africans in 1990. Pieter Groenewald had been 'on the run' for eleven years when he was arrested in 2002. President Chissano reacted in the Mozambican state-owned publication *Noticias*, where he declared that Groenewald's claims were 'absurd and only designed to avert attention from the true culprits'. In February 2004, Jacob Zuma, Deputy President of South Africa, speaking at a memorial service in Maputo commemorating the deaths of ANC members killed by the apartheid state, 'promised Mozambicans the truth would be uncovered' about the death of Samora Machel.[48]

Dulcie September, the ANC representative in Paris, was murdered on 29 March 1988. She was 'hit by a volley of five bullets fired at close range' in front of the ANC office. In the weeks before September's assassination, there had been two attempts on the life of Godfrey Motsepe, the ANC's representative in Brussels. On 2 February, a masked man fired two bullets through Motsepe's office window, and on 27 March, two days before the murder of Dulcie September, a 17 kg bomb was planted in the ANC Brussels office; it did not explode. Motsepe suggested that the would-be assassin was Joseph Klue, who had been a military attaché in Britain in 1982 (see page 186). It was later reported that following his return to South Africa in 1982, Klue was posted to Southern Cape Command and the SADF Infantry school in Oudtshoorn, where he was in June 1988.[49] Klue's denial of involvement in the assassination attempt appeared to be well-founded. Responding to September's murder, Pik Botha declared that she was the victim of a conflict within the liberation movements: 'Government cannot be held responsible for this deed. Although details concerning the assassin are not known yet, government must point out that serious differences appeared among the members of organisations that used violence to achieve political goals.' Political scientist Tom Lodge told the *Weekly Mail* that 'there is enough circumstantial evidence that one way or another the attacks against the ANC can be traced back to South Africa . . . Who else would want ANC people out of the way?' President Mitterand, according to *New York Times* foreign affairs specialist Anthony Lewis, 'called the South African Ambassador to his office and demanded an explanation. He said the murder made the question of sanctions "still more burning".'[50]

A week after September's death, while reports in the French press suggested that French right-wingers might be responsible for the murder, 'British, Belgian, French and United States intelligence officers based in Paris' briefed *Le Monde*. The ensuing headlines in South Africa screamed: 'Z-Squad Unmasked' and 'SA's "secret" Z-Squad killers'. It was either a vindication of Gordon Winter's revelations in *Inside BOSS* seven years earlier or a cunning example of intelligence 'spin'. The Johannesburg *Star* stated: 'The South African Government has a top secret weapon known as "Z-Squads Incorporated" – a group of professional highly trained hitmen . . . It is an obvious reference to the Mafia's "Murder Incorporated" but the sources claimed that the South African version is much deadlier and has a virtually unlimited range of action and operation funds.' A French intelligence officer reportedly continued: 'We believe the NIS often uses its Z-Squads without clearing their actions with the Government first.' The reporters had been informed that Dirk Stoffberg, an arms dealer famously described by *Private Eye* in 1982 as 'the world's worst spy', and by the *Village Voice* in 1992 as being 'as bad as a motherfucker', had been questioned at Heathrow airport with another South African. They were in possession of an NIS 'hit list of 20 ANC members and sympathisers'.[51]

The South African coverage of the murder of Dulcie September had intensified because of the attempted assassination of Albie Sachs in Maputo on 7 April. MID operative Henri van der Westhuizen later testified before the TRC that the car-bomb that maimed Sachs was the creation of a special-forces covert operation intended to kill ANC diplomat Indres Naidoo.[52] However, the resurrection of the 'Z squad' name and the reported involvement of foreign intelligence agencies demonstrated that something rather dramatic was happening. The reappearance of Dirk Stoffberg is equally odd. On 24 September 1982, in the immediate aftermath of the arrest of Aspinall and Casselton (see page 184), *Private Eye* had carried a small piece on Stoffberg which noted that he 'claims to be a Colonel with . . . South African intelligence . . . British intelligence sources think that his recent trip to London was to recruit mercenaries.' The story was censored from copies of *Private Eye* delivered to South Africa. Jacques Pauw later interviewed this melodramatic cross between a confidence trickster and a pantomime villain and revealed that Stoffberg claimed that following adventures related to Ronald Reagan's 'October Surprise' in Iran in 1980, 'he became a Security Branch agent [in South Africa] at the end of 1982'. By 1987, he claimed to have started work for MID, while also being 'a member of a criminal gang in Europe [the Adler Group] that specialised in assassinations, blackmail, arms smuggling and money laundering'. Stoffberg, who was murdered with his seventh wife in July 1994, told Pauw:

> that towards the middle and end of the 1980s, [MID] increasingly used the services of the Adler Group. They wanted a list of names and addresses of ANC operatives in Europe and asked Stoffberg to find out where the ANC's bank accounts were held and what the account numbers were . . . He said the assassins [of Dulcie September] were two former French legionnaires . . . 'She was an easy target. We knew where she lived and worked and what her movements were. There was no particular reason. I did not even know who she was. I didn't decide to have her killed either. I just had to pay the killers [£20,000 each].'[53]

The French investigation into September's murder concluded that she was 'killed in the context of a plan by the South African state to eliminate senior ANC figures in Europe'. The French investigation named a former French soldier, François Rouget, as the leader of a group in Paris that was gathering information on ANC representatives in the months before September's death. In 1985 Rouget had been employed by the

Presidential Guard in the Comores, while that 'outfit [was] funded by South Africa'. In 1987 Rouget moved to the Republic where he worked for the Europe–Africa Export company. Eugene de Kock added that the assassination was a CCB operation which employed Jean-Paul Guerrier, a member of the Comoran Presidential Guard as the assassin. The CCB's European intelligence was provided by Eeben Barlow (see page 377). Christoffel Nel, the CCB's head of intelligence, informed the TRC that the CCB viewed September's killing as success for the organisation but he could not name the assassin.[54]

In 2002, Riaan Labuschagne published *On South Africa's Secret Service* in which he claimed that, in late 1986, the NIS established a covert structure known as 'Directorate K'. He announced that K was controlled by Mike Kuhn, who had joined BOSS in the 1970s: 'Directorate K was tasked to conduct any covert action required by [the NIS] or the [SSC]. Its operational ambit extended far beyond that of any other arm of the South African security and intelligence forces – except probably the military's covert [CCB].' Labuschagne described K as 'a mirror image of the [NIS] and the private intelligence service of President P.W. Botha and his inner circle'. It is tempting to place embittered former NIS spook Labuschagne in the same category as numerous other South African purveyors of paranoid spooky conspiracy literature. But in August 1991 the former BOSS–NIS agent Martin Dolinchek gave an interview to the *New Nation* in which it was stated: 'Perhaps one of the most secretive ["divisions" of the NIS] is Division Z, also known as the "special ops" division. "During my time, they carried out assassinations inside and outside the country" . . . Among the victims of Division Z agents was student leader Abraham Tiro [see page 81], who was killed in a parcel bomb explosion . . . among those responsible for his death were a Mike Kuun [sic] and Dries Verwy.' Either Labuschagne was recycling Dolinchek's, and perhaps Gordon Winter's, stories or the NIS did possess a covert capacity that has not yet been fully examined. Labuschagne believed that September's assassination had been the work of the CCB. He reported: 'A former member of Special Forces who became an operational team leader in the CCB, was in Paris at the time of the incident. He was accompanied by members of his team.' This appeared to be a reference to Eeben Barlow. Labuschagne added that 'Members of Directorate K were also in Paris at the time. On their return to South Africa they expressed dismay at the timing of September's murder as it had endangered them and complicated their further actions in Europe.'[55]

Evelyn Groenink, who is married to the former ANC intelligence operative and current South African Revenue Service (SARS) head of investigations Ivan Pillay, has spent many years examining the murder of Dulcie September, with substantial assistance from friends within the current South African intelligence services. Her unpublished manuscript on the subject is a somewhat incoherent romp through a series of loosely sourced conspiracy theories, but she makes a handful of useful points. In 1989, Aziz Pahad told Groenink that the ANC's London office considered September to be 'a bit of a drama queen . . . She always had those stories of people spying on her, trying to kill her . . . She was a bit paranoid . . . After the murder, we did think it was done by a Western government – probably the French. But as [the] ANC, what power [did] we have to investigate?' In 1992, Craig Williamson firmed up the French angle for Groenink, by explaining that in late 1987, early 1988, 'We needed all the arms we could get. It was a crucial time . . . We were losing at Cuito Cuanavale. The French sold us loads [of weapons] . . . I won't be surprised if you [find] that the French at least helped to [murder September]. The military co-operation took place [at] the highest level.'

In 1995, Groenink spoke again to Aziz Pahad, South Africa's Deputy Foreign Affairs Minister, who replied to a question suggesting that September was killed because she had discovered that France and apartheid South Africa were trading in nuclear materials: 'Dulcie stumbled over "nuclear matters", of course, of course . . . It looks like she found out about a nuclear deal with France.' Groenink added one strange story, the tale of Swedish investigator Jan-Ake Kjellberg, who was employed by the TRC to examine 'the special subject of [the] murders of South Africans on foreign soil'. It was Kjellberg who had discovered Nigel Barnett while he was examining the Olof Palme case for the TRC. He was also tasked with investigating the case of Dulcie September. In November 1997, he visited Paris with Wilson Magadhla, the special investigations head of the TRC, in order to examine various aspects of the case. Following the trip, Kjellberg was removed from the inquiry because, he said, the TRC 'had received complaints about me from my own people in the Swedish Embassy . . . They were worried about my coarse approach, about my upsetting the French.' He informed Groenink that none of this was true. When he returned from France, he brought a copy of the French police file on the Dulcie September case. The TRC never bothered to have it translated although Stephen Ellis who read the file recalls that 'it pointed strongly to September having been killed by French mercenaries from the Comoran Presidential Guard'. In

2001, South African History Archive researchers requested a copy of the file from the National Intelligence Agency (NIA), which now controlled it, and where incidentally, Groenink reports, Magadhla then worked. In 2003, an incomplete summary of the report was released and South Africa's Department of Justice declared 'the investigation into the murder of Dulcie September still active and therefore sub judice'.[56] Curious and curiouser.

10

Janus I: Negotiation

We could see no light at the end of the tunnel. It was just a question of sooner or later, there is going to be a huge conflagration. We realised there had to be a total change of direction, otherwise we were simply going to fight to the last man, and whoever inherited this country would inherit a wilderness. And we knew that the longer we waited, the more difficult it was going to be to climb out of this hole – that it would be better to start negotiating while the government of the day still had some power, while South Africa was still a going concern . . . It was clear that politically and morally we were losing. Everything we tried to put up – schools, water tanks, taps – were destroyed because people saw them as attempts to delay their liberation.

Mike Louw, cited in Patti Waldmeir, *Anatomy of a Miracle*, 1997[1]

APARTHEID HAD BEEN engaged in an ideological retreat since the children's revolt of 1976 but it was forced to face its redundancy by the insurrection which started in September 1984 and persisted until the end of 1986. The inability of BOSS and the police to contain the unrest in 1976 had led inexorably to van den Bergh's fall in 1978; in a similar style, the failure of the MID and the police quickly to stem the insurrection of the mid-1980s and the disaster of Cuito Cuanavale in Angola destroyed the supremacy of the MID and reopened the door to Niel Barnard and the NIS, the civilian successor to BOSS. As *Africa Confidential* said of Barnard in 1992: 'By the time the [MID] Generals regarded him as a threat, it was too late.'[2] It would be the NIS that handled the negotiations both with Nelson Mandela in prison and with the ANC in exile.

The Emergency State

From 12 June 1986, the Republic of South Africa had effectively been an 'emergency state'. The first partial 'state of emergency' since 1960 had been declared on 21 July 1985, the day after Matthew Goniwe and his colleagues were buried in the Eastern Cape. It applied to the Vaal Triangle, the Witwatersrand and the Eastern Cape; three months later, the Western Cape was added. The second emergency was all encompassing – instituting, as Anton Harber disclosed in the *Weekly Mail*, 'A massive and little known network of over 500 committees, effectively controlled by the military and police'. The model for the National Security Management System (NSMS) had been established in August 1979 as an embryonic mechanism to execute the will of the State Security Council (SSC). During the early 1980s, political power had become increasingly centralised within the office of the prime minister; this development was set in stone by the constitutional changes of 1983 which established an executive presidency in place of the former cabinet government system. However, the constitutional transformation which included a tricameral parliament designed to incorporate Indian and Coloured South Africans was comprehensively rejected by the Indian and Coloured electorates. The constitutional proposals led directly to the emergence of the United Democratic Front (UDF), which launched on 20 August 1983, uniting hundreds of community organisations, women's groups, civic associations and youth groups in opposition to the apartheid state and in response to Oliver Tambo's call for 'one front for national liberation'.[3] Although the UDF was representative of the exiled ANC interests within South Africa, it was more than just a front organisation, it was the third voice – the first and second voices of the party being the exiled ANC and the prisoners on Robben Island. The UDF and the violent unrest which reappeared in 1984 would prove to be an insurrectionary cocktail.

As the rioting and 'ungovernability' persisted through 1985, it became obvious that the 'total strategy', which had boiled down to increasingly ineffective counter-insurgency brutality accompanied by limited, ad-hoc reforms, had patently failed. South African researchers explained that 'the turning point came in May 1986 when P.W. Botha and the generals decided to scuttle the Eminent Persons' Group's (EPG) proposals by bombing three capitals of Frontline states. Instead of negotiating with the black opposition . . . the state moved to smash it by declaring a nation-wide state of emergency and activating the NSMS at all levels'. The EPG was a team of seven veteran Commonwealth politicians, including Lord Barber, the former British Chancellor, General Obasanjo, the ex-President of Nigeria, and Malcolm Fraser, a former Australian premier. The EPG visited Mandela in Pollsmoor Prison and was developing negotiating positions when the destructive side of apartheid showed its face. As a 'former top security official' told *Newsweek*: 'It was all there . . . All we did with the state of emergency was to hit the switch'. The NSMS, which had been a dormant organisation during the early 1980s, was utilised to facilitate something approaching a 'securotocracy' under the direct control of the Office of the State President. The securocrats adopted a 'counter-revolutionary' strategy which made its priority the restoration of law and order, with secondary attention being given to investment in the most insurrectionary townships. Restoring law and order would eventually involve a permanent state of emergency, mass censorship, the arrest of more than 30,000 people and the 'banning' of thirty-four organisations.[4]

Intelligence and security dominated the NSMS system from the SSC at 'macro policy' level to the 500 regional, district and local Joint Management Centres (JMC). Securocrats on the SSC included the chief of the SADF (General Jannie Geldenhuys), the heads of the army, navy, air force and military medical services, the chiefs of the NIS and MID, the commissioner of police, the head of the Security Police and the director of security legislation. More than half of the permanent members of the SSC held security briefs. The Secretary of the SSC between 1985 and 1988 was the former head of the MID, Lieutenant-General van der Westhuizen, who had concluded his seven-year term a few days after the announcement of the 1985 state of emergency. He was later appointed ambassador to Pinochet's Chile. Each JMC possessed a co-ordinating body and four administrative committees: communications, welfare, security and intelligence. The communications committees, essentially public relations propaganda and censorship, were run from the Bureau for Information, where the former MID Director Major-General Groenewald was national head of planning and research. The welfare committees were concerned with co-ordinating the civilian administration and attending to township development. The intelligence and security committees provided a snapshot of life in a militarised society:

> Each intelligence committee gathers and interprets the intelligence on which co-ordinated state activities are based. Staffed by representatives of military intelligence, the security police and the NIS, it seeks to promote unity of effort between these traditionally competing intelligence agencies. The security committee, the repressive arm of the NSMS, acts on the intelligence provided by the intelligence committee. Staffed by a combination of riot police officers, military officers, security branch officers and officers of

the municipal police, kitskonstabels [instant constables], and commando and civil defence units, it co-ordinates the implementation of security strategies laid down by the SSC.[5]

The Strategic Communications wing of the SSC, known as Stratcom, was established in 1984 (see page 114). It appears to have been an early attempt to develop strategic planning to guide the activities of South Africa's various intelligence agencies (NIS, MID, Security Police and Foreign Affairs): 'A Centre for Strategic Research was created as an arm of the [SSC] which reported directly to the Cabinet.' Kevin O'Brien has suggested that, at a deeper level, Stratcom was the 'nexus between the SSC and . . . various covert units'. The TRC report explained the national role that Stratcom played, describing a '1985 telex directive from the Secretariat of the SSC and the Stratcom branch to regional JMCs' which was concerned with 'advancing ideas and suggestions for further inflaming situations of conflict'. Paul Erasmus was seconded to Stratcom (at the 'security branch head office') in the late 1980s. He recalled: 'There were two types of Stratcom: "*Sagte Stratcom*" (soft stratcom) . . . and "*Harde Stratcom*" (hard stratcom). Hard Stratcom included assassination, sabotage, breaking and entering, theft, the planting of evidence, blackmail and other illegal activities in the "national interest".' Soft Stratcom was 'projects with defined and "legal" aims' such as propaganda, disinformation and 'dirty tricks'. Stratcom also set up front companies, student organisations and trade unions.[6]

Despite the weary programme of winning hearts and minds (WHAM) that the NSMS claimed as its central objective, it was clear that the impetus within the system was towards further repression and control. In September 1987, Professor Willie Breytenbach accurately summarised the situation: 'Where once there could be no security without reform, now there can be no reform without security.' However, only six months earlier, forty senior civil servants had put their names to a document which 'criticised the way government was handling reform . . . snubbed the securocrats and . . . predicted revolutionary conflict if steps were not urgently taken by government to change its attitude to the liberation forces and political change'. The document recommended universal suffrage, the return of the 'independent' homelands to the Republic, the scrapping of discriminatory laws, the withdrawal of troops from the townships, the lifting of the state of emergency and the 'initiation of negotiations'. The *Mail & Guardian* later accused NP politician Roelf Meyer and NIS chief Niel Barnard of suppressing the proposals.[7]

*

In 1992, Niel Barnard informed *Die Burger* that as early as 1984 he had 'become convinced that the South African government had to strike a deal with the ANC "before our backs were against the wall"'. Barnard's position was a variation on what General Constand Viljoen later told Patti Waldmeir he had learned from the Rhodesian peace process: that Ian Smith 'eventually settled for much less than he could have got if he had settled earlier'.[8] It would be simplistic to suggest that Barnard and the NIS had seen the light and embraced the possibility of a non-racial South African democracy. The agency was undoubtedly keen to exploit the divisions within the ANC and thereby 'reform' apartheid South Africa before 'revolution' became inevitable, and it could be claimed that that is what was achieved. It is also important to emphasise that before 1989 no more than a handful of senior NIS officers and National Party politicians had any idea that tentative negotiations were in progress.

Niel Barnard has been described as the 'éminence grise' of the late apartheid era. He was everywhere and nowhere: he assisted the process towards negotiations by secretly meeting Mandela, but he also chaired the KIK which established TREWITS, suspected by the TRC of 'targeting' people for assassination; he reportedly attacked the South African Council of Churches during a speech at the Day of the Vow celebrations at Blood River in December 1986, but he also gave *in camera* evidence at P.W. Botha's trial in 1998 'that his agency became aware that political figures were being murdered and that this was being approved by the [SSC] which Mr Botha chaired: "We were very upset and worried."' A personal and peculiar story about the man 'the Cubans and Angolans saw . . . as a sort of Afrikaner Dr Strangelove' can be found in Max du Preez's memoirs. In February 1990, *Vrye Weekblad*, du Preez's radical publication, described Barnard, inaccurately, as 'the "superhawk" who gave [F.W. de Klerk] the wrong advice'. Then the newspaper exposed 'a prominent Stellenbosch academic who . . . used his cover as a Sovietologist to spy on the [SACP]' for the NIS. For this, du Preez was prosecuted under the Protection of Information Act. The case was held *in camera* because the evidence could 'threaten the security of the state'. Du Preez and his lawyer argued that, as the ANC had been unbanned and Mandela released, the story:

> was completely harmless and in fact in the public interest. Then Barnard took the witness stand. The only people allowed in court were the magistrate, the prosecutor, a policeman, my lawyer and myself. Barnard proceeded to inform the poor intimidated magistrate how nothing had really changed;

the ANC was still the enemy of the state – a communist subversive movement. He spoke for several hours. I sat there in disbelief. I seriously contemplated breaking the *in camera* rule by telling the rest of the country what this powerful man had said in court while he was pretending to negotiate with the ANC in good faith . . . Back in open court, the magistrate sentenced me to a fine of R7,000 and two years in jail, suspended for five years . . . A Supreme Court judge later threw out the magistrate's judgement, harshly commenting on his bias and lack of competency.[9]

Niel Barnard was, and is, an enigmatic and contradictory figure. He is reported to be writing an autobiography, which, if his track record is anything to go by, will carefully avoid giving much information away. Like Hendrik van den Bergh, Barnard was on the US side of the Afrikaner intelligence divide; contrary to a popular misconception that the Anglo-Boer war enmities are alive and well in the twenty-first century, there are many former members of BOSS or the NIS who preferred dealing with the British or the Germans. His unwillingness to be interviewed, unless it is on his golden episode, the negotiations with Mandela, has only confirmed his angry and somewhat sinister image. The man that I met in 2002 was nervous and bitter. Before an interview with the BBC, Barnard smoked but tore the filters off his cigarettes – a disconcerting habit which symbolized a controlling personality. But in the same interview it was also apparent, as former US Assistant Secretary of State Chester Crocker commented of Barnard, that: 'Once you peeled away a tough hide, he represented the emotions, fears, and hopes of Pretoria's establishment.'[10]

From the early 1980s, two officials of the NIS encouraged Niel Barnard to consider the option of negotiation. It would probably be more accurate to state that their mix of relentless pragmatism and idealism eventually wore down the resistance of the austere academic. Mike Louw, born in 1939 in the Western Cape, was the son of a farmer. He studied political science at the University of the Orange Free State and worked for the Department of Labour for two years before being transferred to the DMI. He joined BOSS at its inception in 1969 and for a number of years wrote the agency's annual 'intelligence estimate'. As the Johannesburg *Sunday Times* noted in 1992, on the occasion of his appointment as head of the NIS, Louw's 'forte has always been research and analysis'. He told the Johannesburg *Star* in 1995: 'I'm a civil servant. I have been all my life.' In the mid-1980s he was the special adviser to Niel Barnard, and from January 1988 he held the post of deputy Director-General. Mike Louw was a resourceful man with a good sense of humour, who memorably welcomed Patti Waldmeir to his office in 1992 with the words: 'Take any seat, they're all bugged.'[11]

Maritz Spaarwater was a little younger than Louw, and had been part of the short-lived radical movement among Afrikaner students in the late 1960s that debated the theological morality of apartheid. He told Howard Barrell in 1999 that 'his disillusion with apartheid had taken root in 1978 when it became clear . . . that NP politicians' claims that government policy would reverse the influx of black people to the cities was nonsense'. He served in the MID in the 1970s, eventually reaching the rank of colonel before being recruited by Louw to the NIS, where Spaarwater later recalled 'there was more room for flexible thinking'. During the 1980s, he was 'the government's contact man' with Kenneth Kaunda and also played a role in assisting Barnard in the negotiations that led to Namibian independence. By the time negotiations commenced, Spaarwater was chief director of operations at the NIS – effectively number three in the agency. Of all the senior NIS officials, Spaarwater was the most interested in politics; in the 1990s he would join a succession of different parties attempting to find his natural political home. As Barrell explained, Louw and Spaarwater 'fought a long and lonely battle . . . in the 1980s for an accommodation with the ANC and other liberation movements'.[12]

Negotiations Chronology

By the end of the 1970s, the prison officials, who had watched Mandela's debates with the black consciousness militants in the aftermath of the Soweto uprising and were obviously aware of the 'Free Mandela' campaign launched by the A–AM in London in 1978, were finally recognising the qualities of Nelson Mandela, the man *and* the developing icon. In June 1980, the Deputy Commissioner of Prisons, former police psychologist Jannie Roux, talked with Mandela for two-and-a-half hours and reported, as Anthony Sampson disclosed, that 'Mandela took strong exception to being called a "self-confessed communist" by . . . P.W. Botha . . . [Mandela] appeared to see a place for white people in a future South Africa but not as the holders of political power; he had in mind a five year transition.' The Prisons Service in apartheid South Africa possessed a disguised intelligence capacity, like the Department of Foreign Affairs or the Railway Police, and Roux would later be appointed head of the Cabinet Secretariat in the Office of the Prime Minister. Dan O'Meara explained that 'Jannie Roux soon developed into one of Botha's closest confidants . . . Roux's role as P.W. Botha's gatekeeper resembled that played by Bob Halderman in the Nixon White House.' The new Minister of Justice, Kobie Coetsee, requested further information on Mandela in February 1981. The resulting psychological profile was a revelation, not least because it avoided the usual racial pettiness which was such a feature of the apartheid bureaucracy:

> Mandela is exceptionally motivated and maintains a strong idealistic approach . . . He is a practical and pragmatic thinker who can arrive at a workable solution on a philosophical basis . . . He has an unbelievable memory, to reproduce things in the finest detail . . . He has an unflinching belief in his cause and in the eventual triumph of African nationalism . . . There exists no doubt . . . that Mandela commands all the qualities to be the Number One black leader in South Africa. His period in prison has caused his psycho-political posture to increase rather than decrease, and with this he now has acquired the characteristic prison-charisma of the contemporary liberation leader.[13]

Fourteen months later, Nelson Mandela, Walter Sisulu and two others were removed from Robben Island and imprisoned in Pollsmoor. Whether the prison authorities were removing the leaders in a desperate attempt to decapitate the ANC structures on the Island, or whether the government had intervened in order to purchase a little 'reinsurance' of its own, the recognition of the real Mandela was an important development. Nearly three years later, following the eruption of unrest in the Vaal Triangle, Winnie Mandela commented: 'Things are cracking up. They are losing control.' Quiet overtures to the ANC had been made immediately after the re-emergence of anti-apartheid violence in September 1984. The NIS is reported to have made 'tentative contact' with the ANC in Geneva, and Hendrik Willem van der Merwe, the head of the Centre for Conflict Resolution at the University of Cape Town, travelled to Lusaka in September 'for talks' with Oliver Tambo, Thabo Mbeki and Kenneth Kaunda. Van der Merwe was clearly a pivotal figure. Terry Bell described him as 'ever the facilitator. He also kept open contacts to every sector of South African society and . . . was well aware of the realities of Afrikaner power politics.' Van der Merwe returned to South Africa, where he was permitted to visit Mandela in Pollsmoor prison in October, an indication that the NIS, at least, approved of the contact. He also got in touch with leading 'liberals' within the Broederbond to suggest that they too should cross the metaphorical Rubicon.[14]

At the beginning of 1985, Oliver Tambo's New Year message declared, 'Render South Africa Ungovernable'. The South African government automatically connected the township unrest with the ANC in exile and the political prisoners, even though the reality was far more chaotic. Tambo's statement could more accurately be described as an attempt to hoist the ANC aboard a fractious revolution. In Washington, Chester Crocker 'spent hours closeted with . . . Magnus Malan and [NIS] chief Niel Barnard'. The State Department urged massive reform of apartheid but not, significantly, the release of the prisoners and a move towards a genuine democracy. On 31 January, P.W. Botha announced in parliament that Mandela could have his freedom if he 'unconditionally rejected violence'. Mandela responded in a powerful speech delivered by his daughter Zindzi at a rally in Soweto: 'I am not a violent man . . . Let Botha show that he is different to Malan, Strijdom and Verwoerd. Let him renounce violence.' According to Kobie Coetsee, Botha summoned him soon afterwards and said: 'We have painted ourselves in a corner. Can you get us out?'[15]

As the insurrection intensified during 1985, numerous sectors of South African society began to investigate 'escape routes' from the intractable condition that the country appeared to be in. Harry Oppenheimer, in November 1979, had given Anglo American's blessing to P.W. Botha's marriage of reform apartheid and free-market capitalism during a conference at the Carlton Centre in Johannesburg. Responding to a speech by P.W. Botha, Oppenheimer had said that he now saw 'greater reason for real hope in the future of the country than I have felt in many years'. By 1985, Anglo American, which was reported to control 54 per cent of the Johannesburg stock exchange, responded to both the insurrection and the collapsing economy with studied ambiguity. In January of that year, David Willers of the South Africa Foundation (SAF), essentially an Anglo American propaganda organisation, met with two ANC officials, Seretse Choabe and Solly Smith. Willers assured the ANC men that South African business 'preferred the ANC to be legalised'. In April 1985, South African Associated Newspapers, controlled by Anglo American, closed the *Rand Daily Mail*, which although losing money had a long history of opposition to apartheid.[16]

The declaration of the 1985 state of emergency led eleven days later to an equally significant development: the decision by the American Chase Manhattan Bank, which had lent the apartheid state $500 million and had been the first bank to reinvest after the Sharpeville 'crash', to stop 'rolling over its loans'. Sampson wrote that this 'was disastrous for Pretoria. Other banks began to withdraw credit, the rand began falling, and the South African Reserve Bank had to renew loans from Swiss and German banks, at much higher interest rates . . . foreign bankers would never regain their confidence in South Africa's future under apartheid . . . the bankers' withdrawal would exert decisive pressure on Pretoria to reach a settlement.' President Botha was due to give a speech at the National Party Congress in Durban on 15 August. Behind the scenes, 'modernisers' fought with 'hawks' to define the Republic's response to the crisis. But P.W. Botha, as ever, was unpredictable and difficult to influence; he later claimed that he had written the 'Rubicon' speech himself and read it beforehand to the cabinet, and 'none of them complained'. Foreign Minister Pik Botha later wrote that he had composed a draft speech 'which promised to begin to dismantle apartheid and to release Mandela, and which included the phrase "today we have crossed the Rubicon" '. Pik Botha also encouraged Chester Crocker to expect 'momentous announcements'. It was not to be, as Crocker later recalled: 'P.W. Botha fell into the Rubicon he had promised to cross . . . it was an angry man who appeared on television sets around the world, reacting against the demands of his critics.'[17]

Botha's ranting admonition, 'Don't push us too far,' was the final signal that the money markets needed. On 'Black Tuesday', 27 August 1985, the economic meltdown became apparent: 'the rand started plunging. By the close of business the rand was down to half its value against sterling compared to a year before.' As the traders rushed to the safe haven of gold, pumping up the value of the local stock market in the process, one stockbroker said: 'The share values reflect what South Africans are thinking: that everything is OK. The rand reflects what the world thinks, and it's saying God Help You.' Behind the scenes, as documents later revealed, the South African government halted work on a number of aspects of the nuclear weapons programme but continued to research 'implosion technology and . . . more advanced devices'. In September, a small party of South African businessmen and journalists – Gavin Relly (the chairman of Anglo American), Tony Bloom (chairman of the Premier group of mills, bakeries and shops), Peter Sourer (SAF), Zach de Beer (a former Progressive Party MP and a director of Anglo), Harold Packendorf (the editor of the Afrikaans-language *Die Vaderland*) and Tertius Myburgh (editor of the Johannesburg *Sunday Times*) – travelled to Lusaka for a friendly meeting with an ANC party which included Oliver Tambo, Thabo Mbeki, Mac Maharaj, Pallo Jordan and Chris Hani. The Afrikaner multimillionaire Anton Rupert, who had intended to make the trip to

Lusaka but dropped out when it became public knowledge, 'fearing the anger of the president', told the Johannesburg *Star* on 29 September: 'Apartheid is dead, but the corpse stinks and must be buried and not embalmed.'[18]

In October, Anthony Sampson arranged a 'small private gathering' at his Ladbroke Grove home between Oliver Tambo and a number of British bankers, industrialists and businessmen. In the next few days, Tambo spoke at Chatham House, gave evidence to the House of Commons Foreign Affairs Committee, had tea with Tory MPs, dined with 'bankers and entrepreneurs, and was welcomed by the two biggest banks, Barclays and Standard'. But the situation remained ambiguous, especially as far as Anglo American was concerned. In November 1985, Harry Oppenheimer advised the 'American Chamber of Commerce that businessmen should offer "neither moral support nor material support" for the ANC, since they want "an economic system that would destroy everything that we in this room stand for"'. Meanwhile, Mandela was admitted to hospital for surgery on an enlarged prostate gland. On a flight to visit her recovering husband, Winnie Mandela was greeted by the Minister of Justice, Kobie Coetsee. In typical impetuous style, Winnie Mandela marched into the first-class section of the aeroplane and sat next to the minister for most of the flight; 'by the time the plane landed, Coetsee had decided to visit Mandela in the hospital'. Accompanied by General Willemse, the Commissioner of Prisons, Coetsee met the famous prisoner; the Justice Minister was surprised by Mandela's 'complete command of the situation'. P.W. Botha later said of Coetsee: 'A funny little man. If you ask me what he did in my cabinet, I don't know . . . I always felt after talking to him about Mandela [that] it was a case of confusion worse confounded.'[19]

When Mandela was recuperating he was given a single cell some distance from his colleagues. Coetsee told a former editor of the *Rand Daily Mail* Allister Sparks that the confidentiality essential for talks with Mandela involved clandestine manoeuvres: 'In a sense this is material for Le Carré.' Nevertheless, it was a start. A few months later, on 13 April 1986, Winnie demonstrated the risk of delay when she declared 'We have no guns – we have only stones, boxes of matches and petrol. Together, hand in hand, with our boxes of matches and our necklaces we shall liberate this country.' The 'necklace' was a rubber tyre which was placed over the body of the victim, trapping the arms. It was then doused in petrol and lit. Like the exiled ANC, she was keen to identify with the violent resistance; unlike the ANC's leaders in Lusaka or London, she was living *through* the revolution.

Mandela understood all of this, although he too was very distant from the epicentre of the violence, when he gave his support on 19 May. Ismail Ayob's notes, buried in a file in the Oliver Tambo archive, revealed that 'NM approved of WM's necklace speech.'[20]

On 3 March 1986, the SSC created a 'Special Committee' to investigate the question of 'The Possible Release of Mandela'. The committee included Niel Barnard, General Willemse, General Johan Coetzee, Lieutenant-General P.W. van der Westhuizen and the Director-Generals of Justice and Foreign Affairs. The issue was discussed at the SSC on 17 March. The memorandum prepared for the meeting of the SSC noted that 'the release of Mandela . . . will have to be done proactively by the government . . . Action in reaction to international and/or internal pressure . . . will be considered to be the action of a weak government.' The SSC examined nine 'options' prepared by the special committee. Option 1 was 'Unconditional release'. The perceived advantages were said to include the possibility that 'Mandela's martyr image will be damaged and may even disappear' and that 'evolutionary political reform [in South Africa] will be strengthened, and the responsibility for unrest will . . . be placed on the revolutionaries'. Disadvantages were that 'Buthelezi's role as a moderate leader in the eyes of the international community will fade' and the security forces will be unable 'to stop the revolutionary momentum that will be released'. The second option was 'Release subject to limitations'. Examining Option 3, 'Release in exile (outside South Africa)', the committee suggested ominously that 'an information advantage may emerge'. Of the fourth option, 'Release to the Transkei', it was noted: 'if it can be enforced, Mandela will be denied direct communication with the local population'. Turning to Option 5, 'Continued imprisonment with possible release at a later stage', the committee declared:

Advantages

a. The RSA retains its image of strength and credibility.

b. It buys some time for release at a later stage when circumstances are more conducive.

c. The possibility that his health will deteriorate to such an extent, that if he is released at a later stage, he will only be able to perform leadership functions for a short time should not be excluded . . .

e. The position of Buthelezi [leader of the Zulu 'cultural organisation' Inkatha and of the KwaZulu bantustan] and other TBVC [independent homelands Transkei, Bophuthatswana, Venda and Ciskei] political leaders will not be threatened immediately.

f. The government has time to break Mandela down psychologically, and to discredit him before release . . .

Disadvantages . . .

b. There is a possibility that Mandela may die in prison and the consequent implications thereof.

The sixth option was 'Indeterminate/continued imprisonment'. Option 7 repeated Option 6 but added, 'in household circumstances (luxury villa on Robben Island)'. A disadvantage of this was that it 'makes a joke of the SA legal system. Mandela is a criminal and not a political prisoner.' Option 8, 'Conditional release: release on the condition that violence is abandoned', had already been offered by P.W. Botha in January 1985. The final option, 'Release as a quid pro quo for something else (exchange for other prisoners)', included the disadvantageous 'possibility that his family will leave SA to join him in exile'. This would be 'an important piece of propaganda. Their activities overseas will also cause problems.' The recommendation of the SSC, signed by its secretary, former MID boss P.W. van der Westhuizen, was:

> Option 5 . . . if the following conditions are met:
> a. The timing and circumstances should be suitable for the SA government.
> b. Mandela must be released in exile.
> c. Mandela should be in a relatively bad physical condition so that he will not be able to act as leader for a long time.
> d. A well-planned, proactive psychological action plan should be launched before, during and after the release.[21]

Professor Pieter de Lange, the *verligte* (progressive) chairman of the Broederbond, distributed a document in the mid-1980s which argued that 'the exclusion of effective black participation in the political process is a threat to white survival, which cannot be offset with the maintenance of the status quo or of a further consolidation of power in white hands . . . the scrapping of statutory discrimination . . . [is] a condition for the continued existence of the Afrikaner . . . The biggest risk which we run today is to take no risk at all.' In June 1986, de Lange took the risk and travelled to New York for a conference at the Ford Foundation in order to meet Thabo Mbeki, Mac Maharaj and Seretse Choabe. The three ANC leaders adopted differing positions: Mbeki the charming 'lay psychologist', Maharaj the mediator and Choabe the passionate freedom fighter who shouted, 'I'll shoot you, you Broederbonder,' at de Lange at one point during the conference. Mbeki, who had no history in the ANC's intelligence wing, proved to be both the master of strategy and a diplomat of genius. He won over de Lange because, as Patti Waldmeir observed, '[Mbeki] was shrewd enough to understand that behind the façade of the Afrikaner bully dwelt an almost pitiful yearning to be understood, loved and accepted by Africa. Only the subtlest of ANC minds could recognise the truth: that petting, coddling, and cajoling the Afrikaner would pay enormous dividends.'[22]

The ANC–SACP in exile had relished the insurrection within South Africa, recognising that it carried the potential to cripple apartheid in a way that MK guerrilla activity never could. In 1985, Joe Slovo, whom most white South Africans have always believed, somewhat ridiculously, was a 'full colonel in the KGB', told Waldmeir in 1985 'that he believed whites were losing confidence in their ability to dominate forever . . . [and] that Africans had finally developed the one quality without which no revolution could succeed, "contempt for death"'. By late 1986, the leaders of the ANC–SACP were becoming nearly as fearful of the millenarian township violence (which Sampson with a dash of hyperbole described as 'a [potential] black anarchy ruled by a Khmer Rouge of ruthless schoolboys') as of the government. Joe Slovo, at the SACP's sixty-fifth anniversary celebrations, condemned the 'Pol Pot philosophy' which argued that the ANC could 'pole-vault into socialism and communism the day after the overthrow of white rule'. Afterwards, Slovo told Sampson: 'If the government digs in its heels, chaos may make negotiation impossible, and a bloody struggle would leave a lot of historical debts to be paid . . . there are manifestations which we don't like . . . There are lots of situations which have no control.'[23]

In June 1986, following P.W. Botha's decision to launch air raids on Gabarone, Lusaka and Harare and simultaneously destroy any possibilities that might have arisen from the visit of the Eminent Persons' Group, Mandela informed Kobie Coetsee that he wanted to meet with P.W. Botha. But again, as Mandela wrote in *Long Walk to Freedom*, 'nothing happened'. Botha's government was bent on demonstrating that repression could achieve what it believed talking could not. Over the next year, there were marginal improvements in Mandela's life: he was, for example, taken out on drives around Cape Town. He recalled that 'they wanted to acclimatize me to life in South Africa'. There was also a number of meetings with Kobie Coetsee, who was under instruction from P.W. Botha 'to probe Mandela more closely and report back . . . but not to breathe a word to other cabinet ministers'.[24] In August 1987, Frederik van Zyl Slabbert, the former leader of the opposition who had resigned from parliament in February 1986, having announced the need for a negotiated settlement, organised a meeting in Senegal between sixty-two Afrikaner intellectuals and eighteen members of the ANC–SACP. Thabo Mbeki opened the talks with the declaration, 'My name is Thabo Mbeki, I'm an Afrikaner.' It was a cunning ploy both to identify with and to flatter the isolated Afrikaners. The Dakar meeting, which had been quietly supported by the NIS, represented according Chris Alden 'a watershed event in the shaping of the political destiny' of South Africa: 'The joint communiqué issued at the end of the meeting calling for a negotiated settlement, the unbanning of the ANC and the release of all political prisoners testified to the emerging consensus between the two parties.'[25]

In 1984, Hendrik van der Merwe had carried an invitation to a number of Broederbond 'modernisers' from the ANC in Lusaka. Two academics, Sampie Terreblanche and Willie Esterhuyse, who had intended to make the trip to Lusaka, were summoned to see P.W. Botha in February 1985 and ordered to desist. In June 1986, Rudolph Agnew, the London chairman of the mining company Consolidated Goldfields, agreed to finance meetings between the ANC and the Afrikaners arranged by his 'political adviser' and head of communications Michael Young. On the recommendation of Fleur de Villiers, a former Johannesburg *Sunday Times* journalist then working at De Beers, Young approached Esterhuyse and Terreblanche. While preparing for the meetings, Esterhuyse was contacted by Niel Barnard: 'I didn't ask him how he found out . . . He told me the government wanted an informal contact with the ANC . . . and he asked whether I would be willing to report to him on the discussions we were going to have.' Professor Esterhuyse felt as if he was being asked to behave as a spy when he would have preferred to play the role of a go-between.[26] Eight meetings eventually took place between up to twenty Afrikaner academics, including F.W. de Klerk's brother Willem, and a number of ANC 'diplomats', including Jacob Zuma, Aziz Pahad and Thabo Mbeki, who attended nearly every one. The meetings, which were held between October 1987 and July 1990, started at a hotel in Henley, were consolidated at Eastwell Manor in Kent and eventually settled at a stately home in Somerset. The Esterhuyse channel seems to have worked effectively. Esterhuyse told Patti Waldemeir that he explained the situation to Mbeki and 'was relieved to find that this was exactly what the ANC leader wanted'. The NIS were originally interested in divisions within the ANC and the possibility of splits but Esterhuyse also recalled:

many hours of stimulating discussion in NIS 'safe houses' throughout the country, with an intelligence team whose bona fides he came to accept . . .

[He] also remembers somewhat sheepishly, the efforts of NIS agents to teach him rudimentary counterespionage techniques, such as how to detect a car bomb. In the end, he had to tell them that spying was not his métier.[27]

Although Govan Mbeki was released from prison in November 1987, ostensibly for compassionate reasons, P.W. Botha remained in thrall to the MID 'solution' of extreme repression, military efficiency and regional control. His public response to the Dakar trip had been that 'the ANC is laughing up their sleeves at the naivety of "useful idiots" who . . . can be used to further the aims of the revolution'. On 2 September 1987, a significant event had occurred in Angola which would not be reported in South Africa but which would have a major impact on the negotiating process: 'a South African Bosbok spotter plane had been shot down by SAM-8 missiles'. As Hilton Hamaan explained: 'It took the South Africans completely by surprise and shook the SADF hierarchy . . . It was a harsh wake up call to the quality of the Soviet equipment.' Over the next nine months, the SADF battled in Angola, attempting to defeat a better-equipped MPLA–Cuban–Soviet force, but the arms sanctions had finally had their effect. The last gasp of the hawkish securocrats who had held sway at the top of the South African government since 1978 was the banning of seventeen anti-apartheid organisations on 24 February 1988. The secret operations, dirty tricks and killing would continue for a few more years but the heart had stopped beating. This was demonstrated by the conclusion drawn in mid-1988 by P.W. van der Westhuizen's successor as secretary of the SSC, Lieutenant-General Charles M. Lloyd: 'We can actually destroy our military enemies . . . But bullets kill bodies not minds.'[28]

The detail of what happened in Angola in 1987–8 remains a matter for South Africa's numerous military historians, but the political impact of the battle of Cuito Cuanavale, 'the largest conventional battle in Africa since World War II', was instant. The effect of losing air superiority (the SAAF [South African Air Force] 'lost anywhere from five to 42 of its outdated but irreplaceable . . . versions of the Mirage combat aircraft'), the death of 'unacceptable' numbers of white conscript soldiers and the mutiny of several battalions led P.W. Botha to shift 'away from his generals for the first time since 1986'. Political researcher Mark Swillings later noted that 'P.W. Botha made the decision on the basis of a carefully considered cost-benefit analysis by a senior intelligence officer.'[29] On 13 December 1988, South Africa signed the Brazzaville Protocol with Angola and the Cubans, under the aegis of the US State Department, which would lead to the withdrawal of South

African and Cuban troops from Angola, the closure of the ANC's camps in Angola, and the independence of Nambia in 1990. The entire process was a disaster for the MID. Chester Crocker, in *High Noon in Southern Africa*, suggested that Major-General Cornelius van Tonder, the head of MID, remained 'a leading proponent of a "forward strategy" in Angola and Mozambique', but his position had been badly damaged by the death of William Casey (the hawk-like Director of the CIA); van Tonder 'viewed [the Angola negotiations] with suspicion'. In contrast, Niel Barnard negotiated one of the side-issues: the removal of the ANC from Angola.[30]

Jan Breytenbach, one of the most celebrated figures in South African military history, gave his interpretation of what happened at Cuito Cuanavale to *Die Suid-Afrikaan* in 1992. He declared that the war had been lost because Pik Botha and Magnus Malan had returned from the international negotiations and said that 'there would be no winners and no losers. There were definitely losers, and it wasn't the Cubans and FAPLA [the MPLA's army].' The interviewer asked why the SADF communications officers had briefed 'that the battle of Cuito Cuanavale had been won, and that SWAPO had been neutralised'. Breytenbach answered: 'They were chaps concerned with influencing the climate of opinion. Basically, this means that they were engaged in lying. Pure propaganda.' To the question was the war 'a fruitless undertaking', he replied: 'It was unnecessary because we achieved absolutely sweet bugger all.' In an astutely observed passage in *High Noon*, Chester Crocker judged that 'the isolated South Africans knew little about Soviet thinking and their expertise on the Cubans was the stuff of comic books. Castro knew dangerously little about South African politics or the baronies that made up its national security establishment.'[31] Far too much South African military writing remains determined to merge cartoon warfare with patriotic nostalgia. It misunderstands the fragile underbelly of colonial warfare. The responsibility for 'defeats' like the Tet Offensive in Vietnam (1968), Angola (1976), Angola (1988) and even perhaps Iraq (200?) was consistently unclear but the domestic political effect was immediate. After Tet, Lyndon Johnson announced his decision not to stand for re-election and the Democrat Party won only one election in the next twenty years; after Angola (1975), there followed the Soweto uprising and the quiet coup that was the Information scandal; and after Angola (1988), the democratisation of South Africa began.

The first formal meetings between Mandela and the government team, which included Kobie Coetsee, Niel Barnard, General Willemse and Fanie van der Merwe, the Director-General of the Prisons Department, started in May 1988 as the political repercussions of the battle of Cuito Cuanavale reverberated through the Afrikaner establishment. Mandela had balked at the inclusion of Niel Barnard but eventually capitulated because he feared that, if he had refused, it 'would alienate Botha'. In the event, Mandela thought Barnard was 'exceedingly bright, a man of controlled intelligence and self-discipline', but he was less impressed with the spy chief's knowledge of the ANC. Mandela recalled that 'most of his information [on the party derived] from police and intelligence files, which were in the main inaccurate and sullied by the prejudices of the men who had gathered them. He could not help but be infected by the same biases.'[32] Barnard told *Die Burger* in 1992 that the meeting 'was [not a] political debate but an effort on the part of knowledgeable persons to establish "how Mr Mandela's head worked" '. The discussions were on three themes: 'to establish whether [Mandela] was truly interested in a peaceful solution to South Africa's political problems; to establish if Mandela himself was a communist or not; and to establish whether he would support the protection of minority group rights in a future constitutional dispensation'. There would eventually be forty-seven meetings between Mandela and the group, which soon included Mike Louw, Barnard's deputy. Barnard told the BBC that the bulk of the meetings involved only Mandela, Louw and himself. Some of the meetings lasted 'up to seven hours'. Barnard also sounded vaguely ashamed in later interviews when he admitted that Mandela conducted the first meeting in prison clothing: 'I found it a little humiliating for him.' The other meetings were more informal, often over dinner.[33]

In *Long Walk*, Mandela added that they asked him about the issue of nationalisation. 'I referred them to an article I wrote in 1956 for *Liberation* in which I said that the Freedom Charter was not a blueprint for socialism but for African-style capitalism.' Little did Mandela know that, in the collection of his speeches and essays published in 1965 and edited by Ruth First, the key sentences (which ended 'private enterprise will boom and flourish as never before') in his *Liberation* essay had been cut. If Mandela had needed a political test, the prison inquisition would have been it.[34] Barnard observed that Mandela was a 'wily politician . . . [with] a lot of charisma in a very strange way'. He added that Mandela possessed 'a lot of craft and . . . skill for a man who had been in prison for 27 years . . . in that sense, Mr Mandela is no icon, he's a typical politician. He can argue his way around many difficult issues.' On one level, the meetings were an adjunct to the preparations for Mandela's release. The NIS were well aware that 'the Old Man', as they called him, required time to adjust to the modern world. Knives and forks (prisoners ate with spoons), communications devices, even car-door handles, all needed getting used to. Barnard, in particular, was exercised by the possibility of an ayatollah effect upon Mandela's release. The 'preparation' was an attempt to avoid Mandela being overrun by forces beyond his control in the outside world. There is no doubt that Niel Barnard and Mike Louw grew to respect *and* like Nelson Mandela. As far as the NIS was concerned, the secrecy of the meetings and the fact that the cabinet were not informed was critical to the process. Niel Barnard told the Canadian Broadcasting Corporation (CBC):

> I'm glad that it was not shared with the Cabinet . . . There were members of the Cabinet who were incapable of keeping such information . . . to themselves . . . If we had kicked off the programme . . . by informing CNN, the London *Times*, the *New York Times* . . . it would have been a non-starter from the beginning . . . P.W. Botha asked me many times: 'When should I inform the Cabinet?' And I said: 'Sir, with due respect, you know the members of your Cabinet. If we now make public what has been going on it will be a disaster.'[35]

In December 1988, Nelson Mandela was moved from Pollsmoor to comfortable isolation in a warder's house at Victor Verster Prison. It was a sign that the negotiations were about to move up a gear. The transformative moment appeared when P.W. Botha suffered a stroke on 18 January 1989. Members of his family insist to this day that he was in fact poisoned by traitors within his own cabinet! One month after being rushed to hospital, Botha announced that he intended to separate the position of state president from the leadership of the National Party. In effect, he intended to establish a premiership which would function beneath the grander presidency. Of course, it was bound to fail. In February 1989, F.W. de Klerk, the right-wing candidate, won a tight leadership election to secure control of the party, and on 13 March he won the support of the NP for the leader of the party to 'occupy the office of State President'. P.W. Botha grudgingly agreed to retire following the September 1989 general election and proceeded to engage in a five-month 'sulk' before suddenly announcing on television on 14 August that 'since he was "being ignored" by his Cabinet, he had "no choice" but to resign'. The *Groot Krokodil* (Great Crocodile), who had dominated South African defence policy for twenty-three years, was no longer a force in Afrikaner politics. F.W. de Klerk was immediately sworn in as 'acting president'.[36] The extraordinary interregnum between

January and September 1989 allowed time to consider the implications of 'crossing the Rubicon'.

Or was the crossing already planned? The South African reporter Ivor Powell later revealed that 'the Namibian elections were explicitly treated as a dress rehearsal for a similar kind of scenario in South Africa where the National Party would be taking on the ANC. This is in line with a secret document prepared by the [NIS] in 1988 and presented to an arm of the security council. It outlines a plan for simultaneous negotiations and a destabilisation strategy vis-à-vis the ANC.' The Canadian academic Robert D'A. Henderson noted reports that 'Barnard [had] produced a 1987 secret government discussion paper which argued that the ANC was "unbeatable" as long as it remained in exile, but a "legalized ANC" could be weakened through a protracted negotiations process and drawn into a future coalition government.'[37] It is quite possible that lower-level intelligence and political officials were told that the negotiations were part of an impenetrable plot, whereas the mandarins understood that the process was a one-off deal. However, the events in Namibia, and the chaos that ensued, certainly implied that the South African state was trying to ride two horses at the same time (see page 250).

In June 1989, Niel Barnard decided that it was time to begin intelligence talks with the ANC in exile. He instructed Professor Esterhuyse to liaise secretly with Thabo Mbeki in London – they talked in a pub – to facilitate a meeting between NIS officials and ANC intelligence chiefs. The meetings, which were given the NIS codename Operation Flair, were held over a period of three months. Meanwhile, Barnard arranged for Nelson Mandela to meet P.W. Botha. Both leaders had wanted to meet for some time, but Niel Barnard was to be the ringmaster. He told Allister Sparks that 'I spent an hour with [P.W. Botha] telling him there was no way he could lose out . . . If the meeting goes wrong . . . you will still be remembered as the one who tried to keep things moving forward to a solution. But if it goes well it will be the beginning of South Africa's settlement . . . and history will acknowledge you for that.' The meeting was set for 5 July, although Mandela was given less than twenty-four hours' notice.

The gathering at Botha's official residence included, among others, the President, the prisoner, Neil Barnard and Kobie Coetsee. Mandela later recalled that, only minutes before the meeting, the commander of Victor Verster prison, Major Marais, nervously retied the prisoner's shoelaces. The shoelace story was turned into a parable by Allister Sparks; the distinction in Sparks's story is that Barnard kneeled before the prisoner to lace his shoes properly. Barnard has also confirmed the story in television interviews. But Mandela in a handwritten commentary on Sampson's manuscript clearly stated that Marais had tied his shoelaces. Perhaps, they needed lacing twice. The meeting was 'convivial', although Mandela managed to introduce the proposal that Walter Sisulu should be released on compassionate grounds. Barnard and Mandela clashed during the drive back to Victor Verster because Mandela had ignored the spy chief's request that he should avoid 'controversial issues'; Barnard believed the Sisulu request was controversial. Mandela retorted that Barnard 'was a civil servant whose duty it was to carry out the president's instructions, not to question them'. Barnard told the CBC that he replied: 'Sir, you might in the near future be president of this country [but] if I might give you some advice, please don't appoint people around you who don't tell you the truth.'[38]

P.W. Botha had the famous meeting secretly recorded, perhaps to employ in his continuing struggle with his successor, F.W. de Klerk. Later, the tape recording would become the subject of a furious row between Botha and Barnard. In fact, Barnard had recognised the potential damage that a secret recording could do to the 'trust' that his NIS negotiators were attempting to develop with the ANC. He told his deputy, Mike Louw, that 'he did not ever want to have access [to the tapes] again'; Louw burned the tapes in a wheelbarrow in his garden. Botha claimed that the NIS chief 'had stabbed me in the back'.[39] A myth has built up around the lost tapes. A police intelligence report passed to Mangosuthu Buthelezi in 1995 reported: 'It is possible that [Winnie Mandela] may have tape recordings of conversations between President Mandela and P.W. Botha . . . [The tape] was probably given to her by a member of the old NIS who was intent on causing a rift in the ranks of the ANC.' A single photograph remains, taken by P.W. Botha's private secretary, of the extraordinary encounter between the prisoner and the President; it shows Mandela and Botha laughing, with Niel Barnard in the middle smiling. Mandela, apparently, hates the picture.[40]

F.W. de Klerk and the Namibian 'Dress Rehearsal'

On 16 August, the SSC, chaired for the first time by 'Acting President' F.W. de Klerk, approved an innocuous resolution carefully drafted to provide authorisation of the first NIS–ANC meeting: 'It is necessary that more information should be obtained and processed concerning the ANC, and the aims, alliances and potential approachability of its different leaders and groupings. To enable this to be done, special additional direct action will be necessary, particularly with the help of the National Intelligence Agency functionaries.' Neither de Klerk nor the SSC had any idea that they were approving the first secret negotiation between the NIS and the ANC in Switzerland. Niel Barnard told *Die Burger* that:

> for the NIS to meet the ANC in Europe was no easy matter . . . These were not chaps who could meet openly in some hotel. We knew that, when we travelled abroad, we were being watched. The same applied to the ANC persons. We had to use quite interesting methods to evade observation by other intelligence services. The fact that we did it without alerting anyone proves we were able to do it professionally.

Following the re-election of the National Party on 6 September 1989, Mike Louw ('Michael James') and Maritz Spaarwater ('John Campbell') met Thabo Mbeki ('John Simelane') and Jacob Zuma ('Jack Simelane') at the Palace Hotel in Lucerne on 12 September. Switzerland was the only European country, except for Britain, that still had South African diplomatic representation and didn't require an entry visa. As Sparks disclosed: 'Three [NIS] field agents waited at Geneva airport to monitor the ANC men's arrival, then tailed them all the way to Lucerne. It was a measure of the mutual suspicions surrounding the meetings.' In fact, Zuma and Mbeki travelled with only one person, a driver. It was an understandably tense situation when the ANC group arrived, as Mike Louw recalled:

> How can we expect these guys to trust us?. . . I mean, we might have been sitting there with guns and the moment they opened the door just blown them away. So we opened the door so that they could see in, and we stood there in full view. We could hear them coming, talking, and then they came around the corner and they could see us standing there. Thabo walked in and said, 'Well here we are, bloody terrorists and for all you know fucking communists as well.' That broke the ice, and we all laughed, and I must say that from that moment on there was no tension.[41]

Despite the bravura performance, Thabo Mbeki was nervous: he whispered to Jacob Zuma in Zulu, 'Sitting here with the enemy I feel my stomach moving.' But he covered it well. It was a successful meeting, and they talked long into the night, basing their discussion on the form of 'an investigation, not a negotiation'. Louw recalled that Mbeki talked of an African renaissance: how the wealth and expertise of South Africa would be able to 'raise' the rest of the continent. Louw explained that the South African economy was almost bankrupt.[42] It must have been a depressing occasion as well as an exhilarating one. Patti Waldmeir suggested later that 'clandestine talks were taking place between NIS officials and the ANC' from as early as May 1988, but no solid evidence has ever emerged. She reported that 'British intelligence picked up evidence of meetings in London, and US diplomats and Zambian officials say they believe contact was also made in Zambia where Barnard journeyed often, sometimes in disguise.' The September meeting happened without Mandela's knowledge or approval, and it is possible that the same was true of earlier meetings. As Louw explained to Waldmeir: 'We were getting worried that [Mandela] was losing the confidence of those outside, so we had to do something to get the other side on board. But we were afraid that it could backfire on the Mandela talks.' The NIS officials returned to South Africa bearing good news: 'The ANC was willing to negotiate.' When Louw briefed de Klerk, the new President was disappointed that he had not been informed of the negotiation. Louw produced a copy of the SSC resolution and explained that the mission had essentially been an 'investigative' foray: 'From that moment on . . . he took the ball and ran with it.'[43]

With an electoral mandate, F.W. de Klerk was able to act decisively. His brother, the political commentator Wimpie de Klerk, had told *Africa Report* earlier in the year that '[F.W.] will be more dependent on national intelligence, not on military intelligence.' And so the pattern of the previous twenty-five years continued: just as Vorster had the 'insurance' of RI–BOSS, and P.W. Botha had the DMI–MID, F.W. de Klerk would adopt the NIS. The distinction, of course, was that Vorster had created RI when he was Minister of Justice and Botha had been Minister of Defence for so long (twelve years) when he was elected prime minister that he effectively 'owned' the MID. F.W. de Klerk did not have a security history as a politician and, far from adopting the NIS, was, in effect, adopted by Niel Barnard. For an ambitious and talented forty-year-old 'master spy', the opportunity to handle the levers of power rather than analyse and influence from the shadows must have been irresistible. As Barnard told me in 2002: 'Making peace is like making love, no one can do it on your behalf.' Although he was ostensibly referring to attempts by Sir Robin Renwick and Margaret Thatcher to muscle in on the southern African negotiations during the late 1980s, he was also subconsciously referring to his own role. This was borne out when he resigned from the NIS in December 1991 to take up what he imagined would be the historic role of Director-General of the Constitutional Development Service.[44]

F.W. de Klerk's final NP government had something of John Major's 'cabinet of the chums' about it. Barnard remembered one of the new President's first private statements as being that he intended 'to reinstall cabinet government in its full glory in this country'. The 'new broom' immediately swept through South Africa's security culture: the NIS and the Bureau for Information were placed under the control of the Office of the State President. De Klerk ordered a review of the functions of the SSC and the National Security Management System (NSMS). Finally, the cabinet decided to dismantle South Africa's nuclear programme and decommission the Pelindaba uranium-enrichment plant; by 1989, it was later admitted, six functioning nuclear weapons had been built. A massive protest march in Cape Town on 13 September, which de Klerk permitted, emphasised the need for change. Terry Bell observed waspishly that activists noticed significant changes from demonstrations in the past: 'not only were the police absent . . . new faces [were] vying to get to the front of the march', among them a whole detachment from the ('liberal') Democratic Party.' On 15 October, Walter Sisulu and seven other veteran ANC political prisoners were released. Mandela believed that the fact that the men 'could speak in the name of the ANC . . . [showed] that the ban on the organisation had effectively expired'.[45]

By one account, South Africa's 'intervention' in the Namibian Assembly elections of November 1989 cost in excess of R180 million. The primary aim of the secret South African expenditure was an attempt to reduce the expected SWAPO majority. As in the later South African election, there was a determination on the part of the South African government to keep the majority below the two-thirds limit required to permit the winning party to compose the nation's constitution without consultation. The (dying) apartheid state in Namibia employed a barrage of different tactics to this end. Politically, the MID had enjoyed a long relationship with the conservative Democratic Turnhalle Alliance (DTA); support was also given through the Security Police-funded Namib Foundation to nine minority parties.[46] Enormous sums of money were invested in MID propaganda. Major Nico Basson, who later told his story to the press, was paid more than R1 million for his role in Operation Agree. The central themes of Agree were: building up support for the DTA; exploiting the scandal of SWAPO torture camps; and developing anti-SWAPO resentment, especially with regard to cross-border military incursions. Basson ran the African Communication Projects from the Kalahari Sands Hotel and doubled as the media liaison officer for the DTA. He later told the *Windhoek Observer* that 'he was involved in smear campaigns aimed at prominent SWAPO members and sympathisers . . . [and that South African] Foreign Affairs officials, including Sean Cleary, funded dozens of front organisations'.[47] The inimitable Terry Bell revealed that:

> In a 'Top Secret' [Treasury] document, of which only ten copies were made, the auditor-general laid down strict rules of accountability for R185.5 million in secret funds. The army got R125 million, the police R26.5 million, [NIS] R3 million, Department of Foreign Affairs and the [Bureau] of Information R15 million each. However, the auditor-general also noted: 'In the light of the percentage increase that the above amounts bring to bear on the accounts concerned, it is necessary that the Treasury gives further attention to this with the object of preventing any unnecessary public disclosure' . . . The [SSC] approved the budgets on 2 May 1989.

On 1 April 1989, the United Nations Transitional Assistance Group, which included UN troops, was tasked to begin implementation of the process leading to elections in Namibia. On the same day, 600 SWAPO guerrilla fighters crossed the border from Angola. SWAPO insisted that their return was 'in accordance with the agreement'. The SADF declared that it was a SWAPO 'invasion'. Chester Crocker later pronounced the movement of SWAPO troops a 'ploy to gain UN-recognised "bases" inside the territory'.[48] Pik Botha, according to British Ambassador Sir Robin Renwick, 'was adamant that the South Africans would have to take the law into their own hands and call in air-strikes'. Margaret Thatcher, who was visiting Windhoek on the day in question, supported Botha but argued that without UN approval 'The whole world will be against you – led by me!' Koevoet, with support from the SADF, intercepted the SWAPO soldiers. Peter Stiff's history of Koevoet revealed that the majority of the SWAPO 'insurgents' on 1 April 'neither adopted a threatening attitude nor opened fire'. Over the next two days, Koevoet's helicopter gunships 'reduced the stock of cannon ammunition . . . to a critical level'. By 9 April, when the SWAPO incursion was finally repelled, nearly 300 guerrillas had been killed.[49]

If Nico Basson's operations sound like the Info scandal revisited, the behaviour of the intelligence agencies also replicated the chaos of the late 1970s. Extending the comparison, the assassination of the Secretary-General of SWAPO, Anton Lubowski, on 12 September 1989 reflected aspects of the murder of the Smits, in the sense that nobody has been convicted of the crime. Robin Renwick believed that 'this exploit was the work of undeclared elements of South African intelligence'. Basson later revealed that he had attempted to recruit Lubowski with a bribe of R250,000. More than five months after Lubowski's death, General Malan informed the South African parliament that the SWAPO lawyer had been a 'paid agent of Military Intelligence'. Malan continued by observing that the CCB could not have killed him because 'The Chief of Staff Intelligence, General Witkop Badenhorst, would consequently not have approved any action against Lubowski.'[50] Malan's statement is, of course, an indirect admission that the head of MID *could* approve actions of this sort.

Anton Lubowski, a thirty-seven-year-old advocate, had long been subjected to vilification because of his public support for SWAPO. He was shot dead outside his own home. The police, acting on a tip-off, arrested 'an Irish criminal and hitman', Donald Acheson, who soon pointed the police in the direction of the CCB. Acheson denied murdering Lubowski but revealed in his statement that he had been employed by the CCB 'to kill Ms. Gwen Lister, the editor of *The Namibian* newspaper . . . He was to use "slow acting poison which could be injected into her toothpaste, placed on her Tampax or put into anything she would eat or drink." '[51] The Johannesburg *Star* reported in May 1990 that 'the murder charge against [Acheson] was dropped . . . because of lack of evidence. He was freed after Namibian prosecutor-general Hans Heyman had tried in vain to get South Africa to procure evidence from four witnesses who had refused to go to Namibia to testify, despite an indemnity.' Donald Acheson, who is reported to have fought as a mercenary in the Rhodesian war in the 1970s, travelled to South Africa before being sent to a hideout on the island of Crete. He returned to the Republic but was a frightened man. He told Jacques Pauw: 'They are out to get me. Man, I know these people. They want to kill me.' Acheson was deported to Britain in March 1991. The TRC later attempted to find him but he has proved untraceable. In June 1994, the Namibian Supreme Court found that Acheson had murdered Lubowski; the 144-page judgement named nine former members of the CCB as Acheson's accomplices.[52]

Robin Renwick expected that 'we would witness a final attempt by South African [MID] to disrupt' the election. The form the 'final attempt' took in early November was feeble. Pik Botha received intercepted messages that SWAPO was planning another 'invasion' with the support of

Kenyan soldiers within the UN force. Renwick commented that it took no more than 'three hours' to demonstrate that Botha was the recipient of disinformation: 'A furious Pik Botha had been misled by his own intelligence services.' Botha was forced to apologise to Sam Nujoma, the soon-to-be President of Namibia. SWAPO won the election but with less than two-thirds support.[53]

As in 1978–9, the election of a new leader in South Africa carried in its wake a maelstrom of intelligence revelations and inter-agency 'warfare'. The MID 'invasion' scare and the revelations of Dirk Coetzee in *Vrye Weekblad* were just the most dramatic and the most embarrassing. In his memoirs, de Klerk wrote that 'I gave instructions for the investigation of all secret covert operations of the security forces with a view to determining whether their continuation could be justified in the light of my commitment to reform, transparency and cabinet rule.' Towards the end of November, he announced that the NSMS would be 'dismantled and replaced by more conventional and civilian-orientated coordinating mechanisms'. The SSC was downgraded and a National Security Committee established. Barnard later explained that 'the country's intelligence effort was eventually resolved through the creation of this "initially weekly, then bi-weekly and currently monthly" meeting of intelligence department heads'.[54] As far as the security state was concerned, well-informed articles in the South African press captured the mood. The *Weekly Mail* noted that the NIS 'is said to have some 5,000 employees [and] . . . has recently moved into a new R63 million headquarters in Pretoria', while the Johannesburg *Star* quoted Stellenbosch Professor Hennie Kotze's assertion that the NIS was 'laughing up its sleeve because it is not in the firing line'. The *Weekly Mail* concluded mysteriously: 'The world is unlikely to be fooled by sudden roundups of far-right fanatics. The worms have burrowed deep, but their tracks are unravelling, and they lead not to the entrails of white society but to the heart of power itself.'[55]

On 13 December 1989, more than three months after his election victory, F.W. de Klerk finally met Nelson Mandela. Niel Barnard, Kobie Coetsee and General Willemse introduced the prisoner to the President. Two new members of the gathering were Mike Louw and Gerrit Viljoen, the former chairman of the Broederbond who had recently been appointed minister of constitutional development. As de Klerk recalled: 'After the usual greetings and pleasantries, the others withdrew and left Mr Mandela and me to hold private talks.' The pair would never be friends, but they decided that they 'could do business with each other'.[56] As the 1980s became the 1990s, all the ingredients were in place: the collapse of the South African economy (1985); the US Comprehensive Anti-Apartheid Act (1986), – a dramatic rebuff for President Ronald Reagan and an important signal that apartheid had become internationally unacceptable; political–mechanical defeat at Cuito Cuanavale (1988); and the fall of the Berlin Wall (9 November 1989). De Klerk told his brother Willem: 'It was as if God had taken a hand – a new turn in world history . . . We had to seize the opportunity. The risk that the ANC was being used as a Trojan horse by a superpower had drastically diminished.' On 2 February 1990, de Klerk informed the South African parliament of his intention to release Nelson Mandela unconditionally and 'unban' the ANC, SACP and PAC.[57]

I I

Janus II: The Third Force

The extent of the challenge posed by the internal unrest and the ANC
can be gauged by a special meeting convened by the KIK in October
1985 to discuss whether it was possible to avoid a settlement with the
ANC. Attended by top-level generals and intelligence personnel . . .
the consensus was that any negotiation should take place from a position of strength, not weakness and a settlement should be avoided
until the balance of power could be shifted. In the words of General
Groenewald: 'This is the stage when one can negotiate from a position of strength and can afford to accommodate the other party, given
that it has largely been eliminated as a threat.'

TRC, *Report*, Vol. 2, 1998.[1]

IN THE EIGHT-YEAR period from 1986 to 1994, between 18,000 and
20,000 people died as a result of political violence in South Africa.
Before 1990, most of this violence was concentrated in KwaZulu–Natal;
from July 1990, the violence spread to the townships of the Vaal Triangle
in the Transvaal. On the surface, this was a low-intensity civil war between
ANC-supporting and Inkatha-supporting Zulu South Africans, but during
1990 it began to develop into a direct conflict between the ANC and the
Inkatha Freedom Party (IFP). Commentators at the time, members of the
security forces and the TRC have all declared that a 'Third Force' played
a significant role in the conflict. But what was the 'Third Force'?

Nelson Mandela in *Long Walk* reminded readers that he had given a
speech in September 1990 in which he had said that 'there was a hidden
hand behind the violence and suggested that there was a mysterious "Third
Force", which consisted of renegade men from the security forces who
were attempting to disrupt the negotiations'. F.W. de Klerk in his autobiography, *The Last Trek*, acknowledged that 'from the inception of my
Presidency there were persistent rumours and reports that hit squads,
constituting a shadowy third force operating within the security forces,

were responsible for the instigation of violence'. In January 1990, before Mandela's release, Magnus Malan informed de Klerk that he had 'just discovered' the existence of the CCB: '[he] appeared to be as shocked as I was'. De Klerk appointed the Harms Commission to 'investigate alleged incidents of murder and other unlawful acts' but he remained 'convinced that by far the greatest part of the conflict in the country was the result of the struggle between the ANC and the IFP in the province of Natal'. He visited the White House on 24 September 1990, and recorded proudly in his memoirs: 'I was the first South African head of government to pay an official visit to the United States since Field Marshal Jan Smuts forty-five years earlier.' The autobiography did not record that President Bush's first statement of substance during the meeting was 'I am concerned about evidence on a "third force".'[2]

Theory and Practice

Between 1985 and 1986, the State Security Council (SSC) discussed the establishment of a Third Force ('parallel to the SA Defence Force and the SA Police') on a number of occasions. The subject was first discussed on 4 November 1985 when a Third Force Committee was established; the members of the committee were Deputy Minister of Law and Order Adriaan Vlok, General Jannie Geldenhuys (SADF), General Johan Coetzee (Commissioner of Police) and the Secretary of the SSC, Lieutenant-General P.W. van der Westhuizen. Additional members added to the committee were Niel Barnard and Lieutenant-General Willemse (the Commissioner of Prisons). Later that month, an NIS 'discussion document' considered 'contra-mobilisation':

> The activities of the Comrades should be rendered inoperative by the neutralisation of the leadership by means of an operation called '*vasvat*' (to take a firm grip), or, in a clandestine manner, to make them the targets of the 'vigilantes' or 'mabangalala'. . . The action against intimidation from anarchists and revolutionaries by the so-called 'vigilantes' and 'mabangalala' should, taking in consideration an organisation such as Inkatha, in a clandestine manner, be reinforced, extended and portrayed as a natural resistance by moderates against anarchy.[3]

On 9 May 1986, the Secretariat of the SSC circulated a document entitled 'Creation of a Special Counter-Revolutionary Capacity (Including a Third

Force)'. The document defined 'special capacity' as 'specifically organised, equipped and trained to plan, co-ordinate and set up counter-revolutionary actions to fight internal unrest and terrorism'. The document was discussed on 12 May, a minute of which records that 'The Third Force must be mobile with a well trained capacity to effectively root out terrorists . . . It must be prepared to be unpopular and even feared without marring the image of the SA Defence Force or the SA Police. It must stand under very strong authority.' It was later claimed that the Third Force discussed by the SSC was never established, and there is documentary evidence to suggest that as a formal structure within the security forces the claim is accurate.[4] However, the development and the implementation of a covert form of the Third Force continued apace . . .

Stephen Ellis, in his brilliant analysis of the 'historical significance' of the Third Force, acknowledged the elastic meanings and interpretations of the expression but opted 'to use the term to designate a substantial, organised group of security officials or former officials intent on perpetrating violence in the service of a counter-revolutionary strategy'. Having already discussed the South African death squads in Chapter 9, I prefer to interpret the Third Force in the central context of the apartheid state's attempts to facilitate and exploit the political tension between the UDF–ANC and Inkatha which had been developing in Natal since 1980 and had started to escalate in 1986. The John J. McCuen pamphlet (see page 148), popular among South African military theorists, proposed under the heading 'Counter Guerrillas':

> CONCEPT . . . The development of a counter-revolutionary guerrilla force which is employed according to guerrilla tactics to annihilate revolutionary guerrillas and take control over the population.
> DEVELOPMENT . . . Government forces can form counter-guerrilla gangs by sending in military teams to get minority or dissident groups together, to arm and train them and even to assume command over them.[5]

*

The South African security forces had first experimented with deploying Zulu migrant workers against anti-apartheid activists during the Soweto uprising of 1976. The hostels in which most migrant workers lived made ethnic mobilisation a relatively simple prospect. Two African *Rand Daily Mail* journalists, Nat Serache and Jan 'Gabu' Tugwana, achieved the scoop of the uprising when they overheard white policemen, on 25 August, instructing Zulu workers at the Mzimhlope hostel to fight the students: 'You are warned not to continue damaging the houses because they belong to the West Rand Administration Board. If you damage houses, you will force us to take action against you to prevent this. You have been ordered to kill only these troublemakers.' During Christmas 1976, a similar collusion occurred in Nyanga near Cape Town, but it received minimal coverage. One hundred and five people died in the violence between the hostel dwellers and the students. The American press, in particular, concentrated on what would later be known as 'black-on-black violence'. The *Chicago Tribune*, for example, editorialised: 'South Africa's troubles are no longer simply a matter of blacks rioting . . . We now find blacks fighting blacks . . . This is the clearest refutation yet of the myth of Black solidarity.'[6] Anthea Jeffrey, a researcher at the South African Institute of Race Relations, once a liberal institution, by the mid-1990s a hotbed of neo-conservatism, concluded:

> The Mzimhlope and Nyanga incidents in 1976 were 'harbingers of things to come' in terms of conflict between the ANC/SACP alliance and Inkatha. They involved coercion of hostellers (many of whom supported Inkatha) by township youth to compel participation in protest action; a backlash by hostel residents against militant youth; retaliation by hostellers entirely disproportionate to the scale of the original attack; and the development of a cycle of attack and counter-attack which rapidly attained a self-sustaining momentum. The Mzimhlope incident was also *said* to have involved the police, and to have demonstrated that the force was quick to take advantage of tensions between hostellers and youth to feed internecine conflict [my emphasis].[7]

Jeffrey's use of the word 'said' is instructive. Black journalists in South Africa during apartheid were consistently censored by white editors and suspected of lacking balance. The most substantial difficulty that the ANC would face on the issue of the Third Force was breaking through the controlling white discourse. Soweto, and to a lesser extent Cape Town, had demonstrated to the Security Police the possibilities, in both physical terms ('ethnic' conflict) and propaganda terms (black-on-black violence), that the manipulation of Zulu politics could unleash. It also showed a reluctance on the part of Chief Buthelezi to involve himself in attempting to control the violence. As Alan Brooks and Jeremy Brickhill asked in 1979: 'Why did Buthelezi himself – despite protestations of concern and appeals for calm – stay away from Soweto for the first three days of the backlash, only arriving on the Friday to address the hostel-dwellers?'[8]

It seems likely that the Afrikaner political establishment had recognised as early as 1949, during the anti-Indian riots in Durban which left 142 dead, the devastating potential threat that Zulu ethnic nationalism posed to the ANC's non-racial agenda. Mandela wrote in 1978 that the 1949 riots were 'an unforgettable experience for those who have given their lives to the promotion of inter-racial harmony'. Even in Natal in 1949, there had been reports that 'whites had encouraged the riots by transporting Zulus to the scene'. The ancient imperial strategy of 'divide and rule' possessed huge attraction in apartheid South Africa where the division itself appeared to confirm both the inherent logic of Afrikaner nationalism and the dangers of unregulated race relations. Of course, Verwoerdian 'grand apartheid', the idea that all Africans could be redefined as belonging to a single ethnic group – Zulu, Xhosa, Venda, Tswana and so on – and could therefore, technically, be allotted to a series of 'bantustans' or, later, the nominally 'independent homelands' was also a form of divide and rule. Connie Mulder famously said in 1978: 'If our policy is taken to its logical conclusion . . . there will not be one black man with South African citizenship.'[9] The Balkanisation of a society weakens the smaller ethnic groups but strengthens the potential, at least, of the larger groups. Zulu speakers represented the largest language group in South Africa.

Mangosuthu Buthelezi and Inkatha

Over more than forty years, Chief Mangosuthu Buthelezi has shown himself to be, in Shula Marks's subtly ambiguous description, 'an ambitious ethnic entrepreneur'. He exploited the cracks in the grand apartheid façade to develop a strong power base in Natal without surrendering to the full ethnic captivity of an 'independent homeland'. Utilising the mythologised history of the Zulu people while claiming kinship with the exiled ANC, he won the support of both the domestic and the foreign press by the early 1970s. Due to his cunning interplay between compliance – the agreement to accept the establishment of the KwaZulu Legislative Assembly (bantustan) in 1972 – and resistance – the invocation of the exiled ANC – Buthelezi became something of 'a thorn in the government's side'. But there were weaknesses in his complicated 'fence sitting', not least the fact that his interpretation of politics was elite-driven. He believed that he spoke for all Zulus and he had little inclination to tolerate the natural divisions of political debate.

In 1973, following the Durban strikes and Buthelezi's tentative support for aspects of the black consciousness philosophy, as personified by Steve Biko, BOSS and the Department of Information intervened in KwaZulu's politics by creating an opposition to Buthelezi: Chief Charles Hlengwa's 'Shaka's Spear'. The party did not survive for long. In June 1974, Hlengwa accused Buthelezi of being 'an aspirant dictator' and announced that he was preparing a motion of 'no confidence' to be put before the Assembly. Buthelezi declared 'that Shaka's Spear had been founded and financed by BOSS in the person of Mr François Fouché, a BOSS officer stationed in the Empangeni area'. Two weeks later, Grinith Mageba, an executive member of Shaka's Spear, admitted that Buthelezi's allegation was true. She revealed that the party had been created following a meeting in 1973 with a Department of Information employee. The BOSS official, Fouche, had instructed Mageba and her brother that they 'should go out to the chiefs and persuade them to join the opposing ranks against Chief Buthelezi'. Mageba said, 'Despite all the denials . . . BOSS is the founder of Shaka's Spear – they wrote its constitution, its press releases, and even funded it. It was done with one reason – to get rid of Chief Buthelezi.'[11]

In August 1991, Martin Dolinchek, the former BOSS–NIS agent who had 'defected' to the ANC in 1986, informed the *Weekly Mail* that BOSS had 'set up an office in Empangeni, not far from Ulundi, in 1974 with the object of providing direct security and surveillance services' to Buthelezi. The BOSS office was run by Charles Scoombe. Dolinchek continued: '[The office] was staffed by three people and this was later raised to nine. They were basically a liaison office between Chief Buthelezi's Ulundi office and the Pretoria office of BOSS. They undertook any investigation of an intelligence nature which emanated from Chief Buthelezi's office.' The article noted that 'efforts to contact Inkatha's media representative, Walter Felgate, were . . . unsuccessful.' In 1998, Felgate, Buthelezi's erstwhile speechwriter and confidant, told an *in camera* hearing of the TRC that Buthelezi had received monthly intelligence briefings from the South African intelligence agencies from as early as 1973. The BOSS liaison officer in that year was Captain Olckers, whose 'cover' was that he worked for the Natal Tanning Extract company, which also employed Felgate. Buthelezi continued to receive intelligence briefings, including police intelligence documents that reported on the ANC, until 1995, one year after the election of Mandela and the ANC.[12] A number of the documents quoted in this chapter were selected from Felgate's copies of the Buthelezi security papers.

In 1975, Mangosuthu Buthelezi revived Inkatha YaKwaZulu, a cultural nationalist organisation which had been active in the 1920s. In this action, he had the support of ANC President Oliver Tambo, and Buthelezi adopted the black, green and gold ANC colours and the party's anthem, 'Nkosi Sikelel' iAfrica'. However, his statement in the KwaZulu parliament that 'all members of the Zulu nation are automatically members of Inkatha . . . no one escapes being a member as long as he or she is a member of the Zulu nation' should have warned observers that Inkatha was an ethnic nationalist project. As Shula Marks commented: 'The KwaZulu government and Inkatha rapidly became synonymous, as Inkatha members filled all the seats in the Legislative Assembly and dominated the executive and the bureaucracy . . . Effectively, KwaZulu become a one party mini-state.'[13] The Soweto uprising in June 1976 created an immediate problem for KwaZulu's Chief Minister as it did for the entire apartheid system. Either Buthelezi could offer tacit support to the students or he would be perceived as a 'stooge' of the government. At the end of July, he criticised students who had engaged in arson in KwaZulu 'and approved the idea of vigilante groups being formed'. A few weeks later, when Buthelezi attended the University of Zululand to receive an honorary doctorate, his car was stoned. In September 1976, a student leaflet declared: 'If we are still looking for favours . . . to recognise us as matriculants, it simply means that we are not independent but servants of the system like Gatsha Buthelezi who is paid by Vorster.' As the South African journalist John Kane-Berman commented: 'The position of Gatsha Buthelezi . . . has been seriously and perhaps irretrievably undermined by the upheavals.'[14]

In his manuscript, 'Mangosuthu Buthelezi: The Iago of South African Politics', Walter Felgate noted that 'Buthelezi had no sympathy for Biko. I was the one who told him of Biko's death and I know what his reaction was. The misfortunes of Buthelezi's detractors did not perturb him.' In March 1978, the Chief was stoned and spat upon by a crowd of mourners at the funeral of former PAC leader Robert Sobukwe. While he was being trumpeted by the *Citizen* as 'the most popular political figure in South Africa', based upon slightly dubious opinion polls, he was also being criticised by radical political activists for collaborating with the apartheid state.[15] In the KwaZulu elections of that year, Inkatha won a clean sweep of the seats on a turn-out of 38 per cent. Doctoral student Bella Schmahmann, who analysed the results of the election, commented on reports of 'intimidation': 'If these reports are indicative of such a spirit encouraged by the movement, it is an indictment of its leadership . . . The danger is . . . that should support for Buthelezi and his movement wane, the machinery with which he could maintain his dominant position, and the anti-democratic methods by which it could work, will have been established.' In October 1979, following a meeting in London with Oliver Tambo and the ANC, the detail of which was leaked to the South African press, Buthelezi cut the link with what he would afterwards call the 'ANC mission in exile'. He later claimed that the reason for the split was his unwillingness to allow Inkatha to become 'an internal surrogate of the ANC'. Buthelezi positioned himself and Inkatha as South Africa's 'moderate'— anti-sanctions, anti-armed struggle – black opposition, willing and capable of entering into negotiations with P.W. Botha's government.[16]

One of the most significant distinctions between those bantustans that opted for 'independence' and those that remained 'self-governing territories' was that the independent homelands were able to create security forces and intelligence agencies. These hotbeds of spookery were often manned by retired white intelligence officers, primarily from the South African and Rhodesian security services. Eugene de Kock, for example, noted that Vlakplaas had to 'get permission' from Brigadier Flip Loots of the Bophuthatswana Intelligence Service before it was permitted 'to launch an attack' in Bophuthatswana. The hypocrisy of apartheid bureaucracy was surely one of the wonders of the southern world. In 1980, Buthelezi received the approval of the South African government to create a police service for KwaZulu. In addition to his functions as chief minister, he retained the police portfolio from soon after the foundation of the KwaZulu Police (KZP) in 1981 until the closure of the service in 1993. It would soon become apparent that the KZP 'was a highly politicised, biased and partial police force and was openly supportive of' Inkatha.[17]

During May 1980, a new wave of student protests emerged in Cape Town and spread to Durban. On 18 May, KwaZulu's Chief Minister informed a political rally in KwaMashu: 'Evil political forces thought that they could attack Inkatha . . . We can identify the political riff-raff . . . We will shake them and drive them out from our midst, and if they are not careful they may find that they run risks . . . one of which may be having their skulls cracked, as none of us can predict what form the anger they raise takes.' The following day, Inkatha vigilantes assaulted boycotting students. This was explained as the action of 'angry parents' determined to '[thrash] the would-be intimidators'.[18] In July 1980, Buthelezi informed the Inkatha central committee 'of a broadcast monitored by the South African Security Police "in which the ANC said they would kill him", and he accused the ANC of promoting a civil war against African people . . . The [Johannesburg] *Sunday Times* of the same day reported that Brigadier [Johan] Coetzee . . . had confirmed the threat and promised to protect Buthelezi.' Police intelligence documents from the late 1980s to 1995 regularly flagged up assassination threats against the leader of KwaZulu. It would seem that the apartheid state had an ongoing project to feed and inflame Buthelezi's paranoia. *Africa Confidential* reported that in 1981 Inkatha Secretary-General Oscar Dhlomo visited Israel, where he requested funds and personnel 'to aid in the establishment of a paramilitary wing, including a camp for "something like ten thousand trainees"'.[19]

One of the myths about Buthelezi in ANC–SACP circles was that he received substantial financial support from international and South African business interests and ideological support from foreign intelligence agencies, especially the CIA. Interviews with Buthelezi's advisers have suggested that these myths were false. Mario Ambrosini, a right-wing American 'who was linked to the Cuban anti-Castro resistance movement in Miami and various [US] covert operations in Latin America' before becoming a strategist for Inkatha, told me in 1999 that the IFP would have welcomed assistance from the CIA but it was not forthcoming. Walter Felgate has confirmed that funding was a constant source of concern to Buthelezi. He explained that from the late 1970s left-wing international funding organisations and international Church groups would provide funds only with the approval of the ANC. In 1978, for example, Buthelezi visited Geneva to met Craig Williamson and Lars Gunnar Eriksson at the IUEF (see page 137). Felgate recalled: 'the ANC would give [Inkatha] substantial support in return for some kind of ANC control over the projects on which this money was going to be spent. Buthelezi walked out of the meeting . . . and said that he would not be bought.'[20]

Despite the regular overseas trips to Britain, Germany and the United States and a mastery of public relations, Buthelezi remained a mercurial figure: neither hare (serious opposition) nor hound (government or 'independent' state). It was difficult for capital to see how investing in Inkatha could generate profit, although the Konrad Adenauer Stiftung (the overseas representation of West Germany's Christian Democrats) was reported to have funded the Inkatha Institute. The TRC reported that 'as early as 1982, the SADF [had] proposed to the SSC that it should "exploit and encourage the division between the ANC [and] Inkatha"'. The creation of the UDF in 1983, the eruption of rioting in 1984 and the foundation of the Congress of South African Trade Unions (COSATU) in 1985 directly challenged Inkatha's shaky supremacy in KwaZulu and confirmed *Africa Confidential's* assessment that Buthelezi was 'increasingly isolated in black politics'.[21] Meanwhile, eruptions of violence and militaristic speeches were becoming common features of the Inkatha polity. On 29 October 1983, some 500 Inkatha supporters attacked students at the University of Zululand, who had opposed permitting Chief Buthelezi to use the university facilities for ceremonies to commemorate the anniversary of the death of King Cetshwayo. The TRC later recorded that '[Inkatha-supporting] attackers broke down locked doors behind which students were hidden, dragged them out and assaulted and stabbed them with traditional weapons.' Four students and one Inkatha supporter were killed. On 28 May 1984, Buthelezi informed the KwaZulu Assembly that the development of a paramilitary capacity was essential: 'I believe that we must prepare ourselves not only to defend property and life, but to go beyond that and prepare ourselves to hit back with devastating force at those who destroy and kill.'[22]

Walter Felgate told the *Mail & Guardian* in 2003 that by the mid-1980s Buthelezi was receiving 'all kinds of information and misinformation about assassination attempts by the ANC'. Felgate suggested that Buthelezi's self-image had been damaged by the crisis of the mid-1980s: 'Everyone was rallying around the ANC, which had established diplomatic missions around the globe. Buthelezi had in the past been described as the possible first black president of South Africa.' But although Buthelezi might have felt under threat in KwaZulu, internationally he was still acknowledged as a powerful player. The US Defense Intelligence Agency, traditionally more conservative than the CIA, stated in a report in May 1985 that Buthelezi was a 'political heavyweight' and possessed 'an absolute claim to representation of the six million Zulus in South Africa'. In 1998, Felgate informed the TRC that a former soldier, Kobus du Toit Bosman, had played the role of middleman in the conspiratorial process that would follow. Bosman had told Inkatha that 'although he wasn't in the military on a full-time basis . . . he was on active call for special task-force work'. Inkatha appointed Bosman to be 'an adviser with a special responsibility for liaison with the apartheid government'. KwaZulu's Chief Minister swallowed his pride and 'approached Malan for assistance to set up a "home guard" '.[23]

A memorandum dated 27 November 1985 from the head of MID, Vice-Admiral A.P. 'Dries' Putter, to the chief of the SADF, Jannie Geldenhuys, reported a meeting between Buthelezi and General Tienie

Groenewald during which the Chief Minister of KwaZulu requested assistance with the training of a paramilitary force. The memo noted Buthelezi's comment that 'the ANC must realise that if it uses violence against KwaZulu, the Zulus are also in position to take violent steps against the ANC'. Groenewald remarked on Buthelezi's desire 'to take the struggle to the ANC in Lusaka'. The document concluded with 'a hand-written note at the foot of the last page [which called] for the document to be destroyed after reading. It indicated further that a copy . . . had gone via the Minister of Defence to the State President.' A few days later, the *Financial Mail* declared that Chief Buthelezi was 'Man of the Year'. The business magazine informed its readers: 'Who can deliver SA to a new era of conciliation and relative harmony? (We use the adjective "relative" advisedly; it would be naive to believe that anything short of a smoking ruin would satisfy many of those now fomenting violence. They will have to be put down) . . . One name comes easily to mind . . . Chief Mangosuthu Buthelezi . . . a man of compromise . . . he eschews violence . . . against disinvestment . . . an unabashed free marketeer.'[24]

In the mid-1980s, as part of the internalisation of the destabilisation policy that had been applied to the front-line states through support for UNITA, RENAMO and the Lesotho Liberation army, the SADF developed two programmes of action to address and manipulate unrest in the Transkei–Ciskei and KwaZulu. Colonel John More was involved in both operations which were known as Operation Katzen and Operation Marion. Katzen was launched by the MID's Directorate of Special Tasks in 1986. It was a response to the intense and seemingly unstoppable power of local UDF–ANC resistance in the Eastern Cape. The plan in essence was an attempt to create a greater Xhosaland which would involve the merging of the Transkei and the Ciskei, two 'independent homelands', under the leadership of President George Matanzima, the leader of the Transkei. The operation was conceived by Brigadier C.P. 'Joffel' van der Westhuizen, the commanding officer in the Eastern Cape who had ordered the murder of Matthew Goniwe (see page 210). Van der Westhuizen was later appointed head of the MID in the early 1990s. The SADF soldiers deployed in Operation Katzen were mainly former Rhodesian Selous Scouts from the 'Hammer Unit' of the SADF, set up by van der Westhuizen in 1983 'as a kind of "recce unit" for the Eastern Cape, which had no special forces of its own'.[25]

Operation Katzen was approved by the SSC: at the meeting, P.W. Botha 'issued orders for the unrest in the country to be halted "by the end of December 1986"'. The MID plan involved the 'permanent removal' of President Lennox Sebe of the Ciskei and an invasion of his 'country' by the Transkei Defence Force, which was led by former Selous Scout commanding officer 'General' Ron Reid-Daly. One document said of Lennox Sebe: '[He] has for a long time been an embarrassment to our government, the SP [State President] has himself said so. He will be got rid of with the implementation of this plan.' Preparatory work would require the escape from prison of Lieutenant-General Charles Sebe, the President's brother; the creation of a political opposition and military 'resistance' (Iliso Lomzi) which would eventually be commanded by Charles Sebe but supported by the SADF; the development of Ciskeian 'hit squads'; and psychological operations to destabilise the Ciskei. Most of the plan was put into practice, but the invasion failed. Katzen was quietly dropped in 1987.[26]

Joe Lelyveld, in his majestic work of foreign reporting *Move Your Shadow*, recalled Charles Sebe when he had been the Ciskei's Director of State Security: 'a flamboyant black cop who sometimes wore a black Stetson with his smoked glasses and Christian Dior suits'. Xhanti Charles Sebe's history was certainly remarkable: born in the Eastern Cape in 1934, he joined the SAP in 1957, and played a role in the defeat of the PAC military wing, Poqo, in the early 1960s. He joined BOSS in 1973, under the supervision of Johan Coetzee, and spied on Steve Biko. In 1977, he founded the Ciskeian Intelligence Service with three men. By the time of his arrest in 1983, he held the rank of 'commander general [and was] in control of all the armed forces in Ciskei, a total of about 4,500 men'. The arrest was on the direct orders of his brother, the President, and 'may have had something to do with a woman'. Charles Sebe was shot dead by Ciskeian soldiers in February 1991. The *Guardian* reported in 1993 that 'there is considerable evidence that he was the victim of a hoax concocted by [an MID] agent, Jan Niewoudt, who appeared out of the blue to set up a Ciskei intelligence agency for President Gqozo. It is believed Mr Niewoudt persuaded Charles to return to the Ciskei to lead a coup against President Gqozo, and then set up an ambush for him.'[27]

Operation Marion, the training of a paramilitary offensive capacity for Inkatha, had longer-lasting effects in South Africa than the clumsy Operation Katzen. The name of the operation reflected its deeper function: 'marion' was a shortened form of the English and Afrikaans word 'marionette': a 'puppet moved by strings'. On 19 December 1985, General

Tienie Groenewald sent a memorandum to Magnus Malan passing on Buthelezi's request for paramilitary offensive training for an Inkatha unit which could be deployed 'to act against the ANC'. A second document, prepared by Brigadier Cor van Niekerk (MID), suggested that 'indemnity from prosecution for steps taken against members of the ANC and UDF' would be needed and 'warned of the possible creation of a "potential monster" should Buthelezi's attitude towards the government change'. This document, entitled 'SADF Support to Chief Minister Buthelezi and Bishop Lekganyane [the head of the conservative Zion Christian Church, or ZCC]', is transparent in its cynicism:

> It is important that a large portion of the black population is currently not prepared to accept the expansion of the Charterist [UDF–ANC] movement and is willing to actively resist this activity. If the Charterists succeed in neutralising Inkatha, it is unlikely that the other groups will be able to withstand the pressure against them. The end result of this will be that the government will only have the whites as a bastion against the revolutionary onslaught . . . Inkatha and the ZCC's willingness to actively resist revolutionary elements provides a golden opportunity for the State to pull a meaningful and influential section of the black population into a counter-insurgency and mobilisation programme . . . Open SADF support to Chief Buthelezi and Bishop Lekganyane will clearly have a negative impact on their power base . . . Any support must be clandestine or covert. Not one of the leaders must, as a result of SADF support, be branded as marionettes of the South African government by the enemy.[28]

At an 'extraordinary meeting' of the SSC on 20 December attended by twenty-four people including President P.W. Botha, Pik Botha, F.W. de Klerk, General Malan, Lieutenant-General P.W. van der Westhuizen, General Johan Coetzee and General Jannie Geldenhuys, three government ministers 'were authorised to assist Buthelezi in establishing a "security force"'. Niel Barnard was not present at the meeting. On 9 January 1986, Buthelezi attended a meeting of an SSC subcommittee in Cape Town in which he 'called for the power to issue fire arms licences . . . He advised that he was training 500 men at the Amatigulu Youth Camp as members of the KZP and that he required finance . . . He required not only a strong police force but also a military force.' The report of an SSC meeting in Ulundi on 14 January noted: 'Chief Buthelezi is concerned that open special support will destroy his political credibility, therefore it must be "considered and discussed with him thoroughly". He must not be seen as a "puppet of the RSA government".' At an SSC subcommittee meeting on

16 January, Niel Barnard and Dr Van Wyk, of the Department of Constitutional Planning and Development, 'objected to the creation of an offensive paramilitary unit, insisting that it be authorised at the highest political level and that Buthelezi must clarify exactly what he wanted'. Barnard, in particular, was concerned by the dangers of such a development. A report of the meeting states: 'Dr Barnard . . . made major objections to the creation of such a force and indicated that the political risks associated with it were so great that he could not support it.' Johan Coetzee, who had worked closely with Hendrik van den Bergh in RI in the 1960s, argued in favour of the proposal. On 17 January, a letter from Jannie Geldenhuys to Malan explained that the 'establishment of a paramilitary element must be investigated at the highest political level *and* clarified with the Chief Minister [Buthelezi]'. The SSC meeting on 3 February 1986, at which Barnard was present, supported the 'creation of the paramilitary element' for KwaZulu. The final decision was taken at 'the highest political level', which was President P.W. Botha. General Tienie Groenewald told the *Mail & Guardian* in 1995: 'At the time . . . it was imperative to boost organisations like the IFP if we were to have a multi-party system.'[29]

On 10 February, a communication between Putter and Geldenhuys indicated that approval had been granted for Operation Marion. Two days later, Groenewald met Buthelezi and it was agreed that 200 members of Inkatha would be given paramilitary training: 'three capacities were listed: contra-mobilisation, offensive and intelligence'. On 17 February, Malan, Groenewald, Geldenhuys, P.W. van der Westhuizen and Bosman met to resolve an argument over whether MID or Special Forces would run the Marion 'project'. It was concluded that MID would administer Marion through the Directorate of Special Tasks (DST). The 'Liebenberg Report', prepared by General André 'Kat' Liebenberg, dated 27 February 1986, confirmed that the Inkatha requirement was:

A para-military capacity which includes the following:
i. A Contra-mobilisation capacity to neutralise the UDF . . .
ii. A Defensive element organised along military lines which would include a full time leadership element organised alongside the existing Inkatha structure . . .
iii. A small full-time offensive element that will covertly act (*aangewend*) against the UDF/ANC (approximately 30).
iv. Assistance with the training of an Inkatha group for the protection of Buthelezi and senior Inkatha leaders.

v. The extension and development of an Intelligence capacity to give Inkatha the capacity to collect and use intelligence.

Liebenberg was appointed chief of the SADF in 1990. A memorandum on 16 April 1986 indicated that 'salaries for a year' would cost R900,000; 'training equipment', R200,000; and 'weapons and ammunition', R200,000. Between April and November, around 200 members of Inkatha, under the command of Buthelezi's personal assistant M.Z. Khumalo, were transported to 'Camp Hippo' on the Caprivi Strip in South West Africa–Namibia for paramilitary training conducted by the Special Forces arm of the SADF. The *Mail & Guardian* reported in 1995 that Khumalo had been an employee of South Africa's Department of Information during the 1960s.[30] According to Captain Gerhardus Jacobs, the commander of Camp Hippo: 'The eventual goal of the training . . . was to enable the resistance movements to operate independently of the SADF.' During May, Kobus Bosman argued with MID and 'was bought out of the project in order not "to make an enemy" out of him'. Walter Felgate's testimony before the TRC explained the lack of a distinction between 'offensive' and 'defensive' elements: 'To put it simply, nobody in those days could think of defence as a passive thing. Defence meant pre-emptive action.' On the question of the bodyguard ('protection') training, Felgate revealed: 'If Buthelezi really wanted a VIP protection, he had no further to look than the [KZP] . . . [but] his information was that that's where his greatest danger lay because they would be infiltrated . . . He didn't trust his own security people.'[31]

The MID through the DST 'supplied on the ground support to the paramilitary groups, including the offensive group'. One of the first attacks by the Inkatha 'hit squad' was in January 1987 on the home of UDF activist Victor Ntuli. Having checked that Ntuli was neither a military nor a police source, Colonel John More instructed two DST instructors 'to collect ten AK47 rifles from a secret DST base in Natal'. The instructors supplied the weapons to the Caprivi trainees who had been selected for the operation and, outside Ulundi, 'the attack was planned and simulated'. Before the attack took place, the commanding officer of Natal Command was informed and medical back-up (for the killers) was provided. The police were also briefed and it was agreed that 'patrols [would be] diverted from the operational area'. The attack proceeded as planned and resulted in the massacre of thirteen people, mostly women and children, in KwaMakutha township. Victor Ntuli was not at home but was murdered later, in January 1990. After the attack, the DST instructors collected the weapons and handed them to a counter-intelligence officer. The weapons were taken to Pretoria and smelted. The 'political commissar' and commander of the Caprivi trainees, Daluxolo Luthuli, informed the TRC: 'During this period, there were literally hundreds of incidents where attacks were launched against UDF people, property and homes. It is impossible for me to record the extent of these attacks. The comrades responded by attacking us with equal vigour.'[32]

Further Operation Marion training took place in November 1987. By late January 1988, Vice-Admiral Putter, the head of MID, following 'discussions' with Buthelezi, recorded that the Chief Minister had requested that 'more Inkatha members be trained in order to swing the struggle in the townships in his favour'. A second document stated that the estimated cost of training Inkatha members for Operation Marion was 'R600,000 per 100 men per year, including salaries'. An MID report a few days later explained: 'The security situation in Natal is not favourable. Inkatha is on the retreat. The Chief Minister has been politically and securitywise painted into a corner. We must be careful that he does not throw in the towel and join the enemy.' The report continued: 'Attempts must be made to give the Chief Minister more means to control the neutral masses and to provide purposeful security force action that can address the core of the problem, and not be preoccupied with a factional conflict.' A memorandum of a meeting between Malan and Buthelezi on 21 March quoted the Minister of Defence as saying: 'The threat is serious . . . we must climb in.'[33]

On 30 August 1988, M.Z. Khumalo visited General Malan, 'on the instruction of Chief Minister Buthelezi'. The report of the meeting recorded Khumalo's comments that 'Since the objectives which gave rise to Marion have not been reached, Dr Buthelezi does not want Marion to go backwards or be dissolved. He . . . has the perception that certain SADF liaison . . . officers "do not have their heart and soul in the matter".' In October 1988, the Chief of the SADF dispatched a memorandum to Malan entitled 'Operation Marion: Liaison' which questioned whether members of the SADF, especially those in 'planning', could be 'charged with capital offences'. It is difficult not to imagine that concerns of this sort, while obviously repugnant in that they demonstrate that the SADF was well aware of the moral crime in facilitating the 'civil war' in Natal, reflected wider fears in the Afrikaner polity: whispers of negotiations with the ANC and the depressing news from Angola. Captain J.P. Opperman's 'duty sheet', dated 31 October 1988, contained

Sir Percy Sillitoe: MI5 chief, and midwife to the South African security service, addresses a press conference in the USA, 1951

John Vorster and Gordon Winter enjoy drinks and information, early 1960s

Jean La Grange: BOSS spy, Gordon Winter's wife and Charlie Richardson's lover, 1970

Peter Hain (*far right*) attends an early demonstration in London against sporting links with apartheid South Africa, July 1968

Hendrik van den Bergh, Eschel Rhoodie, Yitzhak Rabin and Shimon Peres cooking up a bomb in Israel, April 1974

General Magnus Malan (*left*), P. W. Botha (*centre*), and Admiral Bierman (*right*) in the Caprivi Swamps, Namibia, 1975

Hendrik van den Bergh: the Boss in his office, 1976

Eschel Rhoodie and Hendrik van den Bergh discuss 'tea leaves'
(South Africa and Israel's nuclear collaboration) in Paris in March 1979

Lieutenant-General P. W. van der Westhuizen: a very rare photograph of the Chief of Staff Intelligence, Military Intelligence, 1979

Niel Barnard: the éminence grise of South African spookery, 1980

Gerard Ludi enjoying life after BOSS – pioneering in the private sector, 1981

Dieter Gerhardt and Ruth Johr: GRU agents and South Africa's most successful spies prepare for a long prison sentence, 1984

Craig Williamson, without his customary beard, waves grenades around at a press conference, 1985

Almond Nofemela (*left*) and Dirk Coetzee (*right*): the askari and the death-squad leader's refusal to 'take the pain' assisted the exposure of the death squads. Pictured here at the TRC hearings, 1997

Eugene de Kock, the death-squad leader nicknamed 'Prime Evil', tells all at the TRC hearings, 1999

Gideon Nieuwoudt, the Eastern Cape's 'Angel of Death', at the TRC finally attains the 'fame' he promised his victims

Mac Maharaj relaxes after receiving his
indemnity from prosecution for
Operation Vula, 1992

Mike Louw, the former Director-General
of the NIS, prepares for life as the first
head of SASS, January 1995

Mo Shaik, Operation Vula's intelligence
chief, exerted a powerful influence over
the transformation of South Africa's secret
service in the 1990s, no date

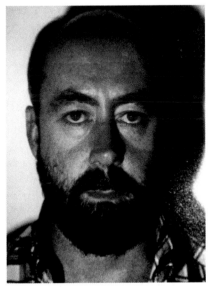

Wouter Basson: the darkest secrets of
apartheid intelligence related to chemical
and biological weapons, March 1999

General Meiring (*left*), Ronnie Kasrils (*centre*) and Joe Modise (*right*): the men in charge of the SANDF, November 1997

Bheki Jacobs (*centre*) with two ANC comrades outside Lenin's mausoleum in Moscow, early 1990s

the instructions issued to the MID liaison officer from Colonel M.A. van den Bergh (DST):

12. *Assurance*: You are already familiar with the sensitivity of this operation. The following is brought to your attention for compliance . . .
(e) Do not give a cover story in a situation where not necessary.
(f) Avoid situations which will test your cover story if possible . . .
(g) Although you are in the service of Reeva [M.Z. Khumalo] you must still maintain a low profile . . .
15. *Offensive Actions*: Must only be carried out by trained cells under strict control. Authority must be granted by DST-2 beforehand. Targets must be approved by Reeva, SAP . . . and SADF. Criminal prosecution of participants must always be taken into account. Highly professional actions are the key to success . . .
18. *Liaison*: . . . You must manipulate matters in such a way that Reeva, and where possible the President of Inkatha, cannot wash their hands of [the paramilitary force] at the expense of the SADF.

On 28 November, Brigadier Buchner, the head of the Pietermaritzburg Security Police, who was one of the founders of Vlakplaas and later the Commissioner of the KZP, referred during a meeting to the selection of 'targets'. An MID officer, who attended the same meeting, wrote in his diary: 'Must we not rather go for lower level targets that make less waves?' There was obvious concern within the MID that too many Inkatha paramilitary-unit members were having to be hidden because their activities were attracting unwanted attention. The fears about military 'legality' were also growing. In the same month, it was decided to move the emphasis of the SADF support for Inkatha from 'offensive' capacity to mobilisation support.[34] Documents from Walter Felgate's archive provide a fascinating insight into the culture of distrust and paranoia which surrounded Mangosuthu Buthelezi in late 1988. A security report dated 26 October from the 'Office of the Head of Operations' warned that UDF and ANC 'elements are planning to assassinate the Hon. Dr M.G. Buthelezi on the 30.10.88'. The report, quoting 'a very reliable source', revealed that the assassination was to take place 'during a ceremony which will be held at Kamsane to commemorate the late King Shaka'. The assassin, named in the document, 'is a person called Mike Thobela, [also known as] Mike Ngidi . . . who is said to be a member of the KwaZulu Police'. It also alleged that 'Thobela' was one of Buthelezi's 'aides'. Less than two months later, an anxious letter, dated 20 December 1988, dispatched by the National Chairman of the Inkatha Youth Brigade, Musa K. Zondi, later the Secretary-General of the IFP, to Chief Minister Buthelezi revealed the degree to which Third Force and vigilante activity was hidden from some party officials:

> I am deeply concerned by reports of the rising spate of violent con-flicts between our members and the supporters of the UDF-COSATU alliance. My deepest concern stems from reports which allege Inkatha to be on the forefront of these ugly things. For instance . . . attacks . . . in the Inanda Area . . . which resulted in several people being killed and no less than ten children of plus or minus 2 years old savagely killed with spears, axes and pangas . . . It is further alleged that Inkatha was assisted by the police in clashes . . . I am terribly concerned about the image of the Movement under the circumstances. It really is at stake. While we uphold the position that it is our inalienable right to defend ourselves when attacked, I do not believe there was a case of self-defence in the Inanda incidents. If it is true that children were killed, just how does one defend oneself against babies of two years or so? I submit that I might be ill-informed, but pending information to the contrary I now strongly believe that some of our members have found a pastime in killing other people as long as those people are not Inkatha.

Buthelezi's handwritten comment on the above letter reads: 'This dis-turbs me if some of our people are now beginning to swallow our enemies' propaganda.'[35] In May 1989, a report on an ANC–UDF meeting in Harare in December 1988, apparently typed up from notes taken by a spy, was delivered through intelligence channels to the Chief Minister. The sub-stance of the meeting addressed the need to end the violence in Natal, but the report stated that:

> there has been increasing collusion between . . . Inkatha Warlords and the Security Forces. In [KwaMakutha] they collaborate with the [K]ZP; in Inanda it is the SADF; and in Mpumalanga they have used the Kitskonstables to murder UDF and Cosatu activists and terrorise the community. Inkatha Chiefs and Warlords have become almost totally dependent on the state (security forces) for their existence. They have in turn become the tool . . . of the state strategy to smash the UDF and prevent it . . . taking control over these areas.[36]

The final training of Operation Marion took place in 1988, and in June 1989 the paramilitary unit was demobilised and the members were incorp-orated into the KZP as 'instant constables'. It is important to emphasise that although the Natal ANC also engaged in violent action against

Inkatha, the evidence suggested that the substantial majority of the human rights violations were engineered by Inkatha. The TRC report recorded that 'the number of acts [of severe ill treatment] attributable to Inkatha [in KwaZulu between 1983 and 1989] was double the number attributed to the police and more than three times the number attributed to the ANC'. Nevertheless, ANC violence, including plans to assassinate Buthelezi, grew during the decade. The veteran Stalinist Harry Gwala, 'the Lion of the Midlands', behaved like a local warlord, gathering 'around himself a group of "strongmen" who intimidated and threatened people . . . on occasion, he ordered assassinations'. Anthea Jeffrey produced a useful table of the 'number of people killed in violence in KwaZulu/Natal' in her book *The Natal Story: 16 Years of Conflict*. The table showed that the increase was dramatic, from 9 people killed in 1984 to 117 in 1985, from 451 in 1987 to 912 in 1988. The number peaked in 1990 at 1,811 and averaged 1,480 through the early 1990s.[37]

In 1989, in the course of which 1,279 people died from political violence in KwaZulu–Natal, David Webster (see page 213) and Maggie Friedman examined Inkatha as a prime example of what they described as 'South African Contras': 'It is tribalist in ideology, regards Natal as its fiefdom, and is intolerant of other organisations which are operating in its sphere of influence . . . Over the last two years Inkatha members have been involved in one of the most sustained periods of brutality ever witnessed in the Natal region.' On 31 October 1989, Buthelezi met with two MID officers, Colonel van Niekerk and Colonel M.A. van den Bergh, whose memorandum of the meeting recorded Buthelezi's concern 'at the situation in Mpumalanga and the fact that he was losing the "armed struggle". He referred to the "cell" idea for offensive action which did not get off the ground.'[38]

By the beginning of 1990, the situation in Natal and KwaZulu was critical, as the CIA noted in a heavily censored intelligence report dated 19 January 1990:

> Black-on-black violence in KwaZulu–Natal has accounted for more than half of the deaths from political upheaval in South Africa since 1984 . . . *What is Pretoria's Role?* Many observers charge that the government has encouraged the KwaZulu–Natal violence as a means to split the black opposition and eliminate key anti-apartheid activists. We believe South African security forces have trained and armed Inkatha paramilitary groups. Reporting from a variety of sources suggests that, at a minimum, government forces aided Inkatha by selectively allowing the violence to continue:

security forces intervened less frequently in political violence in KwaZulu–Natal than in other parts of the country.[39]

Two weeks after the CIA report was distributed, de Klerk announced the unbanning of the ANC–SACP. Leading strategists within the government believed that a possible NP–IFP alliance could establish a right-of-centre political force which might be capable of defeating the left-of-centre ANC–SACP–COSATU alliance at the polls. It was a pipedream, not least because, as many securocrat politicians would later testify, Buthelezi was extremely difficult to deal with. One MID officer told the TRC: 'In 1989 there was a strategy of counter-revolution . . . in 1990 after the F.W. announcement . . . we all thought: this is it, fuck the kaffirs, this is the time to sort them out'.[40]

Following the unbanning of the ANC in February 1990, the sporadic civil war in Natal intensified. One of the worst incidents occurred during the last week of March, when more than two hundred people died in what became known as the Seven Day War in the greater Edendale Valley in the Pietermaritzburg area. Three thousand houses were destroyed and more than 30,000 people made homeless. This 'reign of terror' by Inkatha supporters was facilitated and encouraged by the KZP and the SAP. Witnesses who testified before the TRC had watched the KZP provide 'buckets of ammunition to the armed attacking combatants'. One member of the SAP Riot Unit watched as 'special constables attacked, burnt and looted houses at KwaShange . . . and [returned] with stolen property [which] was loaded onto a police vehicle'.[41] Meanwhile, Buthelezi continued to meet MID officials. A memorandum from the chief of the SADF to the new head of MID noted that 'On request from the Chief Minister, the liaison channels which were established during Op Marion, are still maintained. This includes periodic visits by CSI [the head of MID].' Financial support for Inkatha during 1990–1 was approximately R200,000.[42]

In July 1990, Inkatha launched as a national political party: the Inkatha Freedom Party (IFP). Simultaneously political violence erupted in the townships of the Vaal Triangle. Nelson Mandela recalled that 'the ANC received information that hostel-dwellers belonging to the [IFP] were planning a major attack on ANC members in Sebokeng township . . . on 22 July'. The ANC warned the authorities, who, in Mandela's words, 'sat on their hands'. The TRC recorded that twenty-seven people died (de Klerk suggested twenty-four, Mandela thirty) at the hands of the IFP on

22 July. Mandela visited the site of the slaughter: 'At the morgue were bodies of people who had been hacked to death; a woman had both her breasts cut off with a machete. Whoever these killers were, they were animals . . . We had no doubt that men at the highest levels of the police and security forces were aiding the Third Force.' F.W. de Klerk commented in his autobiography: 'I reject without qualification that my government was ever behind the violence . . . We . . . regarded many of Mandela's representations as the height of hypocrisy – given the ANC's own deep involvement in violence in Natal and throughout the country – as well as its apparent unwillingness to rein in members and supporters who were clearly involved in violence.'[43]

The Transvaal chairman of the Inkatha Youth Brigade, Themba Khoza, was arrested at the scene of the Sebokeng massacre after his car was found loaded with weapons. Charges were later dropped because there were no fingerprints on the guns. Khoza claimed that somebody had borrowed his car and put the weapons there. Vlakplaas operatives would later apply for amnesty for supplying the weapons that were used at Sebokeng. It also transpired that Khoza was a spy for both the police and the NIS, and that his bail had been paid and his car supplied by Vlakplaas. Eugene de Kock, who apparently received his nickname 'Prime Evil' from a *Ghostbusters* television cartoon, later confirmed that 'The black-on-black violence – Inkatha versus the ANC – that we encouraged was a handy propaganda tool because the outside world could be told with great conviction that the barbaric natives, as might have been expected, started murdering each other at every opportunity.'[44]

The 'train violence' – on the Johannesburg-Soweto line – that started in July 1990 led to the deaths of more than 550 people over the next three years. The TRC suggested that 'it aimed predominantly at causing general terror, rather than at achieving a clear, direct, political objective'. A policeman, Wayne Swanepoel, applied for amnesty on the basis that in 1988 he had been 'involved in throwing people from the trains . . . in an attempt to cause the ANC and the IFP to blame each other'. He had worn a balaclava and darkened his skin with paint. The most horrific example of a 'train attack' was the Benrose massacre on 13 September, during which twenty-six people were killed and a hundred injured 'by two gangs of men wielding a range of weapons including pangas, knives, sharpened instruments and guns'. The Johannesburg *Star* described the carnage: 'Moving from carriage to carriage, the black attackers shot, stabbed and hacked their way through the passengers . . . Some were slain where they sat, or hacked as they tried to flee. The killers shouted as they carried out the slaughter.' In previous days, 'unidentified black men driving a minibus' had randomly machine-gunned people waiting at taxi ranks. Evidence submitted to the TRC alleged that the train violence had been executed by members of 5 Recce and RENAMO, who had been briefed at Vlakplaas.[45]

Until the end of September 1990, M.Z. Khumalo received financial support of R6,500 a month from MID. On 8 October, a memorandum prepared for the head of MID reported: 'Claims are being made in the media (*Weekly Mail* and others) that the SADF was involved in Inkatha training and Inkatha/RENAMO co-operation. The reports are currently of a low-profile and are not carried by all newspapers.' Meetings between the Chief Minister and MID officials continued until 16 July 1991. On 17 September 1990, Buthelezi was visited in Ulundi by an American diplomat. The leader of the IFP complained that the US government 'is biased against funding for Inkatha'. When it was suggested to him that it was puzzling that he didn't 'use the influence of his leadership to end the violence', Buthelezi 'gave a 20-minute commentary on the history of violence in South Africa: the sum of which was that the ANC, UDF and COSATU – not Inkatha – are responsible for the current level of killings. (*Looking very serious*).' Four months later at the beginning of 1991, a State Department report of a two-and-a-half-hour meeting between Buthelezi and a diplomat from the American Embassy revealed an extraordinary degree of paranoid vanity. Having given the diplomat a 'six-page, single-spaced "confidential memorandum"', the Chief launched into his grievances with the United States:

> In summary, he expressed his frank concern 'that the ANC/SACP alliance has been singled out for special consideration by representatives of the US [government] and that the US is sending out a worldwide signal that it believes one organization is more deserving than others'. He said . . . that President Bush speaks 'about Nelson Mandela as though the South African situation was . . . to be decided by F.W. de Klerk and Dr Mandela' . . . that President Bush personally phoned Mandela to brief him on the de Klerk visit; that 'I am being told that I am "out of favor" at your Embassy'; that 'briefings about me are prejudiced'.[46]

The violence between the ANC and the IFP would continue intermittently until the late 1990s. The TRC recorded details of eleven 'major massacres' between July 1990 and May 1993, of which the worst was the Boipatong massacre on 17 June 1992, during which forty people lost their lives. Violent attacks appeared to be particularly intense whenever negotiations between the ANC and the government were in progress. Mark Shaw's doctoral research shows that the more clinical killing such as hit-squad activity, train attacks and 'massacres – defined as the killing of five or more people in a single incident' declined from July 1992 when the NP began to abandon its relationship with the IFP. By this point, of course, the 'monster' which had concerned MID officials in 1985 had been unleashed, as the continuing ANC–IFP conflict demonstrated. Walter Felgate's memoirs captured the complicated personality of Mangosuthu Buthelezi: 'On the one hand, he believed he was right . . . [and] he was sure the ANC would fail . . . On the other hand, he genuinely hated and opposed apartheid. These two pulls in different directions characterised much of what he did and said . . . In one mode, he could offer the genuine rhetoric of the revolutionary. In the other mode, he spoke as the despised collaborator.'[47]

The question of the Third Force has always been subject to angry debate, which has often disagreed as to whether the term encapsulated a 'hidden hand' engaged in 'hit-squad' activity or a concentrated attempt by elements within the security state to act as agents provocateurs in order to inflame the growing enmity between Inkatha and the UDF–ANC. At different times and in different places it was probably both. In its first stage between 1986 and 1989, the Third Force was clearly a formal conspiracy. Later, it was somewhat more amorphous. Eugene de Kock, to his credit by far the most informative killer to testify before the TRC, discussed supplying weapons to the IFP at a Vlakplaas 'function' with Police Generals Englebrecht and van Rensburg in 1990. They in turn discussed the subject with General Basie Smit, and de Kock was given 'permission' to distribute the weapons and to 'generate funds in the usual manner'. John Carlin's relentless pursuit of the Third Force in the *Independent*, and the *Weekly Mail* and the *Guardian*'s simultaneously published 'Inkathagate' revelations of state funding to Buthelezi in July 1991, served to destroy the South African government's phoney stance of neutrality. As Stephen Ellis noted, from 1989 the Third Force's 'senior command and control system were gradually eroded until 1992. Thereafter it was effectively privatised.'[48] The TRC report, published in 1998, found that:

> while there is little evidence of a centrally directed, coherent or formally constituted 'Third Force', a network of security and ex-security force operatives,

acting frequently in conjunction with right-wing elements and/or sectors of the IFP, were involved in actions that could be construed as fomenting violence and which resulted in gross violations of human rights . . . Such networks functioned at times with the active collusion and/or knowledge of senior security force personnel, and that the former government, either deliberately or by omission, failed to take sufficient steps to put an end to such practices.[49]

Professor Richard Wilson has observed that the problem with the TRC's findings on the Third Force was historical 'periodization'. The TRC based its analysis of the Third Force on the period from 1990 to 1994, while Wilson suggested that it should have recognised the 'continuity between 1980s structures and 1990s violations'. His alternative analysis offered a history of the Third Force, part one, from 1985 to 1992: an NP–IFP political relationship which employed covert violence in an attempt to weaken the ANC and increase its chance of establishing 'the hegemony of an apartheid conservative alliance'; and part two, from 1992 onwards: following the collapse of the NP–IFP relationship, 'another political alliance gelled between units of the security forces, and ex-security forces, the IFP and the white right . . . which sowed random terror and sought to trigger a civil war and derail the first democratic elections'.[50]

On 20 May 1991, two months before the publication of the *Guardian*'s Inkathagate story, South Africa's most determined Third Force-denialist, John Kane-Berman, the long-standing head of the South African Institute of Race Relations (SAIIR), had briefed US 'diplomats' for two hours 'on the violence'. According to a State Department telegram, Kane-Berman stated that the ANC's 'policies are inherently confrontational, a final bid to destroy Inkatha as a serious political player. The ANC has lost the war and is now asking the SAG [South African Government] to disarm Inkatha unilaterally; it won't work. A war against the Zulus cannot be won.' The US Embassy found this hard to take: 'Despite a well-known anti-ANC, pro-Inkatha bias, Kane-Berman remains one of South Africa's most respected sociological analysts and commentators. His views are influential in the white liberal establishment, in business circles, in the media and in government. Where we disagree with his current analysis is his emphasis on ANC intimidation and coercion as a major source of today's violence on the Reef.'[51]

By 1993, Kane-Berman's analysis of violence in South Africa had become more nuanced: 'the demonisation of the state and the romanticisation of the behaviour of its victims – two sides of the same coin – have helped to prolong the violence'. Six years later, he developed the theme, claiming in the foreword to a pamphlet entitled *The Truth about the Truth Commission*, that there was a moral equivalence between the 'Third Force', which he admitted involved the 'security force and IFP members conspir[ing] to commit acts of violence', and the 'people's war', which he blamed on the ANC's invocations to 'render South Africa ungovernable'. In 2001, in an article wearily entitled 'Whither the Third Force?', Kane-Berman concluded:

> The 'Third Force', once blamed for all political violence in South Africa, seems to have disappeared without so much as a whimper, let alone a bang . . . Ludicrous as the Third Force theory was, it served a useful purpose in allowing all violence to be blamed on the then government and its supposed allies while entirely exonerating the ANC. It was a critically important tool in the ANC's propaganda armoury.[52]

Sadly, John Kane-Berman's work is what passed for intellectual thought in South Africa's morally culpable, white 'liberal' society: it is, and has always been, somebody else's fault. In 1986, the ANC was an exiled, imprisoned and banned group of people who attempted, successfully, to 'ride the tiger' of millenarian rage; the NP government and Inkatha were functioning national and regional political organisations with access to weapons, who colluded in a despicable attempt to undermine the liberation struggle. The key to understanding the role of the Third Force is the recognition that the 'black-on-black' political violence and the so-called 'tribal conflict' between the Zulus and the Xhosas, regularly promoted in apocalyptic terms in the domestic and the international media of the 1990s, virtually disappeared within a few years of the 1994 election. As Shula Marks memorably announced, it had been 'the dog that did not bark'.[53]

The Millionaire Tribalists and the Guru

Perhaps, the most ridiculous aspect of the Third Force story was the role played by the South African novelist Laurens van der Post and a group of maverick right-wingers in London. In the mid-1980s, while South Africa was racked by violent unrest, van der Post emerged as Buthelezi's channel to Margaret Thatcher. The writer and the Chief Minister had met only once previously in Johannesburg in 1977, after which van der Post had commented: 'I feel you are the only statesman of stature to stand for a future of the totality of all South Africans.' In 1984, they resumed a correspondence which led to Buthelezi dining with the British Prime Minister in August 1985. During the same period, van der Post engineered meetings between Buthelezi and Sir Geoffrey Howe, the Foreign Secretary, Charles Powell, Thatcher's foreign policy adviser, and the heir to the British throne, Prince Charles. Buthelezi also attracted support and found friends in West Germany, especially the Chancellor, Helmut Kohl. During the second half of the 1980s, van der Post lobbied relentlessly on Buthelezi's behalf. As a gatekeeper to Mrs Thatcher, he blocked progressive interpretations of the South African situation gaining a fair hearing. In July 1988 and October 1989, further meetings were held between Buthelezi and Thatcher.[54] At no time during her premiership did Margaret Thatcher deign to meet Oliver Tambo, the President of the ANC.

Following the release of Mandela, a group of rich, maverick right-wingers became increasingly vocal in their support of what they perceived as 'the Zulu cause'. In July 1990, as the terroristic Third Force violence erupted in the Transvaal, Buthelezi spoke to the Centre for Policy Studies, Thatcher's favourite think-tank, where he declared that the British had 'an unfinished job to do in South Africa'. The Conservative journalist Bruce Anderson 'complained that the Zulus were not being violent enough'. In November, John Aspinall, the eccentric zoo-keeper and casino-owner, who believed himself to be a 'White Zulu', organised a 'banquet' for Buthelezi with the millionaire asset-stripper Sir James Goldsmith, the aristocratic investment banker Jacob Rothschild and Marc Gordon, executive director of the International Freedom Front's London office. The *Mail & Guardian* revealed in 1996 that Gordon was an MID agent. He was later employed as a 'spin doctor' by the IFP during the 1994 elections and as a 'field organiser' by Goldsmith's Referendum Party in Britain's 1997 general election. In November 1992, van der Post met Aspinall, and the pair made common cause. Soon van der Post was included in Aspinall's club of 'tribalists' who had adopted Buthelezi with the affection that right-wing Americans in the 1980s had reserved for the Angolan UNITA leader Jonas Savimbi.[55] Additional members of the pro-IFP club were two media tycoons from Canada and Australia, Conrad Black and Kerry Packer. Black's autobiography, published in Canada in 1993, provided a glimpse of an April 1991 visit to Ulundi:

At dinner, Buthelezi and his king, Goodwill Zwelathini, and their principal collaborators appeared in their leopard skins and Aspers, on demand, gave them an address whose peroration called upon the Zulus to 'burnish your shields, sharpen your spears, and remember Shako [sic] the Great' . . . On this occasion, Buthelezi assured me that the tall, spear-carrying, fierce-countenanced young men who accompanied him and the king were 'not warriors. They are boy scouts. We have no warriors.' I asked how many 'boy scouts' he had. 'About 100,000' . . . The course of . . . the township violence clearly suggested that the Afrikaner government didn't altogether discourage the Zulus from resisting too complete or authoritarian a township takeover by the ANC.

Conrad Black, who later fell on hard times following an investigation by the US Securities and Exchange Commission which reported how he had transformed his own company into a 'corporate kleptocracy', concluded his assessment of Buthelezi with the following words, which one can only assume were some sort of in-joke: 'Gatsha . . . Buthelezi . . . and his powerful tribe are the third force in South Africa, after the ANC and the National Party government.'[56] A few weeks after Black's visit to Ulundi, the now ex-Prime Minister Margaret Thatcher gave a supportive speech in the region's Holiday Inn during which she declared: 'I am a Zulu'. Aspinall, Goldsmith and Packer eventually gave Buthelezi £1,000,000 before the 1994 election, but the dominant reason for the Chief's endless communication with Sir Laurens van der Post was a fantasy that Prince Charles would announce his support for Buthelezi and the IFP. On 1 May 1993, Prince Charles had a private meeting with Buthelezi at his Highgrove home. J.D.F. Jones, in his entertaining authorised biography of van der Post, *Storyteller*, commented that 'the consequences of support from the heir to the British throne for the Zulu leader before the multi-racial elections . . . would have been disastrous for the Prince as well as for British policy . . . The Foreign Office, should they have known any of this, would have been frantic.' Prince Charles did not make any statement.[57]

12

Shuffling the Pack

John Vorster may mock the term 'police state', but the fact remains that a pervasive uneasiness and fear underlie South African life in all sectors of the community, even triumphant Afrikanerdom. The uneasiness and fear are a direct result of the rigidly harsh policies of the Government. Not all those policies can be excused simply by blaming somebody or something else, the English, the past, the Bantu, the UN, the Communists, or what have you. Many of them are attributable to sheer, direct, personal stupidity, intolerance and lack of imagination on the part of those who make the laws and those who enforce them. It is time for them to face up to the fact that if you want a nation to live, you cannot destroy its decencies and wither its hopes forever. You have got to grow up and be worthy of your trust. You have got be brave enough to be human. You have got to stop creating more fear because you yourself are afraid. You have got to acquire the self-confidence to relax and be decent.

Allen Drury, *A Very Strange Society*, 1967[1]

SOUTH AFRICA WAS not transformed by the decision to release Mandela from prison in February 1990. The structural problems that plagued the dying apartheid state continued to threaten the negotiations process of the early 1990s, the election of 1994, the Mandela and Mbeki governments, and will continue to pose a problem in South Africa for many years to come. In brief, these problems are: rampant unemployment, anarchic violence, astounding levels of wealth disparity and a historical legacy of corruption, organised crime and a morally bankrupt paternalist polity. What did change adroitly was the intelligence culture of the Republic, at least on the surface. The policy grip of the hawkish securocrats had been loosening from May 1988, and by December 1992 it was effectively broken. In its place, a void appeared. This would eventually be filled by the victor of the Afrikaner intelligence wars, the NIS; by the ANC, which possessed a very different intelligence tradition; and by a massive private sector of both international and domestic security analysts, investigators, soldiers and spies.

ANC Traditions of Intelligence, 1969–1986

Vladimir Shubin, in his book *ANC: A View from Moscow*, made great play of attacking the factual errors and woolly thinking in apartheid South Africa's intelligence and media reports on the ANC, the SACP and the Soviet Union. It is quite correct to assert that the 'experts' on communism in the Security Police, DMI–MID and BOSS–NIS were often surprisingly ignorant of basic factual detail. Equally, South African intelligence information on the liberation movements was distinctly patchy. The NIS, for example, had no knowledge of ANC intelligence chief Joe Nhlanhla when they met him during one of the final Geneva negotiations in early 1990.[2] But the exiled ANC were no better prepared for the collision of modernity and tradition that awaited South Africa. Within half a dozen years, the Republic would throw off the shackles of an isolated, backward, besieged mindset and be transformed into a contemporary version of an entrepôt: a portal between the southern and northern worlds, between East and West, Africa and Europe, rich and poor, and past and future. Visitors would never again be sure whether they were travelling in a lost bubble of the colonialist 1950s (an innately racist, semi-feudal society) or the science-fiction 2050s (random brutality, ultra-capitalism and ubiquitous security).

The ANC's submissions to the TRC revealed an organisation that was subjected to decades of penetration by both South African and Western intelligence agencies. In a refreshingly honest and straightforward style, one submission admitted that 'in the 1960s, cadres were carefully recruited or selected by ANC branches inside the country before being sent abroad for military training. This screening and selection process inside the country resulted in a degree of complacency in the ANC's mission in exile.' In April 1969, at the Morogoro Conference in Tanzania, perhaps inspired by the failure of the Wankie campaign launched by Umkhonto we Sizwe (MK) (see page 50), a Department of Intelligence and Security (DIS) was proposed and accepted. Moses Mabhida was appointed the head of the DIS, a position he shared with his other responsibility as secretary of the Revolutionary Council ('the organ charged with implementing decisions made by the [ANC's National Executive Committee] in both the political and military domains').[3] Born in 1923 and active in communist politics since 1942, Moses Mabhida was a seasoned ANC–SACP politician. He had served as commander of MK before 1969 and he would be elected general secretary of the SACP in 1979, a position he would hold until his death from a heart attack in 1986. Mabhida appears to have attracted the ire of Temba Mqota, who would later be expelled from the ANC in October 1975 as a member of the anti-communist 'Gang of Eight'. Stephen Ellis noted that soon after Morogoro:

> Mqota wrote a letter to Wilton Mqwayi, the [MK] commander until 1964, who was then imprisoned on Robben Island. He told him that the organisation had been taken over by what Mqota termed boys and *tsotsis*. The former was a reference to Moses Mabhida. It is not in the Zulu tradition to require young men . . . to undergo a manhood circumcision ritual: the description of Mabhida as an uncircumcised 'boy' was clearly an insult, and a tribal one at that. The mention of *tsotsis*, the township gangsters, was a disparaging reference to [Joe] Modise who, in his younger days, had a reputation as one of the toughest street-fighters in Alexandra and was even accused by his enemies of having been a member of the notorious Msomi gang.[4]

Mabhida's first major intelligence project was Operation J, which he planned with Joe Slovo and Oliver Tambo. The idea of using a ship to transport MK soldiers to South Africa had originally been proposed in 1963 by Arthur Goldreich. Four years later, Joe Slovo visited Moscow in order to request assistance. In October 1970, the Politburo of the Soviet Union agreed, after successful reconnaissance by an MK team including Alex Moumbaris, 'to assist in acquiring a vessel, supplying the necessary equipment, including radio equipment, and training the landing party'. MK cadres received training at the Soviet naval base in Baku. The ANC purchased a ship, *Aventura*, which travelled to Somalia, refuelling on the way in Cape Town and Durban. The plan was for between twenty-five and forty-five MK guerrillas to land on the Eastern Cape coast. But then everything started to go awry. The ship's engines 'seized up off Mombasa' and the naval side of the plan was abandoned. It is possible that Operation J and *Aventura* was the 'Soviet plan' linked to Robert Gordon Bruce's attempt to release Mandela in 1969–70 (see page 45).

The ANC–MK was determined to persevere with the concept of taking the war to South Africa, and so the Operation J guerrillas were flown into Botswana and Swaziland and infiltrated across the border. Ronnie Kasrils, an important figure within the SACP, recalled that 'one of their number surrendered himself to the police' and Moumbaris and the others were captured and later imprisoned. The Russian historian Vladimir Shubin concluded that a Soviet GRU agent, Nikolay Chernov, who had been turned by the CIA in 1963 and was not exposed until 1974, was probably responsible for the failure of Operation J. Among Chernov's responsibilities was 'keeping in order the passports and visas of the guests of the Communist party', so he would have had access to the names and photographs of the MK cadres trained in Baku. The CIA, especially Angleton, would almost certainly have traded this information with BOSS. Shubin also suggested that Ahmed Timol's arrest in 1971 (see page 79) could have been facilitated by Chernov, as Timol had studied at the Lenin School in Moscow in 1969.[5]

During the early 1970s, the DIS concentrated on bureaucratic tasks such as gathering intelligence on potential 'inanimate' MK targets within South Africa, developing routes back into the Republic and providing security for senior members of the Congress. The DIS, at this stage, was a police force and an intelligence agency, responsible for both military and 'civilian' activity. One of the most impressive anti-apartheid espionage operations of the 1970s was the theft of nine files of classified material, concerning South African–West German nuclear collaboration, from the South African Embassy in West Germany. In September 1975, the ANC published a glossy pamphlet entitled *The Nuclear Conspiracy* which reproduced documents and correspondence from the classified files. The incident was extremely embarrassing for the South African government and the Ambassador in Bonn, Donald Sole: the ANC had shed the first light on South Africa's nuclear weapons programme *and* damaged South African–West German diplomatic relations. Hendrik van den Bergh rushed to Bonn to supervise the investigation into the leak. Lieutenant-General Günther Rall, the German Military Representative to the NATO Military Council, was dismissed by the German Defence Minister for making a clandestine 'private' visit to a South African nuclear research centre.[6] But who had been responsible for this 'intelligence' coup? In 1984, Breyten Breytenbach revealed that his 'kernel of a political formation . . . Okhela' had

> managed, *inter alia*, to penetrate the South African embassy in West Germany and to lay our hands on enough secret material . . . to show conclusively that there was collaboration with the Germans enabling the South Africans to start their own programme manufacturing, ultimately, nuclear arms . . . I am not so sure that we, at our level, in our context, were not at least as effective as the officially established anti-apartheid groups.[7]

Oliver Tambo's biographer Luli Callinicos confirmed Breytenbach's association with the ANC, noting cautiously that his 'record of achievements was in a very sensitive realm'. By the time the documents were published, Breytenbach was under arrest in South Africa (see page 42). In the late 1970s, Simon Makana headed the DIS. Representative of the younger generation of ANC–SACP leaders, Makana, who was in his thirties, had recruited Chris Hani into the ANC while the pair were students at Fort Hare. As the ANC's submission to the TRC revealed, the large influx of new recruits which followed the Soweto uprising was welcomed but 'fraught with danger since the [apartheid] regime was quick to exploit the situation by sending in several agents to infiltrate the Movement'. Vladimir Shubin wrote that in 1977 the 'screening' of new recruits was the responsibility of the Department of Work and Planning, but that this crucial task would be soon be handed over to the DIS. In 1978, around 500 ANC cadres were poisoned in the 'infamous Black September episode' at the MK Nova Catengue camp in Angola, popularly known as 'the University of the South'. That there were no deaths was due to the swift action of local Cuban doctors.[8]

In 1979, Oliver Tambo informed the party's NEC in Lusaka that 'major Western intelligence services held the view that the only way to defeat the revolutionary forces in South Africa was to infiltrate the ANC and transform it from within'. The conjunction of the threat of apartheid spies and Western interference led to a transformation in ANC intelligence. In 1980, the DIS was renamed the Department of National Intelligence and Security (NAT) and was organised into three sections: Intelligence, Security and Processing of Information. The organisation quickly assumed 'the roles of Military Intelligence, Counter-Intelligence, Military Police, VIP protection, and correctional services in a relatively ad hoc fashion'. In addition, according to the TRC submission, the NAT began to develop a 'strategic intelligence capacity, capable of forewarning the leadership of enemy moves'. Selected cadres were sent to the Soviet Union and East Germany (the German Democratic Republic, or GDR) for 'specialised training in security and intelligence . . . [the] training emphasised that the use of force was counterproductive, and stressed the use of the intellect'. Ronnie Kasrils confirmed that 'Whatever might be thought about interrogation methods in communist countries, I found that Soviet and East German training emphasised the need to depend on brain work and not beatings to arrive at the truth.'[9]

Mzwai Piliso, whose name would later adorn the post-apartheid National Intelligence Agency's Academy, was appointed as the third head of ANC intelligence in 1981. His deputy, Joe Gqabi, was assassinated in Harare later in the year (see page 152); Gqabi was replaced by Peter Tshikari. Simon Makana had been reassigned as head of Processing and Information, the section that BOSS–NIS would have called 'Evaluation'. Meanwhile, the ANC had established a system of Regional commands (both political and military). These included 'Organs' in Mozambique, Botswana, Lesotho and Angola. The NAT Security section, known within MK as Mbokodo ('a Xhosa word designating a stone used for grinding maize, generally regarded as "a euphemism for the harshness with which the Department treated its victims"'), would later be cited as a major reason for the mutinies which swept the Angolan camps in the mid-1980s.[10]

The problem was twofold: the MK cadres in the camps were eager to return to the 'war' in South Africa because news of 'spectacular' MK operations in the Republic had created a sense of false optimism (see page 159); and paranoia was rife within the ANC as a result of cadres, rightly, suspecting that apartheid spies operated at all levels, including the highest echelons of the organisation. Albie Sachs later explained: 'People were being sent to kill us . . . it was said at the time that we were paranoid . . . We were anxious and untrained and did not know how to respond.' This situation had been exacerbated by the discovery of a major apartheid spy-ring in March 1981. The NAT had launched an investigation into the death of an MK cadre which had resulted from a beating ordered by 'Kenneth Mahamba' (Timothy Seremane, brother of Joe Seremane later a Democratic Alliance MP), the commander of the MK camp at Quibaxe.[11] The investigation 'facilitated a major breakthrough with the discovery of an extensive network of infiltrators . . . some of whom were linked not only to Pretoria, but also to the intelligence services of some Western powers'. Stephen Ellis reported that an apartheid Security Police spy, 'Piper', had been uncovered in Lusaka. Piper's story is informative: he served time in the MK camps in Angola before being sent to the Lenin School in Moscow to study politics. Shubin revealed that Piper 'was so highly regarded by some SACP and ANC leaders that he was invited to an enlarged meeting of the Central Committee [of the SACP], which took place in the GDR'. Another apartheid agent confessed that he had poisoned the food at Nova Catengue in 1978. Ellis suggested:

There is no doubt that the climate their unmasking created was used by some in the ANC for blatantly personal and political purposes, and to rid themselves of rivals . . . Mbokodo men set to work detaining anyone suspected of espionage . . . They were given full powers to beat and torture suspects. In the pervasive atmosphere of suspicion, almost any action by a cadre . . . could become grounds for investigation. Men and women who complained about the quality of food in the camps, or who complained about the lack of military activity in South Africa itself, were labelled as suspects and held for interrogation.[12]

MK certainly faced very serious problems in the early 1980s. One of the spies who was detained by Mbokodo but escaped was Joe Mamasela, a car thief who had been recruited by the Security Police and instructed to join the ANC in Botswana; he returned to South Africa and was employed by Vlakplaas as an askari (see page 205). Shubin disclosed that sixty people 'confessed to contacts' with South Africa intelligence in the early 1980s which, if true, is a shocking indication of the scale of the infiltration. The central figure in the crisis that developed was Andrew Masondo, who had been severely beaten while serving his twelve-year sentence on Robben Island and was remembered by Mandela as 'a volatile fellow'. Ironically, Masondo's favourite passage in Shakespeare's work was from *Julius Caesar*: 'O! pardon me, thou bleeding piece of earth, That I am meek and gentle with these butchers.' Having travelled to the Soviet Union for 'specialised military training', he was appointed the ANC national commissar, described by Oyama Mabandla as 'the critical nexus between the [political] commissars and *Mbokodo*. The two were to work in harness as the Praetorian Guard of orthodoxy and "ideological correctness" in the movement. Their task was clearly to defend the movement from both "ideological subversion" and espionage penetration.'[13]

In June 1983, Pallo Jordan, a 'free-thinking intellectual' within the ANC, was arrested and held for six weeks. One Mbokodo officer was reported to have said of Jordan: ' "This American-trained intellectual is uppity" – and thus in need of straightening out.' Pallo Jordan later became a cabinet minister in the Mandela and Mbeki administrations. The MK mutiny started in December 1983, peaked in February 1984, leading to the ANC's Stuart Commission of Inquiry, and continued intermittently until June 1984 when seven mutineers were executed by firing squad following a hastily assembled military tribunal headed by Sizakele Sigxashe, later to be the first Director-General of the NIA. The Stuart Commission was scathing about the role played by Andrew Masondo, who was

demoted and redeployed to the post of director of the Solomon Mahlangu
Freedom College in Tanzania. Masondo later became a general in the
South African National Defence Force (SANDF) and was responsible for
the integration of MK cadres into the SANDF until his retirement in
2001. He is now the chairperson of the 'Vlakplaas Project' which is transforming the Vlakplaas farm into a National Centre for Traditional Healing
and Reconciliation.[14]

Although the Stuart Commission found that the brutality of Mbokodo
had 'seriously hampered' the organisation's 'major task of being the "eyes
and the ears" of the Movement', it concluded: 'Was there a plot, [a] conspiracy by enemy agents . . . to subvert the organisation, to seize power
within MK and dictate to the leadership? . . . The Commission has no
doubt that enemy agents . . . did exploit genuine grievances and fanned
the disturbances.' But it also stated that 'we have not uncovered any evidence that enemy agents organised the disturbances from the beginning'.
On the issue of enemy agents, the Commission recommended: 'Suspects
should be given trial missions . . . The NEC must adopt a coherent policy
with regard to captured enemy agents.' The Skweyiya Commission (1992),
established by the ANC, found former ANC intelligence chief Mzwai
Piliso 'directly responsible' for the establishment of Quatro, the worst of
the MK prison camps. Piliso 'candidly admitted his personal participation
in the beating of suspects in 1981 . . . [He] justified this treatment on the
basis that he wanted information . . . "at any cost".'[15]

The ANC's submission to the TRC concluded that the overreaction
by Mbokodo was 'probably almost inevitable – but by no means excus-
able' given the lack of 'clearly defined lines of authority', lack of training
in prison service and 'the very limited resources' available. At one level,
the tension between the young veterans of the Soweto uprising and the
older members of the ANC–SACP was similar to the tension between the
'young lions' attending 'the university of' Robben Island and the veterans
of Rivonia. The substantial difference was that, on the Island, Mandela
and Sisulu *had* to debate the issues with the young men, and the Robben
Islanders were faced with the (spying) apartheid prison authorities but not,
as far as we know, spies within their own structures. At another level, the
conflict between the MK mutineers and MK's leadership and security
structures reflected the problems involved in attempting to channel and
control millenarian rage. Ronnie Kasrils, who was chief of Military
Intelligence, a newly formed post, from 1983 to 1989, described Jabu
Nxumalo (Mzala), later to be the author of an eviscerating book on

Buthelezi, as 'militant even by June 16 [1976] standards'.[16] The 'children' of the Soweto uprising were very difficult revolutionary soldiers to discipline.

The Skweyiya Commission's report on 'complaints by former [ANC] prisoners and detainees' stated: 'We were left with an overall impression that for the better part of the '80s, there existed a situation of extraordinary abuse of power and lack of accountability.' The ANC later suggested that there had been bureaucratic difficulties in Angola caused by the fact that between 1983 and 1986 the NEC had 'declared Angola a military zone' which therefore 'fell under' MK command. MK Military Intelligence, Stephen Ellis reported, 'was widely regarded as being staffed by whites and Indians rather than black South Africans'. Kasrils portrayed the situation slightly differently: by his account, until 1987 MK's military intelligence was researched by Bill Anderson 'from a flat behind King's Cross station . . . [where] the two largest rooms had been converted into a virtual operations centre. The walls – and even the windows – of one room were completely covered in chipboard, on which were tacked maps and deployment charts.'[17] Following the Kabwe Conference (June 1985), the civilian wing of ANC espionage resumed control of intelligence in Angola. In a related decision, Mzwai Piliso was retired in 1986 and the intelligence department was administered by an 'interim directorate' which included Alfred Nzo, Joe Nhlanhla, Jacob Zuma and Sizakele Sigxashe. Although the ANC was forced to abandon its camps in Angola in 1989, a prison camp in Uganda continued to function until 1991. South African intelligence, especially the MID, made maximum use of the propaganda value of the MK prison camps during the early 1990s, as they had done with SWAPO's equivalent Angolan camps in the late 1980s.[18]

The ANC–SACP had, since 1961, been less concerned with 'intelligence' than with military action and security. It is, however, instructive to note that the political problem with the Gang of Eight in the early 1970s was linked, in part, to the establishment of the intelligence structure in 1969, and that the mutinies in Angola were made worse by Mbokodo rather than pre-empted by incisive intelligence work. MK terrorism ('armed propaganda') within South Africa had continued through the 1980s, but none of the actions possessed the panache of the SASOL bombings in 1980 or the destructive capacity of the Church Street bomb in 1983. Indeed, most MK activity was rapidly superseded by the violent unrest of the mid-decade. There can be little doubt that the assassination and murder, often with the 'necklace', of African spies, informers (*izimpimpi*) and policemen, which surely included a number of people who were innocent of the charges levelled against them, destroyed the apartheid intelligence networks so carefully established by van den Bergh and RI–BOSS in the 1960s and 1970s. It is possibly also true that many people recognised that the apartheid state was disintegrating and therefore were unwilling to assist the security forces. The Institute of Strategic Studies in Pretoria, considered by reporters to be close to the NIS, recorded 136 MK attacks in 1985, a further 230 'incidents of insurgency' in 1986 and 234 in 1987.[19]

One significant intelligence breakthrough in 1983 was engineered by Roland Hunter, a conscripted corporal in the MID, who leaked a substantial number of MID Directorate of Special Tasks documents detailing the SADF's support for RENAMO in Mozambique to ANC supporters Derek and Patricia Hanekom. The MID realised that it had a spy in its midst when in negotiation with the Mozambicans it became apparent that 'FRELIMO had a lot of information about its operations.' Later, evidence emerged, in the Wouter Basson case, that Hunter had been considered as a possible target for poisoning (see page 328).[20] In the media, the ANC had also been developing 'friends'. Howard Barrell, for example, outed himself in the *New Statesman* in February 1990. He disclosed that since 1980 he had 'worked clandestinely' for the ANC–SACP within the 'South African commercial press'. He had attempted to 'redefine the agenda of news in South Africa' by winning 'sustained' news coverage, either positive or negative, for the party. He recalled 'years of necessary deception, of lying, of projecting sometimes five or more personae . . . a measure of paranoia was indispensable [to his work]: you or more likely someone else could be dead without it'. Barrell also later admitted that his 'brief and lamentable career in intelligence with the [ANC] in the mid-1980s' had taught him three things:

> One: anyone who wants to join an intelligence outfit is probably unfit to do so. Entry should be granted only to those contemptuous or aggressively sceptical of the business and its practitioners. Two, a second requirement of admission should be a prodigious capacity to endure boredom – without having to resort to fantasy to maintain interest in the job. And three, women are better at intelligence work than men. They get on with the job quietly.[21]

A second ANC–SACP journalist–spy was Gavin Evans, who for a period in 1989 was targeted for assassination by the CCB. Evans, who has told his story many times, appeared in *Leadership* magazine in 1994 as 'the unlikely spy catcher', reporting that he had spied on Security Police agent Joy Harnden in 1984. Evans, like many of the apartheid spies, had emerged from the furious intelligence activity within South Africa's white student union, NUSAS. Harnden was later betrayed by Olivia Forsyth, another apartheid spy, when she was unmasked by the ANC and imprisoned in Quatro in 1986. Following her escape in 1988, Forsyth sought refuge at the British Embassy in Luanda. Back in South Africa, she claimed that she had been recruited by the ANC in the form of the Harare-based journalist Howard Barrell, who she claimed was 'known to be paranoid and highly suspicious'.[22] According to Evans, anti-apartheid activists in South Africa 'took to wearing "I never slept with Olivia" buttons'. The *Guardian* later reported that, according to Forsyth's own statement, in order to make herself ideologically acceptable 'her controllers gave her "a free hand to belittle South African Parliamentary politics, with the proviso that public officials at cabinet level could not be discredited under any circumstances"'. The world of South African student and media espionage was byzantine in its complexity, but the successes of the ANC in the mid-to-late 1980s demonstrated that South Africa's intelligence penetration of the anti-apartheid opposition was slowly being reversed.[23]

The importance of the intelligence changes effected at the Kabwe Conference, including the reversal of the structure's name from the NAT to the Directorate of Intelligence and Security (DIS), should not be underestimated. To a significant extent, Kabwe represented the ANC's response and adoption of the 'People's War' that had already started in South Africa. Joe Slovo told *Marxism Today* in 1986 that 'the ruling power bloc and its support constituency in the white community . . . know they cannot hold on for very much longer'. The ANC–SACP was therefore eager to exploit the possibilities that the insurrection of the mid-1980s had exposed. Howard Barrell's doctoral thesis noted the strategies being debated within the higher echelons of the ANC in 1986:

> The more innovative of the ANC's strategists [suggested that] ANC strategy [should] henceforth depend, in effect, entirely upon ordinary people's energies. The ANC should abandon any thoughts of leading a gradual build-up of forces as entailed in the people's war [strategy]. Rather, it should hold out the perspective of decisive popular insurrection against the state, a sort of quick fix of one or another degree of spontaneity. Whereas some in the ANC (like Slovo) maintained the ANC could not hope even to provide significant leadership to such an insurrection, which would be entirely spontaneous, others (like [Mac] Maharaj and [Ronnie] Kasrils) argued it could

and must be led in ways suggested by the [underground warfare – Military and Combat Work] approach.

Joe Nhlanhla's appointment as director of the DIS was confirmed in 1987. In late 1987, the 'President's Committee' was created to support Oliver Tambo. Its members included Alfred Nzo, the Secretary-General of the ANC, Thomas Nkobi, the Treasurer-General, Joe Modise, the Army Commander of MK, and Nhlanhla, representing the DIS. Jacob Zuma was confirmed as deputy director of the DIS and head of Intelligence in 1988; Sigxashe had been appointed head of the Central Intelligence Evaluation Sector: Processing and Analysis in 1985.[24]

One of the interesting aspects of the dual-intelligence history of South Africa is the fact that the three key moments in the history of ANC intelligence closely mirrored developments within the apartheid structures. It is possible that the creation of the original DIS following the Morogoro Conference in April 1969 was a response to the announcement of the establishment of BOSS in South Africa. The creation of NAT in 1979–80 could also be seen as a reaction to the Information scandal and the MID takeover in 1978. The increasing militarisation within South Africa was quickly reflected in the dominance of Mbokodo in the Angolan camps during the early 1980s. The decision in 1985 to transform ANC intelligence once again could be compared to the secret debates within South Africa which intensified the brutality and illegality of the apartheid security forces. Until the mid-1980s, the ANC's intelligence system had effectively shadowed the apartheid structures; from 1986, while retaining certain similarities (not least the secrecy), Operation Vula would move in a dramatically different direction from the NIS's slow progression towards negotiation.

The Vula Boys

The decision to launch Operation Vul'indlela (translated from Zulu as 'Open the way', hereafter 'Vula') was taken in 1986 by a meeting of the ANC's NEC. In a replica of the SSC's later acceptance of the NIS's 'permission' to meet the ANC in exile (see page 248), Chris Hani and Jacob Zuma proposed to the NEC that a special committee which comprised Oliver Tambo and Joe Slovo should be established to investigate methods of smuggling senior ANC leaders into South Africa, and that, in Maharaj's words, 'they are empowered to conduct this work without reporting to the

NEC, they may choose the moment at which they wish to report progress; and they are given a blank cheque'. The proposal was approved. The ANC later explained that Vula was designed 'to undertake the task of relocating senior members of the movement – including members of the NEC – in the country to create on-the-spot integrated political–military structures charged with the task of giving day-to-day leadership to the struggle'. The senior commanders of Vula were Mac Maharaj (recruiting and in-country command), Siphiwe Nyanda (deputy to Maharaj) and Ivan Pillay (administration and 'project co-ordination' in Lusaka). Mac Maharaj was a fascinating figure who had served twelve years on Robben Island between 1964 and 1976 and in exile was elected to the NEC of the party in addition to taking responsibility for the ANC's underground structures within South Africa. He would later be appointed minister of transport in Mandela's first government.[25]

Vula was shrouded in secrecy – those involved were determined that it should not be penetrated and compromised like so many secret operations in the past. In 1985, for example, Operation Butterfly, which had involved a number of people who would later be involved in Vula, had attempted to smuggle in 'middle-ranking' leaders and was immediately exposed by a Security Police spy. Another factor that directly contributed to Vula's secrecy was the ongoing transformation within ANC intelligence: the leader of MK, Joe Modise, was not informed of the operation, but Ronnie Kasrils was quickly recruited. In late 1986, Kasrils and Ebrahim Ismael Ebrahim approached the Dutch A-AM chairperson, Conny Braam, to inform her that the ANC needed to recruit white Europeans and North Americans to move to South Africa and the frontline states in order to develop 'safe houses' from which ANC activists could operate. Ebrahim said:

> Don't forget that a white face has many advantages . . . It means that fewer questions are asked; salaries for whites are mostly higher, they have better houses – even in Swaziland. They're less likely to be stopped at roadblocks. They are just not so likely to be suspected of helping us. Whites are still very much a protected species in southern Africa. We must use that fact to our advantage.[26]

Mac Maharaj later made it clear that the foreigners were 'coming to serve, albeit in an infrastructural level, and [were] not engaged in the actual [armed] struggle'. Nyanda added: 'The foreigners were very peripheral to the actual project.' During 1987 and 1988, a number of Dutch, Canadian,

British and American nationals, who had agreed to 'serve' the
ANC–SACP, established 'covers' in southern Africa. One of the most
intriguing Vula operatives was a Dutch airline hostess, 'Antoinette', who
in a neat reversal of the 'Airline spies' incident more than a decade earlier
(see page 42) would smuggle messages, money and equipment to the Vula
leaders in South Africa.[27] Since the early 1980s, Tim Jenkin, who had been
imprisoned and had escaped from Pretoria in 1979, and Ronnie Press, a
South African exile, had been experimenting with communications systems. As Jenkin noted in a series of articles for *Mayibuye*: 'Poor communications had determined the shape of our struggle. It was because our . . .
cadres could not communicate with the leaders and between themselves
that the underground never developed and People's War never became a
reality.' By 1987, Jenkin had developed a system that, using computer
programs and very primitive modems, could dispatch encrypted messages
through telephone lines. Working closely with Braam, Maharaj and Jenkin
sent a 'playboy type that no one would suspect of being a "spy"' to South
Africa where he investigated the South African phone system: 'He photographed public telephones, located nearly every suitable phone in
Johannesburg and Durban and brought back a number of "samples" that
he pulled out of the sockets and ripped out of phone booths!. . . He [also]
found out that radio telephones had just been introduced in South Africa.'

In July 1988, Mac Maharaj, Siphiwe Nyanda (Gebhuza) and two others
departed for Moscow. Their covers were that Maharaj was awaiting a
kidney transplant and Nyanda was to attend a Soviet military training
course. Within a few weeks, they had infiltrated South Africa in disguise,
and contacted London from Durban using the new communications technology. Over the next few months a system would be developed which
linked the Vula operatives and the ANC in Lusaka ('the spokes') to London
(Jenkin's 'hub'). It was an impressive achievement, the technology of which
was constantly improved and updated. Over the next two years, Vula would
build an underground intelligence structure. Vula activities are said to have
included: 'propaganda', meetings with the Mass Democratic Movement
(MDM – the successor to the UDF) leaders, plans to set up a reception
committee for Mandela upon his release, and the stockpiling of weapons.
By April 1989, Charles Nqakula, the Vula commander in the Western
Cape, had devised a method whereby Mandela in a warder's house in the
grounds of Victor Verster prison could communicate with the ANC in
Lusaka through the use of written messages hidden inside undetectable
compartments in books. Jenkin, in London, noted that Tambo and

Mandela 'were now talking in confidence for the first time since the early
'60s . . . I thought how the regime's chiefs [imagined] they were entirely
in control of the situation. They wanted to create the impression that they
were talking to Mandela alone and that his responses were his personal
opinions. Little did they know that they were talking to the collective.'[28]

Maharaj wrote on the subject of his cover to his friend Vladimir Shubin
in Moscow: 'Keep well and keep telling effective lies about me . . . (Oh,
how one lie will lead to a lifetime of lies).' In July 1989, Maharaj briefly
visited Moscow and London because, as Jenkin said, 'the stress of the situation was beginning to take its toll'. In an interview with *Mayibuye*, Nyanda
later revealed that 'Our primary concern was carrying out underground
political work . . . this was to provide us with the capacity to organise MK
structures with specialisation in combat, intelligence etc. . . . We were only
beginning to create viable military structures.' The Vula network that was
created between 1988 and 1990 involved many figures who would play a
significant role in ANC politics and intelligence over the next decades:
Janet Love, later an ANC MP; Mo Shaik, an East German-trained intelligence operative who headed Vula's intelligence structure; Dipak Patel,
Director-General of Transport from 1997 to 1999; Pravin Gordhan, the
Commissioner of the South African Revenue Service; Raymond Lalla,
later head of the reformed South African Police's Crime Intelligence division; and Billy Nair, later an ANC MP. In early 1990, Ronnie Kasrils flew
into South Africa, in disguise, to join the Vula team.[29]

In her account of the Vula story, Conny Braam revealed that in the
summer of 1988 one of the ANC operatives being prepared to be infiltrated into South Africa was suspected of 'working for South African security'. Braam provided a glimpse into the paranoid world of exile resistance:

> The invisible monster gnawing away at the organisation had been partially
> exposed. After a little while the anxiety grew again of its own accord. The
> spies were there, all right. But where? And who? The terrible truth was of
> course that the ANC had indeed been infiltrated, probably on a large scale.
> This was known. So everybody was preoccupied by the question of who
> could be trusted, and who were the villains. But in that very complex situ-
> ation who could prove they could be trusted when the worst came to the
> worst? And who could claim the right to throw the first stone?[30]

Tim Jenkin observed in his account of Vula that 'the only way [the
communications] system could be cracked was if the enemy somehow got
hold of the "key" disks and made copies . . . After a while it was clear that

nothing of the sort was happening. If the enemy was reading the messages then they would surely have acted on the information.' Despite the fear of penetration, Vula operatives actually managed to develop a number of 'moles' within the Security Police, the SADF and the NIS. The Canadian academic Robert D'A. Henderson reported that Mo Shaik recruited a 'senior [NIS] official – codenamed "Nightingale" – who . . . became an agent-in-place, passing on considerable classified material outlining the extent of the government's intelligence on the ANC and its underground networks within the country'.[31] In July 1994, Maharaj released 'a three-volume dossier' of DONS–NIS material, from 1979–1980, gathered on himself. The Maharaj files were, according to the Johannesburg *Star*: 'at times chilling and sinister, at others bumbling and childish'. Most of the information had been compiled by Karl Edwards, an associate of Craig Williamson. Maharaj said that he had released the dossier because 'I am aware that files are being destroyed . . . I am signalling that we have the capacity to compare information and know what they have.' The documents were amateur and littered with spelling errors, but they contained a confirmation of the fact that the prison authorities bugged the cells on Robben Island: 'The Security Branch of the Department of Prisons co-operates with the Security Police and the NIS by providing raw data collected through mail censorship and listening devices.'[32]

On 6 July 1990, two Vula operatives, Mbuso Shabalala and Charles Ndaba, were arrested. Henderson, citing 'confidential correspondence', suggested that 'one of the two original Vula detainees had previously worked as a Security Police informant'. Nyanda later admitted that 'perhaps we tended to relax after February 2 when the ANC was unbanned. For example, we could have acted much more swiftly after discovering that some of our comrades were missing.' On 11 July, Nyanda was captured and the Durban network raided. Jenkin recalled: 'four "legals" and six underground comrades had been arrested . . . the [operatives] in Durban had violated all the rules of security that we had so assiduously tried to impress upon them . . . The minutes of an entire underground conference were [later] quoted by police as evidence of the plot to overthrow the government.' Five days later, the police pounced in Johannesburg, and on 25 July Mac Maharaj was captured. There is little doubt that the Vula operatives had been lucky to survive the clutches of the Security Police for so long. It later transpired that Maharaj *and* the CCB used the Rosebank Hotel in Johannesburg for meetings; ironically, this was also the hotel that the BBC utilised.[33]

In October 1990, eight Vula operatives were put on trial charged with conspiring 'to create an underground network the task of which would be to recruit, train, lead and arm a "people's" or "revolutionary" army to be used to seize power from the government by means of an armed insurrection'. The defendants were released on bail and later granted indemnities. On 22 June 1991, ten Vula operatives were 'unmasked', including Ronnie Kasrils, who had remained in hiding for eleven months. Nelson Mandela proudly announced: 'For more than two years the Government and its security forces had no inkling of [Vula's] existence [and] had not detected that members of the [ANC] leadership were living and working inside the country.' The TRC later found that Shabalala and Ndaba, the two Vula operatives captured on 6 July 1990, were murdered by the Security Police on 12 July 1990. Kasrils added: 'The execution took place at night on the banks of the Tugela River. Their bodies were wrapped in wire mesh, weighted down and tossed into the shark-infested river mouth, never to be seen again.'[34]

An intriguing US State Department 'confidential' report, dated 26 July 1990, was entitled 'ANC denies conspiracy, but evidence mounts'. The document noted that Mac Maharaj had been arrested on 25 July and 'growing evidence [suggested] that a communist-dominated ANC underground was at work in South Africa preparing for a possible seizure of state power'. The State Department disclosed that its 'press source' believed that Ronnie Kasrils 'will also be arrested soon'. The dynamite in the report detailed a meeting between the unnamed journalist and Maharaj, 'shortly before he was arrested'.

> Our source was astonished that Maharaj admitted off-the-record that:
> – He had indeed been busy caching arms inside South Africa, as police allege;
> – One of the contingency plans of 'Vula' for triggering a 'national insurrection' called for the assassination of Nelson Mandela;
> – The ANC [NEC] in Lusaka, which three years ago authorised creation of an underground command structure in South Africa, had only hazy knowledge of the actual structure and operations of 'Vula'.[35]

While the Americans may well have been misinformed by their source on the alleged plan to assassinate Mandela – the next few years would see a multitude of stories relating to attempts to assassinate South Africa's icon – it is interesting that Maharaj's reported off-the-record statements are accurate on the first and third points. The third point, the ANC's 'hazy knowledge' of Vula, is perhaps the most revealing for its intelligence implications. Tim Jenkin revealed that within two weeks of Mandela's release Mac Maharaj submitted his resignation and requested to be 'exfiltrated'. Apparently, the Vula operatives felt that their views 'were largely ignored' by the ANC in Lusaka. There was no response to Maharaj's request and, in April 1990, Mandela encouraged him to retract his resignation. In December of that year, Maharaj attempted to resign his membership of the ANC and the SACP but was dissuaded. Jenkin explained that one of the key weaknesses of Vula was that 'no one was supposed to know that they were in the country, making it difficult for those in the know to give much weight to the views emanating from the underground'. But, despite the obvious restraints of a supposed invisible underground structure, the deeper grievances related to the tensions between the Vula operatives and the 'above ground' UDF–MDM and ANC officials. As Jenkin observed: 'It appeared that important decisions relating to internal matters were being taken without consulting [the Vula operatives] . . . internal structures that had not been operating underground . . . appeared to be exerting undue influence.' Mac Maharaj told me in 2002 that Vula operatives had spied on UDF–MDM officials meeting with 'the Israelis' during 1989, and there is some suggestion that the residual UDF–MDM were eager to purchase weapons and receive military training.[36]

Vula was a genuine intelligence operation. Ironically, this is indirectly confirmed by the secrecy that still surrounds its activities and the restricted information that is available on what it actually achieved. Henderson appraised Vula in the following terms: 'After almost 25 years of ANC/MK armed infiltrations and high-profile sabotage attacks, Operation Vula ranked as the only successful ANC/MK clandestine operation to create a functioning nationwide underground structure.' Patti Waldmeir, in her usual forthright style, attempted a deconstruction of Vula: 'Perhaps the Vula project . . . [was intended] to persuade the ANC of its own strength. Perhaps it was an insurance policy, in case negotiations failed. Maybe it was one last tilt at revolution. ANC leaders themselves still dispute Vula's meaning, an issue over which emotion clouds hindsight. No one knows what Maharaj was really up to with Vula.' The operation's deeply problematic contribution to the struggle was that it had established, in addition to DIS and MK's Military Intelligence, a third ANC intelligence network. Maharaj had enjoyed the rare opportunity to select MK and ANC cadres for his secret operation, he had received substantial funding and he had utilised foreign civilians to provide a critically important supportive function. Most significant of all, he had been able to shut out of the process many ANC–MDM members who would not forget the insult. In this sense, Vula was, and perhaps had to be, an 'exclusive' structure in direct contrast to the 'inclusive' tradition of the ANC's non-racial history. Over the next fifteen years, Maharaj's 'Vula boys', as they were named by Sam Sole, even though women made up a substantial component of the Vula team, would exert a significant influence on the development of intelligence in the Republic.[37] Vula's most dominant legacy to the ANC and the new South Africa would be that it cemented one single message into the minds of ANC politicians: the importance of possessing a personal intelligence network.

As the exiled members of the ANC returned to South Africa in 1990, its official intelligence structures were 'assisted by various MDM networks, and contacts within the intelligence services of the regime'. According to the TRC submission, it soon became apparent that 'the extent of [the apartheid intelligence] infiltration of anti-apartheid structures was immense, running to thousands of agents'. There were a few changes at the top of the ANC's intelligence structures at the beginning of the 1990s: in 1989, Keith Mokoape succeeded Kasrils as the head of MK's Military Intelligence; he later became a director of ARMSCOR, the state arms manufacturer. Mokoape was followed in 1992 by Mojo Motau, who is the current head of the SANDF's Military Intelligence. Joe Nhlanhla remained the Director of the DIS until the 1994 election and Jacob Zuma continued as head of the DIS Intelligence section until 1993, when Patrick 'Terror' Lekota was appointed.[38]

There was a fair amount of prejudiced nonsense written in the mid-1990s about 'the KGB, the Cuban DGI, Libyan Intelligence, and the East German SSD (or *Stasi*)' training of the NAT–DIS operatives, which had apparently merged with 'ideological fervour based on the socialist/communist politics' to create 'a complete intolerance for dissenting views . . . and gave an ideological character to the periodic purges carried out within the ANC'. Somehow this fictional representation was supposed to equate with the excesses of apartheid's bantustan, military, police or civilian intelligence, which had been 'developed and trained largely according to Western norms and practices'.[39] The parallel has not been borne out.

The Inheritance Shuffle

A second ANC–NIS meeting was held in Lucerne on 6 February 1990, four days after de Klerk's famous speech: Louw and Spaarwater met Mbeki and Aziz Pahad, in place of Jacob Zuma. Louw recalled that during this meeting, 'We were not feeling each other out any more. Now we were starting to set up structures and make practical arrangements.' Among the concerns were how to return ANC, SACP and PAC personnel back to South Africa in safety; responses from the ANC on de Klerk's statement; issues surrounding definitions of 'political prisoners'; and the preliminary 'talks about talks' that preceded full negotiations. Allister Sparks recorded that working committees were established to address the most urgent problems: 'Group Alpha (Mandela's release), Bravo (the release of detainees), Charlie (setting up discussions at the political level), and Delta (maintaining contact between the NIS and the [DIS])'. Louw and Spaarwater returned to South Africa believing that they were under surveillance from Swiss intelligence. As Spaarwater told Sparks: 'We were there on false documentation, false passports and cover names, which of course constitutes a criminal offence.'

A third meeting, on 20 February, was held in Berne. Niel Barnard and Fanie van der Merwe, both of whom had negotiated with Mandela in prison, attended the third ANC–NIS meeting. The ANC team included its intelligence chief, Joe Nhlanhla, for the first time. As the teams discussed the modalities for the first meeting within South Africa between the government and the ANC's NEC, it became apparent that Barnard was not willing to countenance the involvement of SACP leader Joe Slovo in the ANC delegation. Eventually, having telephoned de Klerk, the NIS chief accepted that the both delegations could choose whoever they wanted. Barnard later commented: 'It may not seem much . . . but it was a big step then.' A fourth meeting took place in Geneva in early March, 'at which a joint steering committee was set up to make detailed arrangements for the return of the exiles and for the first formal meeting between the government and the ANC on South African soil'.[40]

Between March 1990 and April 1994, South Africa experienced a staggered hand-over of power. Intelligence functioned at multiple levels throughout the period. The senior operatives on both sides were directly involved in the negotiations process, but they 'withdrew to the periphery of the process', no longer driving the changes as they had in 1989. On the government side, Barnard and Spaarwater resigned from the NIS at the end of 1991, leaving Mike Louw to become the fourth head of the agency that, although greatly changed, had been started by Hendrik van den Bergh in the 1960s. On the ANC side, Nhlanhla and Zuma continued in their intelligence roles, whereas Thabo Mbeki, who had been perhaps the most successful 'diplomat' in the late 1980s, retreated from the intelligence world in which he had dabbled in 1989 and 1990.

The first period of the transition (from 1990 to September 1992) was dominated by the violence of members of the security forces and the ANC–IFP conflict in Natal and the Transvaal (see page 274). The ANC–SACP position had been clear since at least 1986, when Slovo told Jonathan Steele: 'the bottom line is that there must be an acceptance of the principle of majority rule in a unitary, democratic state'. The NP government's bottom line was 'group self-preservation'. The ANC's central challenge was essentially the same as it had been since the Soweto uprising, containing and controlling the exuberance of its soon-to-be electorate; the government was faced with the task of harnessing the security-force 'monster' that it had created but which appeared in the words of André du Toit to be intending 'to go on playing a central role according to [its] own vision'. De Klerk's stumbling moves to this end were contradictory and clearly limited by his government's weaknesses. He appointed the 'Harms Commission of Inquiry into certain alleged murders' (death squads) on the same day as he unbanned the proscribed organisations and announced Mandela's release, but the Commission's report, delivered in September 1990, was cautious and defensive, although the hearings had been a revelation. A few weeks later, de Klerk appointed General 'Kat' Liebenberg (see page 268) as chief of the SADF. In April 1991, the Special Branch or Security Police was transformed by government legislation into the Crime Intelligence Service (CIS).[41]

By May 1991, as Dan O'Meara explained, 'the NP government had gone a long way to rebuilding the political *élan* it seemed to lose after 1973 . . . the ANC seemed weakened and struggling to define its own role. Many nationalists began to take seriously the prospect of a post-apartheid NP-led government.' Hugo Young, the doyen of liberal commentators in London, declared on 25 April that 'what the blacks need is a leader as competent as de Klerk'. Of course, the ANC was battling with innumerable (and often invisible) opposing forces, not the least of the party's problems being the difficulties attached to establishing a political infrastructure throughout the country capable of mobilising the population and fighting an election. The Inkathagate scandal in July 1991 (see page 277) weakened de Klerk immea-

surably; as Sampson noted: 'Rarely has any news story had such an immediate impact on a government.' The Minister for Law and Order (Police),
Adriaan Vlok, and the Minister of Defence, Magnus Malan, were removed
from their posts and demoted to lesser jobs within the cabinet. De Klerk
later recalled: 'Both ministers had solemnly and repeatedly assured me that
they had no personal knowledge of, or involvement in, the totally unacceptable criminal activities – such as murder, assassination, torture and the
instigation of violence – of which elements within the security forces were
being accused.'[42]

A series of reports by the Goldstone Commission investigating the violent and malevolent activities of the police and defence force, between
November 1992 and April 1994, and the unpublished Steyn Report
(1992–4), which led to the dismissal of twenty-three senior members of
the SADF, 'including two generals and four brigadiers', during the 'night
of the Generals' in December 1992, effectively neutralised institutional
MID and police power. De Klerk's autobiography referred to 'a veritable
rat's nest of unauthorised and illegal activity within military intelligence'.
Mike Louw and the NIS played a crucial role in assisting Air Force General
Pierre Steyn in his continuing attempts to investigate the military. In
October 1992, the NP government had 'steamrolled' the Further
Indemnity Bill through a special session of parliament; this gave indemnity
to those who 'had advised, directed, commanded, ordered or performed
offenses with a political objective prior to 8 October 1990'.[43] This general
amnesty was a clear sign that the settlement was at hand. But containing
the security forces and forging a political consensus would not reveal the
intelligence secrets of the Republic, many of which would retain subterranean political power for many years to come.

The ANC's proposals of a Government of National Unity and the
'sunset clauses' which would permit civil servants to retain their jobs for a
period of five years led in November 1992 to a 'Record of Understanding'
that slowly but surely set the country on the path to the elections of 1994.
There would be many nightmares during the eighteen months before
South Africa's 'rainbow' election: the constant obstructiveness, until the last
days before the election, of Chief Buthelezi and the IFP; the murder of the
SACP General Secretary, Chris Hani, on 10 April 1993 by right-wing
maniacs, which continues to raise significant questions in many quarters;
the emergence of a Volksfront under the leadership of General Constand
Viljoen; and the cartoon buffoonery of the white-supremacist Afrikaner-
Weerstandsbeweging (AWB). But the die had effectively been cast in

November and December 1992. South Africa's general election was held from 26 to 29 April 1994 and President Nelson Mandela was inaugurated on 10 May.[44]

Despite the fact that, in Barnard's words, the NIS had 'melted into the background' after the negotiations of 1989, occasional glimpses appeared. Prior to his resignation in December 1991, Barnard, speaking on behalf of the League of Former Members of the NIS, responded to P.W. Botha's statement that the NIS was 'a corrupt department and a bad lot'. Barnard said that League members were 'upset' and added: 'I would like to put on the record that the service and its people have always been loyal in serving this country and have always been willing to make sacrifices in this regard.' In February 1992, Mike Louw, the new head of NIS, warned the Johannesburg *Sunday Times* 'against the view that one can wind down counter-intelligence operations. He believes South Africa is more vulnerable than ever – particularly through the possibility of foreign manipulation of domestic political processes.' The *Argus* quoted the understated but often informative avatar of transformation as saying: 'It is not easy for us in the NIS to function objectively, rationally and effectively in these times . . . If the referee punishes us, we will accept it. But also remember that a country, a society, which damages its intelligence capability unnecessarily because of political infighting, is in danger of eventually paying a high price for it.'[45]

In April 1992, Sandy Africa published an essay on intelligence which raised most of the questions that would dominate the transformation of the agencies over the next three years. She revealed the astonishing scale of 'intelligence' in apartheid South Africa's thoroughly 'spooked' culture: 'The Department of Foreign Affairs, the SA Prison Services, the National Coordinating Mechanism, Escom, the National Parks Board, the Council for Scientific and Industrial Research, and the Human Sciences Research Council all provide intelligence which is coordinated by the National Intelligence Interpretation Branch of the [SSC].' Africa recommended the suspension of the SSC, the 'pruning' of the MID's 'bloated bureaucracy' and the disbanding of police intelligence. Here was a brave voice that was prepared to take things back to basics, asking: 'Is there a need for intelligence activities?'[46] It was a refreshing question.

In May 1992, the ANC published a list of guidelines designed to facilitate the establishment of a genuinely *national* intelligence service. The document was based on a discussion paper written by former Vula intelligence operative Mo Shaik, and signalled a dramatic paradigm shift in both the

National Party and the ANC's intelligence traditions. Primarily the document declared that 'the National Intelligence agency will be responsible for gathering, collating and evaluating strategic information that pertains to the security of the state and the citizenry'. It stipulated that intelligence would recognise the democratic rights of South Africans to 'engage in lawful political activity' and it assured the public that the agency would be 'politically non-partisan', 'accountable to parliament' and 'regulated by relevant legislation'. The guidelines added that the new agency would be opposed to all forms of prejudice: 'it shall guard the ideals of democracy, non-racialism, and non-sexism, national unity and reconciliation and act in a non-discriminatory way'. Affirmative action would be employed to guarantee that the agency would 'reflect the social and gender composition' of the country. Finally, it announced that 'it should be subject to the right of the public to information gathered by any intelligence institution subject to the limitations of classification consistent with an open and democratic South Africa'.[47] This particular clause appeared to imply a significant extension of 'freedom of information' never previously experienced in the Republic.

At an academic conference organised by the Institute for Strategic Studies on 'Security and intelligence in a post-apartheid South Africa', held in August 1992, Joe Nhlanhla announced that the new intelligence service would 'no longer regard [the population of the Republic] as its enemies'. He declared that the 'professionalism' of the new service would 'be based . . . on the highest moral standards'. He acknowledged the symbiotic relationship that intelligence would need to facilitate in the new South Africa: 'The security of the state depends on the security of the people, and the security of the people depends on the security of the state.' But in a period when negotiations towards a new settlement had broken down, Nhlanhla did not cushion his indictment of the 'distorted features' which he believed were 'deeply rooted' in the apartheid intelligence agencies:

- A militaristic and racist culture where the interests served have been those of the ruling Nationalist government and not those of the people as a whole.
- A culture of secrecy and lack of transparency and a total absence of accountability to the public.
- An undermining of basic human rights and freedoms, including the freedom of speech, thought and action, and the right to privacy.
- Repressive and criminal methods – detention and torture, assassinations, kidnapping – in pursuit of the interests of state security.

- An inward-focused approach where the greatest threat to national security was seen to come from fellow South Africans – those engaged in the liberation struggle.
- The wanton infiltration of organisations, and disinformation against anti-government organisations.
- The deliberate misleading of the public through the use of front organisations to achieve ignoble intelligence objectives.
- The abuse of taxpayers' money, and many more excesses.[48]

On 12 and 13 March 1993, the NIS briefed the DIS 'on how it functioned and the principles to which it subscribed'. At further meetings in May and July, intelligence representatives formed a 'working group' to begin the process of establishing the principles that would underpin the new amalgamated intelligence service. In November 1993, Mo Shaik attended a conference addressing the issue of covert operations, during which he presented a paper which stated: 'My personal view on the issue of covert operations is that for a while, . . . until the people of this country are protected and can live in a stable environment . . . it may be a necessary evil for a period, but . . . we must still have the checks and balances to ensure that it is not open to abuse and will not lead to the kinds of atrocities we have had in the past.' In the same month, the Sub-Council of the Transitional Executive Council was tasked to oversee the negotiations towards an interim constitution, including the development of intelligence principles. Security specialist Mark Shaw explained that 'the first principle agreed was that a single agency be established. Tied to this was an agreement, never officially stated, that it would have a new name: "National Intelligence Agency" appeared to be favoured early on, although "South African Secret Service" was also mooted in mid-1994.' It was also 'agreed that the "constant flow of intelligence should not be disrupted." Current structures would continue until they evolved into something new.'[49]

At the Strategic Studies conference in 1992, Professor W.J. Breytenbach, who had attended the Afrikaner–ANC meetings in London, informed his audience that 'the uncertainties about the security outcomes in South Africa . . . are essentially political in nature. It is therefore a question of the proverbial inheritance of the political kingdom. It can be taken for granted that the political, rather than the practical considerations, will predominate. That means that security controls – including control over intelligence – still depend on power plays.' Although the situation was complicated by the coalition Government of National

Unity, President Mandela confirmed the issue of the 'political kingdom' in an interview with *Time* magazine in May 1994: 'As far as the question of the Third Force . . . is concerned, we have taken over the army as well as the police. Mr de Klerk tried to say, "If you take defense, give us the police. Or if you take the police, give us defense." I said, "No. Those two must be controlled by us. You are not in a position to clean the police force of the elements that are creating this violence."' F.W. de Klerk was eventually granted the chairperson's role in the cabinet committee over-seeing the new intelligence services. Before the election, *Africa Confidential* had pronounced: 'Intelligence capacity is said to be at its lowest since the crisis in the Afrikaner nationalist movement during World War II. The objectives of the [NIS] and associated agencies have not been effectively reoriented since the unbanning of the [ANC].' After the election, the *Mail & Guardian* reported that 'NIS operatives, confi-dent about a bright future under the new government, are referring to their organisation as the "Mo, Joe and Louw show".' [50] The press didn't really have a clue what was going on.

The reorganisation of South Africa's intelligence agencies was finally le-gislated in late 1994. The White Paper on Intelligence, published in October 1994, acknowledged that in the 'new, non-racial, democratic order . . . much weight is given to the rights of the individual'. The document defined 'modern intelligence' as 'organised policy related information'. 'The purpose of intelligence' under an ANC government was 'to provide the policy-makers, timeous, critical and sometimes unique information . . . to identify opportunities in the international environment . . . [and] to assist good governance . . . Intelligence services should tell governments what they ought to know and not what they want to know.' The White Paper interpreted 'national security' as 'peace, stability, development and progress'. The structural reorganisation divided the NIS to create the NIA ('to con-duct security intelligence within the borders of the Republic') and the South African Secret Service (SASS – 'to conduct intelligence in relation to external threats, opportunities and other issues'). The section on 'coord-ination of intelligence' noted that neither the NIA nor SASS would possess 'law enforcement powers'. In addition to a Joint Standing Committee for parliament, the White Paper guaranteed that two inspector-generals would be appointed for review and oversight purposes: 'These two persons will have unhindered access to classified information.'

The creation of a National Intelligence Co-ordinating Committee (NICOC) was intended to function 'as the key link' between the spies and the politicians. One of NICOC's functions would be 'to avoid and to eliminate conflict, rivalry and unhealthy competition between the members of the intelligence community'. A key development in the White Paper was the declaration on 'covert action': 'Measures designed to deliberately interfere with the normal political processes in other countries and with the internal workings of parties and organisations engaged in lawful activity within South Africa, must be expressly forbidden. Intelligence agencies or those within them guilty of such breaches must be disciplined in the severest terms.' The annexure 'Basic Principles and Guidelines of National Intelligence' extended this issue to include 'the principle of political neutrality': 'No intelligence or security service/organisation shall be allowed to carry out any operations or activities that are intended to undermine, promote or influence any South African political party or organisation at the expense of another by means of any acts (eg "active measures" or "covert action") or by means of disinformation.' The White Paper recognised threats that had developed in recent years: 'International extremists have forged links with their South African counterparts, whilst international drug cartels use our country both as a transit route for their trade and as a market.' Particular attention was given to the 'dramatic increase in foreign intelligence activities in South Africa. Apart from classic political and military espionage, other activities of foreign/hostile intelligence services and industrial espionage agents have increased markedly in the economic, technological and scientific fields.'

The document concluded by recognising that South Africa's relationships 'with other African countries must be designed to promote political stability, regional security and our mutual economic growth and development'. Finally, and realistically, the White Paper noted that 'massive socio-economic degradation, with poverty, hunger, homelessness and unemployment . . . will render the political changes meaningless if they are not accompanied by a significant improvement in the quality of our people's lives'.[51] The reorganisation of South Africa's intelligence agencies had involved the need to amalgamate the NIS, the ANC's DIS, the Bophuthatswana Internal Intelligence Service, the Transkei Intelligence Service and the Venda National Intelligence Service. That was by no means a simple task. The wider functions of police intelligence and military intelligence were explained briefly in the National Strategic Intelligence Bill, which provided that 'crime intelligence will be the responsibility of the South African Police Service. The National Defence Force shall conduct foreign military intelligence as well as (under specified circumstances) domestic military intelligence.' The intelligence responsibilities of the security forces were later outlined in the White Paper on Defence, *Defence in a Democracy*, and the South African Police Services Act, both 1995. In theory, the police and the military had been reduced to pre-1969 levels of intelligence capacity. All in all, the White Paper was a strong, if somewhat idealistic, statement of intent. But how much of it would the new agencies be capable of respecting? Chris Hani had warned *Work in Progress*, less than a year before his assassination, of the priority of controlling the security forces:

> Never again in this country should we give (unchecked) powers to the security. Because we know, in a number of countries, even the advanced bourgeois countries, how the security can stifle democracy . . . The state should be defended against subversion . . . but we should never allow a situation with a group of men and women only answerable to an individual minister . . . [the] organs of civil society and parliament should have the right to question the activities of the security. The security must not hide behind the president . . . and refuse to be accountable . . . there must be clear guidelines to avoid the sort of thing that happened to a very small extent in the ANC and a very large extent within the security forces of the [apartheid] regime.

Kevin O'Brien has estimated the number of intelligence agents and officials in South Africa in 1994 as 16,650, which included 4,000 (NIS), 7,000 (MID), 3,500 (Police), 800 (DIS), 500 (MK), and 850 (Bophuthatswana, Transkei and Venda Intelligence); from 1 January 1995, some 6,500 spies occupied the new intelligence structures, which included 2,500 (NIA), 1,500 (SASS), 2,000 (SANDF Intelligence Division – ID), and 500 (Crime Investigation Service – CIS). This was an impressive reduction of approximately 10,000 intelligence operatives. Unfortunately, far from de-spooking the country, the reduction in the size of South Africa's intelligence agencies and the explosion in criminal activity that was such a feature of the 1990s created a boom in the private intelligence and security business (see page 372). The Minister of Intelligence, Joe Nhlanhla, warned in 1995:

> The wholesale demobilisation of trained personnel from the security services, including those from the intelligence services, in an environment of heightened instability can lead to a proliferation of private armies and security agencies. The intelligence agencies, mindful of the wastage that results from pay-out packages, favour the route of retraining and redeployment as a means of rationalisation.[52]

Two SIS Stories

On 19 March 2000, the Scottish newspaper the *Sunday Herald* reported a bizarre and unsubstantiated claim, drawn from Stephen Dorril's *MI6: Fifty Years of Special Operations*, that Nelson Mandela had been an MI6 'agent of influence':

> Nelson Mandela is to be named as an MI6 agent who aided British intelligence officers with operations against Colonel Gadaffi's Libyan weapons programmes, supplied his handlers with details of arms shipments to Ulster terrorists and allowed UK spying operations to be based in South Africa . . . Dorril claims highly placed MI6 officers told him about Mandela's recruitment by the Secret Intelligence Service . . . Sources within the Foreign Office and the intelligence service have said that Dorril's claim 'is entirely credible' . . . One expert on Southern Africa said . . . '[Mandela's] life history shows he would have been attractive to MI6 and MI6 would have been attractive to him . . . British diplomats were central to smoothing the end of apartheid . . . it can not be underestimated how many MI6 and CIA officers were working in this area. Their numbers were colossal.'

The South African government responded with alacrity: 'False and nonsensical allegations against Nelson Mandela appearing in the British media . . . have been repeatedly made in a futile attempt to tarnish his image . . . The allegations are baseless and are motivated by a difficulty in accepting that individuals other than those from the "first world" can play an important part in world affairs.' Nelson Mandela told Anthony Sampson that the MI6 allegations 'show a contempt for Africa'. When Dorril's book was published a few days later, it made little of its mighty 'scoop': 'Whether Mandela was recruited in London before he was imprisoned in South Africa is not clear, but it is understood that on a recent trip to London he made a secret visit to MI6's training section to thank the Service for its help in foiling two assassination attempts directed against him soon after he became President.' Out of more than 800 pages, no more than six concerned South Africa. The *Sunday Herald* had reported that 'Dorril says the assassination attempts . . . probably included one from within a faction of the ANC . . . Another is believed to have been planned by a covert operations wing of the apartheid government's military.'[53]

Sampson's response in the *Guardian* revealed that Lord Renwick, the British Ambassador in 1990, 'asked British intelligence experts to train Mr Mandela's bodyguards and advise on security at his home . . . "But there is no truth in the suggestion that the relationship went deeper than that."

The report that Mr Mandela was recruited is "an absolute travesty".' One British intelligence official told Sampson: 'The idea that we recruited Mandela is crap.' Dorril's letter in the *Guardian* the following day demonstrated circumspection and confusion in equal measure: 'There is nothing implausible in the idea that someone such as Nelson Mandela might have been recruited . . . I quote from MI6 training manuals on the methods used to recruit "agents of influence", who, internal reports state, were often not "conscious" they had been recruited . . . My admiration for Mr Mandela is in no way diminished by this claim made by a former MI6 officer.' In a matter of five days, Dorril's sources had shrunk from a plural to a singular. The source, was in fact the renegade former MI6 agent Richard Tomlinson.

In January 2001, Richard Tomlinson published *The Big Breach* in Russia. He claimed that Mandela had a 'longstanding' relationship with MI6. He alleged that Nelson and Winnie Mandela made a 'clandestine' visit to England in 1990 while travelling in France. They were transported to Kent in a 'special operations helicopter' where they spent the day engaged in 'secret discussions' with MI6. He also claimed that in 1993 an MI6 'agent' within the AWB had exposed a plan to assassinate Mandela. MI6 decided to give the report to Mandela directly rather than depend upon the usual South African intelligence channels: 'Too many of those bastards would like to see Mandela dead . . . and the message might never reach him.' Once again, Mandela entered the fray, describing Tomlinson's allegations as a 'disgraceful fabrication . . . If we had such relations with British or any other intelligence agencies there should somewhere be some evidence of the contract or of payments made.' The allegations 'should be dismissed with the contempt they deserve'. The *Guardian* revealed that in June 1990 Mandela had 'stayed for two days in a house in Kent, arranged by the British government'. The purpose of his trip was to see O.R. and Adelaide Tambo and to rest before visiting the United States.'[54]

A few days after Mandela's furious response, Tomlinson wrote to Sampson: 'I had no intention of causing [Mandela] any distress at all, and am mortified that he has interpreted what I said as a slur.' Tomlinson withdrew the allegation that Mandela had a 'longstanding' relationship with MI6 and suggested that the British officials that Mandela met at the house in Kent in 1990 were MI6 officers posing as diplomats: 'I realise that Mr Mandela may not have been conscious that he was meeting MI6 as opposed to ordinary government officials. I have asked the publisher to remove all mention of Mr Mandela.' The paperback edition of the book contained a single reference to the AWB assassination plot. Tomlinson had clearly been embarrassed by the insupportable allegation against Mandela; MI6 historian Christopher Andrew, commenting on Tomlinson's apologetic letter, gloated in *The Times*: 'Only a fantasist . . . could ever have believed that Mandela would regard it as anything [other than a "slur"]. Whatever Tomlinson's operational skills, his erratic judgement renders him unfit for a career in SIS.'[55]

Perhaps the weirdest intelligence connection in South Africa during the early 1990s was a rock band assembled by the BBC foreign correspondent Fergal Keane. The band was ironically named Total Onslaught. According to one of Keane's numerous newspaper reminiscences, 'Our drummer was a cameraman for German TV, our bass player a sound recordist . . . We were hot. Very hot. We played about four gigs but I am sure South Africa has never forgotten them.' Keane was the singer in the band and, according to a witness who saw the group perform, managed a passable Mick Jagger impression. The guitarist was a British diplomat who Keane had met at a party. 'We got to talking about music,' recalled Keane. 'In a few minutes we'd set up a guitar session and the rest is history.' In another *Independent* article, Fergal Keane noted that his friend was 'a diplomat with a difference: he plays a mean blues guitar.' In reality, Total Onslaught's guitarist *was* a diplomat with a difference: he was the MI6 head of station. The hack and the spook's musical interlude was a marriage made in heaven for the conspiracy theorist: ivory and ivory, the BBC and the SIS in musical harmony. If only somebody had tape-recorded or videotaped a performance of Total Onslaught, what mysteries would be revealed? Keane continued: 'The final epic performance came at the time of the first multiracial election. The week after the votes were cast . . . we performed to a crowd of journalists and politicians in the lush premises of the Transvaal Automobile Club. The new deputy Minister of Defence, Ronnie Kasrils (a famous anti-apartheid activist), joined us on stage. It was a great night in the middle of extraordinary times.'[56] Kasrils was appointed South Africa's third Minister of Intelligence in 2004.

13

Poisonous Influence

If we could learn to look instead of gawking
We'd see the horror in the heart of farce.
If only we could act instead of talking,
We wouldn't always end up on our arse.
This was the thing that nearly had us mastered;
Don't yet rejoice in his defeat, you men.
Although the world stood up and stopped the bastard,
The bitch that bore him is in heat again.
Bertolt Brecht, The Resistible Rise of Arturo Ui, 1945[1]

NEITHER PRESIDENT BILL Clinton nor Prime Minister John Major attended Nelson Mandela's inauguration in Pretoria on 10 May 1994. It was certainly a strange gathering: 'Hillary Clinton and Fidel Castro, Yasser Arafat and President Chaim Herzog of Israel, Prince Philip and Julius Nyerere'. Of one thing we can be certain: Major and Clinton will not miss Mandela's funeral. So why did they stay away in 1994? Was it the left-wing reputation of the ANC or the uncertainty that surrounded the election before the IFP's last-minute decision to take part? Bill Clinton, who was known for his empathetic relationship with African-Americans, has admitted that missing Mandela's inauguration was due to 'some big reason . . . I very much wanted to go'. John Major's autobiography gives no clues to his absence, although he reminded readers that he had visited South Africa in September 1994 and played cricket in Alexandria township: 'I bowled out Steve Tshwete, the South African Sports Minister, with my first ball. It was one of the happiest of visits.'[2] The absences were all the stranger because Britain, the US and France, among others, had been battling for intelligence influence in the new South Africa since 1990. Most of the foreign intelligence agencies understood that those who were there at the birth, like Attlee and Sillitoe in 1949 (see page 9), would be well placed to exert influence for many years to come.

Who Won the Influence War?

The relationships of Britain and the US with South Africa had traditionally been complementary but competitive. Seymour Hersh explained in
1986 (see page 158) that meetings between the CIA and MI6 discussed
'tasking': 'previous intelligence assignments and future targets'. Just as
British and American broadcasters shared film footage, the BBC for example had a long-standing relationship with NBC, the intelligence agencies shared 'information'. The moment of 'carve-up' or 'tasking' was
dependent upon numerous factors, not least the state of relationships with
the domestic agencies and genuine influence with senior politicians. As the
Financial Times commented:

> With its budget severely constrained . . . [MI6] must choose foreign intelli-
> gence targets with care . . . The UK targets countries where it has import-
> ant political and economic relationships; ones that are considered potential
> trouble spots; areas such as Hong Kong where it has historical ties; and coun-
> tries to which it sells military hardware . . . But it also picks targets where it
> knows intelligence will be of use to its US ally, and through which it hopes
> to encourage the US to open [its] intelligence files to the UK.[3]

Between 1949 and 1961, the British (MI5) appeared to have been the
dominant foreign intelligence agency in South Africa. From 1962 until
1975, the Americans seemed to have exerted primary influence. Between
1975 and 1981, MI6 took advantage of US 'local difficulties' in the post-
Angola period; and from 1982 until 1989, the CIA returned to the number-
one position. Intelligence relationships are rarely 'happy marriages' – events
tend to get in the way of long-lasting matrimony. The apartheid state had
important but less dominant relationships with Germany, France, Israel and
Switzerland which were equally subject to fluctuating fortunes. In 2003,
Professor Jeffrey Herbst announced in the respected journal *African Affairs*
that 'the emphasis in the literature on collaboration between US and South
African intelligence agencies is probably too strong'. Having analysed available US intelligence 'estimates' of South Africa over the apartheid period,
1948–94, Herbst concluded that 'the greatest failure was the inability of analysts to "think outside the box" and thus prepare American policymakers
for the possibility of apartheid ending peacefully'.[4]

The problem with Herbst's research, and I have studied many of the same
National Security Archive documents, is that the available CIA material
only takes the historian a certain distance. As one would expect, even under

strong Freedom of Information legislation, the CIA tends only to release documents that show its organisation in a relatively good light. Where are the boxes of documents detailing the close relationship between P.W. van der Westhuizen and William Casey, or indeed Hendrik van den Bergh's 'friendship' with James Jesus Angleton, who, like the Peter Wright faction in MI5, believed that Harold Wilson was a Soviet agent? Herbst's suggestion that anti-communism was not a 'particularly significant' factor in CIA analysis because 'South Africa was not in a primary theatre of the Cold War' ignored the fact that from 1975 Angola became one of the most significant proxy Cold War battlegrounds. The following statement plucked at random from Herbst's essay demonstrates inherent anti-communist bias:

> According to Fred Hitz, former Inspector-General of the CIA, the attitude of the South African security agencies to the CIA station in South Africa was actually hostile from roughly 1955 to the end of apartheid. The South Africans surveilled American officers *as if they were from communist countries*, always suspicious that they were trying to recruit and encourage the ANC [my emphasis].[5]

Chester Crocker's memoirs, which Herbst ignored, painted a brutalist portrait of the conflict inside the White House between the State Department and 'President [Reagan's] own South Africa lobby: Bill Casey, Pat Buchanan, and several aides'. Ronald Reagan's presidential speech on South Africa on 22 July 1986 referred to 'the calculated terror by elements of the [ANC]' and stated bluntly that 'the South African Government is under no obligation to negotiate the future of the country with any organization that proclaims a goal of creating a Communist State'. Crocker suggested that Reagan 'the "great communicator" became the great polariser'; his 'pro-Pretoria tilt' repulsed Republican senators and 'literally forced a split in his party in the Senate'. The historic Comprehensive Anti-Apartheid Act, drafted by two Republican senators, transformed the 'terms of trade' between South Africa and the US. Crocker acknowledged that the retirement of Bill Casey in April 1987 'created a new foundation for the conduct of US foreign policy'.[6]

As late as March 1987, Colonel Opperman (MID) and two colleagues were permitted to visit the United States and liaise with fellow US defence intelligence personnel and the CIA. The *Mail & Guardian* reported that Opperman was determined to 'project South Africa with the "correct" perspective'. Two of the MID officials travelled on first-class tickets. Despite the fact that the CIA almost certainly attempted to back-pedal on the issue of South Africa from mid-1987 onwards, it still needed to work closely with the South African government on Angola and Namibia, as part of Crocker's 'constructive engagement'. As far as the ANC was concerned, the CIA and the State Department had a lot of catching up to do. Until the early 1980s, ANC members were often refused visas to the United States and were permitted to attend the UN only on the condition that they did not violate a twenty-five-mile perimeter.[7] In March 1982, a Senate subcommittee investigating the role of Soviet, Cuban and East German 'Involvement in Fomenting Terrorism in Southern Africa' gave the South African Ambassador, Donald Sole, the opportunity 'to present black South African and Namibian witnesses' and publicise ancient anti-ANC–SACP propaganda. In August 1983, according to Vladimir Shubin, Crocker's assistant Robert Cabelly visited Lusaka for a non-meeting (Cabelly's definition) with Thabo Mbeki: '[Cabelly] insisted that the ANC should renounce its alliance with the SACP and friendly relations with the USSR, stop the armed struggle (which, he alleged, was imposed on the ANC by white communists), and become part of "the policy of reforms" . . . If this was not done, he threatened, the ANC would be "driven" out of the region.'[8]

One sign of the shift in the intelligence relationship between the USA and South Africa was the emergence of stories in American newspapers which reported on South African espionage connections with right-wing Americans. Following Naval Intelligence officer Jonathan Pollard's arrest, and his imprisonment for life in 1987, for supplying intelligence documents to the Israelis, newspapers ignored testimony relating to Pollard's college 'friend', a senior South African intelligence officer; the story eventually emerged in Wolf Blitzer's book on Pollard, *Territory of Lies*. Evidence given at Pollard's trial disclosed that the CIA believed that 'much of what reached Jerusalem was promptly handed over to Pretoria'. The raw intelligence data supplied by Pollard to Israel included details on 'American covert operations in South Africa, which the CIA had neglected to coordinate with South African intelligence'. As Andrew Cockburn reported, this 'gave the South African government the means to identify [CIA] agents and operatives, therefore endangering their lives'.[9]

Inspired by the Comprehensive Anti-Apartheid Act, the US government began to intercept American arms dealers who were trading with South Africa. In 1988, US Customs caught arms traders 'in the act of shipping gyroscopes for missile guidance systems to South Africa. Operation "Exodus" implicated two South Africans, one American arms dealer . . . and Israel Aircraft Industries.' In October of the same year, the *Washington*

Post revealed that a former US army 'clandestine warfare specialist' faced up to ten years in prison for supplying 'scores of classified military documents to the South African regime from 1979 to 1983 . . . He told FBI agents he "believed he was doing for South Africa what the United States should have been doing".' In 1997, the Johannesburg *Sunday Independent* reported that in the mid-1980s MID's Directorate of Counter-Intelligence recruited a US Embassy official in Pretoria in order 'to establish the identities of the United States's "deep cover" agents in the country . . . Because of the close links between the US and British intelligence services, the recruitment was handled in such a manner that the woman was convinced she was working for the British.'[10]

By 1989, Hollywood had been roped in to the desperate repositioning. The motion picture *Lethal Weapon 2* actually featured Afrikaner villains. Unfortunately for the CIA, British intelligence had already developed links with the ANC in Lusaka. Shubin said of this, rather gracelessly, that 'preliminary contacts . . . were made unofficially by some British intelligence officers (posing as diplomats)'. Anthony Sampson noted in the *Guardian* that 'British agents were certainly involved with the exiled ANC in Lusaka, Zambia, before Mr Mandela's release . . . while Mrs Thatcher was supporting the South African Zulu leader, Mangosuthu Buthelezi, as an alternative to the ANC, MI6 agents took the ANC more seriously.' The fact that a number of senior ANC–SACP leaders had been based in London, rather than the United States, was bound, despite the vicissitudes of British politics, to stand British intelligence in good stead when the change in South Africa eventually happened. Ronnie Kasrils noted in *Armed and Dangerous* that 'apart from frequent scrutinies by Customs at Heathrow airport, I never experienced any problems from Her Majesty's intelligence and security forces'. Oliver Tambo detailed the 'two Britains' in a speech at the Greater London Council's Anti-Racist Day on 21 March 1984:

> Our people have known London as the imperial capital that betrayed both its principles and the African people. To this day, the heir to Imperial London continues to see the creature it spawned in 1910 as its ally . . . Tonight, we are meeting with another London . . . [the] People's London . . . This is the London of Fenner Brockway, who met and welcomed Solomon Platje . . . It is the London we have known as the birthplace of the British Anti-Apartheid Movement.[11]

Although apartheid intelligence activity in Britain never returned to the titanic levels of 1976 or the brutal clumsiness of 1982, it continued but in a less blatant form. In July 1985, for example, the A–AM offices in Islington were victim of an arson attack that caused £15,000 worth of damage. In the same year, an 'Irishman' informed the ANC that a South African 'bounty of £100,000 was on offer for killing or kidnapping Slovo'. In 1987, a Norwegian, a Dane and two British subjects were arrested and charged with plotting to kidnap members of the ANC. The four men were, according to *Africa Confidential*, following a plan prepared by South Africa's MID. The plan was to abduct and interrogate Joe Slovo and Thabo Mbeki, 'lay a trail which would throw suspicion on exiled Seychellois and British intelligence' and by extension protect the existing Seychellois government, led by President France-Albert René, who was a collaborator with the apartheid regime. The leader of the alleged kidnap plot was 'Lieutenant-Colonel Frank Larsen' (a Norwegian, Viggo Oerbak). According to documents seized by the police following the arrests, Larsen had worked with the Rhodesian special forces and arrived in the UK in 1982 where he developed a 'legend' as a British army officer. The documents gathered by the police, and later provided to the press, revealed that in 1986 Larsen liaised with a South African special forces officer, Johann Niemoller, who was in contact with the South African military attaché in London, Colonel Rob Crowther.[12]

'Larsen' was arrested for homosexual importuning 'in the lavatories of the Regents Palace Hotel, Piccadilly' on 9 July 1987, and following a search of his 'rented house in Aldershot' – which led, bizarrely, to the discovery of 'large quantities of Masonic literature' – three additional men were also arrested. 'John Larsen' claimed to be Frank Larsen's son but was, in fact, a Danish citizen called Hans Christian Dahl; Jonathan Wheatley was a former paratrooper who had been dishonourably discharged from the British army following the Falklands war; and Evan Dennis Evans was a former MI6 officer, who later ran a 'sub post office in North Wales'. The allegations of a 'kidnap plot' were certainly fishy but so was the behaviour of the authorities in Britain. In October 1987, the Director of Public Prosecutions announced that there was insufficient evidence to continue the case. The *Independent* suggested that the real reason was that 'material relating to national security would have been produced in court had the case gone ahead.' As Richard Dowden and Stephen Ellis speculated: 'Did [British Intelligence] allow the Larsens to operate for the South Africans to find out things for themselves and then call a halt when they realised there were going to be dead ANC people on British territory?' The arrests of Larsen and his associates had immediate diplomatic repercussions: in

September 1985, Britain had withdrawn its military attaché from Pretoria; after the expulsion of Colonel Rob Crowther in 1987 a replacement was not permitted. Ronnie Kasrils wrote in his memoirs that, after the discovery of a 'hit-list of leading apartheid opponents . . . in 1987', Scotland Yard detectives offered regular 'advice and protection . . . We had been reared in a climate of almost paranoid suspicion of Western intelligence agencies. We found in the Scotland Yard officers the very best of British civility.'[13]

In April 1989, Daniel Storm, an ARMSCOR official working under cover as 'an administrative and technical officer' in Paris, was arrested by French intelligence agents attempting to purchase 'a Blowpipe surface-to-air missile unit' from three Ulster Resistance terrorists. The *Independent* reported that an American arms dealer was 'thought to have acted as a go-between'. It transpired that South Africa had already supplied the Loyalist paramilitaries with weapons. Four South African Embassy officials were expelled from Paris and, after a period of indecision, three, selected 'at random', were expelled from the Embassy in London. These included South Africa's final military attaché in Britain. Correspondence in a South Africa Foreign Affairs file which fell into the hands of the *Mail & Guardian* in June 2000 revealed that Mrs Thatcher had instructed the South African government: 'You will make it clear to ARMSCOR and its agents, who incidentally are still trying to recruit missile experts in Northern Ireland, that they should cease forthwith their activities in the United Kingdom.' Another letter confirmed the suspicion that South Africa used 'diplomatic bags' to transport weapons: 'One wonders whether [South African Airways] know what they sometimes transport on the aircraft in sealed [diplomatic] bags?'[14]

Sir Robin Renwick, the British Ambassador to South Africa between 1987 and 1991, was discreet in his autobiography but he could not disguise his distaste for South Africa's MID. He described the CCB, for example, as a 'bunch of killers', and noted that, following F.W. de Klerk's election as the leader of the National Party, he visited him to explain that 'if the security police and military intelligence were allowed to continue their activities unchecked, there was no way any of us were going to be able to help South Africa . . . despite all the disclaimers, South African military intelligence were continuing actively to support RENAMO in Mozambique.' Renwick's grumbles at South Africa's spies cited both the farcical and the sinister:

> A source of constant irritation, though also some amusement, were the . . . antics of the South African intelligence services. Determined to monitor our

telephones, they did so in such inept ways that each [periodic] move of the Embassy [from Pretoria] to Cape Town was followed by the appearance of a group of technicians whose interference with the junction box outside the Embassy gates invariably managed to put it out of action for several hours before it was reconnected and declared fit for us to use. Their efforts were not always so benign. My friend Bob Frasure, political counsellor in the American Embassy [1986–8], was engaged in monitoring the cross-border exploits of the South African Defence Force. As he discovered more about these than military intelligence wished him to know, they retaliated by terrorizing his wife and children during his absences from home, to such effect that Frasure had to be withdrawn. Why the State Department permitted this to happen without publicizing the circumstances, I have never been able to understand.[15]

Mike Louw recalled that when the ANC returned from Lusaka a number of British intelligence operatives 'came with them, promising a lot but delivering very little'. The leading British intelligence man in South Africa in the early 1990s was Anthony Rowell; he had been an FCO [Foreign and Commonwealth Office] counsellor in Nairobi from 1985 to 1990 and was based in Pretoria until 1993, whereupon he left the Foreign Office. Four years later, he joined the private intelligence company Kroll Associates (see page 368). Ronnie Kasrils joked that in July 1991 he was photographed 'sandwiched between diplomats from Britain and the USSR'. One of his colleagues said: 'It's taken the combined forces of the KGB and MI6 to catch you.' Kasrils replied: 'Not at all . . . I've been recruiting them.' The British diplomat was Rowell.[16]

Although the South African spookery in Britain faded after 1990, there were still a few 'apartheid' incidents. In October 1990, for example, the *New Statesman* reported that Harold Wolpe had 'discovered that his telephone has been bugged . . . for at least 15 months'. A man called 'Mike' telephoned the veteran SACP activist and university lecturer to inform him that he had, upon moving into a new flat, discovered two tape recordings of what appeared to be Wolpe's telephone calls. The tapes were authentic and 'Mike' did not want to reveal his identity. In April 1992, MID sent two operatives, Leon Flores and Captain Pamela du Randt, to London to recruit Ulster Loyalists to murder death squad defector Dirk Coetzee. Under the banner 'Project Echoes', the pair were primarily tasked to spread disinformation about ANC relations with the IRA. *Africa Confidential* reported that the 'discovery of the two alleged assassins . . . has created the most serious strain in British–South African relations since De Klerk became President'. Flores, a former Vlakplaas operative, was dismissed by the SADF but du Randt, a former assistant to MID chief General C.P. 'Joffel' van der Westhuizen, was 'found to be innocent'. In July 1992, John Horak, a journalist who for thirty years worked as a police spy, revealed that there were approximately 150 South African agents operating in Britain; he claimed that 'many of the agents were British private detectives sub-contracted to collect information on individuals and organisations'.[17]

Despite the embarrassing mistake he made in connection with Nelson Mandela (see page 311), there are a number of interesting details relating to South Africa in Richard Tomlinson's *Big Breach*. In the first chapter, Tomlinson reveals that he spent his 'gap year' 1980–1, before going up to Cambridge to study engineering, working for De Beers in Johannesburg; the iniquities of apartheid were obviously no more than a minor concern. Tomlinson joined MI6 in 1991 and quickly observed that the service's recruitment figures demonstrated a prejudice against 'equal opportunity . . . only about 10 per cent of the officers were female, there were no black officers whatsoever, only one of mixed Asian parentage, and there were no disabled officers'. In 1991, MI6 'controllerates' addressing the Middle East and Far East were growing in prominence, whereas Africa and the Western Hemisphere (Latin America and the Caribbean) were shrinking. Among his contemporaries on the Intelligence Officer's New Entry Course (IONEC), the lowest-achieving performer was 'posted to [a] . . . desk in the Africa controllerate'. In the early 1990s, one British agent was 'travelling around South Africa as a Zimbabwean chicken-feed salesman, which gave him cover to meet ANC and Inkatha agents in remote rural locations'.

Tomlinson acknowledged that 'the core activity of MI6 is agent-running'. A case in point was South Africa, where MI6 'had been very successful in recruiting a network of informers under the apartheid regime and a lot of these agents were now high up in the ANC'. One British agent commented 'with a touch of sarcasm, "It's amazing how many of them, having spied for years for 'ideological reasons', are now happy to carry on pocketing their agent salaries post apartheid."' Tomlinson described an MI6 agent whose deep cover was that he worked as an investment consultant. This fellow, a friend of Tomlinson's, was sent to Johannesburg in 1993 to handle 'MI6's two most important agents in South Africa, a senior army officer and a senior government official. Both had been recruited early in their careers but had risen to such prominence that no member of the MI6 station in Pretoria could safely contact them.' In November 1995, after Tomlinson had left MI6 in high dudgeon and taken a holiday in South

Africa, the agency had been so 'concerned that in my disaffected state I might be vulnerable to recruitment by South African counter-intelligence [that] they pulled my friend . . . out of the country . . . In fact, the South Africans made no approach.'[18]

Apartheid South Africa had always retained good relations with Switzerland, but, following the collapse of the rand in 1985 and the introduction of US sanctions in 1986, the relationship intensified. By 1989, Switzerland had become the fourth largest trading partner with the Republic, after the UK, the US and Germany. South African involvement in Swiss banking has been so consistent since the 1960s that some investigators have suggested, only partly in jest, that apartheid South Africa might have actually owned a Swiss bank. The two countries also engaged in arms trading. In 2001, Jubilee SA researchers revealed that P.W. Botha had decorated two Swiss industrialists in 1978. Dieter Bührle, an arms manufacturer, was awarded the faintly Ruritanian 'Grand Cross: First Class' and his colleague, Gabriel Lebedinsky, the 'Star of South Africa: Grand Officer Second Class'. The two Swiss businessmen were also directors of the Swiss Bank Corporation, which merged with the Union Bank of Switzerland to create UBS in 1998. Aktion Finanzplatz, a pressure group, which has examined the South African Reserve Bank's archives, announced that 'Swiss investments in South Africa tailed off dramatically after 1993'. Mike Louw recalled with some amusement that the Swiss spooks asked for two years' warning of any substantial political change so that they would have time to get their money out.[19]

Israeli collaboration with apartheid South Africa – one colony of a special type defending and supporting another – was particularly intense between 1973 and the mid-1980s. Indeed, Israeli investment in South Africa's bantustans, especially Bophuthatswana and the Ciskei, and its relationship with Chief Mangosuthu Buthelezi demonstrated Israel's exceptional support for apartheid. Ari Ben-Menashe, who would in December 2001 appear on a video-recording discussing the assassination of Robert Mugabe with Zimbabwean opposition leader Morgan Tsvangirai, claimed in his book *Profits of War* that Israel, through Robert Maxwell's company Degem, gave South Africa access to its 'Promis' computer programs which facilitated the targeting and murder of ANC activists. Apparently, 'black-on-black' violence was known as 'Kushi kills Kushi' within Mossad. Ben-Menashe, whose stories need to be taken with a pinch of salt, noted that Israel–South African relations 'deteriorated [between 1985 and 1988] . . . because South Africa began to sell conventional equipment and missile technology to Iraq'. An undated US Defense Intelligence Agency document stated:

> In March 1987, Israel announced that it would sign no new contracts for military goods with South Africa, its first public admission that military contracts existed with South Africa at all; the announcement came on the eve of the publication of a US Presidential report on worldwide violations of the arms embargo against South Africa. At the same time, Israeli officials admitted to the press that existing arms contracts would be honored and that some of these stretch into the 1990s.[20]

During the summer of 1987, Israel's Prime Minister Yitzhak Shamir 'toured countries in West and Central Africa trying to win back friends lost through the South African liaison'. South Africa's relationship with oil traders like Marc Rich would prove to be the most difficult to break. In 2001, the *Mail & Guardian* reported that 'of 865 identified deliveries by tankers in excess of 50,000 tons from 1979 to 1993, the Shipping Research Bureau found that 149 shipments were linked to Rich' who was indicted in the United States in 1983 'on more than 50 counts of tax evasion, fraud, racketeering and trading with the enemy'. His companies paid $200 million in fines and Rich fled to Switzerland. The Conservative politician Alan Duncan worked as an oil trader for him in the 1980s. Marc Rich was controversially pardoned by President Clinton in January 2001.[21] As if to demonstrate that the relationships of the past continue to influence the present, in the summer of 2005 a political scandal erupted in South Africa, unimaginatively called 'Oilgate', which allegedly involved ANC politicians and businessmen corruptly trading in Iraqi oil with the assistance of the Swiss-based company, Glencore.[22]

The 'influence war', at least between Britain and the United States, was won by the British. In 2002, a former MI6 station chief told friends in London that he had been able to secure a three-hour meeting with President Mbeki during a trip to South Africa. At the opening of the NIA's academy in the same year, the Minister of Intelligence Lindiwe Sisulu publicly thanked the same British intelligence officer, a breach of protocol which upset some of the retired Afrikaner officials who were present. During the same year, an 'MI6 wife' telling her story to the *Guardian* explained that Pretoria and Nairobi were among 'the few MI6 outposts left in Africa'. But the real benefits of the victory in the influence war could be detected in the British share of the R30 billion South African arms procurement deal. As *Punch* explained in September 2001: 'MI6 spends more time and resources helping major British arms companies to secure contracts than perhaps any other business . . . The main beneficiary of MI6 intelligence is British Aerospace plc (BAe).' The other major profiteer in the arms deal was the French, who had been particularly active in South Africa during the early 1990s cultivating ANC politicians and businessmen.[23]

But, as Niel Barnard told me in 2002, it could have been quite different. If 9/11 had happened ten years earlier, the white South African government might have been able to cling on to power. The opportunity to demonise the ANC as 'terrorists' and collaborators with militant Islam would have possessed huge resonance in the international political climate of the twenty-first century, as would white South Africa's eagerness to play the role of colonial outpost. Of course, if apartheid, in one form or another, had survived, the damage inflicted upon the South African economy would have been insurmountable and internal unrest would probably have developed into a full-blown revolution. Perhaps Niel Barnard should have recalled his experiences in the clichéd spy city of Vienna in 1989, when in a desperate attempt to strike a deal with the Soviet Union he met with the KGB. Unlike the West German BND, who according to NIS sources were always ready to assist South Africa, the KGB was unwilling to respond to South Africa's overtures. While Barnard argued that if the Soviet Union could coexist with De Beers it could surely come to an arrangement with the NIS, the KGB declared that apartheid South Africa was already finished. Sitting under a bright light, Barnard is said to have become so stressed that his sweat seeped through his shirt, his waistcoat and his suit jacket.[24]

Dr Death and Project Coast

The deepest secrets of the apartheid regime related to weapons of mass destruction (WMD) and high finance. Accordingly, these were the last secrets to be exposed, and the exposure was never anything but fragmentary. The revelation that South Africa possessed nuclear weapons in the early 1990s was accompanied by a number of mysterious stories about an unknown substance called 'red mercury' and a string of unsolved murders. Arrests continue to be made of South Africans who have attempted to sell nuclear material on the international market. To the regularly asked question, 'Why did apartheid South Africa give up the bomb?', there is only one answer: because they didn't want the blacks to have it.[25]

The origins of the apartheid state's chemical weapons programme are still contested. In 1960, tear gas had been employed during the Pondoland uprising in the Transkei and during the same year 'South African scientists were sent for a course on nuclear, biological and chemical warfare in the United Kingdom.' In the early 1970s, senior generals within the SADF urged the creation of a chemical and biological warfare (CBW) capability. However, at this early stage, it was concluded that a CBW industry would be too expensive; the estimated cost in 1974 was $500 million. This cautious state of affairs was abandoned following three significant events: the Angolan intervention of 1975, the Soweto uprising of 1976 and the primacy of the MID following the election of P.W. Botha in 1978. Lieutenant-General Lothar Neethling told the TRC that the June 1976 riots had triggered the need for a CBW response: 'When the riots started, the South African Police were caught unawares. They had nothing apart from guns, shotguns and sharp point ammunition. Nobody wanted to use that and that's why there was a search for various techniques to be applied . . . I went overseas . . . to Germany, England, Israel [and] America to find the best techniques available.' General Constand Viljoen acknowledged that South Africa needed to develop 'alternative crowd control methods', but he also claimed that the SADF was forced to develop a CBW programme in order to defend its troops against the possible use of CBW by the Cuban forces in Angola.[26]

The most convincing evidence suggests that the South African state either adopted the use of CBW from the Rhodesians in the late 1970s or used the Rhodesian conflict as a laboratory to experiment with CBW. Documents dated June, August and November 1977, uncovered by Marlene Burger and Chandre Gould, revealed that the Rhodesian Special Branch and Selous Scouts employed toxins to poison African opponents. One report referred to a 'decrease in the quantity of materials directed into the field', which was due in part to 'the shortage of necessary ingredients which are to be obtained from South Africa'. Henrik Ellert, a former Rhodesian Special Branch officer, writing in 1989, recalled that the Selous Scouts killed numerous Zimbabwean guerrilla fighters through the use of poisoned clothing, normally blue denim jeans: 'after exposure to the poison for a period of seven days the victim would experience symptoms which included bleeding from the nose and mouth and a rise in temperature'. Death swiftly followed.[27] In 1976, the Selous Scouts experimented with poison ('measured quantities of bacteriological cultures') in the Ruya river near Mozambique. The deaths among local people that followed were attributed to cholera. Another mass poisoning occurred when Scouts infected the reservoir that supplied the

Cochemane administrative centre in the Tete province. A report dispatched to the US Defense Intelligence Agency detailed the intentional poisoning of water supplies with dead bodies by the Rhodesian military and attempts 'to infest the water system with *Vibrio cholerae*'. In 1979 and 1980, more than ten thousand Zimbabweans were infected with anthrax; 182 people died. Before 1978, Rhodesia had averaged only thirteen human anthrax cases a year. Dr Timothy Stamps, former Health Minister in the Zimbabwean government, told Tom Mangold:

> No doubt about the anthrax . . . You only have to look at the figures. No doubt about the cholera either. Cholera was new to this country. Odd isn't it, that it spread so quickly, particularly during a period of hostility when human movements were very, very severely restricted in the Eastern districts of Zimbabwe, where the cholera broke out. Now if these outbreaks had been endemic, we would have expected them to continue and reoccur, especially with our health services in disarray . . . We had a localised out-break of bubonic plague during the dirty wars, and it reoccurred twice more in that area. But why so local? It was a place where there was intense fight-ing between the forces of liberation and the regime . . . Do I have evidence? Only circumstantial. In fact, the Rhodesian security forces were more expert than the Nazis at covering up evidence.[28]

Wouter Basson was born in 1951; 'his father was a police colonel and Rugby official, his mother an office secretary and opera singer'. He trained as a medical doctor and joined the SADF in January 1975. Six years later, having qualified as a specialist physician, Basson was promoted, at the age of thirty, to lieutenant-colonel. Within a few weeks, he was instructed by the Surgeon-General and head of the SADF Medical Service Lieutenant-General Nicol Nieuwoudt to establish a CBW research programme. Following a meeting with General Constand Viljoen, Lieutenant-General Pieter van der Westhuizen (the head of MID) and Lieutenant-General Fritz Loots (the head of the SADF's Special Forces) it was agreed that Basson's 'first task would be to gather as much information as possible about CBW in the international arena'. This activity would obviously involve espionage and 'plausible deniability – under no circumstances was the SADF to be linked to his activities'.[29] In April 1981, 'Project Coast' was formally established. The annual budget, approved by Minister of Defence Magnus Malan, has been estimated at $10 million, employing a staff of 200. In 1982, 'the Delta G Scientific Company began work on chemical war-fare agents . . . The chemicals that Delta G developed for testing were divided into lethal, incapacitating, and irritating agents. Roodeplaat Research Laboratories (RRL) then tested the biological effects of the agents.' The head of RRL between 1982 and 1986 was Dr Daan Goosen. By 1984, scientists associated with Project Coast 'had tested a range of BW toxins and had developed counter-measures to ricin and botulinum. Reportedly, they had acquired anthrax, Plague, cholera, E. coli, staph, necrotising fasciitis, ricin, botulinum, gas gangrene, anti-matter bacteria, and the Ebola, Marburg and Rift Valley viruses.'[30]

The number of 'experimental' exterminations gathered together under the banner 'Operation Duel', but directly linked to Project Coast, defies the imagination and has never been effectively quantified. Evidence given during the trial of Wouter Basson by a number of former Barnacle operatives suggested that as many as 200 SWAPO prisoners were incapacitated with the use of muscle-relaxant pills and thrown from aeroplanes into the sea. Members of the SADF who talked publicly of Basson's clandestine operations were also poisoned. Johan Theron, an MID officer, was the 'chief executioner' of Duel; and the killing, which started in 1979 and lasted until at least 1987, was planned, as Burger and Gould related, 'with customary military precision. Theron visited the SADF's highly sophisticated electronic intelligence command centre at Silvermine in the Western Cape in order to obtain accurate data about tidal movements in the oceans around southern Africa so that he could calculate the chances of "a package" weighing as much as an average man being washed up after it was dumped in the ocean.' He discovered that victims needed to be flown up to 100 nautical miles out to sea before being dropped into the water. In court, Basson's defence advocate described Theron, who testified on behalf of the prosecution, as a 'psychopath . . . a vile and repugnant creature.'[31]

William Finnegan captured Wouter Basson's mercurial role in South Africa's CBW programme in an essay for the *New Yorker*: 'so often described as a "brilliant scientist" or "apartheid's mad scientist", [Basson] actually had little to do with the scientific work performed for Project Coast. He issued orders, but he rarely visited the labs. He was the project's liaison to its funders and overseers in the Army leadership, and to the Special Forces and police operatives who used its products.' Like Eschel Rhoodie, Basson's real genius was for international networking, information-trading and performance. One colleague recalled that he played each role to the hilt: 'Once, he was in London, and he was supposed to be a banker, so he dressed up in everything he thought a banker should wear – a striped Savile Row suit, even a bowler hat.' He also had a voracious sexual appetite: 'Wouter had an issue about strip joints, pornography, and so on . . . Whenever you travelled with him, you ended up in such places. He was not comfortable with women, but he was a great seducer.'[32] And like the former Secretary for Information, his superiors believed that, far from being tried for his crimes, he should have been given a medal. General Niel Knobel told Tom Mangold that Basson had 'the capability of going anywhere and talking to anybody . . . he went all over the place, he went to the cartels in Columbia, he went to Iraq and Iran, he went to the Philippines, to Northern Korea to Croatia, all over the world – and he made friends and contacts and he obtained information'. The *New Yorker* added:

> [Basson] attended international conferences of forensic toxicologists in Western Europe and aerospace medical officers in the United States; befriended key scientists and military men and program administrators, particularly those who seemed interested in his battlefield tales of fighting Communism . . . on the front line in southern Africa; claims to have gained entrance to world-renowned facilities such as Fort Detrick, in Maryland, or Porton Down, in England . . . He learned to play East off West – offering intelligence, however dubious, about the Soviet bloc's biowarfare capacities to Western agents in return for information or equipment he wanted, some of which he could then turn around and trade to a growing list of contacts in East Germany, Czechoslovakia, Poland and the Soviet Union. Basson found that some NATO officials and former officials were as willing to sell their countries' military secrets as their Communist counterparts . . . Some ex-intelligence agents also proved happy to come out of retirement to help defend, for a fee, the last beach-head of white-supremacism in Africa.[33]

In 1989, the Reverend Frank Chikane, an anti-apartheid leader, was poisoned. He fell ill in Namibia on 24 April with 'abdominal pain, nausea, vomiting, diarrhoea, and extreme weakness'. He was taken to hospital and later flown to Johannesburg for further treatment. A diagnosis of acute gastroenteritis was made and Chikane was discharged after four days. On 10 May, he flew to the United States with colleagues for a meeting with President George Bush. Once again, Chikane became sick 'and was admitted to the University of Wisconsin Hospital. This attack was so serious that he lost consciousness, stopped breathing and had to be given artificial ventilation. But he was discharged after a week, again in apparent good health.' He returned to hospital twenty-four hours later suffering from 'profound anxiety, confusion, hyperventilation, respiratory alkalosis, and hypophosphataemia . . . Post-traumatic stress syndrome was diagnosed.' Despite recovering for a third time, Chikane was once again readmitted to hospital with appalling symptoms. After four separate attacks, American doctors 'suggested a diagnosis of organo-phosphate poisoning'. Dr Chikane informed the press in 1989: 'a review of his movements . . . left his baggage as the only common denominator . . . "When I left for the USA I went back to the same baggage with those items." ' The *Lancet* commented in 1999: 'It is important to remember that chemical warfare can be conducted surreptitiously and on a small scale.' Chikane was not alone; Conny Braam was similarly poisoned in 1987 during Operation Vula.[34]

A number of Project Coast's operations appear in retrospect to have been utterly insane. Plans included: the distribution of cans of poisoned beer at roadside stalls; the development of fertility drugs that could be disseminated in the water supply thereby rendering blacks sterile and stemming the high birth rate; a CCB plot to assassinate Ronnie Kasrils and Pallo Jordan in London with the use of a poisoned umbrella, in the style of the Bulgarian assassination of World Service reporter Georgi Markov; the development of 'race-changing drugs' which would 'turn whites into blacks [for a limited period] so that apartheid operatives could infiltrate the ranks of the enemy'; 'cigarettes spiked with anthrax spores and chocolates laced with cyanide'; the crossbreeding of a Russian wolf with a German shepherd to create a 'wolf-dog' and the crossbreeding of a Rottweiler, a Doberman and a bloodhound to create the 'virtually uncontrollable . . . boerbul'.[35] One MID source who had worked on Project Coast, 'Gert', told Tom Mangold that 'there was some HIV tampering . . . I mean all you have to do is get one covert guy, he's HIV positive . . . You get him to infiltrate the whole town, screw the whole lot . . . get him out and shoot him.' In November 1999, two former Vlakplaas operatives applied for amnesty from the TRC on the basis that they had used four HIV-positive askaris 'to spread the disease by infecting prostitutes in two Hillbrow hotels, the Chelsea and Little Rose, in May 1990'. Helen Purkitt and Stephen Burgess explained that 'the many unanswered questions about . . . Project Coast may help to explain why current senior officials in South Africa, including President Thabo Mbeki, expressed so many doubts about the causes of the HIV/AIDS pandemic'.[36]

In 1986, a secret agreement had been formally concluded 'between the Swiss and South African military intelligence services . . . The deal concerned the mutual exchange of information on nuclear, chemical and biological warfare.' The former deputy CSI of MID, Chris Thirion, who believed that he had been unfairly dismissed during the 'night of the generals' in 1992 and now owns a restaurant, Die Werf, near Pretoria, told Swiss researcher Jean-Phillippe Ceppi in 1999: '[The 1986] agreement was very important for us . . . [it] paved the way for Basson.' In one of the rare examples of the new South African intelligence services persecuting a journalist, Ceppi was later arrested by the Crime Intelligence Service on the instruction of South Africa's military Intelligence Division (ID) and held for sixty hours. His only crime was the possession of 'documents that turned out to be part of the truth commission's public record'. The Basson case, which featured Swiss front companies, led to Peter Regli, the former head of Swiss military intelligence, being summoned to appear before a Swiss parliamentary committee regarding the Basson revelations. In August 2001, it was reported that 'Regli had destroyed all his own as well as office documentation and archives relating to secret contacts with members of the former South African security apparatus.' Sixteen months later, an independent inquiry commissioned by the Swiss government 'sharply criticised the country's military intelligence service for [it's] close ties . . . with agents of South Africa's former apartheid regime.' The investigation led by a Swiss academic confirmed that intelligence documents had been destroyed.[37]

In August 1988, SADF and Armscor officials travelled to West Germany and Israel. One of the officials was Uwe Paschke, son-in-law of President P.W. Botha and father of Varenka Paschke, who would later achieve notoriety as the artist whose paintings were attributed to Nelson Mandela and are currently subject to legal action for fraud in the South African courts. A memorandum prepared after the trip recorded:

1. It provided for personal contact with experts in the field of CBW and the establishment of relationships which can be followed up.
2. Access was gained to industries which were formerly inaccessible.
3. A basis was laid for possible co-operation with Israel's [MOD] in the field of CBW . . . the SADF was acknowledged as a partner in the field of defensive CBW, although this will not be announced, especially in Germany.[38]

In the United States, a friend of Project Coast was Dr Larry Creed Ford, a gynaecologist Mormon who doubled as an expert on infectious diseases and CBW. Former SADF Surgeon-General Niel Knobel claimed to have met Ford for the first time at the Beverly Hills home of Gideon Bouwer, the South African trade representative at the Consulate in Los Angeles. Ford was invited to visit the University of the Orange Free State in the mid-1980s. Other sources have suggested that Ford was a regular visitor to apartheid South Africa from the late 1970s. On a number of trips to the Republic,

Ford is said to have been accompanied by an American surgeon 'with extreme views', who claimed to have worked as a 'special forces physician' in the Rhodesian war. The surgeon was famously quoted as saying: 'Every time I leave Africa a disease breaks out.' Gideon Bouwer told an acquaintance, who later became an FBI informant that Ford had given Knobel a briefcase containing 'biological warfare materials'.[39] Ford was reported to be particularly interested in HIV–AIDS research. Although Larry Ford visited Roodeplaat in 1987 to instruct 'scientists working with an SADF front company [on] how to turn teabags, doilies and pornographic magazines into "weapons" . . . using a species of clostridium bacteria', little is known of Ford's role in South Africa's CBW programme. Purkitt and Burgess have reported that Ford travelled widely in South Africa, until mid-1995, gathering amniotic fluid 'from thousands of women in South African military hospitals'. On 2 March 2000, Larry Ford shot himself while the Californian police were travelling to arrest him for the attempted murder of his business partner. After his death, the police discovered more than a hundred weapons, thousands of rounds of ammunition, explosives 'and more than 30 sealed and hand-labelled bottles of suspected pathogens and toxins'.[40]

Although Dr Basson was known to have visited Taiwan in the early 1980s, many aspects of Project Coast's international relationships remain shrouded in mystery. In Britain, Major Roger Buffham, a former military intelligence agent and bomb-disposal expert, became a business associate. Basson and Buffham were reported to have met eight times and entered into a series of financial transactions together. Buffham stated in an affidavit that 'his dealings with Basson had been confined to the supply of electronic security equipment' but he proved to be unwilling to testify in South Africa because 'he feared for his life'. At the time of the Basson trial, Buffham was the head of security at the Jockey Club. The origins of Basson's involvement in Libya are equally obscure. In court, he testified that 'top-ranking SADF officers both knew about and authorised' his interactions with Libyan spies from 1986 and that he was a regular visitor to the country from 1988. The South African prosecutors suggested that Basson's reports of Libyan involvement in Basson's CBW programme were nothing more than 'romantic fantasies'.[41]

The secret Steyn Report in December 1992 unearthed the first evidence of Basson's activities. At the beginning of 1993, South Africa signed the Chemical Weapons Convention. On 31 March 1993, Project Coast was closed down and Basson retired from the SADF. In reality the majority of

Project Coast's front corporations had been privatised two years earlier. In *Armed and Dangerous*, Ronnie Kasrils suggested that 'de Klerk panicked when he received the Steyn Report' because the NIS had earlier given him similar information. Kasrils continued: '[Niel] Barnard . . . resented the political interference and influence of the generals. So in all probability NIS found a way of recycling its own data back to de Klerk.'[42] The South African government ordered the biological 'hardware' (the bacteria and viruses) of Project Coast destroyed. The 'software', the library of knowledge developed under the aegis of Coast, was transferred to a set of CD-ROMs before shredding. Under minimal supervision, Basson stored the software documentation in two trunks in his garage. Basson was immediately employed by Transnet, the South African public-owned transport corporation, and travelled to Libya on at least five occasions on Transnet's behalf. Over the next twelve months, MI6 and the CIA, which appear to have had little idea of South Africa's CBW programme before 1993, worked together to bully the de Klerk regime into action. De Klerk later recalled to Tom Mangold:

'A special meeting was set up through the secret services. My initial reaction, after having listened to the British and the Americans, was to firstly restate the sovereignty of the South African Republic. They were initially quite aggressive'. . . 'They wanted five things,' recalls a senior South African official who was present at every meeting. 'They said: "Destroy all your BW records, destroy all your capability, make a public declaration in this regard, and inform Mr Mandela. We also want access to all your records, we must be able to look through them all"'. . . . Supported by President de Klerk, this official counter-attacked. 'What about your biological warfare stockpiles? . . . We are not going to do what you say. There was a major confrontation,' the official recalls, 'and we refused to see them again. Later they had to come back and eat humble pie and we made friends again.'[43]

General Niel Knobel informed the TRC that 'US and UK representatives urged President de Klerk to close down the program, saying they were concerned that it should not end up in the hands of the [ANC].' On 11 April 1994, less than three weeks before South Africa's general election, the British High Commissioner and the US Ambassador delivered a démarche to President de Klerk which demanded that British experts be briefed on the CBW programme. After the election and his inauguration as president, Nelson Mandela was fully briefed on South Africa's CBW. Tom Mangold reported that Mandela was 'terrified that the South African "Third Force" elements . . . might lay their hands on it. He specifically asked British officials for their assistance and advice.' A joint British–US team interviewed Basson but remained concerned at the continuing visits to Libya. Eventually, it was suggested by both British and American officials and former Afrikaner generals that Basson should be brought 'under control by re-hiring him'. The Johannesburg *Sunday Independent* later reported a British intelligence source who had commented that 'at one point a Western intelligence agency suggested to Pretoria that Basson be killed to prevent his knowledge from falling into the wrong hands'. In May 1995, Basson was rehired as an SANDF surgeon.[44] Meanwhile, the new government continued to investigate the extensive allegations of financial malfeasance related to the CBW programme. As with Eschel Rhoodie, corruption would play a significant role in the downfall of Basson.

Dr Wouter Basson was arrested on 29 January 1997. He was in possession of 1,000 ecstasy capsules and seemed to be attempting to complete a drug deal. A South African intelligence source said that 'The hint came from the Americans . . . The CIA approached us in December, saying that Basson was going to skip town and asked us to make sure it didn't happen.' Project Coast scientists had long been involved in the drugs business. General Lothar Neethling, who played a key role in distributing Basson's poisons (see page 200), also provided the scientists with confiscated LSD, several tons of cannabis, and hundreds of thousands of mandrax pills; mandrax, a depressant, is very popular among Africans, especially when smoked. The scientists had experimented with creating mortar bombs filled with methaqualone, extracted from mandrax pills, in order to pacify rioters. The experiments were abandoned in 1988 because the bombs had the reverse effect.[45] In the early 1990s, extensive experiments with MDMA (ecstasy) were designed to produce an incapacitant. It was later reported at the TRC that MID officials smuggled ecstasy and cannabis 'into Britain in the nose-cone of an aircraft that carried rugby fans to watch the first Springbok test match after sporting ties were re-established [in 1992]'. The *New Yorker* reported that Basson was 'happy to suggest that his dealings with the ANC during the years when he was masquerading as a wealthy, sanctions-busting businessman were extensive. The liberation movement needed connections, especially for arms and intelligence . . . The drugs [Basson] is alleged to have trafficked in? Those were placebos palmed off on the ANC which had no qualms about selling illegal drugs.'[46]

The National Intelligence Agency's counter-intelligence chief, Mike Kennedy, led the investigation into Basson's activities and quickly discovered the two trunks with the Project Coast documents. An unnamed NIA officer told Tom Mangold: 'This was a dirty game . . . both the British and the

Americans have behaved hypocritically over this, but so did the Germans, the Israelis, the Swiss and a large number of greedy academics.' The TRC, which examined South Africa's CBW programme in June and July 1998, declared that 'the hearings revealed a nepotistic, self-serving and self-enriching group of people . . . the CBW programme achieved little of value or of common good. Enveloped as it was by secrecy, threats and fear, opportunism, financial mismanagement, incompetence, self-aggrandisement, together with a breakdown in the normal methods of scientific discourse, the results were paltry.' Basson's trial started in October 1999. He faced sixty-four charges, including twelve for murder and three for attempted murder. The trial was something of a farce, as indeed the KwaMakutha 'Third Force' trial of General Malan and others had been in the mid-1990s. The *New Yorker* commented: 'The scene in the courtroom is pure Old South Africa. Anyone with any standing or authority is white. Virtually everyone . . . is Afrikaans.' As early in the proceedings as February 2000, the state's senior prosecutor Anton Ackerman 'brought an application . . . for the Judge to remove himself from the bench on the grounds of bias [in favour of the defendant].' Judge Willie Hartzenberg dismissed the application for his removal, describing it as 'frivolous, mind-boggling, absurd and unfounded in its totality.'[47]

One of the most shocking revelations during the Basson trial had nothing to do with CBW: on 7 June 1989, Louis Pienaar, the Administrator-General of South West Africa–Namibia had issued an extraordinary but secret proclamation, *Official Gazette* No. 5725. This had stated that 'No criminal procedures may be instituted or continued following the date of this proclamation in any law court against any person . . . in respect of a crime committed by such person at any time prior to the date mentioned, in the territory or elsewhere.' The proclamation covered all members of the South African security forces who 'in the execution of their duties and activities in the territory committed an act or neglected to commit an act which represents a crime'. Therefore neither Basson nor any other South African could be tried for crimes committed on Namibian or foreign soil before June 1989. Basson was, predictably, found not guilty in April 2002. Five former SADF generals, Malan, Viljoen, Joubert, Knobel and Dirk Marais ('who [had] spearheaded the highly successful campaign to dissuade apartheid's warriors from approaching the [TRC] for amnesty'), celebrated the verdict in the court room. It is very likely that Basson will be retried at some future date.[48]

Basson's arrest and trial did not close the chapter on South Africa's adventures in the global CBW market. In October 2001 during the anthrax attacks in the United States, Basson's former colleague Dr Daan Goosen contacted the Pentagon offering his knowledge of anthrax strains and vaccines. He was referred to a private company, Bioport, in Michigan, which he visited in January 2002. 'But interest from the US side evaporated quickly,' as the *Washington Post* later remarked. Upon his return to South Africa, Goosen was introduced by a mutual acquaintance to a former MID Officer, Major-General Tai Minnaar. Minnaar convinced Goosen that he could sell vials of the bacteria that produce anthrax, plague, botulism, salmonella and other genetically modified bio-weapons to the American government in exchange for $5 million and nineteen US immigration permits. Minnaar, who claimed to have worked with the CIA in Cuba in 1976, contacted the Americans. Over a period of two months, two former CIA agents, Don Mayes and Robert Zlockie, assessed the validity of Goosen's claims. Mayes owned a company, the ICT Group, that specialised in the covert procurement of foreign weapons systems. At one point, Zlockie transported a toxic substance (hidden within a modified toothpaste tube) on a commercial flight to the FBI laboratories in the United States.

Documents leaked to the *Washington Post* showed that plans were developed to smuggle the mass of the bio-weapons out of South Africa. These plans involved using a light aircraft to transport '200 ampoules containing deadly organisms' including anthrax strains from their hiding place to Cape Town. The ampoules would then be stored on a private yacht with a liquid-nitrogen cooling unit to keep them freeze-dried. The yacht would then either meet a US Navy ship in the South Atlantic or make the three-week voyage to Florida. After two months of planning between March and May 2002, the Americans abandoned the deal. Although the sample proved to be a genetically modified pathogen, FBI scientists reported that the genetic engineering was dated and that they were not prepared to meet Goosen's and Minnaar's price. The FBI handed their evidence to the South African authorities, which investigated Goosen on two occasions but failed to charge him.[49]

However, it is clear that the American authorities were playing a complicated game. Following the collapse of the Goosen deal, US intelligence agents visited Dr Basson, who admitted that he did not know who controlled the surviving Project Coast bio-weapons. He also described an unknown strain of anthrax that the apartheid scientists had developed and which in tests proved extremely difficult to detect. Basson told the American officials that he had learned the techniques for his 'stealth anthrax' from

Israeli scientists. South African intelligence officials and Daan Goosen believed that the FBI leaked the story in order to expose South Africa as a proliferation risk. Documents linked to the case revealed that Mayes and Zlockie had meetings and correspondence with high-level figures within the FBI, including Barbara Martinez, the head of the Weapons of Mass Destruction Unit. Minnaar continued to search for a purchaser for the WMD. Working with a former South African intelligence agent, Arnold van Eck, he contacted a former Czech agent, Helmut Gaensel, who had made his name as a hunter for hidden Nazi treasure. Gaensel was interested in buying both the serum for anthrax and anthrax spores. Goosen refused to supply anthrax 'for testing the serum'. Minnaar and Van Eck then became entangled in a complicated sting operation launched by South Africa's National Intelligence Agency. The sting involved a fake Arab sheikh in a Johannesburg hotel. Once again, Goosen refused to supply the anthrax. In retrospect, Dr Goosen believed, as he informed the *Mail & Guardian* that he was deliberately set up by the US to make South Africa look bad – a view echoed by officials of the [NIA].'[50]

General Tai Minnaar died in September 2002 in mysterious circumstances. Although he reportedly had a heart attack, it is widely believed that he was murdered. His lover, in whose arms he died, told investigators that Minnaar had vomited before his death 'and that his corpse had swollen rapidly to more than double its normal size'. Such swelling can be characteristic of some of the poisons Minnaar had been attempting to sell. A kilogram of potassium cyanide was found among other chemicals in his home by the police. His lover hired a private detective to investigate the case. The detective noted that documents had been stolen from Minnaar's office following his death. In a further bizarre twist, the Commissioner of Police, Jackie Selebi, admitted that he had had a meeting with Minnaar some weeks before the latter's death. US sources informed the *Mail & Guardian* that the former CIA agents Mayes and Zlockie were so concerned by Minnaar's death that they made contact with the *Washington Post*, fearing for their own safety. In May 2003, Vusi Mavimbela was asked whether he could guarantee that the NIA had 'sufficient controls to prevent proliferation' of WMD. Mavimbela replied: 'I believe there is sufficient control. But at the same time there are many scientists who are not working with the government of the day, and some who have even left the country. We can't lock them all up.'[51]

14

National Intelligence

In the public mind, and among those who claim to interpret it, [intelligence] has come very close to being identified with 'truth', that will-o'-the-wisp which trails in its wake the broken reputations of countless epistemologists. Intelligence, it seems, will tell us what the state of things really is: it will take the risks out of *virtù* and the dangers out of *fortuna*; it can remove all guesswork from diplomacy. The humble spy has become something like a shaman. Some of this, of course, results from media shorthand which often depends on finding the most common denominator to make complex things look simple. Much of it, also, can be traced to 'political science', where international affairs are still sometimes pictured as a matter of ricocheting interests and rebounding advantages, much on the model of pocket billiards. Those in the intelligence business, however, know it to be a mix of fact and judgement often as uncertain and ambiguous as the human state of affairs it is trying to describe.

James M. Murphy, 'Shaman spies', *Times Literary Supplement*, 22 August 2003[1]

THE FIRST AND most important statement that has to be made on the subject of South African espionage, since the election of Nelson Mandela's ANC, is that it has been dramatically different from the security-dominated intelligence which guided the Republic for thirty years between 1963 and 1993. That is not to claim that it has been more efficient or effective, merely that the average South African citizen no longer feels that he or she is being spied upon. It is also true that South African overseas intelligence activity has completely stopped attracting attention. Whether this means that overseas intelligence, under the control of SASS, has virtually ceased to exist or whether it no longer engages in illegal activities is another question. The secret services in post-apartheid South Africa have continued to be closely linked to the politics of the country, but the violence and criminality of the MID or the Security Police is no longer a permanent feature – the virtual disappearance of political murders being a case in point. The biggest problem facing South African espionage in the years since 1994 has been the intelligence legacy of the past, not least the fact that because it was impossible to 'wipe the slate clean', and the TRC was not tasked to launch 'mole hunts' in order to unearth double agents, the whispers and rumours relating to both apartheid South Africa and the ANC networks continue to possess substantial power.

Suspicious Spies

Two of the NIS's 'progressives', the former Director-General Mike Louw and the head of intelligence operations until 1991, Maritz Spaarwater, offered interesting observations on the transformation of intelligence. Louw said that, in the early 1990s, during the negotiations with the ANC regarding intelligence consolidation, he had offered Thabo Mbeki, Jacob Zuma and Joe Nhlanhla an arrangement that he hoped would be in the best interests of the Republic. He said that he had reason to believe that the ANC had been penetrated by foreign intelligence agents; he recommended that the ANC should 'declare' those people it suspected of being spies to the NIS and then both parties would destroy the evidence. The NIS would assist the ANC by revealing compromising information from its files on foreign agents which, he hoped, would assist in neutralising the problem. Of course, such an arrangement would have required reserves of trust that were just not available after so many years of opposition. Strategically, it made sense that Louw should have sought such a deal – after all, it was likely that the ANC would become the hegemonic political power in South Africa for many years in the future. Louw recalled that the response of the ANC negotiators was interesting: Mbeki sucked his pipe and smiled, Zuma laughed and Nhlanhla expounded for twenty minutes on why the ANC's intelligence structures had not been penetrated by any foreign agency.[2] A more important 'exchange' would have been if the ANC and the NIS could have disclosed their intelligence penetration of each other. There is no evidence that any such discussion was ever contemplated.

In the early 1990s, members of the ANC quietly admitted that the former ANC chief representative in London, Solly Smith, and Dr Francis Meli, a former editor of the ANC magazine *Sechaba* and author of a history of the ANC, had been spies for the apartheid regime. The truth emerged after both men, who were alcoholics, had died. In June 1994, the Johannesburg *Sunday Times* published an interview with two former members of the MID's Directorate of Covert Collection (DCC) who claimed to possess 'a great deal of secret information . . . including the names of many informants', a number of whom were senior members of MK. In February 1996, the *Mail & Guardian* reported that DCC operative Commandant Anton Nieuwoudt's compensation claim against the SADF for unfair dismissal in December 1992 was settled *in camera* on the eve of the 1994 election. Documents attached to Nieuwoudt's claim included an MID memorandum in September 1992 which referred to Agent 241/222 (an ANC source and MK regional commander), who:

> is prepared to have a secret meeting with the defence force along with: J. Modise (MK commander), L. Moloi (chief of operations, MK), M.K. Zakes (regional commander PWV [Pretoria, Witwatersrand, Vaal]), M.K. Maincheck (commander of MK outside South Africa) and J. Mnisi (commander Pretoria) . . . This meeting could be instrumental in beginning to neutralise the SACP/Hani/Kasrils faction.[3]

Joe Modise, the Minister of Defence, told the *Mail & Guardian*: 'I want to state clearly that I never attended a meeting that you referred to in your questions.' In March 1997, the story emerged again when a lawyer representing five senior police officers who had applied for amnesty at the TRC announced: 'There are people in current government . . . high-profile people who were informers.' Former askari Joe Mamasela informed the *New Nation* that five ANC cabinet ministers had been spies for the apartheid government. Nelson Mandela, during a state visit to Malaysia, told the press: 'We want to know who [the spies] are, not necessarily because we want to take action against them but because, if they had been informing on behalf of the apartheid regime, there is the likelihood that they are doing that today.'[4] In April 1997, an ANC leader in the Midlands district of KwaZulu–Natal, Sifiso Nkabinde, was expelled from the party when it emerged that he had been in the pay of the security forces from 1988. Nkabinde later joined Bantu Holomisa's United Democratic Movement (UDM) and was assassinated in January 1999. On 22 October 1997, under parliamentary privilege, the impetuous but respected PAC politician Patricia de Lille said that Nelson Mandela and Thabo Mbeki had a list of twelve spies, of whom she named eight. The *Sowetan* published the names:

> Those who stand accused include
> Defence Minister Mr Joe Modise,

Minister of Minerals and Energy Affairs, Mr Penuell Maduna,
Minister of Public Enterprises, Ms Stella Sigcau,
Deputy Minister of Environment Affairs and Tourism, Mr Peter Mokaba,
Deputy Minister of Intelligence Services, Mr Joe Nhlanhla,
Eastern Cape Premier, Makhenkesi Stofile,
Mpumalanga Premier, Matthews Phosa,
and Ricky Nkondo [of the NIA].[5]

Mandela denied that he had any list of spies, but a few days later Bantu
Holomisa informed the *Mail & Guardian* that Mandela had told an NEC
meeting in January 1996 that 'they should not forget that he now has access
to [the intelligence] files [of members of the NEC]. He reminded us that
we shouldn't talk too much because he knows some of us were working
for the state . . . He could not just have said that. It means [Mandela]
knows.' The allegations of additional members of the ANC, not included
on de Lille's list, having worked for the apartheid security forces have continued to reverberate ever since. It later emerged that in May 1997 the
ANC had 'handed a list of spies and informers to the [TRC] but requested
that the list be kept secret'. At the same time, Niel Barnard 'made a confidential submission to the TRC . . . saying various people – some in
prominent leadership positions – had supplied the NIS with information
in the 1980s. Barnard declined to name any informers, but the ANC
insisted, saying refusal to do so "implied a continuation of those structures".' The submission and the ANC list were repossessed by the NIA
when the TRC closed its offices in 1999.[6]

Maritz Spaarwater's story is equally informative. I asked him how many
of the agents or assets that the NIS had funded were genuine and not
conmen. He explained that this question had always concerned him; in the
late 1980s, he had decided that he would try and meet all the people that
the NIS was paying money to. Spaarwater did not care how he met his
spies: in his office, at a social occasion or even in more clandestine circumstances. The point of the exercise was that he wanted to look into the
eyes of his spies, so that he could decide whether or not they were authentic. I asked, 'How many did you manage to meet?' Spaarwater replied:
'About 50 per cent.' I continued: 'And how many were genuine?' The
answer: 'About 50 per cent.' He admitted: 'I have begun to believe that
intelligence is a somewhat pointless exercise.' The former spymaster's
declining faith in the value of espionage could easily be interpreted as
another sign of the slow withdrawal of white South Africans from the
political and intelligence scene, but I believe it was something more sig-

nificant. I think that Maritz Spaarwater had come to the realisation that intelligence agencies are much weaker and less knowing than lower-level spies always insist.[7] His realisation that the NIS was extremely vulnerable to the crooks, conmen and fantasists that occupy the 'frontiers' in South Africa must have been very depressing indeed.

Tom Mangold's book *Plague Wars* provided one of the earliest pictures of the full scale of Wouter Basson's Project Coast; it also contained a snapshot of the paranoid world of post-apartheid politics and intelligence in the late 1990s. Mangold's references to an ODESSA-like network called Die Organisasie ('The Organisation') were confused with the 'Third Force' (see page 255) and even with a relatively peaceful-sounding network of 'expats now living in the United Kingdom, who *may* support the destabilisation of any black South African government' (my emphasis). Mangold announced that Die Organisasie:

> is a group of white South Africans [and ex-Rhodesians] who wait patiently for the demise of the ANC government and a return to the old days. They are not the mad pseudo-Nazis of the far right, but something far more organized, well-financed, and patient . . . We [were] to hear of them time and again from ex-soldiers . . . all the way up to South Africa's deputy defence minister, Ronnie Kasrils. Significantly, files have been opened up by MI5 in London, where Die Organisasie is recognised as a small, potent, and potentially significant union of like-minded South African right-wingers.

Mangold added: '[Die Organisasie] remain a troubling point of political focus to Pretoria, where both the [NIA] and the Ministry of Defence also take them very seriously indeed.' In reality, Mangold had stumbled into the confusing world of post-apartheid 'fear and loathing'. As I explained in Chapter 11, in South Africa during the 1990s the term 'Third Force' was rapidly applied to any anti-ANC phenomenon for which there was no easy explanation. The term 'the organisation' was sometimes employed by former CCB operatives to describe old colleagues who continued to engage in freelance activities.[8] Throughout the second half of the 1990s, members of the South African public who cared to read newspapers, watch the television news or follow the proceedings of the TRC became increasingly aware of what had actually occurred during the horrific death throes of the decaying apartheid state. As the politicians and intelligence officials of the ANC gradually assumed control of the levers of the extensive state machine, the sense that an evil guiding-hand lay behind every mishap, and in particular the boom in random violent crime, was in a peculiar way reassuring.

After all, that had been a profound belief for the majority of South Africa's people during the previous decades. No reliable proof has ever been produced to demonstrate that Die Organisasie was ever anything more than a nightmare.

The New South African Intelligence Services

South African intelligence since January 1995 has endured an extended period of attempting to discover who and what it is. Like a psychiatric patient undergoing a long period of counselling after an episode of mental illness, the South African secret services have spent most of the years since 1995 attempting to come to terms with themselves. It was always going to be difficult to practise intelligence in a democratic country with an inquisitive, if often amnesiac and sensational, press and a history of institutional malfeasance which was being examined on a daily basis in the late 1990s at the Truth and Reconciliation Commission. The sunset clauses which protected civil servants' jobs for a five-year period after the 1994 election and the integration of former intelligence officials from the liberation movements and the former 'independent' homelands led to the 'mixed marriage' from hell. The Government of National Unity which attempted to wed the victorious ANC, the IFP and the NP in an inclusive administration survived only until May 1996, three months after the TRC started. The intelligence agents were not permitted to seek a divorce, and so the dysfunctional relationship continued, stymieing almost any form of serious investigation as it did so.

The 'compromise' that created the short-lived 'rainbow nation' avoided the brutal reckoning that normally follows massive social upheaval, but it also cemented a compromised bureaucratic culture into place. This was particularly true in the intelligence agencies, which had a long history of minimal accountability and nepotism (Hendrik van den Bergh's son, Johan, worked for the National Intelligence Agency until the late 1990s). The NIA must have been a very strange institution in the late 1990s, with Dirk Coetzee – the former death squad commander who told the *Sowetan* in 1996, 'I am not a spy and will never be one' – working alongside former CCB operatives and Sizwe Gabriel Mthembu, commander of the Quatro punishment camp from 1979 to 1982. 'Ann', a white NIA agent, who worked for BOSS, the NIS and the NIA from 1975 to 1999, believed that:

There is no difference between what the ANC is doing in the Intelligence Service and what the previous dispensation did. It is the same narrow-minded perspective . . . There is far less open debate now in the Intelligence Service than there was under the Nationalists . . . If you don't allow differing opinions within the Intelligence Service, it is going to rot. I didn't leave because I had a political problem. It [was] just a narrow-minded way of looking at things and also incompetent bosses . . . They must close that place down (the NIA and SASS) and start from scratch . . . It is becoming totally irrelevant and you cannot have a politically-laden intelligence service.[9]

Certain features of the new South African intelligence culture became apparent within a few years. There would be no 'strongman' or 'master-spy' figures; in fact, intelligence ministers or officials rarely remained in their posts for extended periods: this was in keeping with ANC intelligence history but in direct contrast to the Afrikaner tradition. Intelligence, in effect, became a rung on the ladder of political, bureaucratic or business advancement. While on one level this development was encouraging in so far as it made abuse of intelligence power less likely, it also damaged the efficacy of the agencies and ruined the sense of institutional collective memory. A significant continuity from the previous intelligence dispensation was the intermittent inter-agency conflict: this would get progressively worse as the government established alternative structures that dabbled in intelligence, in order to bypass what was perceived as the incipient chaos within the established institutions, and as the senior ANC politicians mobilised and activated their personal intelligence networks.

The four official intelligence agencies, the NIA (domestic intelligence), South African Secret Service (SASS – foreign intelligence), Defence Intelligence (ID – military) and the Crime Intelligence Service (CIS – police), in theory reported to the Provincial Intelligence Co-ordinating Committees (PICOC) and the National Intelligence Co-ordinating Committee (NICOC). NICOC reported to the Minister of Intelligence and was overseen by the Joint Standing Committee on Intelligence and the Inspector-General of Intelligence, a post that has only been sporadically filled since 1995. In the ensuing years, a further four intelligence-like institutions have been either created or exposed: the Scorpions (see page 358); the Presidential Intelligence Unit, established by Thabo Mbeki; the South African Revenue Service (SARS), which is believed to be running a makeshift intelligence structure within its investigatory wing; and the Department of Foreign Affairs, which possessed an intelligence capacity during the apartheid era and is thought to possess one now.[10] The state expenditure on the South African intelligence agencies, excluding military intelligence, has grown rapidly in the post-apartheid period. In 1993–4, the budget was R435 million; two years later, in 1995–6, this had increased to R714 million. As the international value of the rand dropped at the beginning of the twenty-first century, so the budget grew: in 2002–3, South African intelligence cost R1.3 billion (R868 million for the NIA; R362 million for SASS; and R76 million for Crime Intelligence). For the tax year 2004–5, the amount allocated for intelligence was R1.978 billion.[11]

Leadership and oversight within the new South African intelligence culture has remained problematic. There have been three ministers of intelligence during the Mandela and Mbeki administrations: Joe Nhlanhla (1994–2000), Lindiwe Sisulu (2001–4) and Ronnie Kasrils (2004–). All three had been involved in DIS and MK intelligence in exile. Nhlanhla, despite appearances, was one of the longest-serving intelligence chiefs in South African history: at the time of his retirement, due to ill health following a stroke, he had served at the helm of ANC–DIS and state intelligence for thirteen years. In 1997, during a visit to the NIA's new offices, President Mandela lammed the agency, which had recently lost ten [mini]buses and computer equipment during a robbery: 'How can you claim with any measure of integrity that you are competent to protect the country if you cannot secure your own premises?' Four years later, Mandela revealed: 'As President for five years I know that my intelligence services many times didn't inform me before they took action. Sometimes I approved, sometimes I reprimanded them.'[12]

Lindiwe Sisulu, a former chairperson of the parliamentary Joint Standing Committee on Intelligence and the daughter of Walter and Albertina Sisulu, perhaps the most revered family in ANC history, led South African intelligence without attracting too much attention or conflict. In an interview with the *Financial Mail* she criticised the ANC's intelligence activity in exile: 'We took our cue from the intelligence services of the apartheid state. We were a law unto ourselves. We felt comfortable with that because we were fighting fire with fire.' Sisulu was a moderniser who opened the new Intelligence Academy, promoted the civilian agencies in advertisements and established websites which helped to publicise the NIA's and SASS's work. Her transfer to the Ministry of Housing in 2004 had not been predicted. Sisulu's successor, Ronnie Kasrils, who remained a senior member of the SACP, had long been considered a safe pair of hands by the ANC. One of the longest-serving government ministers, he had previously been Deputy Minister of Defence (1994–9) and Minister of Water Affairs and Forestry (1999–2004). Observers suggest that Kasrils is very keen on Cuban solutions to ANC intelligence problems. His relationship with South Africa's Jewish community has been tense because of his outspoken opposition to Israeli government policy towards the Palestinians – a position which when held by a Jew is viewed as virtual heresy by South Africa's overwhelmingly zionist Jewish community.[13]

In 1996, Ronnie Kasrils was unwittingly used in an extremely unethical FBI sting operation. Two American communists, Kurt Stand and Theresa Squillacote, whose names had been discovered in the records of the East German intelligence service, the Stasi, were placed under surveillance by the FBI. Squillacote worked in the Pentagon's Office of Acquisition Reform. The FBI secretly searched the couple's apartment and downloaded the contents of their computer. The computer's memory revealed a letter that Squillacote had sent Ronnie Kasrils after reading his autobiography, *Armed and Dangerous*. They also discovered a Christmas card that Kasrils had sent in reply. The FBI dispatched a letter to Squillacote as if from Kasrils, suggesting that she should meet one of South Africa's 'special components' (intelligence agents). Squillacote met an FBI agent and gave him five relatively innocuous Defense Planning documents. She was particularly keen that South Africa should pass the information on to Vietnam and Cuba. Squillacote and Stand were convicted of espionage and conspiring to transmit documents and information relating to the national defence. Theresa Squillacote was sentenced to twenty-three years imprisonment and her husband Kurt Stand received seventeen years. The FBI agent who entrapped Squillacote appreared to be riddled with the prejudices of the Cold War. He 'testified that apartheid was only "occasionally" brutal to Blacks; that he believed Nelson Mandela to be a communist; and that South Africa "is a member of the Communist Bloc"'. Ronnie Kasrils discovered the deceit when the case was reported on the South African news. He angrily referred to the FBI as the 'Federal Bureau of Idiots' and demanded an apology for the 'misappropriation of the South African flag, my name and office'. He told the *Independent*: 'Quite frankly, I feel for the people entrapped using my name . . . people who thought they were helping the Democratic Republic of South Africa.'[14]

The first Director-General of the NIA, Sizakele Sigxashe, had been the chief intelligence analyst of ANC intelligence from 1984 and had played a significant role in suppressing the mutiny in the ANC's Angolan camps. He caused some embarrassment to the agency when police were called to his home in 1995 to deal with a domestic situation in which he had thrown a plate of food at his wife and, according to reports, threatened to shoot her. The appointment of Sigxashe's successor, Vusi Mavimbela, was announced in October 1999, a few months after President Mbeki's election. Mavimbela had been Mbeki's political adviser and special adviser on intelligence and security between 1994 and 1999. The *Mail & Guardian* quoted an intelligence insider's assessment that 'South Africa can hardly claim to have an intelligence capability at the moment'.[15] Mavimbela, who had been trained by the East German Stasi, resigned less than five years later, and was swiftly hired by ANC businessman–politician Tokyo Sexwale's Mvelephanda. Sexwale is a South African version of the Russian oligarchs. The fact that he is assembling experienced intelligence operatives around himself signals a continuing interest in political activity and quite possibly a campaign for the Presidency. Billy Masetlha, the third Director-General of the NIA, had enjoyed a complicated intelligence career in the post-apartheid period. He had been the deputy DG at SASS between 1995 and 1996 and thereafter head of the agency until 2000. He survived a brief period as the Director-General of Home Affairs, a treacherous spying posting where his central role was to keep a close watch on the Minister, Mangosuthu Buthelezi. Masetlha then headed Thabo Mbeki's newly formed Presidential Intelligence Unit between 2001 and 2004, before ascending to the top spy post in the country.[16]

According to an interview with Sigxashe in 1995, the NIA was divided into seven directorates: 'domestic collection, research, counter-espionage, security, corporate resources, technology and intelligence academy'. Mike Louw was honoured for his role in the transformation of South Africa's intelligence agencies by being appointed Director-General of the foreign intelligence service, SASS, in 1995. His first duty, he recalled, was to inform President Mandela how his agency had been conned out of substantial funds while attempting to establish a presence in Nigeria. Louw retained his pragmatic optimism and in a revealing interview in the Johannesburg *Star*, headed 'Memoirs of an invisible man', defended the need for an intelligence *service* in the new South Africa:

'A good intelligence service is the cheapest defence a country can have'. . . Suddenly, unexpectedly, the real-life spymaster quotes from a fictional character, John le Carré's immortal Smiley, musing the *The Secret Pilgrim*: 'All history teaches us that today's allies are tomorrow's rivals. Fashion may dictate priorities but foresight doesn't. For as long as rogues become leaders, we shall spy. For as long as there are bullies and liars and madmen in the world, we shall spy. For as long as nations compete, and politicians deceive, and tyrants launch conquests, and consumers need resources, and the homeless look for land, and the hungry for food, and the rich for excess [our] chosen profession is perfectly secure . . .' For Mike Louw, that says it all. 'Convince me that such conditions do not exist, here at home and internationally, and I will agree that we do not need an intelligence service.'[17]

In 2000, the Stasi-trained Hilton Dennis succeeded Masetlha to the top post in SASS. Dennis took some of the praise in 2004 for halting Simon Mann's and Mark Thatcher's attempt to execute a coup in Equatorial Guinea (see page 385), informing the Johannesburg *Star* that: 'There were many interests involved, but people don't give the actions of the intelligence service the credit they deserve.' He was a little less vocal on the Zimbabwean CIO's discovery of a SASS 'spy-ring' in January 2005. As he had advised the *Star*, 'Not getting caught is the name of the game.'[18]

NICOC has had four intelligence co-ordinators since 1995. Although it was originally imagined that this role would be tantamount to being 'South Africa's new intelligence supremo', that is not what has happened in practice. Shaun McCarthy reported that Niel Barnard 'made a bid for the position [but] did not succeed'. Mo Shaik, whose brothers Schabir and Shamin would later be active agents in South Africa's defence procurement programme, served as the temporary co-ordinator of NICOC between 1995 and 1996 before moving through a series of posts in the Department of Foreign Affairs, including ambassador to Algeria. He resigned from the public service in 2005. Shaik was followed by two relatively invisible intelligence co-ordinators: Linda Mti served in the post from 1996 to 2001 before being appointed national commissioner of Correctional Services (Prisons). Jeff Maqetuka, who held the post between 2001 and 2005, had previously been deputy DG of both the NIA and SASS. He proceeded to the Director-Generalship of Home Affairs. Barry Gilder, a former MK cadre and 'career spy', has held exactly the same positions at different times in his career as his predecessor Maqetuka.[19] Five-year time limits for the post of NICOC intelligence co-ordinators and the DGs of the various intelligence agencies have effectively halted the development of intelligence barons, but the constant reshuffling of spy chiefs has facilitated the spreading of intelligence practices throughout the South African civil service.

By 1999, all the senior positions within South African intelligence were held by appointees who had intelligence backgrounds within the ANC. Meanwhile, independent oversight had barely developed from the idealistic designs of the White Paper of 1994. Lewis Skweyiya, who had investigated human rights abuses in the ANC's Angolan camps in 1992, was appointed the first Inspector-General in 1996 but resigned due to 'prolonged and delayed negotiations' and a dispute over his salary before he had actually taken office. The post remained empty for five years before former Truth Commissioner Dr Fazel Randera was appointed in May 2000; he was not actually 'sworn in' until June 2001. Randera resigned after six months, citing 'personal reasons'. *Africa Confidential* pointed out that he 'did not issue a single public report suggesting he had completed any investigations'. It would be three more years before the third Inspector-General, Zolile Ngcakani, was appointed. Unlike Skweyiya and Randera, Ngcakani was an intelligence insider who had served in the ANC's DIS in the early 1970s before training as an environmental engineer. He worked in the Intelligence Ministry from 1996 until 2004 and claimed: 'I have an advantage in knowing, or having been in, the intelligence services because there are things that I would be able to see which an outside person would take some time [to discover].'[20]

Niel Barnard remained as Director-General of Constitutional Affairs until 1996, although his new minister, Valli Moosa, had attempted to engineer his resignation in 1994. He was then appointed Director-General of the only remaining National Party-controlled region, the Western Cape – a post he held until December 2001. During that time 'he chaired regular meetings of police, army, intelligence and government officials' in the midst of a campaign of local Islamic terrorism. In 2002, the Desai Commission of Inquiry investigated alleged bugging and corruption in Western Cape politics and revealed that Barnard was so convinced that the local government offices were bugged that he held meetings in a reinforced storeroom, where he sat on plastic-coated aluminium garden furniture, 'to which no bugging device could be attached', while utilising a bizarre device called 'the Watchdog, which could detect bugs and snoop on conversations 4 km away'. The head of the Community Safety Department said 'he had not come across anything like it "in all my 30 years as a civil servant"'. Barnard also hired former BOSS–NIS agents as freelance spies and employed a private security company to 'bug-proof' his offices. The company was owned by Stephen Whitehead, who while employed as a member of the Security Police in 1982 had interrogated the trade unionist Neil Aggett, who was later subjected to an 'induced suicide' (see page 213).[21] Like any ex-spy, Barnard had established a spy-ring, or what was more politely called the Western Cape 'information unit'.

P.W. van der Westhuizen, the former CSI of MID, retired from the public service in 1991 after three years as Ambassador in Chile. Van der Westhuizen avoided testifying to the TRC and is reputed, in the years since, to have made a fortune in import–export with Latin American countries. In June 2003, an Intelligence Services Council was created by Lindiwe Sisulu; three former intelligence chiefs were invited 'to make recommendations . . . on human resource policies, improved salaries and fringe benefits for members of the civilian intelligence community'. The Council's chairperson was Sizakele Sigxashe, the first NIA Director-General. Richard Knollys, a former member of the Bophuthatswana Intelligence Service, was appointed deputy chairperson and Mike Louw was asked to serve in a part-time capacity. With the blessing of the South African state, which had offered similar assistance to Northern Ireland in the late 1990s, Niel Barnard and Mike Louw met with Israeli intelligence officials in 2002 and 2003 to offer advice on the peace process. Niel Barnard is reported to be working on his memoirs and was a guest at the luncheon following Minister of Intelligence Kasrils's budget speech in May 2005.[22]

Early snapshots of the new South African secret services were few and far between. Gillian Slovo visited Joe Nhlanhla and Mo Shaik in the mid-1990s at the Plein Street offices of the NIA. Slovo was seeking files on her parents, Ruth First and the recently deceased Joe Slovo. She described Nhlanhla's office: 'His desk top was . . . discreet, devoid of paper . . . the whole office was a document-free zone.' Mo Shaik apparently referred to the NIA's offices 'affectionately . . . as his world of spooks'. A second portrait emerged from a public relations exercise on 10 February 1997 to which thirty journalists were invited. *Africa Confidential* described this 'impressive, if slightly bizarre, demonstration of open government'. The hosts for the evening were Nhlanhla, Mo Shaik, Linda Mti and the NIA's Media Director, Willem Theron. A fragment of captured conversation demonstrated that 'South Africa's intelligence culture is unique . . . "He was trained by Langley (CIA)," a new era officer gestures towards an old era officer, "and I was trained in Moscow, and we've got good contacts in both places." '[23]

In early 1998, the dark side of South Africa's intelligence culture was demonstrated when residual elements of the old MID, hidden within the South African National Defence Force (SANDF)'s ID, levelled one final attack on the ANC government. The final surviving securocrat, Lieutenant-General Dirk Verbeek, the MID's head of counter-intelligence from January 1988 to 1993 and then CSI of both MID and ID, informed General Georg Meiring, the Chief of the SANDF, that he had a source 'very near Winnie Mandela who'd given information about a plan to usurp the power of the government'. On 5 February, Meiring, by most accounts, bypassed Joe Modise, the Minister of Defence, to hand an intelligence report directly to President Mandela; Meiring claimed in *Days of the Generals* that he *had* consulted Modise before contacting Mandela. The ID report alleged that a group of black leaders, including Winnie Mandela and Bantu Holomisa, were engaged in a plot with 'Cuban and American diplomats' and ex-MK officers in the SANDF, primarily Lieutenant-General Siphiwe Nyanda (see page 294), 'to assassinate Mandela, murder judges, occupy Parliament and key institutions and overthrow the government prior to the 1999 general elections'. As Ronnie Kasrils, then Deputy Minister of Defence, later explained: '[the] report stretched credulity to the limits for these were the officers Modise had announced . . . would be promoted to the most senior posts of the SANDF during 1998–1999.' Mandela was also 'sceptical' but 'bided his time'.[24]

A secondary figure named in the report was Robert McBride, a former MK guerrilla who had earned the undying hatred of white South Africans on 14 June 1986 when he had car-bombed two Durban bars, the Why Not, 'frequented by off-duty members of the security forces', and Magoo's Bar, which was directly opposite. The bomb killed three people and injured sixty-nine. The TRC later stated that McBride's 'reconnaissance . . . was of a highly amateurish nature'. He was captured, convicted and sentenced to death before being released as part of the negotiations in the early 1990s. In 1998, McBride was working for the Department of Foreign Affairs and was a representative on the National Intelligence Estimates Board, a section of the NIA. On 11 March 1998, more than a month after the Meiring report was given to Mandela, Robert McBride was arrested in Mozambique and charged with gun-running. Reporter Wally Mbhele campaigned with determined passion on behalf of McBride while the South African press swallowed the disinformation. Mbhele's paper, the *Mail & Guardian*, stated in an editorial:

> The first sniff that there was another reality behind McBride's arrest was the unseemly haste with which police Assistant Commissioner 'Suiker' Britz rushed to Maputo and announced . . . that the young diplomat was guilty . . . But then in an oh-so-familiar way, the smears began mysteriously appearing. McBride was a buddy of the East Timor dissidents; he was in cahoots with the [IRA] . . . To cap it all, [MID], through their chosen

mouthpiece, *The Citizen* (nothing changes), announced that they had been keeping McBride under surveillance for two years.[25]

Four months earlier, McBride had been contacted by Vusi Mbatha, a military intelligence and police informer. Mbatha claimed that MID officials were continuing to smuggle weapons into South Africa from Mozambique. McBride had told the NIA about his freelance investigation, but, as his biographer noted, 'after his arrest . . . neither the South African government, nor the NIA, nor his department, nor the ANC would acknowledge that he was in [Mozambique] on official business'. Meiring informed Hilton Hamaan that the MID 'source' was Mbatha and that 'we were trying to get [McBride] to buy arms with cash we'd tagged and then planned to follow [him] and see where [he] went. We had people waiting at the border posts . . . to tag the ship or lorry with a transmitter.' President Mandela appointed a judicial inquiry, headed by Chief Justice Ismail Mohamed, which quickly dismissed the Meiring report as flawed. Meiring retired on 6 April 1998 to 'restore trust', and Verbeek, who later testified at the Basson trial that he was aware of Project Coast's offensive CBW programme from 1987, was replaced by Mojo Motau, an MK military intelligence official, in June 1998. Siphiwe Nyanda, aged thirty-eight, was appointed the first MK chief of the SANDF. He retired in 2005 and entered business. Ronnie Kasrils said in his memoirs that he looked 'forward to recounting my perspective on the episode when I am able to'.[26]

Robert McBride remained in prison in Mozambique for six months until September 1998. The *Mail & Guardian* suggested that the Deputy President Thabo Mbeki had been 'greatly angered' by McBride's 'private enterprise'. Mbeki wrote in a letter to Paula McBride: 'Your husband was arrested in Mozambique, he having taken himself to Mozambique of his own volition . . . We will not act in any manner, which . . . suggests that Mozambique is no more than a bantustan of democratic South Africa.' In October 2003, McBride was appointed chief of the Ekurhuleni Metro Police Department. He is currently suing the *Citizen* over an editorial which claimed that because of his background he was 'blatantly unsuited' to become head of a police force.[27] In September 1998, the SANDF and, in particular, Defence Intelligence had been further damaged by a poorly prepared intervention, ordered by 'Acting President' Mangosuthu Buthelezi, in the mountain kingdom of Lesotho. As Anthony Sampson recalled: '[The SANDF] took several days to impose order, and in the process destroyed much of the capital, Maseru, while looters emptied the shops . . . the bungled operation made South Africa look like a clumsy bully.'[28] Lesotho stands as the only cross-border operation of the post-apartheid era.

In September 1998, the parliamentary Joint Standing Committee on Intelligence reported that military intelligence remained 'dominated by apartheid operatives.' It also noted the scale of MID's destruction of records. *City Press* reported in November 1999 that in the wake of the Meiring report 'dozens of mistrusted senior military intelligence operatives were edged out in what amounted to a silent purge . . . Another "purge" followed the intervention of the South African military in neighbouring Lesotho – where the SANDF troops found themselves in a conflict situation for which their intelligence had failed to prepare them.' David Beresford summed up the popular impression of South African spies in the aftermath of the Meiring–McBride episode: 'The apartheid spy agencies were infamous but they enjoyed a degree of respect in the intelligence world – exchanging assets with Israel's Mossad, playing cat and mouse with the CIA and trading blows with the KGB. Four years after the collapse of apartheid, the agencies' failures have left their political masters staggering virtually blindfold around the quagmires of foreign policy.' The philosophy lecturer Dr Anthony Holiday emphasised the point:

> It is an open secret that South Africa no longer possesses anything approaching what a developed nation would regard as a genuine intelligence capacity and certainly nothing like the flow of confidential information which P.W. Botha could command in the high days of the 'total strategy'. There are indeed intelligence-gathering organisations, like the [NIA]. But they are leaky, ramshackle contraptions, crippled by inefficiency and Byzantine office intrigues, as a new breed of [ANC] analysts and operatives struggle to wrest control from apartheid-era survivors. In consequence (and doubtless also because of the friendly disposition Pretoria has evinced towards the likes of Cuba's Fidel Castro, Palestine's Yasser Arafat and Libya's Moammar Gadaffi), foreign intelligence agencies, like the CIA and MI6, no longer supply us with 'feed' from their spy satellites – something they readily did before apartheid died.[29]

*

In retrospect the despair of 1998 was the low point. Over the next few years the new secret services secured control of South African intelligence. Sadly, the intelligence high jinks did not disappear but switched from the 'old era–new era' tension to political conflicts within the ruling party. Early in President Thabo Mbeki's first term there was a brief flurry of media coverage which discussed so-called plots against the Presidency. In August 2000, South African newspapers alleged that ANC politician turned businessman Cyril Ramaphosa was engaged in a plot with British and American businessmen to replace Mbeki because of 'dissatisfaction over Mbeki's handling of the Zimbabwe and HIV/AIDS issues'. The *Guardian* reported that the allegations were based upon 'a confidential [NIA] report'. A few weeks later, Mbeki was reported by Howard Barrell of the *Mail & Guardian* as having told the ANC's parliamentary party caucus on 28 September 2000 that 'he and his government were the target of a hostile campaign by powerful international forces, including the CIA and the big multinational drug companies. This was because he questioned the link between HIV and AIDS and South Africa was challenging the world economic order.' Aziz Pahad, the Deputy Minister of Foreign Affairs, wrote to the newspaper to complain about Barrell's journalism being based upon anonymous sources:

> I attended the caucus meeting and can categorically state that the president never said that . . . 'the CIA is working covertly along with the big pharmaceutical manufacturers to undermine him' . . . To erroneously suggest that the president of South Africa had made such foolish statements can only be an attempt to create tensions, distrust and divisions between developed countries and the South African government.[30]

By 22 April 2001, the 'plots' against Mbeki merged with allegations about his personal life, ancient rumours about his connections with foreign intelligence agencies in exile and whispers about the role of senior ANC politicians in the murder of Chris Hani to create a perfect storm of paranoia and panic. The Minister of Safety and Security, Steve Tshwete, alleged in the Johannesburg *Sunday Times* that the plotters intended to 'physically harm' the President: 'As far back as last year, we picked up clandestine activities involving certain individuals and we are monitoring this on a day-to-day basis to ensure that the president is safe.' On 24 April, Tshwete named the plotters on an SABC television station as Cyril Ramaphosa, Tokyo Sexwale and Mathews Phosa. Mbeki described the situation as 'a conspiratorial thing'. Nelson Mandela swiftly emerged from retirement to demonstrate his support for the accused. Mark Gevisser informed the *Financial Times* that there was no evidence for the alleged plot.

Tshwete's and Mbeki's action 'has had the desired effect. The three potentially most dangerous opponents of the president have been forced to publicly declare that they will not mount a challenge against him.'[31]

In reality, it was all a little more chaotic than Gevisser's cynical but intri-
cate conspiracy theory suggests. Tshwete's source for the plot allegations
was revealed to be a former ANC Youth League leader, James Nkambule,
an impressive spinner of tall tales and a troublemaker. Rather than approach
the NIA, Nkambule had taken his allegations directly to an unofficial and
previously unknown ANC party intelligence unit. The allegations were
taken seriously by the Commissioner of Police, Jackie Selebi, and this
encouraged Tshwete to act. Nkambule, who at the time faced criminal
charges relating to the embezzlement of more than R1 million from the
Mpumalanga Parks Board, had in 1999 given evidence against Phosa, the
premier of the Mpumalanga region, which had led to his removal by
Mbeki. In June 2001, Mbeki informed television viewers that Tshwete had
been 'wrong' to name the accused before the investigation against them had
been completed. In August, Nkambule resigned from the ANC and more
than a year after the allegations had been made, Steve Tshwete completely
exonerated Phosa, Sexwale and Ramaphosa. It had been a strange episode,
but one which demonstrated, as *Noseweek* magazine explained, that the
ANC government was 'dogged by its exile culture – a leadership built
around personalities, each with their own shady intelligence and money-
making networks – and dogged, too, by the unfinished business of those
in its ranks who were allegedly apartheid agents'.[32]

In June 2005, the South African journalist Patrick Laurence wondered, in
a typically patronising tone, whether the South African intelligence services 'are alert and competent enough to succeed in thwarting would-be
assailants . . . fanatical extremists . . . particularly those linked to, or
inspired by, Osama Bin-Laden's *al-Qaeda*.' Laurence drew a parallel
between South Africa and London, New York and Madrid. A more accurate comparison would be Bali in Indonesia. The obvious al-Qaeda target
in South Africa is Cape Town: a multi-racial city where Western tourists
enjoy the pleasures of the Third World. South Africa had actually experienced Islamic terrorism, in the form of People Against Gangsterism and
Drugs (PAGAD) in the late 1990s. During August 1998, for example, the
Planet Hollywood restaurant in Cape Town was subject to a bomb attack
which killed two and injured thirty. But the wilder elements of PAGAD
were effectively contained by the efficient action of the NIA, the Scorpions

and the South African Police before 9/11. Khalfan Khamis Mohamed, one of the al-Qaeda bombers responsible for the bombing of the US Tanzanian Embassy, had been captured in Cape Town in October 1999 and extradited to the United States. In August 2004, two South African citizens, Zubair Ismail and Feroze Ganchi, were arrested in Pakistan, and the South African press reported that they had been interrogated by the CIA as suspected al-Qaeda operatives. South African government sources informed the *Sowetan*: 'The Americans leaked the information to embarrass us because they are not happy with the stance we took on Iraq.'[33] South Africa refused to support the invasion of Iraq, and Thabo Mbeki and Nelson Mandela had been outspoken critics of the American and British action.

In October 2004, the CBS television programme *60 Minutes* cited a CIA report to allege that al-Qaeda operatives were resident in South Africa. Ronnie Kasrils warned the media to be 'wary of scaremongering'. Two months earlier, the then NIA chief Vusi Mavimbela had informed the *Sowetan* that '"it would be naive for any country to believe that it is immune to terrorism" . . . On the question of whether there were any al-Qaeda operatives in South Africa, Mavimbela said the presence of such individuals did not necessarily mean that South Africa was target for terror attacks.' Informed observers have suggested that an al-Qaeda cell is active in Cape Town but prefers to retain access to South Africa's banking and communications networks while recognising an unstated tacit agreement that its members will not be persecuted as long as they avoid terrorist activity within South Africa. During the May 2005 budget debate, Kasrils declared: 'We do not discern any imminent threat [from international terrorism].'[34]

On 31 October 2002, a group of disaffected Afrikaner reactionaries launched a short-lived terrorist campaign which killed one person and injured two. The NIA was particularly active investigating and assisting the prosecution of the obscure group responsible, the Boeremag. The Minister of Intelligence at the time, Lindiwe Sisulu, said, 'For as long as mad right-wingers threaten our peace, we will ensure that they rue the day they were born.' Despite the hyperbole in the media – even *Africa Confidential* headlined an article on the subject 'The right wing explodes' – the NIA and associated agencies handled this potentially dangerous situation very well indeed.[35] Militant reactionaries have learned that, far from establishing a new Afrikaner republic, the only thing they are likely to secure is a substantial prison sentence.

★

In the new South Africa, the ridiculous intelligence stories have rubbed up alongside the sinister. Silly spookery included the discovery in November 1999 by German counter-espionage operatives of a poorly hidden video camera in a tree opposite the German Embassy in Pretoria, from which wires ran to a rubbish bin. The story was a case study in incompetence. Apparently, in 1995, the BND had tried 'to recruit agents both in and outside intelligence circles'. In response, the NIA 'tried to recruit a woman working inside the German Embassy to spy on any South African "traitors"'. The woman refused. Some months later, 'the very same NIA operative . . . decided to rent the house opposite the German Embassy to keep it under surveillance. The operation was blown when the . . . woman happened to see her potential NIA recruiter loitering outside the house opposite the Embassy.' In April 2002, the NIA drew further mockery when it proposed 'security-competence tests' for 'journalists applying to join the presidential press corps', including polygraph tests, information on the applicant's sexual life, copies of bank statements and psychiatric diagnoses. In October 2004, the Johannesburg *Sunday Times* announced that the NIA had been called in to 'screen people involved in [administering] the matric [GCSE/A-levels] exam'.[36] The impartial observer might have imagined that South Africa's spies had something more significant to do with their time.

In addition to the continuous 'spy versus spy' stories, reports of sinister spookery also occasionally emerged. In October 1995, Muziwendoda Mdluli, a former commander in the PAC's army, APLA, was discovered dead in his car; he had been shot in the head. The range of speculation included allegations that Mdluli 'was on the track of "Third Force" hit squad men linked to [MID] and that he had been murdered' to the suggestion that 'he committed suicide rather than face the disgrace of being exposed as a double agent'. The *Sunday Independent* disclosed that Mdluli had been investigating the possibility of former NIS agents being involved in an attempted coup in the Comores. Nobody was charged with Mdluli's 'murder'. In January 1996, Werner van Gruenen alleged that he had been hired by the NIA 'to spy on National Party members in local government and report on "unconstitutional activities which threatened the government"'. In September 1999, Joe Nhlanhla disclosed in an answer to a parliamentary question that in the previous five years 115 NIA and SASS employees 'had been charged with misconduct – ranging from smuggling platinum and illegal dealing in gold to murder'. In February 2000, NIA agents monitored events during an unofficial strike at the Volkswagen plant in Uitenhage. One agent said that the strike 'posed a threat to national security'.[37]

In August 2000, newspapers publicised the fact that Defence Intelligence operatives had approached Adrian Hadland, political editor of the Cape *Argus* and the author of a biography of Thabo Mbeki, and David Bristow, the editor of the travel magazine *Getaway*: 'Hadland said [it was] indicated to him that a number of journalists were already on the books and . . . had agreed to pass on information to the cloak-and-dagger brigade. In exchange the journalists were to get tip-offs from defence intelligence as well as invitations to select briefings by operatives on the inside.' In July 2001, it was reported that the NIA had been summoned to investigate the South African Reserve Bank after documents were leaked to a 'London financial institution'. Governor Tito Mboweni said that 'Bugs were found.'

Two months later, ANC MP Andrew Feinstein and IFP MP Gavin Woods reported that they had been approached by 'intelligence agents' regarding South Africa's controversial 'arms deal' announced by the government in November 1998. The original costing, which inflated rapidly as the Rand crashed over the next three years, suggested that for R29.8 billion South Africa would receive four German frigates, three German submarines, four British helicopters, forty Italian helicopters, twenty-eight Anglo-Swedish Gripen fighter planes and twenty-four British Hawk fighter planes. In addition, it was reported that more than 64,000 badly needed jobs would be created through European 'offsets'. Commentators wondered why South Africa, which didn't face any obvious enemy, required such a huge investment in arms. Cynics believed that the 'arms deal' represented the corrupting of the new ANC government.

In August 2002, the *Sunday Independent* reported that NIA agents had investigated plans by the Landless People's Movement to 'disrupt' the World Summit on Sustainable Development soon to be held in Johannesburg. The *Financial Mail* reported that Vusi Mavimbela 'and three of his operatives paid a surprise visit to the offices of the Anti-Privatisation Forum in downtown Johannesburg . . . and questioned its secretary, Trevor Ngwane, a former ANC member'. Three years later, following violent protests over the failure of local government 'delivery' in the Free State, the NIA was reported to be investigating 'the causes of unrest'. Ronnie Kasrils told the Johannesburg *Sunday Times*: 'Our ongoing mandate is to assess anything in the country that could be a threat to public order.'[38]

*

An undated confidential NIA document entitled 'Re-understanding NIA's domestic intelligence mandate' demonstrated that the agency had moved a long way from the White Paper of 1994 (see page 307). The edict reminded operatives: 'Domestic Intelligence is proactive and predictive intelligence (on any internal activity, factor or development) . . . on any issues that may affect national security and stability.' Most of the document addressed subjects close to the hearts of most South Africans: corruption, organised crime, terrorism and smuggling. But a number of the 'areas of interest' were a little odd, such as 'Special events', which, the document explained, was 'To monitor and give support to special events inside the Republic of national or international significance that impact on: domestic security . . . foreign/diplomatic relations (impact of event . . . on strained/sensitive relations with other countries) . . . Possibility of SA hosting similar events in future and effect on the international stature of SA.' The linking of certain issues is also strange: the Zimbabwean Movement for Democratic Change would not be pleased, for example, to discover that under the subject 'Imported Issues . . . the use of SA soil by foreign groups', it is listed alongside RENAMO, the Tamil Tigers and 'O Bin Laden support'. The problem with memorandums of this sort is that they can easily be misunderstood or abused. Under 'Political processes and dynamics . . . Theme: Governance', the document declared:

> *To monitor and investigate* factors/issues/developments undermining and/or subverting the process of governance;
> – Any issue, development or factor directed at undermining the ability of government to function and deliver effectively, eg
> – corruption of government officials (including NIA members),
> – gross mismanagement,
> – mis- and disinformation (including the misuse of media for negative anti-South African reporting),
> – identification of security breaches,
> – links of government officials with organised crime and hostile intelligence services.[39]

Scorpions and Elephants

President Thabo Mbeki announced the establishment of the Scorpions, officially the Directorate of Special Operations (DSO), in the aftermath of his election victory in 1999. As researcher Jean Redpath later commented:

'from the beginning, one of the motivating factors behind the creation of the Scorpions appeared to be to raise public confidence in the ability of government to fight crime . . . the Scorpions were launched with all the paraphernalia of a well-managed media campaign including T-shirts and baseball caps emblazoned with their catchy name and logo'. The new organisation was swiftly mythologised as South Africa's version of the 'Untouchables': an FBI to complement the South African Police Service (SAPS). John Carlin described the Scorpions as 'South Africa's first post-liberation police force' and explained the nickname in the following terms: 'a scorpion can bring down an elephant'. The crime-fighters' motto, 'feared by the criminals and loved by the people', would prove difficult to live up to in a country suffering an explosion of post-apartheid criminal activity.[40]

In reality, the Scorpions represented a desperate attempt to step above the post-apartheid squabbling and incompetence of the existing police force and the NIA. The boom in violent crime, organised crime and corruption that had accompanied the transition period during the 1990s was one of the dominant issues during the 1999 election. But the creation of an 'elite' force of 'intelligence agents, detectives and prosecutors', an innovation in South Africa, was bound to attract severe criticism. For the concept to work, it would need assistance from the existing security forces and time to establish a structure that could prove its worth. The original intention was to recruit 'new' South Africans, untainted by the country's appalling security history, who would receive training in the latest crime-detection methods from respected international institutions, such as the FBI and the Metropolitan Police. But the pressure to act against the criminals was too great. While some Scorpions were dispatched abroad for training, others learned their craft by watching Kroll Associates training videotapes. Bulelani Ngcuka, the Director of Public Prosecutions, who effectively controlled the Scorpions, was questioned by Carlin about the racial composition of the new force. Carlin wondered why 'almost all the juniors are black [and] almost all the senior investigators will be white'. Ngcuka's reply encapsulated the pressure he was under: 'My problem is that I have to do two things. Number one: I have to deliver, and I have to deliver yesterday, not today. I don't have time. Number two: I have to deal with this national question of transformation . . . I will go with my white guys to solve my crime today. In terms of the transformation, it will happen, it will. But I am prepared to bide my time.'[41]

Tensions between the police and the Scorpions were apparent from the beginning. *Business Day* noted in August 2001 that 'every time the Scorpions claim a success, a detective squad rises up to protest that the elite unit has stolen hard-won police work and claimed it as its own'. The new agency also suffered as its 'white guys' disappeared at an early stage. 'Incorruptible cop' Frank Dutton, 'the sting in the Scorpions' tail', announced that he was likely to retire with ill health before the DSO had even passed through the legislative process. Observers who hoped that the Scorpions would tackle South Africa's longest-standing mysteries such as gun-running by IFP members or the business interests of alleged Mafia don Vito Palazollo, who had lived a protected life in apartheid South Africa from 1986, were to be disappointed. Nor would the Scorpions be immune from the ridiculous difficulties that plagued the other security agencies: in July 2002, three computer hard-drives were stolen from the offices of the Scorpions following a break-in. The legislation to create the DSO was rushed through at the end of 2000 and the Scorpions were sent into action in January 2001.[42]

As early as August 2001, the DSO had announced that it was investigating South Africa's controversial and politically poisonous arms deal 'with a view to carrying out prosecutions for any criminal wrongdoing it might uncover'. In October 2001, the Scorpions launched an 'intensive day-long raid on the Durban offices of Nkobi Holdings (Pty) Ltd, the group of companies owned by Schabir Shaik . . . Shaik is the brother of Shamin "Chippy" Shaik, head of the Defence Department's acquisitions and procurement programme.' The *Mail & Guardian* reported that 'In France, the offices of Thales International and the residence of Alain Thétard, the managing director of Thomson-CSF Holdings South Africa, were [also] raided.' By November 2002, it was apparent that the Scorpions were 'actively investigating Deputy President Jacob Zuma for an alleged attempt to secure a bribe of R500,000 a year from French defence giant Thomson-CSF'. While the DSO was achieving success as an investigation and prosecution unit and winning the support of many South Africans, it had strayed into dangerous political territory with the arms deal. The Scorpions boss, Leonard McCarthy, characterised the investigation into Zuma in the following terms: 'When you shoot at the king, make sure you don't miss.'[43] But Zuma and his close associate Mo Shaik were former intelligence chiefs and they were willing to deploy all their espionage knowledge to protect Zuma's route to the Presidency.

In retrospect, the Hefer Commission, established by President Mbeki to investigate allegations that had been made against Bulelani Ngcuka, seems like a strange aberration, but it had been coming for a long time.

Former TRC researcher Professor John Daniel declared in the *Mail & Guardian* that 'the "informer issue" has hung like a Damoclean sword over South African politics since the end of the apartheid era'. As the DSO investigation got closer to Jacob Zuma, it also threatened ex-Minister of Transport and former Vula chief Mac Maharaj. There had been attempts to smear Ngcuka in the press in June 2003, including a report that he was 'about to resign to join mining giant, de Beers'. Ngcuka blamed 'well-connected . . . criminals masquerading as comrades'. Mo Shaik later revealed that he had 'handed his reconstructed spy dossier' to Zuma in December 2002. The dossier, assembled during Operation Vula's investigation into apartheid spies known as Operation Bible, revealed that Ngcuka, who had been a clerk in the office of Griffiths and Victoria Mxenge in the early 1980s (see page 201), was granted a passport while he was in detention and that an NIS database appeared to identify the Director of Public Prosecutions as Agent RS452.[44]

Like a dam bursting, the events associated with the 'Ngcuka affair' came thick and fast over a six-week period in 2003. On 27 July, the Johannesburg *Sunday Times* reported that 'Mac Maharaj and his wife Zarina . . . are being investigated in connection with their relationship with Shaik and Nkobi [and] payments and gifts worth R500,000.' Ngcuka's opponents immediately attempted to place the spy story in the Johannesburg *Sunday Times*, but the biggest-selling newspaper in South Africa balked. On 19 August, Maharaj and Shaik gave interviews to e tv 'confirming the 1989 [Vula] investigation and spy finding against Ngcuka. e tv also interviews three unidentified ex-security branch members at Shaik's home who confirm elements of the allegations.' The television film was not broadcast. On 23 August, Maharaj met President Mbeki to urge him 'to conduct a confidential investigation into the spy claims against Ngcuka'. On the same day, Ngcuka held a press conference in which he announced there was a prima facie case against Jacob Zuma but that he would not be prosecuted. On 7 September, *City Press*'s front page screamed the headline: 'Was Bulelani Ngcuka ever a spy?' Mac Maharaj repeated the allegation on television. On 14 September, a spokesman for the Scorpions informed selected journalists that '[Agent] RS452 was a "white woman lawyer from the Eastern Cape".' On 16 September, death squad killer Gideon Nieuwoudt, who had been paid R40,000 for 'flights, hotels, travel and legal expenses' by Mo Shaik, appeared in an e tv documentary to state: 'Ngcuka was an agent from [the NIS].' On 19 September, President Mbeki appointed the Hefer Commission.[45]

The Commission opened on 13 October 2003 and Mac Maharaj and Mo Shaik were represented by the fourth Shaik brother, Yunus. The anti-Ngcuka case was severely damaged a few days later when Vanessa Brereton, resident in south London, revealed to Terry Bell that she had been Agent RS452. Brereton, a human rights lawyer, had spied for the Security Police between 1985 and 1991 and had been recruited by her lover, BOSS–NIS agent Karl Edwards (see pages 134 and 267). Brereton had been involved in Operation Crocus, a project to spy on the 'white left'. The NIA, represented by George Bizos, refused to provide intelligence files to the Commission. Bizos suggested that Maharaj and Shaik should provide their own Vula–NIS documents. Mac Maharaj has privately described Bizos's action as the biggest disappointment of his life.[46] The *Mail & Guardian* explained that the pair 'were likely to resist producing the documents, as they were copies and the originals were in the possession of state agencies. They could face prosecution if they illegally possessed state documents.' Mo Shaik testified for three days at the Commission, revealing Oliver Tambo's motto that 'spy information must be as "true as the Bible"', but without the NIA files he was incapable of proving that Ngcuka had been an apartheid spy. During the hearings, it emerged that Shaik had employed Michael Snow, a former British MI6 agent, and Mike Kuhn, the former head of the NIS's Directorate K, responsible for overseas intelligence. Shaik eventually admitted that Kuhn had claimed that 'the buzz in the intelligence community was that Ngcuka had worked for [the apartheid state]'.[47]

When it was over, Mac Maharaj declared incoherently that 'those who will benefit are the carpetbaggers of the new SA'. He added, 'In the world of intelligence you will seldom find direct evidence.' The Hefer Commission's report found that 'Messrs Maharaj and Shaik's allegations of spying have not been established. Mr Ngcuka probably never acted as an agent for a pre-1994 government security service.' President Mbeki stated in his internet 'Letter from the President': 'None of us should ever again seek to win whatever battles we are waging by labelling others as having been apartheid spies.'[48] The allegations regarding Bulelani Ngcuka were an accident waiting to happen. The new South Africa's unwillingness to face the truth about its compromised, intelligence-saturated past will continue to poison the security and political culture for many years to come. Terry Bell declared in the Johannesburg *Sunday Times*:

> The furore that has erupted over allegations of apartheid spies highlights one
> of the great and lingering dangers in our society. It is a suppurating cancer

buried deep within the body politic that could damage the lives and careers of innocent and guilty alike. For the sake of a democratic future, it must be excised. And the only way this can be done is to expose it to the full analytical glare of the public.[49]

It was an encouraging thought, but it was not going to happen. Rather than open the wounds of the past, South Africa's post-apartheid secret services preferred to bind them tight and pretend that the culture of allegation didn't really exist. The wounds would continue to weep. The whispers about the future of Bulelani Ngcuka and the Scorpions predated the Hefer Commission and they intensified afterwards. In 2004, the parliamentary Joint Standing Committee on Intelligence announced that it was concerned that the Scorpions 'may be undertaking intelligence gathering – and that this undercover work is being done without the necessary oversight by parliament'. The Johannesburg *Star* reminded readers: 'According to South African law, only the president can establish an intelligence service . . . and he must do this as head of the national executive in terms of national legislation.' Bulelani Ngcuka resigned as head of the National Prosecution Authority [NPA] in July 2004 and retreated into business, where he struck up an alliance with millionaire ANC businessman Saki Macozoma and joined the board of a security company, Stallion Security, which employed a number of former apartheid operatives.[50]

Ngcuka was replaced in January 2005 by Vusi Pikoli, the former Director-General at Justice who had led an unpublicised investigation into the failings of South African intelligence in the late 1990s. In a very strained security and political climate, Pikoli was believed to be 'the only person acceptable to everyone'. Schabir Shaik was found guilty on 2 June 2005 and Judge Squires sentenced him to two terms of fifteen years' imprisonment for corruption, and one term of three years for fraud, to be served concurrently. President Thabo Mbeki dismissed Vice-President Jacob Zuma on 14 June. Zuma's trial for corruption is scheduled to commence on 31 July 2006.[51] Four months after the dramatic political effects of the arms deal investigation had played out, the Khampepe Commission considered the future of the Scorpions. A thirty-two-page confidential submission to the Commission by Billy Masetlha, the Director-General of the NIA, alleged that the Scorpions directorate 'interacts with foreign intelligence agencies to the detriment of national security; is controlled by former apartheid prosecutors; and leaks sensitive and classified information to the media'. Ironically, Masetlha's submission was leaked to Johannesburg's *City Press*. At the hearings, George Bizos, the lawyer for the NIA, argued against the conclusions of his client, the agency's Director-General.[52]

David Bruce (see page 48), a senior researcher at the Centre for the Study of Violence and Reconciliation, spoke for many when he noted that 'the Scorpions model of a special unit, comprising investigators and prosecutors employed by the prosecution authority, is in some ways unique to SA. The strongest argument for maintaining the Scorpions may not be drawn from the examples of other countries, but from the vigorous and dynamic investigative role they have played at home.' On 24 November 2005, President Thabo Mbeki gave the address at the Intelligence Services Day 10th Anniversary Awards Ceremony and did not disguise his concern about the 'quality' of intelligence work in the new South Africa: 'I must say that for many years now I have been concerned about the quality of a significant proportion of the intelligence information I have been provided . . . Our intelligence family must understand that the only way in which its members will continue to retain their jobs is by producing reliable and timely quality intelligence products that help our government . . . to improve the safety and security of our country and people.'[53]

15

The Private Sector

'The country isn't half worked out because they that governs it won't let you touch it. They spend all their blessed time in governing it, and you can't lift a spade, nor chip a rock, nor look for oil, nor anything like that, without all the Government saying, "Leave it alone, and let us govern." Therefore, such *as* it is, we will let it alone, and go away to some other place where a man isn't crowded and can come to his own. We are not little men, and there is nothing that we are afraid of except Drink, and we have signed a Contrack on that. *Therefore*, we are going away to be Kings.'

'Kings in our own right,' muttered Dravot . . .

'We have slept over the notion half a year . . . They call it Kafiristan . . . They have two-and-thirty heathen idols there, and we'll be the thirty-third and fourth' . . .

'And that's all we know, except that no one has gone there, and they fight; and in any place where they fight, a man who knows how to drill men can always be a King. We shall go to those parts and say to any King we find, "D' you want to vanquish your foes?" and we will show him how to drill men; for that we know better than anything else. Then we will subvert that King and seize his Throne and establish a Dy-nasty.'

Rudyard Kipling, *The Man Who Would Be King*, 1888[1]

THE REAL VICTORS of the transformation in South Africa were the rulers of the dynastic mining monarchy, the Oppenheimers. Anglo American and its sister company, De Beers, have gone from strength to strength after the ANC government permitted Anglo to repatriate funds to the United Kingdom and obtain a listing on the London Stock Exchange. Anthony Sampson summarised Anglo American in *Who Runs This Place?*: 'still the most powerful company in South Africa with its own web of subsidiaries, farms, estates, ships, planes, police force and intelligence system'. Anglo and

De Beers have hidden in the margins throughout this book: seeking Sir Percy Sillitoe's advice in the 1950s, victims of Fred Kamil and Hendrik van den Bergh's machinations in 1976 and negotiating with the ANC in 1985, and they continue to exert political influence in the new South Africa. Working in close conjunction with British intelligence, Anglo stands a good chance of watching its favoured candidate, Cyril Ramaphosa, secure the Presidency in 2009, which if it happens will be the first time since Jan Smuts in the 1940s that the mining conglomerate has been able to enjoy such a friendly relationship with the state.[2] Most of the intelligence power in South Africa since 1994 has followed the lead of Anglo American and De Beers and migrated to the private sector.

Privatised Intelligence

Between 1997 and 2003, while the South African intelligence services appeared to be in hibernation, a number of private foreign 'intelligence' companies grabbed the opportunity to establish a beachhead in the new South Africa. The most influential of these companies were 'the undisputed industry leader', Kroll, UK-based Control Risks and Michael Oatley's CIEX. Kroll Associates was founded in New York by Jules B. Kroll in 1972, beginning life as an upmarket private detective company, or as the *New York Times* described it in 1985: 'Wall Street's Private Eye'. The company's work focused upon corporate intelligence: researching takeover target companies, 'due diligence' cases (checking companies and executives before a deal is struck) and investigating corporate raiders. Kroll was certainly expensive to employ: in 1985 it charged $5,000 to $25,000 for 'due diligence' and $50,000 to $500,000 for studies of corporate raiders. It used a variety of professionals on investigations: 'former FBI and law enforcement officers, business executives, lawyers, Ph.D's skilled in research and several former investigative reporters'.[3] During the 1970s and 1980s, while the orthodox intelligence agencies concentrated on the Cold War, Kroll worked in what amounted to economic intelligence. During the 1990s, as the CIA and MI6 among other national agencies announced that they were primarily concerned with economic intelligence, Kroll Associates increasingly began to involve itself in international affairs. In March 1991, Jules Kroll appeared on CBS's *60 Minutes* and announced that his company had discovered more than $10 billion removed by Saddam Hussein from the Iraqi Treasury and stashed in bank accounts and front companies throughout the world. *New York* magazine reported that:

> In a world in which contacts are everything, Kroll has nurtured loyalties and friendships that seem to reach everywhere . . . Through his special brand of hard work and self-promotion, Kroll has acquired a clout that no other private-eye firm can match. Not only does each new case bring new contacts and sources, but the information in Kroll's files has long since reached a kind of critical mass at which the files alone become reason enough to hire the firm.[4]

Between 1985 and 1991, Kroll Associates had quadrupled in size. Although Jules Kroll explained that his investigators engaged in 'plain old investigative journalism . . . We work very hard at developing solid, accurate, and reliable information,' it would be more correct to say that the company employed many former intelligence agents who retained useful links with their erstwhile colleagues stationed around the world. By 1991, Kroll Associates had overseas offices in London, Paris and Hong Kong. During the 1990s, Kroll expanded its operations to include penetration of the organised crime networks of Moscow. In France, the company was criticised by politicians for its links with MI6 and the CIA. In 1997, Kroll Associates merged with O'Gara of Ohio, manufacturers of armoured cars. By 1999, Kroll-O'Gara Co. was listed on the Nasdaq exchange and had combined annual sales of $200 million. The merger, which had intended to take advantage of the potential synergy of providing software (intelligence) and hardware (security), failed. Kroll and O'Gara went their separate ways in 2001. Following the terrorist attacks on New York and Washington DC on 9/11, Kroll's shares doubled in value.[5]

The speed of Kroll's expansion in the 1990s – by 1999 the company had more than 1,000 'associates' – naturally led to tensions. In 1997, more than twenty Kroll employees established a rival company, the Risk Advisory Group, led by Kroll's former European operations director, ex-SAS man Arish Turle. A former associate told *EuroBusiness* in 1999: 'a lot of us believed that Jules had gone over-the-top and had diversified our product range into areas that would have been foreign to us five years before. The exclusivity of Kroll was sadly diminished, which is why so many of us left. To be honest, Kroll lost its flair, and although it pains me to say this, it had become boring.' So how did Kroll become involved in South Africa? In the 1980s, Kroll Associates was instrumental in convincing Minorco to abandon its bid for Consolidated Goldfields. In 1997,

Kroll visited South Africa on behalf of Western clients 'to weigh how much was being done to prevent the country going the same way as Russia'. The company's prognosis was not promising: Johannesburg was rated as one of the most dangerous cities in the world, on a par with Bogotá and Algiers. Among the senior Kroll 'associates' who visited South Africa were Norb Garrett (ex-CIA), Anthony Rowell (ex-MI6 – see page 320), Steve Vickers (ex-head of criminal intelligence for the Hong Kong police) and Tom Cash (ex-head of the US Drug Enforcement Administration in Miami).[6]

In May 1998, the South African government announced that it had hired Kroll Associates, as reported in the *Financial Times*, to 'train members of the South African police, [the NIA and SASS] and the prosecution services. It is working with the NIA's own training academy on the programme.' The Johannesburg *Sunday Times* reported:

> The Minister of Safety and Security, Sydney Mufamadi, said yesterday the decision to hire Kroll had been prompted by the severe economic damage done by some 190 criminal syndicates operating in and through South Africa. He would not disclose the cost of the contract. 'It's estimated the country is losing R17 billion a year in revenue from our ports because of their porousness . . . Compare that to my R13.2 billion police budget and you see how these syndicates are running our country into the ground.'[7]

However, Kroll was not merely engaged in a 'year-long programme of seminars for the security forces', as the *Financial Times* explained. A few days before the announcement by the South African government, two white South Africans visited a professor of African Politics at London University's School of Oriental and African Studies (SOAS). They told the Professor that they worked for Kroll Associates and that they were enquiring as to whether Sydney Mufamadi would be able to study for a degree in African Politics 'by post' (that is, from South Africa). The men explained to the Professor that Mufamadi needed the qualification because he was likely to be made minister for foreign affairs during the Presidency of Thabo Mbeki. In July 2004, Fholisani Sydney Mufamadi was awarded an MSc in State Society and Development by SOAS.[8]

During the next five years, Kroll's activities in South Africa went far beyond 'seminars'. The company became embroiled in the investigations into the Reserve Bank (1998–9), trained the Scorpions (1998–2000) and investigated both the Strategic Fuel Fund (2000–1) and the Post Office (2001). It appeared that whenever the South African government had a problem or a subject that required investigating, it called for Kroll. In July 2000, Kroll advertised in the *Guardian* for research associates to be based in London with 'additional opportunities to work in other Kroll offices in Frankfurt, Paris, Milan, Moscow *or Johannesburg*' (my emphasis). The fact that no other African or Asian bureaus were listed in the advertisement emphasised the importance of the South African relationship to Kroll. Seminars held by SOAS and the Royal Institute of International Affairs in London have been attended regularly by Kroll representatives. In 2001, Kroll was employed by the UN Security Council to investigate UNITA's overseas assets. In 2002, the *Sunday Telegraph* reported that the British Foreign Office had hired Kroll 'to lead the hunt for Mr Mugabe's overseas assets'.[9]

If Kroll was only employed on a one-year contract, why was the contract renewed? Sources suggest that the ANC was very pleased with Kroll's work, which was considered to be thoroughly professional; perhaps more importantly, Kroll's work was not perceived as being tainted with the history and politics which have plagued South African intelligence. But there was an obvious problem: Kroll Associates had its own agenda – generating profit – and while that might not appear to be at odds with healthy governance in South Africa, it may come back to haunt leading ANC politicians. To take a hypothetical example: what if Kroll gathered information during an investigation that was not directly pertinent to the matter in hand and what if that information at some future unspecified date was desired by a third party? Kroll cannot forget the information it gathers; after all, one of the major reasons companies and countries employ it is because of its long track record. As Jules Kroll told *New York* magazine in 1991: 'We're very careful about how we handle the stuff we come up with. Sometimes we don't even tell the client everything we learn.' The *Observer* noted in 2004, 'A firm's "hinterland" of contacts is what gives it the edge – and in some cases, may provide potential for sharp practice.'[10] In essence, we are back to the old question of 'who polices the police?' With a private company employing foreign and domestic ex-intelligence agents, the question is even more ominous.

Observers suggest that Kroll's activities in South Africa have gone far beyond the international company's usual financial detective work. Journalists who have been employed by or interviewed in the course of Kroll investigations testify to the company's efficiency. But efficiency costs money and Kroll is notorious for being, as *Private Eye* put it, 'amazingly expensive'. Like any private sector company, Kroll was very talented at promoting itself. American commentators point out that Jules Kroll is a master at winning positive news coverage. One 'disaffected former employee' told the *Observer* that companies like Kroll and Control Risks do 'not very much, a lot of the time . . . They pull up documents that any journalist would know how to find – a set of company accounts, or a newspaper cutting from the LexisNexis database – then charge clients 10 grand for it.'[11]

Following the invasion and conquest of Iraq in 2003, Kroll, Control Risks and their global competitors shifted the bulk of their interest towards the Middle East. Control Risks secured a profitable contract to provide 'private security' to the British Foreign Office. In 2003, a Control Risks employee stated: 'Private security can't take over from the troops . . . Private companies will never have the remit to run a private army.' Eighteen months later, Nick Clissitt, a director of the company, had adjusted the message: 'Governments are not really set up to be agile . . . the private sector has much more agility.' Kroll was involved in a scandal in London when Richard Chang, aged forty-eight, an Abbey National employee, 'fell from the fifth-floor balcony at the bank's Triton Square headquarters in central London . . . "minutes" after he was quizzed by Kroll'.[12] In May 2004, Jules Kroll sold his company to Marsh and McLennan for $1.9 billion 'in cash'; his personal shareholding was valued at $110 million. In March 2005, it was revealed that Kroll had declined an invitation from the US government to run Guantanamo prison as a privatised facility. A few days later, it was reported in South Africa that Kroll had lobbied for a contract 'to "sweep" government departments and parastatals' for bugs. But if the career trajectory of the former head of Kroll operations in South Africa, the former ANC intelligence operative, NIA Deputy Director-General and Scorpion Pete Richer, is anything to go by, power has already shifted. Richer is now happily ensconced with former Vula spook Ivan Pillay in the South African Revenue Service (SARS).[13]

Another figure who played a mysterious role behind the scenes in the new South Africa was former MI6 officer and Kroll Associates operative Michael Oatley. Described by Liam Clarke as an 'Irish Lawrence of Arabia', Oatley played an important role over eighteen years in Northern Ireland developing secret channels through which MI6 could communicate with the IRA. In 1994, Oatley's company, CIEX, was employed by British businessman Julian Askin in his battle with ABSA Bank. Frank

Welsh's excellent book, *Dangerous Deceits*, revealed that Oatley's 'early years with MI6 . . . had been [as] an African specialist, and his last overseas post was in Zimbabwe'. In addition, Oatley 'had spent more time on African issues than any other member of MI6 [and] was one of the half-dozen or so most senior officers concerned with understanding and activating intelligence penetration of the apartheid regime'.[14]

In August 1999, the *Sunday Times* carried an interview with former MID operative Chris Clark, who had been 'dispatched to Britain by military intelligence to work undercover in 1988, [when] he was ordered to monitor the London headquarters of the ANC'. Clark claimed that he had broken into the ANC's offices 'to repair a faulty bug'. In 1991, he was engaged in the surveillance of Dirk Coetzee. 'I knew the intention was to murder him. My job was to watch him, to see what his daily routine was' (see page 320). Clark claimed to have 'tipped off a former MI6 officer', Michael Oatley, whom he first met in 1991 in the boardroom of Kroll Associates in the former Curzon Street headquarters of MI5. Over the next eight years, Clark worked for Oatley. As he told the *Sunday Times*: 'I am the port of last resort. I get called in when all other lines of investigation are exhausted. I do the dirty work that reputable organisations can't afford to be seen to get involved in.'[15]

In 1998, Deputy President Thabo Mbeki and Tony Seedat (SASS) agreed a contract with Oatley's CIEX worth ' "several million pounds" to uncover apartheid-era crimes and secret projects'. The Johannesburg *Sunday Times*, which had studied Chris Clark's affidavit, reported that 'CIEX had been paid to gather information about former Finance Minister Barend du Plessis and the SA Reserve Bank's role in awarding a R90 million "lifeboat" to ABSA [Bank] . . . CIEX was [also] briefed by Mbeki to gather information about the drug-smuggling operations in Britain of Wouter Basson.' A few weeks later, *City Press* recorded that the South African government had employed 'a British-based outfit . . . [and] a South African private intelligence firm, run by top agents of the Security Police and [MID] who left the service before the 1994 elections'. When I spoke to Michael Oatley in 2002, he was surprisingly bitter about Kroll's dominance in the South African private intelligence market.[16]

In conjunction with the international intelligence organisations, former members of the apartheid security forces followed the trail blazed by Gerard Ludi (see page 141) and Craig Williamson (see page 189) into the private security business. It would perhaps be more accurate to report that the apartheid spies had been engaging in a complex process of self-privatisation since the late 1980s. Roy Allen, for example, whose name has been linked to a number of death-squad killings, found work with Fidelity Guards, taking care of security at Johannesburg International airport, always an important site for spookery. Later, he emigrated to Australia. As South African crime spread into previously white areas, a legion of companies were ready to exploit people's fears. In 1997, Linda Mti, the NICOC co-ordinator, announced that 204 new security companies had registered with the Security Officers' Board in January 1997. As of 21 October 1998, a total of 5,939 companies were registered in the Republic, with 136,310 employees. By 2004, South Africa boasted 'one of the largest private security industries in the world . . . [consisting] of approximately 260,000 active registered security officers and more than 4,100 security businesses . . . [the industry] is estimated to be worth R14 billion per year . . . [and] outnumbers the [SAPS] and the [SANDF] in terms of human resources'.[17]

One of the first local private intelligence agencies was Panasec Corporate Dynamics established by former NIS officers, including Maritz Spaarwater and Daan Opperman, who had been expelled from the US for spying in 1982 (see page 157). Spaarwater explained that the company was attempting to exploit the market later seized by Kroll: 'Our focus is on business intelligence and private security . . . We will be engaged in conventional industrial investigation which will include among other things, internal fraud . . . We do not want to have any connection with political parties.' Panasec did not prosper but the more mysterious Associated Intelligence Networks (AIN) and Orion Professional Management (OPM) did. In March 2001, *Africa Confidential* reported that OPM's 'expertise in counter-espionage could threaten the effectiveness of state surveillance operations'. OPM was controlled by the Strategic Resource Corporation, the holding company of Executive Outcomes (see page 377) and was 'chasing contracts with [SARS] and the [NIA]'. OPM was also connected to Alfred Oosthuizen, the former head of apartheid Security Police counter-intelligence, who had 'formed a security company, Ukukhula, as a joint venture with some of his erstwhile enemies including individuals who had been part of Operation Vula'. Warren Goldblatt's AIN was, according to the *Financial Mail*, 'accused by its enemies of using bribery and other illegal means to dig into people's private lives'. In 2001, the *Mail & Guardian* revealed that AIN had been raided by the South

African Police in a fraud investigation. Nevertheless, charges have not been brought and AIN remains in business.[18]

In October 2001, the South African government proposed plans to limit foreign involvement in the private security industry. The *Financial Times* reported that 'foreign companies, mainly from the UK, have invested about R2.5 billion . . . over the past year in companies like Sentry Security, Gray Security and BBR Security. Securicor, Chubb, Group 4 and ADT have [also] made acquisitions of local security companies.' After a meeting between the Minister of Safety and Security, Steve Tshwete, and representatives of the British companies, the South African government swiftly removed the proposed legal amendment. By 2005, the giant British companies had been thoroughly South Africanised, employing former apartheid operatives and building defensive political relationships with current and former ANC politicians. Despite Minister of Intelligence Lindiwe Sisulu's inconsequential commission set up to examine the ownership, function and control of security companies – she was reportedly concerned that certain 'security and risk analysis companies may be fronts' for MI6 or the CIA – there is clearly a need for much tighter regulation of South Africa's private security companies.[19]

Wild Geese and Dogs of War

South Africa is a land of 'frontiers': between developed and developing worlds, between East and West, between Europe and Africa and between ancient and modern. Perhaps it is fitting that the number of frontiers has inspired a mercenary military culture. The most famous of modern mercenary leaders, Mike Hoare, first came to public attention in the Congo in the early 1960s. An odd feature of recent mercenary history is that, although South Africa has regularly been the base for mercenary escapades, the leaders of the operations have often, like Mike Hoare, not actually been South Africans. It must be the echoes of a fading colonial heritage in the Republic that allows the excitable European immigrant to imagine a continental interior where anyone can be king. European mercenaries in the Congo came from all types of backgrounds: the old Harrovian Alastair Wicks; the Afrikaner Jeremiah Puren; the Irish adventurer 'Mad' Mike Hoare; the Belgian *colon* 'Black Jacques' Schramme; and the Gascon Bob Denard. Wicks and Hoare had emigrated to Rhodesia and South Africa after the Second World War; Schramme had grown up in Belgium and arrived in the Congo aged eighteen to 'run a family plantation'; Denard had fought in Indochina and Algeria; only Puren had no personal military history. The first batch of recruits to Mike Hoare's Five Commando were 'mainly Germans from South West Africa'. But the quality of the 'soldiers of fortune' in the Congo was not, in Hoare's opinion, very high:

> The general standard was alarmingly low. There was too high a proportion of alcoholics . . . bums and layabouts, who were finding it difficult to get a job anywhere else and thought this was a heaven-sent opportunity to make some easy money . . . I discovered to my horror, that there was a fair sprinkling of dagga [cannabis] smokers and dope [heroin] addicts, many of whom were beyond recall. Perhaps the greatest surprise of all, and it was to remain so right through the three six-month contracts we served, was the incidence of homosexuals.[20]

Five Commando's reputation, such as it was, originated in the impression that the mercenary force had stepped into the breach, where the United Nations had failed, to protect Western values. But, as Jeremy Harding explained, the 'anti-Communist ideology had a useful subsuming role: greed, adventurism and some brusque racial views were comfortably rolled up into a defence of the free world'. A surprised Anthony Mockler, for example, noted in *The New Mercenaries* that Five Commando's 'enemy', the Simbas, proved to be 'the only armed bands that showed any restraint' when it came to looting and plunder. The mythology and glamour of Hoare and his compatriots were entirely due to their friends in the press corps. The veteran reporter Chris Munnion acknowledged in his memoir: 'Foreign correspondents and mercenaries have much more in common than either group would like to admit.' The failure of the mercenaries who opposed the Nigerian army during the Biafran war inspired Frederick Forsyth to comment that 'far from consolidating the position of the mercenary in Africa, [Biafra] has completely exploded the myth of the Congo's "White Giants" . . . most have been revealed as little more than thugs in uniform'.[21]

In the Angolan war, the SADF played the role of a mercenary force until reality arrived. The FNLA, with the covert encouragement of the CIA, recruited mercenaries in London. The most notorious 'soldier of fortune' in Angola was Costas Georgiou, 'Callan'. Georgiou, a Cypriot who had emigrated to the UK in 1963 at the age of twelve, was a former paratrooper. He had been court-martialled, given a dishonourable discharge and sentenced to five years in prison following his involvement in the armed robbery of a post office in Northern Ireland. He arrived in Zaire in

December 1975 as a medic and within little more than a month had been appointed 'Field Commander' of the FNLA. John Stockwell, then head of the CIA task force, later told the Callan story:

> Agency officers flying in and out of northern Angola took note of an Englishman named George Cullen ... who had somehow become [Holden] Roberto's field general ... [CIA] Kinshasa, reporting favourably on his activities, wanted to recruit him as an in-place observer of the fighting ... Almost singlehandedly, he had ambushed and routed a small MPLA column ... Cullen, a native of Leeds ... spoke Greek, Arabic, English, and some Portuguese. Altogether, a good man, it seemed. Only days later, Cullen seemed much less of a good thing. Incredible tales concerning him began filtering out of the war zone. Cullen was beating up blacks; Cullen was murdering blacks; Cullen had stripped, beaten, and humiliated Zairian officers; Cullen was a psychopath. On February 1, 1976, a mobile patrol of twenty-five mercenaries went on a reconnaissance operation ... on the way back they attacked a forward defence post of their own men ... Then they fled to São Salvadore. Two days later, Cullen having tracked them down, lined fourteen of the malefactors beside the road, and gunned the whole lot down. Stripping their bodies, he left them in the sun as an example to others and disappeared into the bush.[22]

Stockwell's version is accurate in spirit but littered with errors of detail. Anthony Mockler composed a more nuanced account which filled in the background: Callan (not Cullen) spent his teenage years in north London; there is no evidence that he spoke Arabic or Portuguese; it was not a 'small MPLA column' but an MPLA column of 600 soldiers, of whom sixty were killed, with a number of Soviet tanks and rocket launchers destroyed. Mockler suggested that Callan 'was a complex personality: in many ways he was a primitive murderous lout ... [But] he had a certain heroic stature.' Costas Georgiou was tried by an Angolan court, found guilty and executed by firing squad in July 1976.[23] It is difficult to decide which is more disturbing, Callan's Kurtz-like behaviour and psychopathic command or the former CIA officer's inability to report basic facts; obviously, the CIA didn't bother gathering basic intelligence on British mercenaries, even when they had paid for them.

One of the last flights of the 'wild geese' was Mike Hoare's attempted coup d'état in the Seychelles in 1981. Soldiers of fortune were traditionally known as 'dogs of war' or 'wild geese'; and when it came to his mercenary activities, Mike Hoare was especially fond of tradition. The Seychelles had attained independence from Britain in 1976, and within months Eschel

Rhoodie and his Info associates were embracing Sir James Mancham, the pro-Western President. Reports of luxurious holidays by Info staff in the Seychelles formed part of the coverage during Muldergate. In June 1977, Mancham was overthrown in a coup and replaced by the ostensibly left-wing President Albert René. In 1978, a BOSS officer, Martin Dolinchek, liaised with Seychellois exiles in South Africa. As plans to launch a coup in the Seychelles developed, there was the usual tension between the MID and DONS–NIS as to who was planning the operation. This confusion would prove to be emblematic of the entire episode. The sixty-three-year-old Mike Hoare was selected to launch the coup and on 25 November 1981 he landed in the Seychelles with a gang of forty-five mercenaries (members of South African special forces and Rhodesians) disguised as tourist 'members of a drinking-club . . . ye Ancient Order of Frothblowers'. Weapons, which had been supplied by the SADF, were hidden in cricket and golf bags.[24]

At the airport, an AK47 was discovered in one of the mercenary's bags and a shoot-out ensued. The mercenaries would later argue over who was and who wasn't inebriated during the coup. Seven mercenaries were captured, including Dolinchek and the Congo veteran Jeremiah Puren. The remainder hijacked an Air India aeroplane and returned to South Africa. The *Sunday Tribune* reported that the attempted coup 'had been backed by the . . . [CIA]'. Hoare's crew was arrested in South Africa and tried in Durban. The majority received six-month prison sentences, but Mike Hoare was sent to prison for a punitive ten years; he was released after three. It later emerged that Hoare had been assisted by Jimmy Claasens, the Deputy Director-General of the NIS, and Major-General Charles Lloyd, who in 1987 would become secretary of the SSC. In mid-1983, the government of the Seychelles returned the captured mercenaries after South Africa secretly paid René a ransom of $3 million. Mike Hoare joked: 'I should have taken Richard Burton and Roger Moore along with me and we'd have had a happy ending.'[25]

The Seychelles 'invasion' was the end of an era. It didn't need to be as amateur and chaotic as Hoare's mercenaries made it. Within a few years, South African intelligence (in the oversized form of Craig Williamson) would secure control of the Seychelles without a single shot being fired. This was achieved through the ministrations of Giovanni Mario Ricci, the Italian millionaire businessman who controlled President René's security. In 1986, Williamson was appointed the managing director of Ricci's company, GMR, in South Africa. The Seychelles, under the control of the MID, and the Comores, ruled for nearly ten years between 1978 and 1988 by the French mercenary Bob Denard, and then controlled directly by South Africa were extremely useful to the apartheid regime, situated as they were 'in the middle of the sea-lanes and air-routes carrying weapons from South Africa to the Gulf and oil in the opposite direction'. As Stephen Ellis commented: 'in matters of strategic deception, the South African secret services had made considerable advances from the ham-fisted bribery of the Department of Information and the 1981 mercenary fiasco'.[26]

From the 1981 raid on Maputo by a force of ex-Rhodesian special forces, the SADF and the MID slowly began to incorporate the full range of mercenary activity into their destabilisation programme in the front-line states. Following the return of insurrectionary rioting in 1984, the lawless quality of the mercenary was let loose within the Republic by the state. It appeared to many observers that the old-fashioned world of the 'mercen-ary for hire' had finally disappeared. Eeben Barlow, a former captain in the SADF's 32 Battalion, had led the CCB's operations in Western Europe. Al Venter wrote that 'Barlow was well known to British intelligence . . . he had been involved with them in Rhodesia and had used his links to London for sanctions-busting operations while in the CCB.' In 1989, he created a company designed to exploit what he later described as 'a niche in the market'. Executive Outcomes (EO) was originally intended to be 'a counterintelligence consultancy firm'; among its earliest clients was De Beers. It grew rapidly and found a ready pool of employees among the former SADF special forces operatives who were at something of a loose end as South Africa moved towards full democracy. EO discovered that the end of the Cold War had created an untapped market for its services; by 1991, the company was engaged in mine security and the penetration of international crime syndicates and had even been employed in the 'war on drugs' in Latin America. Leading members of EO were the former Koevoet operative Lafras Luitingh and Nik van den Bergh, an ex-member of 1 Recce.[27]

In January 1993, UNITA seized the oilfields of the former Special Boat Service operative Tony Buckingham's Heritage Oil and Gas in Angola and shut down production. Buckingham and his colleague, the old Etonian, former SAS officer and risk-assessment consultant Simon Mann, hired EO, who with a team of fewer than a hundred men recaptured the fields. After EO departed, the fields were once again captured by UNITA. The Angolan MPLA government appealed for assistance to the

Canadian company Ranger Oil, which operated Angola's offshore oil-fields. Ranger gave Buckingham and Mann $30 million to recruit a force of at least 500 men; they returned to EO, who recruited the soldiers, including twenty-four SADF officers.[28] The Angolan war had been raging for eighteen years when EO intervened in 1993. The irony, of course, was that the EO engagement was an archetype of mercenary behaviour: most of EO's African 'footsoldiers' had previously fought in support of UNITA as members of Koevoet and the 32 Battalion. In reality, the EO–Heritage relationship represented a post-modern form of imperialism: EO was paid in cash whereas the Heritage Group received mining and oil concessions. At the time EO was launching its new mercenary operations in Angola, the former leader of the British Liberal Party Sir David Steel was a director of Heritage Oil and Gas, and Tony Buckingham, whose name according to *Africa Confidential* was a *nom de guerre*, recruited Rupert Bowen, a British 'diplomat' previously stationed in Namibia to join the Heritage empire.[29]

According to a 'UK Eyes Alpha' British Defence Intelligence Staff report, compiled in 1995 and later reported in the *Observer*, the ANC did not oppose the EO engagement because 'it would remove from South Africa a number of personnel who might have had a destabilising effect on the forthcoming multiracial elections'. The EO intervention, however, caused extreme irritation in MID circles in South Africa, although it is not clear whether this was from envy or from residual loyalty to UNITA. Before the end of 1993, MID secret documents on EO were being circulated within the SADF. One stated: 'So successful has EO proved itself to be, the OAU may be forced to . . . offer EO a contract for the management of peace-keeping continent wide.' Eeben Barlow summed up the tone of the material: EO apparently 'was of grave concern to the SADF . . . we should be shut down as quickly as possible . . . we were lying to people in our recruitment by saying they were going to protect oil wells . . . we were contravening exchange control laws . . . every possible law . . . unit commanders must advise all members of their units not to apply for work in [EO].' One of Barlow's EO colleagues told Jim Hooper: 'Fortunately, Eeben is a very capable intelligence officer himself, and had . . . friendly chats with people inside military intelligence . . . as a result we were kept up to speed on some of the machinations.' The mercenary engagement eventually forced UNITA to negotiate a peace accord in November 1994. The *Observer* summarised the British Defence Intelligence report as follows:

[EO] 'is acquiring a wide reputation in sub-Saharan Africa for reliability and efficiency', with a particular appeal to 'smaller countries desperate for rapid assistance' . . . There 'is every likelihood' that the company's services . . . 'will continue increasingly to be sought'. But the document warns that . . . [this would be] a cause for concern because the company is able to barter its services 'for large shares of an employing nation's natural resources and commodities . . . On present showing, [EO] will become ever richer and more potent, capable of exercising real power, even to the extent of keeping military regimes in being. If it continues to expand at the present rate, its influence in sub-Saharan Africa could become crucial.'[30]

One of the most impressive features of EO and its successor companies was their mastery of public relations. Jeremy Harding noted that 'Barlow has a way of speaking about the company's benefits to civilians as though he were running a Christian outreach project . . . [he] likes to stress that his company undertakes no work for rebel movements; EO's services are available only to "legitimate" governments; he also says that he will seek to encourage the growth of democracy wherever EO works – a slightly chilling remark from a former CCB operative.' It is less easy to find references to the accusations of serious human rights abuses that occurred in Angola'. These reportedly included looting and the use of napalm, cluster bombs and fuel-air explosives ('bombs that, on detonation, suck out oxygen in a massive fireball, killing all life within a one square mile radius'). Under pressure from the Clinton administration, the Angolan government terminated EO's contract in December 1995.[31] Meanwhile, Valentine Strasser, the President of Sierra Leone, invited EO to join the war against the Revolutionary United Front (RUF). Once again, EO was victorious; one mercenary described the engagement in comparison to Angola as 'child's play'. EO left Sierra Leone in January 1997, having defeated the RUF for a total cost of $35 million – as P.W. Singer explained, that was 'just one-third of the government's annual military budget.'[32]

In 1997, Barlow and the Falklands war veteran Lieutenant-Colonel Tim Spicer were 'guests of honour' at a United States Defense Intelligence Agency symposium on 'Privatization of National Security Functions in Sub-Saharan Africa' held in Virginia. One year later, EO was disbanded following the passage of the Regulation of Foreign Military Assistance Act in South Africa, which declared: 'No person may within the Republic or elsewhere recruit, use, train, finance or engage in mercenary activity.' But Tony Buckingham had prepared for the eventuality of government legislation in South Africa. As Duncan Campbell observed, 'in the mid-1980s,

EO blended into Sandline International'. In October 1996, Buckingham and Mann had approached Tim Spicer, who had recently retired from the directorate of Special Forces in the British army. According to Spicer's autobiography, *An Unorthodox Soldier*, Buckingham and Mann had decided that EO 'carried a lot of political baggage' and that 'it would be better to make a fresh start' in the mercenary business. Spicer agreed to set up the new organisation.[33]

Sandline International's first operation, in Papua New Guinea in 1997, was a disaster: 'Spicer and his South African mercenaries were arrested and jailed soon after they arrived . . . the charges were set aside after [Spicer] agreed to face questioning by a government commission of enquiry'. In London, Sandline's PR company was busy promoting the description 'private military company' to replace the old-fashioned and pejorative 'mercenary'. Meanwhile, a second intervention, this time in Sierra Leone, covertly supported by Britain's Foreign Office, drew further criticism. The 'Sandline affair' provided an uncomfortable moment for the new Labour Foreign Secretary, Robin Cook. Britain's interventionist Prime Minister Tony Blair took a different view: 'When people say "run an ethical foreign policy", I say Sierra Leone was an example of that, not an example of not doing it. It is up on the high ground.'[34] Despite Blair's messianic support, by the end of the century it looked as if the new wave of mercenaries had been nothing more than a historical blip. It was difficult to challenge Alex Vines's assessment in 1999:

> none of these firms have shown the ability to provide anything but short and localised respites from conflict. They certainly have not enhanced stability or encouraged business confidence. Indeed their poor human rights record, their lack of transparency, their engagement in arms transfers, their training in psychological warfare against civilians, their erosion of national self-determination and sovereignty in situations of crisis and their use of people with track records of human rights abuse does not bode well for the upholding of international law . . . the foreseeable rivalry between oil and mineral companies and their accompanying private security companies could signify a dangerous step towards the 'privatisation of warfare', which also raises the question whether peace is in the interest of such companies.[35]

But Vines had not imagined 9/11 and the ensuing wars in Afghanistan and Iraq. By 2003, the United States needed a supply of 'private security' operatives who could perform front-line tasks in Iraq and thereby reduce the threat to American and British troops. The US companies Halliburton, Bechtel and Lockheed Martin, providers of support services and defence equipment, secured the largest contracts in Iraq in 2004, closely followed by Tim Spicer's Aegis Defence Services, which was awarded a $293 million contract in June 2004 'to co-ordinate security operations among thousands of private companies, making it the biggest private security company in Iraq'. Aegis was criticised in 2005 by US government investigators for failing 'to verify that employees were properly qualified for the job'. As the 'peace' in Iraq revealed itself to be nothing more than Orwellian code for continuing 'war', the need for battle-hardened former special forces soldiers and counter-insurgency policemen intensified. More than 5,000, mainly white, former apartheid 'stormtroopers' are understood to have enlisted for 'tours of duty' during which mercenaries have been reported to be earning up to £800 per day.[36]

In January 2004, two South Africans employed by the South African–British security company Erinys International were subjected to a bomb attack in Baghdad. François Strydom, a former member of Koevoet, was killed, while Deon Gouws was maimed. Gouws was a former Vlakplaas operative who had been granted amnesty by the TRC for 'between 40 and 60 petrol bombings of political activists' houses . . . a car bombing in 1986 that claimed the life of homeland cabinet minister and ANC activist Piet Ntuli' and the extrajudicial murder of another fourteen people. Gouws later said: 'To go to Iraq is to sign a death warrant . . . People do not want us there . . . No amount of money is worth it.' Erinys International, originally founded by an apartheid-era diplomat, Sean Cleary, had been awarded a contract worth $39.5 million 'to train 6,500 Iraqis to guard oil pipelines, wellheads and refineries'. In November 2004, the *Observer* published a photograph which showed 'two employees of Erinys restraining [a] 16-year-old Iraqi with six car tyres around his body.' The newspaper had been told that the boy 'was left was left immobile and without food or water for more than 24 hours'. Erinys admitted that the photograph was authentic but claimed that the 'process lasted for approximately three minutes.' Erinys also confirmed that the French mercenary François Rouget (see page 223), who had been convicted and fined in Johannesburg under the Foreign Military Assistance Act in 2003 for recruiting South Africans to fight in the Ivory Coast, was an employee of the company. A senior director of Erinys International, Alastair Morrison, a 'former SAS officer who won the Military Cross for storming an airliner of hostages in Mogadishu in Somalia in 1977', had recently resigned to become the chief executive of Kroll Security International in London.[37]

By March 2005, thirteen South Africans had been killed in Iraq. Seven months later, Nicholas 'Fink' Haysom, a former senior legal adviser in President Mandela's office, informed the Johannesburg *Sunday Times* following a six-month tour of duty in Iraq on behalf of the United Nations that he estimated there were more than 7,000 South Africans in Iraq. He claimed that they were 'highly regarded' and reported that 'those South Africans bearing arms in Iraq' are 'low-key, competent and highly professional, not trigger-happy', unlike their US counterparts. Haysom added that South Africans 'are restrained and professional, much more approachable and conversant with the conditions'. British publications provided a slightly different portrait of South African mercenaries in action. In March 2004, the *Economist* commented on the 'stressed and sometimes ill-trained mercenaries [who] operate in Iraq's mayhem with apparent impunity, erecting checkpoints without authorisation, and claiming powers to detain and confiscate identity cards. A South African company guarding a Baghdad hotel put guns to the heads of this correspondent's guests.'[38]

In February 2005, the London *Sunday Times* observed: 'There is a large South African contingent. "No one likes the Afrikaners," says one combatant. "They walk around completely gung-ho, bristling with four guns each, even beside the swimming pool. They point them at waiters, which is a really stupid thing to do. They go around in these large American vehicles and wear their own khaki uniform."' One South African company, Meteoric Tactical Solutions, has been very successful in Iraq, securing 'a big contract [in 2003] to train a private Iraqi security force to guard important buildings and other important sites currently protected by US soldiers'. In August 2004, South African newspapers reported that Louwtjie Horn, Meteoric's 'representative for Iraq', and Harry Calse, the company's 'former director for the Middle East', had been arrested at Harare airport with Simon Mann, from where they were planning to launch a coup in Equatorial Guinea.[39]

Mark Thatcher's Big Adventure

After Executive Outcomes closed down, the main players went their separate ways. Simon Mann, whose South African grandfather was a director of De Beers, invested in a gold company in Guyana and acted in Paul Greengrass's television film *Bloody Sunday* while subsisting on the $10 million or so he had earned while working for EO. In mid-2003, he decided in the style of a great performer returning to the stage for a final show – echoes of Mike Hoare in 1981 – that he should execute a coup d'état in oil-rich Equatorial Guinea. As if by design, Mann's plan was nearly identical to the plot of Frederick Forsyth's *The Dogs of War*, which featured the mining magnate Sir James Manson declaring: 'Knocking off a bank or an armoured truck . . . is merely crude. Knocking off an entire republic has, I feel, a certain style.' Anthony Mockler suggested in *The New Mercenaries* that Forsyth's novel was 'very possibly the thinly disguised account of a real mercenary *coup* planned and financed by Forsyth himself'.[40]

Mann believed that Equatorial Guinea's corrupt dictatorship would crumble at one glimpse of his askari 'army' and that he would be able to appoint a puppet ruler, Severo Moto, who would tolerate the demands of Mann and his backers. Mark Hollingsworth obtained documents dated 22 July 2003 which outlined the agreements between Mann and Moto. Mann ('Captain F') was to be paid £10 million and his four lieutenants £1 million each; 'the mercenaries would be paid $3,000 . . . after the coup, they would receive a $30,000 bonus and guaranteed jobs in the presidential guard'. The rewards for Mann and his merry band made the risks worthwhile:

> [They] were promised a series of lucrative contracts as well as a share of the oil royalties. A company would be set up with Mann as the CEO, and he would retain a 33 per cent stake. The firm's first task would be to recover 'all the national capital that has fled due to the illegal activities' of President Obiang and they would receive 30 per cent of any assets recovered on a 'no cure no pay' basis plus their costs. It would also be in charge of the intelligence agencies and armed forces and oversee the outsourcing of security contracts for the police, customs, tax and environmental control . . . Mann viewed Moto as someone who could be manipulated. 'We'll have a problem with him but once we've put him in power, we'll change things,' he told a friend.[41]

Documents leaked to the London *Sunday Times* 'by South African intelligence sources' revealed that the plotters intended to establish a trading company, the Bight of Benin Company, to run their 'private colony': 'The company would have controlled the country as a private fiefdom, modelled on the British East India Company.' Mark Hollingsworth reported that Mann's backers were Ely Cahill, a Lebanese trader born in Nigeria, Greg Wales, a British businessman, and three other Lebanese and British investors. Lord Archer was reported to have deposited $134,000 in the bank account that financed the projected coup. All the named backers have denied involvement in any conspiracy. A memorandum written by Simon Mann on 12 January 2004 remarked of Mark Thatcher: 'If his involvement is known, the rest of us and project is likely to be screwed – as a side issue to people screwing him. It would particularly add to a campaign, post-event, to remove us. Ensure doesn't happen.' It also revealed Mann's deeper concerns: 'This is potentially a very lucrative game. We should expect bad behaviour: disloyalty, rampant individual greed, irrational behaviour (kids in the toy-shop types), back-stabbing, bum-fucking and similar ungentlemanly activities.'[42]

Mark Thatcher had long been a visitor to South Africa and enjoyed friendships with both General Magnus Malan and Jean-Yves Ollivier, a businessman and representative of Thomson-CSF, the French arms manufacturer involved in South Africa's arms deal. In 1995, he had settled in Cape Town, which he found suited his need for privacy: 'There are no local paparazzi . . . For the most part the local press here are fast asleep.' Beyond an ill-judged microloan business venture, he had remained relatively quiet for nine years. Simon Mann recruited Nick du Toit, whose company Military Technical Services had been, according to one South African researcher, originally established by General Tai Minnaar (see page 334), and Crause Steyl, a pilot who had worked with Executive Outcomes. The coup plot was engineered through Mann's company, Logo Logistics. Eccentric meetings were held to plan the coup in places like a Wimpy café in Centurion near Pretoria and 'a holiday caravan park just east of Pretoria [where the plotters] held an impromptu barbecue'.[43]

On 7 March 2004, a US-registered Boeing 727 landed in Harare. Simon Mann and sixty-nine mercenaries were arrested, despite the fact that Mann offered the 'Zimbabwean chief intelligence officer . . . $10,000 "to look the other way"'. Nick du Toit, thirteen other mercenaries and four locals were arrested in Equatorial Guinea. On 21 March, Mann sent a letter to his wife from prison:

> They [his lawyers] get no reply from 'Smelly' [Cahill] and 'Scratcher' [Thatcher] . . . What we need is maximum effort – whatever it takes – now . . . It may be that getting us out comes down to a large splodge of wonga [cash] . . . What will get us out is MAJOR CLOUT. We need heavy influence of the sort that . . . David Hart [can exert] and it needs to be used heavily and now. Once we get into a real trial scenario we are F–d.[44]

The reference to David Hart, a former adviser to Margaret Thatcher and Michael Portillo, who played a significant role in breaking the miners' strike in 1984–5, has never been explained. On 22 July, Simon Mann was found guilty on two counts of the illegal purchase of firearms; he was sentenced to seven years in jail, reduced to four years. He will be released in 2006. Meanwhile, Mark Thatcher had been quietly whispering to South Africa's NIA. 'But I've been co-operating,' he is reported to have said when he was arrested by South Africa's Scorpions on 25 August 2004. He was charged at Wynberg Magistrates' Court, had his passport confiscated and was released on bail of R2 million. A senior Scorpions official later told the Johannesburg *Sunday Times*: 'It was a question of "Who was your mother again? We don't really care." '[45] Some strange intelligence connections emerged as the British media investigated the case. The London *Sunday Times* revealed that the nephew of former MI6 chief Sir Richard Dearlove, Justin Longley, 'was working closely with Mann on goldmining, forestry and engineering ventures in Africa. He visited the continent as a representative of Logo Logistics.' The *Mail on Sunday* suggested that Michael Oatley had been asked to 'help plan the coup'. Oatley had 'turned the plotters down . . . [but] denied passing details of the coup attempt to the Foreign Office'. In August 2004, the *Observer* speculated:

> Many in the intelligence community are asking whether a hidden hand was played by Western powers. Some suggest American, Spanish and British interests offered their backing to exiled leader Severo Moto. On the other side were the French, who believed a successful coup would have cemented US domination in the country where US oil giant Exxon Mobil already enjoys the most important drilling concessions. British intelligence sources have suggested that the French learned of the plot and helped to sabotage it.[46]

*

On 7 January 2005, Mark Thatcher agreed a plea bargain with the South African state. The ten-page document that later emerged was risible. Mark Thatcher's version of events started in November 2003 when he was approached by his friend Simon Mann who 'enquired whether [Thatcher] could assist him by chartering a Bell Jet Ranger III helicopter' to be used in a 'transport venture' in west Africa. Mann also mentioned that 'he was considering becoming involved in a mining transaction in Conakry, Guinea Bissau'. Thatcher 'indicated . . . that he would be interested'. A few weeks later, Thatcher discovered that two Alouette II helicopters were for sale in Wellington and told Mann. At this time, on Mann's instructions, he had a meeting with Crause Steyl at Lanseria airport, Johannesburg. Mann contacted Thatcher to say that the Alouette II helicopter was not suitable but that he 'had found an Alouette III helicopter that could be chartered for a minimum of three months on approximately the same financial terms as previously discussed'. (The plea bargain didn't provide any information on the previous financial terms.) The document continued:

> [In] late December 2003 to early January 2004, the accused [Thatcher] began to doubt Mann's true intentions and suspected that Mann might be planning to become involved in mercenary activity in the West African region. The accused began to suspect that the helicopter might in fact be intended for use in such mercenary activity . . . Despite his misgivings the accused decided to invest money in the charter of the helicopter . . . Shortly before 9 January 2004 the accused was requested by Mann to make a payment of US$20,000 to AAA Aviation (Pty) Limited, a company controlled by Steyl, as a payment to reserve the helicopter.

On 16 January 2004, Thatcher made a second payment 'of US$255,000' on Mann's instructions. Steyl chartered a helicopter 'which was flown from East London to Walvis Bay, Namibia, where it sat for a period of three weeks'. Although the helicopter was not 'used in any mercenary activity', Thatcher accepted his guilt because he had 'realised, prior to the dates on which the payments were made . . . that the helicopter might be used for mercenary activity . . . consequently [he had] . . . attempted to finance mercenary activity.'[47] Mark Thatcher had broken South African law as set out in the Regulation of Foreign Military Assistance Act. He was fined R3 million, which was paid by his mother, and given a four-year suspended prison sentence. As Thatcher declared on the steps of the court: 'I am willing to pay any price to be reunited with my family and I am sure all of you who are husbands and fathers would agree with that.'[48] The words 'any price' would resonate in South Africa.

In one of his final columns for the *Independent* before his death, Anthony Sampson noted that the South African government *had* to 'move against the networks of mercenaries which are the most dangerous legacy of the previous apartheid governments and have been the most difficult to overcome . . . the continued presence of mercenaries threatened the effectiveness of [South Africa's] own army and intelligence services'. It was certainly a cunningly executed trick by the South African secret services to permit the mercenaries to leave South Africa, while contacting Presidents Obiang and Mugabe and thereby destroying the coup. It was particularly cunning because it removed the dogs of war from South African soil and from the responsibility of South African justice. Allowing Mark Thatcher to pay a fine and walk free, however, left a bitter taste in the mouth. In January 2005, Crause Steyl informed the *Mail & Guardian* that 'We knew from early December that the plan had been leaked and that the South African authorities knew something was going to happen, but it was not until shortly before we left that they sprang into action . . . Up to that point, their attitude was one of watch and wait, and both Mann and Du Toit were convinced that if we pulled it off, Pretoria would be perfectly happy.' Steyl claimed that a last-minute telephone call 'from Paris to Pretoria' had inspired the South African intelligence services to intervene. He added that Mark Thatcher 'knew a lot more' about the coup plot than he admitted in his plea bargain.[49]

The rumour in intelligence circles in South Africa was that Thatcher actually gave a full and complete statement to the Scorpions. I was told that his affidavit stretched to more than sixty pages. He apparently named a senior ANC politician turned businessman and a senior member of South Africa's intelligence community as having, personally, blessed the coup. I could not ascertain whether he had made any reference to the coup's European backers.[50] It would make sense that Simon Mann would not have gone ahead with the operation unless he had some form of local insurance. If Thatcher did provide such a statement, he is even more stupid than most people suspect. Documents rarely stay buried for long in the new South Africa. In an interview with *Vanity Fair* magazine, published in the same month as Thatcher achieved his plea bargain, he was misquoted as saying that 'I just feel in this particular case like a corpse that's going down the Colorado River.' He later informed the *Sunday Telegraph* that he had actually said that he felt like a 'cork'.[51] There are a number of bitter, betrayed men in South Africa who might well like to demonstrate that the original quotation was more accurate. Or perhaps they will display some of the Republic's famous spirit of reconciliation.

Epilogue: Who is 'Comrade Bheki'?

In the summer of 1998, in conversation with Professor Arnold
Feinstein, the subject arose of what exactly contemporary history is . . .
I broke the habits of a lifetime and offered a flippant definition. 'It's
gossip-with-footnotes,' I replied . . .

AF: Gossip is very important. It has a great deal to do with human
consciousness – the need to find out about people who can harm you
or bring you pleasure; the need to find out how they are likely to
behave. Without this characteristic we would be autistic.

PH: So in that sense intelligence – in the sense of intelligence
services – is one of the oldest human activities?

AF: Yes. Exactly.

Peter Hennessy, 'The Itch after the Amputation', in
War, Resistance and Intelligence, 1999[1]

T HE ACTIVITIES OF the South African secret services in 2005 remained
impenetrable to the public as they had for the previous ten years.
Despite the occasional public relations exercises designed to encourage
South Africans to feel that their tax money was well invested, most intelligence officials appeared still to be fighting the traditional inter-agency
battles of their apartheid predecessors. In October 2005, Billy Masetlha,
the Director-General of the NIA, was dismissed by the Minister of
Intelligence, Ronnie Kasrils, after Masetlha made public his belief that the
Scorpions should be subsumed within the police service. The reason given
for the sackings of Masetlha and his colleagues, 'head of operations' Gibson
Njenje and counter-intelligence chief Bob Mhlanga, related to an unauthorised espionage operation aimed at a millionaire businessman, Saki
Macozoma.[2] In reality, the dismissals were linked to the burgeoning con-
flict within the ANC over the question of the presidential succession.
Perhaps South Africans should be relieved that South African intelligence
activity remained preoccupied with internal ANC network and business

politics. The history of South African espionage and 'dirty tricks' does not inspire confidence in what it might become if led by 'strongman' leaders like Hendrik van den Bergh or P.W. van der Westhuizen, or if the 'security of the state' is challenged by violent domestic unrest, as in 1976 or the mid-1980s.

There has continued to be a thriving business in conspiracy theories and bizarre apocalyptic manuscripts which have attempted to sum up the history of South Africa since 1910, especially Afrikaner political and intelligence history. Books such as advocate P.J. Pretorius's *Sell-Out!*, originally published in Afrikaans in 1996, would be genuinely worrying if they weren't so dominated by hysteria and intellectual incoherence. In fact, texts of this sort reflect the inchoate despair of a small number of Afrikaners at the collapse of white-minority rule. Nevertheless, the reader is forced to acknowledge the agonised vulnerability that leads an individual to declare:

> South Africa is being propelled by a number of subversive powers or counterbalances which operate mainly behind the scenes, in order to form a holistic unity with the so-called *New World Order*. The principal actors are mainly the International Monetary Power, the British and American state administrations (especially their Departments of Foreign Affairs and their Intelligence Services), the Freemasons, the *Afrikanerbond* (the AB which was formerly known as the *Afrikaner Broederbond*, although not from the outset), and the Anti-Apartheid movements. In the agendas of the aforementioned actors they all have in common a faceless, characterless, classless, genderless and raceless reality as universal goal with a Socio-Darwinistic ideal for one world government. This was also the vicissitude of South Africa. It is a Neo-colony of the United States of America (*Pax Americana*).[3]

*

The most intriguing intelligence figure in the new South Africa is an accommodating fellow who chooses to work from coffee-bars in Cape Town. 'Bheki Jacobs' or 'Hassan Solomon' is also known as 'Hassan Osman, Hassan Effendi . . . Solomon King, King Solomon, Uranin Vladimir Dzerzhinsky Joseph Solomon . . . Becky Jacobs, Beckie Jacobs'. His date of birth is not clear but is listed in at least one document as 9 June 1962. An ANC ID card issued in Lusaka in 1990 gives his date of birth as 16 December 1961 (the same day as the creation of MK). As a child he was 'classified' as 'Cape Malay' (Coloured) under the Group Areas Act; but his mother later applied for a birth certificate in a different name in order for him to be able to study at a local 'Indian' school. In 1978, he attended

Sastri College in Durban. By 1982, he was active within the ANC. Jacobs asserted in a police statement in 2003 that 'as part of my duty in the organisation I travelled between Swaziland and South Africa whilst working for a youth forum programme run by an organisation known as Diakonia Ecumenical Centre in Durban'. A colleague at Diakonia told *Noseweek* magazine in 2001: 'I worked closely with Jacobs. He was an extremely committed activist . . . He was also extremely intelligent and had a very good grasp of strategic detail.'[4]

On 17 November 1985, the Johannesburg *Sunday Times*'s 'Extra' section headlined a front-page story: 'Missing Activist: Hit Squad Fears. Right-wing assassins may have killed UDF leader, says family'. The report stated that 'Hassan Solomon . . . disappeared on the night of August 11 after telling his family he was travelling with friends to King William's Town to attend the funeral of lawyer and UDF supporter, Mrs Victoria Mxenge.' In January 1986, the South African Broadcasting Corporation reported that Solomon was living with an Indian family on the island of Mauritius: 'He has been studying the constitution of Mauritius and is playing football with local teams.' Hassan Solomon/Bheki Jacobs would remain in exile for more than nine years.[5] A few months later, 'Becky Jacobs' (the name was apparently a ruse to confuse the Security Police into thinking they were hunting a Jewish woman) travelled to Lusaka to join the ANC; *Noseweek* reported that at one point he was imprisoned in 'the notorious Quatro prison, where he spent about five months before being rescued by Ivan Pillay'. By the end of the decade, he was active among the rebellious ANC–MK cadres in Lusaka. Between 1990 and 1994, Jacobs was posted to Russia, where he studied at the Institute of Asian and African Studies, Moscow State University, under the supervision of Professor Apollon Davidson.[6]

Jacobs returned to South Africa in November 1994. A DIS communiqué, signed by Mo Shaik 'on behalf of Joe Nhlanhla', announced: 'The Department of Intelligence and Security kindly requests accommodation for Cde Bheki Solomon who has just arrived from the Russian Federation.' Soon afterwards, Jacobs worked at the ANC's headquarters, Shell House, in the Department of International Affairs, headed by Thabo Mbeki. During June 1995, Jacobs was photographed with Sinn Fein President Gerry Adams, during the Northern Ireland politician's visit to South Africa. The police statement by Jacobs added that in the mid-1990s 'I was . . . registered as an agent of the South African Secret Service under the name of Hassan Osman. I received payments from them, certain of my flights were paid by them and I received communication equipment from them.'[7] In 1995, Bheki Jacobs and a number of colleagues registered Congress Consultants as a private company. *Noseweek* described Congress Consultants 'as a kind of guerrilla intelligence network to give Mbeki independent intelligence on what was happening in the country and in his rival's camps'. A Congress Consultants intelligence report dated 1997 examined the 'Business Front – Anglo America[n]/De Beers/Ramaphosa' and noted that, 'Anglo America[n]/De Beers believe that, since 1993, Thabo Mbeki and the Russian government were jointly planning to destroy the Central Selling Organisation [the diamond-selling cartel operated by De Beers]'.[8]

Jacobs first came to public prominence in March 2001 when Ranjeni Munusamy (Johannesburg *Sunday Times*) broke an agreement to keep his identity secret. The front-page article, headed 'Man poses as Mbeki's "secret agent" ', noted that Jacobs had been an 'ANC intelligence operative in exile' and had supplied ' "intelligence" documents' to officials in Thabo Mbeki's office from 1996; he had been associated with 'the Minister in the Presidency, Essop Pahad, former Intelligence Minister Joe Nhlanhla, Mbeki's international affairs adviser, Thembi Majola, former spokesman Thami Ntenteni and Mbeki's former political adviser, Vusi Mavimbela'. The *Sunday Times* accepted that 'top officials trusted Jacobs and took his information seriously', but also reported that the NIA 'has instructed presidential staff to keep away from a man who, they say, has for five years masqueraded as a secret agent reporting directly to the President'. Jacobs had been employed by the Africa Institute since August 1999 but also 'runs an independent company, Congress Consultants, which . . . "has over 800 people to deliver services" including investigations, political, security and threat analyses, and demobilisation of former combatants'. Of particular importance, the article alleged that Bheki Jacobs was the man who leaked the 'arms deal' documents.[9]

The *Mail & Guardian* magnified the confusion: 'Jacobs, one of the African National Congress's most highly trained intelligence operatives, received his formal intelligence instruction in Moscow. Well-placed intelligence sources . . . gave the *M&G* a range of documents showing Jacobs maintained formal links with South Africa's two main state intelligence agencies until late last year. They said Jacobs had a high credibility rating.' Presidential spokesperson Bheki Khumalo declared that 'Bheki Jacobs has never been an agent of the president', while Professor Tom Lodge, who had employed Jacobs at the Africa Institute, 'said there was nothing . . . that suggested [that Jacobs] was unbalanced. "His work was fine." ' The *Mail & Guardian* commented: 'Jacobs was known for some time in Cape Town political circles as "the other ears of the president" . . . [His] inside information about the government and the ANC has often been uncannily accurate.'[10]

The following month, *Noseweek* added to the story. Describing Jacobs as 'diminutive but remarkable', it observed: 'most of the investigators employed in probing South Africa's tainted arms procurement programme have confidentially consulted him, because of his extensive knowledge of the personalities and processes involved in the deal.' The magazine suggested that the source for the *Sunday Times* was 'none other than Minister Pahad . . . no mean spy himself':

> In the spy world Bheki Jacobs is the real deal – an experienced operative who has, for two decades, worked for the ANC at the highest levels – latterly, even for the Presidency. And Pahad has foolishly committed the cardinal sin of the intelligence community – that of exposing the identity of its operatives. The *Sunday Times* appears keen to ignore the fact that what Pahad has exposed amounts to a private Presidential intelligence network . . . Pahad's attempts to portray Jacobs as some kind of Walter Mitty character does not stand up to even the most cursory scrutiny. Of course, Pahad is relying on the fact that in most cases the world of intelligence really is so bizarre as to seem implausible . . . But Jacobs' career as a trusted intelligence operative is simply too well documented.[11]

Following Mac Maharaj's declaration that Bulelani Ngcuka, the head of the Scorpions, had once been an apartheid double-agent and the subsequent foundation of the Hefer Commission to investigate the allegation, a fascinating document began to be circulated within South Africa's political and intelligence communities. The 'Report to the Honourable Patricia de Lille of the Independent Democrats' was signed by the 'Concerned Patriotic Intelligence Community loyal to the Constitution of the Republic of South Africa'. It announced: 'A silent coup is being engineered in our country.' The leaders of this so-called coup included Mac Maharaj, Mo Shaik, Jacob Zuma, Lindiwe Sisulu, Charles Nqakula (Minister of Safety and Security), Jackie Selebi (Commissioner of Police), Billy Masetlha (Presidential Intelligence Unit), Vusi Mavimbela (Director-General of the NIA) and Raymond Lalla (head of the Crime Intelligence Service). Two businessmen were named as 'providing funding', Brett Kebble and Nico Shefer. The aims of the plotters were alleged to be:

> To undermine and destroy institutions of the state like the Scorpions.
> To divide the ANC and to develop offshoots of leadership.

To play the race card of Zulu vs. Xhosas etc.

To undermine and replace the President of the ANC and the President of the Republic of South Africa (Possible assassination of the President).

To determine the succession after Thabo Mbeki.

To make South Africa ungovernable.

The report claimed that Operation Vula, led by Mac Maharaj, had been penetrated by the NIS; it alleged that in 1985 Mo Shaik had been turned while in detention and would later manipulate Vula under NIS guidance in a project that was known secretly as Operation Bible: 'Jacob Zuma and Mac Maharaj had by now become unconscious agents of the apartheid regime with the ANC Intelligence totally compromised at a strategic level. Mac's overzealousness in trying to be a legend and Jacob Zuma, as head of ANC Intelligence, with his legendary laziness and incompetence helped the process.' The NIS penetration allowed the apartheid intelligence structures to destroy the ANC's underground and weaken its capacity to negotiate 'from a position of strength'. Developing this theory, the document claimed that Mo Shaik, who from 1994 was in charge of integrating ANC–DIS officials into the NIA, 'made sure that the NIS [double-]agents in Vula as well as the NIS operatives were put in control of the new Intelligence Services of the democratic South Africa'. The most dramatic allegation in the document was that 'Charles Ndaba and Mbuso Shabalala . . . were killed by Mo's handlers, so as to protect his identity as an NIS agent.'

The first operation of the 'Vula boys', in conjunction with their networks in the SACP, COSATU, the 'Indian Cabal' and the remnants of the UDF, was an attempt to make Cyril Ramaphosa the first deputy president of South Africa. This 'engagement' failed and Thabo Mbeki was appointed, against the personal wishes of Nelson Mandela. Since Mbeki's election as president, the network:

> has been mobilising and building support and infrastructure for the removal of Thabo Mbeki [in order to] replace him with the compliant Jacob Zuma. They have infiltrated ministries, like the Transport Ministry, Defence Ministry, Intelligence agencies, Armscor, businesses, banks, financial houses, political parties, parastatals, the ANC, Parliament, the Presidency, SARS etc. . . . The one area they [have] failed to get strategic control of is the NPA (Scorpions), therefore they have launched this smear operation to get rid of Bulelani Ngcuka . . . Their motive is simply attainment of political power and self-enrichment. There is no ideology or struggle. The Vula gang, together with their apartheid cronies, are using their political infrastructure

in all levels of state to achieve political control and power . . . Further they are working with foreign multinationals and intelligence agencies to subvert our democracy.

The document assessed the NIA and concluded: 'South Africa does not have an effective intelligence capability.' The report concluded that the 'Mac/Mo/Zuma axis' was running a 'Stratcom strategy' and suggested that 'there is talk in NIA circles to have Bheki [Jacobs] arrested and killed by convicts in a prison or police station, or to have him killed in a car hijacking . . . We fear that when killing of this nature starts, it never ends.'[12] On 22 November 2003, Bheki Jacobs was arrested in Cape Town and flown to Pretoria in Commissioner of Police Jackie Selebi's executive jet. The *Mail & Guardian* reported that the arrest occurred after '[Mo] Shaik forwarded a copy of the "Jacobs dossier" to police out of "serious concern" at its contents.' Shaik contacted the Crime Intelligence Service (CIS) head, Raymond Lala (a former Vula operative), who ordered Jacobs's arrest a few days later. According to Jacobs's colleagues, he was first imprisoned in the same cells as the Boeremag (Afrikaner terrorists) who had been arrested for a number of bombings in 2002. When this failed to achieve its intended effect, the prison authorities put him in a cell with common criminals. Finally, they were forced to place him in solitary confinement.[13]

After five days of imprisonment, Jacobs was charged with possessing multiple passports in different names; he was released on bail. He declared in a police statement dated 27 November 2003: 'I deny that I am implicated in any conspiracy to murder the State President. I have devoted my entire life to the struggle for democracy in South Africa. I would never be involved in any conspiracy against a government to which I have devoted my whole life. I would go out of my way to protect the life of the State President.' Senior Superintendent Selby Bokaba later told the Johannesburg *Star*: 'We have deliberately shied away from, and chose to remain silent on, the current sensationalism that has characterised reporting on this issue.' The Bheki Jacobs case has never been tested in court, although the police retained the hard drives from his computers.[14]

If Bheki Jacobs is a fraud, then he is without doubt the most believable South African confidence trickster since Sir Laurens van der Post. Intelligence operatives who have described him as 'discredited' or 'delusional' should at least recognise that his arrest and subsequent release in 2003 were utterly counter-productive. Many observers have concluded that it is quite impossible to be released from a reported charge of 'conspiring to assassinate the President' without the direct intervention of South Africa's head of state. The 'Report to the Honourable Patricia de Lille' was a wild document, but it was also one of the most complete indications of the extraordinary subterranean tensions between the different factions within South Africa's intelligence communities. I have spoken with Jacobs many times and he is certainly one of the most entertaining and informative sources on ANC politics and intelligence. He also appears to be a victim, although he would never use such a term, of the convoluted history of South African espionage. He informed me on one occasion that he served three masters: 'The Soviet Union, which no longer exists, the ANC, which is slowly disintegrating, and Thabo Mbeki, and I am beginning to believe that he no longer exists.' He added, somewhat ominously: 'The ANC is drowning in greed.'[15]

In May 2005, the *New Yorker* told the story of Pham Xuan An, the only *Time* reporter to remain in Saigon after 1975. It later transpired that An was 'split right down the middle'. From the early 1950s, he had been a spy for the North Vietnamese. The *New Yorker* recalled that he was 'recognised as a brilliant political analyst' and that he 'seemed to do his best work swapping stories with colleagues in Givral's cafe, on the old Rue Catinat. Here he presided every afternoon as the best news source in Saigon.' Veteran reporter David Halberstam added: 'An's story strikes me as something right out of Graham Greene . . . It broaches all the fundamental questions: What is loyalty? What is patriotism? What is the truth? Who are you when you're telling these truths . . . There was an ambivalence to An that's almost impossible for us to imagine.'[16] In a strange way, Bheki Jacobs's story, whoever and whatever he is, raises many of the same issues.

Notes

In order to reduce the number of notes in this book, they have been compacted. Each note number in the text refers not only to the immediate fact or quotation but also to the material in the previous lines or paragraphs since the last note. I have attempted to keep the number of references to 'private information' to the bare minimum but I also have to protect people who told me revealing nuggets of information in confidence. Where South African newspapers, such as the *Star*, the *Sunday Times*, the *Sunday Express* and the *Sunday Independent* share their titles with British newspapers, I have placed 'Johannesburg' before the title. The British *Sunday Times* appears unadorned, as does Britain's *Independent on Sunday*. South Africa does not have a (daily) *Independent*.

PROLOGUE: A LAND OF SPOOKS

1. Walter Benjamin, *Illuminations*, 1970, p. 247. The Theses on the Philosophy of History was written in spring 1940, a few months before Benjamin took his own life. It was published in 1950.

2. Jeremy Cronin, *Inside & Out: Poems from 'Inside' and 'Even the Dead'*, 1999, pp. 131–2.

3. Tony Leon, e-mail to author, 13 April 2006; *Paratus*, March, November 1976; *Wits Student*, 25 August 1980. Voortrekkerhoogte medical hospital included a 'ward 22' where from 1969 the SADF attempted to 'cure' homosexual soldiers. The treatment took the form of electric shocks administered while the victim was shown pictures of naked men. The *Guardian*, 29 July 2000, reported that Dr (Aubrey) Levin 'believed the same treatment could also cure "drug addicts" [and] . . . those who simply did not want to serve in the apartheid military. They were also tagged as "disturbed".' From 1980, aversion therapy for gay men and women was abandoned in favour of chemical castration. See Mikki van Zyl, Jeanelle de Gruchy, Sheila Lapinsky, Simon Lewin and Graeme Reid, *The Aversion Project: Human Rights Abuses of Gays and Lesbians in the South African Defence Force by Health Workers during the Apartheid Era*, 1999. For the

original exposure of Leon's *Paratus* journalism, see Ronald Suresh Roberts, *Financial Mail*, 24 November 2000.

4. *Spectator*, 24 June 1978; Tony Leon, e-mail to author, 13 April 2006.

5. 'About Tony Leon', DA website: www.da.org.za; *Paratus*, March 1976.

6. Tony Leon, e-mail to author, 13 April 2006; Johannesburg *Sunday Times*, 5 April 1992; *Mail & Guardian*, 29 August 1997; *This Day*, 10 August 2004; the NNP was finally laid to rest in April 2005.

7. In 1997, I completed my doctorate, 'A Struggle for Representation: The International Media Treatment of South Africa, 1972–1979', and it was published in 1999 as *South Africa and the International Media, 1972–1979*.

8. *Atlantic Monthly*, February 1998.

9. *Guardian*, 2 October 2003; 7 May 1996.

10. *Daily Telegraph*, 22 October 2003; Michael Herman, 'Ethics and intelligence after September 2001', *Intelligence and National Security*, Vol. 19, No. 2, Summer 2004, p. 345.

11. *Prospect*, June 1997.

12. *Cape Times*, 19 May 1988; *Argus*, 3 March 1990.

13. Stephen Ellis, *Journal of Modern African Studies*, Vol. 42, No. 3, September 2004, p. 470.

CHAPTER 1: REPUBLICAN INTELLIGENCE

1. Graham Greene, *The Human Factor*, 1978, pp. 54–5.

2. 'South African Security Organisation', unsigned document, 1949; Clement Attlee, letter to Dr D.F. Malan, 18 October 1949 [PREM 8/1283].

3. Sir Percy Sillitoe, *Cloak Without Dagger*, 1955, pp. 21–54. Sillitoe served in the BSAP from 1908 to 1920; Sir Percy Sillitoe, letter to L.N. Helsby, 10 Downing Street, 9 November 1949; Sir Evelyn Baring, Minute, December 1949 [PREM 8/1023].

4. Sir Percy Sillitoe, letter to C.R. Swart, 3 December 1949 [PREM 8/1023].

5. G.F. Rumbold, letter to Sir Percivale Liesching, 19 December 1949; Dr D.F. Malan, letter to Clement Attlee, 31 December 1949 [PREM 8/1023].

6. 'Visit by Director-General of the Security Service to South Africa', unsigned document, 14 November 1949 [PREM 8/1023].

7. Mary Benson, *South Africa: The Struggle for a Birthright*, 1985, pp. 129–30; Richard J. Aldrich, *The Hidden Hand*, 2001, pp. 114–15; Philip Murphy, 'Creating a Commonwealth Intelligence Culture: The View from Central Africa 1945–1965', *Intelligence and National Security*, Vol. 17, No. 2, Autumn 2002, p. 142, citing David Maxwell-Fyfe to Churchill, 2 September 1952 [PREM 11/349].

8. Gordon Winter, *Inside BOSS*, 1981, p. 37. A.W. Cockerill, *Sir Percy Sillitoe*, 1975, pp. 188–9, noted that Sillitoe also disbanded the Malayan Security

Service and incorporated it into the Malayan Special Branch (intelligence) at the beginning of the Malayan emergency in 1948. Four years later, he integrated the security services in Kenya during the Mau Mau uprising. As Cockerill observed, 'Sillitoe's ability to expose organisational weaknesses and to offer remedies was his great strength.' On the staggering colonial repression in Kenya during the Mau Mau rebellion, see David Anderson, *Histories of the Hanged*, 2005; Caroline Elkins, *Britain's Gulag*, 2005.

9. Cockerill, op. cit., pp. 193–204; Anthony Hocking, *Oppenheimer and Son*, 1973, pp. 284–7; Edward Jay Epstein, *The Death of the Diamond*, 1983, pp. 128–33; Janine Roberts, *Glitter and Greed*, 2003, pp. 215–16; Stefan Kanfer, *The Last Empire*, 1993, pp. 271–4.

10. Ian Fleming, *The Diamond Smugglers*, 1957, originally published in the *Sunday Times*, September–October 1957; Ian Fleming, *Diamonds are Forever*, 1956, pp. 5–6, 15: 'M' informs Bond, 'You probably saw in the papers that De Beers took on our friend Sillitoe when he left MI5, and he's out there now, working with the South African security people. I gather he's put in a pretty drastic report and come up with plenty of bright ideas for tightening things up.' For an insider's account of IDSO's investigations, see Captain J.H. du Plessis, *Diamonds are Dangerous*, 1960.

11. Sillitoe, op. cit., p. 219; Cockerill, op. cit., pp. 195, 197–204.

12. *Daily Telegraph*, 5 October 2002; Fleming, *Diamond Smugglers*, p. 155.

13. Peter J. Schraeder, *United States Foreign Policy toward Africa*, 1994, p. 198; Sanders, op. cit., p. 164; Anthony Sampson, *Mandela: The Authorised Biography*, 1999, pp. 127, 131. On Sharpeville, see Philip Frankel, *An Ordinary Atrocity*, 2001.

14. Terry Bell with Dumisa Buhle Ntsebeza, *Unfinished Business*, 2003, p. 24.

15. Murphy, 'Creating a Commonwealth Intelligence Culture', *Intelligence and National Security*, Autumn 2002, pp. 146–7, 153, citing De Quehen to Welensky, 30 April 1960 [Welensky Papers 607/1]; Philip Murphy, 'Intelligence and Decolonisation: The Life and Death of the Federal Intelligence and Security Bureau, 1954–1963', *Journal of Imperial and Commonwealth History*, Vol. 29, No. 2, May 2001, p. 119, citing De Quehen to Welensky, 2 August 1962 [Welensky Papers 239/5]. Anthony Verrier, *The Road to Zimbabwe*, 1986, recalled that in April 1960, after Sharpeville, Eric Louw, South Africa's Minister of Foreign Affairs, proposed to de Quehen that 'intelligence liaison between the Union [of South Africa] and the Federation [should be] on a "declared" basis. Without indulging in technicalities, it may be said that such a basis indicates, or is intended to indicate, a degree of trust and co-operation between Governments which provides for intelligence to be shared – up to a point' (p. 103).

16. Interview with Eleanor Emery, 12 December 1996; Anthony Verrier, *Through the Looking Glass*, 1983, p. 252; Sampson, *Mandela*, pp. 145–6.

17. *Guardian*, 5 September 2005; Mary Benson, *A Far Cry*, 1989, p. 60. The liaison with the South African authorities on the subject of the ascetic Michael Scott

was a direct product of Sir Percy Sillitoe's visit in 1949. A letter from Sillitoe to General Palmer, Commissioner of the South African Police, 13 April 1950, admitted that 'at the request of Major du Plooy, whose acquaintance it was a pleasure to me to renew today, I enclose a note which summarises our information about the Reverend Michael Scott. I mentioned to du Plooy that paragraphs 2 and 3 of this note contained material which is derived from highly secret sources which should on no account be compromised.' A note by 'D.B.', dated 3 October 1950, on the 'Minute Sheet' of the first Scott file reveals that 'the [Foreign Office] and Sir Evelyn Baring at Pretoria were . . . opposed to allowing the South Africans the use of information from British sources because of the political objections . . . I said that [Sir Percy Sillitoe's] clearance was given purely from the security point of view and he would, of course, appreciate the political objections raised' [KV2/2052]. By September 1951, Bob De Quehen, covering Central Africa for MI5, was hungrily reporting Scott's visit to South Rhodesia (B.M. de Quehen, 'The Reverend Guthrie Michael Scott', to the Director-General of the Security Service, 26 September 1951) [KV2/2053]. A year later, the South African politician Eric Louw, who would later become the Minister for Foreign Affairs, gave a speech in which 'he said that the Union Government had been officially informed that the Rev. Michael Scott was a past member of the Communist Party, and that he may still be a sympathiser or fellow-traveller'. Sir Percy Sillitoe's successor, whose name is not included in the document, commented that it is 'always . . . embarrassing when confidential Security information is made public without proper authorisation' (Director-General, 'Rev. Michael Scott', to SLO Central Africa, 13 November 1952) [KV2/2054].

18. Stella Rimington, *Open Secret*, 2001, p. 101; *The Times*, 23 July 1998; *Daily Telegraph*, 6 August 1998.

19. G.R. Berridge, 'The Ethnic "Agent in Place": English-speaking Civil Servants and Nationalist South Africa, 1948–1957', *Intelligence and National Security*, Vol. 4, No. 2, April 1989, pp. 257–62, citing 'Defence Equipment for South Africa', a note prepared by the Treasury for a discussion with Dr Steyn on 10 December 1952 [DEFE 7/177]. Berridge singles out Donald Sole, 'a fast-rising diplomat, speaking with excessive frankness to a British diplomat . . . though on a topic of the first importance', citing Wilfred, to Hillier-Fry, 18 February 1955 [FO 371/113479]. Sole later served as ambassador to West Germany and the United States. Richard Cummings, *The Pied Piper*, 1985, insists that Allard Lowenstein was a CIA operative and observes that 'Donald Bell Sole . . . took a liking to Lowenstein' in the mid-1970s. In conjunction with Sean Cleary, Sole felt the American 'could be helpful' (p. 204). His son, Sam Sole, is an investigative reporter for Johannesburg's *Mail & Guardian*.

20. Thomas Borstelmann, *Apartheid's Reluctant Uncle*, 1993, pp. 90, 159, 169.

21. Sampson, *Mandela*, pp. 67–75, 87–9, 91–4, 99, 105–10, 118–21, 143, 171;

Fatima Meer, *Higher Than Hope*, 1990, p. 202; Nelson Mandela, *Long Walk to Freedom*, 1995, p. 372.

22. Johannesburg *Star*, 14 July 1986; Emma Gilbey, *The Lady*, 1993, pp. 304–5: 'Following publication of the *Star*'s story, CBS News ran a report in which they named Don Rickard, the consular officer of the period, as a CIA operative . . . The *National Reporter* [Vol. 10, No. 2, Autumn/Winter 1986], a left-wing monitor of US covert action . . . confirmed that Rickard had been the young American at the party and pointed out that he was listed in *Who's Who in the CIA*.' *Washington Post*, 11 June 1990.

23. *Atlanta Journal-Constitution*, 10 June 1990.

24. Sampson, *Mandela*, p. 172; 'Overt and covert activity by the South African Police within the High Commission territories' [DO 119/1222]; interview with Donald Rickard, 18 October 1997.

25. Sampson, *Mandela*, p. 109; interview with Gerard Ludi, 8 June 1999; *Spy*, March–April 1996: Ludi informed *Spy* that 'The South African intelligence services didn't have decent training manuals . . . It was really pathetic. They asked Millard to update and do a proper training manual.' In the mid-1980s, Shirley was employed by Telkom, South Africa's public sector postal and telephone service, 'to train a special intelligence unit . . . Shirley brought a thick stack of Pentagon "psychological warfare manuals" with him, according to Mike Leach, the former chief of the Telkom spook unit. "The manuals he gave us were for booby traps, poisons, etc. . . . One of the items he gave us was a recipe for prussic acid, a clear compound which, if inhaled, would give a massive coronary. If a doctor's not looking for [it] he'll put [the cause of death] down to natural causes."'

26. T.W. Aston, 'Paul Eckel Memorandum', 23 January 1959 [DO 119/1209].

27. J.B. Ure, 'Note', 25 May 1964 [FCO 371/177122].

28. H.J. Potgieter, *Report of the Commission of Inquiry into Matters Relating to the Security of the State*, 1970–3, pp. 7–9.

29. Bell, op. cit., pp. 42–4; *Rand Daily Mail*, 1 February 1980; Winter, *Inside BOSS*, pp. 13, 35–6.

30. Henry Pike, *A History of Communism in South Africa*, 1985, pp. 368–79; Gerard Ludi, *Operation Q-018*, 1969, pp. 7–9, 13–16, 18, 23, 94–100, 106–22, 138–42, 170. Ludi also worked for the *Rand Daily Mail* while spying for RI.

31. Winter, *Inside BOSS*, pp. 101–4; Stephen Clingman, *Bram Fischer*, 1998, pp. 335–6, 352.

32. Ludi, *Q-018*, pp. 173, 192; interview with Pieter Swanepoel, 3 August 1998.

33. Gerard Ludi and Blair Grobbelaar, *The Amazing Mr Fischer*, 1966, p. 60; Ludi, *Q-018*, p. 214.

34. Winter, *Inside BOSS*, pp. 13, 21, 34–8, 42, 45, 55–6, 65, 81–5, 104; Benjamin Pogrund, *War of Words*, 2000, p. 247.

35. Sampson, *Mandela*, pp. 184–5, 189–90, 194–7; W.H. Young, letter to Guy Millard, 20 May 1964 [FO 371/177122]; Tom Lodge, *Black Politics in South Africa since 1945*, 1983, p. 225. The police raids and ensuing trials are handled well by Glenn Frankel in *Rivonia's Children*, 1999. For a reactionary account of the crushing of the ARM, see Miles Brokensha and Robert Knowles, *The Fourth of July Raids*, 1965. For a personal testimony by a member of the ARM who gave evidence for the state against his colleagues, see Adrian Leftwich, 'I Gave the Names', *Granta*, 78: 'Bad Company', June 2002. For an account of life in a South African prison by an ARM prisoner, see Hugh Lewin, *Bandiet*, 1976.

36. Winter, *Inside BOSS*, pp. 93–4, 96–98; Bell, op. cit., pp. 47–8, 51; *To the Point*, 4 June 1976.

37. Winter, *Inside BOSS*, pp. 95, 100; Bell, op. cit., pp. 49–50; Pogrund, op. cit., pp. 248–9. The *Guardian*, 1 November 1995, noted that Lloyd had assured Hugh Lewin that he would not give evidence against him: 'The next day he stood as a state witness and did exactly the opposite . . . He effectively put the noose around John Harris's neck.' John Lloyd was deselected as a Labour candidate for the 1997 British general election following newspaper coverage of his role in the Harris trial. Peter Hain, aged fifteen, read the address at a ceremony following Harris's execution.

38. Colin Wilson, *A Criminal History of Mankind*, 1985, p. 581; Robert Parker, *Rough Justice*, 1981, pp. 162–9, 217–20, 245–9; Charlie Richardson, *My Manor*, pp. 173–82. Charlie Richardson described South Africa as 'a country ruled by dull-brained Boers who looked like the oxen that pulled their carts' (p. 172).

39. Parker, op. cit., pp. 249–51, 262–5; Winter, *Inside BOSS*, pp. 134–8.

40. *Sunday Telegraph*, 20 November 1966; Parker, op. cit., pp. 271–2, 285–7; *Sunday Times*, 4 October 1981: Jean La Grange arrived in the UK in 1966 and continued to spy for RI. From June 1968, she worked on a voluntary basis for Christian Action. During 1969, she was employed by Canon Collins's Defence and Aid; in late 1969, the Home Office intervened: 'The grounds given to Canon Collins were her connection to the Richardsons but [the *Sunday Times* has] learned that the then Home Secretary, Jim Callaghan, was told Christian Action had been "infiltrated" by BOSS.' Collins later categorically denied that La Grange had ever worked for Defence and Aid, before admitting that she had worked for the organisation 'for a few weeks'. The *Sunday Times* also 'established that long before Richardson confessed to Robert Parker, he told the prison authorities. As a result, Richardson claims, he was interviewed in jail by British intelligence officers.' See also Winter, *Inside BOSS*, pp. 293–7; Denis Herbstein, *White Lies*, 2004, p. 143.

41. Winter, *Inside BOSS*, pp. 139–40; C. Richardson, op. cit., pp. 210–12; Parker, op. cit., pp. 338, 344. See also Eddie Richardson, *The Last Word*, 2005 and the motion picture, *Charlie*, 2004, directed by Malcolm Needs and

starring Luke Goss. This is the only film that features a portrayal of Hendrik van den Bergh.

42. John D'Oliveira, *Vorster – The Man*, 1977, pp. 177–80; *Guardian*, 12 September 1983; Helen Suzman, *In No Uncertain Terms*, 1993, p. 69. Perhaps the best study of Demitrios Tsafendas is Henk van Woerden, *A Mouthful of Glass*, 2000.

43. Hilton Hamann, *Days of the Generals*, 2001, pp. 5–6; Dan O'Meara, *Forty Lost Years*, 1996, p. 151.

44. Bell, op. cit., pp. 58–9.

45. *Citizen*, 20 October 1976; Winter, *Inside BOSS*, pp. 476–9; Gordon Winter, 'Report on Doreen Bilson' to David Beresford, 8 September 1998 [Gordon Winter Papers]; Johannesburg *Sunday Express*, 8 October 1961; on *The Manchurian Candidate*, 1962, directed by John Frankenheimer, starring Frank Sinatra, see Greil Marcus, *The Manchurian Candidate*, 2002. For a full-blown conspiracy theory on the assassination of Verwoerd, see P.J. Pretorius, *Sell-Out!*, 1997, pp. 169–80.

46. Barbara Carr, *Spy in the Sun*, 1969, pp. xix, 1–5.

47. Tom Mangold, *Cold Warrior*, 1991, pp. 209–19; *Rand Daily Mail*, 1 February 1980.

48. Mangold, *Cold Warrior*, pp. 26–8, 220–3, 225–6; Mike Geldenhuys commented: 'This Loginov thing – there's going to be a big stink about it, isn't there?' (p. 29). Surprisingly, the truth about Loginov was ignored in South Africa. *Cape Times*, 10 March 1984; David Leigh, *The Wilson Plot*, 1988, revealed that Angleton had attended a British public school, Malvern College in Worcestershire, 'where he was a corporal in the Officers' Training Corps' (p. xii).

49. Christopher Andrew and Oleg Gordievsky, *KGB: The Inside Story*, 1990, pp. 385–6; *Cape Times*, 5, 7 March 1984. See also Karl Anders, *Murder to Order*, 1965.

50. Sampson, *Mandela*, p. 269, citing Oliver Wright, memo to P.W. Carey (Board of Trade), 17 October 1964 [PREM 13/092]; Paul Foot, *The Politics of Harold Wilson*, 1968, p. 261; Ben Pimlott, *Harold Wilson*, 1992, pp. 377, 379.

51. *Guardian*, 7 April 1997; Ken Flower, *Serving Secretly*, 1987, p. 91; Roger Morris, *Uncertain Greatness*, 1977, p. 119.

52. Sampson, *Mandela*, p. 146; conversation with Anthony Sampson, 21 January 1999.

53. Foot, *The Politics of Harold Wilson*, pp. 277, 280–3, citing Hansard, 21 April 1966; Sampson, *Mandela*, pp. 222, 270; *The Times*, 1 January 1998.

54. *Guardian*, 7 April 1997; conversation with William Gutteridge, 27 November 1999; Flower, op. cit., p. 91; John W. Young, 'The Wilson Government's Reform of Intelligence Coordination, 1967–68', *Intelligence and National Security*, Vol. 16, No. 2, Summer 2001, pp. 135, 138–41. On the original 'Oilgate', see Martin Bailey, *Oilgate: The Sanctions Scandal*, 1979; and 'Harold Wilson: The Letter and the Lie', BBC Radio 4, 26 September 2002. Verrier, *The Road to Zimbabwe*, described the relationship between British military intel-

ligence and 'the South African Government' as co-operative 'throughout the entire region south of the Zambeze, including Angola and Mozambique . . . South Africa's departure from the Commonwealth . . . made no difference to this liaison' (p. 112); he also suggested that as early as September 1961 the United States employed South Africa as a proxy in Angola: 'The South African Government has met our request to conduct secret military operations [in Angola]' (p. 141); Verrier is particularly acute on the shifting mood in Whitehall during the 1960s: 'Illogically, but perhaps not unnaturally, Whitehall found sense among the hard men in Salisbury and Pretoria. As the Foreign Office came to absorb the Colonial and Commonwealth Relations Office, Whitehall lost its remnant of commitment to black Africa south of the Zambeze' (p. 149).

55. James Bamford, *The Puzzle Palace*, 1983, pp. 213–14; Jeffrey Herbst, 'Analyzing Apartheid: How Accurate were US Intelligence Estimates of South Africa, 1948–1994?', *African Affairs*, Vol. 102, No. 406, January 2003, pp. 92–3; State Department, 'The White Redoubt', 28 June 1962.

56. Kenneth Mokoena (ed.), *South Africa and the United States: The Declassified History*, 1993, pp. 189, 194; Kevin Danaher, *The Political Economy of US Policy Toward South Africa*, 1985, pp. 79–80.

57. Ed Stanley, 'France and Africa, 1944–90', unpublished doctoral thesis, 2004, pp. 110, 236, 243, citing Ministère des Affaires Etrangères, reply to aide-mémoire, Ambassador de SA Paris, 30 June 1965; South African aide-memoire, 18 June 1965; interview with Gerard Ludi, 8 June 1999.

58. Anthony Sampson, *Black and Gold*, 1987, p. 139.

CHAPTER 2: BUREAU FOR STATE SECURITY (BOSS)

1. Phillip Knightley, *The Second Oldest Profession*, 1986, p. 392.
2. D'Oliveira, op. cit., pp. 84–7; *To the Point*, 4 June 1976.
3. *Daily Telegraph*, 19 August 1997; *To the Point*, 4 June 1976; *BOSS: The First 5 Years*, 1975, p. 16; Flower, op. cit., p. 155.
4. D'Oliveira, op. cit., pp. 140–1; *To the Point*, 4 June 1976.
5. *To the Point*, 4 June 1976; note of a telephone interview with Hendrik van den Bergh, December 1978 [Anthony Sampson papers]; John Nicholls, 'The Bureau for State Security', to Michael Stewart, 12 August 1969 [FCO 45/306/1].
6. *Observer*, 21 January 1979; O'Meara, op. cit., p. 211; Bell, op. cit., p. 49.
7. *To the Point*, 4 August 1978.
8. Max du Preez, *Pale Native*, 2003, p. 87; *Guardian*, 21 August 1997; see also *Mail & Guardian*, 22 August 1997; interview with Benjamin Pogrund, 27 September 1995.
9. Flower, op. cit., p. 156.
10. Interview with Gerard Ludi, 8 June 1999; Winter, *Inside BOSS*, p. 562; R.B.P.

Erasmus, *Report of the Commission of Inquiry into Alleged Irregularities in the Former Department of Information*, December 1978, p. 91; *To the Point*, 4 August 1978. *Washington Post* journalist Jim Hoagland saw a different side of Hendrik van den Bergh in 1970 when he 'met the head of BOSS by accident . . . van den Bergh is a tall, thin, bookish-looking man who appeared to be much more of an introvert than most Afrikaners I met. We chatted, he seeming almost as nervous as I was, and then he left, saying he had to get on with business' (Jim Hoagland, *South Africa*, 1973, p. 138).

11. Potgieter, *Report*, pp. 12, 44; John Nicholls, 'The Bureau for State Security', 12 August 1969 [FCO 45/306/1]; *To the Point*, 4 June 1976. In October 1968, the Johannesburg *Sunday Times* described van den Bergh as 'the second most powerful man in State service in South Africa – second only to Mr Vorster' (Brian Bunting, *The Rise of the South African Reich*, 1986, p. 414).

12. John Nicholls, 'The Bureau for State Security', 12 August 1969; Martin Berthoud, 'Special Powers in Northern Ireland', to John Macrae, 8 July 1969; John Macrae, 'The South African Bureau of State Security', to Martin Berthoud, 31 July 1969 [FCO 45/306/1].

13. Paul Killick, 'The Bureau for State Security', to John Macrae, 2 December 1969 [FCO 43/306/1].

14. Potgieter, *Report*, pp. 10, 12, 34, 36–8, 41–4.

15. *BOSS: The First 5 Years*, p. 22; *Africa Confidential*, 16 June 1972; Potgieter, *Report*, pp. 13–27, 31–2, 44.

16. *Cape Times*, 19 June 1978; *Daily Telegraph*, 26 July 1979; Henrik Ellert, *The Rhodesian Front War*, 1989, pp. 54–5.

17. *Rand Daily Mail*, 4 February 1980.

18. Breyten Breytenbach, *The True Confessions of an Albino Terrorist*, 1984, pp. 18–19, 40. Pike, op. cit., pp. 477–8: 'During his trial . . . Breytenbach entered a plea of "guilty" to all charges laid against him and gave a full confession . . . among his plans, he had plotted a "missile attack on a Rhodesian airliner, to demolish Beit Bridge, and [to free] Nelson Mandela from Robben Island by submarine".' Breytenbach was sentenced to nine years in prison (South African Institute of Race Relations, *Survey of Race Relations in South Africa: 1975*, 1976, pp. 64–5). *Rand Daily Mail*, 13 July 1977, revealed that in June 1976, as the Soweto uprising started, Breytenbach had written a letter to Mike Geldenhuys, in which he had agreed to spy for BOSS in Europe if he was released from prison and deported from South Africa. Gordon Winter suggested in the Dutch edition of *Inside BOSS* (*Geheim agent voor Zuid-Afrika*, 1981) that Breytenbach intended to accept the BOSS 'offer' and then doublecross the intelligence agency. Winter claimed that Geldenhuys had tricked Breytenbach into writing the letter of agreement, and following publication, 'Breytenbach's credibility was wiped out in the eyes of nearly all liberally-minded South Africans and his image was . . . tar-

nished overseas' (p. 478). Breytenbach's colleague, Barend Schuitema, the founder and former secretary of the Dutch Anti-Apartheid Movement, who had been suspected of being an 'agent provocateur' following his escape from South Africa in the wake of Breytenbach's arrest, reportedly told the Johannesburg *Sunday Times*, 3 February 1980, that he had been 'politically shattered . . . by the written offer in 1977 from Breytenbach to the Commissioner of Police, General Geldenhuys, to act as a spy . . . in exchange for his release from prison'. The report claimed that Schuitema had started working for the Security Police in 1978. This could have been a complicated smear designed to destroy the credibility of another anti-apartheid campaigner.

19. Ivor Wilkins and Hans Strydom, *The Broederbond*, 1979, p. 181; Johannesburg *Sunday Times*, 16 March 1975; J.H.P. Serfontein, *Brotherhood of Power*, 1979, pp. 154–5. See also Ernest G. Malherbe, *Education in South Africa,* Vol. II, 1977, pp. 663–90; Charles Bloomberg, *Christian-Nationalism and the Rise of the Afrikaner Broederbond,* 1990, edited by Saul Dubow. Bloomberg wrote a series of important articles on the Broederbond for the Johannesburg *Sunday Times* in 1963 and died in exile in 1985 (*Weekly Mail*, 4 April 1986). His American wife, Hope Edinburgh, whom Bloomberg 'married on his death-bed' (Bloomberg, op. cit., p. x), later played a role in the ANC's Operation Vula (see page 293) before her death (Ronnie Kasrils, *Armed and Dangerous*, 2004, pp. 232–40). Kasrils added that 'Charles Blumberg [sic] . . . had worked for me as an intelligence operative before his death' (p. 240).

20. R. Morris, op. cit., pp. 111–12, 115, 117, 119; *The Kissinger Study of Southern Africa*, 1975, pp. 66, 81; Sampson, *Mandela*, p. 271.

21. Herbst, 'Analyzing Apartheid', *African Affairs*, January 2003, p. 98; *Cape Times*, 26 July 1977; John Stockwell, *In Search of Enemies*, 1978, p. 188.

22. Ellen Ray, William Schaap, Karl van Meter and Louis Wolf (eds), *Dirty Work 2*, 1979, pp. 274–5; *Southern Africa*, June 1974; Mangold, *Cold Warrior*, p. 407; 'Opmerkings oor sekere aspekte van Suid-Africa se buitelandse beleid deur 'n senior Franse amptenaar', 1970 [South African National Archives, BTS 1/30/3]. Dr Ed Stanley drew this document to my attention.

23. *The Times*, 18 March 1969; interviews with Robert Gordon Bruce, 12 July 1998, 18 June 2002.

24. Winter, *Inside BOSS*, pp. 264–71.

25. Forum World Features, 6 September 1969; Johannesburg *Star*, 26 June 1969, 17 September 1981; Winter, *Inside BOSS*, pp. 274–7; 'Charles Metterlink' (R.G. Bruce), letter to 'Florrie' (G. Winter), 26 April 1970 [Gordon Winter Papers].

26. Winter, *Inside BOSS*, p. 277; 'Charles Metterlink' (R.G. Bruce), letter to 'Florrie' (G. Winter), 12 April 1970; 'Florrie' (G. Winter), letter to 'Charles Metterlink' (R.G. Bruce), 19 May 1970 [Gordon Winter Papers]; *Guardian*, 2 February 2000; Herbstein, *White Lies*, p. 189.

27. 'Dennis' (R.G. Bruce), letter to 'Margaret Brears' (G. Winter), 5 July 1970; 'Charles Metterlink' (R.G. Bruce), letter to 'Florrie' (G. Winter), 26 April 1970 [Gordon Winter Papers].

28. Winter, *Inside BOSS*, pp. 278–9; 'Charles Metterlink' (R.G. Bruce), letter to 'Margaret Brears' (G. Winter), 18 August 1970 [Gordon Winter Papers]; Gordon Winter, 'Inside BOSS and After', *Lobster*, No. 18, 1989.

29. 'Charles Metterlink' (R.G. Bruce), letter to 'Margaret Brears' (G. Winter), 3 September 1970 [Gordon Winter Papers]; Winter, *Inside BOSS*, p. 280.

30. Johannesburg *Star*, 18 September 1981; *The Times*, 26 July 1988; interview with Robert Gordon Bruce, 12 July 1998.

31. *BOSS: The First 5 Years*, p. 5; Johannesburg *Sunday Times*, 5 May 1974, 22 October 1978.

32. *BOSS: The First 5 Years*, p. 17; Flower, op. cit., p. 153; *Observer*, 13 January 1980; *Now*, 5 October 1979; Winter, *Inside BOSS*, p. 558; Hamann, op. cit., p. 9. James M. Roherty, *State Security in South Africa*, 1992, p. 88: MID criticism of van den Bergh and BOSS included the assessment that 'van den Bergh was simply a policeman' and 'the police are dressed up in uniforms and calling themselves generals'.

33. Potgieter, *Report*, p. 10. This was clearly connected to the plan noted by Bob de Quehen in August 1962 (see page 14).

34. Hamann, op. cit., p. 7; Flower, op. cit., p. 154.

35. Annette Seegers, *The Military in the Making of Modern South Africa*, 1996, p. 138; Hamann, op. cit., p. 9; Eugene de Kock, as told to Jeremy Gordin, *A Long Night's Damage*, 1998, p. 58.

36. Mervyn Rees, interview with Eschel Rhoodie, transcript, 1979; Winter, *Inside BOSS*, p. 296; Al J. Venter, *War Dog*, 2003, p. 278.

37. Christopher Andrew and Vasili Mitrokhin, *The Mitrokhin Archive II*, 2005, pp. 442–3; Rees, interview with Rhoodie, transcript, 1979.

38. David Martin and Phyllis Johnson, *The Struggle for Zimbabwe*, 1981, pp. 127–9; Georgina Sinclair, '"Settlers' men" or policemen? The ambiguities of "colonial policing", 1945–80', unpublished doctoral thesis, 2002, p. 139; Rees, interview with Rhoodie, transcript, 1979; Pogrund, op. cit., p. 289.

39. O'Meara, op. cit., p. 220; Hamann, op. cit., p. 16. Studies of the Angolan war, 1975–6, include: Piero Gleijeses, *Conflicting Missions*, 2002; Edward George, *The Cuban Intervention in Angola*, 2005. See also Fred Bridgland, *Jonas Savimbi: A Key to Africa*, 1986; Jan Breytenbach, *Forged in Battle*, 1986, and *They Live By The Sword*, 1990.

40. Hamann, op. cit., pp. 16–17; Henry Kissinger, *Years of Renewal*, 1999, p. 795.

41. Kissinger, op. cit., pp. 806–8; Hamann, op. cit., p. 23; Stockwell, op. cit., p. 75.

42. Hamann, op. cit., p. 24; Sanders, op. cit., pp. 135, 140; O'Meara, op. cit., p. 220.

43. Gleijeses, op. cit., p. 301; Stockwell, op. cit., pp. 185–6; Rees, interview with Rhoodie, transcript, 1979.

44. Gleijeses, op. cit., pp. 308–11, 320–1; Sanders, op. cit., pp. 141–4; Stockwell, op. cit., p. 202; Hamann, op. cit., pp. 37, 39.

45. Sanders, op. cit., p. 145; Deon Geldenhuys, *The Diplomacy of Isolation*, 1984, pp. 80–3; Rees, interview with Rhoodie, transcript, 1979; O'Meara, op. cit., pp. 221–2; Hamann, op. cit., p. 44; Rhoodie, *REAL Information*, p. 146. See also A.P.J. van Rensburg, *The Tangled Web*, 1977, p. 107.

46. *Daily Mail*, 22 December 1976; *Private Eye*, 7 January 1977; Margaret Thatcher, *The Path to Power*, 1995, p. 361; *Spectator*, 15 November 1975. See also Robert Moss, *Chile's Marxist Experiment*, 1973 and *The Collapse of Democracy*, 1975.

47. *Sunday Telegraph*, 30 January-20 February 1977; Robert Moss, 'Friends in Need: Five Good Reasons for Standing by South Africa', *Politics Today*, No. 3, May–June 1978, p. 25; Interview with Robert Moss, 23 October 1997. See also Arnaud de Borchgrave and Robert Moss, *The Spike*, 1980, and Robert Moss, *Dreamgates*, 1998. The 'About the Author' section of *Dreamgates* informed the reader: 'Robert Moss is a lifelong dream explorer, a shamanic counsellor, a best-selling novelist, and a student of the Western Mystery traditions . . . He teaches innovative programs in dreamwork, shamanism, and creativity in Europe and Australia as well as across the United States. He was guided by dreams to his present home near Albany, New York.'

48. Stockwell, op. cit., pp. 181, 187.

49. *To the Point*, 5 December 1975; *Newsweek*, 17 May 1976.

CHAPTER 3: THE BRITISH DESK

1. Alan Judd, *Short of Glory*, 1984, pp. 16–17. The novelist and motoring correspondent of the *Spectator*, 'Alan Judd' is the pseudonym employed by former MI6 official Alan Petty (Stephen Dorril, *MI6: Fifty Years of Special Operations*, 2000, p. 750).

2. Simon Berthon, *Secret History: Harold Wilson, the Final Days*, Channel 4, 15 August 1996; *Independent on Sunday*, 18 August 1996; Simon Freeman with Barrie Penrose, *Rinkagate*, 1996, p. 232.

3. Mark Israel, *South African Political Exile in the United Kingdom*, 1999, p. 184.

4. Matthew Nkoana, *Crisis in the Revolution*, 1969, pp. 8–9, 24, 27–8; Paul Rose, *The Backbencher's Dilemma*, 1981, pp. 167–9. *BBC History*, September 2003, reported that documents discovered at the Public Record Office have revealed that A.K. Chesterton, the director of propaganda for the British Union of Fascists in the 1930s and the founder of Britain's National Front in 1967, was in regular correspondence with van den Bergh. The relationship started when RI built links with Chesterton's League of Empire Loyalists. In 1964, the League disrupted meetings of the A-AM. Chesterton, who regularly wintered

in the Republic, employed the League to spy on South African exiles in Britain and gather intelligence on the financial backers of the A-AM. In particular, Chesterton helped RI assemble a dossier on Sir Robert Birley. The documents were not, in fact, government papers but part of a private collection that had been bequeathed to the Public Record Office. They have not yet been made available to the public.

5. Israel, op. cit., p. 185; Wade's unpublished history has disappeared from the Anti-Apartheid Archive at Rhodes House, University of Oxford. Winter, *Inside BOSS*, pp. 155–6, 158–9, 163–8, 171–5, 180, 182–4.

6. Rose, op. cit., pp. 163–5; Nkoana, op. cit., pp. 18–19; *Observer*, 12 December 1971.

7. *Observer*, 12 December 1971; *The Times*, 26 July 1967, 1 January 1998. Robin Blackburn told Detective Superintendent Gilbert during questioning that 'I am involved with South African Intelligence and that's all I have to say.' Apparently, Rhodesia could no longer afford £125 a month with expenses and the South African Jan Van Tonder 'is my boss at the moment'. Blackburn had been asked to investigate 'African organisations' and 'Terry Bell, the communist barred from South Africa' (Robin Blackburn, Police Statement, to Detective Superintendent Gilbert, 25 May 1962) [CRIM 1/4718].

8. *Observer*, 12 December 1971; Rose, op. cit., p. 165. Fairer-Smith was not named during the Blackburn–Keenan court case. On Argen in the 1970s, see *Private Eye*, 28 November 1975; *Time Out*, 19 August 1977.

9. *World in Action*, ITV, December 1971; 'Twenty Four Hours: South African Spies', BBC 2, December 1971; *Observer*, 14 November, 12 December 1971; *Sunday Times*, 7 January 1973; Rose, op. cit., p. 176.

10. *Guardian*, 26 March 1973; Michael Morris, *Terrorism*, 1971, pp. 125, 175. Morris had been discovered after Eric Abraham had photographed him watching a demonstration outside South Africa House.

11. Rose, op. cit., pp. 172–5; 'During the course of an internal investigation into an alleged leakage of information to BOSS . . . it came out that Donker had three unreported meetings with Bouwer. Donker . . . said that there were only two and that they were both entirely innocent . . . At the time of Donker's demotion, his colleagues felt that other policemen were in an even more compromising position concerning their relationships with the South Africans'; *Guardian*, 15 March 1972; *Sunday Times*, 7 January 1973; Winter, *Inside BOSS*, p. 281.

12. *Sunday Times*, 15 May 1977; William Raynor and Geoff Allen, 'Smear – The Thorpe Affair', unpublished manuscript, 1978, p. 89; Barrie Penrose and Roger Courtiour, *The Pencourt File*, 1978, pp. 23–4.

13. Barbara Castle, *The Castle Diaries*, 1990, pp. 734; Raynor, op. cit., p. 90.

14. Penrose, op. cit., p. 13; Raynor, op. cit., pp. 92–3.

15. *Sunday Times*, 15 May 1977; Penrose, op. cit., pp. 4, 9, 13.

16. Penrose, op. cit., p. 409; *Morning Star*, 28 March 1979; Freeman, op. cit., pp. 309-10.

17. *Sunday Times*, 12 February 1978; *Listener*, 9 February 1978; Pimlott, op. cit., p. 696; Philip Ziegler, *Wilson: The Authorised Life*, 1995, p. 501. See also *The Times*, 2 February 1978.

18. *London Review of Books*, 2 March 1989.

19. Peter Wright, *Spycatcher*, 1987, pp. 369-72; Paul Foot, *Who Framed Colin Wallace?*, 1989, pp. 32-43. Colin Wallace's 'Clockwork Orange' notes, compiled in 1974, included a list of 'Labour policies which endanger Britain'. The first five items on the list were '1), Defence Budget cuts. 2). Nuclear weapons. 3). South Africa. 4). Anti-Arab. 5). Anti-South Africa/Rhodesia' (p. 43); Stephen Dorril and Robin Ramsay, *Smear! Wilson and the Secret State*, 1991, p. 304; *Rand Daily Mail*, 2 July 1979; *The Times*, 8 June 1981. Chapman Pincher, *Inside Story*, 1978, revealed that Wilson had privately admitted 'that his evidence for the South African interference was first based on information given to him by the Cabinet Office from MI5. "There had been suspicions that people used by BOSS had been paying attention to certain black Commonwealth diplomats in London . . . As regards Thorpe, MI5 could not say that the South Africans were guilty but they could not say they were innocent either"' (p. 368). Pincher continued: 'Caryl de Wet, the South African Ambassador in London at the time, was a personal friend of mine and he assured me after inquiries in Pretoria that no such embarrassing information existed and that the South African government and its Intelligence agency were totally at a loss to explain Wilson's behaviour' (p. 370). Chapman Pincher, *The Truth About Dirty Tricks*, 1991, p. 125, disclosed that Wilson was 'extravagantly suspicious' of BOSS and 'when one of his senior advisers told him that burglars had stolen his longcase clock Wilson replied, "South Africa without a doubt. You'll find it in the South African Embassy."' Leigh, op. cit., p. 235, gave little credence to the South African connection, claiming that 'Wilson . . . became lost in conspiracy theories – he launched a bizarre attempt to blame his misfortunes, and those of the Liberal leader Jeremy Thorpe, on South African Intelligence. He was encouraged in this belief by MI6.'

20. Raynor, op. cit., p. 15; Jeremy Thorpe, *In My Own Time*, 1999, pp. 139-40, 146, 174-5; Peter Bessell, *Cover-Up*, 1980, pp. 98, 268; Joe Haines, *Glimmers of Twilight*, 2003, p. 147; Winter, *Inside BOSS*, pp. 394-411, 414, 447-8.

21. Bessell, op. cit., pp. 375-6, 482; Raynor, op. cit., pp. 65, 68; Cyril Smith, *Big Cyril*, 1977, pp. 194-5, 205-6.

22. *Private Eye*, 17 December 1978, 15 May 1987; Bessell, op. cit., pp. 44-6, 125-31, 330, 415, 552, 563; Winter, *Inside BOSS*, p. 620; interview with Gordon Winter, 28 September 2005; interview with William Raynor, 29 October 2005; Arnold Goodman, *Tell Them I'm On My Way*, 1993, pp. 73-7, 219-25.

23. There are numerous accounts of the Thorpe trial, in addition to Bessell's

Cover-up, Lewis Chester, Magnus Linklater and David May, *Jeremy Thorpe: A Secret Life*, 1979, and Auberon Waugh's *The Last Word*, 1980, are useful. The committal process at Minehead is handled well by Peter Chippindale and David Leigh, *The Thorpe Committal*, 1979, p. 95.

24. *The Times*, 3 March 1990.

25. Waugh, op. cit., pp. 124–5; Gleijeses, op. cit., pp. 301–2; Sanders, op. cit., p. 140; Hain, *Sing the Beloved Country*, 1996, pp. 100–2.

26. Hain, op. cit., pp. 74, 102. Ross McWhirter, who was later active in the right-wing National Association for Freedom, with Robert Moss (see page 54), was famous, with his twin brother Norris, for the *Guinness Book of World Records*, and the BBC television programme *Record-Breakers*. Ross McWhirter was killed in 1975 by the IRA. For an account of both the sports campaign and the 1972 prosecution, see Derek Humphry, *The Cricket Conspiracy*, 1975.

27. Hain, op. cit., pp. 103–6; Peter Hain, 'South African Agent Disruption of Liberal Party' (memorandum), 24 February 1976; Raynor, op. cit., pp. 80–1.

28. Hain, op. cit., pp. 106–7, 109–10; Raynor, op. cit., p. 114.

29. Winter, *Inside BOSS*, pp. 460–1, 465; Hain, op. cit., p. 122.

30. Epstein, op. cit., pp. 132–3, 137; *Rand Daily Mail*, 18 May 1976.

31. *Rand Daily Mail*, 18–19, 21 May 1976; Epstein, op. cit., pp. 137–8. On the hijacking, see Hocking, op. cit., pp. 447–60; Fred Kamil, *The Diamond Empire*, 1979, pp. 186–99.

32. Epstein, op. cit., p. 138; *Rand Daily Mail*, 19–20 May 1976; *Time Out*, 26 September 1975; Raynor, op. cit., p. 88; Kamil, op. cit., p. 231.

33. Raynor, op. cit., p. 87; Kamil, op. cit., pp. 232, 234–5, 238; Hain, op. cit., pp. 103–4; *Time Out*, 30 April, 14 May 1976.

34. *Time Out*, 14 May 1976; *Rand Daily Mail*, 21 May 1976.

35. Kamil, op. cit., p. 243: 'I felt no responsibility for Wyatt [and] Anita Sassin . . . They had been acting on their own without any instruction from me'; Raynor, op. cit., p. 88; Hain, op. cit., p. 107; Winter, *Inside BOSS*, p. 107; Johannesburg *Sunday Express*, 25 March 1973.

36. Bessell, op. cit., p. 292; *Daily Mirror*, 31 January 1976. There is some suggestion that when Harold Wilson contacted Barrie Penrose in May 1976 in order to facilitate an investigation of the South African connection, he had intended to speak with *John* Penrose, the author of the *Mirror* exclusive on Gordon Winter. Winter published his version of the Thorpe–Scott relationship in the Johannesburg *Sunday Express*, 22 February 1976.

37. *The Times*, 21 May 1976.

38. Winter, *Inside BOSS*, p. 474; *Guardian*, 30 June 1979; Chester, op. cit., p. 160. The *Mail on Sunday*, 18 January 2004, described Lee Tracey as 'a long-serving MI6 agent . . . [who] was first named . . . over his involvement with the Profumo scandal of 1963'.

39. *Guardian*, 15 May 1976; *Sunday People*, 23 May 1976; Penrose, op. cit., p. 41.

40. *The Times*, 21 May 1976; *Guardian*, 24 May 1976; Raynor, op. cit., p. 144; *Time Out*, 21 May 1976.

41. *Sunday People*, 23 May 1976; *Guardian*, 24 May 1976.

42. *Time Out*, 6 August 1976; Penrose, op. cit., pp. 44–54; *Daily Express*, 20 May 1976.

43. *Sunday Telegraph*, 23 May 1976; Gordon Carr's previous work included a television film, broadcast on the BBC in 1973, and book, *The Angry Brigade*, 1975, on Britain's anarcho-terrorists; Raynor, op. cit., pp. 158, 161–2; Penrose, op. cit., p. 55. Peter Deeley, who had investigated BOSS for the *Observer* in 1971, commented in *The Times*, 22 May 1976: 'During the campaign to expose BOSS . . . we came across individuals prepared to tell totally fraudulent stories for publication. Three times in as many weeks we were "fed" false information which, if it had been published, would have destroyed the credibility of the case we had built up.'

44. Hain, op. cit., pp. 111–12; Winter, *Inside BOSS*, pp. 467–72; *Private Eye*, 9 July 1976.

45. Chester, op. cit., pp. 357, 359; Peter Cook's parody of Sir Joseph Canley OBE, the Honourable Mr Justice Cantley, the judge in the Thorpe case, was acute: 'We have been forced to listen to the pitiful whining of Mr Norma St. John Scott, a scrounger, parasite, pervert, a worm, a self-confessed player of the pink oboe. A man, or woman, who by his, or her, own admission chews pillows. It would be hard to imagine, ladies and gentlemen of the jury, a more discredited and embittered man, a more unreliable witness' ('The Secret Policeman's Ball', 27–30 June 1979). See also *News of the World*, 31 May, 6 June 1981.

46. Sanders, op. cit., p. 202: Ian Wright, the *Guardian*'s foreign editor in 1976 recalled that the newspaper was 'deeply scarred by [the experience]. I thought we've got to be careful with those bastards'; The *Observer*, 7 September 1980, reported that 'according to one source, BOSS had an informer – known only as "110" – inside a leading anti-South African movement in London for around 10 years, passing on membership names and information about funding and internecine splits. That [also] ended in 1976.' The *Observer* explained that an example of 'common interest' was that in September 1978 'at a critical moment in Rhodesia, the British wanted South Africa to play the role of intermediaries . . . Two senior BOSS men arrived secretly in Britain for discussions with British security officers and were housed in a large country home near the South Coast'; *Lobster*, No. 40, Winter 2000–1; Simon Berthon, *Secret History: Harold Wilson, the Final Days*, Channel 4, 15 August 1996.

47. Foot, *Who Framed Colin Wallace?*, p. 252; Hain, op. cit., pp. 120, 123.

48. Bessell, op. cit., p. 178. The BBC film, connected to the Pencourt project and supervised by producer Gordon Carr, was abandoned; as was Penguin's publication of William Raynor and Geoff Allen's 'Smear'. In March 2006, the

BBC screened a docu-drama which featured interviews with, and portrayals of, the Pencourt journalists. The 90-minute film ignored the South African connection (Paul Dwyer, *The Plot Against Harold Wilson*, BBC2, 16 March 2006).

49. *Citizen*, 27 May 1977; interview with William Raynor, 29 October 2005.

50. Winter, *Inside BOSS*, pp. 457-9; interview with William Raynor, 29 October 2005.

CHAPTER 4: THE Z SQUAD

1. John le Carré, *The Spy Who Came in from the Cold*, 1963, p. 19.

2. Mervyn Rees and Chris Day, *Muldergate*, 1980, p. 186; O'Meara, op. cit., p. 193.

3. Sanders, op. cit., p. 168; *Mail & Guardian*, 29 November 1996; *Weekly Mail*, 13 June 1986.

4. *Rand Daily Mail*, 17 August 1976; *Citizen*, 27 October 1976.

5. Stephen Ellis and Tsepo Sechaba, *Comrades against Apartheid*, 1992, pp. 82-4; Alan Brooks and Jeremy Brickhill, *Whirlwind Before the Storm*, 1980, pp. 248, 250, 256, 260; Thomas Karis and Gail M. Gerhart, *From Protest to Challenge*, Vol. 5, 1997, p. 168, citing an estimate by the Cillie Commission, noted 'by the end of February 1977, unrest deaths stood officially at 575 – 491 Africans, 75 Coloureds, two whites and one Indian'. In May 1977, the South African Institute of Race Relations estimated that 618 people had died. Brooks and Brickhill recorded that during the eleven weeks from 16 June to 30 August the police in Soweto admitted firing '16,433 rounds of ammunition (made up of 8,702 rounds from R1 automatic rifles, 732 rounds from .38 revolvers, 1,750 from .32 calibre weapons, 2,650 from 9 mm parabellums and 2,529 from shotguns)' (p. 255). Peter Magubane, an African photographer, who captured one of the iconic images of the Soweto uprising, told me that the greatest picture that he failed to get was of South African policemen being photographed, clutching their weapons, standing on top of a mound of dead bodies, as if they had been on a hunting trip. Magubane recalled hiding in the boot of a car, attempting to steal a snap of this grotesque celebration of colonial violence (interview with Peter Magubane, 20 May 1995). The only other places that I have heard of such an inhuman glorification of death being practised were equally neo-colonial: Vietnam, Israel and Iraq, post-2003.

6. Gavin Cawthra, *Policing South Africa*, 1986, p. 19. Jimmy Kruger claimed that the South African police had visited the US 'to study riot control', but this was denied by the US State Department (*Washington Post*, 6 November 1976).

7. Truth & Reconciliation Commission, *Truth and Reconciliation Commission of South Africa Report*, Vol. 2, 1998, pp. 205-9; Madeleine Fullard, 'State repres-

sion in the 1960s', South African Democracy Education Trust, *The Road to Democracy in South Africa*, Vol. 1: *1960–1970*, 2004, p. 363, reported that there were twenty deaths in detention between 1960 and 1969. Fullard added that there were 101 executions for 'sabotage and terrorism' between 1961 and 1968. All those executed were men of whom only one, John Harris (the 1964 Station bomber), was white. All the executions related to incidents during the period 1960–4 and sixty-one of the executed were affiliated to the PAC. Between 1968 and 1979, no South Africans were executed for 'sabotage and terrorism' (pp. 381–2); Winter, *Inside BOSS*, pp. 589–97; George Bizos, *No One to Blame?*, 1998, p. 37. See also Imtiaz Cajee's examination of the murder of his uncle, Ahmed Timol, *Timol: A Quest for Justice*, 2005.

8. TRC, *Report*, Vol. 2, pp. 205–9, 211.

9. *Guardian*, 8 March 1977.

10. TRC, *Report*, Vol. 2, pp. 195–6; Ellert, op. cit., p. 80. The fact that DMI operatives received their interrogation training in Italy provides some explanation for why General Gianadelio Maletti, the 'commander of the counter-intelligence section of the [Italian] military intelligence service from 1971 to 1975', has lived since 1980 in South Africa (*Guardian*, 26 March 2001).

11. Winter, *Inside BOSS*, pp. 307–9, 312; *Rand Daily Mail*, 30 June 1979, 4 February 1980; Rose, op. cit., p. 166; *Private Eye*, 28 November 1975: South African journalist Bob Hitchcock, who discovered Wallace's body, recalled: 'His revolver, which he always carried with him – "I keep it under the pillow at nights" he once told me – was missing.' *Rand Daily Mail*, 2 February 1980, revealed that in 1969 an antique restorer in Oxford, England had claimed on a British television programme that he was a 'double agent' for Kenya and South Africa. He had claimed that South African intelligence had been involved in the assassination of Kenyan Cabinet Minister Tom Mboya.

12. *Private Eye*, 28 November 1975.

13. TRC, *Report*, Vol. 2, pp. 18–19, 99–100; Winter, *Inside BOSS*, pp. 563–4; *BOSS: The First 5 Years*, p. 37.

14. 'Dr Robert van Schalkwijk Smit' election leaflet, November 1977; 'Biographical Statement: Robert van Schalkwijk Smit', undated [Johannesburg *Star* Newspaper Library]; *Financial Mail*, 23 January 1976.

15. Rees and Day, op. cit., pp. 13–14; *New York Times*, 24 November 1977; Winter, *Inside BOSS*, pp. 500–1; *Citizen*, 25 November 1977.

16. Gordon Winter, 'Smit Memorandum', originally written in 1979 for Jacobus Kemp, later supplied to Allister Sparks, *Rand Daily Mail* [Gordon Winter Papers]; conversation with senior police detective, 8 June 1999.

17. *Cape Times*, 21 November 1980; Winter, 'Smit Memorandum' [Gordon Winter Papers].

18. Johannesburg *Sunday Times*, 27 November 1977; *Financial Mail*, 23 March 1979; Rees and Day, op. cit., p. 16.

19. *Rapport*, 18 May 1978; *Rand Daily Mail*, 20 November 1978; *Euromoney*, June 1978; interview with James Srodes/Lewis James, 11 April 1996.

20. Johannesburg *Sunday Express*, 5, 19 November 1978; Johannesburg *Star*, 17 November 1978; Stefan Aust, *The Baader–Meinhof Group*, 1987, pp. 535–40. In West Germany's Stammheim prison, Baader–Meinhof Gang members Andrea Baader, Gudrun Ensslin and Jean-Carl Raspe were either murdered or committed suicide on 18 October 1977, a little over a month before the murder of the Smits; *Rand Daily Mail*, 21 November 1978.

21. *Rand Daily Mail*, 21 November 1978; Erasmus, *Report*, December 1978, pp. 83, 91; Winter, *Inside BOSS*, p. 559; Rees and Day, op. cit., pp. 16–17.

22. Johannesburg *Sunday Times*, 25 May 1980.

23. Ken Owen, evidence to the Erasmus Commission, 1979 [South African National Archives]; *Argus*, 20 March 1979; *Guardian*, 21 March 1979; *Daily Telegraph*, 22 March 1979.

24. Rees and Day, op. cit., p. 176; *Daily Telegraph*, 19 June 1979; *Guardian*, 26 February 1980.

25. *Financial Mail*, 23 March 1979; Winter, *Inside BOSS*, pp. 502–3.

26. Winter, *Inside BOSS*, pp. 511–13; *Rand Daily Mail*, 9, 11 September 1980; 25 February 1981.

27. Johannesburg *Star*, 6 December 1992.

28. *Mail & Guardian*, 22 August 1997; *Noseweek*, No. 2, July 1993.

29. Conversation with Martin Welz, 13 October 2004; interview with Mike Louw, 3 December 2003.

30. TRC, *Report*, Vol. 2, pp. 268–9. None of the named men responded to the TRC's findings as the *Report* recorded: 'the commission received no amnesty applications in respect of the Smit's killings.'

31. Johannesburg *Star*, 6 February 1999; Jerry Dan, *Ultimate Deception*, 2003, p. 360.

32. Interview with Deneys Rhoodie, 3 April 1999.

33. *Sunday Times*, 15 January 1978; *Newsweek*, 23 January 1978; *Independent on Sunday*, 15 July 1989; Richard Turner, *The Eye of the Needle*, 1978, originally published in 1972.

34. TRC, *Report*, Vol. 3, p. 182.

35. Winter, *Inside BOSS*, pp. 564–5; *Independent on Sunday*, 15 July 1989.

36. *Independent on Sunday*, 15 July 1989.

37. Breytenbach, op. cit., p. 296.

CHAPTER 5: MULDERGATE: A QUIET COUP

1. *Capetonian*, Vol. 1, No. 3, February 1979.

2. Sanders, op. cit., pp. 55–7, 73; D. Geldenhuys, op. cit., pp. 84–5; *Daily Telegraph*, 29 July 1993; Eschel Rhoodie, *The REAL Information Scandal*, 1983, pp. 570, 627; interview with Mervyn Rees, 9 May 1995.

3. Rees and Day, op. cit., pp. 163–4.

4. Paul Blackstock, *The Strategy of Subversion*, 1964, p. 303; Winter, *Geheim agent*, p. 399; Sanders, op. cit., p. 56; Eschel Rhoodie, *The Paper Curtain*, 1969, pp. 10, 186.

5. Les de Villiers, *Secret Information*, 1980, pp. 77–8.

6. Sanders, op. cit., pp. 55, 57–9; Rhoodie, *REAL Information*, p. 63; Rees and Day, op. cit., p. 172.

7. de Villiers, op. cit., pp. 65–6; D. Geldenhuys, op. cit., pp. 85–7; Rees and Day, op. cit., p. 219.

8. de Villiers, op. cit., pp. 50, 110; Rees and Day, op. cit., pp. 57, 174; O'Meara, op. cit., pp. 212, 216, added that 'the original (black) "Pangaman" perpetrated a series of brutal rapes and murders of white courting couples in the Pretoria area in the late 1950s and early 1960s. He was later hanged.'

9. Interview with Les de Villiers, 18 April 1996; Rees and Day, op. cit., p. 6, described what emerged from the Information scandal as 'a picture of moral hypocrisy in which absolute power acted as an aphrodisiac to men who used their influence to seduce women both in South Africa and abroad'; interview with James Srodes/Lewis James, 11 April 1996.

10. *Capetonian*, February 1979.

11. O'Meara, op. cit., p. 214; Sanders, op. cit., pp. 60, 66–7; Hendrik van den Bergh, evidence to the Erasmus Commission, 1978 [South African National Archives]; *Rand Daily Mail*, 16 May 1980.

12. Rees and Day, op. cit., pp. 10, 84–6; *Leadership*, November 1995.

13. Rees and Day, op. cit., pp. 197, 199; David Abramson, evidence to the Erasmus Commission, 1978 [South African National Archives].

14. Rees and Day, op. cit., pp. 49, 190. Motion pictures suspected of being Info-manipulated include *Gold*, 1974, directed by Peter R. Hunt, starring Roger Moore and Susannah York; and *Zulu Dawn*, 1979, directed by Douglas Hickox, starring Burt Lancaster and Peter O'Toole; Rhoodie revealed that *Tigers Don't Cry*, 1978 (also known as *Target of an Assassin*, *African Rage*, *The Long Shot* and *Fatal Assassin*), directed by Peter Collinson, and starring Anthony Quinn; and *Game for Vultures*, 1980, directed by James Fargo, starring Richard Harris and Joan Collins, had included Info investment. The greatest of all the Info-connected films, *The Wild Geese*, 1979, directed by Andrew McLagen, starring Richard Burton, Richard Harris and Roger Moore, included a photograph of Moise Tshombe in the main titles which had been taken by Info operative Karl Breyer. Tshombe was the Congolese politician who led the secessionist Katanga province in the early 1960s.

15. Sanders, op. cit., pp. 60, 67; Rhoodie, *REAL Information*, pp. 391–4.

16. Rees and Day, op. cit., pp. 198–9; *Nation*, 14 April 1979, 19 April 1980; Karen Rothmyer, 'The McGoff Grab', *Columbia Journalism Review*,

November–December 1979; Hillary Rodham Clinton, *Living History*, 2004, pp. 445–6; Karen Rothmyer, 'Citizen Scaife', July/August 1981.

17. Rees and Day, op. cit., pp. 194, 198; *Guardian*, 13 December 1978; Milchan has never hidden his role in the Israel–South Africa relationship of the 1970s. In 1993, he told *Premiere* magazine that his involvement with apartheid South Africa had been at the request of the Israeli government. However, he added that after visiting the Republic he came to the conclusion that 'a Jew cannot live with apartheid' (*Premiere*, June 1993). Seven years later, he told CBS television that in the 1970s: 'I was playing an important role in the system of collecting money from South Africa' (CBS, *60 Minutes: Who is Arnon Milchan?*, September 2000); Sanders, op. cit., p. 68; Rees, interview with Rhoodie, transcript, 1979. Mulholland told me that he had not been informed of this prospective employment (interview with Stephen Mulholland, 30 September 1996).

18. O'Meara, op. cit., p. 214; Rees and Day, op. cit., pp. 188–9, 199–200, 203; Rees, interview with Rhoodie, transcript, 1979; *Private Eye*, 13 April 1979. See also Dr Ferry A. Hoogendijk, 'Muldergate: The Eschel Rhoodie Story', *Elseviers*, 28 July–18 August 1979, news agency transcript.

19. Rees and Day, op. cit., p. 200; Rees, interview with Rhoodie, transcript, 1979; Interview with Donald deKieffer, 12 April 1996; *Southern Africa*, September 1976, pp. 14–15.

20. de Villiers, op. cit., pp. 59, 97–8; Johannesburg *Sunday Times*, 17 November 1991, included extracts from former South African Ambassador to the United States Donald Sole's unpublished political memoir. Sole criticised the 'pusillanimity' of Foreign Affairs 'in its attitude to the former Department of Information . . . His ire was particularly raised in March 1978 when [a] Cabinet Minister . . . visited the US under the auspices of the Department of Information without any consultation with the embassy at all . . . Incredibly, Mr Sole was never informed about the scale or intentions of South African military activities in Angola, and . . . had to rely on information from press briefings and the US State Department and National Security Council to establish what was really happening.' Rees and Day, op. cit., pp. 180–1; *Observer*, 21 January 1979.

21. Rees and Day, op. cit., pp. 182–3; on Lejeune, see Stanley, 'France and Africa, 1944–90', thesis, 2004, p. 260, citing Jacques Marchand, *La Propagande de l'apartheid: comment l'Afrique du Sud se crée une image de marque*, 1985, p. 183; de Villiers, op. cit., pp. 94–5: Albie Geldenhuys was Mike Geldenhuys's son: 'Albie came from France, a pale, debonair youth with a bulging briefcase full of pseudonyms and front organisations . . . This brilliant young man, who not only spoke fluent French, but had also adopted French ways, was obviously so involved with Information's activities that he had no time for BOSS. Soon Eschel organised it so that he worked for us alone.' Rhoodie, *REAL Information*, pp. 122–31; D. Geldenhuys, op. cit., pp. 38–9; O'Meara, op. cit., p. 192; Rees, interview with Rhoodie, transcript, 1979.

22. Rhoodie, *REAL Information*, pp. 181–90; *New York Times*, 21 October 1977; Chris Logan, *Celebrity Surgeon*, 2003, p. 241: 'The truth was that Barnard had been an enthusiastic ally of Eschel Rhoodie . . . and a willing tool of the apartheid regime.' Gary Player also needed little encouragement. For a summary of his political philosophy, see *Grand Slam Golf*, 1966, pp. 7–13; *To the Point*, 2 April 1976; *Financial Times*, 5 December 2001.

23. *Daily Telegraph*, 13 August 2001; Rees, interview with Rhoodie, transcript, 1979; General Sir Walter Walker, *The Bear at the Back Door*, 1978.

24. Eschel Rhoodie, *P.W. Botha*, 1989, p. 29; Retief van Rooyen, Les de Villiers, evidence to the Erasmus Commission, 1978 [South African National Archives]; *Rand Daily Mail*, 16 May 1980; interview with Gerard Ludi, 8 June 1999. For a full list of the Information Department's secret projects, see Sanders, op. cit., pp. 233–7. See also Julian Burgess, Esau du Plessis, Roger Murray, Peter Fraenkel, Rosanne Harvey, John Laurence, Peter Ripken and Barbara Rogers, *The Great White Hoax*, 1977; John C. Laurence, *Race Propaganda and South Africa*, 1979; Derrick Knight, *Beyond the Pale*, 1982.

25. Sanders, op. cit., pp. 62–3; de Villiers, op. cit. p. 152.

26. Rees and Day, op. cit., p. 2; Erasmus, *Report*, December 1978, p. 32.

27. Rhoodie, *REAL Information*, p. 420; interview with Gerard Ludi, 8 June 1999; Rees and Day, op. cit., pp. 7, 8, 15.

28. Rees and Day, op. cit., p. 111; O'Meara, op. cit., pp. 233, 237.

29. Rees and Day, op. cit. pp. 18, 20, 26, 112.

30. Sanders, op. cit., p. 64; Rees and Day, op. cit., pp. 22, 28.

31. *Citizen*, 16–18 May 1978, 4 November 1980; *Rand Daily Mail*, 24, 26–28 June 1978, 15 May 1980; *Cape Times*, 22 October 1980; Hendrik van den Bergh, evidence to the Erasmus Commission, 1978 [South African National Archives].

32. O'Meara, op. cit., pp. 234–5; Rees and Day, op. cit., pp. 68–9, 73; *Die Transvaler*, 23 September 1978; Erasmus, *Report*, December 1978, p. 83.

33. O'Meara, op. cit., pp. 237–40; Rees and Day, op. cit., p. 72; Rhoodie, *P.W. Botha*, pp. 42–6.

34. *Rand Daily Mail*, 3 November 1978; Rees and Day, op. cit., pp. 99–101, 121, 138, 150.

35. Erasmus, *Report*, December 1978, pp. 68–74, 91.

36. Rees and Day, op. cit., pp. 132, 154–210, 214; *Rand Daily Mail*, 4 June 1979; David Harrison and David Dimbleby, *Tonight Special: Interview with Eschel Rhoodie*, BBC 1, 21 March 1979.

37. R.B.P. Erasmus, *Interim Report of the Commission of Inquiry into Alleged Irregularities in the Former Department of Information*, March 1979, pp. 11, 18, 20; O'Meara, op. cit., p. 243; R.B.P. Erasmus, *Supplementary Report of the Commission of Inquiry into Alleged Irregularities in the Former Department of Information*, June 1979, p. 10.

38. Rees and Day, op. cit., pp. 182–84. Eschel Rhoodie revealed that 'the cork in

the bottle' was his and van den Bergh's 'term' to describe the role of John Vorster – 'he was stopping the flow of development'.

39. Rees and Day, op. cit., pp. 72, 184; David Harrison, *The White Tribe of Africa*, 1981, pp. 245–6; Johannesburg *Star*, 25 September 1988.

40. *Daily Telegraph*, 14 August 1976; Sanders, op. cit., p. 62, citing Department of Information, *Report for the Period, 1 January 1976 to 31 December 1976*.

41. *Newsweek*, 25 October 1976.

42. Sanders, op. cit., pp. 200, 206; *To the Point*, 29 October 1976; Pogrund, op. cit., p. 290.

43. Rees and Day, op. cit., pp. 215–22; Rhoodie, *REAL Information*, p. 8.

44. Pogrund, op. cit., p. 289; Winter, *Geheim agent*, p. 398.

45. Rees and Day, op. cit., pp. 163–4, 195; Jim Hougan, *Spooks*, 1979, pp. 126–7; *Indianapolis Star*, 23–27 March 1980.

46. Rees and Day, op. cit., pp. 195–6; Frances Stonor Saunders, *Who Pays the Piper*, 1999, p. 311; Brian Crozier, *Free Agent*, 1993, pp. 20–1, 55, 63, 66–7, 85–90, 225.

47. Peter Janke, 'Southern Africa: End of Empire', *Conflict Studies*, No. 52, December 1974; *Time Out*, 5 September 1975; Rees, interview with Rhoodie, transcript, 1979; Paul Lashmar and James Oliver, *Britain's Secret Propaganda War*, 1998, pp. 167–8; Crozier, op. cit., p. 176. Jonathan Bloch and Patrick Fitzgerald, *British Intelligence and Covert Action*, 1983, p. 54: 'MI6 showed a marked reluctance to supply the 1974–9 Labour government with complete reports from Southern Africa as they believed that a number of ministers were sympathetic to nationalist movements in the region, possibly jeopardising the position of their agents.'

48. Hoogendijk, *Elseviers*, 28 July–18 August 1979; *Sunday Independent*, 2 June 1997; *Africa News*, 16 December 1985, revealed that John Sears, a former Republican campaign manager who had 'directed' Ronald Reagan's presidential campaigns, unsuccessfully in 1976 and successfully in 1980 (*Rand Daily Mail*, 20 February 1981) was employed as a lobbyist by the South African Embassy for an annual fee of $500,000 with $30,000 for expenses.

49. Rhoodie, *REAL Information*, pp. 522, 524.

50. *Observer*, 25 March 1979; *City Press*, 28 March, 18 April 1993.

51. *Africa Confidential*, 4 February 1994; *Weekly Mail & Guardian*, 11, 18 February 1994; William E. Burrows and Robert Windrem, *Critical Mass*, 1994, p. 451; Arthur Jay Klinghoffer, *Oiling the Wheels of Apartheid*, 1989, p. 60; *Washington Post*, 12 July 1974, 16 February 1977. See also *Sunday Independent*, 4, 11 May 1997, originally published in Israeli newspaper, *Ha'aretz*: 'Those close to [van den Bergh] have recounted . . . [that] he spoke with affection and longing for the "house on the hill" . . . The "house" . . . that the general missed so much was the residence in the north of Tel Aviv used to secretly accommodate certain official guests of the state of Israel.'

52. *Financial Times*, 14 December 1978; *Los Angeles Magazine*, April 2000; Burrows,

op. cit., pp. 457–9. See also *The Middle East*, No. 90, April 1982, on the Kimche brothers; *Africa Confidential*, 10 June 1977, noted that 'Israeli Defence Minister General Moshe Dyan ... visited South Africa in September 1974 [and] told South Africans, "I am one of your admirers, and I believe you have very many friends ... You have first class troops and good installations in your country" ... He said there were many similarities between South Africa and Israel; nobody could fail to be impressed by the "tremendous civilisation" that was being created in South Africa.'

53. *Guardian*, 19 May 2001; Anthony Sampson, *The Arms Bazaar*, 1977; Sampson's essay on Milchan was an extract from his unpublished autobiography. Amazingly, Shawn Slovo, the daughter of South African communists Joe Slovo and Ruth First, was employed as a secretary by Milchan in 1977, this appears to provide both the link to Anthony Sampson and correlate with the beginning of Milchan's disillusionment with apartheid South Africa (*Los Angeles Magazine*, April 2000). Milchan-produced Hollywood films include: *The King of Comedy*, 1983; *Once Upon a Time in America*, 1984; *Brazil*, 1985; *Pretty Woman*, 1990; *JFK*, 1991; *Natural Born Killers*, 1994; *Heat*, 1995; and *Fight Club*, 1999.

54. Naomi Chazan, 'The Fallacies of Pragmatism: Israeli Foreign Policy Towards South Africa', *African Affairs*, Vol. 82, No. 327, April 1983, pp. 172–3; Zdenek Cervenka and Barbara Rogers, *The Nuclear Axis*, 1978, p. 311; Daniel Yergin, *The Prize*, 1991, p. 613; see also Anthony Sampson, *The Seven Sisters*, 1975; Rhoodie, *REAL Information*, pp. 114, 117.

55. Rhoodie, *REAL Information*, pp. 115–16; Andrew and Leslie Cockburn, *Dangerous Liaison*, 1992, p. 299; Chazan, 'The Fallacies of Pragmatism', *African Affairs*, April 1983, p. 170; United Nations General Assembly Resolution 3379, 10 November 1975.

56. Rhoodie, *P.W. Botha*, pp. 20–1, 95; O'Meara, op. cit., p. 307.

57. Johannesburg *Star*, 14 June 1986; *City Press*, 24 February 1991; *The Times*, 20 July 1993; Interview with Katie Rhoodie, 12 May 1999. There was some irony in Rhoodie's death on a tennis court. During his regular visits to South Africa, he had often dined with his journalistic nemesis Mervyn Rees and lectured him upon his smoking. Rees was later told by Info operative Stuart Pegg that 'we discussed the possibility of framing you. I wanted to get them to send a girl into your hotel room, get her to shout rape, rip her clothes, that sort of thing' (Harvey Tyson, *Editors Under Fire*, 1993, p. 237). It is particularly strange that Rees retained an affection for the subject of his greatest investigation. Following Rhoodie's fatal heart attack, Rees told the Johannesburg *Star*, 25 July 1993: 'In a funny sort of way, I got to like him. He was very bright and had charm, but was utterly humourless. Go easy on him.'

58. Rees and Day, op. cit., p. 136; Johannesburg *Star*, 3 February 1981; *Sunday Independent*, 6 August 1985. Van den Bergh's manuscript remains unpublished.

CHAPTER 6: INTELLIGENCE INTERREGNUM

1. Blackstock, op. cit., p. 62. See also Knightley, op. cit., pp. 297–9: 'Defectors are the lifeblood of Western intelligence agencies . . . Almost every major counter-intelligence coup since the war in the United States, France, Britain, Germany, Scandinavia and Australia has been sparked off by a defection . . . But defectors, rewarding though they may be, are also both dangerous and difficult. They are dangerous because of the need to decide whether they are genuine or acting under orders as part of a plan to plant a mole, however briefly, in your service, or to confuse and confound you with disinformation. A defector who arrives unexpectedly, who "walks in", is therefore regarded with great suspicion. Western intelligence services prefer a defector they have targeted themselves, worked on for a long while, and who comes reluctantly, preferably kicking and screaming. Even then, suspicion lingers. It is an exaggeration, but not a great one, to say that defectors are *never* trusted, and few ever achieve total acceptance from all sections of the service. The rationale is simple and cynical: if he can be "turned" once, he can be "turned" again.'

2. *To the Point*, 4 August 1978; CIA 'confessions' included Victor Marchetti and John D. Marks, *The CIA and the Cult of Intelligence*, 1974; Philip Agee, *Inside the Company: CIA Diary*, 1975; Philip Agee and Louis Wolf, *Dirty Work: The CIA in Western Europe*, 1978; and Stockwell, op. cit.; *Rand Daily Mail*, 4 February 1980. Kenneth W. Grundy, *The Militarization of South African Politics*, 1986, p. 43, noted that 'BOSS grew from five hundred to over a thousand full-time employees in the decade of its existence.'

3. 'Bureau for State Security Act', *Government Gazette*, 30 June 1978, pp. 13, 15.

4. Johannesburg *Sunday Times*, 24 July 1977, 1 June 1980; interview with Mike Louw, 2 December 2005.

5. Johannesburg *Sunday Times*, 24 July 1977. One former BOSS–DONS analyst recalled that during 1979 a group of DONS officials became keen on gambling on the horses. They would skive off work to place bets on Wednesday afternoons. On one occasion, they bumped into Alec van Wyk, who said nothing more than 'I hope you are having a good day, boys.' When van Wyk retired, he was said to have made a substantial sum from his extracurricular activities at the race track (private information).

6. *Guardian*, 22 June 1978; *Observer*, 13 January 1980; Johannesburg *Sunday Times*, 22 October 1978.

7. *Observer*, 13 January 1980; *Now*, 5 October 1979. On Fullerton and MI6 see www.johnfullerton.com/bio

8. *CIA: The Pike Report*, 1977, pp. 10–12; *New York Times*, 16 April 1977; *The Times*, 21 May 1977.

9. Herbst, 'Analysing Apartheid', *African Affairs*, January 2003, p. 99; Lutfullah Mangi, 'US Policy towards South Africa c.1960–c.1990: From

Political Realism to Moral Engagement', unpublished doctoral thesis, 1994, p. 213.

10. *The Times*, 19 June 1978; *To the Point*, 4 August 1978; *Observer*, 21 January 1979.

11. Aida Parker, *Secret US War against South Africa*, pamphlet, 1977; Johannesburg *Sunday Times*, 2 March 2003; interview with Aida Parker, 3 April 1999; *The Times*, 13 December 2002; for further information on Ted Shackley, see *Vanity Fair*, January 1990 and Theodore Shackley, *The Third Option*, 1981; interview with Pieter Swanepoel, 15 December 2003.

12. A. Parker, op. cit., pp. 18–19.

13. Sanders, op. cit., pp. 201, 206; Richard Pollak, *Up Against Apartheid*, 1981, p. 87; *The Times*, 30 August 1978.

14. A. Parker, op. cit., pp. 10, 57.

15. *Citizen*, 31 January, 11 February, 8 August 1977, 17 February, 30 September, 4, 9 October 1978; Kinsolving, a syndicated journalist, broadcaster and clergyman denied 'being an "apologist" for apartheid . . . "but you can certainly describe me as a Friend of South Africa. I've visited it twice as a guest of [the South African] Government."' (*Citizen*, 11 February 1977). The *Washington Post*, 27 January 1977, reported that Kinsolving, had countered anti-apartheid campaigners by attending shareholders' meetings of major US companies. The shares in the companies which permitted him to attend had been purchased on his behalf by the South African Department of Information's Washington law firm. The *Post* noted that the US State Department Press Correspondents' Association stated 'Members of the press galaries shall not engage in lobbying or paid advertising, publicity, or promotion work.' Kinsolving told the *Citizen* that '"the truth is that after I attended each meeting I was told to cash the $200 worth of shares which had been bought in my name" . . . [he] added that he had spoken at dozens of rallies held to raise Israeli bonds. "I was paid in Israeli bonds for those speeches, but nobody accused me of being an Israeli agent".' Rees, interview with Rhoodie, transcript, 1979; *Sunday Tribune*, 8 October 1978. Based upon information supplied by Aida Parker, Gordon Winter reported in *Inside BOSS* that 'Jordan . . . was the head of the CIA's special operations in South Africa. A personal friend of . . . van den Bergh, he spent his Sundays driving a tractor around [van den Bergh's] farm' (p. 552).

16. Sally Shelton, letter to Shun Chetty, 3 August 1978 [Gordon Winter Papers]; Johannesburg *Star*, 4 February 1979; 18, 19 May 2000; *Citizen*, 2 February 1979; *Observer Foreign News Service*, 27 September 1979. The Arlington National Cemetery Website (www.arlingtoncemetery.net/wcolby), noted that Colby, who 'had directed Operation Pheonix [in Vietnam] pooling US intelligence resources to identify and "neutralise" Vietcong leaders, ultimately resulting in as many as 20,000 deaths' was director of the CIA between September 1973 and January 1976 (that is, during the coup d'état in Chile which overthrew President Salvador Allende, and during the Angolan war).

Colby died in April 1996 'from drowning and hypothermia after apparently collapsing from a heart attack or stroke and falling out of his canoe'. He was seventy-six years old. See also the *Guardian*, 7 May 1996.

17. Johannesburg *Sunday Times*, 15, 22 April 1979; *New York Times*, 14 April 1979.

18. *Daily Telegraph*, 30 April 1979; Flower, op. cit., pp. 228–9. Ian Smith, *The Great Betrayal*, 1997, pp. 308–10, recalled that the visit to Washington by Flower and Muzorewa in July 1979 was the result of the capture by the Rhodesian police of 'three CIA agents spying . . . they were also operating in South Africa and Kenya'. The spies confessed and were returned to the United States in exchange for Muzorewa's trip and a meeting with President Carter.

19. James Adams, *The Unnatural Alliance*, 1984, pp. 188, 195; *Los Angeles Times*, 26–28 October 1979; *New York Times*, 28 October, 1 November 1979; the *Observer*, 27 January 1980, suggested that Dr Christie's arrest, on his return to South Africa from a period studying at Oxford University's St Antony's College, had been based upon documents supplied by police spy Craig Williamson which 'alleged that [Christie] had links with the [ANC] and apparently included a letter from Ms Frene Ginwala . . . asking Christie to collect information about South Africa's nuclear programme'; *The Times*, 5 April 1980; *Daily Telegraph*, 31 January 1980. Seymour M. Hersh, *The Samson Option*, 1991, asked a 'former Israeli official' why Israel facilitated the apartheid nuke. The official gave four reasons: 'One: to share basic resources. South Africa is a very rich country and Israel is poor. Two: the supply of raw materials. Three: testing grounds. Try to do a [nuclear] test and all hell breaks loose. In South Africa it's different. Four: there is a certain sympathy for the situation of South Africa among Israelis. They are also European settlers standing against a hostile world' (p. 265). Three days after the 'double flash of light', P.W. Botha informed a Cape National Party congress meeting that 'If there are people who are thinking of doing something . . . I suggest they think twice about it. They might find out we have military weapons they do not know about' (*Rand Daily Mail*, 26 September 1979).

20. *Rand Daily Mail*, 30 June 1979; *Guardian*, 30 June 1979.

21. *Citizen*, 2 July 1979.

22. Winter, *Inside BOSS*, pp. 607–8, 611–17; interview with Gordon Winter, 23 June 1997.

23. *New African*, December 1979, pp. 40–1; *Guardian*, 31 December 1979.

24. *Observer*, 30 December 1979; *Cape Times*, 7 May 1980; *Rand Daily Mail*, 11 August 1981.

25. *Observer*, 6, 13 January 1980; *Rand Daily Mail*, 26 January 1980. Copies of the McGiven documents were published in the *Cape Times*, 23 February 1980.

26. *Cape Times*, 1 January 1980; Herbstein, *White Lies*, p. 216; *Rand Daily Mail*, 26 January 1980.

27. *Observer*, 27 January 1980; *Cape Times*, 7 January, 2 February 1980; Bell, op. cit., p. 123. The Johannesburg *Sunday Express*, 3 February 1980, concluded:

'Members of the IUEF now believe that Arthur McGiven timed his first article in the *Observer* as a warning to Captain Williamson that his cover was about to be blown . . . Suspicion continued overseas – and in some circles here – that McGiven remains on DONS' payroll.' In the post-McGiven–Williamson spy frenzy in South Africa, one victim was American political scientist Professor Robert Rotberg who was indirectly accused in parliament by P.W. Botha of being 'Mr X . . . someone in the service of a foreign agency' who had been using Helen Suzman's letter-headed paper. Rotberg denied that he was a spy (*Cape Times*, 14 February 1980).

28. *Guardian*, 31 January 1980.

29. *New Statesman*, 15 August 1980: the cover photograph of the magazine featured Ben van der Klashorst, 'South Africa's top BOSS man in Britain'; Johannesburg *Sunday Times*, 10 October 1982.

30. *New Statesman*, 15, 22 August 1980; Johannesburg *Sunday Times*, 17 August 1980.

31. Johannesburg *Sunday Times*, 17 August 1980; *Observer*, 17, 31 August, 7 September 1980.

32. S.W. Boys Smith (Home Secretary's private secretary), letter to Mr Robert Hughes, 3 November 1980 [A-AM Archive]; *New Statesman*, 5, 12 September 1980.

33. Herbstein, *White Lies*, pp. 216–17; *Observer*, 6 January 1980; Bell, op. cit., p. 123.

34. Herbstein, *White Lies*, p. 217; *Guardian*, 23 January 1980.

35. Bell, op. cit., pp. 85–90, 94–6, 98–9; see also the *Observer*, 6 February 2000; Kasrils, op. cit., p. 93.

36. Bell, op. cit., pp. 107–8, 110, 113–15, 117–23; Herbstein, *White Lies*, pp. 208–16; *Weekly Mail & Guardian*, 24 February 1995.

37. Don Foster, Paul Haupt and Maresa de Beer, *The Theatre of Violence*, 2005, p. 188; *Africa Confidential*, 28 January 1981.

38. *Guardian*, 1 April 1981; *Sunday Times*, 8 February 1981; *Sunday Independent*, 6 April 1997.

39. *Rand Daily Mail*, 1–5 February 1980; Johannesburg *Sunday Express*, 28 June 1981.

40. Johannesburg *Sunday Express*, 28 June 1981; *Financial Mail*, 1 January 1982. See also Johannesburg *Star*, 3 July 1981.

41. Winter, *Inside BOSS*, jacket sleeve; *Argus*, 30 October 1981; *Observer*, 25 October 1981.

42. Winter, *Inside BOSS*, p. 10; Winter, 'Inside BOSS and After', *Lobster*, No. 18, 1989.

43. *Guardian*, 29 October, 10 November 1981; *Morning Star*, 2 November 1981.

44. *Argus*, 18 September 1981; *Observer*, 1 May 1983: Peter Bessell was pacified with an 'erratum slip before publication' although 'Peacourt' in the *Daily*

Mirror (3 February 1978) had reported that Bessell 'had spied for the USA'; Adelaide Tambo's £150 in legal costs was paid and a correction was included in 'all copies still in the warehouse, in which she denied categorically saying anything to Winter or showing him any documents which could have been of any assistance to the South African security service'; Barney Zackon also had his legal costs paid and received a promise 'that allegations made against him in the book would be omitted in the next edition'; *Rand Daily Mail*, 16 May 1984: PAC founder-member Nana Mahomo won 'an undisclosed sum in damages' in the High Court in London; *Cape Times*, 9 July 1984: Stan Winer received 'substantial' damages and an apology from Penguin Books 'in an out-of-court settlement . . . following two years of litigation'.

The Times, 2 November 1984: former Conservative MP Harold Soref 'accepted "substantial" damages in the High Court in London'. In 1965, Harold Soref co-authored with Ian Greig *The Puppeteers*, which claimed on its cover to be 'an examination of those organisations and bodies concerned with the elimination of the white man in Africa.' On pp. 95–6, the ANC was reported to 'have long ceased to be an indigenous and autonomous body but it is a willing tool of the Communists having the avowed aim to massacre the 3,000,000 whites in South Africa'. On the night of 19 May 1986, South African special forces destroyed a house in Harare 'which was supposed to be occupied by the [ANC]'. In reality, the house was owned by Harold Soref, who contacted the South African Embassy in London demanding compensation: 'As I was always rather pro-South Africa, you would have thought the South African government would have adopted a different attitude . . . but I have not received a farthing in compensation' (*Independent*, 22 April 1989).

New Statesman, 18 April 1986: Ben Turok received an apology and damages in May 1985; in February 1986, Richard Gibson, was 'paid "a suitable sum" . . . for passages saying he had worked for the CIA'; Matthew Nkoana, a PAC activist (see page 58), 'fought his case for nine days in the High Court and won. The jury awarded him £12,000, which was rather less than Penguin paid their lawyers'; Denis Herbstein reported that 'Penguin company secretary, Mr Gordon Byard, said *Inside BOSS* was "the biggest problem book we had, in time and effort, and we have thick files to show for it".'

45. Winter, 'Inside BOSS and After', *Lobster*, No. 18, 1989; *New Statesman*, 18 April 1986.

46. *Rand Daily Mail*, 5 February 1980; interview with Gordon Winter, 14 January 2001. None of the four defectors returned to live in South Africa, either during the dying days of apartheid or after 1994, which confirms their claims to be 'genuine' defectors. Winter and McGiven live in the United Kingdom; Himmelhoch is believed to live in Australia; and Lambert has not been heard of for many years.

CHAPTER 7: THE MID SOLUTION

1. Sun Tzu, *The Art of War*, c. 500 BC, pp. 52–3.

2. Gavin Cawthra, *Brutal Force*, 1986, pp. 27, 30; South African Institute of Race Relations, *A Survey of Race Relations in South Africa: 1977*, 1978, p. 89; Philip H. Frankel, *Pretoria's Praetorians: Civil–Military Relations in South Africa*, 1984, p. 46.

3. O'Meara, op. cit., pp. 259–61; André Beaufre, *An Introduction to Strategy*, 1965, p. 125. See also Frankel, op. cit., pp. 46–60.

4. Samuel Huntington, 'The Clash of Civilisations?', *Foreign Affairs*, Vol. 72, No. 3, Summer 1993; O'Meara, op. cit., p. 263; Samuel P. Huntington, 'Reform and Stability in a Modernising, Multi-Ethnic Society', *Politikon*, Vol. 8, No. 2, Dec. 1981, pp. 11, 17, 19–20; Rhoodie, *P.W. Botha*, p. 131. Huntington returned to South Africa in 1986, where he was 'impressed with "reform by imposition from the top" in this unique setting' (Roherty, op. cit., p. 63, citing Samuel Huntington, 'Whatever Has Gone Wrong with Reform', *Die Suid-Afrikaan*, Winter 1986).

5. Frankel, op. cit., p. 70; Stephen Ellis, 'The Historical Significance of South Africa's Third Force', *Journal of Southern African Studies*, Vol. 24, No. 2, June 1998, pp. 270, 275.

6. John J. McCuen, 'The Art of Counter-Revolutionary War' samizdat pamphlet, pp. 6–7, 19, 23, 62; TRC, *Report*, Vol. 2, p. 16; John J. McCuen, *The Art of Counter-Revolutionary War*, 1966, pp. 78, 189. See also pp. 141–3, 'Police Action', which noted that 'the strategy of counter-terrorism must [include the] use of police action to destroy or neutralise the revolutionary politico-administrative network . . . It is vital that the police expand their intelligence network and information contacts . . . accurate and timely intelligence on the revolutionaries is the very foundation of effective counter-action . . . the police must carry the major burden of collecting and processing this decisive internal intelligence . . . during counter-terrorist operations the police are probably best qualified to chair intelligence committees'; pp. 54–7, 'Mobilizing the Masses', observed that Chairman Mao considered 'mobilizing the masses [to be] a science and a fundamental principle of revolutionary warfare.' McCuen understood that 'mobilization' carried dangers: 'It may initially require some force and sanctions being applied against the population itself . . . Force . . . will soon alienate the population and world opinion and will erode the morale of troops and police involved – all critical revolutionary war defeats. Nevertheless, study of recent wars suggests that these may be required in extreme instances to break an iron revolutionary grip on the people. These are hard words, but it is human nature to react to what one fears most. Force and sanctions – *not torture and terror* – may be the quickest and most human methods of neutralzing fear of the

terrorists' [my emphasis].' Robert Thompson, *Defeating Communist Insurgency*, 1966, pp. 85–6, 89, stated: 'The best organization to be responsible for all internal security is the special branch of the police force . . . It is a great advantage if intelligence officers have police powers . . . If it can possibly be avoided, the army should not be responsible for internal security intelligence . . . In an insurgency the army is one of the main consumers of intelligence, but it should not be a collector . . . Perhaps nearly as bad as no intelligence organization, or a multiplicity of intelligence organizations, is an overloaded one . . . Good intelligence leads to more frequent and more rapid contacts. More contacts lead to more kills.'

7. 'Total war in South Africa: Militarisation and the Apartheid State', NUSAS report, 1982, pp. 12, 17; O'Meara, op. cit., pp. 224, 227–8; Johannesburg *Star*, 7 May 1980; *Cape Times*, 12 May 1980; Frankel, op. cit., p. 89. In March–April 1976, Professor Milton Friedman, the father of monetarist economics and guru of Margaret Thatcher, visited South Africa and Rhodesia. In an article, 'Suicide of the West', published in the Johannesburg *Sunday Times*, 2 May 1976, he declared: 'The actual situation in both South Africa and Rhodesia is very different from and very much more complex than the Black–White stereotypes . . . Neither country is an ideal democracy – just as America is not. Both have serious racial problems – just as America has. Both can be justly criticized for not moving faster to eliminate discrimination – just as America can; but both provide a larger measure of freedom and affluence for all their residents – Black and White – than most other countries of Africa. Both would be great prizes for the Russians – and US official policy appears well designed to assure that the Russians succeed in following up their victory in Angola through the use of Cuban troops by similar takeovers in Rhodesia and South Africa.' See Meyer Feldberg, Kate Jowell and Stephen Mulholland, *Milton Friedman in South Africa*, 1976, with a foreword by Anton Rupert.

8. TRC, *Report*, Vol. 2, pp. 28, 50, 52; Howard Barrell, 'The Turn to the Masses: The African National Congress' Strategic Review of 1978–79', *Journal of Southern African Studies*, Vol. 18, No. 1, March 1992, pp. 80–9; Bell, op. cit., pp. 79–80, 290; see Jan-Bart Gewald, 'Who Killed Clemens Kapuuo?', *Journal of Southern African Studies*, Vol. 30, No. 1, September 2004, for an examination of the murder of the paramount chief of the Ovaherero, and leader of South West Africa-Namibia's Democratic Turnhalle Alliance, on 27 March 1978. Operation Reindeer was launched less than a month later.

9. TRC, *Report*, Vol. 2, p. 29; Foreign Affairs intelligence was later explained in a document printed in a limited edition of 30 in April 1987. W.P. Steenkamp's 'The RSA Intelligence Community and the Department of Foreign Affairs' revealed that the department was a 'prominent founding member' of the South African intelligence community (Johannesburg *Weekend Star*, 4 March 1995).

10. Bell, op. cit., p. 222; Craig M. Williamson, 'Memorandum on Aspects of State

Counter-revolutionary Warfare Principles and Strategy: Republic of South Africa in the 1980s', presented to the TRC, 9 October 1997.

11. Frankel, op. cit., p. 72; South African Institute of Race Relations, *Race Relations Survey: 1988/89*, 1989, p. 518; Paul Els, *We Fear Naught But God*, 2000, pp. 8–9, 14; Kevin A. O'Brien, 'Special Forces for Counter-Revolutionary Warfare: The South African Case', *Small Wars and Insurgencies*, Vol. 12, No. 2, Summer 2001, p. 91.

12. Els, op. cit., pp. 20, 43–4, 96; O'Brien, 'Special Forces for Counter-Revolutionary Warfare', *Small Wars and Insurgencies*, Summer 2001, p. 93; Seegers, op. cit., p. 185.

13. Els, op. cit., pp. 44–5; TRC, *Report*, Vol. 2, pp. 89, 135, 323–4; O'Brien, 'Special Forces for Counter-Revolutionary Warfare', *Small Wars and Insurgencies*, Summer 2001, pp. 92–5. On 32 Battalion, see Piet Nortje, *32 Battalion*, 2003. Johannesburg *Sunday Times*, 11 May 1980, reported: 'Members of Zimbabwe's controversial and much-feared former crack army units – the Selous Scouts and the Special Air Services – are joining the [SADF] in large numbers.' Verrier, *The Road to Zimbabwe*, recorded the decadence of the Rhodesian special forces in the late 1970s: 'They degenerated into *banditti* when the war reached the decisive stage . . . A Combined Operations Headquarters . . . was forced to arbitrate quarrels among the commanders of these private armies as to who should be allowed to organise slaughter of "terrs" [terrorists], and in which particular area of Rhodesia, Mozambique, Zambia – or Botswana' (pp. 233–4). He added that 'all CIO files were dispatched from Salisbury to Pretoria immediately the result of the February 1980 election was known' (p. 311).

14. Hanlon, pp. 27, 136; Stephen Ellis and Tsepo Sechaba, *Comrades Against Apartheid*, 1992, p. 107.

15. TRC, *Report,* Vol. 2, pp. 103–4; Johannesburg *Sunday Times*, 18 April 2004; Peter Stiff, *Cry Zimbabwe*, 2000, pp. 59–66, described the assassination of Gqabi but preferred to disguise Branfield as 'Major Brian'.

16. TRC, *Report*, Vol. 2, pp. 135–43; see also two State Security Papers: 'BSB (CCB) Presentation to Head of Military: Head of Military Comments', 28 April 1997: '<u>Methods that are applied</u>: The Head of the Military does not see the actions as murder and defines it as follows: an attack on individual enemy targets with non-standard weaponry in an unconventional manner not to affect innocents . . . Elimination of specific targets. A channel to handle these matters must be established . . . The CCB may suggest targets but these must go directly to the Head of the Military'; 'CCB Year Plan: 1987', undated: 'Through covert operations the CCB must disrupt any enemy operations inside or outside the country to the maximum . . . 24-hour CCB integrated citizens communications systems should be established.'

17. TRC, *Report*, Vol. 2, pp. 320–1.

18. *Now*, 5 October 1979; Frankel, op. cit., p. 43; Crocker, op. cit., pp. 116–17. Roherty, op. cit., pp. 144–5, provided a more friendly portrait of van der Westhuizen: 'Energetic, almost driven, widely travelled, widely read, *verlig* [progressive], he was the ideal choice for a military figure in the highest echelon of the "security-cum-welfare" program of counterrevolution . . . Somewhat jokingly General van der Westhuizen . . . remarked to the author in 1983 that "under Vorster we [the SADF] were on the shelf, now under P.W. we are being co-opted; I don't know which situation is worse!"'

19. *Rand Daily Mail*, 16, 19 March 1981; *New Statesman*, 5 November 1982; Crocker, op. cit., p. 90.

20. Chester A. Crocker, 'South Africa: Strategy for Change', *Foreign Affairs*, Vol. 59, No. 2, Winter 1980–1, pp. 334, 343–5.

21. Herbst, 'Analyzing Apartheid', *African Affairs*, January 2003, pp. 100–1; Cockburn, op. cit., pp. 301, 303–6. Bull served a four-and-a-half month prison sentence for arming apartheid South Africa. On Gerald Bull, see also William Lowther, *Arms and The Man*, 1991; Hersh, op. cit., pp. 216–17; Burrows, op. cit., pp. 168–9, 177; *Sunday Independent*, 11 May 1997, originally published in *Ha'aretz*.

22. *Covert Action*, No. 13, July–August 1981; Seegers, op. cit., p. 236; *Sunday Independent*, 15 March 1998; Sampson, *Mandela*, p. 321. Six months earlier, P.W. Botha had been visited by former CIA Director Stansfield Turner, who took 'a special tour of [the] war zone in Northern Namibia' (Kevin Danaher, *In Whose Interest?*, 1984, pp. 164, 169).

23. Crocker, op. cit., p. 289; Bob Woodward, *Veil: The Secret Wars of the CIA, 1981–1987*, 1987, p. 437; *Washington Post*, 3 November, 21 December 1982.

24. Crocker, op. cit., pp. 215–16. Ros Reeve and Stephen Ellis, 'An Insider's Account of the South African Security Forces' Role in the Ivory Trade', *Journal of Contemporary African Studies*, Vol. 13, No. 2, June 1995, p. 233: Colonel Jan Breytenbach described MID officials as being 'a civvie who's put on a uniform . . . They get a degree . . . and he joins the Defence Force and he puts a uniform on and now he's a colonel, or he's a major, or he's a brigadier, or he's a corporal, or whatever. But now he's got status. But he's not a fighter.'

25. Herbst, 'Analyzing Apartheid', *African Affairs*, January 2003, p. 102; *International Herald Tribune*, 26 December 1984; *Weekly Mail*, 18 July 1986.

26. *New York Times*, 23 July 1986; see also *New Statesman*, 1 August 1986. Testifying before the Senate Foreign Relations Committee, Secretary of State George Shultz 'said that William J. Casey, Director of Central Intelligence, had told him this morning "categorically that that was not true and had not been true during the course of this Administration and to his knowledge before that"'. CBS News reported 'from "knowledgeable sources" that the [NSA] had spied

on the [ANC] "for several years" and passed the information on to British intelligence. "The British, in turn, are said to have given the information to the South African secret police" ' (*New York Times*, 24 July 1986).

27. 'Further Submissions and Responses by the ANC to Questions raised by the Commission for Truth and Reconciliation', 12 May 1997; Ellis and Sechaba, op. cit., pp. 105, 111; Gillian Slovo, *Every Secret Thing*, 1997, pp. 241–3.

28. Ellis and Sechaba, op. cit., pp. 111–12.

29. TRC, *Report,* Vol. 2, pp. 323, 328; Jacques Pauw, *Into the Heart of Darkness*, 1997, p. 43; private information.

30. Stephen Ellis and John Daniel, 'State Security Policy', unpublished paper, 1996, p. 31; TRC, *Report*, Vol. 2, pp. 57–8; *Economist*, 14 August 1982.

31. TRC, *Report*, Vol. 2, pp. 89–92; *Washington Post*, 22 October 1989; Hanlon, op. cit., pp. 35, 113, 219.

32. Johannesburg *Star*, 14 November 1979; *Africa Confidential*, 20 March 1992; *Cape Times*, 15 January 1980.

33. Johannesburg *Star*, 14 November 1979; Johannesburg *Sunday Times*, 18 November 1979; *Pretoria News*, 27 June 1990; *Newsweek*, 10 December 1979.

34. Private information; Ellis and Daniel, 'State Security Policy', unpublished paper, 1996, p. 31; Crocker, op. cit., p. 116. See also Signe Landgren, *Embargo Disimplemented*, 1989, p. 167: '[Barnard's] main piece on South African nuclear strategy is entitled "the deterrent strategy of nuclear weapons", written in Afrikaans in the mid-1970s . . . Barnard proposed that South Africa should no longer try to rely upon the West for its security, since the Western states were pathetically defensive in the face of communism . . . He advocated preparation, including developing a nuclear weapons capability immediately, for when the onslaught came it would be too late to prepare. Finally, he declared that the "value of nuclear weapons lies in their deterrence. This in turn relies upon the perception of that capability. Hence, South Africa must not only develop nuclear weapons, but must also announce to the world and convince the world that it possesses such capability." '

35. Johannesburg *Sunday Express*, 13 December 1981; *Rand Daily Mail*, 6, 7 May 1982; Johannesburg *Sunday Times*, 9 May 1982; Antony Altbeker, *Solving Crime: The State of the SAPS Detective Service*, Institute for Security Studies Monograph No. 31, November 1998.

36. *Financial Mail*, 4 June 1982; *Rand Daily Mail*, 12 May 1982.

37. Dr L.D. Barnard, C.R. Swart Lecture: 'National Intelligence Work in International Relations', 2 September 1983. Under the heading 'Covert Human Intelligence Operations', Barnard revealed that 'Covert human sources of information have little in common with the James Bond syndrome. Success in this field is the result of patient and time consuming planning, fearless acceptance of the risks involved and the meticulous execution of the intelligence operation. Successful intelligence operators are individuals who have

mastered the art of acting and operating inconspicuously and thus doing, as the saying goes, what the Romans do in Rome.'

38. Johannesburg *Sunday Times*, 26 January 1992; *Pretoria News*, 27 January 1990; *Africa Confidential*, 20 March 1992; Crocker, op. cit., p. 274.

39. Johannesburg *Star*, 24, 25 May 1982; *Rand Daily Mail*, 25 June 1982; Pieter Wolvaardt, *A Diplomat's Story*, 2005, pp. 100–2.

40. *Sun*, 25 May 1982; *Daily Mail*, 25 May 1982; Johannesburg *Star*, 25 May 1982.

41. *Financial Times*, 26 May 1982; *Citizen*, 2 June 1982; Wolvaardt, op. cit., p. 108.

42. *Daily Express*, 26 May 1982; *Observer*, 30 May 1982; Sanders, op. cit., pp. 109–11; *Guardian*, 12–16 March 1973.

43. Johannesburg *Sunday Express*, 30 May 1982.

44. *Citizen*, 2 June 1982; Johannesburg *Star*, 1 June 1982.

45. Johannesburg *Sunday Times*, 11 May 1982; Rees, interview with Rhoodie, transcript, 1979; *Africa Confidential*, 10 June 1977; O'Meara, op. cit., p. 255.

46. *Africa Confidential*, 12 March 1980; Johannesburg *Sunday Times*, 11 May 1982; Arthur Gavshon and Desmond Rice, *The Sinking of the Belgrano*, 1984, p. 17. After the Falklands war and Argentina's return to civilian government, the relationship with South Africa declined in significance. Meanwhile, the Republic's trade with Chile intensified and Anglo American invested $300 million in Brazilian gold mines, summoning up the concerning image of 'Oppenheimer as Fitzcarraldo' (David Fig, 'South African Interests in Latin America', South African Research Service, *South African Review II*, 1984, p. 243).

47. Adams, op. cit., pp. 102–3, 208; Johannesburg *Star*, 9 July 1982.

48. Wolvaardt, op. cit., pp. 104, 108–9.

49. Johannesburg *Star*, 20 July 1983; Landgren, op. cit., p. 109, citing *Defense & Armament*, No. 11, September 1982; *Afrique-Asie*, July 1983.

50. Johannesburg *Star*, 20 July 1983; Landgren, op. cit., pp. 109–10, citing *African Defence*, September 1993; *Aerospace Daily*, 28 November 1983.

51. Anti-Apartheid Movement, 'Britain, South Africa and the Falklands', November 1983 [A-AM Archive].

52. *Mail & Guardian*, 1 September 2000.

53. Daniel Korn, *Exocet*, BBC 2, 1 July 2001.

54. William Wilson, 'Visit by Colonel Cockbain', to Mr Bottomley, 8 December 1969. See also M.A. Robb, 'South African Navy', to William Wilson, 27 February 1969 [FCO 45/281] which noted that Vice-Admiral Biermann, the head of the South African Navy, would be visiting London 'at his own expense', having accompanied P.W. Botha and his wife to a submarine launch in France. Biermann 'has said that he hopes to see [the British] Admiral Bush'. A handwritten note on the document states: 'The Admiral and his wife are very nice people and good friends of ours. The Admiral is on very good terms with Admiral Sir John Bush.'

55. Interview with Tienie Groenewald, 28 June 1999.

56. Crocker, op. cit., p. 289; Steven Emerson, *Secret Warriors*, 1988, p. 222.

57. Interview with Tienie Groenewald, 28 June 1999; *Independent*, 9 June 1988.

CHAPTER 8: SPY GAMES

1. Joseph Conrad, *The Secret Agent*, 1907, pp. 62–3.

2. TRC, *Report*, Vol. 6, pp. 248–9.

3. *Rand Daily Mail*, 10 September 1982; *Guardian*, 11 September 1982; Johannesburg *Sunday Times*, 12 September 1982. On Caroline de Crespigny's imprisonment, see the *Listener*, 18 August 1966.

4. *Guardian*, 11 September 1982.

5. Johannesburg *Sunday Times*, 12 September 1982; *Rand Daily Mail*, 16 September 1982.

6. Johannesburg *Sunday Times*, 26 September 1982; *Argus*, 4 December 1982; *Daily Telegraph*, 2 September 1983, 24 January 1984.

7. Interview with Pieter Swanepoel, 3 August 1998; 'Top Secret Report', 7 August 1961 [Gordon Winter Papers]. Gordon Winter gave me a copy of this report in early 1998, which he had 'borrowed' from Piet Swanepoel's office at BOSS headquarters in the 1970s. I discovered Swanepoel's whereabouts by telephoning the numerous P. Swanepoels in the Pretoria telephone directory and asking: 'Are you the Pieter Swanepoel who used to be a BOSS agent?' Eventually, one P. Swanepoel replied: 'Ah, you would be looking for my father.' Piet Swanepoel senior confirmed that the document had been stolen from his office and furnished me with a sixty-four-page manuscript he had written on the subject.

8. Pieter Swanepoel, 'The De Crespigny Mystery', unpublished, undated manuscript, pp. 13, 16–17, 28–35; *Ramparts*, April 1967.

9. Swanepoel, op. cit., pp. 37–44, 46, 48, 52–9.

10. Randolph Vigne, *Liberals Against Apartheid*, 1997, p. 146.

11. Magnus Gunther, 'The National Committee of Liberation (NCL)/African Resistance Movement (ARM)', SADET, *The Road to Democracy*, Vol. 1, pp. 216–18, citing Geoffrey Bing, *Reap the Whirlwind*, 1968, p. 402. Gunther ignores substantial problems posed by Bing's autobiography, not least the fact that John Lang didn't require Rubin to mediate with the Ghanaian authorities on his behalf: 'At the Law School [at the University of Accra], John Lang's second-in-command was Leslie Rubin, a recently arrived white South African lawyer' (p. 324). In contrast, Gunther recorded that 'Lang was released from prison [in South Africa] at the end of June 1960 . . . [Rubin] was offered a post at the University of Accra's law faculty, and by June 1960 was settled in Accra' (Gunther, SADET, op. cit., p. 217). Bing recalled that 'after Sharpeville in 1960 my wife was to pioneer an organized rescue attempt by which [South

African] refugees of all colours were collected in Bechuanaland and airlifted over the Federation of Rhodesia . . . The total number which she brought out was small – only twenty-four' (p. 326). There is no mention of John Lang or the nascent ARM in this context. However, the Johannesburg *Sunday Express*, 24 November 1963, reported that John Lang, 'who fled South Africa in 1961 for political reasons, was . . . reported to be on his way to Bechuanaland . . . on "an important mission" . . . It is understood that Mr Lang's visit concerns refugees from South Africa.'

12. *Noseweek*, No. 30–3, August 2000, February, April and June 2001; *Mail & Guardian*, 20 October 2000.

13. *Mail & Guardian*, 20 October, 3 November 2000.

14. Johannesburg *Sunday Times*, 22 October 1978.

15. Interview with Anthony de Crespigny, 14 September 1998. William Raynor accompanied me to meet de Crespigny and also questioned him; *Noseweek*, No. 31, February 2001, reported that de Crespigny had been married four times. *Noseweek*, No. 33, July 2001, carried a letter from Lolly de Crespigny which disclosed that 'De Crespigny has been married 5 times – I was his fifth.'

16. Conversation with Randolph Vigne, 24 October 2000; Randolph Vigne, e-mail to author, 19 August 2004; Gunther, SADET, op. cit., p. 221. Alan Paton, *Journey Continued*, 1988, p. 224, described Vigne as being 'in so far as a white South African can be – without racial fear or prejudice'. But he also recalled that '[Vigne] had an imperious personality . . . [and] a quality of ruthlessness'.

17. Interview with Neville Rubin, 9 December 2000. Progressive white South Africa in the early 1960s was a tiny world. C.J. Driver, 'Used to be Good Friends', *Granta 80: The Group*, December 2002, is a thoughtful reminiscence on 'a photograph of a twenty-first birthday party in the late winter of 1962'. Among the eleven people featured in the photograph are ARM member Alan Brooks; Stephanie Kemp, who later married and divorced Albie Sachs and later still was Joe Slovo's lover; Rick Turner, murdered in 1978 (see page 90) and Barbara Follett. John Clare, whose birthday party it was, became education editor of the *Daily Telegraph*, his 'then wife, Sheila Robertson, had been briefly a member of the ARM'. C.J. Driver was the Liberal President of NUSAS. He noted that although not a member of the ARM he was a fellow traveller. In 1961, he 'had been persuaded to open a post office box in a Cape Town suburb under [a] false name, for . . . clandestine purposes'. Driver recalled that NUSAS was 'fortunate in having as an ally Robert Birley . . . who had come out to the University of the Witwatersrand as a visiting professor of education' (see page 47).

18. Bell, op. cit., p. 115; *Observer*, 19 December 1982; *Guardian*, 18 December 1982.

19. TRC, *Report*, Vol. 2, p. 157; Pauw, *Heart of Darkness*, p. 215. Casselton told Jacques Pauw that the ANC office 'had a sophisticated alarm system'. In order to practise disabling the alarm, he broke into a Kensington art gallery that had an 'identical alarm system'. Standing inside the gallery, 'I saw a painting of a

Boer general on his white horse and I decided to take the painting' which was later dispatched to South Africa 'and presented to . . . Johan Coetzee. It was placed in [his] lounge and it became one of the best in-jokes in Section A of the Security Branch' (p. 216).

20. TRC, *Report*, Vol. 2, pp. 157–8; de Kock, op. cit., pp. 83–6; *Observer*, 19 February 1995.

21. Williamson, 'Memorandum on Aspects of State Counter-revolutionary Warfare', 9 October 1997; *New Statesman*, 27 August 1982; TRC, *Report*, Vol. 7, 2002, pp. 114–15; *Observer*, 19 February 1995; *Mail & Guardian*, 24 February 1995.

22. TRC, *Report*, Vol. 2, p. 107; Slovo, op. cit., p. 261.

23. *Observer*, 19 December 1982; *Guardian*, 18 December 1982; *Daily Telegraph*, 18 December 1982.

24. 'Court sequel to break-ins at the London offices of SWAPO and the ANC', undated document [A-AM Archive].

25. *Observer*, 26 September 1982.

26. 'Court sequel to break-ins', undated document [A-AM Archive]; *Observer*, 3 October 1982; Johannesburg *Sunday Times*, 10 October 1982.

27. *Guardian*, 19 October 1982.

28. *Anti-Apartheid News*, November 1982.

29. *Guardian*, 17, 18 December 1982; *Argus*, 16 December 1982.

30. *Observer*, 19 December 1982; *Sunday Times*, 19 December 1982: the editorial, entitled 'No allies, they', admitted 'The charge has been made for many years that the South African Embassy in London houses security agents who are aggressively active . . . Numerous incidents of burglary, harassment and worse, against South African exiles here, have supported this suspicion. On most occasions, the charge is not taken seriously by British authorities . . . Because South Africa is an ally, it has been argued, her agents should not have to live by the same rules as the agents of a hostile power . . . If the US [CIA] patrolled London in pursuit of enemies, there would be an outcry. South Africa merits less fraternal treatment than the US'; *Rand Daily Mail*, 20 December 1982.

31. Michael Crick, *The Right to Know*, BBC Radio 4, 27 September 2005.

32. *Guardian*, 8 April, 27 June 1983; *Morning Star*, 4 May 1983.

33. TRC, *Report*, Vol. 2, p. 107; TRC, *Report*, Vol. 7, p. 764; *Observer*, 19 February 1995; Williamson, 'Memorandum on Aspects of State Counter-revolutionary Warfare', 9 October 1997.

34. *Work in Progress*, No. 55, August–September 1988, p. 40; *Rand Daily Mail*, 26 January 1980; *Guardian*, 25 January 1994. Journalist and police spy John Horak said of his handler Johan Coetzee: '[he] is a brilliant man. He gave many lectures to the CIA and FBI . . . He's been many times to [the CIA headquarters at Langley Park] to lecture' (June Goodwin and Ben Schiff, *Heart of Whiteness*,

1995, p. 337). General Johan Coetzee died in 2004. His final years had been dominated by tragedy. He had suffered prostate and throat cancer. His son Ernest committed suicide in 2002 and his wife Yvonne committed suicide in 2003 (*Daily Dispatch* online, 30 April 2004: www.dispatch.co.za).

35. *Leadership*, February 1986.

36. *Observer*, 16 July 1995; *Weekly Mail & Guardian*, 4 October 1996, 20 January 2006.

37. *Observer*, 16 July 1995. The MID did not start *Aida Parker's Newsletter*, but by 1984 an SSC document noted that '[the police] are currently using it and much success is being achieved with propaganda against the ANC' (*Weekly Mail & Guardian*, 24 February 1995). On the IFF, see also *Weekly Mail & Guardian*, 16 August 1995.

38. *Washington Post*, 29 December 2005, 4 January 2006; *Mail & Guardian*, 20 January 2006.

39. On Williamson and Ricci, see *Africa Confidential*, 15 April, 13 May 1987; Johannesburg *Sunday Star*, 19 April 1987, 7, 28 February 1988. Marius Schoon said of Williamson in 1995: 'I want him charged. I am completely opposed to amnesty. The people who committed these sorts of crimes should be brought before the courts . . . I don't feel that knowing who did it means that there can be forgiveness. These were unforgivable crimes' (*Observer*, 19 February 1995); *Mail & Guardian*, 15 December 2000, Johannesburg *Star*, 15 May 2002, stated that the families of Ruth First and Jeanette Schoon were attempting to have Williamson's TRC amnesty, which had been granted in 2000, overturned. *Africa Analysis*, 20 February 2004, reported that 'Having agreed to a large cash settlement to the families of three of his victims . . . Craig Williamson has failed to honour the commitment.'

40. *Sunday Independent*, 24 January 1995; Conrad, op. cit., p. 221: 'The Embassy people. A pretty lot, ain't they! Before a week's out I'll make some of them wish themselves twenty feet under ground . . . I wish I could get loose in there with a cudgel for half an hour. I would keep on hitting till there wasn't a single unbroken bone left among the whole lot. But never mind, I'll teach them yet what it means to throw out a man like me to rot in the streets. I've a tongue in my head. All the world shall know what I've done for them. I am not afraid. I don't care. Everything'll come out. Every damned thing. Let them look out!'

41. Ronen Bergman, 'Treasons of Conscience', *Mail & Guardian*, 11 August 2000, originally published in the Israeli newspaper *Ha'aretz*, 7 April 2000; Mervyn Rees, 'The Spy who knew it all', *Mail on Sunday*, 20 November 1983.

42. *Mail & Guardian*, 11 August 2000; *New Nation*, 14 March 1997.

43. Janet Coggin, *The Spy's Wife*, pp. 76–8, 85, 114, 119, 121, 137–8, 148–9, 179, 220–7; Johannesburg *Sunday Times*, 4 April 1999.

44. *Mail & Guardian*, 11 August 2000; *Mail on Sunday*, 20 November 1983; *Los Angeles Times*, 27 August 1977.

45. *Mail & Guardian*, 11 August 2000.
46. 'The Jericho Weapon System', 21 March 1975 [South African History Archive].
47. *Mail on Sunday*, 20 November 1983; *Mail & Guardian*, 11 August 2000; *The Times*, 2 January 1984; *Vrye Weekblad*, 4 September 1992.
48. *Mail on Sunday*, 20 November 1983; *Mail & Guardian*, 11 August 2000.
49. *Mail & Guardian*, 11 August 2000; *The Times*, 2 January 1984. On the Kozlov spy-swap, see *Financial Times*, 30 January 1981; *Guardian*, 13 May 1982.
50. *Mail on Sunday*, 20 November 1983; interview with Mervyn Rees, 4 April 1999.
51. *The Times*, 21 November 1983.
52. Interview with Mervyn Rees, 4 April 1999; *Washington Post*, 12 June 1984.
53. *Servamus*, February 1992; Johannesburg *Star*, 25 February 1992.

CHAPTER 9: 'TAKE THE PAIN'

1. Jacques Pauw, *In the Heart of the Whore*, 1991, p. 22.
2. Hamann, op. cit., p. 122.
3. Pauw, *Heart of the Whore*, pp. 35–7; Dirk Coetzee, 'Vlakplaas and the Murder of Griffiths Mxenge', in Anthony Minnaar, Ian Liebenberg and Charl Schutte (eds), *The Hidden Hand*, 1994, p. 178.
4. Pauw, *Heart of the Whore*, pp. 37–8, 40–1, 43–7.
5. Ellis and Sechaba, op. cit., pp. 97–8; Pauw, *Heart of the Whore*, pp. 47–8, 50.
6. Pauw, *Heart of the Whore*, pp. 1, 31–5; TRC, *Report*, Vol. 7, p. 361.
7. David Goodman, *Fault Lines*, 1999, pp. 95–6; Pauw, *Heart of the Whore*, pp. 52–5; Martin Meredith, *Coming to Terms*, 1999, pp. 83–5.
8. Pauw, *Heart of the Whore*, pp. 2–6; *Weekly Mail*, 20 October 1989.
9. Pauw, *Heart of the Whore*, pp. 16–18, 60, 65–6, 68; Jacques Pauw, *Into the Heart of Darkness*, 1997, pp. 156–8. Welz had introduced Coetzee to Pauw, 'I discovered years later that [he] had told Welz in much more detail about his involvement and had also mentioned the existence of death squads to some very prominent parliamentary politicians'. At one point, Coetzee decided he would kill Welz 'by unscrewing the bolts of a front wheel on his car'. This plan was later abandoned (*Whore*, pp. 18, 68).
10. Pauw, *Heart of the Whore*, pp. 22, 70; *Guardian*, 7 December 1989; *Weekly Mail*, 9 March 1990.
11. *Vrye Weekblad*, 17 November 1989; Pauw, *Heart of Darkness*, pp. 161, 163–6; *Sowetan*, 19 January 1996; Antjie Krog, *Country of My Skull*, 1999, pp. 90–1.
12. de Kock, op. cit., pp. 43–4, 49, 57–8, 60, 63, 71–2; Pauw, *Heart of Darkness*, pp. 34–6.
13. Denis Herbstein and John Evenson, *The Devils are Among Us*, 1989, pp. 63–4.
14. Hamann, op. cit., pp. 64–5; Peter Stiff, *The Covert War*, 2004, pp. 96, 149; de Kock, op. cit., pp. 74, 87.

15. Herbstein, *The Devils*, p. 76; Stiff, *Covert War*, pp. 488–9; *Mail & Guardian*, 29 September 2000. For an alternative view of Koevoet, see Jim Hooper, *Beneath the Visiting Moon*, 1990. Hooper was an American 'adrenaline junkie' who found his 'Vietnam' as a photo-journalist in South West Africa-Namibia. He recalled 'the ego trip of being with Koevoet . . . whenever we stop at an army base, I enjoy the looks we get . . . I find myself swaggering right along with the rest of them, trying to look tough and wearing my dirt like some kind of badge. I know I am supposed to keep myself detached but it's damned difficult when you get to know them' (p. 177). Although Hooper defends Koevoet – 'they're no bunch of choir-boys, but they hardly fit their popular image of cold-blooded psychopaths' (p. 171) – he admits that Koevoet 'invaded [Angola] *looking* for someone to chase' (p. 56).

16. de Kock, op. cit., pp. 106–8; Pauw, *Heart of Darkness*, pp. 45–6; Ellis and Sechaba, op. cit., p. 169.

17. de Kock, op. cit., pp. 117, 122–3, 126–8; Ellis and Sechaba, op. cit., pp. 165–6.

18. de Kock, op. cit., pp. 102–3, 110–3, 116–20, 129; *Mail & Guardian*, 2 February 1996: the murder of Maki Skosana by a mob on 20 July 1985 was the direct result of Vlakplaas distributing booby-trapped grenades. As David Beresford explained: 'She was attending a funeral at Duduza when a crowd of mourners inexplicably turned on her. They chased her across the veld, beat her, stoned her, tore her clothes off, set her on fire, put a huge rock on her so that she couldn't get up and . . . rammed a broken bottle into her vagina. Her death was filmed by [international] television cameras and the ghastly footage was broadcast at length . . . in what was clearly seen by the authorities . . . as a propaganda triumph – a demonstration of the barbaric savagery of township residents.' In late June 1985, askari Joe Mamasela had distributed booby-trapped grenades to ANC students who later blew themselves up when they pulled the pins on the grenades. A rumour began to circulate in the township that Maki was Mamasela's girlfriend. She died at the funeral of the grenade victims. De Kock had told Mamasela that 'it would be a first for the terrorists to blow themselves up'.

    In 1977, Helmoed-Römer Heitman, the veteran correspondent of *Jane's Defence Weekly*, contributed an article entitled 'Some Possibilities in Counter-Insurgency Operations' to the South African magazine, *Militaire*. It stated that 'operations can include the sabotage/doctoring of discovered arms . . . The resultant difficulties will sap confidence and morale as well as creating distrust between the insurgency and its suppliers . . . Such operations should not be overdone so as to avoid creating suspicion.' Heitman gave as an example, 'the placing of instant detonation fuses in . . . every 10th handgrenade' (*Weekly Mail*, 24 November 1989).

19. Ellis and Sechaba, op. cit., pp. 168–9; de Kock, op. cit., pp. 132–5.

20. de Kock, op. cit., pp. 111, 136, 143–4, 151, 189; TRC, *Report*, Vol. 2, pp. 291–2.

21. de Kock, op. cit., pp. 244–6, 274; Pumla Gobodo-Madikizela, *A Human Being Died That Night*, 2004, p. 135; F.W. de Klerk, *The Last Trek*, 1998, p. 317; *Guardian*, 4 June 1998.

22. *Mail & Guardian*, 15 January 1999; Johannesburg *Sunday Times*, 21 August 2005; *Guardian*, 31 March 1998; TRC, *Report*, Vol. 2, p. 225. Nieuwoudt sadistically informed his victims: 'I'll make you famous.'

23. TRC, *Report*, Vol. 2, pp. 37–8, 176, 226–7.

24. *Mail & Guardian*, 15 January 1999; TRC, *Report*, Vol. 2, p. 227; *New Nation*, 14 May 1992.

25. *Weekly Mail*, 5 July 1985; *Mail & Guardian*, 28 May 1999. See also Christopher Nicholson, *Permanent Removal*, 2004, a thorough account of the murder of the Cradock Four and the long campaign through two inquests and TRC hearings which eventually ended in justice for the surviving families. At the second inquest in 1993, the SADF was represented by Anton Mostert, formerly Judge Mostert (see page 108), who had headed the Mostert Commission which contributed to the downfall of Eschel Rhoodie, Connie Mulder and Hendrik van den Bergh. As Nicholson explained, Mostert left the bench in January 1980 and returned to private practice. 'The Johannesburg bar accepted his readmission as there were "exceptional circumstances". His successful return to practice made him a natural choice for counsel for the Defence Force' (p. 107).

26. *Guardian*, 11 August 1985; Pauw, *Heart of the Whore*, pp. 6, 8–10; TRC, *Report*, Vol. 2, pp. 229–30.

27. TRC, *Report*, Vol. 6, pp. 241–2.

28. TRC, *Report*, Vol. 2, pp. 274, 276, 278, 280–5, 287–9.

29. *Guardian*, 14 April 1982; *Weekly Mail*, 22 August 1986; see also *Mail & Guardian*, 3 March 2000.

30. *Independent*, 2 May, 15 July 1989; David Webster and Maggie Friedman, *Suppressing Apartheid's Opponents*, 1989, pp. 22–4, 30, 33. Since the mid-1980s, David Webster had become the leading academic authority on apartheid state violence. See Max Coleman and David Webster, 'Repressions and Detentions in South Africa', South African Research Service (eds), *South African Review 3*, 1986, pp. 111–36; David Webster, 'Repression and the State of Emergency', Glenn Moss and Ingrid Obery (eds), *South African Review 4*, 1987, pp. 141–72, which noted: 'The "success" of the emergency has been achieved at the expense of enormous repression in the form of army and police state patrols. And it has been bought at the price of massively alienating township residents' (p. 172); David Webster and Maggie Friedman, 'Repression and the State of Emergency: June 1987-March 1989', Glenn Moss and Ingrid Obery (eds), *South African Review 5*, 1989, pp. 16–41, was published posthumously.

31. *Independent*, 3 May 1989; Johannesburg *Saturday Star*, 23 January 1993; TRC, *Report*, Vol. 2, p. 233.

32. TRC, *Report*, Vol. 2, pp. 271–2; de Kock, op. cit., pp. 165–6, 170–2;

Johannesburg *Sunday Times*, 21 August 2005; Nicholson, op. cit., pp. 92–5; *SA Barometer*, 15 December 1989.

33. Jan Bondeson, *Blood on the Snow*, 2005, pp. 2, 4–5, 9, 11, 118, 128, 140, 142; *Guardian*, 30 September 2004; *Argus*, 9 September 1986.

34. Bondeson, op. cit., pp. 171–2; SAPA-AFP, 30 January 2003; Klaas de Jonge, 'Truth Commission Files', November 1997 (www.contrast.org/truth/html/olof_palme).

35. Bondeson, op. cit., pp. 88–9, 92, 97, 173; *Observer*, 6 October 1996; de Jonge, op. cit.; SAPA-IPS, 4 October 1996.

36. *Independent*, 27 September 1996; *Observer*, 6 October 1996.

37. *Observer*, 6 October 1996; *Cape Times*, 13 January 1990; de Kock, op. cit., p. 84; Pauw, *Heart of Darkness*, pp. 218, 220.

38. TRC, *Report*, Vol. 2, p. 99; Bondeson, op. cit., p. 173.

39. Bell, op. cit., pp. 304–9; *Mail & Guardian*, 17 July 1998; the name 'Nigel Barnett' appears on the Rhodesian Roll of Honour website: www.mazoe.com/ROH_A_C; *Africa Analysis*, 7 February 2003. In January 2003, there was a flurry of press coverage of the South African connection to the Palme assassination. Mysterious documents, which later proved to have been forged by former apartheid operatives, suggested that Roy Allen, a reported former member of the Z Squad, was in Stockholm on the day of the assassination. Allen, who had emigrated to Australia, was cleared of suspicion by Swedish police investigators (SAPA-AFP, 30 January 2003).

40. TRC, *Report*, Vol. 2, pp. 494–7; Iain Christie, *Samora Machel: A Biography*, 1989, pp. xiii, xv; *Guardian*, 10 July 1987. See C.S. Margo, *Report of the Board of Inquiry into the Accident to Tupelov 134A-3 Aircraft C9-CAA on 19th October 1986*, 1987.

41. Christie, op. cit., pp. 112, 116–17; Hanlon, op. cit., pp. 37, 144, 147–8; Ellis and Sechaba, op. cit., pp. 137–8; Brian Pottinger, *The Imperial Presidency*, 1988, pp. 223–4: 'The European trip represented the pinnacle of achievement in Botha's first decade'; see also Margaret Thatcher, *The Downing Street Years*, 1993, pp. 514–15. The South Africans appear to have been particularly keen on lobbying the Pope: Eschel Rhoodie in the 1970s also visited the Vatican (Rees, interview with Rhoodie, transcript, 1979).

42. *Mail & Guardian*, 10 July 1998.

43. *International Herald Tribune*, 26 October 1986; *Guardian*, 23 October, 10 November 1986.

44. Iain Christie, op. cit., p. xiv; *Guardian*, 13 November 1986.

45. *Africa Confidential*, 21 December 2001; TRC, *Report*, Vol. 2, pp. 496–7, 500–2.

46. *Sowetan Sunday World*, 12, 19 January 2003; *Mail & Guardian*, 10 July 1998.

47. Christie, op. cit., p. xvi; Jane Hunter, *Israeli Foreign Policy*, 1987, p. 48, reported that the South African authorities had admitted that 'Machel's heart and brain were "not present due to the violence of the accident"', citing SAPA, 22 January 1987; *Sowetan Sunday World*, 6 April 2003.

48. Conversation with Mpikeleni Duma, 29 November 2005; SAPA, 19 March 2003; SAPA-AFP, 11 April 2003; *Daily Telegraph*, 16 February 2004.

The Republic of South Africa has a long and inglorious history of suspicious plane crashes. Craig Williamson informed the TRC that 'covert action, leading to mysterious explosions, deaths etc. cannot be said to be unusual in SA political life since 1961. A long list of incidents could be compiled, starting with the explosion aboard the aircraft sent to Botswana in the early 1960s to uplift Goldreich and Wolpe to safety' (Williamson, 'Memorandum on Aspects of State Counter-revolutionary Warfare', 9 October 1997). In addition to the Samora Machel crash, three aeroplane crashes since 1960, which are linked to South Africa, raise more questions than answers. Former RAF 24 Squadron pilot and commander and 'committed Zionist' Judge Cecil Margo investigated or held inquiries into all three crashes (Johannesburg *Sunday Times*, 26 November 2000), in addition to the Board of Inquiry into the Machel crash.

1) The *Albertina* crash, 17 September 1961. The death of Dag Hammarskjöld, the Secretary-General of the United Nations, and fifteen others while travelling from Leopoldville in the Congo to Ndola in Katanga province has always been considered suspicious. The best account of the crash can be found in Arthur L. Gavshon, *The Last Days of Dag Hammarskjöld*, 1963. The Rhodesian and UN investigations into the crash were inconclusive. Conor Cruise O'Brien and George Ivan Smith, both of whom had been UN officials involved with the Congo crisis in 1961, declared in a letter to the *Guardian* (11 September 1992) that 'Hammarskjöld's death was "no accident". They contend that the "European industrialists who controlled Katanga" arranged for two aircraft (piloted by mercenaries) to intercept the Secretary-General's flight.' O'Brien's declaration was 'based on 20 interviews with former mercenaries that were taped by a senior French diplomat in the 1970s' (David N. Gibbs, 'Dag Hammarskjöld, the United Nations, and the Congo Crisis of 1960–1: A Reinterpretation', *Journal of Modern African Studies*, Vol. 31, No. 1, March 1993, pp. 163–4). In 1998, obscure documents bearing the letterhead of the equally obscure South African Institute for Maritime Research (SAIMR) were released by the TRC. The documents suggested that MI5 and the CIA had colluded with the SAIMR in a plot to assassinate Hammarskjöld (*Mail & Guardian*, 28 August 1998; *The Times*, 20 August 1998). The existence of the SAIMR was first revealed in 1990 in connection with a number of mercenary escapades (Johannesburg *Sunday Times*, 11 November 1990). An investigation by a Norwegian researcher, Bodil Katarina Naevdal, suggests that Hammarskjold was murdered after the crash by a 'South African mercenary named Swanepoel', based upon an interview with a former mercenary (*Mail & Guardian*, 1 December 2000).

2) The *Rietbok* crash, 13 March 1967. The plane was flying to East London

when it disappeared; the 'authorities . . . maintained that neither the wreck, nor any bodies, were found.' In fact, the plane crashed into the sea and was swiftly discovered by navy divers. Among the victims of the crash were Professor J.P. Bruwer, the acting head of the Broederbond, and Audrey Rosenthal, an American anti-apartheid activist. Bruwer's children have claimed that at the time of the crash their father 'had started publicly to denounce apartheid as racial discrimination and told them that he would be killed'. In 1998, historian Martin Legassick disclosed that he had recruited Rosenthal to work for Defence and Aid. She had been in South Africa for five weeks meeting 'secretly with the remnants of the underground movements and [helping] them . . . receive desperately needed payments from the fund'. Before her death, Rosenthal wrote to Legassick 'that she thought she was being followed'. Former Security Police detective Donald Card recalled that 'his police superiors [were] obsessed with Rosenthal' (*Mail & Guardian*, 9 April 1998). Cecil Margo, who chaired the commission of inquiry, concluded on the 'balance of probabilities that the pilot had been the victim of a heart attack'. In his autobiography *Final Postponement: Reminiscences of a Crowded Life*, 1998, Margo suggested that 'structural failure' had been responsible for the crash (*East London Daily Dispatch*, 20 April 2001).

3) The *Helderberg* crash, 28 October 1987. The *Helderberg*, a Boeing 747, was a commercial plane which was travelling from Taiwan to South Africa when it 'crashed into the sea off the coast of Mauritius' with the loss of 159 lives. The Margo Commission found that 'the crash was caused by a fire on board, but that the cause of the fire was undetermined'. Relatives of the dead and investigative journalists took up the case to no avail, although circumstantial evidence suggested that 'SAA passenger flights were used to courier arms components and explosives in sanctions-busting activities by the parastatal ARMSCOR.' The TRC investigated the *Helderberg* case and concluded that 'Questions raised throughout the investigation process indicated that the investigators of the Margo Commission had not followed correct procedures . . . It is clear that further investigation is necessary before this matter can be laid to rest' (TRC, *Report*, Vol. 2, pp. 503–9). The *Mail & Guardian*, 15 June 2000, revealed that a 'hand-written [Department of Foreign Affairs] memo' dated 1989, questioned: 'One wonders whether SAA knows what they sometimes transport on the aircraft in sealed bags? Mindful of the Helderberg incident, an accident can also expose something.' In March 2001, TRC investigators 'had access to the unscrambled flight recording from the ill-fated aircraft, which indicated that when the captain told crew members after takeoff about the cargo contents, they said it was "madness" to carry that kind of freight' (Helen E. Purkitt and Stephen F. Burgess, *South Africa's Weapons of Mass Destruction*, 2005, pp. 78–9). For the alternative view that the Machel and *Helderberg* crashes were innocent accidents, see South African 'satirist' and former pilot Robert Kirby, *Mail & Guardian*, 1 September 2000.

49. TRC, *Report*, Vol. 2, p. 119; Johannesburg *Sunday Times*, 12 June 1988.

50. *Business Day*, 30 March 1988; *Weekly Mail*, 31 March 1988; *International Herald Tribune*, 11 April 1988.

51. *Weekend Argus*, 9 April 1988; Johannesburg *Sunday Star*, 10 April 1988; *Private Eye*, 22 October 1982; Pauw, *Heart of Darkness*, pp. 297, 309.

52. *Weekly Mail*, 8 April 1988; TRC, *Report*, Vol. 2, p. 121.

53. *Private Eye*, 24 September, 3 December 1982; Pauw, *Heart of Darkness*, pp. 297, 300–1, 306.

54. TRC, *Report*, Vol. 2, pp. 119–21, 140. The TRC *Report* admitted that it was unable to corroborate the evidence against Rouget and Guerrier and concluded that: 'The Commission believes on the basis of the evidence available to it that [Dulcie September] was a victim of a CCB operation involving the contracting of a private intelligence organisation which, in turn, contracted out the killing'.

55. Riaan Labuschagne, *On South Africa's Secret Service: An Undercover Agent's Story*, 2002, pp. 178–80, 229–30; *New Nation*, 9 August 1991.

56. Evelyn Groenink, *Dulcie: Een vrouw die haar mond moest houden*, 2001, English translation provided by the author; Evelyn Groenink, 'Murder Inc.: killing for business in southern Africa: The assassinations of Dulcie September, Anton Lubowski, and Chris Hani', unpublished manuscript, 2005, pp. 26, 35, 38, 44–6; see also *Mail & Guardian*, 9 January 1998, 5 April 1992; Bell, op. cit., pp. 296–7; Stephen Ellis, email to author, 10 March 2006.

CHAPTER 10: JANUS I: NEGOTIATION

1. Patti Waldmeir, *Anatomy of a Miracle*, 1997, pp. 49, 51. See also Hermann Giliomee, *The Afrikaners*, 2003, p. 625.

2. *Africa Confidential*, 20 March 1992.

3. *Weekly Mail*, 3 October 1986; Mark Swilling and Mark Phillips, 'The Powers of the Thunderbird', *South Africa at the End of the Eighties*, 1989, pp. 35, 46; Sampson, *Mandela*, pp. 330–2; Sampson, *Black and Gold*, p. 207.

4. Mark Swillings and Mark Phillips, 'The Emergency State: Its Structure, Power and Limits', Glenn Moss and Ingrid Obery (eds), *South African Review 5*, 1989, p. 76; Sampson, *Mandela*, pp. 342, 343, 348, 350–1; *Newsweek*, 20 June 1988; Swilling and Phillips, 'Powers of the Thunderbird', *South Africa at the End of the Eighties*, pp. 48–9.

5. Swilling and Phillips, 'Powers of the Thunderbird', *South Africa at the End of the Eighties*, pp. 50–3, 64; Swilling and Phillips, 'The Emergency State', *South African Review 5*, pp. 85–6; *Africa Confidential*, 8 July 1987, 17 June 1988.

6. Paul Erasmus, 'Confessions of an Apartheid Killer', *Observer*, 6 October 1996; O'Brien, 'The Use of Assassination (Part II)', *Terrorism and Political Violence*,

Summer 2001, pp. 116–17; TRC, *Report*, Vol. 2, p. 299; *Mail & Guardian*, 23 June 1995.

7. Swilling and Phillips, 'The Emergency State', *South African Review* 5, p. 80; *Work in Progress*, No. 55, August–September 1988, pp. 40–1; Mark Swilling and Mark Phillips, 'State Power in the 1980s: From "Total Strategy" to "Counter-revolutionary Warfare"', Jacklyn Cock & Laurie Nathan (eds), *War and Society*, 1989, p. 145; *Mail & Guardian*, 11 October 1996.

8. Chris Alden, *Apartheid's Last Stand*, 1998, p. 267, citing *Die Burger*, 19 February 1992; Waldmeir, op. cit., p. 35.

9. *Africa Analysis*, 14 December 2001; *Argus*, 12 February 1987; *Guardian*, 2 June 1998; Crocker, op. cit., p. 407; du Preez, op. cit., pp. 188–9. See also Piers Pigou, 'The Apartheid State and Violence: What Has the Truth and Reconciliation Commission Found?', *Politikon*, Vol. 28, No. 2, June 2001, pp. 216–17: 'Barnard acknowledged that he received stories and rumours that the police or the military were involved in illegal operations, and that he raised them with fellow [KIK] members. He said that their response was to ask him to bring evidence of such actions to the table. Unable to do this, he took his concerns to President P.W. Botha and left it at that, assuming that these concerns "would be dealt with on a political level" . . . Barnard insisted that the objective of the NIS throughout the 1980s was a peaceful political solution to the crisis facing the country . . . This position, however, did not mean that strong-armed tactics were precluded: "giving over was never an option . . . the South African government had to protect the physical integrity of the State and its citizens, the structures of the Security Management system, and their tasks".'

10. *Noseweek*, No. 68, May 2005; interview with Niel Barnard, 29 October 2002; Crocker, op. cit., p. 407.

11. Interview with Mike Louw, 7 July 2002; Johannesburg *Sunday Times*, 23 February 1992; Waldmeir, op. cit., p. 49.

12. Interview with Maritz Spaarwater, 9 July 2002; *Mail & Guardian*, 8 October 1999.

13. Sanders, op. cit., pp. 97–8; Sampson, *Mandela*, pp. 276–82, 298–9; Fran Buntman, *Robben Island and Prisoner Resistance to Apartheid*, 2003, pp. 206–8, 214–16; O'Meara, op. cit., p. 278.

14. Sampson, *Mandela*, p. 324; Buntman, op. cit., pp. 223–4; Sampson, *Black and Gold*, p. 210; Crocker, op. cit., p. 274; Alden, op. cit., p. 267; Bell, op. cit., pp. 250–1.

15. Sampson, *Mandela*, pp. 334–6; Crocker, op. cit., pp. 273–4; Mandela, *Long Walk*, p. 622.

16. O'Meara, op. cit., p. 294; Sampson, *Black and Gold*, pp. 251–4.

17. Sampson, *Mandela*, pp. 338–9, 341; Crocker, op. cit., p. 275.

18. Sampson, *Black and Gold*, pp. 43–4, 255; Sampson, *Mandela*, p. 340; *Weekly Mail & Guardian*, 18 February 1994; Bell, op. cit., p. 255.

19. Sampson, *Black and Gold*, pp. 258–62; Luli Callinicos, *Oliver Tambo*, 2004, p. 586; Robert Harvey, *The Fall of Apartheid*, 2001, pp. 15–16;

Sampson, *Mandela*, pp. 243, 364; Allister Sparks, *Tomorrow is Another Country*, 1995, pp. 21, 24.

20. Sampson, *Mandela*, p. 345; Sparks, *Tomorrow*, pp. 25–6; 'Memorandum: File No. MC/M353 Nelson Mandela Charitable Trust', 19 May 1986 [O.R. Tambo Papers]. See also Harvey, op. cit., p. 118.

21. State Security Council, 'The Possible Release of Mandela', 3 March 1986; 'Strategic Advice with Regard to the Options for the Release of Mandela', 17 March 1986. The second document also stated: 'Mandela is already perceived to be the Messiah who will free the black man from white oppression . . . Mandela is a symbol of the unification that will overthrow the SA government . . . Mandela is considered the unquestionable leader of the ANC and he definitely has the leadership abilities to escalate the revolutionary struggle to a point of no return . . . Mandela's release, no matter how it is done, will result in increased pressure on the SA government, and the pressure will simply move to another area because of the impression that the government is busy folding under revolutionary pressure.' Mike Louw explains that the 'Options' document 'was typical of the time (1986) when conflicting views were forced to compromise' (Mike Louw, e-mail to author, 10 December 2005). Both of the SSC documents emerged during the TRC process but this is the first time that they have been publicly quoted or cited. My particular thanks to the research specialist who made them available to me.

One conceivable victim of the 'proactive psychological action plan' was Winnie Mandela. While it appears that human right abuses occurred between May 1987 and February 1989 under the aegis of the Mandela United Football Club, a strange gathering of disturbed young men at Winnie Mandela's home in Soweto, it is also clear from Paul Erasmus's statements to the *Mail & Guardian* and to the TRC that 'the Security Police were involved in a concerted disinformation campaign against the ANC and the [SACP], and that Ms Madikizela-Mandela was a prominent target . . . Security policemen from Soweto admitted that she had been under constant electronic surveillance by means of telephone taps and bugs' (TRC, *Report*, Vol. 2, pp. 578–9). Winnie Mandela had always been subjected to extraordinary attention by the South African security forces. In 1981, Gordon Winter recalled that he had spied on Winnie Mandela in the 1960s: 'Pretoria has tried to frame, bribe and harass Winnie for years . . . van den Bergh's "Dirty Tricks" department planted a rumour round Johannesburg that Winnie was actually a BOSS agent. That "explained" why she always got acquitted whenever she was charged' (*Inside BOSS*, pp. 228, 237). In 1972, Winnie Mandela was arrested with her friend the *Rand Daily Mail* journalist John Horak (Gilby, op. cit., p. 98). Horak left journalism in 1985 and re-emerged as a major in the Security Police (Johannesburg *Sunday Star*, 14 June

1992). While questions remain about aspects of Winnie Mandela's life both in internal exile at Brandfort and from 1986 in Soweto, it is possible that the events of 1987-9 were permitted by the Security Police, which possessed a number of informers within the Mandela United Football Club, because the security forces intended to exploit the information in the future. Paul Erasmus masterminded the Stratcom propaganda operation to supply the foreign media with anti-Winnie Mandela material: '"We would work out a million stories for a million occasions." He said Stratcom dogma was the propaganda of the type should be based on 70 percent fact and 30 percent fiction. "You create a perception. Even when some of it can be disproved, since some of it is true people think all of it is true"' (*Mail & Guardian*, 30 June 1995). See also Paul Trewhela, 'The Trial of Winnie Mandela', *Searchlight South Africa*, Vol. 2, No. 3, July 1991; 'The Mistrial of Winnie Mandela: A Problem of Justice', *Searchlight South Africa*, Vol. 3, No. 1, August 1992; 'Mrs Mandela, "Enemy Agents!" . . . and the ANC Women's League', *Searchlight Africa*, Vol. 3, No.3, October 1993; *Vanity Fair*, October 1990; Fred Bridgland, *Katiza's Journey*, 1997; *Focus*, No. 9, January 1998; *Gaurdian*, 25 March 1999.

22. Waldmeir, op. cit., pp. 52-3, 63-4, 67-8; Herman Giliomee, '*Broedertwis*: Intra-Afrikaner Conflicts in the Transition from Apartheid', *African Affairs*, Vol. 91, No. 364, July 1992, p. 360; Hermann Giliomee, 'Surrender Without Defeat: Afrikaners and the South African "Miracle"', *Daedalus*, Vol. 126, No. 2, Spring 1997, p. 132, citing Broederbond circular, 'Political Values for the Survival of the Afrikaner', 1986. See also the *Guardian*, 5 February 1987, 18 September 1989. *Africa Confidential*, 21 January 2000, examining the Afrikanerbond (the organisation renamed itself during the transformation of South Africa), found that 'The Bond is still exclusive, with around 14,000 members grouped around (nowadays lower rank) decision-makers. Formerly all were invited, male, Protestant Afrikaners but they now include 700 women and 200 "people of colour".'

23. Ellis and Sechaba, op. cit., p. 58; Vladimir Shubin, *ANC: A View from Moscow*, 1999, pp. 238, 274-5; Waldmeir, op. cit., pp. 65-6; Sampson, *Black and Gold*, pp. 263-4, 324-5. Willie Esterhuyse told the annual congress of the Afrikaans Studentebond in Potchefstroom in July 1986: 'It is an illusion to think the release of Mandela . . . will bring instant peace in black townships . . . "We are not even sure that the ANC 'controls' the Comrades"' (Johannesburg *Star*, 15 July 1986).

24. Sampson, *Mandela*, pp. 351-2; Mandela, *Long Walk*, pp. 632-5; Sparks, *Tomorrow*, p. 36. On the EPG, see the Commonwealth Group of Eminent Persons, *Mission to South Africa*, 1986.

25. Sampson, *Mandela*, p. 363; Waldmeir, op. cit., p. 74; Alden, op. cit., p. 267.

26. Bell, op. cit., pp. 250-1; Sampson, *Mandela*, p. 363; Sparks, *Tomorrow*,

pp. 77–9; Harvey, op. cit., provides the most detailed account of the Afrikaner–ANC meetings which Rudolph Agnew financed at a cost of 'between £500,000 and £1 million' (p. 20).

27. Harvey, op. cit., pp. 127, 132, 225; Waldmeir, op. cit., pp. 77, 80. The story of a South African individual who attempted to create a private channel between the ANC and the South African government is told in Richard Rosenthal, *Mission Improbable*, 1998.

28. Sampson, *Mandela*, p. 364; Alden, op. cit., pp. 267–8; Hamann, op. cit., p. 90; *Africa Confidential*, 17 June 1988. P.W. van der Westhuizen had demonstrated his uncertainty at the transformation that was beginning to happen in Afrikaner politics in an interview with James Roherty in March 1987: 'van der Westhuizen was anything but his ebullient self. "What you are doing is incomprehensible . . . the posture adopted by Washington in the past year is not just a mistake in *tactics*; it is a mistake in *principle* . . . The RSA is 'Africa's State of the Future' . . . There will be a new dispensation here, which *we* shall work out . . . *cannot Washington understand that?*" ' (original emphasis). Six months later, it was announced that van der Westhuizen had been appointed ambassador to Chile. As Roherty commented: 'the point may well have been reached where it was deemed best to send the energetic general abroad' (Roherty, op. cit., pp. 196, 205).

29. O'Meara, op. cit., pp. 377–8; Swilling and Phillips, 'Powers of the Thunderbird', *South Africa at the End of the Eighties*, p. 65. For histories of the battle of Cuito Cuanavale, tilted towards the military interpretation rather than the political, see George, op. cit. pp. 213–35; Fred Bridgland, *The War for Africa: Twelve Months that Transformed a Continent*, 1990; Jannie Geldenhuys, *A General's Story: From an Era of War and Peace*, 1995; Helmoed-Römer Heitman, *War in Angola*, 1990; Roherty, op. cit. p. 166. Ellis and Sechaba, op. cit., pp. 185–8, offers the alternative interpretation. See also *Africa Confidential*, 18 November 1987: 'Malan's problem is that increasingly his boys are returning from combat zones in Angola in plastic bags.'

30. Crocker, op. cit., pp. 406–7, 432–3, 441–5.

31. *Colin Legum's Third World Reports*, 27 January 1993; Crocker, op. cit., p. 368.

32. Sparks, *Tomorrow*, p. 36; Mandela, *Long Walk*, pp. 636–7, 640.

33. Johannesburg *Star*, 19 February 1992, citing *Die Burger*, 18 February 1992; Alden, op. cit., pp. 268–9, citing *Die Burger*, 19 February 1992; Sparks, *Tomorrow*, p. 36; David Dimbleby (BBC), interview with Niel Barnard, 29 October 2002, transcript. In contrast to Allister Sparks, Niel Barnard suggests that there were forty-eight meetings (Robin Benger [CBC], interview with Niel Barnard, January 2003, transcript).

34. Mandela, *Long Walk*, p. 642; 'In Our Lifetime', *Liberation*, June 1956, pp. 4–8; Mandela, *No Easy Walk to Freedom*, 1965, pp. 55–60; Sampson, *Mandela*, pp. 95, 594.

35. Dimbleby, interview with Barnard, 29 October 2002, transcript; interview with Mike Louw, 7 July 2002; Sampson, *Mandela*, p. 403; Benger, interview with Barnard, January 2003, transcript. In August 1988, Esterhuyse, Terreblanche and Willem de Klerk carried an exciting message to Mbeki, Pahad and Tony Trew in Britain: 'the release of Mandela [was scheduled] to happen after [the] local government elections in October but before Christmas 1988' (Harvey, op. cit., p. 148). This is an indication of how complicated and fluid the negotiations process was.

36. Sampson, *Mandela*, p. 381; private information; O'Meara, op. cit., pp. 388–92.

37. Ivor Powell, 'Aspects of Propaganda Operations', in Minaar, op. cit., p. 338; Robert D'A. Henderson, 'South African Intelligence Under de Klerk', *International Journal of Intelligence and Counterintelligence*, Vol. 8, No. 1, Spring 1995, p. 84.

38. Sparks, *Tomorrow*, pp. 54–6, 109–10; Sampson, *Mandela*, op. cit., pp. 382, 390–92; Mandela, *Long Walk*, p. 658, contradicts Mandela to Sampson: 'Dr Barnard looked down and noticed that my shoelaces were not properly tied and he quickly knelt down to tie them for me'; Dimbleby, interview with Barnard, 29 October 2002, transcript; Benger, interview with Barnard, January 2003, transcript.

39. Sampson, *Mandela*, p. 392; interview with Mike Louw, 3 December 2003; Mile Louw, e-mail to author, 10 December 2005.

40. 'Analysis: Winnie Mandela', 1995 [Walter Felgate Security Papers]: The photograph of the prisoner and the President is included in David Harrison, *Mandela: The Living Legend*, parts 1 and 2, BBC 1, March 2003; and Robin Benger, *Madiba: The Life and Times of Nelson Mandela*, CBC, April 2004; Benger, interview with Barnard, January 2003, transcript: 'Mr Mandela never liked that photo . . . He believed that . . . in the picture one can see him in a . . . subservient physical mode.' The original South African edition of Allister Spark's *Tomorrow is Another Country*, published by Struik in 1994, included the photograph but it was removed from the international Heinemann edition (Buntman, op. cit., pp. 214–15). Verne Harris and Carolyn Hamilton, *A Prisoner in the Garden*, 2005, p. 207, displays a different photograph: 'Minister Kobie Coetsee gives Mandela a briefcase as a gift before his release from Victor Verster. Between the two of them is Niel Barnard.'

41. Sparks, *Tomorrow*, pp. 110–13; Johannesburg *Star*, 19 February 1992, citing *Die Burger*, 18 February 1992.

42. Allister Sparks and Mick Gold, *The Death of Apartheid*, BBC 2, 1994; interview with Mike Louw, 3 December 2003.

43. Waldmeir, op. cit., pp. 145–46; Sparks, *Tomorrow*, pp. 113–14.

44. *Africa Report*, July–August 1989, p. 36; Willem de Klerk, *F.W. de Klerk: The Man in His Time*, 1991, pp. 54–5, adds that following the inauguration of his brother, 'I went at his request to see a top man in the [NIS]. At that meet-

ing I had my arm twisted to stop visiting the ANC because it "lent prominence to an organisation on its knees", one that "could never play a role in negotiations".' F.W. de Klerk had been 'outraged and disturbed' when he discovered Willem de Klerk's continuing role in talks with the ANC in Britain. The President described the secret channel as 'hobnobbing with terrorists'; *Africa Confidential*, 20 March 1992, reported that 'Willem de Klerk has told friends that he doesn't understand what his brother . . . sees in Barnard.' Interview with Niel Barnard, 21 October 2002; Harvey, op. cit., p. 168; Percy Cradock, *In Pursuit of British Interests*, 1997, pp. 144–58; Johannesburg *Star*, 22 January 1992.

45. John Major, *The Autobiography*, 1999, p. 209; Benger, interview with Barnard, January 2003, transcript; de Klerk, op. cit., p. 153; Henderson, 'South African Intelligence Under de Klerk', *International Journal of Intelligence and Counterintelligence*, Spring 1995, pp. 56–7; Sampson, *Mandela*, p. 397; Bell, op. cit., pp. 277–8, 280; Mandela, *Long Walk*, pp. 661–2.

46. Bell, op. cit., pp. 265, 267–8, 271.

47. *Argus*, 23 March 1991; *Guardian*, 11 July 1991; *Windhoek Observer*, 25 May 1991; *Work in Progress*, No. 79, December 1991. For Basson's propaganda, see Nico Basson and Ben Motinga, *Call Them Spies*, 1989. Two ANC spies within South Africa's Bureau of Information told their Namibian story in *Sechaba*, December 1989, pp. 18–23.

48. Bell, op. cit., pp. 266–8; Crocker, op. cit., p. 484.

49. Robin Renwick, *Unconventional Diplomacy in Southern Africa*, 1997, p. 133; Stiff, *The Covert War*, pp. 373, 397; Bell, op. cit., p. 266.

50. Renwick, op. cit., p. 134; *Windhoek Observer*, 25 May 1991; Louis Harms, *Report of the Commission of Inquiry into Certain Alleged Murders*, 1990, p. 163.

51. Pauw, *Heart of the Whore*, pp. 133–4, 190–1; du Preez, op. cit., p. 124; Pauw, *Heart of Darkness*, p. 232; TRC, *Report*, Vol. 2, p. 83.

52. Johannesburg *Sunday Star*, 13 May 1990; Pauw, *Heart of the Whore*, pp. 131, 190–1; conversation with Tori Pretorius, 8 June 1999; Pauw, *Heart of Darkness*, pp. 234–5; TRC, *Report*, Vol. 2, pp. 82–3. For Evelyn Groenink's entertaining but conspiratorial take on the murder of Anton Lubowski, see *Mail & Guardian*, 16 July, 1 October 1999. Peter Stiff, *Warfare by Other Means*, 2001, p. 412: 'It appears highly likely that once he was overseas, Acheson was hunted down and murdered. He posed too much of a danger to the [CCB] to be allowed to live.'

53. Renwick, op. cit., pp. 134–5; Henderson, 'South African Intelligence Under de Klerk', *International Journal of Intelligence and Counterintelligence*, Spring 1995, pp. 57–8; Bell, op. cit., pp. 270–1.

54. de Klerk, op. cit., p. 152; Henderson, 'South African Intelligence Under de Klerk', *International Journal of Intelligence and Counterintelligence*, Spring 1995, pp. 57–8; Bell, op. cit., p. 59.

55. *Weekly Mail*, 8 December 1989; Johannesburg *Star*, 10 December 1989.
56. de Klerk, op. cit., pp. 157–8; Mandela, *Long Walk*, pp. 663–5.
57. Waldmeir, op. cit., pp. 136–7; Sampson, *Mandela*, p. 402.

CHAPTER 11: JANUS II: THE THIRD FORCE

1. TRC, *Report*, Vol. 2, p. 38.
2. Keith Gottschalk, 'The Rise and Fall of Apartheid's Death Squads, 1969–93', Bruce Campbell and Arthur Brenner (eds), *Death Squads in Global Perspective*, 2000, pp. 244–5; TRC, *Report*, Vol. 6, p. 579; Mandela, *Long Walk*, p. 703; de Klerk, op. cit., pp. 188–9, 193–5; Department of State, 'Memorandum of Conversation: One-on-One Meeting with FW de Klerk', 24 September 1990 [National Security Archive].
3. TRC, *Report*, Vol. 2, pp. 177, 298–9; Civilian Support Component, 'The Apparatus of State-orchestrated Violence in Apartheid South Africa', unpublished report, February 1997, p. 21.
4. TRC, *Report*, Vol. 2, p. 178; Civilian Support Component, 'The Apparatus of State-orchestrated Violence', unpublished report, February 1997, pp. 22, 24–5.
5. Ellis, 'The Historical Significance of South Africa's Third Force', *Journal of Southern African Studies*, June 1998, p. 263; McCuen, 'The Art of Counter-Revolutionary War', samizdat pamphlet, p. 37.
6. Sanders, op. cit., pp. 175–6; Anthea Jeffrey, *The Natal Story*, 1997, p. 29.
7. Jeffrey, *The Natal Story*, p. 29.
8. Sanders, op. cit., pp. 176–7: Patrick Laurence, from 1977 the *Guardian*'s correspondent in South Africa and a *Rand Daily Mail* journalist, now the editor of the Helen Suzman Foundation's *Focus*, demonstrated the paternalist tendency in South African liberalism, informing a student researcher in 1978: 'Blacks were less inclined to question eye-witness accounts and were more likely to give credibility to police brutality'; The situation was much the same during the mid-1980s. William Finnegan, *Dateline Soweto*, 1995, p. 119, discussed the Vaal Triangle uprising with a white Johannesburg *Star* reporter: 'The only people surprised in this building . . . were the white sub-editors who had been relegating all the warnings they were getting from black reporters to [the African edition] . . . Whites hardly knew that anything was up'; Brooks, op. cit., p. 217.
9. Sampson, *Mandela*, p. 53; O'Meara, op. cit., p. 202.
10. Shula Marks, ' "The dog that did not bark, or why Natal did not take off": Ethnicity & Democracy in South Africa', in Bruce Berman, Dickson Eyoh and Will Kymlicka (eds), *Ethnicity & Democracy in Africa*, 2004, pp. 185, 190–1; Gerhard Mare and Georgina Hamilton, *An Appetite for Power*, 1987, pp. 57–8, 60.
11. TRC, *Report*, Vol. 3, p. 166; Mare, op. cit., p. 150; *BOSS: The First 5 Years*,

pp. 34–5. See also *Christian Science Monitor*, 14 May 1974.

12. *Weekly Mail*, 2 August 1991, 27 November 1998; Walter Felgate, 'Section 29' testimony at the TRC, November 1998; interview with Walter Felgate, 10 December 2000.

13. Mare, op. cit., pp. 45–54, 137; Marks, ' "The dog that did not bark" ', Berman, op. cit., pp. 190–1.

14. Brooks op. cit., pp. 65–6, 127, 130–1, 224.

15. Walter Felgate, 'Mangosuthu Buthelezi: The Iago of South African Politics', unpublished manuscript, 1999; Mare, op. cit., pp. 153, 168, 178–9; Sampson, *Mandela*, p. 356; Robert Sobukwe's story is well told in Benjamin Pogrund, *How Can Man Die Better*, 1990; Sampson, *Black and Gold*, p. 140: '[In 1970], Sobukwe of the PAC was under house arrest in Kimberley . . . When I visited him . . . we drove in a hired car as we talked, but a police car was following us after a few minutes . . . [Sobukwe] suffered from paranoia after his long isolation and he was convinced the police had inserted a listening device into his body.' Sampson was tempering the truth: Robert Sobukwe believed that the South African intelligence services had implanted a microphone in his rectum so that they could listen to his conversations (conversation with Anthony Sampson, 3 October 1997).

16. Mare, op. cit., pp. 85–7, 145, citing Bella Schmahmann, 'KwaZulu in Contemporary South Africa: A Case Study in the Implementation of the Policy of Separate Development', unpublished PhD thesis, University of Natal, 1978; Jeffrey, *The Natal Story*, pp. 34–7; Felgate, 'Mangosuthu Buthelezi', unpublished manuscript, 1999; Marks, ' "The dog that did not bark" ', Berman, op. cit., p. 191.

17. de Kock, op. cit., p. 169; Mare, op. cit., pp. 214–15: the KZP were responsible for the rural areas and most of the townships excepting the largest townships near 'the largest concentration of white inhabitants in Natal'; TRC, *Report*, Vol. 2, p. 470. Barry Streek and Richard Wicksteed, *Render Unto Kaiser*, 1981, p. 45, explained that following Transkeian 'independence', the Transkei Intelligence Service (TIS) was established as a model of BOSS and took over the agency's functions within the independent homeland. The TIS was headed by a former BOSS employee and had white advisers. Chief George Matanzima said in a parliamentary debate that he had 'recently been talking to . . . General van den Bergh, whom he described as "a man of high integrity" '.

18. Mare, op. cit., pp. 185–7; Anthea Jeffrey, *The Natal Story*, pp. 47, 132.

19. Mare, op. cit., p. 147; Felgate Security Papers; *Africa Confidential*, 7 January 1987; Walter Felgate, 'Section 29' testimony, November 1998.

20. *Africa Confidential*, 26 July 2002; interview with Mario Ambrosini, 15 June 1999; interview with Walter Felgate, 18 June 1999; Felgate, 'Mangosuthu Buthelezi', unpublished manuscript, 1999; Felgate, 'Section 29' testimony, November 1998.

21. *Mail & Guardian*, 15 September 1995; TRC, *Report*, Vol. 2, p. 299; *Africa*

Confidential, 30 October 1985; Marks, '"The dog that did not bark"', Berman, op. cit., pp. 190–1.

22. TRC, *Report*, Vol. 2, p. 459; Howard Varney, 'The Role of the Former State in Political Violence, Operation Marion: A Case Study', unpublished paper, March 1997, p. 58.

23. *Mail & Guardian*, 14 February 2003; Defense Intelligence Agency, 'Defense Intelligence Estimate – South Africa in Transition: Prospects for Internal Political Moderation and Regional Stability', May 1985 [National Security Archive]; Walter Felgate, 'Section 29' testimony, November 1998. Kobus Bosman had previously been the head of the SADF's Directorate of Public Relations or as the *Rand Daily Mail* titled him, 'The man who controls what you know'. Bosman had effectively been the chief censor. He told the newspaper: 'In my experience . . . we [have] prohibited so few things that they are really not worth mentioning. The media in South Africa has a very good understanding of what should not be published . . . [I] think that over the years we have built up a very good relationship with our military correspondents' (*Rand Daily Mail*, 2 November 1981).

24. Varney, op. cit., pp. 58–9, citing Vice-Admiral Putter, memorandum prepared by General T. Groenewald, to General J. Geldenhuys, 27 November 1985; Mare, op. cit., p. 176, citing *Financial Mail*, 6 December 1985.

25. TRC, *Report*, Vol. 2, pp. 436, 439–40; *Guardian*, 12 March 1993; Gert Hugo and Stef Snel, *Military Intelligence and the Counter Revolutionary War in the Eastern Cape*, 1998, p. 50; Sam Sole, 'The Hammer Unit and the Goniwe Murders', Minnaar, op. cit., pp. 278–9.

26. TRC, *Report*, Vol. 6, pp. 435–40; Hugo, op. cit., pp. 50–1. See also the *Independent*, 25 August 1992. After Sebe's death, the Port Elizabeth *Evening Post* revealed that Colonel Jan Breytenbach had been recruited by the MID-dominated International Research-Ciskei Intelligence Service to command 1 Ciskei Parachute Battalion (28 September 1991).

27. Joseph Lelyveld, *Move Your Shadow*, 1986, pp. 157–8, 168, 175, 177; Johannesburg *Sunday Express*, 15 November 1981; TRC, *Report*, Vol. 2, p. 436; East London *Daily Dispatch*, 18 September 1991; *Guardian*, 20 March 1993.

28. *Mail & Guardian*, 8 March 1996; Varney, op. cit., p. 53, citing General Groenewald, 'SADF Assistance to Chief Minister Buthelezi and Bishop Lekganyane', to General Malan, 19 December 1985.

29. Varney, op. cit., pp. 54, 67, 69–70, 72–3, 76, 78, citing H.J.R. Myburg, 'Special Support to Chief Minister Buthelezi', 14 January 1986; General Geldenhuys, memorandums prepared by General Groenewald, to General Malan, 16, 17 January 1986; *Mail & Guardian*, 10 November 1995, 8 March 1996. The government ministers selected to assist Buthelezi were Magnus Malan, Louis Le Grange and Chris Heunis (Constitutional Development).

30. Varney, op. cit., pp. 79–80, 82, 85, 93–4, 96–8, 109, citing Vice-Admiral Putter,

memorandum, to General Geldenhuys, 10 February 1986; General Groene-wald, memorandum, to Vice-Admiral Putter, 14 February 1986; General Groenewald, 'Discussions with the Minister of Defence on 17 February 1986 in connection with military assistance to KwaZulu', to Vice-Admiral Putter, 18 February 1986; General Liebenberg, 'The Liebenberg Report', to General Geldenhuys, 27 February 1986; Vice-Admiral Putter, memorandum, to General Geldenhuys, 16 April 1986; *Mail & Guardian*, 8 December 1995.

31. Varney, op. cit., pp. 98–9; Walter Felgate, 'Section 29' testimony, November 1998.

32. Varney, op. cit., pp. 109–10; TRC, *Report*, Vol. 7, p. 696; TRC, *Report*, Vol. 3, p. 225. The *Mail & Guardian*, 8 December 1995, added that on 5 December 1986 three union shop stewards were murdered by members of the Inkatha hit squad 'on a lonely road near Mpophomeni'. Daluxolo Wordsworth Luthuli was a fascinating figure: the grandson of ANC leader and Nobel peace prize winner Albert Luthuli; a former MK veteran and Robben Island prisoner (Pauw, *Heart of Darkness*, p. 132).

33. Varney, op. cit., pp. 113–18, citing Vice-Admiral Putter, memorandum, to General Geldenhuys, 28 January 1988; report, to General Geldenhuys, 3 February 1988; Howard Varney and Jeremy Sarkin, 'Failing to Pierce the Hit Squad Veil: A Critique of the Malan Trial', *South African Journal of Criminal Justice*, 1997.

34. Varney, op. cit., pp. 54–6, 121–2, 131, 134, 136, citing Signal report 'marked exclusive for Geldenhuys and Putter', 31 August 1988; Colonel M.A. van den Bergh, 'Duties and Responsibilities: S03(ST) Op Marion', to Captain J.P. Opperman, 31 October 1988; General Geldenhuys, 'Operation Marion: Liaison', to General Malan, October 1988; Brigadier Jac Buchner, 'Operation Marion: Liaison with SAP Security', to General Neels van Tonder, 28 November 1988; Brigadier Cor van Niekerk, Diary, 28 November 1988.

35. Unsigned, 'A Planned Attempt on the Life of Inkosi Buthelezi', to the Office of the Head of Operations, 26 October 1988; Musa K. Zondi, 'The Rising Spate of Violence in the Durban–Pietermaritzburg Area' to H.E. Inkosi Dr M.G. Buthelezi, 20 December 1988 [Felgate Security Papers].

36. 'Harare Meeting – December 1988', delivered on 13 May 1989 [Felgate Security Papers].

37. Varney, op. cit., p. 141, citing General Jannie Geldenhuys, 'Operation Marion: SADF Support to Inkatha', to General Neels van Tonder, April 1990; TRC, *Report*, Vol. 3, pp. 190, 214; Stephen Ellis, e-mail to author, 13 January 2005; Jeffrey, *Natal Story*, pp. 1–2.

38. Webster and Friedman, *Suppressing Apartheid's Opponents*, p. 26; Varney, op. cit., pp. 56, 140, citing General Neels van Tonder, 'Op Marion: Liaison with the Chief Minister', to Admiral Putter, 6 November 1989.

39. CIA, 'Africa Review – South Africa: Political Violence in KwaZulu-Natal', 19 January 1990 [National Security Archive].

40. Ellis, 'The Historical Significance of South Africa's Third Force', *Journal of Southern African Studies*, June 1998, p. 283; interview with Pik Botha, 11 December 2000; TRC, *Report*, Vol. 2, p. 693.

41. TRC, *Report*, Vol. 2, pp. 625–6; TRC, *Report*, Vol. 3, pp. 259, 264.

42. Varney, op. cit., p. 141, citing General Jannie Geldenhuys, 'Operation Marion: SADF Support to Inkatha', to General Neels van Tonder, April 1990.

43. Mandela, *Long Walk*, pp. 703–5; TRC, *Report*, Vol. 3, p. 676; de Klerk, op. cit., pp. 202–203.

44. TRC, *Report*, Vol. 2, pp. 608–9; de Kock, op. cit., pp. 100, 237; Pauw, *Heart of Darkness*, pp. 62, 127. Themba Khoza, who avoided prosecution and represented the IFP in the post-1994 South African parliament, died of 'AIDS-related illnesses' in May 2000. As the *Mail & Guardian* commented: 'Khoza could lay legitimate claim to a place among the top 10 mass murderers in South Africa's history' (2 June 2000). During the early 1990s, an intriguing fellow who worked with the IFP was Philip Powell, a former member of the Security Police. De Kock recalled Powell once telling him, 'with tears in his eyes, how tired he was of walking among the bodies of his people; how upset he was that his people were seriously lacking in training and, because of that, were being mown down by the ANC' (de Kock, op. cit., p. 242). On Powell, who is reported to be living in Britain (*City Press*, 1 August 2004), see *Mail & Guardian*, 7 March 1997, 18 June 1999, 20 June 2000, 10 October 2003.

45. TRC, *Report*, Vol. 3, pp. 704–5, 707; Johannesburg *Star*, 13, 14 September 1990; *Cape Times*, 7 September 1990.

46. Varney, op. cit., pp. 57–9, citing Brigadier van Niekerk, memorandum on 'SADF Involvement', to CSI, MID, 8 October 1990; handwritten, undated memorandum: 'Inkatha: Op Marion: SADF Involvement'; Department of State, 'C.G. Myrick's First meeting with Chief Minister Buthelezi', 17 September 1990; Department of State, 'Meeting with Buthelezi', 7 January 1991 [National Security Archive].

47. TRC, *Report*, Vol. 3, p. 676; Mark Hugh Shaw, 'South Africa's Other War: Understanding and Resolving Political Violence in KwaZulu-Natal (1985–) and the PWV (1990–)', unpublished PhD thesis, March 1997, pp. 220–5; Felgate, 'Mangosuthu Buthelezi', unpublished manuscript, 1999. On the Boipatong massacre, which has been subject to substantial examination, see Rian Malan, *Mail & Guardian*, 28 May 1999, *Frontiers of Freedom*, June 1999, March 2001; and Piers Pigou, *Mail & Guardian*, 21 May 1999, 6 October, 1 December 2000. A heavily censored CIA report commented in 1992: 'We have no reporting that indicates President de Klerk or senior security officials ordered the 17 June attack at Boipatong . . . We doubt – but cannot rule out – the direct participation of rogue police or soldiers . . . We believe isolated secu-

rity mavericks are exacerbating black feuding in some areas to weaken the ANC and undermine negotiations' (CIA, 'South Africa: The Boipatong Massacre and Reining in the Security Forces', 28 August 1992 [National Security Archive]). Bill Berkeley, *The Graves Are Not Yet Full*, 2001, demonstrated that in the late 1990s Buthelezi, Groenewald and Buchner felt little remorse for their actions. Buthelezi told Berkeley: 'I've always espoused nonviolence . . . I've always been a proponent of peaceful change' (p. 185). When asked whether he had been a 'puppet' or a 'stooge' of the apartheid security forces, Buthelezi replied: 'I'm not going to respond to the propaganda of my enemies . . . I'm not going to get into these insults! Everybody knew that I was anti-apartheid' (pp. 188–9). Major-General Jac Buchner, the head of the KZP in the late 1980s, proudly informed Berkeley: 'Our training was mostly from you guys, and the Brits. By that I mean American techniques . . . It's a brotherhood – we in the police of the various intelligence offices overseas, including ones in Washington' (p. 180). And Groenewald announced mysteriously: 'Don't underestimate the involvement of foreign intelligence in Third Force operations: MI6, the CIA . . . South Africa was a pawn in the struggle between the big powers' (p. 172).

48. de Kock, op. cit., pp. 235–6; Pauw, *Heart of Darkness*, p. 125; *Independent*, 19, 26 July 1991; *Weekly Mail*, 19 July, 9 August, 13 December 1991, 10 January 1992; *Guardian*, 19, 25, 26 July 1991; Ellis, 'The Historical Significance of South Africa's Third Force', *Journal of Southern African Studies*, June 1998, p. 293.

49. TRC, *Report*, Vol. 2, p. 709.

50. Richard A. Wilson, *The Politics of Truth and Reconciliation in South Africa*, 2001, pp. 62, 79.

51. Department of State, 'John Kane-Berman on the Violence', 20 May 1991 [National Security Archive].

52. John Kane-Berman, *Political Violence in South Africa*, 1993, p. 88; John Kane-Berman, Foreword, Anthea Jeffrey, *The Truth About the Truth Commission*, 1999, p. 4; *Frontiers of Freedom*, March 2001, p. 9.

53. Marks, ' "The dog that did not bark" ', Berman, op. cit., pp. 183–4.

54. J.D.F. Jones, *Storyteller*, 2001, pp. 415–18 – I researched the van der Post, Buthelezi, Aspinall material for this book; Sampson, *Mandela*, pp. 356, 396, 440. On Aspinall, Goldsmith and Lord Lucan's 'Clermont set', see John Pearson, *The Gamblers*, 2005.

55. Sampson, *Mandela*, p. 441; *Weekly Mail & Guardian*, 18 October 1996: Gordon was later 'a member of a British team of "spin doctors" brought in by Inkatha to advise' during South Africa's 1995 local government elections. In 1996 Tim Martin, a spokesman for the (British) Referendum Party was ' "very pleased that Marc Gordon joined the party to work with us". They had looked into the South African links before he joined the party and were satisfied with the results'; *Private Eye*, 20 September 1996; Jones, op. cit., pp. 420, 428.

56. Conrad Black, *A Life in Progress*, 1993, pp. 492, 495–6; Anthony Sampson,*Who Runs This Place?*, 2004, p. 235.

57. Margaret Thatcher, Speech at Ulundi, 12 May 1991; interview with Walter Felgate, 18 June 1999; *Independent*, 24 June 1993; Jones, op. cit., pp. 420–3.

CHAPTER 12: SHUFFLING THE PACK

1. Allen Drury, *'A Very Strange Society'*, 1968, pp. 455–6.

2. Vladimir Shubin, *ANC: A View from Moscow*, 1999, pp. 82, 102, 219–20; Sparks, *Tomorrow*, p. 118. For the archetype of the ill-informed anti-communist, see 'right-wing American clergyman' (Ellis and Sechaba, op. cit., p. 2) Henry Pike's *A History of Communism in South Africa*, p. xvi: 'Sincere thanks to Gerard Ludi . . . and to General H.J. van den Bergh (retired) for a long interview in which he gave me a full summary of communism during his long tenure as head of South Africa's Security Police and Intelligence Service.'

3. ANC, 'Further Submissions and Responses by the ANC to the TRC', 12 May 1997; Ellis and Sechaba, op. cit., p. 61.

4. E.J. Verwey (ed), *New Dictionary of South African Biography*, Vol.1, 1995, pp. 146–8; Ellis and Sechaba, op. cit., pp. 61, 63–4.

5. Shubin, op. cit., pp. 45–6, 102–7; Kasrils, op. cit., pp. 87–8.

6. ANC, 'Further Submissions and Responses by the ANC', 12 May 1997; ANC, 'The Nuclear Conspiracy', September 1975; *Sechaba*, November–December 1975; Cervenka, op. cit., pp. 4–5; Johannesburg *Sunday Times*, 17 November 1991: Donald Sole commented in his unpublished autobiography, 'When the embassy was moving from one building to another in Bonn, top secret documents about South African and German collusion on nuclear technology were put in a non-secret file and left in an unlocked basement. The document was pilfered and led later to a massive public exposure.' See also the *Observer*, 5 October 1975, 14 August 1977.

7. Breytenbach, op. cit., pp. 78–9.

8. Callinicos, op. cit., pp. 343–4; ANC, 'Further Submissions and Responses by the ANC', 12 May 1997; Shubin, op. cit., p. 205; Ellis and Sechaba, op. cit., pp. 47, 87, 117.

9. Shubin, op. cit., p. 205; ANC, 'Further Submissions and Responses by the ANC', 12 May 1997; Kasrils, op. cit., p. 193.

10. ANC, 'Further Submissions and Responses by the ANC', 12 May 1997; *The Times*, 1 March 2002; Stephen Ellis, 'Mbokodo: Security in ANC Camps, 1961–1990', *African Affairs*, Vol. 93, No. 371, April 1994, p. 285.

11. *Work in Progress*, No. 82, May–June 1992, p. 15; ANC, 'Further Submissions and Responses by the ANC', 12 May 1997; Ellis and Sechaba, op. cit., p. 116.

12. ANC, 'Further Submissions and Responses by the ANC', 12 May 1997; Ellis and Sechaba, op. cit., pp. 116–19; Shubin, op. cit., p. 226.

13. Ellis, 'Mbokodo', *African Affairs*, April 1994, pp. 288, 290; Shubin, op. cit., pp. 174, 227; Mandela, *Long Walk*, p. 516; Sampson, *Mandela*, p. 234.

14. Ellis, 'Mbokodo', *African Affairs*, April 1994, p. 294; James Stuart, 'Stuart Commission Report into Recent Developments in the People's Republic of Angola', 1984, but not released until the 1990s; see 'Profiles of Awardees: Profiles of the National Living Treasures Awards candidates for 2005' (www.nhc.org.za/index.php?pid=136&ct=1).

15. Stuart, 'Stuart Commission Report', 1984; Adv. T.L. Skweyiya, 'Report of the Commission of Enquiry into Complaints by Former African National Congress Prisoners and Detainees', 1992.

16. ANC, 'Further Submissions and Responses by the ANC', 12 May 1997; Sampson, *Mandela*, pp. 276–82; Kasrils, op. cit., p. 141; Mzala, *Gatsha Buthelezi: Chief with a Double Agenda*, 1988.

17. Skweyiya, 'Report of the Commission of Enquiry', 1992; ANC, 'Further Submissions and Responses by the ANC', 12 May 1997; Ellis and Sechaba, op. cit., p. 149; Kasrils, op. cit., p. 199. Ellis revealed that one of the bones of contention in MK's military intelligence related to access to a television during the 1986 football world cup: 'A group of white and Indian ANC members gathered to watch the games on television in an ANC military intelligence safe house in Lusaka whose existence was not even known to many African Military Intelligence officials. Some ANC members, ultra-sensitive to any suggestion of discrimination on racial grounds, felt moved to complain . . . since it seemed to confirm the widespread belief that some of the white ANC leaders generally felt more comfortable with Indians or with other whites than with blacks' (p. 149).

18. ANC, 'Further Submissions and Responses by the ANC', 12 May 1997; Ellis, 'Mbokodo', *African Affairs*, April 1994, p. 283; the scale of attention given to the human rights abuses in MK's prison camps is vastly greater than any equivalent examination of the apartheid regime's prison institutions. See *New Statesman*, 28 February 1986; Nico Basson and Ben Motinga, *Call Them Spies*, 1989; 'A Namibian Horror', *Searchlight South Africa*, Vol. 1, No. 4, February 1990; ANC, 'Report of a Commission of Inquiry Set up in November 1989 by the National Working Committee of the African National Congress to Investigate the Circumstances Leading to the Death of Mzwakhe Ngwenya (also known as Thami Zulu or TZ)', March 1990; 'Inside Quadro', *Searchlight South Africa*, Vol. 2, No. 1, July 1990; *Aida Parker Newsletter*, No. 141, January–February 1991; Amnesty International, 'South Africa: Torture, Ill-Treatment and Executions in African National Congress Camps', December 1992; IFF, 'The Report of the Douglas Commission 1993', January 1993; 'The ANC Prison Camps: An Audit of Three Years, 1990–1993',

Searchlight South Africa, Vol. 3, No. 2, April 1993; Samuel Motsuenyane, 'Report of the Commission of Enquiry into Certain Allegations of Cruelty and Human Rights Abuse against ANC Prisoners and Detainees by ANC Members', August 1993. See also Mwezi Twala and Ed Benard, *Mbokodo: Inside MK*, 1994; Thula Bopela and Daluxolo Luthuli, *Umkhonto we Sizwe*, 2005. Mike Hoare, who was imprisoned in South Africa for his part in the 1981 attempted Seychelles coup (see page 375), wrote of the apartheid prison system: 'The Prisons Department was completely separate from the South African Police. They were a law unto themselves . . . No criticism of the Prisons Department was permitted by the press . . . and it was an offence punishable by law to print any comment whatsoever about the conditions in prisons in South Africa or the way they were run . . . South African prisons as represented by Pretoria Central are sixty to seventy years behind the times . . . Not only in their establishments, which are woefully outdated, but also in their thinking, they lag behind the remainder of the world in penal reform' (Mike Hoare, *The Seychelles Affair*, 1986, pp. 207, 243–244).

19. ANC, 'Further Submissions and Responses by the ANC', 12 May 1997; Swilling and Phillips, 'The Emergency State', *South African Review 5*, p. 75.

20. Johannesburg *Sunday Express*, 15 July 1984; *Guardian*, 31 July 1984; *Weekly Mail*, 29 September 1989; *Sunday Independent*, 3 December 2000; Marlene Burger and Chandre Gould, *Secrets and Lies*, 2002, p. 76. The RENAMO connection was something of a weak link for the apartheid intelligence services, see Gottschalk, 'The Rise and Fall of Apartheid's Death Squads', Campbell, op. cit., pp. 247–8: 'When the Zimbabwean army overran a base of the SADF-supplied RENAMO . . . in Mozambique, it captured papers of one of the South African military liaison officers . . . These included an [MID] assessment of every member of the contemporary South African cabinet. The [MID] assessment included words to the effect that in any future major crisis, Mr R.F. "Pik" Botha, then Minister of Foreign Affairs, was the cabinet minister most likely to betray the Afrikaner volk – and in such circumstances should be eliminated. When he was shown this particular captured document on his next visit to Mozambique, the Mozambican minister noted that Pik Botha "turned as white as a sheet".' See also Robert Davies, 'The SADF's Covert War against Mozambique', Cock, op. cit., pp. 104–5.

21. *New Statesman*, 16 February 1990; *Mail & Guardian*, 26 November 1999.

22. *Leadership*, June 1994; *Business Day*, 17 November 1988; *Argus*, 3 February 1989; Kasrils, op. cit., pp. 194–5, 216–17, 'Like her one-time mentor, Craig Williamson, [Forsyth] had cool nerves and considerable courage, but we had never been taken in by her because of her bloodless lack of passion for the anti-apartheid cause . . . Infiltrators have the problem of finding a convincing balance between tight self-control and exaggerated passion.' On spies in NUSAS, see *Weekly Mail*, 27 March 1986. The *Guardian*, 8 July 1996,

NOTES TO PAGE 292

reported that 'emerging literary talent, Mark Behr, who defied the National Party government as a student leader [at Stellenbosch University] . . . has disclosed he was a police agent'. Behr's novel *The Smell of Apples*, 1993, was 'shortlisted for the 1995 Guardian Fiction Prize'. On Evans's numerous accounts, *Arena*, September 1997, *Independent*, 31 October 1998, *The Times*, 26 October 2002.

23. Gavin Evans, *Dancing Shoes is Dead*, 2002, p. 208; *Guardian*, 4 February 1989. See also *Africa Confidential*, 26 November 1986: '[The ANC] claims to have penetrated government security networks. In a sensational court case, two black security policemen were recently charged with being ANC spies'; *Guardian*, 5 May 1987; *Natal Mercury*, 4 December 1987: 'Miss Odile Harrington . . . was sentenced to 25 years' imprisonment in Zimbabwe for being a foreign agent. [She] was nothing more than an "enthusiastic amateur".'

The South African media had been riddled with spies and informers since the early 1960s, of whom the most famous were Gordon Winter and Gerard Ludi. Winter revealed in *Inside BOSS*, p. 578: 'In 1976 H.J. van den Bergh told me that BOSS had thirty-seven South African journalists on its payroll. Three of these were parliamentary correspondents, one was an editor in chief, and eight worked on news desks in one capacity or another.' The editor in chief is understood to have been Tertius Myburgh, the former editor of the Johannesburg *Sunday Times*.

John Horak, a 'committed Christian' and former chief sub-editor of the Johannesburg *Sunday Express*, ended his media career as Morning Group manager of South African Associated Newspapers (SAAN) in 1985. He admitted that 'for 27 years he had led a life of deceit and double-dealing as he spied on his newspaper colleagues at [SAAN]'. He told American author June Goodwin that during the Information scandal Eschel Rhoodie revealed to Allister Sparks that Tertius Myburgh was a police spy. As Sparks was believed to be intending to expose Myburgh, Horak received a telephone 'call from [General] Johan Coetzee . . . saying "Go to Myburgh and offer him assistance . . . and defend him at all costs." . . . I said, "How far must I go?" . . . [A] few minutes later, I got a call giving me an instruction to defend Myburgh to the extent that even if my cover is blown . . . I must defend Myburgh' (unpublished interview with June Goodwin, 4 May 1992). See also Tony Heard, *The Cape of Storms*, 1991, p. 143. Myburgh surrounded himself with a strange group of people, including Bruce Louden (*Daily Telegraph*) who had been dismissed by the *Financial Times* in 1974 following publication in Portugal of letters that he had written to the former Portuguese dictatorship's Secretariat of State for Information and Tourism, offering to work as a propagandist (Sanders, op. cit., pp. 149–50; *Time Out*, 6 February 1976). Fleur de Villiers, the political editor of the Johannesburg *Sunday Times* under Myburgh, and later editorial writer on southern Africa for *The Times* (of London),

abandoned journalism in 1988 to work as a 'Public Affairs Consultant' for De
Beers and Anglo American (www.iiss.org/biogs.php?staffID=62).

Horak told the TRC in 1997 that 'informers in the SAAN group were "two
a penny" and that about 50 staffers, including assistant editors, had approached
him, wanting to take part [in spying] . . . After the elections, the ANC asked
him to help found the [NIS] . . . Horak said there was more telephone tapping and infiltration of the media by government agents [in 1997] than there
had been under the National Party . . . [he added] that the agents did not spy
on the newspapers but used them as a cover for intelligence gathering.
Claiming this was standard practice around the world, he said: "In 1970 I was
in contact with an MI5 individual and by then more than three-quarters of all
[British] foreign correspondents were in some way sponsored by the British
intelligence services because it was so prohibitively expensive to put a man in
the field" ' (*Guardian*, 17 September 1997). In May 1997, Johannesburg *Star*
senior journalist Norman Chandler was accused by Craig Williamson and
former operative Vic McPherson of spying for the Security Police in the
1980s. The *Mail & Guardian*, 2 May 1997, reported that during the early 1980s,
'while Chandler was employed at the *Rand Daily Mail* . . . he reported on his
colleagues and on "foreign visitors" to the newspaper'. In 1985, while he was
managing director of the Lesotho newspaper, the *Nation*, Chandler was 'a
"useful" agent' supplying 'important intelligence on the movement of South
African refugees in and out of Lesotho'.

In 1997, a Security Police document was released by the TRC which detailed
how news of anti-apartheid activist Allan Boesak's extramarital affair with an
official of the South African Council of Churches was fed to 'long-standing
regional office/head office confidants' in the press. The confidants included
Aida Parker, Horak, Chandler, Tony Stirling (the *Citizen*) and Cliff Saunders of
the SABC (*Mail & Guardian*, 19 September 1997). In February 2000, Saunders
revealed that he had spied for both the NIS and the post-apartheid South
African Secret Service (SASS). Saunders's strange career 'came to light when
[he] submitted a demand to the secret service for more than £10,000 in unpaid
expenses'. He later told *Rapport*, 'I was not a spy. Work I did, for whomever,
was designed to promote the welfare, stability and security of the country and
further afield' (*Guardian*, 17 February 2000; *Focus*, No. 17, March 2000).

24. ANC, 'Further Submissions and Responses by the ANC', 12 May 1997;
Marxism Today, December 1986; Howard Barrell, 'Conscripts to their
Age: African National Congress Operation Strategy, 1976–1986', unpub-
lished DPhil thesis, 1993.

25. Robert D'A. Henderson, 'Operation Vula against Apartheid', *International
Journal of Intelligence and Counterintelligence*, Vol. 10, No. 4, Winter 1997–8,
pp. 418, 424; Barrell, 'Conscripts to their Age', unpublished DPhil thesis,
1993; Nelson Mandela, 'Press Statement . . . on the Operation Vulindlela and

the indemnification of ANC members', 22 June 1991. For an account of Mac Maharaj's Robben Island imprisonment, see S.R. 'Mac' Maharaj, 'Robben Island', 1978, Nelson Mandela, *The Struggle Is My Life*, 1994, pp. 234–56.

26. Barrell, 'Conscripts to their Age', unpublished DPhil thesis, 1993; Henderson, 'Operation Vula', *International Journal of Intelligence and Counterintelligence*, Winter 1997–8, pp. 425–6; Conny Braam, *Operation Vula*, 2004, pp. 23, 25–6.

27. Henderson, 'Operation Vula', *International Journal of Intelligence and Counterintelligence*, Winter 1997–8, p. 428; *Mayibuye*, December 1990; Braam, op. cit., pp. 161–4, names the airline hostess 'Elise'.

28. Tim Jenkin, *Escape from Pretoria*, 1987; Tim Jenkin, 'Talking to Vula: The Story of the Secret Underground Communications Network of Operation Vula', *Mayibuye*, May–October 1995; Shubin, op. cit., pp. 334–6; Henderson, 'Operation Vula', *International Journal of Intelligence and Counterintelligence*, Winter 1997–8, pp. 430–2. Mike Louw responds that Jenkins's assertion that the NIS had no idea of Mandela's ability to communicate with Oliver Tambo is 'Simply not true. We accepted that Mandela would have means to communicate with the ANC, but did not mind' (Mike Louw, e-mail to author, 10 December 2005).

29. Shubin, op. cit., pp. 336–8; Jenkin, 'Talking to Vula', *Mayibuye*, May–October 1995; *Mayibuye*, December 1990; Braam, op. cit., p. 271; Henderson, 'Operation Vula', *International Journal of Intelligence and Counterintelligence*, Winter 1997–8, p. 433; *Slate*, 7 April 2004; SAPA, 10 August 1999; Kasrils, op. cit., pp. 1–3, 230, 259. A comprehensive list of those involved in Operation Vula is still to be produced.

30. Braam, op. cit., pp. 141–3.

31. Jenkin, 'Talking to Vula', *Mayibuye*, May–October 1995; Henderson, 'Operation Vula', *International Journal of Intelligence and Counterintelligence*, Winter 1997–8, p. 438. 'Nightingale' was mysteriously 'a walk-in' (that is, someone who contacted Mo Shaik).

32. Johannesburg *Star*, 29 July 1994; *Weekly Mail*, 29 July 1994. The 'Maharaj files' have been deposited at the Mayibuye Centre archive at the University of the Western Cape. One document noted that the NIS believed in 1980 that the ANC was 'in an admirable condition [and] had moved into an excellent strategic position'. The NIS also expressed concern at the 'very little inside information' on the new generation of Indian ANC activists.

33. Kasrils, op. cit., pp. 230–1, 242; Henderson, 'Operation Vula', *International Journal of Intelligence and Counterintelligence*, Winter 1997–8, p. 445; *Mayibuye*, December 1990; Jenkin, 'Talking to Vula', *Mayibuye*, May–October 1995; conversation with Mac Maharaj, 11 June 2002; Pauw, *Heart of Darkness*, p. 232.

34. Jenkin, 'Talking to Vula', *Mayibuye*, May–October 1995; Mandela, 'Press Statement . . . on the Operation Vulindlela', 22 June 1991; TRC, *Report*, Vol. 7, p. 780; Kasrils, op. cit., p. 310.

35. US State Department, 'ANC denies conspiracy, but evidence mounts', 26 July 1990 [South African History Archive].

36. Jenkin, 'Talking to Vula', *Mayibuye*, May–October 1995; conversation with Mac Maharaj, 11 June 2002; Slovo, op. cit., pp. 136–8: 'Vula [was] first mooted in 1981 . . . by the time [it] closed down it had . . . three score and ten people as full timers.' She recalled an angry meeting between her father Joe Slovo and the Vula leaders: 'They needed to hit out and they did – at Joe. He bore the full brunt of their outrage . . . for the way the negotiations were going, and in particular, for concessions they saw the ANC making over the question of indemnity for political acts . . . Such was the force of their fury that, after a while he just sat, head bowed, as those with whom he'd had the very closest working relationships accused him of betraying their cause.' The most dramatic Mandela assassination plot was planned for the day of the new President's inauguration. The assassination weapon, a 'rifle, with a .50 calibre bore – the size of an anti-aircraft shell – and with an accurate killing range of one kilometre, was equipped with an infra-red aiming equipment'. Mandela was inaugurated behind a 'large bullet-proof glass screen'. The plot was uncovered, and the rifle seized, by André Lincoln, an ANC intelligence operative who told his story when he was arrested for 'fraud and theft' (*Mail & Guardian*, 27 February 1998, 9 November 2001; *Sunday Times*, 8 March 1998; Johannesburg *Star*, 9, 10 July 2002); Lincoln was found guilty 'on 15 counts of fraud' (SAPA, 19 November 2002).

37. Henderson, 'Operation Vula', *International Journal of Intelligence and Counterintelligence*, Winter 1997–8, p. 441; Waldmeir, op. cit., p. 82, adds: 'Vula had never flourished, and by July 1990, it existed far more powerfully in the mind of Maharaj than in fact' (p. 162); *Noseweek*, No. 37, November 2001.

38. ANC, 'Further Submissions and Responses by the ANC', 12 May 1997; *Mail & Guardian*, 18 August 2000.

39. Kevin A. O'Brien, 'South Africa's Evolving Intelligence and Security Structures', *International Journal of Intelligence and Counterintelligence*, Vol. 9, No. 2, Summer 1996, pp. 208–9.

40. Sparks, *Tomorrow*, pp. 115–19.

41. Mark Shaw, 'Spy Meets Spy: Negotiating New Intelligence Structures', in Steven Friedman and Doreen Atkinson (eds), *South African Review 7: The Small Miracle*, 1994, p. 261; *Natal Mercury*, 22 January 1992; Henderson, 'South African Intelligence Under de Klerk', *International Journal of Intelligence and Counterintelligence*, Spring 1995, pp. 61, 86; *Marxism Today*, December 1986; O'Meara, op. cit., pp. 405–7; de Klerk, op. cit., pp. 194, 203–4; Louis Harms, *Report of the Commission of Inquiry into Certain Alleged Murders*, 1990.

42. O'Meara, op. cit., pp. 409–10; *Guardian*, 25 April 1991; Sampson, *Mandela*, p. 443; de Klerk, op. cit., pp. 209–10. Mike Louw offered a heartfelt appeal for F.W. de Klerk: 'I have a much more positive opinion of the man . . . He did what nobody believed could be done . . . I witnessed some of these inci-

dents at first hand. I have nothing but admiration for the steadfast way he kept the process going – even when his senior ministers panicked and wanted to opt out' (Mike Louw, e-mail to author, 10 December 2005).

43. There were more than a dozen reports issued by the Goldstone Commission. The most important are Richard Goldstone, *Commission of Inquiry Regarding the Prevention of Public Violence and Intimidation: Report to the Commission by the Committee Appointed to Inquire into Allegations Concerning Front Companies of the SADF and the Training of Inkatha Supporters at the Caprivi in 1986, 1992; Report of the Committee into Allegations of a Third Force,* May 1993; *Interim Report on Criminal Political Violence by Elements within the South African Police, the KwaZulu Police and the Inkatha Freedom Party,* March 1994. See also *Mail & Guardian,* 7 July 1995. The Steyn Report has never been published. For well-informed speculation as to its contents, see *Africa Confidential,* 23 September 1994; *Mail & Guardian,* 17 December 1996, 31 January 1997; Hamann, op. cit., p. 191; de Klerk, op. cit., p. 262; *Africa Confidential,* 31 July 1992; Henderson, 'South African Intelligence Under de Klerk', *International Journal of Intelligence and Counterintelligence,* Spring 1995, p. 76.

44. Sampson, *Mandela,* pp. 466–8, 470–2, 479–87; on the mysteries surrounding the murder of Chris Hani, see *Mail & Guardian,* 31 January, 7 February, 4 April 1997; *The Times,* 1 February 1997; *Sunday Times,* 2 February 1997. An amusing documentary film on Eugene Terre'Blanche, the ridiculous leader of the AWB, was Nick Broomfield's *The Leader, His Driver and the Driver's Wife,* 1991.

45. Johannesburg *Star,* 2 December 1991, 19 February 1992; Johannesburg *Sunday Times,* 23 February 1992; *Argus,* 23 February 1992.

46. *Mayibuye,* April 1992. See also Sandra Africa, 'Intelligence, Accountability and Democracy: Prospects for SA', *IDASA Occasional Paper 45,* July 1992.

47. Roger Southall, 'Restructuring Intelligence for Post-Apartheid South Africa', *Strategic Review for Southern Africa,* Vol. XIV, No. 2, October 1992, p. 13, citing ANC, 'ANC Policy Guidelines for a Democratic South Africa', May 1992.

48. Joe Nhlanhla, 'The Modalities of Combining the SATNVC and Liberation Movements' Intelligence Services in a Changing South Africa', *Strategic Review for Southern Africa,* October 1992, pp. 67–8, 76.

49. Shaw, 'Spy Meets Spy', Friedman, op. cit., pp. 263–5; Mo Shaik, 'Panel: Policy Formation', Minaar, op. cit., p. 451.

50. W. Breytenbach, 'Security and Intelligence Structures in "New" South Africa with Special Reference to Regionalism within the Context of the Federal/Unitary Debate', *Strategic Review for Southern Africa,* October 1992, p. 34; Harvey, op. cit., p. 126; *Time,* 16 May 1994; *Guardian,* 15 September 1994; *Africa Confidential,* 18 February 1994; Mail & Guardian, 20 May 1994.

51. Republic of South Africa, *White Paper on Intelligence,* 1994, pp. 2–5, 12, 14–19, annexure: pp. 5–6.

52. Republic of South Africa, *National Strategic Intelligence Bill*, 1994; *Draft White Paper on National Defence: Defence in a Democracy*, 1995; *South African Police Services Act*, 1995. *Work in Progress*, June 1992; O'Brien, 'South Africa's Evolving Intelligence and Security Structures', *International Journal of Intelligence and Counterintelligence*, Summer 1996, pp. 196–7, 213.

53. *Sunday Herald*, 19 March 2000; *Guardian*, 23 March 2000; Dorril, op. cit., p. 722.

54. *Guardian*, 23, 24 March 2000, 27 January 2001; *The Times*, 26 January 2001.

55. *Guardian*, 2 February 2001; Richard Tomlinson, The *Big Breach*, 2001, p. 140; *The Times*, 15 February 2001. In June 2002, *Eye Spy*, No. 10, repeated the allegation: 'South Africa's President Emeritus and Nobel Prize winner Nelson Mandela is an MI6 agent.' Obviously, the spooky scribes of *Eye Spy* don't read the *Guardian*.

56. *Independent*, 19 November 1999, 23 September 2000; private information; the *Observer*, 18 September 2005, quoted Keane recalling that 'the guy who used to dance on stage with us is now defence minister of South Africa', which implied that either Patrick 'Terror' Lekota, South Africa's Defence Minister, had also been associated with Total Onslaught or that Keane is unaware that Kasrils is now Minister of Intelligence.

CHAPTER 13: POISONOUS INFLUENCE

1. Bertolt Brecht, *Der Aufhaltsame Aufstieg Des Arturo Ui* [*The Resistible Rise of Arturo Ui*], 1957, Epilogue, written in 1945. This is quite a free translation used in an American performance of the play. See also Hannah Arendt, *Eichmann in Jerusalem*, 1965, pp. 246–7, extract from the judgment: 'These crimes were committed en masse, not only in regard to the number of victims, but also in regard to the numbers of those who perpetrated the crime, and the extent to which any one of the many criminals was close to or remote from the actual killer of the victim means nothing, as far as the measure of his responsibility is concerned. On the contrary, in general, the degree of responsibility increases as we draw further away from the man who uses the fatal instrument with his own hands.'

2. Sampson, *Mandela*, p. 493; Bill Clinton, interview with Paul Woolwich (BBC), 12 December 2002, transcript; see also Bill Clinton, *My Life*, 2005, p. 596, which provides no information on the 'big reason', merely noting that it was 'announced . . . that Al and Tipper Gore, Hillary, Ron Brown and Mike Espy would head our delegation to President Mandela's inauguration . . . It was just another week in the office'; Major, op. cit., pp. 509–10.

3. *New York Times*, 23 July 1986; Sanders, op. cit., p. 40; *Financial Times*, 7 July 2004.

4. Herbst, 'Analyzing Apartheid', *African Affairs*, January 2003, pp. 104, 107.

5. Mangold, *Cold Warrior*, p. 303; Herbst, 'Analyzing Apartheid', *African Affairs*, January 2003, pp. 104, 106.

6. Crocker, op. cit., pp. 322–3, 343.

7. *Mail & Guardian*, 13 June 2003: documentation which was discovered by the South African History Archive also revealed that 'a trip under the auspices of "Project Cake" took place in 1982 in connection with . . . naval research vessels. A reference to another visit to West Germany in 1984 is contained in a file entitled "Project Thoroughbred".' Shubin, op. cit., p. 264; Callinicos, op. cit., p. 504.

8. Shubin, op. cit., pp. 220, 264–5: Donald Sole admitted in his unpublished autobiography that 'We had engineered the establishment of the Committee'; see *The Role of the Soviet Union, Cuba, and East Germany in Fomenting Terrorism in Southern Africa: Hearings before the Subcommittee on Security and Terrorism of the Committee on the Judiciary, United States Senate, Ninety-seventh Congress, Second Session*, 1982.

9. Wolf Blitzer, *Territory of Lies*, 1990, pp. 42, 58–9: Pollard visited Paris in the mid-1970s where he 'met and befriended some white South Africans'. At the same time, according to his father: 'he learned how to read and speak Afrikaans'. In 1978, at the Fletcher School of Law and Diplomacy at Tufts University in Boston, where Pollard was studying for a post-graduate degree, he 'developed a close personal friendship with a South African naval officer'. In 1981, while working for Naval Intelligence, he asked for permission to open a 'back channel' to his old friend: 'Pollard claimed that as a result . . . US and South African officials began to talk to each other "for the first time in two years" '; Cockburn, op. cit., pp. 306–7.

10. Cockburn, op. cit., p. 307; *Washington Post*, 12 October 1988; *Sunday Independent*, 23 February 1997. South African desperation can be detected in a speech that Major-General Tienie Groenewald was reported to have given on 'a mysterious, "semi-official" visit to America in 1987', when he spoke to a 'closed meeting of the American Conservative Caucus'. *Noseweek*, No. 15, April–May 1997, reported that Groenewald told the Americans: 'We have relied greatly on foreign capital, and as a result of that, South Africa is one of the few countries in which there is no control whatsoever over foreign capital . . . Any foreigner can, with no restriction, either bring money into South Africa – whether it is hot money or not, does not matter . . . or take it out. There is no restriction whatsoever on the flow of capital.'

11. Sampson, *Mandela*, p. 394; Shubin, op. cit., p. 266; *Guardian*, 23 March 2000; Kasrils, op. cit., p. 173; Callinicos, op. cit., p. 509.

12. Israel, op. cit., p. 193; *New Statesman*, 12 October 1990; *Africa Confidential*, 4 November 1987. See also the *Independent*, 23 October 1987, which provided

a thorough 'anatomy of a conspiracy' and quoted an Anti-Terrorist Squad officer as saying: 'A Smiley novel looks dead simple after this.'

13. *New Statesman*, 15 January 1988; *Africa Confidential*, 4 November 1987; Israel, op. cit., pp. 199–200; Kasrils, op. cit., p. 220.

14. *Independent*, 29 April 1989; *Guardian*, 24 April 1989; *The Times*, 6 May 1989; *Mail & Guardian*, 15 June 2000. See also *Noseweek*, No. 14, February–March 1996.

15. Renwick, op. cit., pp. 136, 140.

16. Interview with Mike Louw, 3 December 2003; *Who's Who, 2005*, p. 1931; Kasrils, op. cit., pp. 256–7.

17. *New Statesman*, 12 October 1990; *Africa Confidential*, 31 July 1992; Israel, op. cit., p. 197; *Pretoria News*, 25 August 1992; *Argus*, 15 July 1992.

18. Tomlinson, op. cit., pp. 16–17, 51, 73, 60, 95, 129–31, 206.

19. *Southscan*, 28 June 1992; conversation with Martin Welz, 29 January 2005; *Guardian*, 20 March 1998; interview with Mike Louw, 3 December 2003.

20. Hunter, op. cit., pp. 71–7; Ari Ben-Menashe, *Profits of War*, 1992, pp. 136, 139–40, 211. General P.W. van der Westhuizen, who became the ambassador to Chile in 1988, appears to have facilitated the trade to Iraq through Latin American channels (pp. 286–7, 304–5); Defense Intelligence Agency, 'Israel: Military and Nuclear Cooperation with South Africa', undated document [National Security Archive].

21. *Listener*, 6 August 1987; *Sunday Independent*, 11 May 1997, originally published in *Ha'aretz*, reported that 'at the beginning of 1997, the Israeli defence ministry closed its office in South Africa'. *Mail & Guardian*, 23 March 2001; *Guardian*, 4 May 2001; *New York Times*, 18 February 2001. Paul Foot claimed that Bill Clinton explained on the Geraldo Rivera 'chat show' the 'influences' that inspired him to pardon Marc Rich: 'Israel influenced me profoundly.' Foot continued that Clinton 'had been profoundly moved by a letter from Shabtai Shavit, the former head of the Israeli intelligence agency Mossad. Mr Shavit described the fugitive financier as "a fine and generous individual" who had "used his extensive network of contacts . . . to produce results" for Mossad' (Guardian, 20 February 2001). On Marc Rich's sanctions-busting on behalf of South Africa, see also *Africa Confidential*, 7 January 1987; Klinghoffer, op. cit., p. 67.

22. *Mail & Guardian*, 20 May, 10 June 2005.

23. Private information; *Guardian*, 2 October 2002; Sampson, *Who Runs This Place?*, 2004, pp. 293–4; *Punch*, 12 September 2001, the article continued: 'Now, when an MI6 officer sets off for a meeting with an agent, he carries, discreetly tucked into his jacket, not a gun but a large envelope stuffed with cash. MI6 officers, are in effect, government officials who are "licensed to bribe".' For a slightly wild journey through the activities of the French with regard to post-1986 South Africa see Evelyn Groenink, 'Murder Inc.', unpublished manuscript, 2005.

24. Interview with Niel Barnard, 29 October 2002; private information.

25. Peter Hounam and Steve McQuillan, *The Mini-Nuke Conspiracy*, 1995, provides a thorough, if somewhat conspiratorial, outline of the 'red mercury' mystery; *Sunday Times*, 17 July 1994. On South Africa's nukes, see J.W. de Villiers, Roger Jardine and Mitchell Reiss, 'Why South Africa Gave Up the Bomb', *Foreign Affairs*, No. 72, Vol. 5, November–December 1993; Verne Harris, Sello Hatang and Peter Liberman, 'Unveiling South Africa's Nuclear Past', *Journal of Southern African Studies*, Vol. 30, No. 3, September 2004; Peter Liberman, 'The Rise and Fall of the South African Bomb', *International Security*, Vol. 26, No. 2, Fall 2001; *Africa Confidential*, 4 March 1994, 17 November 1995. *Sunday Times*, 25 February 2001, claimed that apartheid South Africa had supplied Iraq with uranium for a nuclear weapon. A senior Iraqi official stated that 'Negotiations began in 1986 and the delivery was made in 1988.' The *Sunday Times* contacted a 'former intelligence official under the apartheid regime who had helped procure components for his country's nuclear weapons programme on the black market. "The story is true . . . about 50kg were sold to the Iraqis."' On post-apartheid nuclear transactions, see *Mail & Guardian*, 10 September, 1 October 2004; *Mother Jones*, May–June 2005.

26. Purkitt and Burgess, *South Africa's Weapons*, p. 88; Burger, op. cit., p. 14; Chandre Gould and Peter I. Folb, 'The South African Chemical and Biological Warfare Program: An Overview', *The Nonproliferation Review*, Vol. 7, No. 3, Fall–Winter 2000, p. 11.

27. Burger, op. cit., pp. 15, 221–2; Ellert, op. cit., p. 111.

28. Tom Mangold and Jeff Goldberg, *Plague Wars*, 1999, pp. 218–20; Ellert, op. cit., pp. 112–13.

29. *New Yorker*, 15 January 2001; Burger, op. cit., p. 17.

30. Purkitt and Burgess, *South Africa's Weapons*, pp. 98–100; Helen E. Purkitt and Stephen Burgess, 'South Africa's Chemical and Biological Warfare Programme: A Historical and International Perspective', *Journal of Southern African Studies*, Vol. 28, No. 2, June 2002, pp. 241–2; Mangold, *Plague Wars*, p. 242.

31. Burger, op. cit., pp. 56, 59–60, 62, 64–8, 191; see also *Mail & Guardian*, 26 May 2000, which reported that SWAPO claimed that Basson 'was responsible for the long-standing emotive issue of the "missing Namibians."' An organisation of former SWAPO detainees 'distributed a list of 700 people as evidence that many Namibians disappeared while in the hands of SWAPO during the liberation war'.

32. *New Yorker*, 15 January 2001.

33. Mangold, *Plague Wars*, pp. 240–2; *New Yorker*, 15 January 2001.

34. *Guardian*, 9 June 1989; *Lancet*, 18/25 December 1999; Mangold, *Plague Wars*, pp. 227–30; Braam, op. cit., pp. 108–14.

35. Danie Phaal, testimony at the Wouter Basson trial, 8 May 2000 (ccrweb.ccr.uct.ac.za/archive/cbw/20); Mangold, *Plague Wars*, pp. 244, 255, 257, 263; Pauw, *Heart of Darkness*, pp. 243–4; Purkitt and Burgess, *South Africa's Weapons*, p. 101; *CovertAction Quarterly*, No. 63, Winter 1998; *Mail & Guardian*, 15 December 1994, 27 June 1997; *New Yorker*, 15 January 2001.

36. Mangold, *Plague Wars*, p. 253; Agence France-Presse, 12 November 1999; Purkitt and Burgess, *South Africa's Weapons*, p. 113.

37. *Southscan*, 5 October 2001, 28 June 2002; Hamann, op. cit., pp. 195–207; Foster, op. cit., pp. 168–70; *Business Day*, 10 March 1999; AFP, 20 December 2002.

38. Gould and Folb, 'The South African Chemical and Biological Warfare Program', *Nonproliferation Review*, Fall–Winter 2000, p. 20; *Noseweek*, No. 66, April 2005, No. 67, May 2005.

39. *Los Angeles Magazine*, July 2001; Burger, op. cit., p. 141; *Sunday Telegraph*, 2 December 2001; Purkitt and Burgess, *South Africa's Weapons*, pp. 85, 110–11, 267; 'Dr Death – South Africa's Biological Weapons Program', CBS *60 Minutes*, 3 November 2002.

40. Purkitt and Burgess, *South Africa's Weapons*, pp. 108–9, 111; *Los Angeles Magazine*, July 2001; Burger, op. cit., pp. 145–6; *Sunday Telegraph*, 2 December 2001. See also the reports on Steven Jay Hatfill, an American 'expert on bio-terrorism' who tricked 'his way into America's highest security bio-defence installation, Fort Detrick, in Maryland'. Hatfill lived in South Africa from 1983 to 1993 and was described by the US authorities as 'a person of interest' (a suspect) in the American anthrax attacks of 2001. Hatfill has always maintained his innocence and has not been charged with any crime (Johannesburg *Star*, 1 July 2002; *New Statesman*, 5 August 2002; *Mail & Guardian*, 16 August 2002; *Observer*, 1 June 2003).

41. Gould and Folb, 'The South African Chemical and Biological Warfare Program', *Nonproliferation Review*, Fall–Winter 2000, p. 19; *Observer*, 7 June 1998; Burger, op. cit., pp. 113, 210; *Mail & Guardian*, 10 August 2001.

42. Mangold, *Plague Wars*, p. 267; Gould and Folb, 'The South African Chemical and Biological Warfare Program', *Nonproliferation Review*, Fall–Winter 2000, pp. 14–15; Purkitt and Burgess, *South Africa's Weapons*, p. 161; Kasrils, op. cit., p. 321.

43. Mangold, *Plague Wars*, pp. 269–71, 279–80; Purkitt and Burgess, *South Africa's Weapons*, pp. 161–2.

44. *Nonproliferation Review*, Fall–Winter 2000, p. 21; Mangold, *Plague Wars*, pp. 272–3; *Sunday Independent*, 2 March 1997. British and American officials were equally concerned with closing down South Africa's nuclear programme. Mark Urban, *UK Eyes Alpha*, 1996, p. 119, reported that 'South Africa was a major SIS target: the agency ran one of its biggest operations there, staffed by

five officers. But it probably comes as no surprise . . . to find that Britain did not know whether South Africa had the bomb: . . . "We were suspicious of them, but we were under-informed." '

45. Mangold, *Plague Wars*, p. 276; *Sunday Independent*, 2 March 1997; Purkitt and Burgess, *South Africa's Weapons*, p. 116; Burger, op. cit., p. 80.

46. *Observer*, 29 June 1997; *New Yorker*, 15 January 2001.

47. Mangold, *Plague Wars*, pp. 279–81; TRC, *Report*, Vol. 2, pp. 520–21; Gould and Folb, 'The South African Chemical and Biological Warfare Program', *Nonproliferation Review*, Fall–Winter 2000, p. 21; *Guardian*, 12 October 1996; *New Yorker*, 15 January 2001, Burger, op. cit., pp. 95, 187, 212; Mike Kennedy is the *only* former South African intelligence officer who cited South Africa's equivalent to the Official Secrets Act when I asked him whether he would be prepared to talk with me.

48. Burger, op. cit., pp. 189, 191; SAPA, 25 February 2005; Gould and Folb, 'The South African Chemical and Biological Warfare Program', *Nonproliferation Review*, Fall–Winter 2000, p. 21. One of the more startling conspiracy theories involving apartheid South Africa concerns the Lockerbie bombing. The UN Commissioner for Namibia, Bernt Carlsson, died in the crash of Pan Am 103 on 21 December 1988. If he had survived, Carlsson would have supervised the independence of Namibia. Incredibly, Pik Botha, Magnus Malan, the CSI of MID Admiral van Tonder and twenty other South African officials were also booked on Pan Am 103. They were travelling to New York for the final signing ceremony of the agreements relating to the Angolan–Namibian peace process. Botha and his team arrived early in London on an SAA flight which 'inexplicably cut out the scheduled Frankfurt stopover'. Botha and five members of his team were hastily booked on the morning Pan Am 101 flight; the remaining seventeen South African delegates did not use their tickets on Pan Am 103 but returned to South Africa. (Patrick Haseldine, 'Lockerbie Trial: A *Better* Defence of Incrimination', 2005.) The Swedish newspaper *iDAG*, 12 March 1990, reported that Carlsson had been due to return to New York on 20 December but was 'persuaded' to visit De Beers in London and therefore was forced to take Pan Am 103 in order to be present at the signing ceremony. A Reuters news report, 12 November 1994, confirmed that the South African party had been booked on Pan Am 103, as did South African Minister of Justice Dullah Omar when he was asked in the South African parliament on 12 June 1996 whether Pik Botha and his entourage had 'had any plans to travel on [Pan Am 103]'. The second parliamentary question: 'Whether the South African intelligence service had any reason to be concerned about or was aware of concerns expressed by the intelligence services of the [USA] or the [UK] about a threat of a possible terrorist attack on Pan Am Flight 103?', drew a 'curiously equivocal' response from the Minister: 'As far as I could ascertain, the answer to both those questions is no' (*Private Eye*, 2 April 1999). On Patrick Haseldine, the

Foreign Office diplomat who was dismissed after writing a letter to the *Guardian* in which he criticised Mrs Thatcher for operating a 'double standard' on South African state terrorism, see the *Guardian*, 7, 17 December 1988, 3 August 1989.

49. *Washington Post*, 20 April 2003; *Mail & Guardian*, 9 May 2003.

50. *Washington Post*, 21 April 2003; *Mail & Guardian*, 24 January, 25 April, 9 May 2003.

51. *Mail & Guardian*, 24, 31 January, 25 April, 9 May 2003.

CHAPTER 14: NATIONAL INTELLIGENCE

1. *Times Literary Supplement*, 22 August 2003.

2. Interviews with Mike Louw, 12 August 2002, 2 December 2005.

3. *Searchlight South Africa*, Vol. 3, No. 4, June 1995; ANC, 'Further Submissions and Responses by the ANC', 12 May 1997: 'The apartheid regime did not hesitate to get rid of its own agents when it appeared they were about to change sides or give the ANC damaging information. The ANC is convinced that both Solly Smith and Francis Meli were poisoned in order to silence them'; Francis Meli, *South Africa Belongs to Us: A History of the ANC*, 1988; Johannesburg *Sunday Times*, 12 June 1994; *Mail & Guardian*, 23 February 1996.

4. *Mail & Guardian*, 1 March 1996; *Daily Telegraph*, 10 March 1997.

5. *Guardian*, 15 April 1997; *Mail & Guardian*, 11 April 1997, 19 February 1999, 24 March 2000; *Sowetan*, 24 October 1997. The seven politicians and the single intelligence operative named by de Lille have never admitted that they spied for the apartheid regime.

6. *Mail & Guardian*, 31 October 1997; *Financial Mail*, 12 September 2003.

7. Interview with Maritz Spaarwater, 11 December 2003. Spaarwater's disillusion was partly due to the lack of 'seriousness with which politicians generally regarded strategic intelligence inputs.' He felt the attitude was 'wait until things blow up, in which event the police and army would be there to control things' (Maritz Spaarwater's e-mail to author, 24 March 2006).

8. Mangold, *Plague Wars*, pp. 250, 278; TRC, *Report*, Vol. 2, p. 140.

9. Sampson, *Mandela*, pp. 467-8; 534-5; interview with Pieter Swanepoel, 14 December 2003; *Sowetan*, 19 January 1996; *Mail & Guardian*, 12 January 1996, 25 July 1997, 3 December 1999; Pauw, *Heart of Darkness*, p. 166; Foster, op. cit., p. 198.

10. *Noseweek*, No. 67, May 2005.

11. RSA Parliament, 'Questions and Answers 11.166: Secret services expenditure highlighted', question asked, 1 March 1997; answered, 10 June 1997 [SAIRR Library]; *Southscan*, 22 February 2002, 25 June 2004.

12. *Leadership*, April 1997; Johannesburg *Star*, 1 August 2000; *Focus*, No. 17, March 2000; *Guardian*, 9 February 2001.

13. *Africa Insight*, Vol. 28, No. 1/2, 1998; *Financial Mail*, 23 February 2001; *Business Day*, 25 January 2001; *Sunday Independent*, 4 February 2001; *The Times*, 1 March 2002; South Africa's *Mail & Guardian* and the DA opposition have a peculiar tradition of publishing an annual 'report card' on the government during the Christmas vacation. Neither the newspaper nor the political party seem to recognise that the grading of the ANC's cabinet ministers by politicians who have never held political office, and ill-informed journalists, demonstrates exactly the form of unreconstructed patronising racism which the new South Africa has supposedly abandoned. As an example, the *Mail & Guardian* awarded Lindiwe Sisulu for her work as Minister of Intelligence: C+ (20 December 2001); B (20 December 2002); and C (19 December 2003). One day, the ANC will realise that all that would be required to halt this silly tradition is for them to issue a single report card on the South African media. Private information; Kasrils, op. cit., pp. 320–4: in 2001, Kasrils took part in a parliamentary debate, during which he 'condemned Israel's intransigence . . . in the process of an ongoing discourse I experienced greater abuse and vilification from sections of the Jewish community than I encountered from white South Africans during the apartheid years.'

14. *CovertAction Quarterly*, No. 66, Winter 1999. One of the Defense documents was 'DOD Interaction with the Republic of South Africa'; Kasrils, op. cit., p. 323; *Guardian*, 17 October 1997; *Independent*, 12 October 1997.

15. *Mail & Guardian*, 20 October 1995, 29 October 1999.

16. *Financial Mail*, 18 February 2000; *Business Day*, 24 January 2005; *Mail & Guardian*, 6 September 1996, 28 September 2001; Johannesburg *Sunday Times*, 6 February 2005.

17. *Sowetan*, 12 December 1995; interview with Mike Louw, 3 December 2003; Johannesburg *Weekend Star*, 28 January 1995.

18. *Financial Mail*, 18 February 2000; Johannesburg *Star*, 29 January 2005; *Africa Confidential*, 21 January 2005.

19. Shaun McCarthy, 'South Africa's Intelligence Reformation', *International Journal of Intelligence and Counterintelligence*, Vol. 9, No. 1, Spring 1996, p. 66; *Financial Mail*, 31 January 1997; *Business Day*, 3 March 2005; *Mail & Guardian*, 6 September 1996; *Noseweek*, No. 30, August 2000.

20. *Africa Insight*, Vol. No. 1/2, 1998; *Business Day*, 24 March 2000, 28 January 2002; *Africa Confidential*, 8 February 2002; *Sunday Independent*, 15 February 2004.

21. Allister Sparks, *Beyond the Miracle*, 2003, pp. 124–5; *Mail & Guardian*, 9 November 2001, 24 May, 14 June 2002; Johannesburg *Sunday Times*, 26 May 2002. At the Desai Commission, Hennie Bester, the former Western Cape community safety MEC (Member of the Executive Council, essentially a cabinet minister of the regional administration), was 'asked why a private firm would be used rather than a government counter-intelligence agency'. He

replied: 'Our suspicion was we were being surveilled [sic] by agencies of the national Government' (*Sowetan*, 22 May 2002).

22. Private information; *Mail & Guardian*, 20 June 2003; interview with Mike Louw, 3 December 2003; *Noseweek*, No. 66, May 2005; *Focus*, No. 39, September 2005.

23. Slovo, op. cit., pp. 249–50; *Africa Confidential*, 28 February 1997.

24. Hamann, op. cit., pp. 230–1; Sampson, *Mandela*, pp. 576–7; *Jane's Intelligence Review*, January 1999; *Mail & Guardian*, 1 May 1998; Kasrils, op. cit., p. 332.

25. TRC, *Report*, Vol. 2, pp. 330–1; Gomolemo Mokae, *Robert McBride*, 2004, pp. 153, 262; *Mail & Guardian*, 13, 20 March, 30 April 1998.

26. Mokae, op. cit., pp. 260–3; Hamann, op. cit., pp. 230–2; Sampson, *Mandela*, p. 577; *Guardian*, 7 April 1998; Lieutenant-General Dirk Verbeek, testimony at the Wouter Basson trial, 6 November 2000 (http://ccrweb.ccr.uct.ac.za/archive/cbw/34); Kasrils, op. cit., p. 334.

27. *Mail & Guardian*, 12 June, 10 July, 21 August, 18 September 1998; Johannesburg *Star*, 26 November 2003; *The Times*, 27 November 2003; *Citizen*, 26 January 2006.

28. Sampson, *Mandela*, pp. 558–9.

29. Johannesburg *Star*, 16 September 1998; *City Press*, 14 November 1999; *Guardian*, 21 September 1998; *Mail & Guardian*, 4 September 1998.

30. *Business Day*, 28 August 2000; *Mail & Guardian*, 1 September, 6, 13 October 2000; *Guardian*, 23 September 2000.

31. Johannesburg *Sunday Times*, 22 April 2001; *Guardian*, 24, 26, 27 April 2001. The *Guardian* reported that 'rumours [were] circulating in the ANC that Mr Mbeki had a hand in the murder of the highly popular Communist party leader Chris Hani in 1993 . . . In the late 70s [Mbeki] was accused by ANC intelligence of being a CIA agent' (26 April 2001); *Financial Times*, 27 April 2001. See also William Mervin Gumede, *Thabo Mbeki and the Battle for the Soul of the ANC*, 2005, pp. 297–8.

32. *Mail & Guardian*, 4 May, 1 June, 17 August 2001; *Noseweek*, No. 33, July 2001.

33. *Focus*, No. 39, September 2005; *Mail & Guardian*, 10 December 1999; *Sunday Independent*, 3 October 2004; *Sowetan*, 5 August 2004.

34. *Sunday Independent*, 3 October 2004; Johannesburg *Star*, 4 October 2004; *Sowetan*, 5 August 2004; private information; Ronnie Kasrils, 'Meeting the Challenges of the 21st Century: Spies, Soothsayers, Sangomas', Budget Vote Address, 17 May 2005. Of course, at a different level, it suits the US to be able to watch and study the individuals involved in South Africa's clandestine terror and nuclear networks.

35. *Guardian*, 30 November 2002; *Africa Confidential*, 6 December 2002.

36. *Sunday Independent*, 13 February 2000; 21, 28 April 2002; Johannesburg *Sunday Times*, 10 October 2004. In 2002, Lindiwe Sisulu launched an AIDS-awareness campaign with the slogan: 'Intelligence officers do it with intelli-

gence ... use a condom.' When questioned at a press conference, she replied: 'When they're with me, they pretend that they don't do it at all' (Johannesburg *Star*, 20 August 2002).

37. *Sunday Independent*, 8 October 1995; *Financial Mail*, 12 January 1996; *Independent*, 26 January 1996; *Citizen*, 21 September 1999; Sakhela Buhlungu, 'From "Madiba Magic" to "Mbeki Logic"', Sean Jacobs and Richard Calland (eds), *Thabo Mbeki's World*, 2002, p. 195.

38. *Mail & Guardian*, 4, 11 August 2000; *Financial Mail*, 13 July, 7 September 2001, 6 September 2002; Terry Crawford-Browne, 'The Betrayal of the Struggle Against Apartheid', 28 September 2000; see also Sam Baqwa, S.A. Fakie and Bulelani Ngcuka, 'Joint Investigation Report into the Strategic Defence Procurement Packages', November 2001; *Sunday Independent*, 11 August 2002; Johannesburg *Sunday Times*, 5 June 2005.

39. NIA, 'Re-Understanding NIA's Domestic Intelligence Mandate', undated document.

40. Jean Redpath, *The Scorpions: Analysing the Directorate of Special Operations*, Institute for Security Studies Monograph No. 96, March 2004, p. 13; *Independent on Sunday*, 23 July 2000. On the deeper roots of crime in southern Africa, see Mark Shaw, 'Organised Crime in Post-Apartheid South Africa', *ISS Papers*, No. 28, January 1998; Stephen Ellis, 'The Historical Significance of South Africa's Third Force', *Journal of Southern African Studies*, June 1998, pp. 295–9; Jean-François Bayart, Stephen Ellis and Beatrice Hibou, *The Criminalization of the State in Africa*, 1999, pp. 49–68; *The World Today*, October 2000.

41. *Business Day*, 24 August 2001; private information; *Independent on Sunday*, 23 July 2000.

42. *Business Day*, 24 August 2001; Jean Redpath, 'Weathering the Storm: Tough Questions for the Scorpions', *SA Crime Quarterly*, No. 8, June 2004; *Sowetan Sunday World*, 26 November 2000; *Observer*, 28 November 1999; *Mail & Guardian*, 3 November 2000; *Sowetan*, 2 July 2002. On Vito Palazollo, see *Noseweek*, No. 9, September 1994; *Mail & Guardian*, 16 October 1998, 19 November 1999, 29 July, 14 September 2001, 12 July 2002, 31 January 2003, 5 November 2004; *Africa Confidential*, 5 February 1999; *Observer*, 30 May 1999; *Guardian*, 3 December 1999.

43. Johannesburg *Star*, 12 October 2001; *Mail & Guardian*, 12 October 2001; *Financial Mail*, 1 August 2003.

44. *Mail & Guardian*, 12 September 2003; Johannesburg *Saturday Star*, 28 June 2003; *This Day*, 24 November 2003; *City Press*, 7 September 2003.

45. Johannesburg *Sunday Times*, 27 July 2003; *Mail & Guardian*, 28 November 2003; *City Press*, 7 September 2003; Johannesburg *Star*, 25 November 2003; *This Day*, 20 November 2003.

46. Johannesburg *Star*, 23 October, 12 November 2003; private information.

47. *Mail & Guardian*, 24 October 2003; Johannesburg *Star*, 22, 26 November 2003.

48. *Financial Mail*, 28 November 2003; Johannesburg *Sunday Times*, 2 November 2003; J.J.F. Hefer, *The Hefer Commission of Inquiry Report*, 2004; Thabo Mbeki, 'Letter from the President', *ANC Today*, Vol. 4, No. 3, 23 January 2004.

49. Johannesburg *Sunday Times*, 14 September 2003.

50. Johannesburg *Star*, 25 September 2004; Johannesburg *Sunday Times*, 25 July 2004; *Noseweek*, No. 66, April 2005, No. 67, May 2005; *Mail & Guardian*, 13 May 2005.

51. *Africa Insight*, Vol. 28, No. 1/2, 1998; *Mail & Guardian*, 28 January 2005; Johannesburg *Star*, 9 June 2005; Thabo Mbeki, 'Statement of the President at the Joint Sitting of Parliament on the Release of Hon Jacob Zuma from his Responsibilities as Deputy President', 14 June 2005.

52. *City Press*, 9 October 2005; *Mail & Guardian*, 14 October 2005. See also www.nia.org.za/SPEECHES/Khampepe – 'Khampepe Commission: NIA Input': 'While putting the [NIA] case to the commission . . . advocate Bizos . . . was misinterpreted by some media. Advocate Bizos is under the brief of the NIA and will not act contrary to the client's instructions.' Billy Masetlha and the NIA recommended 'Relocate the [Scorpions] and change its mandate. This option will go a long way in not only improving oversight and control but also ensuring that functions are performed in a coordinated manner among statutory structures.'

53. *Business Day*, 10 June 2005; Thabo Mbeki, Address at the Intelligence Services Day 10th Anniversary Awards Ceremony and Inauguration of the Wall and Garden of Remembrance: Musanda, Tshwane', 24 November 2005.

CHAPTER 15: THE PRIVATE SECTOR

1. Rudyard Kipling, *The Man Who Would Be King*, 1888, pp. 252–3.

2. Sampson, *Who Runs This Place?*, p. 311; on Anglo American/De Beers, see Duncan Innes, *Anglo American and the Rise of Modern South Africa*, 1984; Roberts, op. cit. There is a great need for a new study of the Oppenheimer empire.

3. *Financial Times*, 2 April 2003; *New York Times*, 4 March 1985.

4. *New York*, 13 May 1991.

5. *New York*, 13 May 1991; *EuroBusiness*, September 1999; *Financial Times*, 27 July 2000, 24 October 2001; *Observer*, 30 September 2001; *Noseweek*, No. 40, August 2002.

6. *EuroBusiness*, September 1999; *Financial Times*, 31 May 1998; *Age*, 16 July 1998; Johannesburg *Sunday Times*, 31 May 1998.

7. *Financial Times*, 27 May 1998; Johannesburg *Sunday Times*, 31 May 1998.

8. *Financial Times*, 27 May 1998; *Mail & Guardian*, 18 June 1999; *Noseweek*, No. 40, August 2002, No. 67, May 2005.

9. *Africa Confidential*, 23 February 2001; *Financial Times*, 9 May 2001; *Business Day*, 10 September 2001; *Guardian*, 3 July 2000; *Observer*, 24 February 2002; *Sunday Telegraph*, 3 March 2002.

10. *New York*, 13 May 1991; *Observer*, 4 July 2004.

11. *Private Eye*, 23 March 2001; *EuroBusiness*, September 1999; *Observer*, 4 July 2004. In 2003 former *Mail & Guardian* editor Phillip van Niekerk demonstrated the significance of Kroll by working for the company before creating his own private intelligence firm.

12. *Independent on Sunday*, 27 March 2005; *Financial Times*, 30 September 2003, 9 May 2005; *Sunday Times*, 15 August 2004.

13. *Financial Times*, 22 May 2004, 26 March 2005; *Business Day*, 11 April 2005; *Observer*, 18 January 2004: 'Undoubtedly the "spook" image helps when it comes to billing clients who are dazzled by the firm's reputation. "Kroll loves giving off an aura of mystery. It makes it seem a bit sexy and dangerous. But the truth is that out of the 100 or so employees in its London office only two or three are from the intelligence agencies. Ex-spooks tend not to make good investigators. They're great when they have the power of a government behind them, but it's completely different when they're operating in private," said one industry veteran . . . [An] intelligence expert [added] "They have feet of clay. A lot of their reports are little more than newspaper cuttings jobs." ' The Scorpion Pete Richer was described by John Carlin as follows: 'with a Lenin beard and high forehead, [Richer] is droll but as sharp as a mamba. He looks every inch the spy he once was, first in exile with the intelligence section of the ANC for 15 years, and then after the 1994 elections, at the new [NIA]' (*Independent on Sunday*, 23 July 2000); See also Johannesburg *Sunday Times*, 28 July 2002. For Richer at SARS, see www.sars.gov.za/Annual%20 Report%202005.

14. Liam Clarke and Kathryn Johnston, *Martin McGuinness*, 2001, p. 255. Father Denis Bradley's first impression of Oatley in the mid-1970s is instructive: 'Oatley in particular was an incredibly sophisticated man . . . but hadn't a clue. When you scraped the surface, underneath all the sophistication you had colonial attitudes' (p. 86); see also Peter Taylor, *Brits: The War Against the IRA*, 2001; Frank Welsh, *Dangerous Deceits*, 1999, pp. 123, 340.

15. *Sunday Times*, 8 August 1999.

16. Johannesburg *Sunday Times*, 15 August 1999; *City Press*, 14 November 1999; interview with Michael Oatley, 18 June 2002.

17. *Mail & Guardian*, 31 July 1998; SAPA-AFP, 30 January 2003; L.M. Mti, 'The Role of the Intelligence Services and Private Security Companies in Crime Prevention and Crime Combating in South Africa', ISSUP *Bulletin*, 5/97; Greg Mills & John Stremlau (eds), *The Privatisation of Security in Africa*, 1999, p. 14; P.J. Visser, 'Legal Changes in the Regulation of the Private Security Industry in South Africa', *Strategic Review for Southern Africa*, Vol. 26, No. 2, Nov. 2004, pp. 1–2.

18. *New Nation*, 17 May 1996; *Africa Confidential*, 23 March 2001; *Mail & Guardian*, 13 July 2001, 7 November 2003; *Financial Mail*, 21 March 2003. See also *Noseweek*, No. 67, May 2005.

19. *Financial Times*, 4 October 2001; *Southscan*, 19 October 2001; *Africa Analysis*, 19 March 2004.

20. Anthony Mockler, *The New Mercenaries*, 1985, pp. 47-8, 56-7, 61, 92; Mike Hoare, *Congo Mercenary*, 1967, p. 66.

21. *London Review of Books*, 1 August 1996; Mockler, op. cit., p. 72; Chris Munnion, *Banana Sunday*, 1993, p. 111; Frederick Forsyth, *The Making of an African Legend: The Biafra Story*, 1977, pp. 115-16.

22. Mockler, op. cit., pp. 163, 168-9, 172; Stockwell, op. cit., pp. 224-5.

23. Mockler, op. cit., pp. 163, 171, 229-31.

24. Rees and Day, op. cit., p. 20; Johannesburg *Sunday Express*, 2 April 1978; James R. Mancham, *Paradise Raped*, 1983, pp. 170-6; Mockler, op. cit., pp. 262, 264-6, 281-2, 285, 288; Stephen Ellis, 'Africa and International Corruption: The Strange Case of South Africa and Seychelles', *African Affairs*, Vol. 95, No. 379, April 1996, pp. 172-3.

25. Mockler, op. cit., pp. 284, 299-301, 309-12, 317-22, 330-1; *Sunday Tribune*, 29 November 1981; *Cape Times*, 10 February 1983; *Rand Daily Mail*, 13 April 1982; Johannesburg *Sunday Star*, 19 October 1986; Ellis, 'Africa and International Corruption', African Affairs, April 1996, p. 173; *Natal Mercury*, 29 July 1992. Mike Hoare's account of his failed invasion and ensuing prison experience is told in Mike Hoare, *The Seychelles Affair*, 1986. Hoare's mercenaries on trial in the Seychelles were defended by maverick Tory MP Nicholas Fairbairn QC, who charged only for his expenses (pp. 183-4).

26. Ellis, 'Africa and International Corruption', *African Affairs*, April 1996, pp. 169-71, 173-9. On South Africa and the Comores, see *Sunday Tribune*, 13 March 1988, 17 December 1989. There is a direct link between South African operations and corruption in the Indian Ocean islands in the mid-to-late 1980s and the growth of the private mercenary companies in the early 1990s. As Ellis explained, ARMSCOR continued actively to trade weapons and broker 'third party deals' long after the demise of the National Party government: 'ARMSCOR continues to be something of a law unto itself, still largely staffed by the personnel of the apartheid era carrying out secretive weapons deals, some of which have embarrassed the ANC government, and making use of commercial networks created in earlier years in both public and private sectors (Ellis, 'Africa and International Corruption', pp. 177-8). See also MID's direct involvement with UNITA and RENAMO in the international trade in ivory and rhino horn (known as Operation Lock). MID was supported by the conservative World Wide Fund for Nature (WWF). Stephen Ellis, 'Of Elephants and Men: Politics and Nature Conservation in South Africa', *Journal of Southern*

African Studies, Vol. 20, No. 1, March 1994, pp. 55–6, explained: '[In the 1970s] operating in remote areas, often along the Mozambican border, Rhodesian soldiers began to acquire ivory . . . According to one former Rhodesian and South African Special Forces officer, it was initially by accident, as the Selous Scouts and other special units would sometimes find dead elephants which had strayed into minefields. The soldiers who stumbled upon these corpses would salvage the ivory and, in order to sell it, would fly to South Africa where they delivered it to their contacts in South African Special Forces or [MID].' By the end of the 1980s, the ivory trade had become a multi-million pound business. See the *Independent*, 8 January 1991; *Africa Confidential*, 27 September 1991, 21 February 1992; Reeve and Ellis, 'An Insider's Account of the South African Security Forces' Role in the Ivory Trade', *Journal of Contemporary African Studies*, June 1995; De Wet Potgieter, *Contraband*, 1995. On the WWF, see Kevin Dowling's series of articles in *Noseweek*, No. 20, December 1997, No. 21, March 1998, No. 22, May 1998, No. 23, July 1998, No. 24, October 1998, No. 25, December 1998, No. 27, September 1999.

27. P.W. Singer, *Corporate Warriors*, 2004, pp. 101–3, 106–7; Venter, op. cit., p. 296; Jim Hooper, *Bloodsong!*, 2002, p. 35; Alex Vines, 'Mercenaries and the Privatisation of Security in Africa in the 1990s', Mills and Stremlau, op. cit., p. 51.

28. Singer, op. cit., pp. 109–10, 117; Duncan Campbell, *Marketing the New 'Dogs of War'*, The Center for Public Integrity, October 2002; *Observer*, 19 January 1997.

29. Singer, op. cit., pp. 108–9; *London Review of Books*, 1 August 1996: Jeremy Harding commented of 'the former president of the Anti-Apartheid Movement' David Steel's relationship with 'some of apartheid's most committed former defenders': 'Steel is aware of the link between Heritage and EO – potentially a source of damage to his reputation – but there is no reason for the subject of EO to be raised at Heritage. Steel's distance from the sharp end of Buckingham's business is probably as good as he can contrive . . . For several years now, Steel's name has been on hand for anyone in the SRC/Branch Energy/EO brotherhood who wants the operation to look like a charitable venture.' Steel eventually resigned from the board of the Heritage Group; *Africa Confidential*, 29 May 1998; Campbell, *Marketing the New 'Dogs of War'*, October 2002; *Sunday Times*, 2 July 2000.

30. *Observer*, 19 January 1997; Campbell, *Marketing the New 'Dogs of War'*, October 2002; Jim Hooper, *Bloodsong!*, pp. 81–2; Singer, op. cit., p. 109.

31. *London Review of Books*, 1 August 1996; Vines, 'Mercenaries', Mills and Stremlau, op. cit., p. 54; Singer, op. cit., pp. 109, 116. Harding added: 'If EO was no longer in Angola by start of 1996, there were scores, perhaps hundreds of its personnel left working in the country under other auspices – a security firm called Saracen . . . another called Alpha 5, and an air charter company called Ibis.'

32. Singer, op. cit., pp. 112–14.

33. *Africa Confidential*, 29 May 1998; Duncan Campbell, *Marketing the New 'Dogs of War'*, October 2002; Vines, 'Mercenaries', Mills and Stremlau, op. cit., p. 49; Lieutenant-Colonel Tim Spicer OBE, *An Unorthodox Story*, 2003, p. 145. Spicer blames the popular image of the mercenary – 'a bunch of thugs attempting to subvert the legally elected government and leaving chaos in their wake' – on Callan in Angola and Mike Hoare's amateur dramatics in the Seychelles (p. 37). In contrast, he saw Sandline and EO as modern capitalist companies: 'Sandline is not a charitable organisation. What we do we do for money and we expect to make a profit out of it. We would argue that PMCs, being profit-orientated, are necessarily cost-effective, unlike many UN operations' (p. 23). The press release accompanying EO's disbanding declared: 'African countries are busy working out solutions in Africa . . . Let's give them a chance' (Singer, op. cit., p. 117).

34. Campbell, *Marketing the New 'Dogs of War'*, October 2002; Vines, 'Mercenaries', Mills and Stremlau, op. cit., pp. 58–9, 61–2; John Kampfner, *Blair's Wars*, 2003, pp. 66–9.

35. Vines, 'Mercenaries', Mills and Stremlau, op. cit., pp. 77–8.

36. *Independent*, 5 January 2005; *International Herald Tribune*, 16 June 2004; *Independent on Sunday*, 1 May 2005; *Sunday Independent*, 6 March 2005. On South African mercenary deaths in Iraq, see also Johannesburg *Sunday Times*, 18 April 2004; *This Day*, 14 October 2004.

37. *Sunday Independent*, 6 March 2005; Johannesburg *Sunday Times*, 7 December 2003, 1 February 2004; *Observer*, 14 November 2004.

38. *Sunday Independent*, 6 March 2005; Johannesburg *Sunday Times*, 16 October 2005; *Economist*, 27 March 2004.

39. *Sunday Times*, 20 February 2005; *Financial Times*, 30 September 2003; *Citizen*, 9 August 2004. By December 2005, at least nineteen South Africans had died in Iraq (SAPA, 19 November, 23 December 2005).

40. Mark Hollingsworth and Paul Halloran, *Thatcher's Fortunes*, 2005, pp. 14–16, 18; *Vanity Fair*, January 2005; Frederick Forsyth, *The Dogs of War*, 1974, p. 146; Mockler, op. cit., pp. 141–6; *Financial Times*, 6 September 2004.

41. Hollingsworth, op. cit., pp. 18–19. Crause Steyl, 'Plea under Section 105A of the Criminal Procedure Act, Act 51 of 1977', 8 July 2004, revealed that the coup plan in December 2003 was: 'a. Luxurious 4 × 4 vehicles would be bought and packed in the back of an Ilyushin aircraft . . . The plan was to use them as decoy and to hand them over as a gift to the President at Malabo airport, EG [Equatorial Guinea]; b. Weapons would also be packed into the Ilyushin aircraft; c. A second freight aircraft would be acquired to fly in armed forces to carry out the coup d'état; d. The aircraft with the vehicles would land at Malabo, EG 20 minutes before the aircraft with Moto and the armed forces; e. While the President was lured to the airport, the armed forces (with Moto) would resist any opposition with force and a switch of Presidents would take place.'

42. *Sunday Times*, 23 January 2005; *Africa Confidential*, 10 September 2004; Hollingsworth, op. cit., pp. 23–4, 27, 32; *Observer*, 18 July 2004.

43. Hollingsworth, op. cit., pp. 16, 18, 22, 25, 329, 337–40, 345; the microloan business involved 'lending relatively small amounts of money . . . at high interest rates' to 'civil servants, court officials, servicemen and women [and] . . . police officers'. Thatcher is reported to have 'lost an estimated £200,000'. Amazingly, he didn't understand that providing microloans to poorly paid and indebted public officials was little more than common 'loan sharking'. He appears to have believed that he was a generous sponsor of the underprivileged. Thatcher informed the *Daily Mail*, 8 August 1998: 'I think the amazing thing is that the people who abused [the generosity] were the guardians of the law in South Africa . . . That's the disappointment to me'; *Mail & Guardian*, 12 March 2004.

44. Hollingsworth, op. cit., pp. 29–30, 35; *Observer*, 18 July 2004.

45. On David Hart, 'a professional anti-communist [and] . . . "conspiratorial . . . somewhat bizarre figure"', see Seumas Milne, *The Enemy Within*, 1994, pp. 364–75; Hollingsworth, op. cit., pp. 36–8; Johannesburg *Sunday Times*, 21 November 2004.

46. *Sunday Times*, 19 September 2004; *Mail on Sunday*, 21 November 2004; *Observer*, 29 August 2004.

47. Mark Thatcher, '[Plea] Agreement in terms of Section 105A of Act 51 of 1977', 7 January 2005.

48. Hollingsworth, op. cit., p. 350; *Guardian*, 14 January 2005.

49. *Independent*, 28 December 2004; *Mail & Guardian*, 21 January 2005.

50. Private information; *Noseweek*, No. 65, March 2005.

51. *Vanity Fair*, January 2005; *Sunday Telegraph*, 28 November 2004.

EPILOGUE: WHO IS COMRADE BHEKI?

1. Peter Hennessy, 'The Itch after the Amputation', K.G. Robertson (ed), *War, Resistance and Intelligence: Essays in Honour of M.R.D. Foot*, 1999, p. 227.

2. *Cape Times*, 21 October 2005; *Sunday Independent*, 23 October 2005.

3. Pretorius, op. cit., pp. 10–12; *Sunday Independent*, 14 September 1997, revealed that Pretorius, who was facing legal suits by generals Viljoen and Groenewald, had applied to the High Court for the release of a 'document, written in 1993 by Mike Louw . . . and sent to Kobie Coetsee', which Pretorius believed 'may show the Afrikaner Volksfront [was] set up by . . . Constand Viljoen and Tienie Groenewald [as] a secret project [of] the State Security Council'; see also Gunther Schickelgruber, 'High Treason: An Intelligence Report on South Africa', unpublished manuscript, 2003.

4. U.V.D.J. Solomon, memorandum to Davidson Badrodien Attorneys, 18 June 2001; Uranin Vladimir Dzerzhinsky Joseph Solomon, Statement to the South

African Police Service, 27 November 2003 [Jacobs Papers]; *Noseweek*, No. 32, April 2001.

5. Johannesburg *Sunday Times*, 17 November 1985, 26 January 1986.

6. Interview with Bheki Jacobs, 12 August 2004; *Noseweek*, No. 32, April 2001.

7. R. Shaik (ANC Department of Intelligence & Security Amalgamation Committee), letter to Cde Malume Manci, 22 November 1994 [Jacobs Papers]; *Noseweek*, No. 32, April 2001; Solomon, Statement to the SAPS, 27 November 2003 [Jacobs Papers].

8. *Noseweek*, No. 32, April 2001; Congress Consultants, 'Business Front – Anglo American/De Beers/Ramaphosa', 1997. A Congress Consultants report of particular interest is 'The Indian Cabal', March 1996, which examines the roles played by Mac Maharaj and Mo Shaik.

9. Johannesburg *Sunday Times*, 11 March 2001.

10. *Mail & Guardian*, 16 March 2001.

11. *Noseweek*, No. 32, April 2001.

12. Concerned Patriotic Intelligence Community loyal to the Constitution of the Republic of South Africa, 'Report to the Honourable Patricia de Lille', unpublished report, 2003.

13. Johannesburg *Sunday Times*, 23 November 2003; *Mail & Guardian*, 28 November 2003; private information.

14. Solomon, Statement to the SAPS, 27 November 2003 [Jacobs Papers]; Johannesburg *Star*, 8 December 2003; interview with Bheki Jacobs, 4 February 2005.

15. *Business Day*, 25 November 2003; interview with Bheki Jacobs, 26 January 2005.

16. *New Yorker*, 23 May 2005.

Select Bibliography

James Adams, *The Unnatural Alliance*, Quartet Books, London, 1984.

Philip Agee, *Inside the Company: CIA Diary*, Penguin, London, 1975.

Philip Agee and Louis Wolf, *Dirty Work: The CIA in Western Europe*, Lyle Stuart, Secaucus, 1978.

Chris Alden, *Apartheid's Last Stand: The Rise and Fall of the South African Security State*, Macmillan Press, London, 1998.

Richard J. Aldrich, *The Hidden Hand: Britain, America and Cold War Secret Intelligence*, John Murray, London, 2001.

Antony Altbeker, *Solving Crime: The State of the SAPS Detective Service*, Institute for Security Studies Monograph No. 31, Pretoria, November 1998.

Amnesty International, *South Africa: State of Fear, Security Force Complicity in Torture and Political Killings, 1990–1992*, Amnesty International, London, 1992.

ANC, 'Statement to the Truth and Reconciliation Commission', August 1996.

ANC, 'Further Submissions and Responses by the ANC to Questions Raised by the Commission for Truth and Reconciliation', 12 May 1997.

Karl Anders, *Murder to Order*, Ampersand, London, 1965.

David Anderson, *Histories of the Hanged: Britain's Dirty War in Kenya and the End of the Empire*, Weidenfeld & Nicholson, London, 2005.

Christopher Andrew and Oleg Gordievsky, *KGB: The Inside Story of its Foreign Operations from Lenin to Gorbachev*, Hodder & Stoughton, London, 1990.

Christopher Andrew and Vasili Mitrokhin, *The Mitrokhin Archive: The KGB in Europe and the West*, Allen Lane, London, 1999.

Christopher Andrew and Vasili Mitrokhin, *The Mitrokhin Archive II: The KGB and the World*, Allen Lane, London, 2005.

Hannah Arendt, *Eichmann in Jerusalem: A Report on the Banality of Evil*, revised and enlarged edn, Penguin, London, 1965.

Kader Asmal, Louise Asmal and Ronald Suresh Roberts, *Reconciliation Through Truth: A Reckoning of Apartheid's Criminal Governance*, David Philip, Cape Town, 1996.

Stefan Aust, *The Baader–Meinhof Group: The Inside Story of a Phenomenon*, Bodley Head, London, 1987, originally published in West Germany in 1985.

Martin Bailey, *Oilgate: The Sanctions Scandal*, Coronet Books, London, 1979.

James Bamford, *The Puzzle Palace: America's National Security Agency and its Special Relationship with Britain's GCHQ*, Sidgwick & Jackson, London, 1983.

Sam Baqwa, S.A. Fakie and Bulelani Ngcuka, 'Joint Investigation Report into the Strategic Defence Procurement Packages', Government Printer, Pretoria, November 2001.

James Barber, 'BOSS in Britain', *African Affairs*, Vol. 82, No. 328, July 1983.

Howard Barrell, 'The Turn to the Masses: The African National Congress' Strategic Review of 1978–79', *Journal of Southern African Studies*, Vol. 18, No. 1, March 1992.

Howard Barrell, 'Conscripts to their Age: African National Congress Operation Strategy, 1976–1986', unpublished DPhil thesis, University of Oxford, 1993.

Nico Basson and Ben Motinga, *Call Them Spies*, African Communication Projects, Windhoek, 1989.

Jean-François Bayart, Stephen Ellis and Beatrice Hibou, *The Criminilization of the State in Africa*, James Currey, Oxford and Indiana University Press, Indianapolis, 1999.

Simon Baynham, 'Security Strategies for a Future South Africa', *Journal of Modern African Studies*, Vol. 28, No. 3, September 1990.

André Beaufre, *An Introduction to Strategy with Particular Reference to Problems of Defence, Politics, Economics, and Diplomacy in the Nuclear Age*, Faber & Faber, London, 1965.

Mark Behr, *The Smell of Apples*, Abacus, London, 1995.

Terry Bell, with Dumisa Buhle Ntsebeza, *Unfinished Business: South Africa, Apartheid and Truth*, Verso, London, 2003.

Robin Benger, *Madiba: The Life and Times of Nelson Mandela*, CBC, April 2004.

Walter Benjamin, *Illuminations*, ed. Hannah Arendt, Jonathan Cape, London, 1970.

Ari Ben-Menashe, *Profits of War: Inside the Secret US–Israeli Arms Network*, Sheridan Square Press, New York, 1992.

Mary Benson, *South Africa: The Struggle for a Birthright*, International Defence and Aid Fund for Southern Africa, London, 1985.

Mary Benson, *A Far Cry: The Making of a South African*, Viking, London, 1989.

Bill Berkeley, *The Graves Are Not Yet Full: Race, Tribe and Power in the Heart of Africa*, Basic Books, New York, 2001.

Bruce Berman, Dickson Eyoh and Will Kymlicka (eds), *Ethnicity and Democracy in Africa*, James Currey, Oxford, 2004.

G.R. Berridge, 'The Ethnic "Agent in Place": English-speaking Civil Servants and Nationalist South Africa, 1948–57', *Intelligence and National Security*, Vol. 4, No. 2, April 1989.

G.R. Berridge, *South Africa, the Colonial Powers and 'African Defence': The Rise and Fall of the White Entente, 1948–1960*, Macmillan Press, London, 1992.

Simon Berthon, *Secret History: Harold Wilson, the Final Days*, Channel 4, 1996.

Peter Bessell, *Cover-Up: The Jeremy Thorpe Affair*, Simons Books, Wilmington, 1980.

Geoffrey Bing, *Reap the Whirlwind: An Account of Kwame Nkrumah's Ghana from 1950 to 1966*, MacGibbon & Kee, London, 1968.

George Bizos, *No One to Blame? In Pursuit of Justice in South Africa*, David Philip, Cape Town, 1998.

Conrad Black, *A Life in Progress*, Key Porter Books, Toronto, 1993.

Paul W. Blackstock, *The Strategy of Subversion: Manipulating the Politics of Other Nations*, Quadrangle Books, Chicago, 1964.

Wolf Blitzer, *Territory of Lies: The Rise, Fall, and Betrayal of Jonathan Jay Pollard*, HarperCollins, New York, 1990.

Jonathan Bloch and Patrick Fitzgerald, *British Intelligence and Covert Action: Africa, Middle East and Europe since 1945*, Junction Books, London, 1983.

Charles Bloomberg, *Christian-Nationalism and the Rise of the Afrikaner Broederbond in South Africa, 1918–48*, ed. Saul Dubow. Macmillan Press, London, 1990.

Jan Bondeson, *Blood on the Snow: The Killing of Olof Palme*, Cornell University Press, Ithaca, 2005.

Thula Bopela and Daluxolo Luthuli, *Umkhonto we Sizwe: Fighting for a Divided People*, Galago, Alberton, 2005.

Thomas Borstelmann, *Apartheid's Reluctant Uncle: The United States and Southern Africa in the Early Cold War*, Oxford University Press, New York, 1993.

Boss: The First 5 Years, International Defence and Aid Fund, London, 1975.

Conny Braam, *Operation Vula*, Jacana, Bellevue, 2004.

Bertolt Brecht, *Der Aufhaltsame Aufstieg des Arturo Ui* [*The Resistible Rise of Arturo Ui*], Suhrkamp Verlag, Berlin, 1957.

Breyten Breytenbach, *The True Confessions of an Albino Terrorist*, Faber & Faber, London, 1984.

Jan Breytenbach, *Forged in Battle*, Saayman & Weber, Cape Town, 1986.

Colonel Jan Breytenbach, *They Live by the Sword*, Lemur Books, Alberton, 1990.

Jan Breytenbach, *Eden's Exiles: One Soldier's Fight for Paradise*, Queillerie, Cape Town, 1997.

Colonel Jan Breytenbach, *The Buffalo Soldiers: The Story of South Africa's 32-Battalion 1975–1993*, Galago, Alberton, 2002.

Fred Bridgland, *Jonas Savimbi: A Key to Africa*, Mainstream Publishing, Edinburgh, 1986.

Fred Bridgland, *The War for Africa: Twelve Months that Transformed a Continent*, Ashanti Publishing, London, 1990.

Fred Bridgland, *Katiza's Journey: Beneath the Surface of South Africa's Shame*, Sidgwick & Jackson, London, 1997.

Victoria Brittain, *Hidden Lives, Hidden Death: South Africa's Crippling of a Continent*, Faber & Faber, London, 1988.

Miles Brokensha and Robert Knowles, *The Fourth of July Raids*, Simondium Publishers, Cape Town, 1965.

Alan Brooks and Jeremy Brickhill, *Whirlwind Before the Storm: The Origins and Development of the Uprising in Soweto and the Rest of South Africa from June to December 1976*, International Defence and Aid Fund for Southern Africa, London, 1980.

Nick Broomfield, *The Leader, his Driver and the Driver's Wife*, 1991, documentary film.

Brian Bunting, *The Rise of the South African Reich*, International Defence and Aid Fund for Southern Africa, London, 1986.

Fran Buntman, *Robben Island and Prisoner Resistance to Apartheid*, Cambridge University Press, Cambridge, 2003.

Marlene Burger and Chandre Gould, *Secrets and Lies: Wouter Basson and South Africa's Chemical and Biological Warfare Programme*, Zebra Press, Cape Town, 2002.

Julian Burgess, Esau du Plessis, Roger Murray, Peter Fraenkel, Rosanne Harvey, John Laurence, Peter Ripken and Barbara Rogers, *The Great White Hoax*, Africa Bureau, London, 1977.

William E. Burrows and Robert Windrem, *Critical Mass: The Dangerous Race for Superweapons in a Fragmenting World*, Simon & Schuster, London, 1994.

Imtiaz Cajee, *Timol: A Quest for Justice*, STE Publishing, Johannesburg, 2005.

Luli Callinicos, *Oliver Tambo: Beyond the Engeli Mountains*, David Philip, Cape Town, 2004.

Bruce Campbell and Arthur Brenner (eds), *Death Squads in Global Perspective: Murder with Deniability*, St Martin's Press, New York, 2000.

Duncan Campbell, *Marketing the New 'Dogs of War'*, The Center for Public Integrity, Washington DC, October 2002.

Barbara Carr, *Spy in the Sun: The Story of Yuriy Loginov*, Howard Timmins, Cape Town, 1969.

Gordon Carr, *The Angry Brigade: The Cause and the Case*, Victor Gollancz, London, 1975.

Barbara Castle, *The Castle Diaries, 1964–1976*, Papermac, London, 1990.

Gavin Cawthra, *Brutal Force: The Apartheid War Machine*, International Defence and Aid Fund for Southern Africa, London, 1986.

Gavin Cawthra, *Policing South Africa: The SAP and the Transition from Apartheid*, Zed Books, London, 1993.

Zdenek Cervenka and Barbara Rogers, *The Nuclear Axis: Secret Collaboration between West Germany and South Africa*, Julian Friedmann Books, London, 1978.

Stephen Chan, *Exporting Apartheid: Foreign Policies in Southern Africa, 1978–1988*, Macmillan, London, 1990.

Naomi Chazan, 'The Fallacies of Pragmatism: Israeli Foreign Policy Towards South Africa', *African Affairs*, Vol. 82, No. 327, April 1983.

Lewis Chester, Magnus Linklater and David May, *Jeremy Thorpe: A Secret Life*, André Deutsch, London, 1979.

Peter Chippindale and David Leigh, *The Thorpe Committal*, Arrow Books, London, 1979.

Iain Christie, *Samora Machel: A Biography*, PANAF, London, 1989.

CIA: The Pike Report, Spokesman Books, Nottingham, 1977.

Jakkie Cilliers and Markus Reichardt (eds), *About Turn: The Transformation of the South African Military and Intelligence*, Institute for Defence Policy, Johannesburg, 1995.

Civilian Support Component, 'The Apparatus of State-orchestrated Violence in Apartheid South Africa', unpublished report, February 1997.

Liam Clarke and Kathryn Johnston, *Martin McGuinness: From Guns to Government*, Mainstream, Edinburgh, 2001.

Nicholas Claxton and Alan Clarke, *The British Desk: South Africa's Intelligence Operations in Britain*, Central Television, 1984.

Stephen Clingman, *Bram Fischer: Afrikaner Revolutionary*, David Philip, Cape Town, 1998.

Bill Clinton, *My Life*, Arrow Books, London, 2005.

Hillary Rodham Clinton, *Living History*, Hodder Headline, London, 2004.

Jacklyn Cock and Laurie Nathan (eds), *War and Society: The Militarisation of South Africa*, David Philip, Cape Town, 1989.

Andrew and Leslie Cockburn, *Dangerous Liaison: The Inside Story of the US-Israeli Covert Relationship*, The Bodley Head, London, 1992.

A.W. Cockerill, *Sir Percy Sillitoe*, W.H. Allen, London, 1975.

Janet Coggin, *The Spy's Wife: A True Account of Marriage to a KGB Master-spy*, Constable, London, 1999.

The Commonwealth Group of Eminent Persons, *Mission to South Africa: The Commonwealth Report*, Penguin, London, 1986.

Concerned Patriotic Intelligence Community Loyal to the Constitution of the Republic of South Africa, 'Report to the Honourable Patricia de Lille', unpublished report, 2003.

'Conference Issue: Security and Intelligence in a Post-Apartheid South Africa', *Strategic Review for Southern Africa*, Vol. 14, No. 2, October 1992.

Joseph Conrad, *The Secret Agent*, Penguin, London, 1963.

Percy Cradock, *In Pursuit of British Interests: Reflections on Foreign Policy under Margaret Thatcher and John Major*, John Murray, London, 1997.

Percy Cradock, *Know Your Enemy: How the Joint Intelligence Committee Saw the World*, John Murray, London, 2002.

Michael Crick, *The Right to Know*, BBC Radio 4, 27 September 2005.

Chester A. Crocker, 'South Africa: Strategy for Change', *Foreign Affairs*, Vol. 59, No. 2, Winter 1980-1.

Chester A. Crocker, *High Noon in Southern Africa: Making Peace in a Rough Neighborhood*, Jonathan Ball, Johannesburg, 1993.

Jeremy Cronin, *Inside and Out: Poems from 'Inside' and 'Even the Dead'*, David Philip, Cape Town, 1999.

Brian Crozier, *Free Agent: The Unseen War, 1941–1991*, HarperCollins, London, 1993.

Richard Cummings, *The Pied Piper: Allard K. Lowenstein and the Liberal Dream*, Grove Press, New York, 1985.

Richard Cummings, 'A Diamond is Forever: Mandela Triumphs, Buthelezi and de Klerk Survive, and ANC on the US Payroll', *International Journal of Intelligence and Counterintelligence*, Vol. 8, No. 2, Summer 1995.

Lt Col. Ron Reid Daly, as told to Peter Stiff, *Selous Scouts: Top Secret War*, Galago, Alberton, 1983.

Jerry Dan, *Ultimate Deception: How Stalin Stole the Bomb*, Rare Books & Berry, Minehead, Somerset, 2003.

Kevin Danaher, *In Whose Interest? A Guide to US–South African Relations*, Institute for Policy Studies, Washington DC, 1984.

Kevin Danaher, *The Political Economy of US Policy Toward South Africa*, Westview Press, London, 1985.

Stephen M. Davis, *Apartheid's Rebels: Inside South Africa's Hidden War*, Yale University Press, New Haven, 1987.

Arnaud de Borchgrave and Robert Moss, *The Spike*, Weidenfeld & Nicolson, London, 1980.

F.W. de Klerk, *The Last Trek: A New Beginning. The Autobiography*, Macmillan, London, 1998.

Willem de Klerk, *F.W. de Klerk: The Man in His Time*, Jonathan Ball, Johannesburg, 1991.

Eugene de Kock, as told to Jeremy Gordin, *A Long Night's Damage: Working for the Apartheid State*, Contra Press, Johannesburg, 1998.

J.W. de Villiers, Roger Jardine and Mitchell Reiss, 'Why South Africa Gave Up the Bomb', *Foreign Affairs*, No. 72, Vol. 5, November–December 1993.

Les de Villiers, *Secret Information*, Tafelberg, Cape Town, 1980.

John D'Oliveira, *Vorster – The Man*, Ernest Stanton, Johannesburg, 1977.

Stephen Dorril and Robin Ramsay, *Smear! Wilson and the Secret State*, Fourth Estate, London, 1991.

Stephen Dorril, *The Silent Conspiracy: Inside the Intelligence Services in the 1990s*, Heinemann, London, 1993.

Stephen Dorril, *MI6: Fifty Years of Special Operations*, Fourth Estate, London, 2000.

'Dr Death – South Africa's Biological Weapons Program', CBS *60 Minutes*, 3 November 2002.

C.J. Driver, 'Used to be Good Friends', *Granta 80: The Group*, December 2002.

Allen Drury, *'A Very Strange Society': A Journey to the Heart of South Africa*, Michael Joseph, London, 1968.

Captain J.H. du Plessis, *Diamonds are Dangerous*, Cassell, London, 1960.

Max du Preez, *Pale Native: Memories of a Renegade Reporter*, Zebra Press, Cape Town, 2003.

Caroline Elkins, *Britain's Gulag: The Brutal End of Empire in Kenya*, Jonathan Cape, London, 2005.

H. Ellert, *The Rhodesian Front War: Counter-insurgency and Guerrilla War in Rhodesia 1962–1980*, Mambo Press, Gweru, 1989.

Nicholas Elliott, *With My Little Eye: Observation along the Way*, Michael Russell, Norwich, 1993.

Stephen Ellis, 'The ANC in Exile', *African Affairs*, Vol. 90, No. 360, July 1991.

Stephen Ellis and Tsepo Sechaba, *Comrades Against Apartheid: The ANC and the South African Communist Party in Exile*, James Currey, London, 1992.

Stephen Ellis, 'Of Elephants and Men: Politics and Nature Conservation in South Africa', *Journal of Southern African Studies*, Vol. 20, No. 1, March 1994.

Stephen Ellis, 'Mbokodo: Security in ANC Camps, 1961–1990', *African Affairs*, Vol. 93, No. 371, April 1994.

Stephen Ellis, 'Africa and International Corruption: The Strange Case of South Africa and Seychelles', *African Affairs*, Vol. 95, No. 379, April 1996.

Stephen Ellis and John Daniel, 'State Security Policy', unpublished paper, 1996.

Stephen Ellis, 'The Historical Significance of South Africa's Third Force', *Journal of Southern African Studies*, Vol. 24, No. 2, June 1998.

Stephen Ellis, 'Review of Terry Bell and Dumisa Buhle Ntsebeza, *Unfinished Business*', *Journal of Modern African Studies*, Vol. 42, No. 3, September, 2004.

Paul Els, *We Fear Naught But God*, Covos-Day, Johannesburg, 2000.

Steven Emerson, *Secret Warriors: Inside the Covert Military Operations of the Reagan Era*, G.P. Putnam's Sons, New York, 1988.

Edward Jay Epstein, *The Death of the Diamond*, Sphere Books, London, 1983.

R.B.P Erasmus, *Report of the Commission of Inquiry into Alleged Irregularities in the Former Department of Information*, Government Printer, Pretoria, December 1978.

R.B.P Erasmus, *Interim Report of the Commission of Inquiry into Alleged Irregularities in the Former Department of Information*, Government Printer, Pretoria, March 1979.

R.B.P Erasmus, *Supplementary Report of the Commission of Inquiry into Alleged Irregularities in the Former Department of Information*, Government Printer, Pretoria, June 1979.

Gavin Evans, *Dancing Shoes is Dead: A Tale of Fighting Men in South Africa*, Doubleday, London, 2002.

Meyer Feldberg, Kate Jowell and Stephen Mulholland (eds), *Milton Friedman in South Africa*, Graduate School of Business UCT, Cape Town, 1976.

Walter Felgate, 'Mangosuthu Buthelezi: The Iago of South African Politics', unpublished manuscript, 1999.

William Finnegan, *Dateline Soweto: Travels with Black South African Reporters*, University of California Press, Berkeley, 1995.

Ian Fleming, *Diamonds are Forever*, Jonathan Cape, London, 1956.

Ian Fleming, *The Diamond Smugglers*, Jonathan Cape, London, 1957.

Ken Flower, *Serving Secretly: An Intelligence Chief on Record – Rhodesia into Zimbabwe, 1964–1981*, John Murray, London, 1987.

Laurie Flynn, *Studded with Diamonds and Paved with Gold: Miners, Mining Companies and Human Rights in Southern Africa*, Bloomsbury, London, 1992.

Paul Foot, *The Politics of Harold Wilson*, Penguin, London, 1968.

Paul Foot, *Who Framed Colin Wallace?*, Macmillan, London, 1989.

Frederick Forsyth, *The Dogs of War*, Viking, London, 1974.

Frederick Forsyth, *The Making of an African Legend: The Biafra Story*, Penguin, London, 1977.

Don Foster, Paul Haupt and Maresa de Beer, *The Theatre of Violence: Narratives of Protagonists in the South African Conflict*, Institute for Justice and Reconciliation, Cape Town, 2005.

Glenn Frankel, *Rivonia's Children: Three Families and the Price of Freedom in South Africa*, Weidenfeld & Nicolson, London, 1999.

Philip H. Frankel, *Pretoria's Praetorians: Civil–Military Relations in South Africa*, Cambridge University Press, Cambridge, 1984.

Philip Frankel, *Soldiers in a Storm: The Armed Forces in South Africa's Democratic Transition*, Westview Press, Boulder, 2000.

Philip Frankel, *An Ordinary Atrocity: Sharpeville and Its Massacre*, Yale University Press, New Haven, 2001.

Sir Lawrence Freedman, *The Official History of the Falklands Campaign*, Vols 1 and 2, Routledge, London, 2005.

Simon Freeman and Barrie Penrose, *Rinkagate: The Rise and Fall of Jeremy Thorpe*, Bloomsbury, London, 1996.

Steven Friedman and Doreen Atkinson (eds), *South African Review 7: The Small Miracle, South Africa's Negotiated Settlement*, Ravan, Johannesburg, 1994.

Arthur L. Gavshon, *The Last Days of Dag Hammarskjöld*, Pall Mall Press, London, 1963.

Arthur Gavshon and Desmond Rice, *The Sinking of the Belgrano*, New English Library, London, 1984.

Deon Geldenhuys, *The Diplomacy of Isolation: South African Foreign Policy Making*, South African Institute of International Affairs and Macmillan South Africa, Johannesburg, 1984.

Jannie Geldenhuys, *A General's Story: From an Era of War and Peace*, Jonathan Ball, Johannesburg, 1995.

Edward George, *The Cuban Intervention in Angola, 1965–1991: From Che Guevara to Cuito Cuanavale*, Frank Cass, Abingdon, 2005.

Jan-Bart Gewald, 'Who Killed Clemens Kapuuo?', *Journal of Southern African Studies*, Vol. 30, No. 1, September 2004.

David N. Gibbs, 'Dag Hammarskjöld, the United Nations, and the Congo Crisis of 1960–1: A Reinterpretation', *Journal of Modern African Studies*, Vol. 31, No. 1, March 1993.

Emma Gilbey, *The Lady: The Life and Times of Winnie Mandela*, Jonathan Cape, London, 1993.

Hermann Giliomee, '*Broedertwis*: Intra-Afrikaner Conflicts in the Transition from Apartheid', *African Affairs*, Vol. 91, No. 364, July 1992.

Hermann Giliomee, 'Surrender Without Defeat: Afrikaners and the South African "Miracle"', *Daedalus*, Vol. 126, No. 2, Spring 1997.

Hermann Giliomee, *The Afrikaners: Biography of a People*, Tafelberg, Cape Town, 2003.

Piero Gleijeses, *Conflicting Missions: Havana, Washington, and Africa, 1959–1976*, University of North Carolina Press, Chapel Hill, 2002.

Pumla Gobodo-Madikizela, *A Human Being Died That Night: A Story of Forgiveness*, David Philip, Cape Town, 2004.

Richard Goldstone, *Commission of Inquiry Regarding the Prevention of Public Violence and Intimidation: Report to the Commission by the Committee Appointed to Inquire into Allegations Concerning Front Companies of the SADF and the Training of Inkatha Supporters at the Caprivi in 1986*, Government Printer, Pretoria, 1992.

Richard Goldstone, *Commission of Inquiry Regarding the Prevention of Public Violence and Intimidation: Report of the Committee into Allegations of a Third Force*, Government Printer, Pretoria, May 1993.

Richard Goldstone, *Commission of Inquiry Regarding the Prevention of Public Violence and Intimidation: Interim Report on Criminal Political Violence by Elements within the South African Police, the KwaZulu Police and the Inkatha Freedom Party*, Government Printer, Pretoria, March 1994.

Arnold Goodman, *Tell Them I'm on My Way*, Chapmans Publishers, London, 1993.

David Goodman, *Fault Lines: Journeys into the New South Africa*, University of California Press, Berkeley, 1999.

June Goodwin and Ben Schiff, *Heart of Whiteness: Afrikaners Face Black Rule in the New South Africa*, Scribner, New York, 1995.

Chandre Gould and Peter I. Folb, 'The South African Chemical and Biological Warfare Program: An Overview', *The Nonproliferation Review*, Vol. 7, No. 3, Fall–Winter 2000.

Graham Greene, *The Human Factor*, The Bodley Head, London, 1978.

Evelyn Groenink, *Dulcie: Een vrouw die haar mond moest houden*, Uitgeverij Atlas, Amsterdam, 2001, English translation provided by the author.

Evelyn Groenink, 'Murder Inc. Killing for Business in Southern Africa: The Assassinations of Dulcie September, Anton Lubowski, and Chris Hani', unpublished manuscript, 2005.

Kenneth W. Grundy, *The Militarization of South African Politics*, Indiana University Press, Bloomington, 1986.

William Mervin Gumede, *Thabo Mbeki and the Battle for the Soul of the ANC*, Zebra Press, Cape Town, 2005.

William Gutteridge (ed), *South Africa's Defence and Security into the 21st Century*, Dartmouth Publishing, Aldershot, 1996.

Peter Hain, *Sing the Beloved Country: The Struggle for the New South Africa*, Pluto Press, London, 1996.

Joe Haines, *Glimmers of Twilight: Harold Wilson in Decline*, Politico's, London, 2003.

Hilton Hamann, *Days of the Generals: The Untold Story of South Africa's Apartheid-era Military Generals*, Zebra Press, Cape Town, 2001.

Joseph Hanlon, *Beggar Your Neighbours: Apartheid Power in Southern Africa*, Catholic Institute for International Relations, London, 1986.

Louis Harms, *Report of the Commission of Inquiry into Certain Alleged Murders*, Government Printer, Pretoria, 1990.

Harold Wilson: The Letter and the Lie, BBC Radio 4, 26 September 2002.

Verne Harris and Carolyn Hamilton, *A Prisoner in the Garden: Opening Nelson Mandela's Prison Archive*, Penguin, London, 2005.

Verne Harris, Sello Hatang and Peter Liberman, 'Unveiling South Africa's Nuclear Past', *Journal of Southern African Studies*, Vol. 30, No. 3, September 2004.

David Harrison, *The White Tribe of Africa: South Africa in Perspective*, British Broadcasting Corporation, London, 1981.

David Harrison, *Mandela: The Living Legend*, parts 1 and 2, BBC 1, March 2003.

David Harrison and David Dimbleby, *Tonight Special: Interview with Eschel Rhoodie*, BBC 1, 21 March 1979.

Robert Harvey, *The Fall of Apartheid: The Inside Story from Smuts to Mbeki*, Palgrave Macmillan, London, 2001.

Tony Heard, *The Cape of Storms: A Personal History of the Crisis in South Africa*, Ravan, Johannesburg, 1991.

J.J.F. Hefer, *The Hefer Commission of Inquiry Report*, Government Printer, Pretoria, 2004.

Helmoed-Römer Heitman, *War in Angola: The Final South African Phase*, Ashanti Publishing, Gibraltar, 1990.

Robert D'A. Henderson, 'South African Intelligence Under de Klerk', *International Journal of Intelligence and Counterintelligence*, Vol. 8, No. 1, Spring 1995.

Robert D'A. Henderson, 'South African Intelligence Transition from de Klerk to Mandela: An Update', *International Journal of Intelligence and Counterintelligence*, Vol. 8, No. 4, Winter 1995–6.

Robert D'A. Henderson, 'Operation Vula against Apartheid', *International Journal of Intelligence and Counterintelligence*, Vol. 10, No. 4, Winter 1997–8.

Peter Hennessy, *The Secret State: Whitehall and the Cold War*, Allen Lane, London, 2002.

Jeffrey Herbst, 'Analyzing Apartheid: How Accurate were US Intelligence Estimates of South Africa, 1948–1994?', *African Affairs*, Vol. 102, No. 406, January 2003.

Denis Herbstein and John Evenson, *The Devils are Among Us: The War for Namibia*, Zed Books, London, 1989.

Denis Herbstein, *White Lies: Canon Collins and the Secret War Against Apartheid*, HSRC Press, Cape Town, 2004.

Michael Herman, *Intelligence Power in Peace and War*, Cambridge University Press, Cambridge, 1996.

Michael Herman, *Intelligence Services in the Information Age: Theory and Practice*, Frank Cass, London, 2002.

Michael Herman, 'Ethics and Intelligence after September 2001', *Intelligence and National Security*, Vol. 19, No. 2, Summer 2004.

Seymour M. Hersh, *The Samson Option: Israel, America and the Bomb*, Faber & Faber, London, 1991.

Christopher Hitchens, *The Trial of Henry Kissinger*, Verso, London, 2001.

Jim Hoagland, *South Africa: Clash of Civilisations*, George Allen & Unwin, London, 1973.

Mike Hoare, *Congo Mercenary*, Robert Hale, London, 1967.

Mike Hoare, *The Seychelles Affair*, Bantam Press, London, 1986.

Anthony Hocking, *Oppenheimer and Son*, McGraw-Hill Book Co., Johannesburg, 1973.

Mark Hollingsworth and Paul Halloran, *Thatcher's Fortunes: The Life and Times of Mark Thatcher*, Mainstream Publishing, Edinburgh, 2005.

Dr Ferry A. Hoogendijk, 'Muldergate: The Eschel Rhoodie Story', *Elseviers*, 28 July–18 August 1979, news agency transcript.

Jim Hooper, *Koevoet!*, Southern Book Publishers, Johannesburg, 1988.

Jim Hooper, *Bloodsong!: An Account of Executive Outcomes in Angola*, HarperCollins, London, 2002.

Gerald Horne, *From the Barrel of a Gun: The United States and the War against Zimbabwe, 1965–1980*, University of North Carolina Press, Chapel Hill, 2001.

Jim Hougan, *Spooks: The Private Use of Secret Agents*, W.H. Allen, London, 1979.

Mike Hough, 'Urban Terror in South Africa: A New Wave?', *Terrorism and Political Violence*, Vol. 12, No. 2, Summer 2000.

Peter Hounam and Steve McQuillan, *The Mini-Nuke Conspiracy: Mandela's Nuclear Nightmare*, Faber & Faber, London, 1995.

David Howarth and Aletta J. Norval (eds), *South Africa in Transition: New Theoretical Perspectives*, Macmillan Press, London, 1998.

Herbert M. Howe, 'The South African Defence Force and Political Reform', *Journal of Modern African Studies*, Vol. 32, No. 1, March 1994.

Gert Hugo and Stef Snel, *Military Intelligence and the Counter Revolutionary War in the Eastern Cape*, Urban Monitoring and Awareness Committee, Cape Town, 1998.

Derek Humphry, *The Cricket Conspiracy*, National Council for Civil Liberties, London, 1975.

Jane Hunter, *Israeli Foreign Policy: South Africa and Central America*, Bertrand Russell Peace Foundation, Nottingham, 1987.

Samuel P. Huntington, 'Reform and Stability in a Modernising, Multi-Ethnic Society', *Politikon*, Vol. 8, No. 2, December 1981.

Duncan Innes, *Anglo American and the Rise of Modern South Africa*, Ravan, Johannesburg, 1984.

Mark Israel, 'Crimes of the State: Victimisation of South African Political Exiles in the United Kingdom', *Crime, Law & Social Change*, No. 29, 1998.

Mark Israel, *South African Political Exile in the United Kingdom*, Macmillan Press, London, 1999.

Sean Jacobs and Richard Calland (eds), *Thabo Mbeki's World: The Politics and Ideology of the South African President*, Zed Books, London, 2002.

Peter Janke, 'Southern Africa: End of Empire', *Conflict Studies 52*, December 1974.

Robert Scott Jaster, *The Defence of White Power: South African Foreign Policy Under Pressure*, Palgrave Macmillan, London, 1988.

Anthea Jeffrey, *The Natal Story: 16 Years of Conflict*, South African Institute of Race Relations, Johannesburg, 1997.

Anthea Jeffrey, *The Truth About the Truth Commission*, South African Institute of Race Relations, Johannesburg, 1999.

Tim Jenkin, *Escape from Pretoria*, Kliptown Books, London, 1987.

Tim Jenkin, 'Talking to Vula: The Story of the Secret Underground Communications Network of Operation Vula', *Mayibuye*, May–October 1995.

Phyllis Johnson and David Martin, *Apartheid Terrorism: The Destabilization Report*, The Commonwealth Secretariat, London, 1989.

R.W. Johnson, *How Long Will South Africa Survive?*, Macmillan, London, 1977.

J.D.F. Jones, *Storyteller: The Many Lives of Laurens van der Post*, John Murray, London, 2001.

David Jordan, *Black Account*, Michael Joseph, London, 1975.

Alan Judd, *Short of Glory*, Hodder & Stoughton, London, 1984.

Fred Kamil, *The Diamond Empire*, Allen Lane, London, 1979.

John Kampfner, *Blair's Wars*, Free Press, London, 2003.

John Kane-Berman, *Political Violence in South Africa*, South African Institute of Race Relations, Johannesburg, 1993.

Stefan Kanfer, *The Last Empire: De Beers, Diamonds and the World*, Hodder & Stoughton, London, 1993.

Thomas Karis and Gail M. Gerhart, *From Protest to Challenge: A Documentary History of African Politics in South Africa, 1882–1990*, Vol. 5: *Nadir and Resurgence, 1964–1979*, Indiana University Press, Indianapolis, 1997.

Ronnie Kasrils, *Armed and Dangerous: From Undercover Struggle to Freedom*, updated edn, Jonathan Ball, Johannesburg, 2004.

Rudyard Kipling, *The Man Who Would Be King and Other Stories*, Oxford University Press, Oxford, 1987; originally published in 1888.

The Kissinger Study on Southern Africa, Spokesman Books, Nottingham, 1975.

Henry Kissinger, *Years of Renewal*, Simon & Schuster, New York, 1999.

Arthur Jay Klinghoffer, *Oiling the Wheels of Apartheid: Exposing South Africa's Secret Oil Trade*, Lynne Reinner Publishers, Boulder, 1989.

Derrick Knight, *Beyond the Pale: The Christian Political Fringe*, Caraf Publications, Leigh, 1982.

Phillip Knightley, *The Second Oldest Profession: The Spy as Bureaucrat, Patriot, Fantasist and Whore*, André Deutsch, London, 1986.

Daniel Korn, *Exocet*, BBC 2, 1 July 2001.

Antjie Krog, *Country of My Skull*, Jonathan Cape, London, 1999.

Riaan Labuschagne, *On South Africa's Secret Service: An Undercover Agent's Story*, Galago, Alberton, 2002.

Signe Landgren, *Embargo Disimplemented: South Africa's Secret Military Industry*, Oxford University Press, Oxford, 1989.

G. Lanning and M. Mueller, *Africa Undermined: A History of the Mining Companies and the Underdevelopment of Africa*, Penguin, London, 1979.

Paul Lashmar and James Oliver, *Britain's Secret Propaganda War, 1948–1977*, Sutton Publishing, London, 1998.

John C. Laurence, *Race Propaganda and South Africa*, Victor Gollancz, London, 1979.

Patrick Laurence, *Death Squads: Apartheid's Secret Weapon*, Penguin Books, London, 1990.

John le Carré, *The Spy Who Came in from the Cold*, Victor Gollancz, London, 1963.

Adrian Leftwich, 'I Gave the Names', *Granta 78: Bad Company*, June 2002.

David Leigh, *The Wilson Plot: The Intelligence Services and the Discrediting of a Prime Minister*, Heinemann, London, 1988.

Joseph Lelyveld, *Move Your Shadow: South Africa Black and White*, Michael Joseph, London, 1986.

Hugh Lewin, *Bandiet: Seven Years in a South African Prison*, Penguin, London, 1976.

Peter Liberman, 'The Rise and Fall of the South African Bomb', *International Security*, Vol. 26, No. 2, Fall 2001.

Tom Lodge, *Black Politics in South Africa since 1945*, Longman, London, 1983.

John Loftus and Mark Aarons, *The Secret War Against the Jews*, St Martin's Press, London, 1994.

Chris Logan, *Celebrity Surgeon: Christiaan Barnard – A Life*, Jonathan Ball, Johannesburg, 2003.

Michael H.H. Louw (ed), *National Security: A Modern Approach*, Institute for Strategic Studies, Pretoria, 1978.

William Lowther, *Arms and the Man: Dr Gerald Bull, Iraq and the Supergun*, Macmillan, London, 1991.

Gerard Ludi and Blair Grobbelaar, *The Amazing Mr Fischer*, Nasionale Boekhandel, Cape Town, 1966.

Gerard Ludi, *Operation Q-018*, Nasionale Boekhandel, Cape Town, 1969.

Gavyn MacFadyen and Laurie Flynn, *The Diamond Empire*, BBC 2, 1994.

Shaun McCarthy, 'Intelligence Services of a Democratic South Africa: Ensuring Parliamentary Control', *Conflict Studies 286*, December 1995.

Shaun McCarthy, 'South Africa's Intelligence Reformation', *International Journal of Intelligence and Counterintelligence*, Vol. 9, No. 1, Spring 1996.

John J. McCuen, *The Art of Counter-Revolutionary War: The Strategy of Counter-insurgency*, Faber & Faber, London, 1966.

John Major, *The Autobiography*, HarperCollins, London, 1999.

Ernest C. Malherbe, *Education in South Africa*, Vol. 2: *1923–1975*, Juta & Co., Cape Town, 1977.

James R. Mancham, *Paradise Raped: Life, Love and Power in the Seychelles*, Methuen, London, 1983.

Nelson Mandela, *No Easy Walk to Freedom: Articles, Speeches, and Trial Addresses*, ed. Ruth First, Heinemann, London, 1965.

Nelson Mandela, *The Struggle Is My Life*, Mayibuye Books, Bellville, 1994.

Nelson Mandela, *Long Walk to Freedom*, Abacus, London, 1995.

N. Chabani Manganyi and Andre du Toit (eds), *Political Violence and the Struggle in South Africa*, Macmillan, London, 1990.

Tom Mangold, *Cold Warrior: James Jesus Angleton: The CIA's Master Spy Hunter*, Simon & Schuster, New York, 1991.

Tom Mangold and Jeff Goldberg, *Plague Wars: A True Story of Biological Warfare*, Macmillan, London, 1999.

Tom Mangold and Peter Molloy, *Plague Wars*, BBC 1, 1998.

Victor Marchetti and John D. Marks, *The CIA and the Cult of Intelligence*, Jonathan Cape, London, 1974.

Greil Marcus, *The Manchurian Candidate*, British Film Institute, London, 2002.

Gerhard Mare and Georgina Hamilton, *An Appetite for Power: Buthelezi's Inkatha and the Politics of 'Loyal Resistance'*, Ravan, Johannesburg, 1987.

C.S. Margo, *Report of the Board of Inquiry into the Accident to Tupelov 134A-3 Aircraft C9-CAA on 19th October 1986*, Government Printer, Pretoria, 1987.

David Martin and Phyllis Johnson, *The Struggle for Zimbabwe: The Chimurenga War*, Faber & Faber, London, 1981.

Fatima Meer, *Higher Than Hope: The Authorized Biography of Nelson Mandela*, Penguin Books, London, 1990.

Francis Meli, *South Africa Belongs to Us: A History of the ANC*, Zimbabwe Publishing House, Harare, 1988.

Martin Meredith, *Coming to Terms: South Africa's Search for Truth*, PublicAffairs, Oxford, 1999.

Cord Meyer, *Facing Reality: From World Federalism to the CIA*, University Press of America, Washington DC, 1980.

Greg Mills and John Stremlau (eds), *The Privatisation of Security in Africa*, South African Institute of International Affairs, Johannesburg, 1999.

Seumas Milne, *The Enemy Within: The Secret War Against the Miners*, Verso, London, 1994.

Anthony Minnaar, Ian Liebenberg and Charl Schutte (eds), *The Hidden Hand: Covert Operations in South Africa*, Human Sciences Research Council, Pretoria, 1994; revised edn, 1998.

William Minter, *King Solomon's Mines Revisited: Western Interests and the Burdened History of Southern Africa*, Basic Books, New York, 1986.

Anthony Mockler, *The New Mercenaries: The History of the Mercenary from the Congo to the Seychelles*, Sidgwick & Jackson, London, 1985.

Gomolemo Mokae, *Robert McBride: A Coloured Life*, SAHO, Pretoria, 2004.

Kenneth Mokoena (ed), *South Africa and the United States: The Declassified History*, The New Press, New York, 1993.

J.D.L Moore, *South Africa and Nuclear Proliferation: South Africa's Nuclear Capabilities and Intentions in the Context of International Non-proliferation Policies*, Macmillan, London, 1987.

Michael Morris, *Terrorism: The First Full Account in Detail of Terrorism and Insurgency in Southern Africa*, Howard Timmins, Cape Town, 1971.

Roger Morris, *Uncertain Greatness: Henry Kissinger and American Foreign Policy*, Quartet Books, London, 1977.

Glenn Moss and Ingrid Obery (eds), *South African Review 4*, Ravan, Johannesburg, 1987.

Glenn Moss and Ingrid Obery (eds), *South African Review 5*, Ravan, Johannesburg, 1989.

Robert Moss, *Chile's Marxist Experiment*, David & Charles, Newton Abbot, 1973.

Robert Moss, *The Collapse of Democracy*, Temple Smith, London, 1975.

Robert Moss, 'Friends in Need: Five Good Reasons for Standing by South Africa', *Politics Today*, No. 3, May–June 1978.

Robert Moss, *Dreamgates: An Explorer's Guide to the Worlds of Soul, Imagination, and Life Beyond Death*, Three Rivers Press, New York, 1998.

L.M. Mti, 'The Role of the Intelligence Services and Private Security Companies in Crime Prevention and Crime Combating in South Africa', *ISSUP Bulletin*, 5/97.

Chris Munnion, *Banana Sunday: Datelines from Africa*, William Waterman Publications, Rivonia, 1993.

Philip Murphy, 'Intelligence and Decolonisation: The Life and Death of the Federal Intelligence and Security Bureau, 1954–1963', *Journal of Imperial and Commonwealth History*, Vol. 29, No 2, May 2001.

Philip Murphy, 'Creating a Commonwealth Intelligence Culture: The View from Central Africa 1945–1965', *Intelligence and National Security*, Vol. 17, No. 2, Autumn 2002.

Mzala, *Gatsha Buthelezi: Chief with a Double Agenda*, Zed Books, London, 1988.

Malcolm Needs, *Charlie*, motion picture, 2004; DVD, 2005.

Christopher Nicholson, *Permanent Removal: Who Killed the Cradock Four?*, Witwatersrand University Press, Johannesburg, 2004.

Matthew Nkoana, *Crisis in the Revolution: A Special Report on the Pan-Africanist Congress of South Africa*, Mafube Publications, London, 1969.

Piet Nortje, *32 Battalion: The Inside Story of South Africa's Elite Fighting Unit*, Zebra Press, Cape Town, 2003.

Kevin A. O'Brien, 'South Africa's Evolving Intelligence and Security Structures', *International Journal of Intelligence and Counterintelligence*, Vol. 9, No. 2, Summer 1996.

Kevin A. O'Brien, 'The Use of Assassination as a Tool of State Policy: South Africa's Counter-Revolutionary Strategy 1979–92 (Part I)', *Terrorism and Political Violence*, Vol. 10, No. 2, Summer 1998.

Kevin A. O'Brien, 'The Use of Assassination as a Tool of State Policy: South Africa's Counter-Revolutionary Strategy 1979–92 (Part II)', *Terrorism and Political Violence*, Vol. 13, No. 2, Summer 2001.

Kevin A. O'Brien, 'Special Forces for Counter-Revolutionary Warfare: The South African Case', *Small Wars and Insurgencies*, Vol. 12, No. 2, Summer 2001.

Kevin A. O'Brien, 'Counter-Intelligence for Counter-Revolutionary Warfare: The South African Police Security Branch 1979–1990', *Intelligence and National Security*, Vol. 16, No. 3, Autumn 2001.

Dan O'Meara, *Forty Lost Years: The Apartheid State and the Politics of the National Party, 1948–1994*, Ravan, Johannesburg and Ohio University Press, Athens, 1996.

David Pallister, Sarah Stewart and Ian Lepper, *South Africa Inc.: The Oppenheimer Empire*, revised and updated edn, Corgi Books, London, 1988.

Aida Parker, *Secret US War against South Africa*, The Citizen, Johannesburg, 1977.

Robert Parker, *Rough Justice*, Fontana, London, 1981.

Alan Paton, *Journey Continued: An Autobiography*, Collier Books, New York, 1988.

Jacques Pauw, *In the Heart of the Whore: The Story of Apartheid's Death Squads*, Southern Book Publishers, Johannesburg, 1991.

Jacques Pauw, *Prime Evil*, SABC 1, 1996.

Jacques Pauw, *Into the Heart of Darkness: Confessions of Apartheid's Assassins*, Jonathan Ball, Johannesburg, 1997.

John Pearson, *The Gamblers*, Century, London, 2005.

Barrie Penrose and Roger Courtiour, *The Pencourt File*, Secker & Warburg, London, 1978.

Piers Pigou, 'The Apartheid State and Violence: What has the Truth and Reconciliation Commission Found?', *Politikon*, Vol. 28, No. 2, June 2001.

Henry Pike, *A History of Communism in South Africa*, Christian Mission International, Germiston, 1985.

Ben Pimlott, *Harold Wilson*, HarperCollins, London, 1992.

Chapman Pincher, *Inside Story: A Documentary of the Pursuit of Power*, Sidgwick & Jackson, London, 1978.

Chapman Pincher, *The Truth About Dirty Tricks: From Harold Wilson to Margaret Thatcher*, Sidgwick & Jackson, London, 1991.

Gary Player, *Grand Slam Golf*, Cassell, London, 1966.

Benjamin Pogrund, *How Can Man Die Better: Sobukwe and Apartheid*, Peter Halban, London, 1990.

Benjamin Pogrund, *War of Words: Memoirs of a South African Journalist*, Seven Stories Press, New York, 2000.

Richard Pollak, *Up Against Apartheid: The Role and Plight of the Press in South Africa*, Southern Illinois University Press, Carbondale, 1981.

Douglas Porch, *The French Secret Services: From the Dreyfus Affair to the Gulf War*, Macmillan, London, 1996.

De Wet Potgieter, *Contraband: South Africa and the International Trade in Ivory and Rhino Horn*, Queillerie, Cape Town, 1995.

H.J. Potgieter, *Report of the Commission of Inquiry into Matters Relating to the Security of the State*, Government Printer, Pretoria, 1970 and 1973.

Brian Pottinger, *The Imperial Presidency: P.W. Botha, the First 10 Years*, Southern Book Publishers, Johannesburg, 1988.

Thomas Powers, *Intelligence Wars: American Secret History from Hitler to al-Qaeda*, New York Review Books, New York, 2002.

Adv. P.J. Pretorius, *Sell-Out!: The Truth behind the History of South African Politics*, self-published, 1997.

Helen E. Purkitt and Stephen Burgess, 'South Africa's Chemical and Biological Warfare Programme: A Historical and International Perspective', *Journal of Southern African Studies*, Vol. 28, No. 2, June 2002.

Helen E. Purkitt and Stephen F. Burgess, *South Africa's Weapons of Mass Destruction*, Indiana University Press, Bloomington, 2005.

Ellen Ray, William Schaap, Karl van Meter and Louis Wolf (eds), *Dirty Work 2: The CIA in Africa*, Lyle Stuart, Secaucus, 1979.

William Raynor and Geoffrey Allen, 'Smear – The Thorpe Affair', unpublished manuscript, 1978.

Jean Redpath, *The Scorpions: Analysing the Directorate of Special Operations*, Institute for Security Studies Monograph No. 96, Pretoria, March 2004.

Jean Redpath, 'Weathering the Storm: Tough Questions for the Scorpions', *SA Crime Quarterly*, No. 8, June 2004.

Mervyn Rees, interview with Eschel Rhoodie, transcript, 1979.

Mervyn Rees and Chris Day, *Muldergate: The Story of the Info Scandal*, Macmillan, Johannesburg, 1980.

Ros Reeve and Stephen Ellis, 'An Insider's Account of the South African Security Forces' Role in the Ivory Trade', *Journal of Contemporary African Studies*, Vol. 13, No. 2, June 1995.

Robin Renwick, *Unconventional Diplomacy in Southern Africa*, Macmillan Press, London, 1997.

Republic of South Africa. *Bureau for State Security Act, 1978*, Government Printer, Pretoria, 1978.

Republic of South Africa, *White Paper on Intelligence*, Government Printer, Pretoria, 1994.

Eschel Rhoodie, *The Paper Curtain*, Voortrekkerpers, Johannesburg, 1969.

Eschel Rhoodie, *The REAL Information Scandal*, Orbis SA, Pretoria, 1983.

Eschel Rhoodie, *P.W. Botha: The Last Betrayal*, SA Politics, Melville, 1989.

Charlie Richardson, *My Manor: An Autobiography*, Pan Macmillan, London, 1992.

Eddie Richardson. *The Last Word: My Life as a Gangland Boss*, Headline Book Publishing, London, 2005.

Jeffrey T. Richelson, *Foreign Intelligence Organizations*, Ballinger, Cambridge, 1988.

Stella Rimington, *Open Secret: The Autobiography of the Former Director-General of MI5*, Hutchinson, London, 2001.

Janine Roberts, *Glitter and Greed: The Secret World of the Diamond Cartel*, Disinformation, New York, 2003.

Ronald Suresh Roberts, *No Cold Kitchen: A Biography of Nadine Gordimer*, STE Publishers, Johannesburg, 2005.

K.G. Robertson (ed), *War, Resistance and Intelligence: Essays in Honour of M.R.D. Foot*, Pen and Sword, London, 1999.

James M. Roherty, *State Security in South Africa: Civil–Military Relations Under P.W. Botha*, M.E. Sharpe, New York, 1992.

The Role of the Soviet Union, Cuba, and East Germany in Fomenting Terrorism in Southern Africa: Hearings before the Subcommittee on Security and Terrorism of the Committee on the Judiciary, United States Senate, Ninety-seventh Congress, Second Session, Government Printing Office, Washington DC, 1982.

Paul Rose, *The Backbencher's Dilemma*, Frederick Muller, London, 1981.

Richard Rosenthal, *Mission Improbable: A Piece of the South African Story*, David Philip, Cape Town, 1998.

James Rusbridger, *The Intelligence Game: The Illusions and Delusions of International Espionage*, The Bodley Head, London, 1989.

Anthony Sampson, *The Seven Sisters: The Great Oil Companies and the World They Made*, Hodder & Stoughton, London, 1975.

Anthony Sampson, *The Arms Bazaar*, Hodder & Stoughton, London, 1977.

Anthony Sampson, *Black and Gold: Tycoons, Revolutionaries and Apartheid*, Hodder & Stoughton, London, 1987.

Anthony Sampson, *Mandela: The Authorised Biography*, HarperCollins, London, 1999.

Anthony Sampson, *Who Runs This Place? The Anatomy of Britain in the 21st Century*, John Murray, London, 2004.

James Sanders, *South Africa and the International Media, 1972–1979: A Struggle for Representation*, Frank Cass, London, 1999.

James Sanders, 'Intelligence, Ignorance and Confusion: Excavating the Remnants of BOSS', unpublished seminar paper, Institute of Commonwealth Studies, University of London, March 1999.

Frances Stonor Saunders, *Who Paid the Piper? The CIA and the Cultural Cold War*, Granta, London, 1999.

Gunther Schickelgruber, 'High Treason: An Intelligence Report on South Africa', unpublished manuscript, 2003.

Peter J. Schraeder, *United States Foreign Policy Toward Africa: Incrementalism, Crisis and Change*, Cambridge University Press, Cambridge, 1994.

Annette Seegers, 'South Africa's National Security Management System, 1972–1990', *Journal of Modern African Studies*, Vol. 29, No. 2, June 1991.

Annette Seegers, *The Military in the Making of Modern South Africa*, I.B. Tauris, London, 1996.

Annette Seegers, 'Secrecy and Accountability in South Africa's Intelligence Agencies', unpublished paper, April 1999.

J.H.P. Serfontein, *Brotherhood of Power: An Exposé of the Secret Afrikaner Broederbond*, Rex Collings, London, 1979.

Theodore Shackley, *The Third Option: An American View of Counterinsurgency Operations*, McGraw Hill Book Co., New York, 1981.

Mark Hugh Shaw, 'South Africa's Other War: Understanding and Resolving Political Violence in KwaZulu-Natal (1985–) and the PWV (1990–), unpublished doctoral thesis, University of the Witwatersrand, March 1997.

Mark Shaw, 'Organised Crime in Post-Apartheid South Africa', *ISS Papers*, No 28, January 1998.

Vladimir Shubin, *ANC: A View from Moscow*, Mayibuye Books, Belville, 1999.

Harold Shukman (ed), *Agents for Change: Intelligence Services in the 21st Century*, St Ermin's Press, London, 2000.

Sir Percy Sillitoe, *Cloak Without Dagger*, Cassell & Co., London, 1955.

Georgina Sinclair, '"Settlers men" or Policemen? The Ambiguities of "Colonial Policing", 1945–80', unpublished doctoral thesis, University of Reading, 2002.

P.W. Singer, *Corporate Warriors: The Rise of the Privatised Military Industry*, Cornell University Press, Ithaca, 2004.

Adv. T.L. Skweyiya, 'Report of the Commission of Enquiry into Complaints by Former African National Congress Prisoners and Detainees', ANC, Johannesburg, 1992.

Gillian Slovo, *Every Secret Thing: My Family, My Country*, Little, Brown & Co., London, 1997.

Cyril Smith, *Big Cyril*, W.H. Allen, London, 1977.

Ian Smith, *The Great Betrayal: The Memoirs of Ian Douglas Smith*, Blake, London, 1997.

Michael Smith, *The Spying Game: The Secret History of British Espionage*, Politico's, London, 2003.

Harold Soref and Ian Greig, *The Puppeteers*, Tandem Books, London, 1965.

South Africa at the End of the Eighties: Policy Perspectives 1989, Centre for Policy Studies, Johannesburg, 1989.

South African Democracy Education Trust, *The Road to Democracy in South Africa*, Vol. 1, *1960–1970*, Zebra Press, Cape Town, 2004.

South African Institute of Race Relations, *Survey of Race Relations in South Africa: 1975*, SAIRR, Johannesburg, 1976.

South African Institute of Race Relations, *A Survey of Race Relations in South Africa: 1977*, SAIRR, Johannesburg, 1978.

South African Institute of Race Relations, *Race Relations Survey: 1988/89*, SAIRR, Johannesburg, 1989.

South African Research Service, *South African Review II*, Ravan, Johannesburg, 1984.

South African Research Service (eds), *South African Review 3*, Ravan, Johannesburg, 1986.

Allister Sparks, *The Mind of South Africa: The Story of the Rise and Fall of Apartheid*, Heinemann, London, 1990.

Allister Sparks, *Tomorrow is Another Country: The Inside Story of South Africa's Negotiated Revolution*, Heinemann, London, 1995.

Allister Sparks, *Beyond the Miracle: Inside the New South Africa*, Profile Books, London, 2003.

Allister Sparks and Mick Gold, *The Death of Apartheid*, BBC 2, 1994.

Ed Stanley, 'France and Africa, 1944–90', unpublished doctoral thesis, School of Oriental and African Studies, University of London, 2004.

Peter Stiff, *See You in November: Rhodesia's No-holds-barred Intelligence War*, Galago, Alberton, 1987.

Peter Stiff, *The Silent War: South African Recce Operations, 1969–1994*, Galago, Alberton, 1999.

Peter Stiff, *Cry Zimbabwe: Independence – Twenty Years On*, Galago, Alberton, 2000.

Peter Stiff, *Warfare by Other Means: South Africa in the 1980s and 1990s*, Galago, Alberton, 2001.

Peter Stiff, *The Covert War: Koevoet Operations Namibia 1979–1989*, Galago, Alberton, 2004.

John Stockwell, *In Search of Enemies: A CIA Story*, W.W. Norton & Co., New York, 1978.

Barry Streek and Richard Wicksteed, *Render Unto Kaiser: A Transkei Dossier*, Ravan, Johannesburg, 1981.

Major-General Sir Kenneth Strong, *Men of Intelligence: A Study of the Roles and Decisions of Chiefs of Intelligence from World War I to the Present Day*, Cassell, London, 1970.

James Stuart, 'Stuart Commission Report into Recent Developments in the People's Republic of Angola', ANC, Lusaka, 1984.

Helen Suzman, *In No Uncertain Terms*, Sinclair-Stevenson, London, 1993.

Pieter Swanepoel, 'The De Crespigny Mystery', unpublished, undated, manuscript.

Peter Taylor, *Brits: The War Against the IRA*, Bloomsbury, London, 2001.

Margaret Thatcher, *The Downing Street Years*, HarperCollins, London, 1993.

Margaret Thatcher, *The Path to Power*, HarperCollins, London, 1995.

Robert Thompson, *Defeating Communist Insurgency: The Lessons of Malaya and Vietnam*, Chatto & Windus, London, 1966.

Jeremy Thorpe, *In My Own Time: Reminiscences of a Liberal Leader*, Politico's, London, 1999.

Paul Todd and Jonathan Bloch, *Global Intelligence: The World's Secret Services Today*, Zed Books, London, 2003.

Richard Tomlinson, *The Big Breach: From Top Secret to Maximum Security*, Cutting Edge, Edinburgh, 2001.

'Total War in South Africa: Militarisation and the Apartheid State', NUSAS report, 1982.

Truth and Reconciliation Commission, *Truth and Reconciliation Commission of South Africa Report*, Vols 1–5, TRC, Cape Town, 1998.

Truth and Reconciliation Commission, *Truth and Reconciliation Commission of South Africa Report*, Vol. 6, TRC, Cape Town, 2003.

Truth and Reconciliation Commission, *Truth and Reconciliation Commission of South Africa Report*, Vol. 7, TRC, Cape Town, 2002.

Richard Turner, *The Eye of the Needle: Toward Participatory Democracy in South Africa*, Orbis Books, New York, 1978, originally published 1972.

Mwezi Twala and Ed Benard, *Mbokodo. Inside MK: Mwezi Twala – A Soldier's Story*, Jonathan Ball, Johannesburg, 1994.

Harvey Tyson, *Editors Under Fire*, Random House, Johannesburg, 1993.

Sun Tzu, *The Art of War*, Wordsworth Editions, Ware, 1998.

Mark Urban, *UK Eyes Alpha: The Inside Story of British Intelligence*, Faber & Faber, London, 1996.

Peter Vale, *Security and Politics in South Africa: The Regional Dimension*, Boulder, Colorado, 2002.

A.P.J. van Rensburg, *The Tangled Web: Leadership and Change in Southern Africa*, Hollandsch Afrikaansche Uitgevers Maatschappij, Cape Town, 1977.

Henk van Woerden, *A Mouthful of Glass*, Granta Books, London, 2000.

Mikki van Zyl, Jeanelle de Gruchy, Sheila Lapinsky, Simon Lewin and Graeme Reid, *The Aversion Project: Human Rights Abuses of Gays and Lesbians in the South African Defence Force by Health Workers during the Apartheid Era*, Simply Said & Done, Cape Town, 1999.

Howard Varney, 'The Role of the Former State in Political Violence, Operation Marion: A Case Study', unpublished paper, March 1997.

Howard Varney and Jeremy Sarkin, 'Failing to Pierce the Hit Squad Veil: A Critique of the Malan Trial', *South African Journal of Criminal Justice*, No. 10, 1997.

Al J. Venter, *War Dog: Fighting Other Peoples' Wars. The Modern Mercenary in Combat*, Casemate, Havertown, 2003.

Anthony Verrier, *Through the Looking Glass: British Foreign Policy in the Age of Illusions*, Jonathan Cape, London, 1983.

Anthony Verrier, *The Road to Zimbabwe: 1890–1980*, Jonathan Cape, London, 1986.

E.J. Verwey (ed), *New Dictionary of South African Biography*, Vol. 1, HSRC, Pretoria, 1995.

Randolph Vigne, *Liberals Against Apartheid: A History of the Liberal Party of South Africa, 1953–1968*, Macmillan Press, London, 1997.

Alex Vines, *RENAMO: From Terrorism to Democracy in Mozambique?*, James Currey, London, 1991.

P.J. Visser, 'Legal Changes in the Regulation of the Private Security Industry in South Africa', *Strategic Review for Southern Africa*, Vol. 26, No. 2, November 2004.

Patti Waldmeir, *Anatomy of a Miracle: The End of Apartheid and the Birth of the New South Africa*, Viking, London, 1997.

General Sir Walter Walker, *The Bear at the Back Door: The Soviet Threat to the West's Lifeline in Africa*, Valiant Publishers, Sandton, 1978.

Auberon Waugh, *The Last Word: An Eye-Witness Account of the Trial of Jeremy Thorpe*, Michael Joseph, London, 1980.

David Webster and Maggie Friedman, *Suppressing Apartheid's Opponents: Repression and the State of Emergency, June 1987 to March 1989*, Southern Africa Research Service/Ravan Press, Johannesburg, 1989.

Frank Welsh, *Dangerous Deceits: Julian Askin and the Tollgate Scandal*, HarperCollins, London, 1999.

Who's Who, 2005, A & C Black, London, 2005.

Ivor Wilkins and Hans Strydom, *The Broederbond*, Paddington Press, London, 1979.

Richard A. Wilson, *The Politics of Truth and Reconciliation in South Africa: Legitimizing the Post-Apartheid State*, Cambridge University Press, Cambridge, 2001.

Gordon Winter, *Inside BOSS: South Africa's Secret Police*, Penguin Books, London, 1981.

Gordon Winter, *Geheim agent voor Zuid-Afrika: 16 jaar in dienst van de BOSS*, Kritiese Biblioteek Van Gennep, Amsterdam, 1981.

Gordon Winter, 'Inside BOSS and After', *Lobster*, No. 18, 1989.

Gordon Winter, 'Vindication is a Dish Still Edible Cold', *Lobster*, No. 48, Winter 2004.

Pieter Wolvaardt, *A Diplomat's Story: Apartheid and Beyond, 1969–1988*, Galago, Alberton, 2005.

Bob Woodward, *Veil: The Secret Wars of the CIA, 1981–1987*, Simon & Schuster, New York, 1987.

Peter Wright, *Spy Catcher: The Candid Autobiography of a Senior Intelligence Officer*, Viking, New York, 1987.

Daniel Yergin, *The Prize: The Epic Quest for Oil, Money and Power*, Simon & Schuster, London, 1991.

John W. Young, 'The Wilson Government's Reform of Intelligence Coordination, 1967–68', *Intelligence and National Security*, Vol. 16, No. 2, Summer 2001.

Paul Yule, *Secret History: White Lies*, Channel 4, 1994.

Philip Ziegler, *Wilson: The Authorised Life*, HarperCollins, London, 1995.

Index

Index